Human Behavior
A Systems Approach

Human Behavior

A Systems Approach

NORMAN W. HEIMSTRA and **VERNON S. ELLINGSTAD**

University of South Dakota

Brooks/Cole Publishing Company
Monterey, California

A Division of Wadsworth Publishing Company, Inc.
Belmont, California

ISBN: 0–8185–0015–8
L.C. Catalog Card No: 79–187501
Printed in the United States of America
1 2 3 4 5 6 7 8 9 10—77 76 75 74 73 72

This book was designed by Linda Marcetti, with technical illustrations by John Foster. It was typeset, printed, and bound by Kingsport Press, Inc., Kingsport, Tennessee.

Preface

Because the majority of people expect a certain number of traditional topics to be included in an introductory psychology textbook, an author has only a few decisions to make about "what" should be covered in his book. Therefore, the decisions about "how" the topics are to be presented are of particular importance in determining its uniqueness. The present text is distinctive in that it uses a model of the behavioral system of man and, within the framework of this model, discusses the traditional topics found in most texts.

Man is viewed as a complex system consisting of a number of behavioral subsystems that interact so that an input is transformed to an output, or behavior. Beginning with a discussion of the characteristics of the input (stimuli), the functions of the various subsystems that transform the input are considered. Thus, chapters are devoted to sensing, identifying (perception), interpreting, learning and remembering, and energizing (motivational) subsystems, as well as the output of the system. Additional chapters deal with man as a subsystem within larger systems (personnel selection and training, human engineering, social behavior), with differences between systems (intelligence, personality), and with system malfunctions (abnormal behavior).

In viewing man as a system, it is possible to analyze him in such a way that the interactions and interdependence of the various subsystems become apparent. Various interacting components and functions and their relationships can be identified. This type of "systems analysis" makes it possible to conceptualize and discuss the complex behavioral system of man at a fairly simple level. The systems approach helps to tie separate human behavioral functions together so that the complete behavioral system can be more clearly understood. The various functions of man as a behavioral system can be considered in terms of their dynamic relationships rather than as static elements, as they are so often treated in introductory psychology books.

To dispense with an unnecessarily complex or confusing array of flow diagrams and charts, we have avoided carrying our analysis of the behavioral system to excessively fine levels and have confined our analysis to three levels. At one level, the functions of the various behavioral subsystems are dealt with in considerable detail. At another level of analysis, the complete system is considered in terms of its output and differences between outputs, and, finally, man's role as a subsystem within larger industrial and social systems is discussed.

This textbook also differs from many others in that it discusses several theoretical positions supported by key empirical investigations, rather than listing a vast number of empirical facts in encyclopedic fashion at one extreme or following only one particular theoretical framework at the other. For most of the major areas that are discussed in the text, there are hundreds or even thousands of studies that have been conducted and published. We have been selective in citing studies in order to avoid another "encyclopedia" and to keep the book at an appropriate length.

We wish to extend our appreciation to the large number of persons who have assisted us in numerous ways in the preparation of this textbook. The critical reviews of William Lambert Gardiner of Sir George Williams University, Robert Sawyer of the University of Missouri at Rolla, David Schum of Rice University, Joseph Sgro of Virginia Polytechnic Institute, and William Uttal of the University of Michigan were particularly valuable. The final version of this book reflects the many comments and suggestions of these reviewers. All of them made suggestions that were invaluable in the final revision of the manuscript. The comments of Arthur McDonald of Montana State University, who reviewed the first draft, and the contributions to Chapter 13 of James Nichols, presently with the United States Department of Transportation, are also appreciated. We are indebted to our graduate students who not only read and criticized the manuscript but who also, on occasion, prodded us into action when pheasant hunting or fishing seemed more important than writing a textbook. A special word of thanks must be extended to Miss Darlene Peterson, who did a first-rate job of typing the manuscript, and to Velda Kilstrom for her assistance in proofreading.

We also wish to express our special appreciation to Bonnie Fitzwater, Adrienne Harris, Linda Marcetti, Pat Cracco, and Anne Phillips of the Brooks/Cole staff for their assistance and supervision during the editing and production steps.

Norman W. Heimstra
Vernon S. Ellingstad

Contents

1

Introduction

The Science of Psychology

If you were asked to visualize the activity in which a psychologist is most likely to be engaged, in all likelihood you would imagine a man in a situation involving a couch and a handful of cards containing an assortment of inkblots or strange pictures. You might see him giving advice to persons with emotional disorders or administering IQ tests; or, if you are a reader of cartoons, the image of a bearded individual in a white coat staring intently at a rat in a maze might appear. Perhaps some of you who watch crime drama on television would visualize the psychologist on a witness stand fielding questions thrown at him by an astute attorney. These are the activities that most people associate with psychology; however, while some psychologists do these things, others are involved in pursuits that might seem quite surprising to those unfamiliar with the diverse subjects that psychology studies.

What is psychology? Psychology is chiefly concerned with human behavior. The term *behavior* is used to mean much more than just the observable physical reactions of people. It includes mental reactions or responses as well as physical reactions. It also includes behavior that we might consider odd or abnormal. In attempting to better understand human behavior, psychologists are often concerned with the behavior of subhuman animals. Perhaps it would be best to define psychology as the scientific study of behavior; however, to most psychologists, the *ultimate* aim of psy-

chology is understanding why people behave as they do and not why
a rat or a monkey behaves in a certain fashion. Consequently, we
will consider psychology as the science of human behavior.

Psychology and Other Sciences

We have referred to psychology as a science, and, if we consider science as being dynamic and as encompassing a method and a
body of organized and verifiable knowledge, then psychology certainly meets this criterion. Let us now consider how psychology
relates to the other sciences.

As new discoveries are continually being made, it becomes
more and more apparent that the divisions of knowledge into areas
such as physics, chemistry, and biology are only divisions of convenience. There is a basic unity in the knowledge that has been
gained over the centuries, and a division of this knowledge into
subject matter areas implies that this unity does not exist. Possibly
one of the most promising trends in science today is the tendency
toward integration and synthesis of knowledge, as reflected in the
development of interdisciplinary fields such as biophysics, bio-
chemistry, psychopharmacology, and psychophysiology. While it
will be necessary to talk about scientific knowledge in terms of the
traditional fields when we examine the relationship of psychology to
other sciences, it should be kept in mind that these various fields
are intimately interrelated.

In attempting to show the relationship of one scientific
discipline to others, the tendency is to construct a type of "hierarchy
of levels," with the various sciences placed at different points on
the hierarchy. Generally, in a hierarchy of this type, psychology is
placed somewhere near the center, with biological sciences below
and social sciences above. The "below" and "above" in this case
does not, of course, imply any type of status rating; rather, it is
based on a concept of *unidirectional dependency.* In order to illustrate this concept, let us consider a typical hierarchy (see Figure
1–1). Unidirectional dependency implies that, at least theoretically,
each discipline could exist without the disciplines above it but could
not exist without the disciplines below it. While there are flaws in
this reasoning, the hierarchy also has some merits. For example, the
disciplines listed above psychology in the hierarchy are concerned
with people and their psychological behavior. Psychology, on the
other hand, is dependent upon physiology, since the physiological
makeup of the individual is an important determining factor of be-

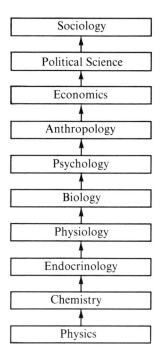

Figure 1–1. Hierarchy of various sciences showing unidirectional dependency. In this type hierarchy, it is implied that a given discipline could exist without those above it but not without those below.

havior. Similarly, physiology is dependent upon chemical reactions, and chemistry in turn is dependent upon physics in that it is concerned with atoms and molecules. It should be kept in mind, however, that in many cases the processes going on at one level of the hierarchy cannot be completely understood unless something is known about the processes taking place at a higher level.

Modern psychology consists of a number of subfields. In an interesting modification of the unidirectional dependency concept, Royce (1957) attempted to show the relationships among various subfields of psychology and closely related fields (Figure 1–2). Note that instead of a vertical hierarchy, Royce utilizes a horizontal arrangement with the unidirectional dependency running from left to right. This scheme implies that philosophy is the "beginning of all science" and that all fields are dependent on philosophy. Further, in this scheme the field of mathematics is shown to underlie all the other scientific fields of knowledge.

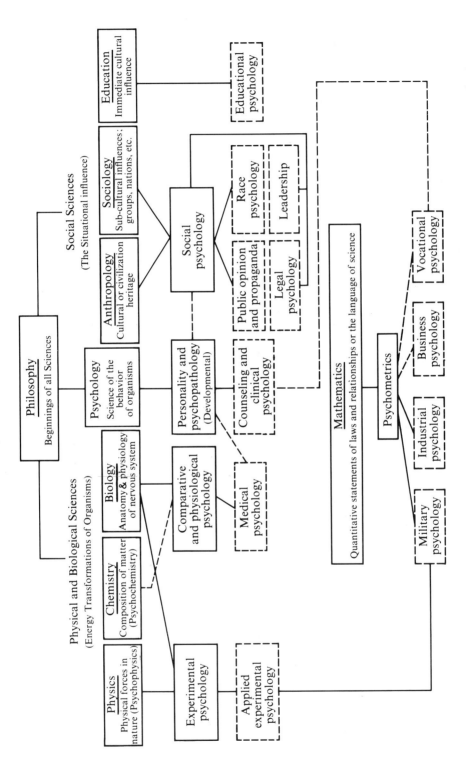

Figure 1-2. Schematic of major fields of modern psychology and other areas of science. Solid rectangles denote basic areas of psychology while broken rectangles denote applied areas. From Joseph R. Royce, Psychology in mid-twentieth century. *American Scientist*, Jan. 1957, Vol. 45, No. 1, pp. 57–73. Reprinted by permission of the author and the publisher.

The influences of various scientific disciplines on the several subfields of psychology can be traced by means of the scheme presented in Figure 1–2. The solid connecting lines represent major influences, while the broken connecting lines denote less important influences. Thus, we see that in the case of comparative and physiological psychology, biology is the major influencing discipline. You will also note that this area of psychology is influenced by chemistry but not to the same degree as by biology. In turn, comparative and physiological psychology exert a primary influence on medical psychology, which is also influenced, to a lesser extent, by the area of personality and psychopathology. The relationships among the other scientific fields and the various subfields of psychology can be traced in a similar manner. Note that the "basic" fields of psychology are designated by means of the solid line blocks, while the "applied" fields are represented by broken line blocks.

Unfortunately, a schematic arrangement such as that shown in Figure 1–2 tends to give the impression that there are clear lines separating the sciences in question. In actual fact, however, it is not possible to clearly divide physics from chemistry, psychology from anthropology, anthropology from sociology, and so forth. In many instances, several of the sciences are concerned with the same subject matter. For example, while a distinction is made on the schematic between psychology and anthropology, both are interested in human behavior. The primary difference is that psychology is usually interested in the individual, while anthropology is generally concerned with cultural and physical characteristics of groups. However, even this distinction becomes obscure when we attempt to differentiate between social psychology and anthropology. Similarly, when we consider psychology and physiology, it becomes apparent that no clear line can be drawn between the two fields. In the final analysis, much of physiology is concerned either directly or indirectly with behavior which, if we were to adhere rigidly to the unidirectional dependency concept, is in the realm of the psychologist. On the other hand, behavior is determined by the underlying physiological and neurological processes, which are properly placed in the field of physiology.

Psychology: A Problem-Solving Science

Much of the research conducted by psychologists is aimed at gaining knowledge that can be put to some practical use. Research of this type is often called applied research and is contrasted to a type of research known as basic research. Generally, if a project goal is to obtain understanding or gain knowledge as an end in itself without any concern about the usefulness of the knowledge gained, it is considered basic research. However, attempts to categorize research as either basic or applied often result in an artificial distinction. Obviously, one never knows when research conducted primarily to satisfy man's curiosity may also be applicable to solving some of man's problems.

Although there might have been a few nineteenth-century psychologists who were interested in some practical aspect of psychology, it was not until the first part of the twentieth century that American psychologists began to apply theory to practice in attempting to answer questions in such areas as tests and measurements, educational psychology, and individual differences. Of particular interest at this time were the psychological problems associated with work and the adaptation of man to various types of work tasks. Hugo Munsterburg, who is often considered the first applied psychologist, published his book *Psychology and Industrial Efficiency* in 1913. Shortly after that, the first journal concerned with the applications of psychology began publication. The *Journal of Applied Psychology* is still published today along with several other journals dealing with applied research. While these journals are primarily concerned with psychology in relation to the technological society surrounding man, there are many others dealing with the other areas of applied psychology such as clinical and counseling psychology. Much of what is written in these journals deals with the problems of modern man and solutions to these problems. It is safe to say that the life of man today is more and more influenced by the science of psychology.

The extent of the applied areas of psychology is shown in Figure 1–2, in which an attempt is made to differentiate between the "pure" and "applied" areas of psychology. Note on this figure that there are considerably fewer "pure" areas than "applied" areas. While this schematic arrangement is arbitrary at best, it does serve to illustrate the pervasive applications of psychology today. It would be interesting to compare this schematic with one prepared 40 or 50 years ago when the applications of psychology were much more restricted. Interest in applying the knowledge that has been obtained in this field has grown—perhaps even faster than the growth of the knowledge itself.

Figure 1–2 shows that five areas of psychology are considered basic, or pure fields: social psychology, personality and psychopathology, comparative and physiological psychology, experimental psychology, and psychometrics. While some psychologists might argue with this breakdown, it provides us with a framework within which we can discuss some of the fields of psychology and their relationships with each other and with other sciences. We will be particularly interested in the practical applications that have developed from these "pure" fields.

Social Psychology

It has already been stated that the basic unit for psychological study is the individual. However, we all belong to groups of one kind or another and our behavior, to a large degree, may depend upon our group affiliations. Social psychology is concerned with the behavior of an individual as part of a group. In recent years a considerable amount of laboratory research dealing with the effects of social variables on various types of behavior has been conducted. While much of this research would be classed as basic, social psychology also has its applied side. As a matter of fact, it may be that the practical aspects of social psychological research will eventually have more impact than any of the other areas of psychology. If you will refer again to Figure 1–2, you can see that there are several applied areas directly influenced by social psychology: race psychology, public opinion and propaganda, leadership psychology, and legal psychology. Each of these areas is of particular importance in today's society.

For example, we are all aware of the racial problems confronting our society. Social psychologists are actively seeking solutions to many of these problems. Research dealing with the underlying causes of prejudice, its development, and its characteristics may eventually help to ease the racial tensions. Government and private agencies have become acquainted with the findings of social psychologists in the area of race psychology and use these findings to develop tactics for reducing intergroup conflict. Similarly, findings of social psychologists who specialize in public opinion polling and attitude measuring are used more and more by the government and by private business as a basis for many important decisions. In some cases, surveys are conducted to determine the attitudes of various groups toward governmental policies, toward other groups, or, for that matter, toward almost anything. Often social psychologists are concerned not only with determining these attitudes but also with changing or modifying them. In this case, the social psychologist might become a "propagandist" in his efforts to bring about these changes. Other social psychologists are involved in studies aimed at gaining a better understanding of leadership behavior. We know that leaders are not "born leaders" but we still do not know a great deal about what characteristics of an individual make him a leader. The military is particularly interested in studies dealing with leadership behavior, but private business and other government agencies are also concerned. While the area of legal psychology is still quite new, social psychologists are working on problems of criminal behavior and how best to handle the criminal. Many city and state agencies employ psychologists to help them combat crime and delinquency.

In recent years some social psychologists have become involved in an area that could have considerable "payoff." We know very little about "aggressive behavior." Efforts are now being directed at determining the causes of aggression and how best to control this form of behavior. Eventually, a better understanding of aggression should help reduce many forms of violence and, hopefully, shed some light on how to control man's tendency toward war.

Personality and Psychopathology

Studies dealing with personality and psychopathology include research of the normal and abnormal personality from birth until death. Thus, this field includes research that is often listed under the heading of "developmental psychology." Psychologists interested in personality and psychopathology represent nearly one half of the psychologists in the United States. In a survey conducted by Lockman (1964), it was found that 37% of the psychologists sampled listed themselves as clinical psychologists, while 11% considered themselves counseling psychologists. As you can see from Figure 1–2, counseling and clinical psychology is the applied area most influenced by the basic personality and psychopathology field.

Clinical psychologists are often confused with psychiatrists. While they may perform similar functions, there are basic differences. First, the clinical psychologist is trained in psychology and, typically, has a Ph.D. in psychology. The psychiatrist is trained in medicine and has an M.D. degree with added training in the diagnosis and treatment of abnormal behavior. Both are capable of the diagnosis of deviant behavior and both are capable of the treatment of deviant behavior, although the clinical psychologist cannot use drugs, shock therapy, or other forms of medical treatment. Possibly the primary difference between the two is that the clinical psychologist is *trained* to conduct research in the area of personality and psychopathology, whereas few psychiatrists have received this type of training.

It would be difficult to present a "job description" for the clinical psychologist since what he does will depend to a considerable extent on the setting in which he is located. Some clinical psychologists spend most of their time administrating research programs, clinics, or hospital wards. Others are involved in the administration, scoring, and interpretation of a wide range of psychological tests. Some may be primarily involved in psychotherapy, while still others may be involved in all of the above. However, the majority of clinical psychologists are, in one way or another, concerned with the diagnosis and treatment of people with "problems."

In general, the counseling psychologist is concerned with individuals who have problems of a less serious nature than those handled by the clinical psychologist. As the name implies, the counseling psychologist "counsels," giving advice ranging from emotional or personal problems to vocational and academic problems. Again, what a counseling psychologist does is largely dependent upon the setting in which he works. Counseling psychologists can be found in private practice, schools, universities, industries, and many other settings.

Psychometrics

Note in Figure 1–2 that the field of psychometrics has a primary influence on industrial and military psychology and also influences several other areas. In a sense, this conclusion is misleading since psychometrics, if we use the term broadly, influences all fields of psychology. Used in a restricted fashion, the field of psychometrics is considered to be involved with the development of tests for measuring human abilities. From this point of view, obviously it would have considerable influence on military and industrial psychology where there is a great deal of interest in the measurement of abilities. However, from a broader point of view we can consider the field of psychometrics as dealing with "measurement" and, of course, this is important in all areas of psychology.

Comparative and Physiological Psychology

Comparative psychology is concerned with describing and understanding the behavior of all species of animals, but for the most part, it has dealt with two sources of data—the white rat and the college sophomore. While some interesting comparisons can be made between the two, the aim of the comparative psychologist is to compare the behavior of one species with that of many others and, hopefully, to arrive at some conclusions about underlying laws governing behavior.

The physiological psychologist deals with the physiological basis of behavior. Consequently, he is particularly interested in the nervous system, although he is also concerned with all internal mechanisms that determine behavior. Much of our knowledge about brain mechanism and behavior has been gained through the research efforts of the physiological psychologists.

The practical applications of comparative and physiological psychology are not so easy to specify as those of some of the other fields. Medical psychology has probably benefited most from the research in these areas. For example, physiological psychologists are concerned with the effects of various types of drugs on behavior. Also, research on the nervous system and its relationship to behavior has contributed a great deal to medical psychology. Studies on the possible physiological basis of mental deficiency and mental illness are also being pursued by physiological psychologists.

Experimental Psychology

It should be pointed out that when we label a field of psychology as "experimental" it is actually a misnomer. Experimental psychology is a method, or approach, rather than a field. However, popular usage of the term has, in a sense, defined what subject areas are involved in the field of "experimental psychology." Thus, the experimental psychologist is usually thought to be interested in basic research in the areas of sensation and perception, learning and memory, and motivation, as well as other areas. He studies these subjects by using the *experimental method*, which will be discussed in detail later in this chapter. This method, however, is not restricted to experimental psychologists. The experimental method is used by comparative and physiological psychologists, by clinical psychologists, and by psychologists in all of the various fields.

There has been a vast amount of basic laboratory research in experimental psychology, and many of the findings have had practical applications. If you refer to Figure 1–2 you will see that experimental psychology has had a direct influence on an area labeled "applied experimental psychology." In recent years there has been a tendency to replace this term and to call this area either *human factors psychology* or *human factors engineering.* While a relatively small percentage of today's psychologists are involved in human factors, it is likely that this field will go through the same expansion that occurred in clinical psychology a few years ago. In many respects this area of psychology best represents the practical application of psychological data and principles to solving problems that confront all of us in our everyday living. Consequently, we will consider the field of human factors psychology in some detail in order to further illustrate the point that psychology is, indeed, a problem-solving science.

Human Factors Psychology

Usually the term *human factors psychology,* or *human factors engineering,* is used to refer to a discipline concerned with improving the performance of men in operating and maintaining machines. In the complex technological age in which modern man exists, man-machine relationships are of great importance in nearly every phase of everyday life and, consequently, improving these relationships becomes increasingly important. However, along with the tremendous increase in the number of machines that man must deal with and, in the complexity of these machines, problems have arisen that are directly related to the machine orientation of our society. An obvious example is our transportation system. Human factors specialists are being called upon to help solve some of the problems of mass transportation as well as other problems that have developed because of the machine age in which we live. Human factors are also involved, however, in mass housing, in the design and administration of hospitals, in educational systems, in automation, and in many other areas. Thus, human factors psychology is concerned with problems other than just those associated with machines, although machines may be responsible, in part, for the problems. Consequently, human factors psychology may better be defined as a professional discipline concerned with man-machine relationships as well as other types of man-environment relationships.

Historically, people have been concerned with human factors since they first began to use tools and implements. Although it is difficult to specify when it became a recognizable specialty, it is the direct descendant of the two major disciplines of psychology and industrial engineering. While industrial engineers and psychologists had for many years been concerned with man's capacity to work and the manner in which his work was influenced by his tools and machines, man was viewed essentially as a source of mechanical power.

However, as the machines became more complex, this view changed. The importance of man as a source of power in the man-machine relationship decreased, and demands on his sensory, perceptual, judgmental, and decision-making capabilities rapidly increased. It quickly became apparent that each of these capabilities has to be considered in the design of equipment. In other words, "human factors" assumed considerable significance. While there was some realization before World War II that these human factors problems existed, the tremendous increases in technological complexity during the war made it apparent that the common-sense approach to solving these problems was not adequate. Consequently, a new group of experts, including a significant segment of the psychological profession, as well as physiologists, anthropologists, and physicians, turned their attention to integrating man into the new and complex machine systems that were developed as part of the war effort. While some engineers were involved, this new group of experts was composed primarily of behavioral scientists. It was largely through the efforts of these men during World War II that human factors psychology emerged as a special discipline.

Obviously, if we compare the complexity of the machine systems that exist today with those existing during World War II, it is immediately apparent that there is even more need today for paying attention to the human factors in these systems. Today, the interest in individual equipment components with individual operators is generally no longer the primary concern of the human factors specialist. Rather, he must think in terms of the problems generated when large numbers of men and *groups* of machines must work together and interact to form an integrated system. This concept of man-machine systems has brought about new techniques and approaches in human factors activity. One of these approaches involves *systems analysis*, which is useful in understanding the often complex interactions between man and machines and man and his environment. The intent of this textbook is to show how this procedure can be used effectively in understanding man and the way he behaves.

Research Methods in Psychology

Psychology, as a science, attempts to explain and to predict a wide variety of phenomena involving the behavior of human, and sometimes subhuman, organisms. The accomplishment of this objective involves a number of more or less discrete stages which, when taken together, can be viewed as a model for any psychological investigation.

> *Stage 1:* The first stage in this model is the systematic observation of behavior. It is assumed that definite rules govern the manner in which behavior is observed.
>
> *Stage 2:* The second step in the process of psychological research is the quantification of observations according to a particular scale of measurement—the measurement of behavior.
>
> *Stage 3:* When observations of behavior have been made and quantified, the psychologist systematically organizes and examines the data, sometimes through the application of statistical techniques. The purpose of examination is to infer the causes and characteristics of behavior in order to come up with an explanation.
>
> *Stage 4:* The fourth step in the research process is the development of ways to predict or to control the behaviors we have studied.
>
> *Stage 5:* The final stage of our model of psychological research links stages 4 and 1. This step in the process is concerned with verification of our predictions and behavioral control techniques by observing more behavior. We can thus revise and improve our predictions of, and controls over, behavior and behaving organisms.

In this chapter we will be concerned with the first stage in the model of a psychological investigation. The other stages within the model are treated in detail in Chapter 15.

Selection of the Behavior to Observe

Each step in the conduct of a psychological investigation involves a number of decisions that are related to the methodological approach and the objectives of that particular study. The first such decision concerns the type(s) of behavior that we will investigate. Behavior can be defined as any activity of an organism, or of systems within an organism, that is observable either directly or with the aid of instruments. Thus, both gross forms of activity, such as lifting weights, and more subtle types of activity, such as the heart beat or the electrical changes within the brain of man, can be considered behavior. The objectives of a given investigation will determine the type(s) of behavior to be observed, and, conversely, the behaviors selected for observation will set limits on the objectives of the study. It is extremely important, therefore, that appropriate behaviors be selected for study.

Instruments of Observation

A decision that closely follows the selection of the types of behavior to be observed concerns the selection of a tool for observing the selected behavior. The experimenter may use tools as simple as a check list or he may use very elaborate and costly equipment. While important research has been, and continues to be, conducted

Figure 1-3. An interior view of the Ford Motor Company's Highway Systems Research (HSR) Car, showing some of the specialized instrumentation designed to monitor and record driver performance measures. The steering wheel of the vehicle is gold plated and serves as a set of recording electrodes to measure the driver's heart rate or GSR. The controls for these physiological measures are located below the dash in the center of the vehicle. The bank of counters and controls mounted in the dash to the right of the vehicle is associated with sensors designed to measure and record a large number of performance variables such as large and small steering movements, vehicular speed, accelerator pedal control, etc. Photo courtesy of Traffic Safety and Highway Improvement Department, Ford Motor Company. Reprinted by permission.

with modest investments of equipment, more and more psychological research requires substantial amounts of equipment. Often, the equipment permits much more accurate and reliable measures of behavior. Sometimes the equipment is designed to be quite versatile and can be used for measuring many different kinds of behavior under a variety of conditions.

In other cases, elaborate equipment is designed to measure a specific kind of behavior. Figures 1–3 and 1–4 show a complicated system of instrumentation that was designed to aid in the observa-

Figure 1–4. A view of the recording system of the HSR Car. This system is housed in the trunk of the vehicle and consists of the two primary units shown in the center of the illustration. The unit on the left is an electronic interface which accepts data from a variety of sensors attached to the steering wheel, accelerator control, and speedometer and converts and organizes these data into a form suitable for recording. The unit on the right is a magnetic tape recorder which is used to record the data from the interface at a high rate of speed. The entire record of a driver's performance during even an extended test session is permanently recorded on magnetic tape. This tape is later "read" by a computer which also accomplishes data analysis. Photo courtesy of Traffic Safety and Highway Improvement Department, Ford Motor Company. Reprinted by permission.

tions of the behaviors characteristic of the driver of a motor vehicle. This device, the Highway Systems Research Car, is designed to record, automatically, a large number of overt driver responses as well as physiological responses of the driver.

The Organization of Behavioral Observations

Of primary importance to psychological research is the manner in which behavior is observed. It is extremely important that the rules governing the way behavior is observed be clearly stated and that the particular set of rules chosen for a given study be appropriate to the questions the investigator seeks to answer. There are four primary methods of observing behavior, or sets of rules governing observations. These methods are *naturalistic observation,* the *case study method, testing,* and the *experimental method.* Each method is suited to particular types of research problems and each has an important role in psychological research.

Naturalistic Observation

Naturalistic observation of behavior is particularly suited to studies seeking to thoroughly describe various types of behavior occurring in a natural setting. If we were interested in the social behavior of children at play, for instance, we would probably use this research methodology. In the application of this technique, the experimenter observes behaving organisms without intruding into the activity in which they are engaged. In some cases, he simply watches organisms behave in a natural environment, through a one-way mirror for instance, and records the types of behaviors which occur. This technique does not, however, rule out the use of sophisticated instruments to quantify the observations. The time and motion studies conducted in industrial plants use the technique of naturalistic observation. The industrial engineer conducting such a study observes a worker operating a particular piece of equipment and makes detailed observations of the time spent during each cycle of a work operation, as well as other behaviors he may engage in. It is similarly possible to equip the worker's machine with sensors that will record worker responses as he performs his routine tasks. All of these diverse types of behavioral observations fall into the category of naturalistic observation because the observation of behavior does not intrude upon the behavior itself and because the behavior is occurring in the natural setting.

Case Study Method

The case study method is perhaps more commonly used in sociology than in psychology, although it is sometimes used in clinical psychology. The case history technique consists of gaining as much information about an individual as possible. In a sense, a case history of an individual is a detailed biography of that individual's behavior. Possibly the most useful instrument of observation for the case study method is the interview. However, other observational techniques can also be useful. The chief limitation of the case study method lies in the fact that much of the behavior about which observations are made has occurred in the past and must be recalled. This limitation thus concerns the quantification of observations and the reliability with which these observations are made.

Testing

The method of testing seeks to measure particular responses to standard stimulus conditions. In a testing situation the organism is presented with a stimulus to which a limited range of responses is possible, and his choice of responses is recorded. The chief advantage to this method of collecting data is in the assessment of similarities and/or differences between large numbers of people, or lower organisms, to identical stimuli.

The Experimental Method

The experimental method of organizing our observations of behavior has at its center the concept of *experimental control*. In studies using this method the situation in which the behavior of interest occurs is under the control of the experimenter. He is free to manipulate or to hold constant various aspects of the situation or antecedents of the behavior in order to determine the effects of these aspects or antecedents on the occurrence and quality of the behavior that is observed. To understand the process of experimental control we must define three key terms related to the process: *dependent variable, independent variable,* and *nuisance variable.* An investigation employing the experimental method will assess the effect of independent variables, which are manipulated, on dependent variables, which are measured, while holding constant or eliminating the effects of nuisance variables.

Dependent Variables.   The dependent variable in an experiment is some quantitative or qualitative index of the behavior we are trying to explain or to predict. Usually an experimenter will pick one aspect of behavior to consider at a time. Thus, in a study of the ability of humans to detect weak and infrequent signals, commonly called a vigilance task, the most logical dependent variable may be the number of missed signals, although we could also record the number of false responses (responses when no signal was present), the time taken to respond, the force of the response, and several other potential responses. Although there are techniques that allow an experimenter to handle, simultaneously, more than one dependent variable, these techniques require rather sophisticated statistical techniques, and the usual procedure is to pick a single dependent variable which represents most closely the particular behavior in which we are interested.

Independent Variables.   The independent variables in a psychological investigation are those aspects of the behavioral situation whose effects on the dependent variable we are trying to assess. A given experiment may attempt to assess the effects of several independent variables on a single dependent variable. For example, in our vigilance study we may be interested in the effects of signal intensity and signal frequency on the number of missed signals. These variables, signal intensity and frequency, are the independent variables in our investigation. To determine their effect upon the dependent variable, the independent variables are systematically varied, and observations of the dependent variable are taken at each value of the independent variables. In our experiment, we might select two levels of signal intensity and two levels of signal frequency. Thus, if the signal is a visual one, the levels of the independent variable, intensity, might be called bright and dim, and for the second independent variable the rates of signal presentation might be called fast and slow. Ordinarily the measurement of the dependent variable will be made under each combination of independent variables. Table 1–1 gives the four possible combinations of independent variables for our example. By organizing our experiment in this manner, we can assess the effects of both independent variables on the number of missed signals, since both variables are under the direct control of the experimenter and both are systematically manipulated.

Nuisance Variables.   In addition to dependent and independent variables, there are potentially a large number of aspects of the experimental situation that may affect the dependent variable. In our example, for instance, the noise level in the experimental room may

Table 1–1. What effect does signal intensity and signal frequency (independent variables) have on signal detection (dependent variable)? With two levels of signal intensity (dim and bright) and two levels of signal frequency (fast and slow), signal detection could be studied under four conditions. The number of correct detections (dependent variable) can be determined with dim signals presented slowly, with bright signals presented slowly, and with dim or bright signals presented rapidly.

		Independent variable I (*Signal intensity*)	
		Dim	*Bright*
Independent variable II (*Signal frequency*)	Slow	Condition 1 Dim-Slow	Condition 2 Bright-Slow
	Fast	Condition 3 Dim-Fast	Condition 4 Bright-Fast

have an effect on the subject's performance. If the situation were such that the room was noisy during the conditions in which the slow signal rate was used and quiet during conditions in which the fast rate was in effect, it would not be possible to determine whether differences in performance were due to differences in signal rate or differences in noise level. To avoid this situation, nuisance variables —that is, variables whose effects we are not interested in—are either eliminated from the experimental situation or are held constant over all experimental conditions. Thus, we could test the subjects in a soundproof room to eliminate the noise problem or, if no such room is available, we could make sure that the noise level is the same for all experimental conditions.

In practice, the four methods of organizing observations of behavior are not mutually exclusive. For example, for a particular study, we may wish to combine the testing method with the experimental method. The four methods are complementary ways in which to order psychological research. In subsequent chapters we will explore other problems in the process of organized behavioral observation.

Man as a System

In recent years the word *system* has become more and more common in the technical journals of psychology and engineering as

well as in the professional journals of many other fields. One would
assume that a word that is common not only in the technical journals but also in everyday conversation would not be difficult to define; however, actually specifying what is meant by a system is not
so simple.

What Is a System?

Pause for a moment and think of the many ways in which we
use the word *system*. We speak of the solar system and of the heating
system in our homes, of social systems, of biological systems, and
of systems for winning at poker or betting on the horses. At first
glance, these systems seem to have very little in common; indeed, if
only the objects, facts, or principles making up the system are
considered, then they may not have much in common. The common-
ality, however, is found in the *relationship* between the objects, facts,
or principles *within* any given system. Thus, at a molar level, a system may be thought of as a set of objects, things, facts, and so forth,
which are related and which, together, form a unity or a whole. In
other words, a whole that functions as a whole because of the interdependence of its parts is called a *system*. We also tend to think of
a system as having some purpose or objective. The important factor
is the *interaction* or relationship between the elements within a system and how these relationships contribute to the objectives or
purposes of the system.

In the study of any system, a key question is *how* the various
elements interact and contribute to the objectives of the system.
One of the primary purposes of a *systems analysis* is to answer this
question. Engineers, in dealing with a complicated piece of machinery or a number of pieces of equipment working together, have
been required to utilize a systems analysis even though they have not
always called their approach by that name. The systems approach
became more formalized when it was recognized that the human
element must also be considered and its interactions with the other
components in a system recognized. By definition, there are many
kinds of systems; however, to further illustrate the systems concept
and systems analysis, we will be primarily concerned with *man-
machine systems*.

Man-Machine Systems

There are a number of definitions of man-machine systems.
However, for our purposes, we will consider a man-machine system

to consist of several elements or components—human and machine —that are designed to work together and to interact in order to achieve a specified goal. These systems can vary from extremely elaborate arrangements of men and machines to relatively simple arrangements. For example, if we consider only systems involved in transportation, the range of complexity becomes apparent. At one end of the range we have the very complicated and elaborate man-machine system used to transport astronauts from the earth to the moon and back. At various levels of complexity we have other transportation systems, such as railroads, aircraft, and automobiles. At a simpler level we have the bicycles, which, while simple in comparison to the other systems, can still be classified as a man-machine system, since the human and machine components work together to achieve a goal.

While most of the man-machine systems that psychologists and engineers are concerned with are much more elaborate than a man-bicycle system, the general pattern or scheme of a "typical" man-machine system can be rather simply illustrated (Figure 1–5). Although the figure is a simplified representation, it does involve the human and equipment, or machine, components. Also, you will note that there is an input to the system and an output. In this case, the output represents the aim or purpose of the system, which, as you will recall, is considered an essential aspect of a man-machine system.

An Example of a Systems Analysis

Basically, then, a man-machine system involves an input, an interaction between man and equipment components, and an output. Further, a system may be made up of a number of subsystems which contribute to the functioning and output of the whole. Our approach to understanding man's behavior is to view man as a system operating within larger systems and consisting of a number of subsystems that have inputs and outputs and that, in one way or another, contribute to the output of the system. This output we commonly call behavior. As we have suggested, a *systems analysis* of man enables us to understand the interactions of the various human subsystems, as well as their functions and their contributions to the output (behavior). To illustrate and clarify this procedure, we will consider in some detail an example of a systems analysis. We will utilize a system, in this case a man-machine system, with which virtually everyone is familiar—the automobile and a driver. In studying the various steps in this analysis, one should keep in mind that in the fol-

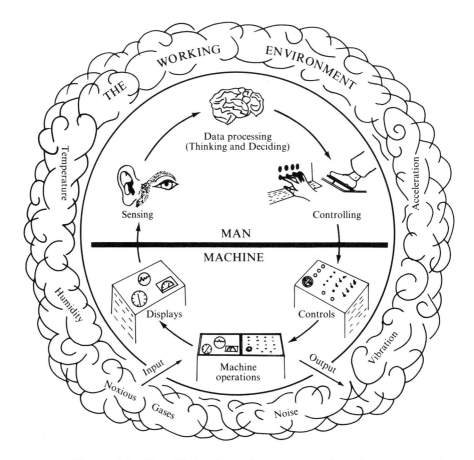

Figure 1–5. Simplified schematic representation of a man-machine system. From A. Chapanis, *Man-Machine Engineering.* Copyright © 1965 by Wadsworth Publishing Company. Reprinted by permission of the publisher, Brooks/Cole Publishing Company, Monterey, California.

lowing chapters a similar procedure will be involved as we attempt to understand man as a system.

The first step in any systems analysis is to determine what goal the system should be designed to accomplish. The goal of the private vehicle transportation system is to transport an individual from one geographic point to another, safely and efficiently. The accomplishment of this goal is the result of the interaction of various system components, or elements, in a prescribed manner. The purpose of a systems analysis is to identify the elements of the system and to determine the manner in which they interact.

Levels of Complexity

It was noted above that many complex systems often include a number of smaller systems called subsystems. When this is the case, it is possible to progress with a systems analysis on several levels of complexity. The first level may treat several relatively complex subsystems as elements and examine the nature of their interrelations. Subsequent levels of analysis might then break these units down into smaller and less complex sub-subsystems or elements.

System Links

It is common practice in systems analysis to graphically depict elements of a system and to indicate the interrelations of these elements with connecting lines. These lines, or links, between elements or subsystems may be either of two basic types. The links between elements may be in the form of information that is transmitted from one element to another (*feedback links*) or in the form of control activities by which one system element may directly influence the status of another element (*control links*).

The Private Vehicle Transportation System

For purposes of illustration we will examine the private vehicle transportation system at a relatively simple level of analysis. Figure 1–6 illustrates the interactions among the elements of three subsystems within the private vehicle transportation system. The first subsystem, *the driver*, consists of three elements or, more correctly, sub-subsystems, labeled *information reception, response processes*, and *knowledge-attitude-skill*. It is readily apparent that each of these elements is, in itself, a relatively complex system that could be further broken down. The second subsystem, *the vehicle*, is comprised of *vehicular controls, vehicular displays*, and *vehicle response* sub-subsystems. The final subsystem, the *highway environment*, consists of two sub-subsystems that include both *traffic characteristics* and *roadway conditions*.

Examination of Figure 1–6 reveals that links between system elements (sub-subsystems, in this case) occur both within a given subsystem and between elements of different subsystems. Thus, the destination of all feedback links in this figure (dashed lines) is the

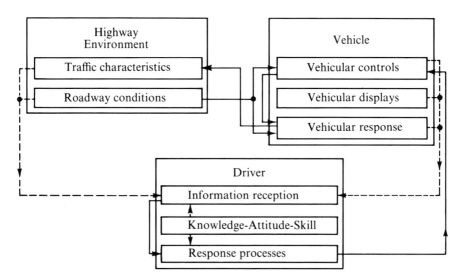

Figure 1–6. Schematic of subsystems in the private vehicle transportation system showing interactions between the subsystems.

information reception sub-subsystem within the driver subsystem. This sub-subsystem is seen to receive information from the other two elements of the driver subsystem, as well as from the elements of each of the other two subsystems. Further examination of this figure reveals that both the highway environment and the response-processes component of the driver subsystem exert control influences (solid lines) over the vehicle, while the vehicular response component in turn exerts some degree of control over the traffic characteristics component of the highway environment.

Advantages of Systems Analysis

It should be apparent from the analysis of the private vehicle transportation system that a systems analysis approach, unlike other available methods, permits us to examine a complicated system and arrive at a better understanding of how the various components making up the system interact and contribute to the final output.

In considering man as a system, we will be using a similar approach. We will see that man can be viewed as a system made up of a number of interacting subsystems, involving both feedback and control links that contribute to the output we call behavior. In our analysis of man we will be asking the same questions about this system as were asked about the transportation system: What does the system do, and how does it do it?

As pointed out by Anatol Rapoport (1968), "the system approach to the study of man can be appreciated as an effort to restore meaning (in terms of intuitively grasped understanding of wholes) while adhering to the principles of *disciplined* generalizations and rigorous deduction. It is, in short, an attempt to make the study of man both scientific and meaningful" (xxii). Rapoport further points out that any organized system, living or nonliving, can be seen from three perspectives. One perspective involves the *structure* of the system, particularly the means by which it can receive, store, process, and withdraw information. Also of concern is the *functioning* of the system—that is, the manner in which, by means of processed and stored information, the system transforms sensory inputs to behavioral outputs. Finally, a system can be viewed in terms of the *evolution* of a systems type.

While the human system's structure and functioning discussed in this text are no different than those covered in most introductory psychology books, they are "tied together" in such a manner that the complete system—man—can be more clearly understood. We have earlier defined a system as a whole that functions as a whole because of the interdependence of its parts. The approach of this text is to classify and discuss these "parts" in such a fashion that their interactions and interdependence become apparent. With this approach, man's functions and structure can be considered in terms of dynamic relationships rather than in terms of isolated elements as is so often the case in books dealing with human behavior. Obviously, man is a dynamic organism, and explaining his behavior in this context will, hopefully, lead to a better understanding of the "whole."

Similarities between Systems

While man-machine systems will differ in complexity, components, and objectives, there are some similarities among the many types of systems. Rather than attempt to discuss these similarities in terms of components or objectives, it is more meaningful to consider the requirements that must be met by man-machine systems in order to ensure adequate performance. While requirements may vary according to the complexity of a system, the following are basic system requirements (Meister & Rabideau, 1965):

1. The system must have the capability of sensing all relevant stimuli originating from both external and internal sources.

2. The system must be such that it can select or filter the stimuli to which it should react.

3. In order to sense and discriminate stimuli, the system

must be "programmed"—that is, it must have instructions, both for analyzing stimuli and directing activities. This implies both a short-term and a long-term memory.

4. The system must also know when to modify its operations, to change their direction, or to stop them completely. This requires that the system must be able to communicate rapidly among the various subsystems which are required to act in coordination.

5. The system must also be able to act effectively on its external and/or internal environment. In other words, it must be able to accomplish specified system goals.

Man, in functioning as a system, meets the requirements listed above by means of complex subsystems involved with sensing, filtering, programming, decision-making, and so on, all of which interact and result in an output. While the functions of these various subsystems will be considered in some detail in the next several chapters, we shall briefly discuss these requirements and how man, as a system, is designed to meet them.

System Requirements and Man

At a very simple level of analysis, man can be considered as a system that is capable of receiving an input, of processing this input, and then of making a response (output) based on the initial input. This basic system is illustrated in Figure 1–7. At this level we have incorporated most of the system requirements previously listed in several subsystems, one concerned with the function of sensing and the others concerned with data processing and output.

The first requirement of a system is that it have the capability of sensing all relevant stimuli (inputs) from sources within and external to the system. In man, the sensing function is accomplished

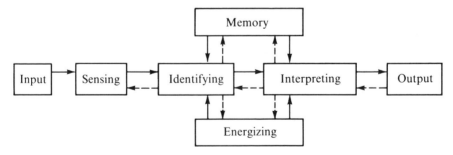

Figure 1–7. A model of the human system showing the various subsystems and their relationships. In subsequent chapters, each of the various subsystems will be considered in detail.

by a highly developed set of sensors, or receptors, that are sensitive to several types of physical energies. As we shall see later, human sensing is restricted to a relatively narrow range of these physical energies, which consist of electromagnetic radiation, mechanical energy, chemical energy, and thermal energy. Receptors, such as the eye and ear, essentially serve as interfaces between the various types of physical energy (stimuli) and the subsystem which transmits information about the stimuli to the brain.

In addition to the sensing subsystem, there are also subsystems labeled identifying, interpreting, memory, and energizing (see Figure 1–7), which perform the functions necessary for meeting all the other listed system requirements with the exception of the last (output). The basic element of these subsystems is the brain and spinal cord. When these subsystems are further analyzed, we shall see how stimuli are selected or filtered by processes that are referred to as *set* or *attention*, how discrimination (which involves the ability to sense a change or difference in some form of physical energy) takes place, and how *short-term* and *long-term memory* are involved. We will also consider how these types of memory are "programmed" by means of a process called *learning*. The process by which the system modifies its operations, changes their directions, or stops them completely is dependent on thinking. The final requirement, that the system must be able to act effectively on its external or internal environment, will be discussed in a chapter dealing with system output.

We have now defined psychology and discussed some of the problems that psychologists attempt to study. We have also considered how man can be viewed as a system and how his behavior can be explained within a systems analysis framework. When we consider the behavioral system of man, however, an important fact should be kept in mind. The science of psychology—that is, the study of behavior—did not just suddenly appear as a full-fledged science. It has a long history, and, in order to better understand why psychology exists as it does today, it is necessary to know something about the forces that have shaped it.

A Brief History of Psychology

The history of psychology began when man first started to observe and think about his own and others' behavior. While we can only speculate as to the nature of these observations and the conclusions drawn, we do know that for as long as man has kept written records he has been interested in human behavior. Generally, however, psychologists tend to think of the beginning of *modern* psychology as dating back to the establishment of the first psychological laboratory in Leipzig in 1879. Our discussion of the history of psychology largely concerns men and events since that date, but it is important to realize that long before 1879 there were ideas and schools of thought that had a profound influence on psychology. For example, the writings of a number of philosophers helped shape and influence the development of psychology as we know it today.

Philosophical and Scientific Influences

Several philosophers and philosophical schools of thought stand out as being particularly important in the history of psychology. The philosophical influences on modern psychology are generally traced back to Descartes (1596–1650). Although there are several ideas of Descartes that are of particular interest to psychology, probably the most far-reaching of these is his view on the relationship between mind and body.

Descartes' reasoning led him to believe that there was a sharp division between the *mind*, which he thought of as the "thinking substance," and *matter*, which he regarded as "extended substance." To Descartes, the body was a machine to which the principles of physics could be applied. He believed that all of the actions of the body—movement, respiration, sensation, and so forth—could be explained according to mechanical principles. The mind (or soul), however, was thought to be completely different from the outer world of matter. Yet the mind, which Descartes felt took up no space and had neither motion nor physical qualities, had the power to direct or alter the mechanical courses of events. Thus, although mind and body were thought to be separate, it was also believed that they nevertheless interacted with each other. The nature of this interaction, and where it took place, Descartes found difficult to explain. He decided that the site of the interaction was the pineal gland, which is located at the base of the cerebrum of the brain. While today no one seriously considers the pineal gland as being a two-way gate between the body and mind, its function is still not clearly understood.

While controversy over Descartes' ideas of the mind-body problem existed for many years, eventually the view prevailed that mind and body should not have been separated in the first place. Even so, Descartes' writings about the mind-body problem as well as his mechanistic views on the actions of the human body had a strong influence on philosophical (and later psychological) thought.

Descartes, like many of the philosophers of his time, believed in the existence of *innate* ideas—ideas that are not derived from experience but, rather, are inherent in man's nature. The rejection of the notion of innate ideas is central to the thinking of another important philosopher in the history of psychology, John Locke (1632–1704). Locke is recognized as the founder of a school of thought, called *empiricism*, whose basic tenet was that ideas are not inborn or inherited but are products of learning or experience. It was Locke's rejection of innate ideas which, essentially, established a groundwork on which the science of psychology could be based. In his "Essay Concerning Human Understanding," in which he compared the infant's mind to a *tabula rasa* (blank tablet) upon which "experience writes," Locke established a tradition which has had a considerable influence on modern psychology. Other important empiricists were George Berkeley (1685–1753) and David Hume (1711–1776).

Closely related to the views of the empiricists were those of the *associationists*. Philosophers such as David Hartley (1705–1757), James Mill (1773–1836), and his son John Stuart Mill (1806–1873) were concerned not only with the question of where ideas come from—that is, are they innate, or based on experience?—but with other questions as well. Thus, they were concerned with how ideas are "associated" with each other, how meaningful "laws of association" could be formulated, and how ideas are compounded.

It has been suggested by several individuals interested in the history of psychology that the ideas of Charles Darwin (1809–1882) probably had more influence on modern psychology than any ideas before or since. While this view might be argued by some, there is little doubt that Darwin's writings have had a considerable effect on psychology as we know it today. What exactly were Darwin's contributions to psychology?

As Heidbreder (1933) points out, Darwin's *Origin of Species* called to the attention of the scientific world the possibility that man could be viewed "not as a special and favorite creation, not as a race set apart, not as an object of special concern in the universe, but merely as one of the many animal species involved in the course of natural events" (pp. 105–106). In other words, man could no longer be considered as having a unique status in the animal kingdom.

With this realization, it became apparent that it was not

enough to study man in and by himself. Rather, man must be thought of as a unit—that is, as a subsystem within a larger, external system—and, as such, must be considered in relation to the many forces that shape him. In this regard, the question of the value of mental activities in helping man adapt to his environment became more important than questions such as how ideas are associated or compounded. Much of the subject matter of psychology today deals, in one way or another, with adaptive capabilities of man.

Darwin's evolutionary theory also gave rise to several other developments in psychology which are still with us today. When he suggested that man inherited his body from animal ancestors, he also raised the question as to whether there is continuity of mind between animals and man. The comparison of the mental capacities of man and other animals is the primary concern of those psychologists working in the field of comparative psychology. Darwin's influence is also seen in another important field of psychology—the study of individual differences. Since man's mental inheritance was thought to have evolved through variation and differential survival, as did his physical inheritance, then individuals' mental abilities should differ as much as their physical characteristics. Out of this notion has grown the whole field of studying individual differences in mental capacities and of psychological assessment by means of mental tests. Indeed, the effect of Darwin's theory on the development of psychology has been tremendous.

While a great deal more time could be spent on the early philosophical and scientific influences on modern psychology, the most important developments in psychology have taken place within the last hundred years or so. As we shall see, during this period of time a number of individuals have contributed to our present understanding of the behavioral system of man.

The Behavioral System from a Historical Perspective

Look again at the behavioral system illustrated in Figure 1–7 and the various behavioral subsystems that are involved. Our understanding of the functions of each of these subsystems is based on the contributions of many individuals, including the philosophers that have already been mentioned. If we were to discuss all, or even most, of the people who have shaped our thinking about the behavioral system of man and who have studied the functioning of the various subsystems, the result would be a comprehensive history of psychology. We are not prepared to undertake such a formidable task. Rather, we will use a sampling technique and present what appear to be the most significant historical figures and developments in each area.

> *The Sensing*
> *and Identifying Subsystems*

When psychology emerged as a science, the subject matter of psychology was sensation and perception ("identifying," as we have labeled it on our illustration). However, a substantial foundation for this new science had already been set down by anatomists and physiologists who were conducting experiments in the areas of sensation, reflexes, nerve excitation and brain functions. These researchers paved the way for the "new" experimental psychology that began in Germany. Three men associated with this emergence are considered most responsible for the establishment of modern psychology—Gustav Theodor Fechner (1801–1887), Hermann von Helmholtz (1821–1894), and Wilhelm Wundt (1832–1920).

Fechner, who was trained as a physicist, is important in the history of psychology because he was the first to apply the experimental methods of physics and physiology to psychological problems. He originated and developed methods of measurement, now called *classical psychophysical methods*, that are still used with only slight modifications in today's psychological research. Helmholtz, who is recognized as one of the greatest scientists of the nineteenth century, was a physicist and physiologist who became interested in psychological research. Known for his work on measurement of the speed of nervous impulses and other physiological research, he also contributed greatly to the experimental psychology of sensation.

While Fechner and Helmholtz worked on psychological problems, Wilhelm Wundt is generally recognized as the first experimental psychologist. Before Wundt, there were physiologists, physicists, philosophers, and others with an interest in psychology, but Wundt defined the subject matter of the field, developed methodologies for studying the subject matter, and set up priorities for the problems to be attacked. He established what is often considered to be the first psychological laboratory in Leipzig, Germany, in 1879, and some of the most important men responsible for the development of modern psychology received their training in this laboratory.

One of Wundt's students, E. B. Titchener (1867–1927), transplanted Wundt's psychology to the United States and was important in a school of psychology known as *structuralism.* Structuralists were interested in analyzing consciousness into various elements— sensations, images, feelings—and determining how these elements were connected. Sensations, to Titchener and other structuralists, were one of three elements of mind (the other two being images and feelings), and he considered sensation to be "an elementary mental process" that had at least four attributes—quality, intensity, clarity, and duration. The important classes of sensation were those associated with the visual, auditory, olfactory, gustatory, cutaneous, and kinesthetic sensory systems. The structuralists, with their emphasis on describing the phenomena of sensation, made outstanding contributions to the area of sensory psychology.

There is, of course, much more to the history of the sensing subsystem than we have outlined above. For example, the school of *behaviorism,* which was founded by John Watson (1878–1958), contributed to the study of sensation. Although this school emphasized the study of behavior as revealed by experimental observation, there was also an interest in determining whether sensory processes could be studied by this method. Various methodologies developed by the behaviorists were found to be useful in studying the neurological correlates of sensory experience.

Most of the investigators who were concerned with sensory functions were also concerned with perception. Thus, Helmholtz, Wundt, Titchener, the empiricists, and the associationists (but not the behaviorists) were all interested in perception. Consequently, a detailed history of perception would include many of the names that were associated with sensory psychology. As you will see in Chapter 4, it is difficult to think of sensation and perception as two separate processes, and, for this reason, their histories are quite similar. However, we will limit our discussion of the history of perception to a school that was not particularly interested in sensation but probably exerted a greater influence on the evolution of modern perceptual psychology than any other group—the *Gestalt* school.

Gestalt psychology had its origin in Germany and began as a revolt against the then current trends toward analysis and synthesis in psychology. Thus, the Gestalt psychologists opposed the reductionistic notion that the mind was made up of elements that were bound by associations. Rather, they felt that experience involved more than the sum of these elements and that there were new emergent properties when the elements were combined. This is the basis for the often quoted Gestalt principle that *the whole is greater than the sum of the parts.* Perceptual experiences are not mere aggregations of sensation but, rather, are organized and meaningful wholes.

Much of the research of the Gestalt psychologists has dealt with how this kind of organization takes place.

In the area of perception, the Gestalt psychologists provided a number of valuable and original contributions. Of particular importance were their principles of the organization of perceptual fields, including the principle of figure and ground, which is fundamental in all perceptual experience, as well as the organizing principles of proximity, continuity, similarity, and closure (see Chapter 4).

While the Gestaltists were initially recognized for their contributions to perceptual psychology, they quickly extended their observations and theories into other areas of psychology such as learning, thinking, and problem solving. There have also been extensions of the Gestalt ideas into the fields of child psychology and social psychology.

The Memory Subsystem

When the memory subsystem is discussed later in the text, it will be pointed out that it involves at least three primary functions or processes: learning, remembering, and forgetting. While the more recent ideas in these areas are discussed in Chapters 5 and 6, we will be concerned here with two important historical figures in the field of learning and forgetting—Hermann Ebbinghaus and Edward Thorndike.

When Locke announced that the human mind at birth is a *tabula rasa* upon which experience writes, he opened the door for the development of a psychology of learning. Hume, Hartley, and other associationists opened the door even wider. The associationists set the stage for the study of learning. A German psychologist, Hermann Ebbinghaus (1850–1909) was the first to make use of this stage.

While Wundt and others pursued investigations into sensation and perception, Ebbinghaus concluded that the methods used by these investigators could be used in attacking the problems of "higher mental processes." Ebbinghaus was particularly interested in studying learning and memory, and his place in the history of psychology was assured by his work in this area. However, he was an active individual in many other areas and is also remembered for founding a new psychological journal, for experimenting on brightness and color, for developing an intelligence test, and for writing a textbook.

In his work on learning and memory, Ebbinghaus made use

of nonsense syllables which he constructed by combining consonants and vowels in such a way as to avoid creating meaningful words. He designed a number of experiments that involved memorizing lists of nonsense syllables under various conditions. In these studies, in which Ebbinghaus served as both subject and experimenter, he was primarily concerned with factors influencing learning and with conditions influencing retention. Much of the data gathered by Ebbinghaus still holds up today and will be discussed in Chapter 5.

The second individual who is very important in the history of learning psychology is Edward Thorndike (1874–1949). When we move from Ebbinghaus to Thorndike we are moving from Germany to the United States. We are also moving from verbal learning involving human subjects to various types of experiments involving animals. What is particularly important about Thorndike is that he offered theoretical explanations and interpretations of the results of his work on learning and forgetting. While we cannot discuss Thorndike's contributions in any detail, he is important in the area of learning for the various laws and principles of learning he developed and advocated. Perhaps it is not appropriate to talk about Thorndike's views of learning in a historical context since his theory is considered by many to be a *contemporary* theory of learning. His ideas are still very influential in the area of learning psychology.

Again, it must be emphasized that there are many other names that could be, and probably should be, mentioned in any history of learning. For example, the *functionalists*, who considered psychology as the study of man's methods of adjustment to his environment, placed great emphasis on learning as a key factor in adaptation. Advocates of this school of thought, such as Harvey Carr (1873–1954), wrote quite extensively on various topics dealing with learning. Similarly, the *behaviorists* actively worked in the area of learning, particularly conditioning. However, Ebbinghaus and Thorndike must be considered as two individuals in the history of learning who made the most significant contributions.

The Energizing Subsystem

The energizing, or motivational, subsystem will energize or activate behavior, it will direct behavior, and it will cause behavior to persist to a goal. Obviously, then, an understanding of motivation is central to an understanding of behavior, and ever since man began to speculate about human behavior, the question of motivation has arisen. However, ideas about motivation remained largely speculative until relatively recently when research on changing physiological states associated with such factors as hunger, thirst, and sex, on emotional states, on habits, sets, and attitudes, and on environmental influences has given us a better idea about motivational processes.

Historically, a significant milestone in the area of motivation is represented by the psychoanalytic system of Sigmund Freud (1856–1939). An important thesis of Freud's theory is that of unconscious motives, which arise from thinking which has been repressed—that is, relegated to unconscious thought because it is too painful for conscious thought. At this unconscious level motives tend to influence a person's behavior and perceptions. Just how these thoughts are repressed and how, through various therapeutic techniques, they are again brought into the conscious realm is discussed in Chapter 11.

Freud's views on unconscious motivation, with some modifications by other theorists in more recent years, still have a strong influence on psychological thought today. However, Freud's psychoanalytic theory was important in the area of motivation for another reason. Prior to Freud, psychology was dominated by structuralistic psychology and, in the structuralist framework, motivation was not considered to be a problem. Consequently, prior to Freud psychologists failed to develop an orientation which was needed to study motivation. With the advent of Freud's psychoanalytic theory psychologists began to turn their attention to the development of techniques that could be used for the quantitative study of motivation.

Another important historical development in motivational psychology was the rise of the *instinct* concept of motivation. With the interest in animal behavior that arose following Darwin's writings, many people became impressed with the repertoire of complex "unlearned" behavior that was demonstrated by various species of animals. The notion that this behavior was based on instincts became popular. Later, some psychologists, such as William McDougall (1871–1938), used the concept of instinct to attempt to explain the motivation behind much of human behavior. Thus, McDougall listed a number of instincts such as flight, curiosity, repulsion, pugnacity, reproduction, and so forth as being important determinants of behavior. While McDougall's system enjoyed initial success, his doctrines are now mainly of historical importance.

Once an interest in motivational psychology arose, a great variety of points of view and diverse approaches developed. One might assume that this field would be one of the best developed areas in psychology. However, this is far from being the case. The field is

characterized by conflicting points of view and, in general, motivational theory remains in an unsatisfactory state.

The Interpreting Subsystem

    In Chapter 8 a number of processes that are associated with
the interpreting subsystem will be discussed in some detail. While
these processes, which include thinking, problem solving, and decision making, will be discussed separately, the separation is one of
convenience. Actually, they should be considered closely related
processes, which, in most instances, are not distinguishable. Thus,
when we refer to problem solving we are referring to a form of
thinking and, of course, the reverse can also be true. These functions must also be considered in relation to the other subsystems
that have been discussed. For example, thinking is closely related
to learning, since concepts, which are learned, are essential tools in
the thinking process. Similarly, a great deal of our thinking is based
on memories and recollections. Thus, much of what we discussed
about the early psychology of learning and perception is equally
applicable to the topic of thinking.
    The various schools of psychological thought and the individ-
uals that have been mentioned in preceding pages all had views on
the nature of the thought processes, although some did not consider
this area as very important. For example, Titchener (a structuralist) assumed that cognitive activities were composed of images and,
like sensations, these images had the attributes of quality, intensity,
duration, and clarity. He held that the thought processes could be
analyzed into elements. In general, however, the structuralists tended
to feel that thinking and other cognitive processes were beyond the
scope of psychology. Similarly, the functionalists also had relatively little to say about thought processes. Thorndike was interested in problem solving but not in cognitive processes *per se*. John
Watson equated thinking with implicit speech and hypothesized
that minute responses of the vocal apparatus were bases for thought.
Anything that could not be verbalized could not be thought about. To
the Gestalt psychologists, thinking was organized according to the
same principles as perception. Much of the work of the Gestaltists in the area of higher thought processes had to do with problem-
solving behavior.
    We could go on and list many more names and schools and
discuss the many different views on cognition and thinking that
have been put forth. However, while this might be informative, the
result would be simply a collection of views on cognition and think-

ing. At present, this area of psychology does not have any satisfactory theoretical offerings and much of the research must be considered exploratory in nature. While progress is being made toward more comprehensive theories of thinking, this progress has been slow.

Summary

1. Psychology is chiefly concerned with the study of behavior. Behavior, in this case, refers to mental reactions or responses, as well as the overt physical responses of an organism.

2. Psychology is more and more becoming a problem-solving science. Much of the research conducted by psychologists is applied research, research aimed at gaining knowledge that can be used to help solve some specific practical problems. Because of the complexity of some of the applied problems, special techniques are required to deal with them. One of these techniques is systems analysis.

3. Psychologists attempt to explain and predict a wide variety of behavior of human and subhuman organisms. This requires different approaches and, consequently, a number of methods of investigation are utilized by psychologists. These methods are naturalistic observation, case study method, testing, and the experimental method.

4. With each of these methods, some aspect(s) of behavior is observed. In many situations the experimental method is desirable because it allows for greater control of the situation in which the observed behavior occurs. When the experimental method is used, three types of variables are important: dependent variables, independent variables, and nuisance variables.

5. Man can be considered as a system and studied by means of the systems analysis approach. With this approach, man's functions can be viewed in terms of dynamic relationships rather than in terms of static elements. By viewing man as a system composed of a number of subsystems, all of which interact and contribute to the final output (behavior), we are better able to answer the question: What does the system do and how does it do it?

6. Psychology, as a science, has a long history. Historically, modern psychology was primarily influenced by philosophers such as Descartes and Locke, by the early German psychologists, by early American psychologists, by other scientific disciplines, and by the various systems of thought that have arisen within psychology.

Selected Readings

Boring, E. G. *A history of experimental psychology* (Rev. Ed.).
New York: Appleton-Century-Crofts, 1950.

Chaplin, J. P., & Krawiec, T. S. *Systems and theories of psychology*. New York: Holt, Rinehart and Winston, 1960.

Lockman, R. F. An empirical description of the subfields of psychology. *American Psychologist*, 1964, **19,** 645–653.

Ross, S., & Lockman, R. F. *A career in psychology*. Washington, D.C.: American Psychological Association, 1965.

Royce, J. R. Psychology in the mid-twentieth century. *American Scientist*, 1957, **45,** 57–73.

2

The Sensing
Subsystem I

Inputs and the Receptor Subsystem

We saw in the previous chapter how, at one level of analysis, man can be considered as a system involving an input, a sensing function, a data-transmission function, and an output. One of the primary research strategies in psychology involves relating the input and the output of an organism and attempting to understand the transformation that takes place between the two. In this chapter and the next we will be concerned with the inputs to the human system, which are called *stimuli,* and with the subsystems that perform the function of sensing—the receptor subsystem (Chapter 2) and the transmitting and processing subsystems (Chapter 3).

In man, the first stage of the sensing function is performed by a complex arrangement of specialized sensors, called *receptors,* that are sensitive to various types of physical energy. Conscious sensations are produced when nerve impulses, traveling from the receptor cells by means of various neural pathways, activate sensory areas in the brain. In order for the receptors to be activated, however, there must first be some form of stimulation (input) from either the internal or the external environment.

Inputs to the System: The Stimuli

The behavior of any organism is elicited and modified by a wide range of internal and external environmental forces (stimuli). In our study of sensation, we are concerned only with those environmental forces that constitute the appropriate sources of stimulation for the various sensory receptors in man.

What is a stimulus? The traditional, technical definition of the term *stimulus,* as it applies to the study of sensation, is: a physical event, or a change in physical energy, that causes physiological activity in a sense organ.

A stimulus may be *effective* in activating certain sensory receptors—that is, it may be a source of stimulation that produces some sensation—and yet not be an adequate, or appropriate, stimulus for the specific sense organ involved. For example, if you exert mechanical pressure (an effective stimulus) on your eyeball, you will experience some sort of sensation, but not the sensation that is characteristic of normal vision. A stimulus that normally elicits a particular sensation is called the *adequate* stimulus for that sensation; a stimulus that elicits a sensory or behavioral response but is not the normal stimulus for the particular sense organ is called an *inadequate* stimulus. Thus, with respect to the receptors in the eye, mechanical pressure is an effective but inadequate stimulus; the effective *and* adequate stimulus, in this case, is a form of electromagnetic radiation known as light.

Limiting our concept of an effective stimulus to some form of physical energy in either the internal or external environment of the human system, we will be dealing with four forms of physical energy that are capable of stimulating the various sensory receptors. These forms of energy are: (1) electromagnetic radiation, (2) mechanical energy, (3) chemical energy, and (4) thermal energy. We will discuss each of these forms of energy in more detail when we consider each component in the sensing subsystem of man.

When a person's sensory channels are all functioning, he is literally flooded with excessive and redundant information (stimuli). Consequently, it must be kept in mind that the sensory subsystem is such that protective mechanisms are required to prevent the brain from being "jammed." As you will see later, this protection is provided at several levels. Through the psychological processes of *set* and *attention,* for example, a person can, by means of instructions, be told what stimulation to attend to in his environment; he learns to "filter out" certain types of irrelevant information. Other protective mechanisms, which will be considered in detail later, enable man to establish priorities among his different senses and select information from his environment.

The Receptor System

You will recall that a system must have the capability of sensing all relevant stimuli originating from both external and internal sources. In man, this capability is provided by a complex arrangement of specialized sensors (receptors). The receptors for the various senses are designed to respond to a specific type of stimulus (called the adequate stimulus), which in humans is restricted to a relatively narrow range of physical energies. Within this range, however, the receptors are remarkably sensitive instruments.

The receptor subsystem may be thought of as an interface between environmental stimulation and the transmitting and processing subsystems. It is the function of the receptors to transform the various types of stimulus energy into a form of electrochemical energy, which we call the nerve impulse. A second function of the receptors is to code the information contained in the stimulus in the form of variations in the spatial and temporal patterns of nerve impulses, which are then transmitted and processed in the central nervous system.

The variety of specialized structures called receptors may be classified in several ways, one of which is based on the source of the stimulus and the location of the receptor. According to this method of classification (called *Sherrington's classification*), receptors are of four types:

> *Proprioceptors* are found in muscles, in tendons and joints, and in the labyrinth. These receptors give us information concerning movements of the body and the position of the body in space.
> *Teleceptors* are located in the eyes, ears, and nose; they give us information concerning changes in the environment which take place at a distance from the body.
> *Exteroceptors* are located in the skin and give us information concerning changes in the immediate external environment.
> *Interoceptors* are located in the visceral organs and tell us about changes in our internal environment.

Receptors may also be classified with respect to the type of energy which is the adequate stimulus for the particular receptor.

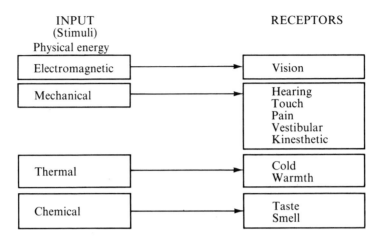

Figure 2–1. Receptors for various sensations and the form of physical energy to which they are sensitive.

According to this categorization scheme, there are *thermal* receptors, *mechanical* receptors, *chemical* receptors, and *photic* (light) receptors.

Before beginning our discussion of the various senses, let us consider the effective stimuli for the receptors that make up the sensing subsystem. Figure 2–1 shows the receptors for various sensations and the type of physical energy to which they appropriately respond. Note that, with the exception of electromagnetic energy, each type of physical energy is capable of stimulating receptors for more than one sensation.

Vision

The effective stimulus for vision is light—a narrow band of radiation on the electromagnetic spectrum. At one end of the electromagnetic spectrum (Figure 2–2) are the extremely short gamma rays; at the other end are the very long electric waves (several miles in length). The particular band of electromagnetic radiation to which the receptors in the eye respond—called the *visible spectrum* —is limited roughly to the wavelengths between 380 and 800 millimicrons.* The receptors do not respond to the energy above or below these points on the spectrum, unless the energy is intense enough to cause damage. Energy of wavelengths between these points, however, has a special characteristic that makes it the effective stimulus for vision in humans.

---

* A millimicron, abbreviated m_μ, is one millionth of a millimeter; the term *nanometer* is often used interchangeably with *millimicron*.

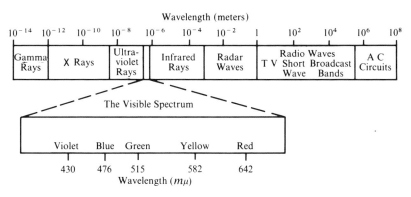

Figure 2-2. The electromagnetic spectrum.

It can also be seen in Figure 2-2 that various points on the visible spectrum are associated with the different colors that we experience. White light includes all wavelengths in about equal proportions; that is, it is a "mixture" of the different wavelengths. The "mixed" nature of white light can easily be seen by means of a prism, which disperses white light and breaks it down into its component colors. These colors form a band ranging from violet at one end of the band through shades of blue, green, yellow, orange, and red. Except under very unusual circumstances, the light that stimulates the receptors in the eye is mixed and consists of many wavelengths. This light can also vary in intensity—that is, the amount of physical energy that is present. The different combinations of wavelengths and intensity reaching the receptors are responsible for all the complicated visual experiences that we encounter.

Measurement of the intensity, or physical energy, of light is called *photometry*. There are several photometric units of measurement for light, but for our purposes it is sufficient to consider only a few of them. The *candela* and *candlepower* are measures of luminous intensity (light at its source); the *footcandle* is a measure of illumination, or the amount of light falling on a surface; and the *footlambert* is a measure of brightness, usually that of light reflected from a surface. *Illumination* refers to the amount of radiant energy incident to a surface; *brightness* refers to how it appears to an observer.

The Visual Sensor: The Eye

The primary function of the eye is to convert patterns of electromagnetic radiation—called light—into a language that can be understood by the brain. This language is in the form of chains of electrical impulses, which are referred to as nerve impulses. We will see how this conversion occurs and how the impulses are transmitted when we take up the transmission subsystem in the next chapter.

Figure 2–3 is a drawing of a cross section of a human eye.

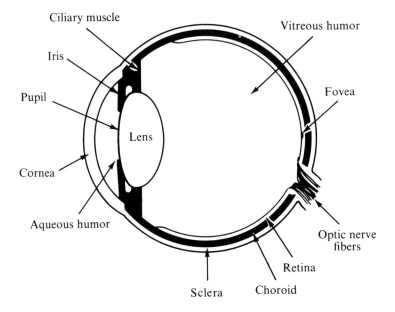

Figure 2–3. Schematic illustration of the human eye. Note the number of surfaces and media the light must pass through before reaching the retina.

The eye is somewhat similar to a camera: both have an adjustable opening that regulates the amount of light entering the structure, both have a lens for focusing the light, and both have a light-sensitive surface that receives the focused image. However, in the case of the eye, the lens actually changes shape in order to help focus the image on the photosensitive material on the inner surface of the eye. In the camera the lens must be moved back and forth in order to provide focus. The most significant difference between the eye and the camera, however, is that the light-sensitive surface of the eye is much more sensitive than the film that is used in cameras. For example, under ideal conditions, the eye is able to detect the light from a match at fifty miles distance.

Considering the path that the light must follow through the eye before it reaches the light-sensitive layer, called the *retina*, it is surprising that the eye is so sensitive. As can be seen in Figure 2–3, the light must pass through several transparent media and at least four surfaces separating these media before it reaches the retina. The transparent media are the cornea, the aqueous humor, the lens, and the vitreous humor. These media are separated from each other and from the air by the two surfaces of the cornea and the two surfaces of the lens. The various surfaces in the eye cause refraction (bending) of the light rays as they pass through the eye. Also, there is some scattering of the light rays, particularly in the vitreous humor. In addition, as you will see when the structure of the retina is considered, the light must pass through several layers of the retina before it reaches the light-sensitive elements. Despite these "obstacles," however, the eye is an extremely efficient sensing device.

Components of the Eye

Cornea. Figure 2–3 shows that light entering the eye first passes through the cornea, which is the transparent outer layer in the front of the eye where the light is bent most to form the image. Actually, the cornea consists of several distinct transparent layers. It is devoid of blood vessels and is very sensitive to noxious stimuli well below the level that could cause damage to the eye. These stimuli are sensed as pain, thus enabling the organism to respond in a way that will prevent the stimulation from reaching a dangerous level.

Iris and Pupil. When comparing the eye with a camera, we pointed out that both have mechanisms for regulating the amount of light that falls on the photosensitive surface. In the eye, this mechanism is called the iris. The iris, which is heavily pigmented (and gives color to your eyes), has a central circular aperture called the pupil, or pupillary aperture. There are two sets of muscles in the iris which serve to dilate the pupil in dim light and to constrict it in bright light. The dilation and constriction of the pupil is our first example in the human system of a *feedback link*, a mechanism that corrects for external change. When light enters the eye and excites the receptors in the retina, a number of neural events take place. Information—some of which concerns the intensity of light—is first transmitted to various parts of the brain, where it is unconsciously "processed" and then passed back to the iris muscles in the form of nerve impulses that cause the muscles either to dilate or to constrict the pupil. To an engineer, this system of feedback links may suggest a neural servomechanism.

While not directly related to the topic at hand, i.e., the structure of the eye, some highly unusual and interesting experiments have been conducted in the last few years which merit a brief discussion. It has been reported by Hess and Polt (1960) that when a person looks at interesting or pleasant materials, in contrast to neutral materials, the pupil dilates. However, looking at distasteful or disliked material produces pupil contraction. Thus it was found that when normal females looked at pictures of nude males, there tended to be a considerable increase in pupil size, while for normal males, looking at the same pictures, there was only a slight increase. However, when pictures of nude women were viewed, the opposite results were obtained. The pupil size of the males increased markedly, while there was only a small increase in the size of the pupils of the females. Since the Hess and Polt study, there has been considerably more work on this interesting "pupil reaction." It appears that the pupillary response is not under conscious control and that a person cannot intentionally manipulate the response.

Lens.   The body of the lens, which is surrounded by a membrane or capsule, is made up of a number of concentric layers somewhat similar to those of an onion. The lens is suspended from a muscle, called the *ciliary muscle,* which by its action can modify the shape of the lens and thereby change the focus of the light passing through the eye. This process is called *accommodation.* The radius of curvature of the lens is increased for distant vision and decreased for near vision. The lens adds to the initial bending of the light produced by the cornea.

Accommodation of the lens is considerably affected by the age of the person. For example, a normal ten-year-old child can clearly see an object that is about three inches from his eye. Such vision requires that the lens be very elastic and that it be capable of maximum curvature. As a person ages, however, the elasticity of the lens decreases so that at age seventy a person must view the same sort of object at a distance of about forty inches in order to see it clearly. This condition can be corrected by convex eyeglasses.

Aqueous and Vitreous Humor.   One of the functions of the aqueous humor is to supply nutrition to, and remove waste products from, several of the structures of the eye, including the cornea and the lens. It appears that there is a continuous formation of the aqueous humor; consequently, methods for drainage have to be present. If drainage does not take place, the increased pressure can endanger the structure and function of the eye. The vitreous humor, which makes up four-fifths of the content of the eyeball, is a thin, transparent, jelly-like substance. Its primary function is to help preserve the nearly spherical shape of the eyeball.

Note on Figure 2–3 that the posterior part of the eyeball is made up of several layers, or coats. The exterior layer, which is called the *sclera*, forms a tough protective coat for the delicate areas within. The *choroid*, which is closely applied to the sclera, consists of a dense network of blood vessels that help to nourish the eye. Since the choroid also contains many pigment cells, it aids in darkening the interior of the eye.

The Retina. The retina is a delicate, almost transparent membrane that contains the light-sensitive receptors as well as a complex network of nerve cells that carry impulses generated by photochemical processes within the receptors. While the retina contains at least ten identifiable layers, we will primarily be concerned with only three: the layer of rods and cones, the layer of bipolar cells, and the layer of ganglion cells. These are shown in Figure 2–4. The rods and cones are the specialized receptor cells; the bipolar and ganglion cells are two different types of nerve cells, or *neurons*, which carry the impulses from the rods and cones.

In referring to Figure 2–4, keep in mind that the light-sensitive elements of the retina are on the inward side. Light must travel through a web of blood vessels, a network of nerve fibers, and the layers of nerve cells and supporting cells before it reaches the rods and cones. The retina thus might be compared with camera film that has been put in backwards. It almost appears that the retina involved a mistake in "design." However, in the part of the retina called the *fovea* (Figure 2–3), the arrangement of the various elements of the retina is such that the light falls almost directly on the receptors—in this case, only cones.

As pointed out above, there are two kinds of light-sensitive receptors in the retina. These are called rods and cones because, under a microscope, they actually look like rods and cones. These receptors show a number of differences in both their anatomical structure and their visual functions. Their distribution in the retina also differs. The rods are found all over the retina except in the fovea, which contains only cones. In passing peripherally from the

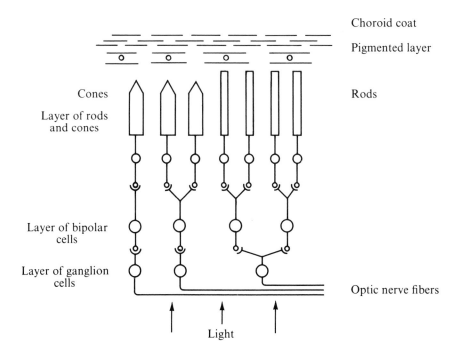

Choroid coat

Pigmented layer

Cones

Layer of rods
and cones

Rods

Layer of bipolar
cells

Layer of ganglion
cells

Optic nerve fibers

Light

Figure 2-4. A schematic showing some of the connections
that can occur in the retina. This is a greatly simplified view
of the retina, which contains a number of identifiable layers
and much more complex interconnections than those shown.

fovea, the cone-to-rod ratio rapidly decreases, although a few cones
occur even at the extreme periphery of the retina.

When light strikes the rods or cones, a photochemical reaction takes place which generates an electrical potential within the
receptor cells. This *generator potential*, the size of which is determined by the amount of photochemical activity in the cell, will then
initiate nerve impulses in the bipolar cells. These impulses then
pass through the bipolar and ganglion cells to the brain by means of
the optic nerve. The nerve fibers (axons) from the ganglion cells
make up the optic nerve. This brings up an interesting point in relation to the number of fibers in the optic nerve and the number of
rods and cones in the retina. We find that there are only about one
million optic nerve fibers and about 130 million rods and cones. Consequently, it is apparent that a single optic nerve fiber may "service" a large number of rods or cones. Careful microscopic examination of the retina reveals that there are two major types of neural
systems in the retina. In one type, there is a single path from an in-

dividual cone to a bipolar cell to a ganglion cell; in the other type, a number of rods and cones converge on bipolar cells, which in turn converge on ganglion cells. In general, the retina is characterized by a vast number of interconnections at all levels. Figure 2–4 shows that there are interconnections at the level of the receptor cells, at the bipolar level, and at the ganglion-cell level.

While the rods and cones are both sensitive to electromagnetic radiation in the form of light, they react differently. According to the *duplicity theory* of vision, the rods are involved in our ability to see things under low levels of illumination, whereas the cones are involved in high levels of illumination. The rods are our night or dim-light sensors. They respond in such a fashion that we experience various shades of gray rather than color. In terms of their ability to respond to minimal stimulation, the rods are more sensitive than the cones. The cones, which function under higher levels of illumination, are most important in relation to our ability to see fine detail (visual acuity) and to see color. Daylight vision involving the cones is called *photopic* vision, whereas vision involving the rods is called *scotopic* vision. These characteristics of the retina determine, to some extent, how we use our eyes. For example, if we wish to discriminate fine detail under good lighting, we look directly at an object so that the image of the object falls on the area of the retina which contains only cones. However, if we wish to see something at night or in dim light, we "look out of the corner of our eye" so that the image falls on a more peripheral area of the retina—an area containing mostly rods. It is for this reason that one looks to one side of an object at night if he wishes to examine it.

The minimal energy required for the human eye to detect light is extremely small. Under ideal conditions, the light from a match can be seen at fifty miles. One of these conditions is that the receptors in the retina are at a stage of maximum sensitivity. The most important factor in determining the sensitivity of the receptors is whether they have recently been exposed to light. Everyone has had the experience of having entered a theater or a dark room and, for all practical purposes, been nearly blind for a moment. After a short period of time in the dark, you are able to make out shapes and, after a longer period, some details of the room. This increase in the sensitivity of the receptors after being in the dark for a time is called *dark adaptation*. Although the cones adapt rather rapidly, dark adaptation of the rods may continue for a long time. Most of the increase in the sensitivity of the rods has taken place after about thirty minutes in the dark, although measurable changes will take place for much longer periods of time. Some idea about the degree of change in sensitivity of the eye can be obtained if we consider that the eye is approximately one million times more sensitive to light after one hour of complete dark adaptation than it is under bright illumination.

The Experience of Seeing

As indicated previously, there are several stages in the sensing function. First, the receptors must be actuated by a stimulus; then the nerve impulse originating from the receptors must be transmitted; and finally the sensory areas of the brain must receive the impulses. When we talk about the experience of seeing, we are actually involved with the last step in the sensory process. We will discuss both the transmitting step and the sensory areas of the brain in the next chapter. Keep in mind, however, that the "experience of seeing" involves each of the required steps in the sensing function. We do not experience the sensation of seeing until the steps are complete.

While there are enough topics under the heading of "seeing" to fill several books, we will be concerned with only two: *visual acuity* and *color vision*. A great deal can also be said about these areas. Consequently, we will limit our discussion to only the basic aspects of visual acuity and color vision.

Visual Acuity

Visual acuity refers to the ability of the eye to resolve detail. It is generally measured and defined by two methods: the *minimum visible* method and the *minimum separable* method. The former measures visual acuity in terms of the narrowest line or thread that can be discriminated from a homogeneous background at a given distance. Visual acuity is also measured by determining the smallest distance by which two lines can be separated without appearing as a single line (the minimum separable method). There are other tests of visual acuity; however, all are simply methods of measuring a basic visual function: detail vision.

There are a number of factors that affect visual acuity. We have already seen that the eye is constructed in such a fashion that the light must pass through several refracting media before it reaches the retina. Thus, visual acuity may be affected by refractive "errors" that impair the formation of a sharply focused image on the retina. In addition to refractive "errors," several other optical conditions affect sharpness of focus—for instance, pupillary size, composition of the light, and random variations of fixation.

Visual acuity is also affected by numerous stimulus factors. Under dim illumination, for example, visual acuity is poor. Although it is adversely affected by glare, visual acuity increases as the illumination falling on the object being viewed is increased. Similarly, the greater the contrast between the object and its background, the finer is the detail that can be seen. The size of the object and the amount of time during which the object can be viewed also affect visual acuity. Only in laboratory settings can each of these factors be controlled; thus, in a man-machine system where good visual acuity on the part of the operator may be important, predicting his acuity under a given set of circumstances may be a complicated process. A reduction in any one of the factors mentioned—size, illumination, contrast, or time—may be offset by an increase in one or more of the other factors. For example, if in the design of equipment it is necessary to reduce the size of an object, then the reduction in visual acuity resulting from this change can be compensated for by increasing the illumination. A considerable amount of research has been conducted to determine how acuity is affected by changes in these variables.

Visual acuity is different on different parts of the retina. We have already mentioned that visual acuity is much better at the fovea, which contains only cones, than in the more peripheral regions of the retina, where rods predominate. It is apparent from Figure 2–5 that visual acuity drops off very rapidly toward the edges of the

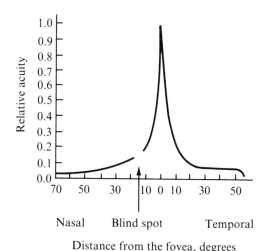

Figure 2–5. Visual acuity is different on different parts of the retina. Acuity is best at the fovea and drops off rapidly toward the periphery of the retina.

Figure 2–6. You can locate the blind spot by means of this simple figure. Holding the book about ten inches from your eyes, close your left eye and stare at the X with your right eye. When you move the book slightly, the spot will vanish. It disappears when it is centered on the blind spot.

retina. Thus, visual acuity only 5 degrees on either side of the fovea (represented by 0 degrees on the figure) is only about half as good as at the fovea.

Figure 2–5 shows that there is a point about 15 degrees from the fovea, on the nasal side of the retina, called the blind spot. This is the area of the retina where the fibers from the ganglion cells course back as the optic nerve. There are also blood vessels coming into the eye at this point. Since this particular area of the eye is absolutely blind, there is a corresponding blind area in our visual field. Normally, we do not notice the blind spot, because the constant movement of our eyes tends to "fill the hole," so to speak. Also, as we have stressed, there are many aspects of our visual field that we do not perceive because of the relationship between eye and brain. The blind spot can be detected, however, by means of the simple test shown in Figure 2–6.

Color Vision

In discussing the visible spectrum, it was stated that the different combinations of wavelengths and intensity which reach the receptors in the eye are responsible for all the complicated visual experiences that we encounter. We see color as we do because of the wavelength and intensity characteristics of the electromagnetic radiation that stimulates the cones in the retina. However, we cannot explain color vision solely on the basis of the physical characteristics, or dimensions, of the stimuli; we must also be concerned with what are called the psychological dimensions of color vision.

There are a number of situations in which attaching a name to a color may be important. This is particularly true for many industrial and engineering purposes, since colors can be very effective in coding information. However, to be useful for coding information, a color cannot be one that could easily be confused with another color, and it should be readily associated with a common color name. These requirements are not as easily met as one might think. Some interesting research on the denotative meaning of various color names showed that, although the human eye is capable of discriminating millions of different colors, there are probably only about 55 usable color names (Chapanis, 1965).

Psychological Dimensions of Color. Color experience depends primarily upon the wavelengths of light entering the eye and is described by two psychological color dimensions: hue and saturation.

Hue is the principal factor in the sensation of color and is what we mean when we say color. Hue is related to the dominant wavelength of light impinging upon the cones.

The psychological dimension of *saturation* refers to the purity of the wave of electromagnetic radiation entering the eye. A highly saturated color or hue is associated with light of a single wavelength. To the extent that the light entering the eye consists of a mixture of wavelengths, the stimulus is less saturated; when an equal mixture of all wavelengths is present, we experience white, or complete desaturation. It might be noted at this point that complete desaturation, or the experience of seeing white, can be accomplished by an appropriate mixture of just two wavelengths of light as well as by a mixture of all wavelengths. For each physical wavelength or psychological hue there exists a *complementary hue* or wavelength such that when the two are mixed in equal amounts the resulting sensation is white or gray. Perhaps the most common complementary pairs of colors are red-blue/green and yellow-blue, although it should again be pointed out that every wavelength in the visible spectrum has its complement.

Mechanisms of Color Discrimination. Historically, two major theories have been advanced to explain the manner in which the visual receptor system discriminates between different wavelengths of light. The *component theory* of color vision postulates the existence of three types of cones, each of which is maximally sensitive to one of three wavelengths of light: red, green, or blue. This theory is based primarily on data that pertain to the laws of *color mixture*. These data show that any color experience can be reproduced by a suitable mixture of three primary colors. For example, if two projectors—one equipped with a red filter and one equipped with a green filter—are focused on the same spot, we will see yellow rather than either green or red. This phenomenon is known as *additive* color mixture and is applicable primarily to the mixing of colored lights. Additive color mixture should not be confused with the process involved when a painter mixes various pigments to produce different colors; this process is subtractive color mixture and is not applicable to the development of the component theory of color vision.

The component theory of color vision suggests that the retina of the eye contains three types of cones: one type sensitive to red, another to green, and the third type to blue. According to this theory, yellow is produced by stimulation of both red and green cones in approximately equal proportions. All other visible colors are produced by the simultaneous stimulation of the appropriate combination of the three types of color-sensitive cones.

The second major theory of color vision is known as the *opponent processes theory*. This theory suggests that there are only two types of color-sensitive cones, each of which reacts to complementary pairs of colors: a red-green pair and a yellow-blue pair. The principal basis for this theoretical position lies in the phenomena of complementary colors discussed earlier.

According to the opponent processes theory of color vision, each of the two types of cones is subject to two distinct types of physiological processes. The first process is called *anabolism*, which is a building up of the photochemical substance within the receptor; the second process, *catabolism*, is the breakdown of the photochemical substance. According to this theory, the red-green receptor reacts to a red stimulus with the process of anabolism and to a green stimulus with the process of catabolism. The color message sent to the brain thus involves both the type of receptor stimulated and the process whereby the receptor reacts to the stimulation. The data relevant to color mixture are handled in the same manner as with the component theory, except that in this case four primary color experiences are used in the mixture.

Within the last several years, several extremely important studies on the photochemistry of color vision have provided unequivocal evidence that the component theory holds true—at least at the level of the fovea of the retina. The first step in this series of research studies was provided by Rushton (1962, 1964), who discovered two distinct types of photosensitive substances in foveal cones. The first of these substances, called *erythrolabe* ("the red catcher"), is most sensitive to wavelengths of light which correspond to the red area of the spectrum. The second cone pigment discovered by Rushton, called *chlorolabe* ("the green catcher"), is maximally sensitive to wavelengths in the green region of the spectrum. Researchers have also identified a third photosensitive cone substance, called *cyanolabe*, which is most sensitive to wavelengths of light corresponding to the blue region of the visible spectrum

(Marks, Dobelle, & MacNichol, 1964). This research also indicated that individual cones contain only one type of photosensitive substance—either erythrolabe or chlorolabe or cyanolabe. Thus, at the level of the retina, there remains little doubt that the component theory explains the process by which color information is coded for transmission and processing in the central nervous system.

In the face of the evidence just cited, it would appear that the opponent process concept might be entirely abandoned, and this is substantially the case insofar as the retinal level of the visual system is concerned. Another line of significant visual research has indicated that the central elements of this theory are true, however, when we follow the visual signal through the optic nerve to higher levels of the central nervous system. At the level of the thalamus, which is the principal sensory relay station of the brain, DeValois (1965) has demonstrated the existence of spectrally opponent cells that respond to the same pairs suggested by the opponent process theory. Although the hypothetical processes of anabolism and catabolism are not involved, it has been demonstrated that individual cells in the visual center of the thalamus respond with an increased firing rate to one member of the opponent process pair and with a decreased firing rate to the other. Four types of opponent process color cells apparently code the color experience at this level of the nervous system. +R−G cells respond with an increased firing rate to red illumination and a decreased firing rate to green illumination, while +G−R cells respond in just the opposite manner. Similarly, there are +B−Y and +Y−B cells that serve to code the blue-yellow opponent pair.

Modern research has thus demonstrated that at least two distinct coding mechanisms are involved in color vision. Although research is continuing in the area, there is as yet no definitive explanation as to the manner in which the component and opponent processes are combined between the retina and the thalamus.

Malfunctions in the Visual System

In many individuals, the visual sensory system does not function as it should. At one extreme are individuals who are completely blind, and at the other are individuals who may have only a minor visual defect. There are many types of defects and abnormalities that may occur in the visual system; some of them can easily be corrected, but others cannot. Uncorrectable defects include malfunctions in color vision.

Three primary types of color vision deficiencies have been

observed in humans. These are, in increasing order of severity, *tri-chromatism, dichromatism,* and *monochromatism.* The labels attached to these forms of color vision malfunction indicate the number of primary colors that these individuals need to match all colors of the visible spectrum. You will recall from the discussion of the component theory of color vision that normal color vision is *tri-chromatic;* that is, three primary colors are required to match any color experience. The first type of color deficiency, trichromatism, also involves three primary colors (red, green, and blue). Trichromats, however, are deficient in one of the three photochemical substances needed for color sensitivity. A green-defective trichromat, for instance, would require a great deal more green in a red-green mixture before he would experience yellow than would an observer with normal color vision. Similarly, a red-defective trichromat—apparently as a result of having a shortage of cones containing erythrolabe—would require an excessive amount of red light in the red-green mixture in order to experience yellow. Trichromats have a color weakness. It must be emphasized, however, that trichromats are *not* color blind; they still require three primary colors to match all of the visible spectrum.

The second form of color vision malfunction is *dichromatism.* This disorder is a form of *color blindness* and is the result of the complete absence of one of the three types of photosensitive pigments. Dichromats require only two primary colors to match all wavelengths of the visible spectrum. A dichromat whose cones do not contain erythrolabe is able to match all colors with only yellow and blue primaries, but he cannot experience those colors which require red in the mixture for normal observers. Similarly, dichromats who lack chlorolabe will use red and blue for every match and are not sensitive to green. Those who lack cyanolabe match colors with red and green and are not sensitive to colors at the blue end of the spectrum.

Monochromatism refers to the complete absence of *at least* two of the cone pigments. Two types of monochromats have been identified. Blue-cone monochromats apparently retain cones containing cyanolabe. Total (rod) monochromats, on the other hand, apparently do not possess cone vision.

Aside from the nuisance value of color blindness in everyday living, it can also be a definite handicap in certain types of occupations. In many man-machine systems, information is conveyed to the human element by means of various types of color coding. These systems require that the operator be able to tell the difference between the colors used in the coding. If he cannot, perform-ance errors that could have serious consequences might result.

One of the primary problems involved with research on color blindness is that the methods of measuring this defect are not ade-quate. The standard measuring device is the *isochromatic chart*. Figures on this chart contain colored numbers that are imbedded in various colored backgrounds. A color-defective individual is unable to see certain of these numbers. Using measuring techniques of this type, it was found in one study that 50 percent of the pilot candi-dates rejected for color blindness by one examiner were accepted by a second examiner (Viteles, 1944).

Vision is perhaps man's most important sensory system, and more is known about vision than about the other senses. For stu-dents who might wish to pursue this topic in more detail than has been possible in this section, a book by R. L. Gregory, called *Eye and Brain: The Psychology of Seeing* (1966), is very much worth reading.

Hearing

Next to vision, our sense of hearing is probably the most im-portant sense by which we receive stimulation from our external environment. Hearing is of great importance in our communication with one another, and it provides us information about our environ-ment ranging from warning signals to soft music. It may also be the sensory system that allows the greatest amount of "annoying" stim-ulation into the system. While we can close our eyes if we wish to eliminate visual sensation, we cannot avoid auditory stimulation.

What Is Sound?

The word "sound" refers both to a form of physical energy and to what we hear; that is, sound has both physical and psycho-logical dimensions. As a form of physical energy, sound consists of variations in air pressure caused by some vibrating body that has set the air molecules in motion. Sound is also what we hear. It is a sensation and can thus be studied as a psychological phenomenon. Sound, in terms of subjective experience, can range from very pleas-ant to highly unpleasant. Whether it is pleasant or unpleasant, of course, depends very much on the person involved. Thus, one man's noise may be another man's music. As we will see, the psychological dimensions of sound are related to the physical characteristics of the stimuli.

The air around us consists of molecules that are constantly moving about in a random fashion. Any object that is more solid than air displaces these molecules, and any vibration of the object causes changes in the density, or pressure, of the air. Thus, when the object moves back and forth, the molecules close to the object are alternately pushed together (*positive pressure*) and then pulled apart (*negative pressure*); the result is a wave of positive pressure moving through the air, immediately followed by a wave of negative pressure. This is the *sound wave*, which is the physical stimulus for hearing.

The back-and-forth movement of the air molecules can be represented mathematically by means of *sine waves*. Shown in Figure 2–7 are three sine waves, each having different physical characteristics. Let us consider these different characteristics and their relation to the psychological dimensions of sound.

Frequency. The first step in the experience of hearing occurs when sound waves strike the eardrum (see Figure 2–9). The pressure waves (the sound waves) cause the eardrum to move in and out, and this vibration is transmitted to other parts of the ear, which eventually help determine what we hear. The rate at which the eardrum moves in and out is an important determinant of what we hear, and the rate of movement is determined by the *frequency* of the sound wave. Frequency refers to the number of cycles per unit of time in a periodic vibration. Figure 2–7 shows that the middle sine wave has a frequency twice that of the upper one. The frequency of a sound wave is primarily (but not completely) responsible for the psychological dimension of hearing known as *pitch,* which refers to how high or low a given tone sounds to us.

Intensity. The frequency of a sound wave determines how *fast* the eardrum moves in and out. The intensity of the sound wave determines how *far* the eardrum moves in and out. In other words, intensity reflects the pressure of the wave. The crest of the sine wave in Figure 2–7 represents the greatest compression of molecules, and the trough of the wave indicates the point of least compression. Intensity is shown as the amplitude of the sine waves in this figure. The amplitude of the bottom sine wave is twice as great as the amplitude of the top two. The psychological correlate of inten-

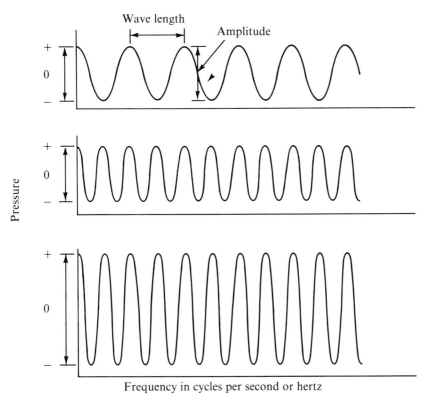

Figure 2-7. This figure shows three sine waves that have different frequencies and amplitudes. The amplitude is the same for the top two sine waves, but the frequencies are different. The bottom sine wave has the same frequency (cycles per given period of time) as the middle wave, but it has twice the amplitude.

sity (amplitude)—that is, the auditory sensation we experience—is *loudness*.

Actually, the physical and psychological dimensions of sound are somewhat more complicated than we have indicated. In the first place, a change in intensity can also cause a perceived change in pitch, while a change in frequency can also result in a change in the perceived loudness. In the second place, it is rare that we encounter a *pure* tone such as represented by the three sine waves. Most tones are complex and are made up of a number of frequencies. This aspect of the physical stimulus results in a third psychological dimension of sound which we call *timbre*, or *tonal quality*.

*The Measurement of Sound
Intensity*

The range of sound intensities which the human ear responds to is so great that sound intensity is measured on a very large scale. The basic unit of measurement of sound intensity is the *decibel*, which is a *ratio expression* indicating the relative difference in in-

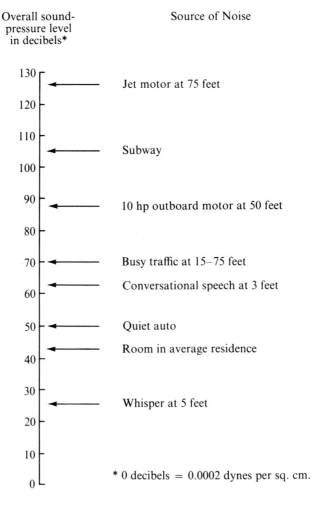

Figure 2–8. Sound-pressure levels for a number of different sounds.

tensity between two sounds. However, a decibel ratio has meaning only if everyone uses the same reference value to compare with the unknown intensity. Since intensity of sound is a measure of pressure, researchers have established an arbitrary reference value of 0.0002 dynes per square centimeter (a dyne is a unit of pressure in the metric system), which is about the lowest change in pressure to which the ear is sensitive. This reference level is the zero point of the decibel scale. When the measurement of sound intensity is made using the standard reference, the decibel scale is referred to as a scale of *sound-pressure level.* Another reference point is sometimes used, however; and on this decibel scale, zero represents the least intense stimulus that can be heard at a frequency of 1,000 cycles per second (the term *hertz* rather than cycles per second is used in much scientific writing).

The decibel scale is a logarithmic scale. Thus, if a sound is 100 decibels more intense than another sound, it is ten billion times more powerful. Figure 2–8 shows sound-pressure levels for a number of sounds. On this scale, the pain threshold is somewhere around 120 decibels; that is, sound pressure at this level will actually cause a person to experience a painful sensation. Extended exposure to the higher sound-pressure levels, even those that are below pain threshold, may result in permanent damage to the ear and in subsequent loss of hearing. It has long been recognized that pilots and workers in certain industries may suffer severe hearing reduction as a result of exposure to loud noise; however, long periods of exposure to loud music may have the same results.

The Auditory Sensor: The Ear

The functional diagram of the ear in Figure 2–9 shows that, in some respects, the ear resembles a funnel. The *external ear*, consisting of the pinna and the external auditory canal, channels the sound waves to the eardrum. The sound waves, which consist of alternating pressure changes, cause the eardrum to move. The frequency of the sound wave determines how fast the eardrum moves, and the amplitude (pressure) determines how far the eardrum moves in and out. Vibrations of the eardrum are transmitted and amplified by means of a set of three tiny bones—the *ossicles.* From the eardrum inward, these bones are called the *malleus,* the *incus,* and the *stapes.* The stapes is attached to a membrane across the entrance (*oval window*) to the *cochlea.* Thus, the amplified vibrations originating at the eardrum and transmitted by means of the ossicles

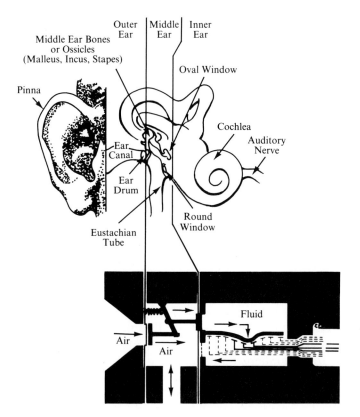

Figure 2–9. Functional diagram of ear. Sound waves impinge on the outer ear and cause the eardrum to vibrate. Vibrations are conducted via the lever action of the middle-ear bones to the oval window, which actuates the fluid-filled inner ear. Portions of nerve endings in the cochlea are selectively excited, and their outputs terminate in the brain. From *Human Engineering Guide to Equipment Design* by C. T. Morgan, J. S. Cook, III, A. Chapanis, and M. W. Lund, Eds. Copyright 1963 by the McGraw-Hill Book Company, Inc. Used with permission of the McGraw-Hill Book Company.

cause further vibration of the membrane across the oval window of the cochlea. As this membrane vibrates, it causes waves of pressure in the fluid-filled cochlea.

Note on Figure 2–9 that, from the exterior, the cochlea resembles a snail shell. The interior of the cochlea houses some rather complex elements, which are illustrated in Figure 2–10. The oval window is located at the end of the *vestibular canal.* Another membrane, the *round window*, extends across a second opening in the cochlea. This second window permits a movement of the fluid in the cochlea; that is, it relieves the pressure generated by the movement of the membrane at the oval window.

The cochlea is divided into two canals by the *basilar membrane,* which runs the length of the cochlea from its base near the oval and round windows to the apex. A second membrane, called the *tectorial membrane,* runs parallel to the basilar membrane but is attached to only one wall of the cochlea. Between these two membranes lies the *organ of Corti,* which contains the receptor mechanism for audition. The organ of Corti is located on the basilar membrane, and the *hair cells* of this structure extend to the surface of the tectorial membrane in which they are embedded. Movement of the fluid in the cochlea distorts the basilar membrane and causes a

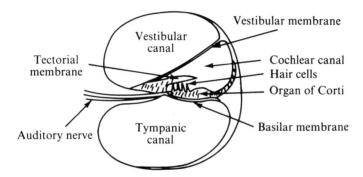

Figure 2-10. A cross-sectional diagram of the human cochlea.

shearing, or bending action, on the hair cells. This movement of the hair cells produces a generator potential, which causes the firing of nerve impulses in the fibers of the auditory nerve. These nerve impulses travel along the auditory nerve to the sensory areas of the brain.

How Do We Hear?

Recall that in the discussion on vision it was pointed out that no completely adequate explanation is available as to how the nervous system can cope with the various physical characteristics of the visual stimuli. The same problem is encountered when we attempt to explain hearing. How are the auditory qualities of pitch and loudness produced by the neural mechanisms of the ear and the brain? As was the case with the eye, the ear is an efficient sensor. The audible range of frequencies is from about 20 to 20,000 cycles per second although the ear is most sensitive to frequencies between about 500 and 4000 cycles per second. Similarly, because of response characteristics of the ear, we are able to experience the sensation of loudness over a very wide range. Obviously, the ear must be capable of dealing with sound waves that vary greatly in terms of frequency and intensity.

As the intensity of a stimulus increases, receptors tend to generate more and more nerve impulses. The more impulses generated by the receptors in the ear and transmitted to the brain, the louder we perceive the sound to be. Although the process is not quite as simple as this explanation might make it appear, basically this is how the nervous system codes the intensity of the sound stimulus so that we experience different sensations of loudness. The more intense the sound stimulus, the greater the number of nerve impulses reaching the auditory area of the brain and the louder the perceived sound (Wever, 1949).

The neural mechanisms related to the perception of pitch are more complex than those related to the perception of loudness. Historically, two major theories have been advanced to explain the phenomenon of pitch—the *place theory* and the *frequency theory.*

The basilar membrane, which runs down the center of the cochlea, consists of numerous transverse fibers that are successively coupled together to form an elastic membrane. According to the *place theory* of pitch discrimination, each of these transverse fibers is "tuned" to a particular frequency. When stimulated by the appropriate frequency, the hair cells associated with the appropriate transverse fiber should generate an electrical potential that causes the discharge of nerve impulses in the auditory nerve. The perceived pitch of a given sound should thus depend upon the particular transverse fiber, or fibers, associated with a particular sound frequency.

The *frequency theory,* on the other hand, considers the ear to be a relatively simple frequency detector. Pitch coding, according to this theory, is dependent upon the total rate at which nerve impulses are produced by the entire organ of Corti. Historically, this theory encountered immediate difficulty when the discovery was made that a single nerve fiber cannot fire at a rate greater than about 1,000 times per second. It had already been known, however, that the ear can discriminate frequencies within a range of 20 to 20,000 cycles per second. To account for this difficulty, Wever and Bray (1937) formulated the *volley principle,* which suggested that frequencies higher than the maximum rate for single nerve fibers were handled by bundles of nerve fibers and that the total firing rate of such a bundle of fibers could follow the frequency characteristics of high-pitched sounds.

A third theory that attempts to explain the ear's ability to code sound frequency is the result of the work of G. von Békésy, who was awarded the Nobel Prize in medicine and physiology in 1961. This theoretical position is based on von Békésy's (1960) work with mechanical models of the cochlea and on his comparisons of these models with human and animal cochleas. Békésy's *traveling wave theory* has demonstrated that, upon stimulation, a pressure wave travels along the basilar membrane. The point of maximum displacement of the basilar membrane is dependent upon the frequency of the stimulating sound-pressure wave, as is the frequency of the traveling wave. The coding of the pitch of a sound stimulus requires aspects of both the place and frequency theories. When sound waves are low in frequency, the entire basilar membrane tends to vibrate as a whole; consequently, frequency coding is necessary. At higher frequencies, where there is a point of maximum displacement on the basilar membrane, both place and frequency serve to code the pitch of the stimulus.

Noise

Everyone is concerned with protecting his eyes from possible damage, and it is relatively rare for a person to look at a bright light source long enough to cause retinal damage. However, thousands of people each year suffer permanent hearing loss because they are exposed to high levels of sound; moreover, since technological developments tend to increase the amount of noise we are exposed to, this problem is assuming major proportions.

Noise, which can be defined as "unwanted sound," can present problems even when it is not intense enough to cause damage to the ear. In industrial settings, for example, noise may have effects on production, worker fatigue, errors, accidents, and so forth. Much of the research on the problem of noise in industry has resulted in equivocal findings, largely because of the difficulty of conducting these studies in actual industrial settings; however, in recent years, carefully controlled laboratory investigations have shed some light on the effects of noise on human behavior. While it was assumed for years that noise has a detrimental effect on a person's performance of a task, it turns out that this is not always the case; in some cases noise has no effect on performance, and in other cases it actually improves performance. For example, in one recent study

(Warner, 1969) it was found that there were fewer errors on a performance task under high-noise levels (up to 100 decibels) than under low-noise and no-noise levels. However, the relationship between noise and performance is a complicated one and may be influenced not only by the nature of the noise itself but also by the type of performance task involved.

The Cutaneous Senses

It is generally assumed that the cutaneous, or skin, sensations are those of *pressure* (touch), *pain, cold,* and *warmth.* Although for humans these sensations are not as important as vision and hearing, each of them gives us some information about our external environment. The receptors associated with these sensations are classified as *exteroceptors;* a number of specific receptors, located at various levels in the skin, are responsible for cutaneous sensitivity. A great deal of effort has been expended in attempting to identify these receptors and to relate a specific type of receptor to a specific sensation; however, the numerous receptors that have been identified are actually variations of only a few broad types. Basically, the skin receptors consist of the endings of nerve fibers. In some cases, there may be a capsule of connective tissue around the end of the nerve fiber, and in other cases there may be "free" nerve endings.

Pressure or Touch (Tactile System)

When a person is touched lightly with some object, the skin is depressed slightly, receptors in the skin are activated, and nerve impulses are transmitted to the brain. Thus, mechanical pressure that deforms the skin is the adequate stimulus for our experience of touch.

How sensitive is the skin to pressure or touch? Research has indicated that certain parts of the body are more sensitive than other parts. Table 2–1 lists, in descending order of sensitivity to pressure, a number of regions of the body. It is apparent that the tip of the tongue and the finger tips are the most sensitive and that the soles of the feet are the least sensitive.

The possibility of using the sense of touch as a communication channel has been receiving increasing attention. Pioneering work in this area by Geldard (1957, 1960) has led to considerable research in recent years. Geldard developed a tactile-communications

Table 2-1. Sensitivity to pressure in various regions of the body. Regions are listed in descending order of sensitivity; that is, the tip of the tongue is the most sensitive region listed while the thick part of the sole is the least sensitive.

PRESSURE SENSITIVITY
Bodily Region
Tip of tongue
Tip of finger
Back of finger
Front of forearm
Back of hand
Calf of leg
Abdomen
Back of forearm
Loin
Thick part of sole

system by means of which his trained subjects were able to learn a tactile code for letters and numbers. Vibrators at different positions on the chest of each subject were used to send the subject signals consisting of changes in duration and amplitude of vibrations. Subjects were able to learn the tactile code and to receive communications at the rate of 38 words per minute. This compares favorably with the reception rate of Morse code. Other investigations have been concerned with the possible use of tactile stimulation in aiding blind persons. Studies using mild (painless) electrocutaneous shock have also demonstrated that this form of tactile stimulation can be used effectively to present information to an operator in a man-machine system (Hofmann, 1968). One can predict that as the various systems in which man must operate begin to "overload" his visual and auditory channels, more and more use will be made of the tactile channel.

Temperature Sensations

The skin receptors for warmth and cold respond when the temperature of the skin is increased or decreased, but they are not activated by an object that is the same temperature as the skin. Although these receptors cannot be differentiated microscopically, it appears that they are of two types—one for warmth and the other for cold. A technique that involves "mapping" the skin reveals that there are separate spots that are sensitive to either warm or cold stimuli but not to both; however, since microscopic examination of these spots has failed to reveal different receptor structures, it appears that the receptors are *functionally* but not *structurally* different. Evidence suggests that free nerve endings are the primary receptors involved in the temperature sense.

Specialized techniques that permit scientists to record the firing of sensory nerve fibers have revealed some interesting facts about the relationship between temperature and nerve firing. For instance, when the skin is cooled, certain fibers increase their rate of firing; when the skin is warmed, the rate of firing of other fibers increases. This has led to the suggestion that there are "warm" and "cold" fibers and that our experience of warmth and cold is based on the rate of firing of these different fibers (Zotterman, 1953, 1959).

Pain Sensitivity

Although pain is a distinct sensory experience, it is difficult in laboratory experiments to separate pain from pressure. Obviously, when a person is stuck with a needle (a common stimulus in experiments), the skin is also deformed so that he experiences touch as well as pain. Consequently, some rather clever techniques have been developed to study the sensation of pain. In some experiments a short electric spark rather than a needle is used as the stimulus. When this spark is applied to the skin, the person experiences either pressure or pain (sometimes both). Areas on the skin that give only the pain response can then be selected and investigated (Bishop, 1944). Another technique for studying pain involves the use of a device that radiates heat to a small area of the skin. When the heat is intense enough, the person reports pain (Wolff & Wolf, 1948).

There is little doubt that the primary receptors for pain are free nerve endings, although overstimulation of virtually any sensory receptor will also produce the sensation of pain. These receptors are spread through all the tissues of the body. There are three kinds of pain: (1) superficial pain, or cutaneous pain; (2) deep pain from muscles, tendons, and joints; and (3) visceral pain. Sometimes pain is also called *prick* pain, which is a bright sensation of short duration. *Dull* pain lasts a relatively long time and is not well localized.

Although the receptors for pain are located throughout the body, the various regions of the body differ in their sensitivity to pain-producing stimuli. By means of an *algesiometer,* which is an instrument with a needle-sharp tip that is pressed against the skin by means of a series of weights, *absolute thresholds* for pain can be determined. An absolute threshold is the smallest amount of a stimulus that can be perceived. Table 2–2 shows the relative sensitivity of various regions of the body. Regions are listed in descending order of sensitivity, based on absolute thresholds for pain. It can be seen from this table that the cornea of the eye is extremely sensitive to pain and that the extremities are relatively insensitive.

Table 2–2. Sensitivity to pain of various regions of the body. Regions are listed in descending order of sensitivity.

PAIN SENSITIVITY TO MECHANICAL PRESSURE
Bodily Region
Cornea
Conjunctiva of the eye
Abdomen
Front of forearm
Back of forearm
Calf of leg
Back of hand
Sole
Fingertip

Consideration of the structural basis for the experience of pain tells us only part of the story. Why is it, for example, that a football player can receive serious injuries during a game and be unaware of any pain until he has left the playing field? Why does the perception of pain vary from culture to culture? Why can fear increase the amount of pain that is experienced? Until we can answer these and many other questions, our understanding of the experience that we call pain will be incomplete.

The Proprioceptive Senses

The proprioceptive senses can be considered as two separate sensory systems, both of which give us information about the position of our body in space. One of these is called the *kinesthetic system,* and the other is known as the *vestibular system.*

The kinesthetic system is critical for normal movement of our body. Through a complex arrangement of receptors and feedback links, the kinesthetic system allows us to automatically coordinate our muscles when we make any type of movement. This coordination, of course, is necessary if we are to walk or to perform any type of skilled movement. It is also necessary for talking and for vision, since muscles are involved in both of these functions. While some types of diseases can affect the kinesthetic system, no one is ever completely lacking in this sense.

The kinesthetic receptors are located in the muscles, in the tendons, and in the joints. There is a complicated interaction between these receptors. For example, some are activated only when a muscle is stretched; others are activated when it contracts. Still others, which are located in the joints, are activated when a limb is moved. It is generally agreed that the perception of movement is associated primarily with the receptors in the joints and that the receptors in the muscles and tendons are of more importance in

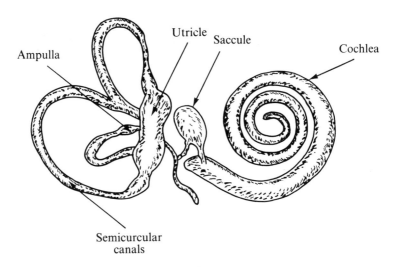

Figure 2–11. A schematic of the vestibular system. The system shown here is enclosed in a bony casing. The three semicircular canals are situated so that one is in each plane of movement. Organs located in the ampullae of the canals respond when the head is rotated or moved. Receptors located in the utricle and saccule are stimulated by gravity and respond to the tilt or position of the head.

telling us when resistance to movement is present. However, all the information from these receptors is utilized by the central nervous system in helping us keep our balance and in keeping our movements coordinated.

The vestibular system is responsible for sensing motion and position of the body. The vestibular system is located in the inner ear (see Figure 2–9) and consists of three organs: the *semicircular canals*, the *saccule*, and the *utricle* (these latter two are sometimes called the *otolith organs*). The vestibular sense organs are shown in Figure 2–11. Each of these organs is filled with fluid. The semi-circular canals and the otolith organs have somewhat different functions. The semicircular canals contain specialized receptors (cells with minute hairs on them) that are moved when movement of the head causes the fluid in the canals to be set in motion. The hair cells in the semicircular canals are activated during a *change* in the position of the head. In fact, this activation occurs only when the change is one of acceleration or deceleration. The receptors in the otolith organs are stimulated by the *position* of the head or by linear acceleration. They can be called static receptors since, unlike the receptors in the semicircular canals, they respond to the position of the head and do not actually need movement for stimulation.

The Chemical Senses

The two chemical senses are smell and taste. Although these senses are generally considered less important than the other senses, they do give us additional contacts with our environment.

Smell (Olfactory System)

The olfactory system is activated when some form of odorous stimulus, in the form of vaporized chemical substances, comes into contact with specialized areas in the upper region of each nostril. These regions consist of *olfactory epithelium*, which contain ol-factory cells (receptors) as well as other cells. The olfactory cells contain the olfactory nerve endings. The outer surface of the epithelium is washed in a mucous fluid, which is secreted by cells in the nasal cavities. It is thought that a gas must be soluble in this mucous fluid in order to stimulate the receptors in the olfactory epithelium.

Exactly what happens when a stimulus excites the olfactory

receptors is not known. While several theories have attempted to account for olfactory sensations, none of the theories is completely adequate. Possibly the best explanation is that certain chemical compounds react with certain substances in the receptors and in this fashion excite the receptors. Whatever the mechanism involved, the sense of smell is extremely sensitive. Studies have shown that only a few molecules of gas have to enter the nose to be detected, and a person who has a normal sense of smell can detect 0.00004 miligram of artificial musk in a liter of air.

Attempts have been made to list the fundamental qualities of smell in the same fashion that the fundamental psychological qualities of vision (hue, saturation, and brightness) and hearing (pitch, loudness, and timbre) have been identified. This attempt has not been very successful. One system lists six qualities of odors: spicy, fruity, burnt, resinous, flowery, and putrid. Whether each of the supposed qualities has separate receptors is unknown.

Taste (Gustatory System)

A person can normally identify four distinct qualities of taste: sweet, sour, salt, and bitter. All other taste sensations are combinations of these four primary taste qualities. The typical stimulus for the taste quality labeled "sweet" is common sugar, for "sour" an acid such as hydrochloric acid, for "salt" sodium chloride, and for "bitter" quinine.

The receptors for taste are located mainly on the top and sides of the tongue, although there are a few in the throat and at the back of the mouth. They consist of specialized epithelial cells situated in little groups, or clusters, called *taste buds*. These buds are embedded in the ridges or bumps (papillae) of the tongue. Just how the taste receptors work is not completely clear. The receptors respond to various chemicals that are in solution in the mouth. The question, of course, is how these receptors code information so that we experience the various taste qualities. If there were one type of receptor associated with each taste quality, the problem would be simplified. However, this is not the case.

Studies dealing with electrical responses from single taste-nerve fibers indicate that nearly all the fibers will respond to more than one taste stimulus. A given fiber may respond most vigorously to salt, for instance, but it may also respond moderately to acid or to quinine (Pfaffmann, 1959, 1964). Consequently, a single fiber may be fired by any number of stimuli. The taste quality that is experienced apparently depends upon the firing of several fibers, and it is the *pattern* of the firing that determines the quality we experience.

Our taste experience, however, is dependent upon more than nerve activity. Actually, what we call "taste" is the result of the interaction of several sensory modalities. The sense of smell is particularly important in determining what we taste. Just as food can be tasteless to someone suffering from a head cold, the taste of food may be affected by temperature or, for that matter, by the food's appearance. Pepper "tastes" as it does because it stimulates some pain receptors as well as taste receptors. *Contrast effects* may also affect our sense of taste. For example, lemonade may taste much more sour than usual if a person eats ice cream first. Obviously, the experience of taste is not as simple as one might assume.

Other Sensory Functions

While there is a great deal more that could be said about the sensory capabilities and functions of man, two topics that were only briefly mentioned previously are of sufficient importance to merit further consideration. These are *sensory adaptation* and *sensory interaction.*

Sensory Adaptation

The sensitivity of a sensory system is modified by the continuous presentation of stimuli. This process of modification is called *adaptation.* Though the physiological mechanisms underlying adaptation vary with different sensory modalities, adaptation as a general process occurs in all the senses when they are exposed to constant stimulation. While it is now recognized that all senses adapt, some adapt much more than others. For our purposes, we will think of adaptation as resulting primarily in a lowering of the sensitivity of the receptors involved; however, as pointed out by Helson (1964), adaptation must be recognized as a two-way process that may involve either heightened or lowered performance of the receptors.

How do we experience adaptation? We have already discussed the visual phenomenon of dark adaptation, which is a case in which the receptors become more efficient during the course of adaptation. In the case of cutaneous adaptation, the receptors become less efficient. Thus, when you first put a heavy sweater on, you may "feel" it on your body; however, you do not feel it for very long. The taste sense also adapts quite rapidly. You only really taste the first bite of food on your plate. Similarly, a room might smell unpleasant when you first enter it; usually, however, you do not notice the odor after a short time.

It was mentioned earlier that the body is constantly bombarded with stimulation and that methods are required which shield the body from excessive stimulation. Adaptation is one of these methods.

Sensory Interaction

One of the questions of concern to those who study human sensation is whether the stimulation of one sensory system has any effect on the sensitivity of another system. Particular interest in this area of research has been shown in the Soviet Union (London, 1954), although psychologists and physiologists in many countries are also studying this phenomenon.

Although the literature on this subject is contradictory, there seems to be little doubt that sensory interaction, or cross-stimulation, does occur. Considering the numerous converging sensory pathways and areas of the brain where sensory impulses "come together," sensory interaction is not a surprising phenomenon; however, the interaction effects that have been demonstrated have been extremely minute and, from a practical point of view, of little significance.

What sort of interaction effects have been demonstrated? Russian studies report that sensitivity of the fovea to white light is increased by mild auditory stimulation. Other studies have reported that auditory stimulation *increases* sensitivity to blue-green light but *lowers* sensitivity to orange-red light. Although their experimental methods and their data have not been open for inspection, Russian psychologists have also claimed that visual acuity is influenced by auditory stimulation (both increased and decreased, depending upon experimental conditions); that olfactory stimulation influences visual sensitivity; and that gustatory stimuli, heat, and cold also affect visual sensitivity. American investigators, whose methods are open for inspection, have also studied sensory interaction. In an investigation by Thompson, Voss, and Brogden (1958), a decrease in auditory threshold was obtained under conditions involving simultaneous visual and auditory stimulation. Although there is still some doubt about the Soviet findings, this study does offer some confirmation.

When we think of sensory interaction as modifying sensory thresholds, we are considering only one aspect of cross-stimulation. Researchers are also interested in learning what happens when more than one sensory channel is used to give a person information concerning his performance on various types of tasks. Such research is generally concerned with the effects of *redundant* information—that is, the same information presented over more than one sensory channel. For example, it has been demonstrated that a person's performance on sonar and radar tasks can be improved by giving him simultaneous visual and auditory displays of information. Performance on other types of tasks has been shown to increase when information is presented not only through visual and auditory channels but also through the sense of touch.

A different type of interaction problem is presented when there are conflicting inputs to the sensory system. Many tasks require that a person pay attention to both visual and auditory information simultaneously. If the information is not redundant, a person's performance may be impaired. Sometimes, however, conflicting inputs will not affect one's performance to any great extent. For example, an experienced telegrapher can receive or send messages while he carries on a conversation.

Sensory Psychophysics

We have seen that the physical properties of stimuli, acting upon the sensors of an organism, are capable of eliciting a variety of sensory experiences or sensations. Each sensor (the eye, the ear, the skin, and so forth) may give rise to a relatively large number of sensations, each of which corresponds to particular properties of the stimulus. Thus, the auditory sense is capable of giving us information about loudness and pitch, as well as about other characteristics of a sound, and the visual sense gives rise to sensations such as saturation and hue (color).

Sensory psychophysics is the study of the relation between the physical properties of stimuli and the quantitative properties (magnitude) of sensations. There are two broad areas of study which have been explored in sensory psychophysics. The first area is concerned with the *physical limits*, or thresholds, of sensation—that is, the smallest amount of physical stimulation required to produce a sensation and the largest amount of stimulation which the sensor will handle. The second area of study is concerned with the construction of *scales of measurement* for subjective sensory experiences. While both of these areas are of importance, we will restrict our discussion to sensory thresholds.

Sensory Thresholds

At the heart of classical sensory psychophysics is the concept of a sensory threshold, or barrier. The threshold is (1) the physical value of a stimulus which must be surpassed for a stimulus to produce a sensation, or (2) the minimum difference in physical stimulus-value between two stimuli of the same type which will produce different degrees of sensation.

Absolute Thresholds

The limits of a given sensation are defined by *absolute* thresholds. The *lower threshold* represents the point at which a sensation will just occur in response to stimulation. It is the smallest amount of stimulation necessary to produce a sensation. Thus, according to classical sensory psychophysics, for the visual sensation of brightness there exists a specific amount of light intensity at which a light is visible; below this intensity, the light is not visible.

Each sense has, in addition to a lower limit below which the sensor will not respond, an *upper threshold*—a point on the physical stimulus-energy continuum above which a sensation will not occur. For some sensations this threshold is not measured because stimuli intense enough to reach this point would damage the sensory mechanism. Thus, sound pressure intense enough to establish an upper threshold for loudness would probably render the subject deaf. For some sensations, however, the upper threshold is meaningful and may be safely tested. For the sensation of pitch, for instance, the audible frequencies of sound range from approximately 20 to 20,000 cycles per second. In this case, the average human observer can hear a sound between these frequency values but not one lower or higher in frequency.

Difference Threshold

Another type of threshold measured in sensory psychophysics is the *difference threshold*. The difference threshold is utilized in the evaluation of a subject's sensitivity to stimuli that differ from one another in degree of intensity. This threshold is the physical difference in amount of stimulation which will be detected as producing a different degree of sensation. The difference threshold is also known as the *jnd* (for just noticeable difference). Thus, if we are measuring difference thresholds for light intensity, the amount of increase in light intensity necessary for an observer to detect a change in the brightness of a light is the jnd, or difference threshold. A problem with the jnd is that it has been found to vary across the scale of intensity for virtually every type of sensation. Thus, for the auditory sensation of loudness, if we find that an increase of .1 decibel (db.) in a 30 db. tone is just detectable, a 90 db. tone may require an increase of .3 db. to produce a jnd. In general, the size of the jnd increases as stimulus values increase.

Threshold Measurement

The ideal observer in psychological experiments on sensation would be absolutely reliable and invariant in his response to stimulation. A light of given intensity would, on every trial, be just detectable to him, and an increment of light intensity of a certain amount would always produce the same value for a jnd. Unfortunately, however, humans do not reach this ideal; their performance is variable and changes over time. At one time, for a given individual, an increment in intensity of .1 candlepower to an initial intensity of 1 candlepower will be the jnd for brightness. At another moment in time, perhaps only half a minute later, it may require an increment of .15 candlepower to produce the jnd. Both the variability in an individual's observations and the even greater variability in observations among people require that we estimate sensory thresholds rather than determine them exactly. A variety of techniques, called *psychophysical methods,* have been developed to arrive at these estimates.

The System So Far

At this point we have not come very far with our systems analysis of the human functions. We have discussed part of the sensing function and have seen how various forms of physical energy are the adequate stimuli for the sensory receptors. Further, it has been emphasized that there are characteristics of the physical stimulus which are of importance in the sensing function but that there are also psychological dimensions of sensation which are related to the stimulus dimensions. There are four important aspects

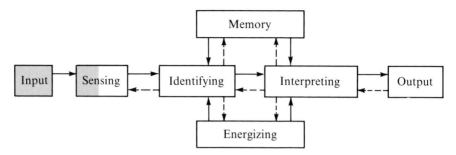

Figure 2–12. The system this far. The inputs to the system
and part of the sensing function have been discussed.

of the sensing function: (1) stimulation in the form of physical
energy, (2) excitation of receptors, (3) transmission of the nerve
impulses from the receptors, and (4) activation of sensory areas of
the brain. We have discussed the first two steps; however, when
we considered the psychological dimensions of sensation, we assumed that all the steps had taken place.

Summary

1. A stimulus, as it is technically defined in reference to
sensation, is a physical event, or a change in physical energy, that
causes physiological activity in a sense organ. The effective
stimulus—that is, one that activates a sensory receptor—is some
form of physical energy—electromagnetic radiation, mechanical
energy, thermal energy, or chemical energy.
2. There are various kinds of receptors associated with the
different senses. Receptors can be classed in several different ways.
One classification, based on the source of the stimulus, classifies
receptors as proprioceptors, teleceptors, exteroceptors, and intero-
ceptors. Categorization in terms of effective stimuli results in
thermal, mechanical, chemical, and photic receptors.
3. The effective stimulus for vision is electromagnetic radiation consisting of wavelengths between approximately 380 and 800
millimicrons wavelength. Receptors in the retina of the eye—
specifically, rods and cones—are stimulated by this type of energy.
Rods function under relatively low levels of illumination (scotopic
vision), and cones function best under high levels of illumination
(photopic vision). The duplicity theory of vision is based on this
differential response.
4. After exposure to light, rods will dark adapt. This greatly

increases their sensitivity (nearly one million times after one hour of dark adaptation). The cones are most important for seeing detail. The fovea, which contains only cones, is the most sensitive area of the eye in terms of ability to see detail.

5. Visual acuity, measured by either the minimum-separable or the minimum-visible method, is dependent upon optical factors of the eye (refraction, pupillary size, variation in fixation, retinal location stimulated) and upon stimulus factors such as size, illumination, contrast, and time of exposure.

6. Color vision is dependent upon the cones. Color experience depends primarily upon the wavelengths of light entering the eye and is described by two psychological color dimensions—hue and saturation. Hue is related to the dominant wavelength of light impinging upon the cones. Saturation refers to the purity of the wave of electromagnetic radiation entering the eye.

7. Sound waves are produced by movements of the molecules in the air caused by a vibrating body. A pure sound wave can be represented as a sine wave. The physical characteristics of the sound stimulus are represented by the frequency, intensity, and complexity of the wave. The psychological dimension associated with frequency is called pitch. The dimensions associated with intensity and complexity are loudness and timbre.

8. The basic unit of measurement of sound intensity is the decibel, which is a ratio measure of the intensity of one sound relative to another.

9. Sound waves strike the eardrum, causing it to move in and out. This movement is transmitted by the ossicles, which are attached to a membrane covering an opening (oval window) in the cochlea. Movement of this membrane causes waves of pressure in the fluid-filled cochlea. The movement of the fluid results in movement of the auditory receptors (hair cells located in the organ of Corti), which generate nerve impulses.

10. Several major theories of hearing have been set forth. These include the place theory, the frequency theory, and the traveling wave theory. None of these is completely satisfactory for explaining how we hear.

11. There are four cutaneous senses: pressure (touch), pain, cold, and warmth. The receptors for these senses are various types of nerve endings, some encapsulated and others free, which are located in the skin. Areas of the body differ in terms of cutaneous sensitivity.

12. The proprioceptive sensory system involves the kinesthetic and vestibular senses. Both of these senses are important in

giving us information about the position of our body in space. Kinesthetic receptors are located in the muscles, tendons, and joints. The receptors for the vestibular sense are located in the cochlea and in the otolith organs of the inner ear.

13. The chemical senses are taste and smell. The number of basic psychological qualities of smell is not known, although six qualities are sometimes identified. There appear to be four qualities for taste: sweet, sour, salt, and bitter.

14. The sensitivity of a sensory system is modified by continuous presentation of stimuli. This process is called adaptation. Sensory interaction refers to a situation in which the stimulation of one sensory system may have an effect on the sensitivity of another system.

15. The most basic concept utilized in psychophysics is that of the sensory threshold. In psychophysical research, we are generally concerned with either an absolute or a difference threshold. The former represents the lowest intensity, or smallest amount, of the stimulus which will give rise to the appropriate sensation. The difference threshold is the minimum detectable difference in intensity between two stimuli of the same type.

Selected Readings

Alpern, M., Lawrence, M., & Wolsk, D. *Sensory processes.* Monterey, California: Brooks/Cole, 1967.

Geldard, F. S. *The human senses.* New York: Wiley, 1953.

Gibson, J. J. *The senses considered as perceptual systems.* Boston: Houghton Mifflin, 1966.

Gregory, R. L. *Eye and brain: The psychology of seeing.* New York: McGraw-Hill, 1966.

3

The Sensing Subsystem II

The Transmitting and Processing Subsystems

We have discussed how receptor cells can be excited by several types of physical energy, and we have seen how this energy is changed, or transduced, by the receptors into generator potentials. Generator potentials, in turn, give rise to nerve impulses. From the receptors these impulses are carried by groups of nerve fibers, which are called *sensory* or *afferent* fibers (in contrast to *motor* or *efferent* fibers), into the central portion of the nervous system. The pathways of fibers leading from the receptors to the sensory areas of the brain are circuitous rather than direct, having "delays" at several relay points in the brain. The information carried by these fibers is eventually analyzed and translated by the brain, enabling us to experience *pitch, loudness, sour, sweet, redness, pain,* and the other psychological qualities of sensation.

In this chapter we will consider the nerve pathways and the areas of the brain that are involved in sensation. We will also discuss the nerve impulse, which transmits information to the brain about changes in the receptors. We will begin our discussion with

an overview of the nervous system, of which the sensory (afferent)
system is only a part.

Overview of the Nervous System

While the neural bases of behavior are extremely complex,
the overall design of the human nervous system can be thought of
in relatively simple terms. Considered anatomically or structurally,
the nervous system consists of the *central nervous system* (*CNS*)
and the *peripheral nervous system* (*PNS*). The central nervous
system includes the brain and the spinal cord, and the peripheral
nervous system includes all the nerve-cell bodies and nerve fibers
outside the brain and the spinal cord. Considered on the basis of
its functions rather than its structure, the nervous system consists
of the *somatic nervous system* and the *autonomic nervous system*.

The Somatic System. Included in the somatic nervous
system are all the peripheral and central nervous system elements
concerned with transmitting impulses from the receptors to the
brain, processing the nerve impulses in the brain, and delivering
impulses from the brain to the striated muscles of the body and
the limbs.

The Autonomic System. As in the case of the somatic
system, the autonomic system includes some components of both
the central and peripheral nervous systems. However, the central
and peripheral components of the autonomic system, which are not
the same as those of the somatic system, also function differently
than those of the somatic system: they serve the internal organs
and the smooth muscles of the body rather than the striated skeletal
muscles.

The autonomic system is further divided into two subsystems—the *parasympathetic* and the *sympathetic*. Most organs
of the body and most smooth muscles receive nerve fibers from
both the parasympathetic and sympathetic divisions of the autonomic nervous system. Generally speaking, the parasympathetic
division is involved in the conservation of bodily resources and in
building up the body. It is active primarily when the organism is
relatively calm. The sympathetic division mobilizes the resources of
the body for use in work and special emergencies. Activity of this
system causes a number of changes in the body that better equip it
to meet an emergency. However, it would be incorrect to assume

that when one of the divisions is active the other is not. Actually, the parasympathetic and sympathetic divisions work together to maintain a balance in the entire system.

At present, we will be most concerned with the somatic nervous system, which is responsible for much of the behavior studied by psychologists. This system consists of a number of subsystems that are shown in Figure 3–1. Although this representation

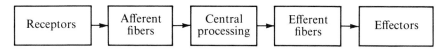

Figure 3–1. Schematic representation of the somatic nervous system.

is a greatly simplified version of the complete somatic division, the basic components of this division are clearly illustrated. The first component is a subsystem of *receptors*, which were discussed previously. The second component is a subsystem of *afferent nerve fibers*, which transmit impulses from the receptors to the *central processing area*. Next are the *efferent fibers*, which transmit impulses from the brain to the *effectors*. Although a system such as this can be conceptualized as consisting of a number of subsystems, a very important fact must be kept in mind. These components may perform different specialized functions but their interactions are such that the output of the system is dependent upon their proper functioning and all their contributions. When we discuss these separately, we are talking about their specific functions in relation to the system as a whole. When a particular subsystem is considered, one must not forget that its functions are dependent on proper functioning of other subsystems.

Neurons

Within the nervous system, the ultimate subsystem is a specialized cell called the *neuron*. The neuron is both the structural and functional unit of the nervous system. Neurons vary in size and shape; however, all have certain characteristics in common. In many ways they are like the other cells of the body. For example, the neuron has a cellular membrane, a nucleus, a protoplasmic-like material, and other elements contained within the membrane. However, the properties of *irritability* and *conductivity* are much more pronounced in neurons than in other types of cells.

Figure 3–2 is a diagram of a neuron that has three main

functional parts: the *dendrite,* the *cell body (soma),* and the *axon.*
The dendrites of a cell are located in such a manner that they can
be excited by stimuli arising from the environment, by other
neurons, or by several types of specialized cells (receptors). The

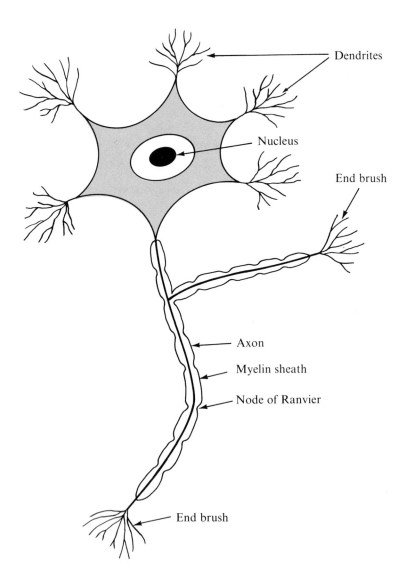

Figure 3–2. Schematic of a neuron. Basic components of
the neuron include the cell body, dendrites, and an axon.

dendrites conduct impulses toward the cell body. These impulses travel to the cell body and then along the axon to another neuron or to an effector such as a muscle. The impulse from one neuron may activate another neuron so that the information carried by the first will continue on through the nervous system. The connection between the axon of one neuron and a second neuron is functional rather than structural; impulses can travel from one neuron to another, but there is actually a small gap between the two. The communication system between the two neurons is called a *synapse*. Some idea about the structure of neurons and about the possible connections between them can be obtained from Figure 3–3.

Some axons are encased in a fatty sheath, called the *myelin* sheath, which is interrupted at regular intervals by constrictions known as the *nodes of Ranvier*. As we will see later, the conduction of a nerve impulse along a myelinated axon is somewhat different than conduction along a nonmyelinated axon.

The dendrites and axons conduct impulses from one point of the nervous system to another. Generally, several nerve fibers (dendrites or axons) run together in a bundle. In the peripheral nervous system, a bundle of fibers is called a *nerve;* in the central nervous system, a bundle of fibers is referred to as a *tract* or *pathway*. Often, a large number of cell bodies of neurons are clustered together. A cluster of this type in the central nervous system is called a *nucleus*. Outside the central nervous system, and associated with the sensory neurons, are clusters of cell bodies known as *ganglia*.

The Spinal Cord

The central nervous system consists of the *brain* and the *spinal cord*. The human spinal cord, which is about 18 inches long and is about as thick as a pencil, rests within a canal formed by the bony arches of the vertebral column. If we were to make a cross section of the spinal cord, we would see that there are two rather distinct areas—one consisting of gray matter and the other of white matter. The gray matter, which consists largely of cell bodies of neurons, forms a central column in the spinal cord. The white matter is made up of the axons and forms the outer area of the cord. This outer area derives its color from the myelin, which is a white, fatty material surrounding the axons. The white matter is made up of ascending (sensory or afferent) and descending (motor or efferent) fiber tracts. These tracts, or bundles of axons, are arranged in an orderly manner depending upon their function. Some

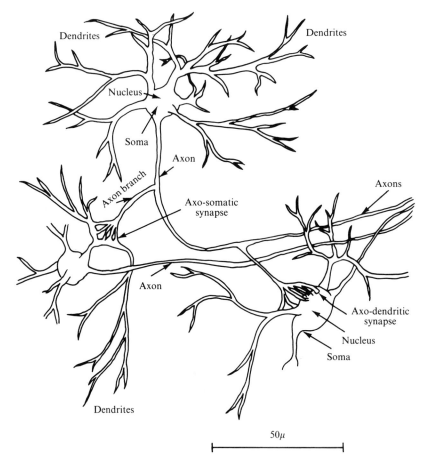

Figure 3–3. Three neurons shown in semischematic form.
Note the various connections between the neurons. From
C. F. Stevens, *Neurophysiology: A Primer.* Copyright 1966
by John Wiley & Sons, Inc. Reprinted by permission of the
publisher.

spinal tracts carry incoming sensory information from the receptors of the body and limbs up to the brain; others carry impulses from the brain down through the cord. It is these latter tracts
which are eventually responsible for activating the muscles of the
body.

The spinal cord is more than a conduction path of sensory
and motor fibers leading to and from the brain: there are also
various interconnections between neurons at the spinal level. Let
us consider one of the simplest of these connections—the *simple
reflex arc.* Shown in Figure 3–4 is a schematic of a cross section of

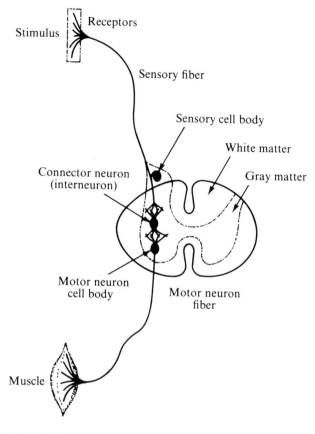

Figure 3-4. A simplified diagram of a reflex arc.

the spinal cord. In this figure, pain receptors are activated by a pin prick (stimulus). These receptors in turn activate a sensory fiber. Note at this point that the cell body for the sensory fiber lies outside the spinal cord. Recall that clusters of cell bodies outside the central nervous system are called ganglia. Thus, the cell bodies of sensory fibers are located in a series of ganglia alongside but outside the spinal cord. The sensory fiber enters the cord and makes a *synaptic* contact with another neuron inside the gray matter of the cord. This second neuron, called a *connector* or *interneuron*, in turn stimulates a motor neuron. Activation of the motor neuron causes the muscle (effector) to contract. This is called a *simple reflex arc* and, indeed, is an oversimplification of anything that actually does happen in the nervous system. For example, with even a simple stimulation such as a pin prick, the picture would be much more complex. Thus the incoming sensory fiber would branch as it entered the spinal cord and would send out both ascending and descending branches. These branches in turn would give off collaterals (other branches) at various levels of the cord, and these collaterals might excite additional motor neurons, thereby producing a large reflex response. In addition, impulses would travel up various pathways in the spinal cord and inform the brain of the presence of the painful stimulus. In response to this message, the brain would send impulses back down the spinal cord. While the interconnections of neurons in the spinal cord are not as complex as those in the brain, the spinal cord is not just a simple bundle of ascending and descending tracts.

The Brain

The brain is a complicated arrangement of about ten billion nerve cells that connect and interconnect in a fantastic number of synapses. An analogy between the brain and a computer is often made, but even the most complex of computers is simple compared to the brain. Actually, of course, the analogy is not a very good one since computers are not made to be like brains. As pointed out by Gregory (1966, p. 64), the brain "is not very similar to actual computers designed by engineers, if only because there are already plenty of brains available at very reasonable cost, and they are easy to make by a well-proved method so that computers are designed to be different." For some functions, the computer is superior. Computers are far better in solving mathematical problems since they can perform thousands of operations in a very short time. However, the brain is superior in solving perceptual problems or problems that require a certain amount of flexibility or versatility in the "programming."

The brain has three major divisions: the *hindbrain*, the *midbrain*, and the *forebrain*. The general locations of each of the three divisions can be seen in Figure 3–5, which is a medial view of the brain; that is, the brain has been sectioned down the middle.

Hindbrain

Two of the most important of the several structures in the hindbrain are the *medulla* and the *cerebellum*. The medulla is often referred to as the vital center of the brain because it contains centers that are concerned with vital functions such as breathing, heartbeat, and blood pressure. However, it also contains relay

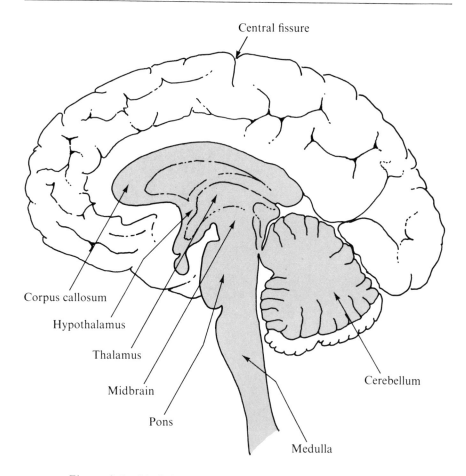

Figure 3-5. Medial view of the human brain.

centers that project sensory impulses arriving from the spinal cord to higher centers of the brain. The cerebellum is a complex structure consisting of many nuclei and pathways. One of its main functions is to aid in maintaining equilibrium and in coordinating voluntary movement. It receives a large volume of neural impulses from the kinesthetic and vestibular sensory receptors.

Midbrain

Essentially, the midbrain forms a connection, or relay station, between portions of the hindbrain and forebrain. However, it does have several sensory nuclei that are lower, or primitive, centers for vision and audition. Motor nuclei are also located in this region.

Forebrain

The structures in the forebrain are largely responsible for the so-called higher mental functions. It is in the forebrain that thinking and perception occur, and it is here that much of what we call "behavior" is determined. Among the major structures of the forebrain are the *cerebral hemispheres*, the *thalamus*, and the *hypothalamus*.

Cerebral Hemispheres. The human brain is divided into two symmetrical halves, which are called the cerebral hemispheres. The hemispheres are connected by a band of fibers called the corpus callosum. The thousands of fibers in the corpus callosum have cell bodies on one side or the other of the two hemispheres and their endings in the opposite side. The surface area of the cerebral hemispheres is called the *cortex*. The cortex presents a rough, rumpled looking appearance because of the numerous ridges, or *gyri* (singular, gyrus), and crevices, which are called *sulci* (singular, sulcus). These can be seen in Figure 3–7. We will consider the cortex in detail later.

Thalamus. Located under the cortex are numerous nuclei and nerve pathways. For our purposes, the most important sub-cortical structure is the *thalamus* (Figure 3–5). The thalamus, which is located just above the midbrain, may be considered as the great sensory relay station of the brain. It is made up of a large number of nuclei that connect with each other, with the lower centers of the brain and spinal cord, and with the higher centers of the brain. In general, these nuclei fall into three categories. There are nuclei with only subcortical connections that do not project fibers to any portion of the cortex. There are other nuclei, called cortical relay nuclei, which receive impulses from ascending sensory pathways and which project these impulses on to the sensory cortex. The third class of nuclei are called association nuclei. These nuclei receive impulses from other nuclei in the thalamus rather than directly from ascending sensory pathways. However, the association nuclei do project impulses to large areas of the cortex, not just to sensory areas.

With the exception of the pathways for the olfactory sense, the sensory pathways for all the senses are interrupted by a synapse in the thalamus before continuing on to the cortex. The thalamus, then, can be thought of as a gateway to the cortex through which passes virtually all the information that we receive from the outside world as well as the information from the sensory receptors inside our bodies.

Reticular Formation. Functions of the *reticular formation* are somewhat similar to those of the thalamus. The reticular formation is a loose collection of neural elements running from the thalamus down into the medulla. Although it is not actually part of the forebrain and is not considered an anatomical entity in the strict sense of the term, it is an important component of the sensory system.

Until fairly recently, the sensory system was thought to consist only of specific pathways that carry impulses to specific nuclei in the thalamus which, in turn, project impulses to special areas of the cortex. In other words, a *specific sensory system.* However, the existence of a second, *unspecific* sensory system involving the reticular formation has now been established. It appears that as the sensory impulses ascend the classical pathways to the thalamus, some of the impulses are "sidetracked" to the reticular formation. The reticular formation projects these impulses on to the cortex, but in a fashion different from the thalamus. Impulses from the reticular formation are projected in such a way that they tend to cause widespread activity in the cortex. Because of its ability to activate the cortex, the reticular system has been called the *reticular activating system (RAS).* One of the primary functions of the RAS is the maintenance of the waking state of the animal.

In considering the thalamus and the reticular formation, it should be remembered that these structures are not concerned with just "one way traffic" of sensory impulses. While the cerebral cortex receives the impulses projected by these structures, the cortex also sends back impulses. The relationship between these subcortical structures and the cortex can be thought of in terms of *closed-loop systems:* thus, impulses from the reticular formation or the thalamus arouse areas of the cortex, but the cortex in turn sends back impulses to these structures which arouse them. Similar feedback systems characterize virtually all structures in the brain. While some structures at lower levels may project impulses to other lower centers and, in turn, receive impulses from these centers, the entire brain involves a system of control and feedback links.

Hypothalamus. The *hypothalamus* is concerned with autonomic functions, although any of the autonomic effects produced by the hypothalamus can also be produced by lower centers in the medulla and in the spinal cord. The hypothalamus is of considerable importance as an integration center, since it coordinates the autonomic responses into patterns of activity that help regulate the body's internal environment. Thus, the hypothalamus plays a role in regulating body temperature, endocrine functions, blood pressure, sexual behavior, and other autonomic functions. The hypothalamus, as part of a system known as the *limbic system*, is of considerable importance in motivation and emotion. The hypothalamus consists of numerous pairs of nuclei, each pair with a rather precise function. The existence of pairs of nuclei is not unique with the hypothalamus and is the case with all structures in the brain. Even when a structure is situated on the midline of the brain, as is true with the hypothalamus, its nuclei are in pairs. When a structure does not exist on the midline, then a similar structure will be found in both halves of the brain.

Some interesting research has been conducted on the functions of the hypothalamus. In studies of subhuman animals, the research techniques usually involve either stimulation of a region of the hypothalamus by means of a mild electric current or destruction of a region by various methods. Either procedure results in some rather bizarre behavior. For example, stimulation of one area of the hypothalamus causes an animal to eat, but stimulation of another area inhibits the animal's eating. Destruction of this latter area, however, causes the animal to eat until it doubles its normal weight. Note that stimulation of an area and destruction of the area bring about opposite results.

Experiments with monkeys and cats have shown that the stimulation or destruction of areas near the hypothalamus also has an effect on emotional behavior. For instance, when the *amygdala* is partially destroyed by means of lesions, male monkeys and cats become so sexually aroused that they attempt to copulate with other male monkeys or cats, with chickens, or with almost any object. Similarly, stimulation of a region of the amygdala makes an animal extremely savage, but removal of the same region makes a wild animal tame. Other emotional responses are also associated with these areas.

Cerebral Cortex. All nerve impulses eventually reach the *cortex*, the structure of the brain which is largely responsible for mental processes. Thinking, willing, memory, emotions, sensations, voluntary control of movement, consciousness—all are results of neural activity of the cerebral cortex. However, it must be remembered that the functioning of the cortex is dependent upon input from other parts of the brain.

The cortex receives nerve impulses from several sources. Figure 3–6 shows that specific sensory pathways carry impulses to nuclei in the thalamus. Some impulses from these pathways also reach the reticular formation. The thalamus projects impulses primarily to the sensory area of the cortex, but it sends impulses to

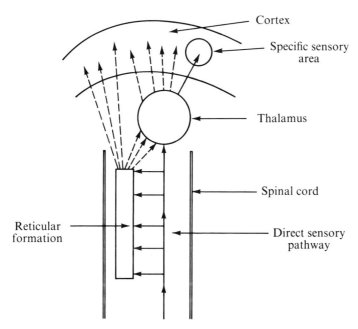

Figure 3–6. Functional diagram of the reticular activating system. The system involves indirect sensory pathways (dotted arrows) to several areas of the cortex. The system receives collaterals from the direct sensory pathway (solid arrows). Not shown are pathways that lead back from the cortex to the reticular system.

other cortical areas as well. As was pointed out previously, the impulses projected by the reticular formation cause widespread activation of the cortex.

Structurally, the cortex of each hemisphere is divided into four sections called *lobes*. In a rough fashion, these divisions or lobes are marked off by several of the larger fissures (sulci). Figure 3–7 shows two prominent fissures—the *central fissure* (*fissure of Rolando*) and the *lateral fissure* (*fissure of Sylvius*). Also shown in the figure are the four lobes of the cerebral cortex. The *frontal lobe* is located in front of the central fissure and above the lateral fissure;

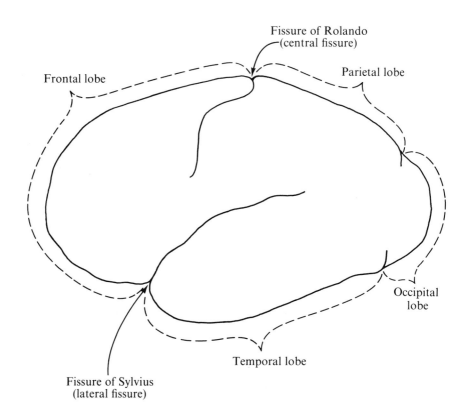

Fissure of Rolando
(central fissure)

Frontal lobe

Parietal lobe

Occipital
lobe

Temporal lobe

Fissure of Sylvius
(lateral fissure)

Figure 3–7. The lobes of the left cerebral hemisphere.

the *parietal lobe* is behind the central fissure, although still partially
above the lateral fissure. The *temporal lobe* is below the lateral
fissure, and the *occipital lobe* is located at the back of the brain.

Over the years, a great deal has been learned about the
microscopic structure of the cortex. Much of the research in this
area has attempted to relate the structure of the cortex, which
differs somewhat in various regions, to the functions of the cortex.
It is generally recognized that there are five types of neurons in the
cerebral cortex and that these neurons can be found in one or
more of the six layers, or strata, of the cortex. Although most
investigators agree that there are six layers of the cortex, it has
been shown that these will vary in different parts of the cortex, and
in some areas one or more of the strata may be reduced or en-

larged. By means of anatomical studies of the brain, anatomists have been able to determine the sensory pathways between the receptors and the brain and to trace the pathways from areas of the brain to the various effectors. However, anatomical research can give us only limited information about the functions of the brain. Other research techniques have been more successful in studying the functioning of the various parts of the brain.

One way of investigating the brain's functions involves studying the behavior of an animal very closely and then *extirpating* (cutting out or destroying) a designated area of the brain to see how the animal's behavior is affected. Similarly, studying the symptoms of patients who are known to have brain lesions of various types has given us some information about brain functions. Another method consists of stimulating certain areas of an animal's brain with mild electric current and then recording behavior changes. With humans, subjective data on brain functions can also be obtained by stimulating some area of the cortex and then asking the subject to report what he feels—for instance, pain or some other sensation. A "reverse" approach is to stimulate some sensory receptors and then trace the nerve impulses to some part of the brain. When these impulses arrive at some area in the brain, there are observable changes in the electrical potential of the brain in that area. These changes can be recorded by means of equipment that is now available in many laboratories. These and other research techniques have given scientists a considerable amount of information about the functions of the brain; however, there is still a great deal to be learned.

Functionally, the cortex is divided into three areas—the *sensory, motor,* and *association areas.* These areas include any parts of the cortex that have not been identified with specific sensory or motor tasks. It has been suggested that the greater the association area of the brain, the greater the degree of behavioral flexibility that will be shown by the animal. The motor and sensory areas of the cortex are mapped on the illustration of the brain in Figure 3–8.

The experience that we recognize as sensation is brought about when nerve impulses, which were generated by the receptors and have traveled over various afferent pathways, reach the sensory areas of the cortex. Figure 3–8 shows that the sensory area of the cortex associated with body sensitivity (the *somesthetic area*) is located behind the central fissure. This area, which is also called the postcentral gyrus, receives impulses which have originated in the receptors for pressure (touch), heat, cold, and pain. Most of the impulses arriving at the postcentral gyrus of one cerebral hemi-

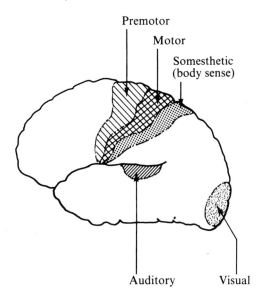

Premotor

Motor

Somesthetic
(body sense)

Auditory   Visual

Figure 3–8. Map of the motor and sensory areas of the
cortex.

sphere originate on the *opposite* side of the body. This phenomenon
is due to the fact that the majority of fibers carrying impulses from
receptors on one side of the body "cross over" at the spinal level
and ascend in tracts on the opposite side of the body. The brain is
characterized by this crossover effect. Thus, if our left arm is
touched, it is "sensed" on the right side of the brain. This is also
true in the case of motor control since many of the efferent fibers
from the motor areas of the brain cross over (*decussate*) at the
level of the medulla.

Various parts of the body are not equally represented, in
terms of amount of area, in the somesthetic region of the cortex.
The representation of a part of the body on the cortex is based not
on the size of the body area but on its sensitivity. Thus, we find only
a very small area of the somesthetic cortex associated with a
region such as the middle of the back, which is relatively insensitive, as compared with the amount of cortical area associated
with the lips and tongue. The area receiving sensory impulses from
the feet is located in the sensory cortex near the top of the central
fissure. The sense organs from the head project impulses to an area
near the bottom of the fissure.

Some idea as to the representation of various parts of the
body on the somesthetic cortex can be obtained from Figure

3–9. This figure, called a "homunculus," shows how much of the cortex is devoted to sensation arising from various regions of the body. Note, for example, the difference between the toes and fingers in the amount of cortical representation. From the "point of view" of the cortex, man is mostly lip, tongue, and fingers.

Each area of the somesthetic cortex represents a particular

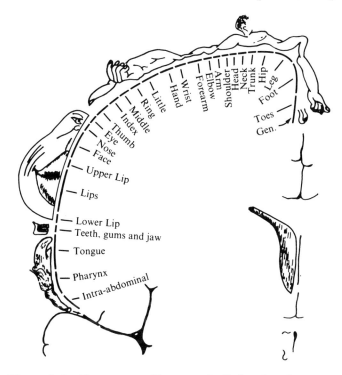

Figure 3–9. The sensory "homunculus" showing the area of cortex devoted to sensation arising from various parts of the body. From Penfield and Rasmussen, *The Cerebral Cortex of Man.* Copyright © 1950 by The Macmillan Company, New York. Reprinted by permission of the publisher.

region of the body. This is called *topographical* representation or topographical arrangement. We find that a topographic arrangement occurs in most of the sensory systems. In some cases, there may even be an arrangement of this type involving subcortical centers. This is the situation with vision. Although the cortical sensory area for vision is found in the occipital lobe of the cortex, the thalamus is also important in vision. By various methods, it has been shown that there are points of the occipital lobe and in the thalamus that represent specific points in the retina. In other words, for any given spot, or point, on the retina there is a corresponding point in the thalamus and on the cortex. This does not imply that the subcortical region (thalamus) is as important for vision as the cortex. If the occipital region of the cortex is destroyed, the individual can still detect light but will not be able to make out any details.

The auditory area of man's cortex (see Figure 3–8), which is located below and behind the lateral fissure, is the projection region for the nerve impulses from the auditory receptors. We still find a type of topographic arrangement which is called *tonotopic projection*. What this means is that a sound of a given frequency will eventually excite neurons in a different part of the auditory area of the cortex than will a sound with another frequency. However, the tonotopic projection does not seem to be as precise as the topographic projection involved in vision and in the somesthetic senses.

Concerning the brain mechanisms responsible for the sensation of taste and smell, very little is known. The difficulty of conducting research with these senses has already been mentioned. Some effort has been directed at localizing the area of the brain involved with the chemical senses and a good idea as to the approximate locations is available. However, the exact areas of the brain responsible for taste and smell are not known with certainty.

Although we are primarily concerned with the sensory aspects of the brain in this chapter, you may have noted on Figure 3–8 that a large area in front of the central fissure (*precentral gyrus*) is marked as motor and premotor area. These areas are responsible for the control of the motor activity, and when part of the motor area is destroyed, there will be a corresponding paralysis in some area on the opposite side of the body. As with the sensory cortex, specific areas on the motor cortex represent specific areas of the body. If one particular point on the precentral gyrus is stimulated, it might result in the movement of a finger on the opposite side of the body. Stimulation of another area will produce movement in the leg, and so forth. As was true in the somesthetic sensory area, different parts of the body are more or less represented in the motor cortex. A "homunculus" of the motor cortex looks very much like that for the somesthetic cortex (Figure 3–9). Areas concerned with movement of the trunk and limbs are quite small, while those for the hands and fingers, lips and tongue are much larger.

On Figure 3–8, the areas involved with sensory and motor functions take up only a small part of the cortex. The remaining areas are called the *association areas* of the cortex and are found in each of the four lobes of the hemispheres—frontal, temporal, parietal, and occipital. An association area is characterized by a vast number of interconnections involving sensory and motor areas, other association areas, and subcortical structures such as the thalamus. In general, what we tend to think of as the higher mental functions are based on the association areas of the brain. For example, an area of the parietal cortex (on only the left hemisphere) is largely responsible for symbolic speech, another part for complex perceptual functions. We also find that the association area in the temporal lobe is involved with visual perception. When parts of this cortex are destroyed, good visual acuity remains, but deficits in the ability to recognize form occur. Some memory functions are also believed to reside in the temporal lobe association areas. Association areas in the frontal lobe are assumed to be involved in a variety of complex response processes, although this has been difficult to demonstrate. The role of the association areas of the occipital lobe is uncertain. Much of what is known about the association areas of the brain is due to the pioneering work of the late Karl Lashley (1929, 1950).

The Nerve Impulse

We have repeatedly mentioned the *nerve impulse*—how it is brought about by excitation of the receptors, how it travels along nerve fibers, how it eventually reaches areas of the brain, and how the brain translates these impulses into our experience of sensation. However, we have not discussed the nerve impulse in terms of what it actually is—*a complicated physicochemical event*. The nerve impulse is actually a rapid voltage charge along a nerve fiber that is called an *action potential*. Let us look at some of the electrical characteristics of a neuron that must be understood before we can meaningfully discuss the nerve impulse.

Electrical Properties of the Nerve Fiber

The neuron has many of the characteristics of other cells, including a cell membrane. However, the membrane is particularly important in the nerve cell since it is intimately involved in the nerve impulse. If we were to use appropriate electrical measuring equipment, we would find that there is a voltage difference between the inside and the outside of a nerve fiber (axon) that is generally referred to as a *potential* difference. This term simply refers to electrical strength. It can be measured in millivolts (1 millivolt =

1/1000 of a volt). The potential difference that exists between the interior of the nerve fiber and the exterior is called the *membrane potential*, simply because the membrane separates this inside-outside voltage.

The membrane potential is the result of a concentration of positive ions outside the axon membrane that is greater than the concentration of positive ions on the inside. Thus, the inside is relatively more negative. The outside of the membrane is characterized by a concentration of sodium and chloride ions, while the inside has more potassium ions. The resulting potential difference is about −50 or −60 millivolts between the inside and outside of the membrane, assuming, of course, that the nerve fiber is at rest. A neuron is "resting" when it is not carrying an impulse. The *resting potential* of a fiber is the same as the membrane potential when the fiber is not active. However, one should not confuse the resting potential and membrane potential. Although they may be the same when the axon is not carrying an impulse, the membrane potential changes drastically when the fiber is active.

Two other terms require definition—*depolarization* and *hyperpolarization*. Since the nerve impulse is mostly concerned with changes in the membrane potential, it is convenient to have terms available to describe these changes. For example, when the change in the membrane potential is such that it is *more positive* than the resting potential (−60 millivolts), then the axon is said to be *depolarized*. Since we are dealing with a negative voltage, if the membrane potential were −20 millivolts instead of −60, we would say that the axon was 40 millivolts depolarized. Suppose, however, the membrane potential were −80 millivolts instead of the resting −60 millivolts. In this case it is *more negative* by 20 millivolts and is said to be *hyperpolarized*. Thus, using the resting potential as a reference point, a decrease in the membrane potential is referred to as depolarization, while an increase is called hyperpolarization. In both cases, the change in polarization is caused by a flow of ions either inward or outward through the fiber membrane. Depolarization occurs when sodium ions flow inward through the membrane while potassium ions move outward. The opposite situation is encountered in hyperpolarization.

The Action Potential

We have already stated that the action potential is a rapid voltage charge along a nerve fiber. We will now consider how this takes place.

It was pointed out that a neuron maintains a *resting potential* due to the different concentration of ions on the two sides of the cell membrane. Because of the greater concentration of positive ions (electrical particles) on the outside of the membrane, the inside is electrically negative in relation to the outside. When the neuron is in a resting stage, the membrane prevents the positive ions from moving to the inside of the membrane and the negative ions from moving to the outside. In other words, the membrane is not *permeable* to these particular ions. However, when appropriate stimulation is applied to the neuron, there is a change in the characteristics of the cell membrane, and, for a brief moment, it "relaxes its guard." There is a rapid exchange of ions between the inside and outside of the membrane with the positive ions (sodium) flowing inward and the negative ions (potassium) outward. If we were to plot this exchange on a time base, we would see that initially the change in permeability of the membrane is for sodium ions which flow inward. Enough of these positive ions flow in so that for a brief instant the polarity of the membrane is reversed— that is, the inside becomes positive and the outside negative with respect to each other. However, the permeability of the membrane of sodium ions lasts for a very short time, and then the permeability for potassium ions increases so that these negative ions move outward through the membrane. This tends to re-establish the ionic balance so that once again the outside of the membrane becomes positive in relation to the inside (Hodgkin, 1958; Hodgkin, Huxley, & Katz, 1949).

Definite changes in the potential differences measured between the inside and outside of the membrane are associated with the inflow of sodium ions and outflow of potassium ions. The entire sequence of these electrical changes, which can be measured in millivolts, is called the *action potential*. During the rapid influx of sodium ions, there is a large *positive* response of the action potential, which is a period of depolarization of the membrane. The depolarization lasts for a very brief time and is followed by a longer period of hyperpolarization as the potassium ions flow outward. If we were to record the changes in the membrane potential associated with these ionic exchanges, it would look something like Figure 3–10. On this figure, it can be seen that the membrane undergoes a large, rapid depolarization which exceeds the magnitude of the resting potential and corresponds to the sodium inflow. As we have pointed out, for a brief period the fiber actually reverses its polarity. This reverse is the *spike potential* component of the complete action potential. Following the spike potential, there is a less rapid

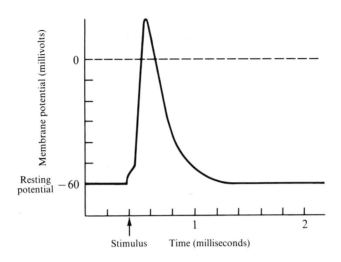

Figure 3–10. Schematic representation of an action potential. The stimulus was applied at the time indicated by the arrow.

return to the resting potential as the potassium ions flow outward—the more gradual downward slope of the spike on Figure 3–10.

Movement of the Nerve
Impulse along a Fiber

The action potential described above does not occur in all sections of the nerve fiber at the same time. If we were to have electrical measuring equipment attached at different points along a nerve fiber, we would see the action potential registering at only one place at a given time. However, we would also see that the impulse was progressing down the fiber. This is accomplished because the leading edge of the active region of the fiber activates the area just ahead of it and causes a spike potential to develop. Thus the process of depolarization goes down the length of the fiber. The action potential might be thought of as an active area of membrane moving down the fiber and depolarizing the area immediately ahead. Just behind it, the polarization of the fiber is restored. The analogy between the nerve impulse and a flame moving down a fuse can be helpful, although one must remember that the nerve fiber is self-restoring, unlike the flame.

In nerve impulse conduction, recording equipment at any point on the fiber would show that the magnitude of the spike potential was the same along the entire length of the fiber. This type of conduction takes place in fibers that are *nonmyelinated*. Recall that myelinated fibers are surrounded by a sheath of fatty material, called myelin, which is interrupted at intervals by constrictions called *nodes of Ranvier*. A different type of conduction takes place in myelinated fibers.

In the myelinated regions between the nodes of Ranvier, the impulse spreads passively down the membrane, decreasing with distance from the node. When the impulse reaches the point on the membrane at which the myelin is interrupted (node of Ranvier), if it is still above threshold it results in a full-blown action potential at the node. This in turn moves along the next myelinated region by passive spread.

In order to better understand this type of conduction, suppose that we were to record the impulse at a number of points along a myelinated fiber. These points would be between and at the nodes of Ranvier as shown in Figure 3–11. It can be seen from this figure that at successive points between nodes we record responses very much like the one at the stimulated node, except they are progressively smaller as we move away from the stimulated node. At the second node, we again record a full-scale action potential. Thus, in a myelinated fiber the impulse "jumps" from node to node, while in the nonmyelinated fiber it "sweeps" continuously along the fiber. The conduction in a myelinated fiber is sometimes called *saltatory conduction* (from the Latin *saltare*—to dance).

How fast does the impulse move along a fiber? Because the nodes of Ranvier act as "boosting stations," conduction speed along a myelinated fiber may be more than ten times as fast as along a nonmyelinated fiber. Actually, the nerve impulse does not travel at a particularly fast rate or speed. The velocity for different fibers will vary from as little as a half meter per second to over 120 meters per second. The speed with which a fiber conducts an impulse depends on several factors, the most important being the diameter. The larger the diameter, the greater the velocity. Thus, since fibers of different diameter carry nerve impulses to the brain, some impulses will be conducted faster than others.

The Excitability of Nerve Fibers

The excitability of a nerve fiber is its responsiveness to a stimulus. Just how "excitable" a fiber is at any given time depends upon several factors. Probably the most important factor is how recently the fiber had been active—that is, how recently a nerve impulse has passed along the fiber.

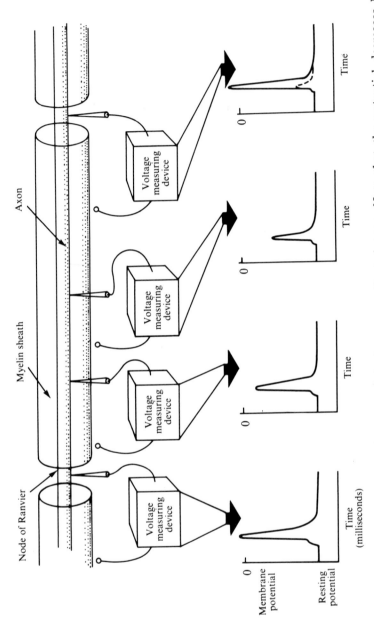

Figure 3–11. Conduction of an action potential along a myelinated axon. Note that the potential decreases between the nodes but is brought up to full "power" at each node. The dotted curve in the right-hand graph indicates the voltage that would have been recorded at that node if the membrane there had not been able to produce an action potential. From C. F. Stevens, *Neurophysiology: A Primer.* Copyright 1966 by John Wiley & Sons, Inc. Reprinted by permission of the publisher.

For example, suppose that electrical stimulation at some point on a fiber results in an action potential. If we stimulate that point again *immediately* after the first action potential, the fiber will not respond, no matter how strong the applied stimulus. This *absolute refractory period* lasts for about one millisecond. Immediately following the absolute refractory period is the *relative refractory period* of several milliseconds during which an action potential can again be initiated, but only by a stimulus that is much stronger than that normally required. These two periods correspond to the times during which the sodium ions are flowing inward (absolute refractory period) and the potassium ions begin to flow outward (relative refractory period).

Stimulation that is not sufficiently strong to generate an action potential may modify the membrane in such a way that it becomes more sensitive. A stimulus of this type, which is called *sub-threshold*, will modify the polarization to such an extent that a second stimulus, which normally would be sub-threshold, will generate an action potential. The change in polarization brought about by a sub-threshold stimulus is referred to as a *local potential* —one that is not conducted along the fiber.

A stimulus that is not of sufficient strength to evoke an action potential is called sub-threshold; a stimulus that is strong enough is called supra-threshold. While one might assume that as a supra-threshold stimulus becomes stronger the resulting action potential will also become stronger, this is not the case. As long as a stimulus is sufficiently intense to evoke an action potential, the amplitude and duration of the action potential will be the same, regardless of the strength of the stimulus. This fact is called the *all-or-none rule*. As is the case with most rules, there are exceptions. However, the all-or-none law does apply for most types of nerve fibers.

Synaptic Transmission

At one time it was thought that there was a physical continuity between the processes of neurons and that nerve impulses were propagated from one neuron to another through the network formed by their intermingled dendrites (McLennan, 1963). New developments in histological techniques, particularly staining methods, showed that the continuity hypothesis was false but that there were points of contact between neuronal processes. Such a point of contact was called a "synapsis" by Sherrington (1897).

It can be seen from Figure 3–12 that, structurally, the

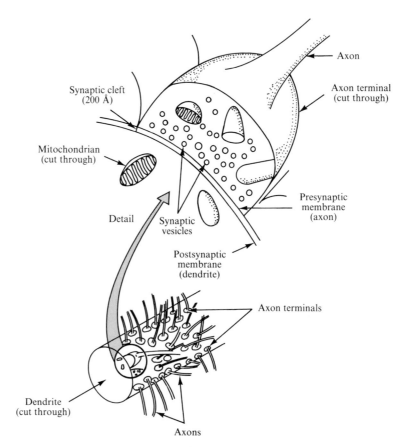

Figure 3–12. An illustration of a synapse. From C. F. Stevens, *Neurophysiology: A Primer.* Copyright 1966 by John Wiley & Sons, Inc. Reprinted by permission of the publisher.

synapse is quite complex. Note the *synaptic cleft*, which is typically about 200 Å wide (1 Å = 10^{-10} meter), that separates the presynaptic membrane (axon) from the postsynaptic membrane (dendrite). Note also the structures, such as the *mitochondria* and *synaptic vesicles*, which are present. The latter are almost always found in abundance adjacent to the presynaptic membrane. It is thought that each of these vesicles holds a minute quantity of transmitter substance that is important in the transmission process.

It is important to keep in mind that each neuron in the nervous system is a separate entity and that there is a tiny gap, the synaptic cleft, between the processes of one neuron and another. Thus, an impulse must bridge the gap between neurons or "die on the vine" so to speak. Just how the gap is bridged is a question that has engrossed researchers for many years. The answers that have been obtained reveal that this process is extremely complex, involving specialized physical structures associated with the synapse, as well as various electrical and chemical events.

The most popular theory of synaptic transmission is a chemical theory. This theory assumes that when the spike potential reaches the ends of the many terminal branches of an axon (*presynaptic terminals*), it causes a chemical to be released across the gap (*synaptic cleft*), which, in turn, evokes a new action potential in the *postsynaptic neuron*. The most obvious questions relating to the chemical theory are concerned with the nature of the released chemical (*transmitter substance*) and how the chemical acts on the postsynaptic membrane to bring about an action potential. Another point that must be taken into consideration is how the transmitter substance is inactivated once it has energized the postsynaptic neuron. *Acetylcholine* is a transmitter substance that has been recognized for some time. This chemical, which has been associated with synapses in the peripheral nervous system, is released at the synapse and, after activating the postsynaptic neuron, is destroyed by an enzyme called *acetylcholinesterase*.

There are several functional characteristics of synapses that are worthy of mention. First, there is a delay in the transmission of the impulse across a synapse; the impulse is momentarily arrested at the synapse. Also, a synapse is a "one-way street." While impulses will travel in both directions within a neuron, synapses are designed in such a fashion that impulses can cross in only one direction. Thus, the impulses will be crossing from the terminals of axons of one neuron to some point on a second neuron. At one time it was thought that the only synapses between neurons were *axodendritic synapses* between the axon of one and the dendrites of others. However, with the advent of the electron microscope it was shown that *axosomatic* synapses also existed. These are synapses between the axon of one neuron and the cell body of another (Eccles, 1957). Some of the possible interconnections between neurons are illustrated in Figure 3-3.

In discussing transmission we have implied that the events that take place are such that the postsynaptic neuron is excited and a new nerve impulse generated. This, indeed, is the case when the membrane of the postsynaptic neuron is depolarized to a sufficient degree. Here, an *excitatory* synapse is involved. However, there are also *inhibitory* synapses that bring about a hyperpolarizing effect on the postsynaptic membrane. This "inhibits" the neuron and tends to prevent the generation of action potentials. Through a combination of inhibitory and excitatory synapses, the excitability of a neuron can be controlled.

The System So Far

In this and the previous chapter we have considered the various elements of the sensing function to make up a subsystem which, in turn, is part of the system that we are concerned with—the human organism. Figure 3–13 shows the relationship of the sensing subsystem to the other subsystems in the complete system.

As you may recall from the example of a system analysis in Chapter 1, an analysis can be made at any of a number of different levels. This is also true of the sensing subsystem. In **Figure 3–13 we**

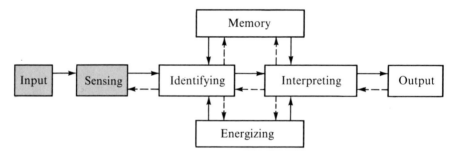

Figure 3–13. The system so far. The inputs to the system and the sensing subsystem have now been considered.

represent this subsystem as a component or element in a larger system. As a first step in further analyzing this subsystem, we can think of it as consisting of receptors, nerve fibers from the receptors, subcortical centers, and the cortex. This type of analysis is shown in Figure 3–14. Beginning at the left of the figure, we have external stimuli exciting receptors. The receptors convert the stimulation to nerve impulses which travel over afferent fibers to the subcortical centers. From these centers the impulses are projected to the cortex. The broken arrows represent pathways from the cortex back to the subcortical centers and back to the area of the receptors.

An analysis of the sensing subsystem such as that shown in Figure 3–14 gives us a better understanding of the subsystem than was available from the simple blocks in Figure 3–13. However, it still does not reveal some of the interactions and relationships that

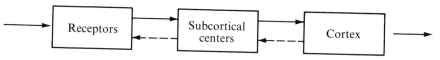

Figure 3–14. A schematic representation of the sensing subsystem.

characterize the various elements in the sensing subsystem. We have seen that the sensing subsystem involves a series of "subsystems within subsystems" which are all necessary for the final output—in this case, our experiencing a sensation of some type. Figure 3–15 represents an analysis of the sensing subsystem that shows some of the more important interactions between the subsystems. As we have emphasized, these subsystems may perform specialized functions, but all contribute to the final objectives or goals of the sensing subsystem.

In Figure 3–15 the various interactions between the elements of the sensing subsystem are shown by means of solid arrows, which represent control links, and broken arrows, which represent feedback links. In order to simplify the schematic, only the most important linkages have been shown. We will briefly review the sensing function by considering each of the subsystems shown and their relationships with the other subsystems.

Receptors. The receptors, which were discussed in the previous chapter, represent the first subsystem within the sensing subsystem. The receptors are specialized collections of cells and nerve endings that are capable of converting some form of physical energy (electromagnetic, mechanical, thermal, or chemical) into nerve impulses—the language of the nervous system.

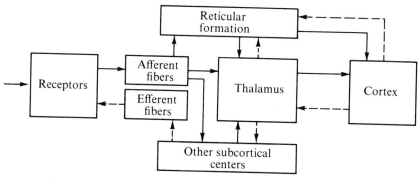

Figure 3–15. A more detailed analysis of the sensing subsystem showing some of the interactions between components of the subsystem.

Afferent and Efferent Fibers. The second subsystem shown on Figure 3–15 is the transmission subsystem. While we are most concerned with the afferent system of nerve fibers, there is also an efferent system that must be taken into consideration. On our schematic, the afferent system carries the nerve impulses from the receptors to various subcortical locations in the brain. Note on the illustration that some of the impulses are "sidetracked" before reaching the thalamus and sent to the reticular formation or to other subcortical centers, such as the centers in the midbrain referred to earlier as primitive visual and auditory centers. In the case of the primitive visual centers, impulses are sent back to the receptor (eye) by means of efferent fibers. These impulses help control the muscles of the iris, and, based on afferent impulses from the retina, the brain will send efferent impulses back to these muscles. Most of the afferent impulses from the various receptors are sent to the thalamus.

Reticular Formation. The reticular formation can be considered as part of the nonspecific sensory projection system, in contrast to the specific projection system which involves the classical sensory pathways through the thalamus to the sensory cortex. Some afferent impulses are sent to the reticular formation and from there to various parts of the cortex. However, rather than projecting to specific areas of the cortex, as is the case with the thalamus, projections from the reticular formation activate larger areas of the cortex. For this reason it is called the reticular activating system and is important in helping maintain the waking state of the individual. Note that the reticular formation receives "feedback" from the brain and from the thalamus.

Other Subcortical Centers. There are a number of centers in the brain that can receive sensory input either directly or indirectly. Since discussion of these centers can further complicate an already complex topic, only two such centers have been mentioned. These are located in the midbrain and receive impulses from both the auditory and visual receptors. On Figure 3–15, linkages between these centers and the thalamus are shown. It is possible that linkages between the cortex and these centers also exist and should be shown on the figure. However, these were omitted from the figure since the extent of these connections, if they exist, is unknown for the sensory pathways.

Thalamus. The thalamus can be considered the great sensory relay nucleus of the brain. Virtually all information from the external and internal sensory pathways passes through the thalamus and is then projected to the sensory areas of the cortex. The thalamus contains a number of nuclei that connect with each other, with lower centers of the brain and spinal cord, and with the cortex. The thalamus is properly considered as the "gateway" to the cortex for most sensory information.

Cortex. Nerve impulses from the thalamus and reticular formation eventually reach various areas of the cortex. It is in these areas that "sensation" is experienced. There are specific areas of the cortex associated with vision, audition, somesthetic sensitivity, and probably for smell and taste. We find that there is typically a topographic representation on the cortex. Thus, in the case of body sensitivity, one area of the somesthetic region will represent the hand, another the foot, and so forth.

On Figure 3–15, we have shown feedback links from the cortex to the thalamus and reticular formation. The information that is sent back to these subcortical centers probably originates in the association areas of the cortex. In other words, for the feedback to the lower centers, more is required of the cortex than just activation of the sensory areas. Activation of these areas in turn produces activity in some of the association areas which, in turn, send impulses back to the lower centers.

Summary

1. The nervous system can be partitioned into a central and peripheral nervous system. This can be considered as a structural scheme. From a functional point of view, the nervous system can be considered as consisting of a somatic and autonomic system. The latter is further divided into a sympathetic and parasympathetic system.

2. Neurons are the structural and functional units of the nervous system. While they are like other cells in many ways, they have specialized properties of irritability and conductivity. Neurons have processes called dendrites, which conduct afferent impulses toward the cell body, and axons, which conduct efferent impulses away from the cell body. Some axons are encased in sheaths consisting of myelin.

3. The brain has three main divisions called the hindbrain, midbrain, and forebrain. The hindbrain consists of the medulla and cerebellum, and other structures. The midbrain is mainly a con-

nection between the hindbrain and forebrain but does contain several nuclei. The forebrain consists of a number of important structures, such as the cerebral hemispheres, the thalamus, and hypothalamus.

4. The thalamus can be considered the main sensory relay station of the brain because most of the sensory fibers reach it. Some incoming sensory fibers go to the reticular formation while still others go to various subcortical centers.

5. The hypothalamus is important in autonomic functions and also plays a role in emotion.

6. The cortex contains the sensory areas that receive the nerve impulses from the thalamus and reticular formation. There are rather specific locations on the cortex for the incoming sensory information for vision, audition, and the skin senses. Topographic representation is the rule in these areas. Association areas are also found on the cortex and are important for the higher mental processes that we normally associate with the cortex.

7. There is a potential difference between the inside and outside of a nerve membrane with the inside negative in relation to the outside. This is called the membrane potential. When the nerve fiber is unexcited, this potential difference is referred to as the resting potential.

8. The membrane potential can change in one of two directions. It can become more positive (depolarized) or more negative (hyperpolarized). These changes are brought about by an inward or outward flow of ions through the cell membrane.

9. The nerve impulse, or action potential, results when a stimulus causes a rapid depolarization of the membrane of the nerve fiber. Sodium ions flow inward and potassium ions outward. This exchange progresses down the fiber, with the resulting electrical changes making up the action potential. The impulse progresses in a different fashion on myelinated and nonmyelinated fibers.

10. The excitability of a nerve fiber will vary at different times. Immediately after a nerve impulse has passed, it cannot be excited by another stimulus (absolute refractory period). Then, for a brief period, a stronger than normal stimulus can set up another action potential (relative refractory period). If not stimulated during these periods, the fiber returns to a normal state of excitability.

11. The axons of one neuron do not make a physical contact with another neuron. Rather, there is a small gap between the two called a synapse. According to the chemical theory of synaptic transmission, a transmitter agent is released at the ends of the

axons of one neuron and will stimulate the membrane of the next neuron and cause an action potential to be generated in the second neuron.

Selected Readings

Butter, C. M. *Neuropsychology: The study of brain and behavior.* Monterey, California: Brooks/Cole, 1968.

McLennan, H. *Synaptic transmission.* Philadelphia: W. B. Saunders, 1963.

Stevens, C. F. *Neurophysiology: A primer.* New York: Wiley, 1966.

4

The Identifying Subsystem

We have seen that the physical world is made up of objects, called stimulus objects, that are capable of producing or reflecting certain forms of energy that stimulate our various sense organs. Nerve impulses generated by the stimulation of the receptors travel to sensory areas of the cortex, which in turn translate these impulses and produce sensations of some kind—touch, sound, color, and so forth. However, man experiences more than bits of color or sound or pressure. The process by which these bits of sensory data are *organized* and given *meaning* is called *perception*. As we will see, this organization is a complex process that is based not only on the incoming sensory information but also on the past experience and present needs of the individual.

For many years most psychologists adhered to the viewpoint that sensation and perception should be considered distinctly separate processes. Perception was thought to arise out of sensation through various associative and compounding mechanisms. However, this view has been abandoned by most psychologists (Helson, 1967), and, as pointed out by Graham and Ratoosh (1962), the use of "sensory" and "perceptual" as different words is a matter of convenience since they are not based on different meanings. There are a number of reasons for the change in the viewpoint toward sensation and perception. Historically, one of the most important reasons was the realization that the sensory process involves more than just a routine "delivery" of nerve impulses to the cortex after which perceptual processes take over. That the sensory process is more complicated than was previously believed is shown by recent neurophysiological research, which indicates that the organism itself will modify the incoming sensory deliveries in a number of ways. This modification may take place by means of efferent impulses from the brain which alter the excitability of the receptors and, consequently, control afferent input. Modifications of sensation also occur through other processes that, in one way or another, affect the sensory input.

What role does perception play in human behavior? Perception can be viewed as a process of identification and can thus be considered man's "identifying subsystem." As we have indicated earlier, the human system can be said to consist of an input, a transformation process, and an output. Although some transformation of input occurs in the sensing subsystem, the primary transformation between input and output begins with the identifying subsystem—that is, with perception.

Definition of Perception

The term "perception" is difficult to define. The problem, as discussed by Zener and Gaffron (1962), is that the verb "perceive" is highly ambiguous and may be used to refer to several specific, but different, processes. What is meant, exactly, when we say that an organism (O) perceives some object, event, situation, or relation (X)? In other words, what happens when "O perceives X"? As Zener and Gaffron suggest, it is more fruitful to examine the different meanings of the statement "O perceives X" than to reconcile the diverse definitions of the verb "perceive." Two meanings discussed by Zener and Gaffron illustrate how divergent the definitions can be.

One meaning of the statement "O perceives X" is that the organism (O) *discriminates* between or among stimuli (X). "Discrimination" in this case refers to the ability of the organism to perceive *differences* among various stimuli. When the organism is able to discriminate (perceive) differences, he makes an experimentally determined response, which serves as an indicator that some sort of "central processing" is going on. Investigators who define the meaning of "O perceives X" in this fashion are not interested in what happens inside the organism during the central discriminatory process; rather, they are interested in the characteristics of the response measure that has been selected. We have already discussed the importance of measurement in psychological research. With this definition, the measurement aspect can be carefully quantified and controlled. Measurement of this sort is advantageous, but it tells us nothing about what the person *experiences* as the perceptual process takes place.

According to Zener and Gaffron, "O perceives X" can also be interpreted to take account of the perceiver's experience in the perceptual process. In this case, the meaning of the statement is: because of some form of stimulation, an *experience* of some type occurs. In other words, because of some specific type of stimulation, a person sees or hears or tastes or feels or smells something. Thus, it is the character of the person's experience rather than the response—verbal or otherwise—that is of central importance to this explanation of the perceptual process. However, the response selected for observation must be such that it gives a good idea of the person's experience. Generally, some form of *verbal report* of the person's experience is the response observed. Although a verbal report may not be a scientifically "neat" form of measurement, it provides more information about the perceiver's experience than can be obtained when the meaning of the statement is "O discriminates X."

As suggested previously, perception can be considered an identifying process; thus, we have called the subsystem responsible for this particular function the "identifying subsystem." We will now consider in more detail why this is an appropriate designation of this process.

Perception as an Identifying
Process

In viewing perception as an identifying process, we borrow from both of the meanings of "O perceives X" that were given above. We have already defined perception broadly (too broadly for technical purposes) as the process by which sensory data are organized and given meaning. What is involved in this organization? Some psychologists believe that perception is the process by which stimuli are organized into *categories* or *classes*. Discrimination is a part of this process, since differentiation among stimuli is a prerequisite to categorizing or classifying. Discrimination, then, is the basic step in the perceptual process. However, the basic process of discrimination must be elaborated upon by the organism, and the sensory information must be placed in classes or categories. Categorization consists of the process of *identification*, which involves placing a stimulus input into a certain class because of its defining attributes (Bruner, Goodnow, & Austin, 1956).

Put in another way, when we identify something, we place it into a category or class with equivalent "somethings" and we exclude it from other categories. For example, when we say that we perceive an apple, we mean that we have identified the environmental referent (stimulus object) of certain sensory signals. We have identified the referent because of various defining attributes such as color, form, size, and texture. By means of these defining attributes, we are able to assign the perception to a class of objects which we label *apples* and not to a class of objects which we label *oranges*. Establishment of these classes is a result of some experience on the part of the organism. Thus, it would not be uncommon for a young child to identify an apple as an orange and to categorize it as such. Perceptual classes are learned, and if the results of certain classifications are not satisfactory for the individual, then through further learning a reclassification takes place.

The attributes of an apple which allow it to be identified and assigned to an *object* class are called *critical attributes*. However, there are many other attributes of the stimulus which are also evaluated in the perceptual process. For instance, a stimulus might also be categorized as *large-small, soft-hard,* and so forth. Based on all these attributes of the stimulus object, the identification, or "placing" of the object in a class, may vary considerably in the richness of its elaboration. Thus, an apple may be categorized not only as an apple but perhaps as a large, red, firm apple. Further, because of previous learning we have a large amount of information about the properties of apples. Once we have identified a particular stimulus object as an apple, we can also anticipate that it tastes sweet or sour, depending upon certain of its attributes (red or green color), and that it may have a worm in it.

Although most of the stimulus objects we perceive in our environment are more complex than apples, the perception of both simple and complex objects consists of the same process of identification and categorization. With increasing complexity, we are forced to deal with more attributes in our identification and, perhaps, to rely more on our past experience with the class of objects encountered. This brings up a rather basic question regarding the concept of perception as an identifying process. When we identify, or categorize, stimuli, we make a decision about the category to which the stimulus should be assigned. Since perception is assumed to be an instantaneous process, some researchers have attacked the view that perception is a process of categorization of stimuli because too much time would be required for the decision making. It has been proposed, however, that even complex stimulus objects might be identified almost instantaneously by neural mechanisms.

While much more could be presented concerning the meaning of perception, for our purposes we will consider perception as the process whereby sensory input is organized into meaningful experience. Meaningful experience is attained by identifying and categorizing the sensory input into separate classes based on various attributes of the stimuli.

Factors Affecting Perception

We have discussed how the identification and labeling, or categorizing, of a stimulus object is dependent upon the attributes of that object. The attributes that a person experiences and utilizes for identifying and categorizing are called *perceived* attributes. However, a stimulus object also has *physical* attributes, which can be measured by means of various instruments and specified in terms of weight, wavelengths, intensity, and so forth. Our perception of an object may be quite different from that which might be expected from an analysis of the physical attributes of the object. For instance, when we view a motion picture, what we perceive is quite different from the physical stimulus that consists of a series of slightly varied static pictures shown rapidly at a certain rate.

One of the problems encountered in the study of perception involves the relationship between the perceived and physical attributes of stimuli. To the extent that the perceived attributes agree with the physical attributes, we say that the relationship is *veridical* or *nonveridical*. Most of our percepts are reasonably veridical; that is, there is a good agreement between the perceived attributes and physical attributes of the stimulus object. Sometimes, however, the relationships are so nonveridical that serious distortions of reality take place.

Numerous factors affect our perceptions of the physical properties of stimuli. In the first place, only a small fraction of the stimulation that bombards the sensory receptors at any given time is ever perceived, because the organism can attend to only a limited amount of sensory stimulation at any given time. Thus, *attention* is an important determinant of perception. Various *stimulus factors* and *personal factors* also affect perception. You will see that perception depends nearly as much on the personal factors (inner factors) as on the stimulus factors (outer factors).

Attention

Attention refers to the process by which a person selects, or attends to, only certain aspects of the stimulation bombarding his sense organs. In attending to some aspects of his environment, a person either ignores or pays "less attention" to other aspects. For instance, someone who is deeply engrossed in an interesting book may notice very little else in his environment.

Stimulus Factors in Attention

Attention is determined in part by personal factors such as motives, interests, and other internal conditions. However, there are also a number of stimulus factors that influence attention. For instance, an *intense* stimulus is more likely to be attended to than a relatively weak stimulus. A bright light against a background of dim lights, or a loud sound among less intense sounds, will tend to attract the attention of an observer. Similarly, the *size* of the stimulus is important in attention. Other factors being equal, a large stimulus among an array of smaller stimuli will attract attention first.

Another stimulus factor that is important in determining the direction of attention is *contrast*. When a stimulus object contrasts with surrounding stimuli, then it tends to be noticed or attended to. For example, a hunter wearing a bright orange jacket stands out from the surrounding terrain because of the contrast. Contrast may be involved in auditory stimulation as well as in the other sensory inputs. Thus, the driver of a car may not notice the noise of the engine until it sounds different for some reason. If the engine misfires, the driver's attention is immediately directed to the sound.

Repetition is another stimulus factor that serves to attract attention. In general, a repeated stimulus is more likely to be noticed than one that is not repeated. However, too much repetition is monotonous and causes a stimulus to become less effective in attracting and holding an observer's attention. Finally, any aspect of the stimulus situation that *changes* is likely to attract attention— for instance, an increase in the intensity of a stimulus, a change in color, a change in contrast, and so forth. *Movement* of a stimulus also attracts attention, and a moving stimulus object stands a better chance of being attended to than a stationary object.

Various stimulus factors may interact with one another to influence the process of attention. For instance, a stimulus of weak intensity that is repeated frequently may be as effective in attracting attention as an intense stimulus that is not presented repeatedly. Similarly, a small stimulus that contrasts sharply with surrounding stimuli may attract attention as effectively as a large stimulus that is low in contrast to surrounding stimuli. In most situations several stimulus factors operate together in determining the direction of a person's attention.

Personal Factors in Attention

There are several personal, or internal, factors that are influential in attracting an individual's attention to various stimuli. Among these factors are *organic* or *biological needs*. A hungry person is likely to notice stimulus objects that are related to food. A thirsty person may be attracted by an illustration of a cold drink but not by other stimuli in his environment. Similarly, stimuli that appeal to the sex drive are quite effective in attracting attention.

Along with organic needs, a person's *interests* play an important role in attention. One is more likely to attend to a stimulus object that, for various reasons, is of interest than to an object that holds no interest. A university instructor who teaches an elective course may hold the attention of his students more easily than the unfortunate instructor teaching a course that is required.

One of the major internal factors that influences attention is *perceptual readiness*, or *set*. Set refers to the disposition of a person to attend to a certain type of stimulus in a particular situation at a given time. For example, as one approaches an intersection while driving an automobile, he is prepared, or "set," to attend to such stimulus objects as traffic lights and other vehicles. Set may be established on the basis of instructions. Perceptual readiness, or set, prepares a person for attending to certain categories of stimulation. In other words, stimulation does not affect a passive receiver but rather a receiver who is "prepared" for certain kinds of stimulation.

A Mechanical Model of Attention

Much of what is known about the external and internal factors affecting attention can be illustrated by means of a mechanical model like the one shown in Figure 4–1. This model, which was invented by D. E. Broadbent in 1957, consists of a Y-shaped tube and several balls that are small enough to pass through the tube. The two branches of the Y tube are wider than the stem, which is only wide enough to take one ball at a time. At the point where the branches of the tube join the stem, there is a hinged flap that normally hangs straight down. However, the flap can be pivoted from its upper edge in such a fashion that it can block either of the branches of the Y.

In Broadbent's model the balls represent incoming sensory information, and the branching arms of the Y represent different

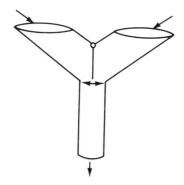

Figure 4–1. A simple mechanical model for attention. From D. E. Broadbent, A mechanical model for human attention and immediate memory. *Psychological Review*, **64**, 1957, 205–215. Copyright © 1957 by the American Psychological Association. Reproduced by permission.

human sensory channels. Thus, the two arms of the Y might represent the two ears, the auditory and visual channels, or any other two channels. In order to influence behavior in any way, a ball that is dropped into one of the arms of the Y must emerge at the bottom of the stem. The operation of this model is analogous to human behavior in several ways.

a. If a ball is dropped into each of the two arms at the same time, the two balls will strike both sides of the flap simultaneously. The flap will not move and the two balls (sensory information) will jam at the junction. A similar process occurs in the human system when two sensory signals are received simultaneously through different sensory channels. Neither signal can be perceived because the two "jam" at some point in the system.

b. If the two balls are not dropped into the arms of the tube at exactly the same moment, the first to arrive at the flap will knock it over and will shut out the other ball. Research on hearing has shown that competing auditory stimuli produce a similar effect in humans.

c. If one ball is thrown violently down the arm, it may push the flap aside even against the weight of another ball arriving at the flap at same time. The violently thrown ball is analogous to an intense sensory stimulus entering the human system. An intense stimulus has an advantage over a less intense stimulus in drawing a person's attention.

d. If a number of balls are to be sent through the tube, it is more efficient to send them through one arm of the Y than to send an equal number of balls through each of the arms. Similarly, information coming rapidly into the human system can be attended to best when it comes in over one sensory channel.

The process that we have referred to as perceptual readiness, or set, can also be illustrated by means of this model. Suppose that the hinged flap is designed so that it can be controlled from outside the tube by means of a handle. When the handle is left alone, the flap moves freely. Suppose, however, that we are alerted to receive one ball or the other. In that case the hinged flap can be moved beforehand so as to pass the desired ball and block the other. The process of adjusting the flap beforehand performs the same function as perceptual readiness, or set.

Physiological Mechanism for Attention

With Broadbent's model, a ball coming through one of the arms of the Y could, under various circumstances, block or jam a ball coming through the other arm of the Y. In other words, one ball represents the stimulus that did gain attention while the other represents a stimulus that did not gain attention. Broadbent's model of attention suggests that under various circumstances, sensory information coming into the system through one channel may block or jam sensory information entering the system through other channels. Evidence that this phenomenon occurs in subhuman animals has been provided by Hernández-Péon and his co-workers (1956).

It has been mentioned previously that when sensory information reaches the cortex there is electrical activity produced at a particular point on the cortex. It has also been pointed out that lower centers of the brain are involved in sensory pathways. With proper techniques, it is possible to record the electrical potentials from regions of the brain of unanesthetized animals without causing them any pain.

In one study by Hernández-Péon, which involved recording

electrical activity from lower auditory pathways in the brain of unanesthetized cats, it was found that auditory clicks brought about distinct electrical activity. When the cat was lying relaxed in its cage, the clicks resulted in a sizable electrical response. However, different responses occurred when a jar containing two mice was placed in the cage with the cat. While the cat crouched in front of the jar and observed the mice, the auditory clicks resulted in virtually no electrical response. This experiment strongly suggests that when attention is directed at sensory input coming through one modality (in this case, visual), incoming information from other modalities (such as auditory) may be jammed. Just how this jamming takes place is not entirely clear, but there is some evidence that the reticular formation plays an important role in this process.

The work of Hernández-Péon has been criticized in a research study by Worden (1966). Worden was unable to replicate the studies of Hernández-Péon and concluded that "there is no solid evidence that attentive states influence the amplitude of auditory potentials at the cochlear nucleus" (Worden, 1966, p. 83). However, this issue is far from being resolved, and research is continuing in this area.

Just as stimulus and personal factors influence the direction of attention, they also influence the perceptual process. Some of these factors and their relation to perception will now be considered.

Stimulus Factors in Perception

What are some of the stimulus factors that influence what we perceive? We are typically confronted with a vast array of stimulus objects in our visual field. However, these stimuli are usually perceived as more than just a chaotic, haphazard, and unstructured collection. Usually, in the perceptual process they are spontaneously seen as being grouped. If the collection of stimulus objects shows groupings within it, then it is said to be *perceptually organized.* In general, stimuli that "belong" together are grouped together. Psychologists are especially concerned with the various stimulus factors that cause us to see objects or figures as "belonging" together—that is, as being perceptually organized. Research, particularly by the Gestalt psychologists, has shown that the stimulus factors that influence organization of perception are figure and ground, similarity, proximity, and closure.

Figure and Ground. Our ability to identify and label a stimulus object results in part from our perception of figure and ground.

When we perceive an object, we perceive it against a background of some type; that is, we perceive distinct objects or parts of objects against a general background rather than an undifferentiated array of unpatterned stimulation.

The figure in any stimulus pattern is the part of the pattern that "stands out" and is most clearly perceived by the observer. The rest of the perceptual field becomes ground. The figure-ground relationship in Figure 4–2 is well defined. In this case, there is no doubt

Figure 4–2. Figure-ground relationships can be well defined. In this illustration there is no question as to where the figure ends and the ground begins.

as to the demarcation between figure and ground. Although the form is meaningless, it is plainly seen as a figure against a background; that is, the figure-ground relationship is not *ambiguous.* This is not always the case. Figure 4–3 shows an ambiguous figure in which the figure-ground relationship reverses itself. Look carefully at the vase in the figure. Now look at the figure again and look for the two faces in profile. You probably saw the vase first because you were told to look for a vase in the figure; that is, the instructions established a "set," which probably caused you to see the vase first.

The concept of figure and ground applies to perceptual phenomena associated with sensations other than visual. For example, a sound that stands out against a background of other sounds can also be considered a "figure." Thus, a person may hear a voice against a background of many other sounds. The figure-ground relationship is much less apparent when one attempts to perceive a single voice against a background of many other voices; however, the same stimulus factors that determine the direction of attention help determine the figure-ground relationship among several sounds. Thus, if one voice were louder than other voices in the same stimulus array, the figure-ground relationship would be much more apparent.

Figure 4–3. An example of a reversible figure-ground relationship. When you look at this figure you can see either a vase or the profiles of two faces. Note how the figure-ground relationship changes back and forth as you stare at the figure.

Similarity. Elements of a stimulus array that are similar to one another tend to be perceived as belonging together—that is, as forming a group or a figure. If a collection of elements in a stimulus array involves two kinds of elements, then subgroups will tend to be formed from these different elements. Figure 4–4 illustrates the influence of stimulus similarity on perceptual organization. Note that the dark circles in this figure tend to be grouped together. The light circles are also grouped together. The overall impression created by these subgroups or subfigures is that of six columns. The same phenomenon is shown in Figure 4–5. The elements in this array tend to organize themselves into three groups because of similarity. There appear to be two squares, one made up of the four

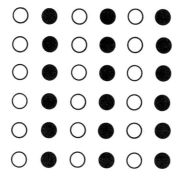

Figure 4–4. Do the circles appear to be arranged in rows or columns? Because of the principle of similarity, the circles are organized into columns.

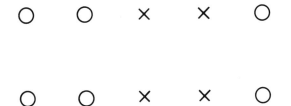

Figure 4–5. Because of the principle of similarity, you tend to see two squares in this figure. One of the squares is made up of the four circles on the left and the second square is made up of the four X's.

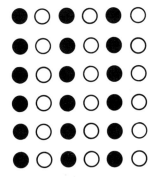

Figure 4–6. Do the circles form rows or columns? Usually, because of the principle of proximity, this figure appears to be organized in rows rather than columns. However, columns can also be seen.

circles on the left and one made up of the X's in the middle. Because of the principle of similarity, one does not see squares made up of two circles and two X's. The principle of similarity applies to both simple and complex arrays of stimuli.

Proximity. Stimuli that are close to one another, either spatially or temporally, are perceived as forming a group or a figure. In an array of stimuli, subgroups tend to be perceived from elements that are spatially close to each other. It should be pointed out that both the principle of proximity and the principle of similarity can be demonstrated most effectively when other stimulus characteristics are held constant. For example, Figure 4–4 illustrates the principle of similarity. Suppose that this figure is modified somewhat. How is Figure 4–6 organized? The organization in this figure tends to favor rows rather than columns, although columns can also be seen. It would appear that, although both types of organization can be perceived, the proximity principle seems to be most dominant in the organization of this figure.

Closure. In perceiving an array of stimuli, a person may add "missing elements" to the array so that he perceives a meaningful, organized figure; that is, he tends to fill any gaps in an incomplete stimulus array. Thus, a drawing consisting of only a few lines may be seen as a complete figure if the lines are positioned in a particular fashion. A figure of a triangle that is outlined by dots will readily be perceived as a triangle and not as a square or a circle.

Personal Factors Affecting Perception

Although the characteristics of the stimulus conditions are important determinants of what we perceive, personal characteristics of the perceiver are also important. Because of the way in which past experience establishes an expectancy, or hypothesis, about what will be perceived in a given situation, a person tends to "see" what he expects to see. Similarly, past experience helps determine what is perceived because of the habits of organization that are acquired from early infancy. Thus, the process of identification and categorizing is, in part, dependent upon past experience. Among the other personal characteristics that influence perception are motives, emotions, immediate needs, attitudes, and values. At any given time, any or all of these personal characteristics may determine what we perceive.

Previous Experience and Perception

When we stress the importance of past experience in perception, we are saying, in effect, that learning is a critical aspect of perception. It was pointed out earlier that the identification and categorization process consists of assigning stimuli to classes such as apples, oranges, chairs, people, and so forth. These perceptual classes are learned from parents, friends, and others, either because certain class responses have been rewarded or punished or because they have assisted a person in adapting to his environment. A person learns not only general classes but also important variations within classes. Thus, he learns not only to categorize an apple as an apple but also to make many more subtle categorizations about the object. Each individual's past experience, then, combines in a complex fashion to help determine his reaction to any stimulus situation. Due to the expectancies a person has developed through past experience, he tends to perceive that situation in a certain way.

Not all psychologists are convinced that past experience plays an important role in perception. There are some who would argue that perception is dependent upon innate characteristics of the organism and that prior experience is of little significance in determining what is perceived. This argument has gone on for years and is by no means resolved. Those who argue that past experience is critical to perception are called *empiricists;* those who claim that perception is the result of the organism's innate properties are called *nativists.* Actually, it appears that perception is determined in part by both factors: some of man's perceptual achievements result from his biological endowment and some result from experience—that is, from learning. Data from various investigations support both points of view.

The importance of experience in perception has been demonstrated by Segall, Campbell, and Herskovits (1966), who studied the influence of culture on visual perception. Individuals from a number of different cultures responded to a series of geometric, or optical, illusions and showed marked differences in susceptibility to these illusions. The authors of the study explained these differences in terms of the extent to which certain classes of experience occur in some cultures and not in others. The optical illusions presented to the subjects were like the vertical-horizontal illusion shown in Figure 4–7. In Figure A the two lines are equal in length, but the vertical line appears to be longer. In Figure B the two lines appear to be about equal in length, but the vertical line is physically shorter than the horizontal.

Segall and his co-workers predicted that an individual whose environment had given him many opportunities for looking at horizontal expanses would be more susceptible to the type of illusion shown in Figure 4–7. This was found to be the case. The investigators found that, in general, plains dwellers proved maximally susceptible and groups that lived in restricted environments, such as equatorial forests, were minimally susceptible.

Other investigations also support the view that experience is important in the development of perception. In some studies, for instance, the eyes of newborn animals were covered for a period of time with translucent shields so that the animals could see light but could not see form. Later, when the animals had matured, the shields were removed and the animals were tested in various ways.

Figure 4–7. The vertical-horizontal illusion. In part A of this figure, the two lines are equal in length, but the vertical line appears to be longer than the horizontal line. In part B, the two lines appear to be equal in length, but the vertical line is actually shorter.

Typically, the animals did not recognize forms and had a great deal of trouble discriminating between even simple forms. The implication of these studies was that experience is important in this type of perception.

Some studies indicate that certain aspects of perception are innate. For instance, it has been demonstrated that, at least in several types of animals, there is an innate ability to perceive depth (Gibson & Walk, 1960). It also seems that figure-ground perception is innate. Although the nativist-empiricist controversy is far from settled, it would appear that a "middle of the road" view is the most reasonable one. Thus, perception is the result of the individual's innate characteristics as well as his past experience.

Other Personal Factors in Perception

In addition to past experience and innate characteristics, there are other personal factors that influence perception. Some of these are transient states of the person; others can be considered as long term factors which, however, are subject to modification. For example, it has been demonstrated that *organic needs* such as hunger affect perception. In one study (Lazarus, Yousem, & Arenberg, 1953) it was found that when slides were exposed for very brief periods on a screen, pictures of food were recognized by hungry subjects more readily than pictures of other miscellaneous objects. In another study, hungry subjects who viewed food objects under various experimental conditions tended to perceive these food objects as being larger than they actually were.

Other studies suggest that internal factors such as *motives, emotions, attitudes,* and *values* help determine perception. One frequently cited investigation that illustrates the importance of values in perception was conducted by Bruner and Goodman (1947), who asked ten-year-old children from either wealthy or poor families to estimate the size of coins of various denominations. The children did this by varying the diameter of a circle of light. It was found that children from poor families tended to overestimate the size of the coins to a much greater extent than children from rich families. Although this study has been criticized because it did not definitely establish that values and needs were the determining factors, other investigations have substantiated these findings.

Most studies of the relationship between personal factors and perception have been conducted in laboratory settings and, by necessity, the stimulus conditions have been relatively simple. It is likely, however, that personal factors such as motives, needs, values, and so forth have their greatest effect in the perception of complex social and interpersonal relationships. Thus, it is not too easy to distort the perception of the size of coins or other concrete objects. However, the more indefinite or ambiguous the stimulus situation is, the more likely these personal factors are to influence the way a person perceives it. Ambiguity is often encountered in social situations and in our everyday relationships with other individuals. Misperception of the comments or behavior of others is not uncommon. Although a certain amount of this type of misperception can be expected, some individuals tend to misinterpret to such a degree that their behavior is considered abnormal.

Social Factors in Perception

Along with the stimulus and personal factors that influence perception, social factors are also important influences. Social factors refer not only to social pressures that may be exerted by groups but also to cultural influences. For instance, there is evidence that culturally determined experience may directly affect perception or may affect it in an indirect manner through specific needs and values associated with particular cultures.

The importance of social factors in perception was demonstrated many years ago in a study by Sherif (1935). In Sherif's study a subject was placed in a dark room and was asked to estimate the degree of "movement" of a small stationary dot of light. (In this situation most subjects think they see the light move even though it is stationary. This phenomenon is called the *autokinetic effect*.) When Sherif's subjects were tested alone, they varied widely in their estimates as to the degree of the imagined movement. However, when they were tested in groups of three and each subject heard the others' estimates of the movement, it was found that individual judgments were very close to the average of the group.

That is, the members of the group established a group average as to the magnitude of the imaginary movement. This experiment demonstrates the influence of other people on an individual's perception in an ambiguous situation.

In a study by Asch (1955), subjects were asked to judge which of three lines on a card was equal in length to a standard line on another card. Cards similar to those used in the study are shown in Figure 4–8. The group condition consisted of one naive subject and six "stooges" who gave wrong answers on a number of cards that were presented. The design of the experiment was such that on the first two trials all the group members agreed as to which of the three lines was equal in length to the standard line. However, on the third trial the stooges deliberately selected a line that obviously was *not* the same length as the standard line.

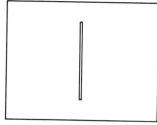 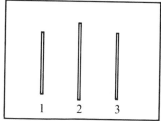

Figure 4–8. Cards similar to those used in the study by Asch. Which line on the right-hand card is closest in length to the line on the left-hand card?

Asch reported that a large number of his naive subjects accepted the wrong judgments of the majority on every trial. However, when the same subjects were not under group pressure, they rarely made incorrect judgments. It would appear from this study, and from other studies as well, that an individual's perceptions can be quite easily modified by the judgments of other people with whom he has contact.

Asch's research suggests that a person's perceptions may be determined, at least in part, by other people. That is, he conforms. Costanzo and Shaw (1966) studied conformity as a function of the age level of the subjects. Stimulus materials similar to those employed by Asch were shown to groups of male and female subjects ranging in age from 7 to 21 years. It was found that conformity was lowest for subjects in the 7–9 age groups and highest for subjects in the 11–13 groups. Conformity decreased for older subjects. The authors of the study concluded that the development of conforming behavior patterns parallels the socialization process. Children in the youngest group were not threatened by the effect of a unanimously wrong majority. However, children in the 11–13 age group were much more aware of their social peers and thus tended to mirror their peers' behavior. Subjects in the older groups had, essentially, learned to rely more on their own judgments and were not influenced as much by the disagreement between their judgments and those of the group.

Perceptual Constancy

The physical nature of the stimulus input may vary over a wide range without disturbing the identifications that are made by the individual. In a broad sense, this is what we mean when we refer to *perceptual constancy*. If it were not for this process, the world we perceive would be a very unstable world at best. Thus, an object looks much the same on different occasions, even though it does not present the same stimulus input to the retina. Perceptual constancy, then, refers to the individual's tendency to perceive a stimulus situation in the same way under a wide range of circumstances. Constancy in perception applies to a number of attributes of a stimulus object. Thus, perceptual constancy involves *shape constancy, size constancy, color constancy,* and *brightness constancy.*

Based on the change of the image projected on the retina of the eye, one would predict that the perceived size of an object would change as an observer approached or withdrew from it. However, this usually does not take place. Instead, the object is perceived as being about the same size even though it may look closer or farther away. This is *size constancy.*

Size constancy can be easily demonstrated. Using two coins of the same denomination, place one coin on your desk about a yard away and the other coin as far away as possible on the desk. Note that the coins appear to be the same size even though they are at different distances from your eyes. However, the retinal-image size of the two coins is quite different. With your hand about halfway between your eyes and the nearest coin, "measure" the coin by lining up your thumb and index finger so that they enclose the edges of the nearer coin. Then, without moving your hand, look at the second coin in the same manner. Based on this rather crude measuring technique, it is obvious that the "size" of the second coin is different than that of the nearer coin. This difference is proportional to the difference in the retinal image provided by the two coins.

Normally, size constancy is demonstrated by adults up to a

distance of 100 feet or more. After that distance, the perceived size of an object changes as its distance from the observer changes. There are several conditions that result in this reduction or loss of size constancy perception. For instance, if the stimuli surrounding an object are removed from view so that the object is seen "out of context," size constancy is reduced or eliminated. Thus, a second important factor in size constancy is past experience. For example, in a study of eight-year-old children, it was found that, for near observation distances, size constancy was similar to that of adults. However, as the observation distance was increased, size constancy decreased. It appears that with added experience the child's size constancy perception begins to develop for distant objects (Zeigler & Leibowitz, 1957).

Shape constancy also tends to stabilize one's perception of the world. Shape constancy refers to a person's tendency to perceive constant shapes of objects regardless of the angle of observation. For example, a rectangular picture on a wall is perceived as a rectangle whether one stands directly in front of the picture or to one side of it, even though the retinal image is that of a trapezoid. Similarly, a square object that is observed from various angles is still perceived as a square object, even though the retinal image is distorted.

The degree of whiteness, grayness, or blackness of a stimulus object also tends to remain constant under various conditions of illumination. This phenomenon is called *brightness constancy*. In bright sunlight a white object might reflect 100 times more light than a black object; however, even in a relatively dark room, the white object still looks white, and the black object looks black. That is, the relative brightness of the two objects remains constant. This is true even though there may be less light reflected from the white square under the dim illumination than there was from the black square in the sunlight. Similarly, snow looks white under most conditions of illumination even though its brightness under dim illumination may be less than that of a black object under bright illumination. One's perception of brightness, then, cannot be predicted on the basis of the physical attributes of the object—that is, the amount of luminous energy reflected from the object. Rather, a person tends to preserve the constant appearance of the brightness of the object. Similarly, the constant appearance of a color is preserved through the process of *color constancy*.

Although scientists have not yet explained the perceptual constancies man exhibits, they do know that perceptual constancy is important in helping man to perceive a stable world. If man's perception was based solely on the retinal images formed by the stimulus objects in his environment, the world would indeed seem chaotic. In considering man as a system, it is tempting to compare various functions of man with functions of machines. Perceptual constancy is one of man's functions that clearly differentiates him from machines. Human perceptual constancy has not yet been built into a machine.

Veridicality Reconsidered

We have stated that if the perceived attributes of a stimulus object correspond to its physical attributes, then the perception is *veridical*. It should now be apparent that many factors determine the degree of veridicality of perception: stimulus factors, personal factors, social factors, and perceptual constancy all affect the relationship between the physical and perceived attributes of stimulus conditions.

Perception of Depth

Man's ability to perceive distance and depth has always been of interest to experimental psychologists. Of particular concern to researchers is the question: how does man perceive three dimensions when the retinas of his eyes are constructed in such a manner that they can "record" only two dimensions? All information that the brain receives is in the form of neural impulses, and these impulses depend upon physical energy from stimulus objects that activate special sense organs. What, then, are the characteristics of the stimulus input that result in depth perception? What are the *cues* that man utilizes in this type of perception?

Stimulus Pattern and Depth Perception

Traditionally, the visual cues for depth perception are classed as either *monocular* or *binocular*. Monocular cues can be utilized by one eye alone; binocular cues require the use of both eyes. Most of the cues that man uses in perceiving depth are associated with characteristics of the stimulus being viewed and are used in both monocular and binocular vision. Among the various cues arising from the stimulus are those of *linear perspective, clearness, light and shadow*, and *interposition*.

Linear Perspective. One of the most important cues for depth perception is linear perspective—a cue that is used by artists to convey the impression of depth in their paintings. Linear perspective is the term used to describe the fact that stimulus objects appear smaller and closer together as their distance from the observer increases.

One of the stimulus conditions that produces linear perspective is the *gradient of texture* of the stimulus array. The term *gradient* in this context refers to a continuous rather than an abrupt change in texture. Most natural surfaces are characterized by a relatively fine appearance as the distance from the observer increases.

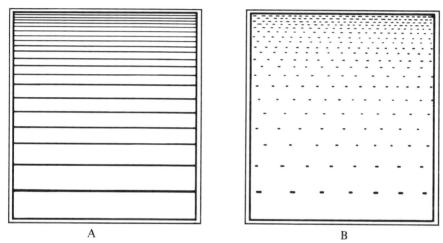

A   B

Figure 4–9. A stimulus condition that produces linear perspective is the gradient of texture. Note how the increasingly finer gradient in both part A and B of this figure gives the impression of depth.

Linear perspective that results from a gradient of texture is illustrated in Figure 4–9. Note that, in both A and B of the figure, the increasingly finer gradient gives the impression of depth.

Clearness. Due to atmospheric conditions, distant objects tend to appear less distinct to an observer than nearby objects. Thus, another cue for depth perception is lack of detail in the object being viewed. If one can see many details of an object, he tends to perceive it as being nearer than an object that appears blurred or indistinct.

Light and Shadow. The manner in which light strikes an object and causes shadows and highlights gives a person important cues for certain depth judgments about the surface of the object. Highlights and shadows tell the observer that the surface of the object is three dimensional; they also tell him something about the depth of the parts of the object being viewed.

Interposition. The way that objects are located in relation to one another often presents cues as to their distance from the observer. Thus, if one object partially blocks from view a second object, then the former is perceived as being nearer the observer.

The cues for depth perception that man obtains from stimulus patterns can be used whether vision is monocular or binocular. Other cues, which result from the structure of the eye rather than from stimulus patterns, are used specifically in monocular or binocular vision.

Internal Cues to Depth Perception

One internal cue used in monocular vision is *accommodation,* the process in which the muscles of the eye cause the lens to change its shape in order to assist in bringing an object into focus on the retina. There are tiny receptors located in the eye muscles which provide feedback as to the accommodation of the lens and other movements of the eye. The information provided the brain about these movements furnishes cues as to the distance of the object from the eye.

In addition to stimulus cues, there are two internal binocular cues for depth perception—*convergence* and *retinal disparity.* When one views objects that are relatively close to him, his eyes converge —that is, they turn inward toward the nose. As the eyes converge, the receptors in the muscles of the eyes pass this information to the brain. This information provides a cue as to the distance of the object. Convergence is useful for viewing objects at relatively close range, but it does not provide distance cues for objects much more than thirty feet away.

The retina of each eye receives a slightly different image of an object because of the spacing between the two eyes. In other words, there is a *disparity* between the two images. Retinal disparity can be demonstrated by means of a simple procedure. First, hold a pencil just a few inches in front of your eyes so that you can see the lettering on it. Without moving your head, look at the pencil with one eye and then the other. Depending on where the lettering is located on the pencil as you hold it in front of you, you will probably see more of the lettering with one eye than you will with the other. The two slightly different, or disparate, retinal images provide us with another cue for the perception of depth or distance.

Depth Perception of Auditory Stimuli

Our discussion of depth and distance perception thus far has been restricted to the visual sensory system. However, man is also capable of perceiving the distance of a source of auditory stimulation as well as the direction of the source. Although this ability may not be as critical for man as his ability to utilize the cues for visual depth perception, it has important adaptive value. We are constantly called upon to estimate the distance of various sounds such as warning signals, sounds of fire engines, ambulances, and so forth. We also judge the direction of sounds of this type.

The cues that we utilize in estimating the distance of a source of sound are based on various characteristics of the stimulus, and these cues can be detected with one ear as readily as with two. The auditory cues to distance are the *intensity* and *frequency composition* of the stimulus. Distant sounds are generally perceived as much weaker, or less intense, than nearby sounds. This implies, of course, that in the identification process we have a category or label available for the sound. In other words, if we have never heard the sound before, it would be difficult for us to judge its distance because we must be familiar enough with the sound to know that the distant sound is weaker than it would be if it were nearer.

The frequencies making up a sound also present us with cues for distance estimates. Low-frequency sounds can be heard at a greater distance than high-frequency sounds, because the latter tend to be absorbed by the air and by objects. Consequently, a complex sound becomes more low pitched as its distance from the listener increases, because more and more of the high-frequency sound waves are absorbed. A person watching a parade hears the low notes of the bass drums before he hears the high notes of the other instruments in an approaching marching band. Again, this cue depends on a person's past experience with the source emitting the sound.

One's perception of the direction of a sound source is dependent, to a large extent, on the use of both ears. Unless a sound emanates from a source directly in front or in back of a person, the sound wave reaches one ear before it reaches the other ear. For instance, a sound wave coming from your left reaches your left ear about 1/1000 of a second before it reaches your right ear. The brain utilizes this *binaural effect* to help localize the source of the sound. A second cue for perceiving the source of a sound that emanates from the listener's left or right is the *intensity differential* between the two ears. If the sound is coming from one side, then the head interferes with the sound waves and absorbs some of the high-intensity sound waves. This results in a slight intensity differential between the ears and provides another cue about the direction of the sound. *Phase difference* is a third cue which is available when the sound consists of low frequencies. Recall that sound waves are represented as sine waves with positive and negative pressures. These waves can stimulate each ear at a different part of the cycle of the sound wave. In other words, the waves at the two ears may be out of phase. This provides the brain with further information that helps to determine the source of a sound.

The auditory cues we have just described do not help a person to locate sounds that are directly in front of or behind the head. Consequently, localization of a sound source is easiest when the sound comes from the left or right and most difficult when it comes from the front or rear. A person very early learns to "scan" with his ears much as he does with his eyes. Head movements help localize a sound source, and we often make these movements without thinking about them.

The Perception of Movement

Although the experience of movement is not confined to the visual sense, man's perception of movement is largely a visual phenomenon. It is generally assumed that our visual perception of movement depends on the successive stimulation of different receptor elements in the retina. In other words, we perceive a visual stimulus to be moving when the image of the stimulus object moves across the surface of the retina. However, we may perceive *apparent movement* even though there is actually no movement of the stimulus pattern over the receptors of the retina. *Real movement* is perceived when the object actually moves through space, stimulating retinal elements at different locations in the retina. This is also a more complex situation which involves higher levels of perceptual organization.

Real Movement

The human observer watching a moving stimulus object usually follows the movement of the object with his eyes. These movements are referred to as *pursuit eye movements*. Early investigators explained the perception of movement by assuming that the observer could follow in an exact fashion the movement of a stimulus object with his eyes. However, if this were the case, then the object itself would not stimulate different retinal receptors since the eye movements would result in the image of the object remaining at the same point on the retina. Thus, perception of movement would be dependent upon the retinal image of the *background* of the stimulus object. In other words, the background rather than the stimulus object itself would stimulate different points of the retina. However, if this were true, then it would be difficult to explain how man perceives an object moving against a homogeneous background. Consequently, early researchers postulated a two-part mechanism to account for the perception of movement. They accepted the moving-background-image explanation for cases in which movement occurs against a nonhomogeneous background. However, they postulated that the perception of motion for objects moving through a homogeneous environment is due to proprioceptive information gained from the optical muscles controlling the eye movements involved in following the stimulus. In other words, one type of visual movement perception was actually dependent upon the muscle senses.

Recent formulations of the problem of determining the physical mechanism of movement perception have been based on two hypotheses (Mashour, 1964, p. 145):

Hypothesis (I)

The eye cannot follow the moving object perfectly and smoothly. Therefore, in contrast to the classical view, the retinal image does not remain stationary in pursuit eye movements.

Hypothesis (II)

Information about the speed of an object is supplied to the higher nervous centers by short frequently occurring pauses during pursuit, causing the image to move at the object's angular speed across the retina.

Extensive research, in which the frequency and amplitude of eye movements were recorded, has shown that these hypotheses are valid statements of the mechanism for movement perception. It appears that the perception of movement occurs when a visual image of the moving stimulus moves across the central area of the retina. The eye movements that accompany the visual pursuit of the moving object simply restrain the movement of the stimulus object to the central area of the retina. These eye movements result in a series of jumps, which reposition the eyes periodically so that the stimulus image moves across the center, or more responsive portion, of the retina. Thus, the human observer is not capable of smoothly following, with eye movements, a moving stimulus object.

Man must constantly make judgments and decisions based on his perception of movement. For example, driving a car in heavy traffic requires one to make many quick decisions based on the perception of movement of other vehicles. A question of some interest to researchers has to do with how accurately individuals can make judgments of this type. Research in the authors' laboratory (Ellingstad, 1967; Ellingstad & Heimstra, 1969) has shown that the accuracy of these judgments may be influenced by a number of variables such as the speed of the moving object, the length of time that the object is in view, and the object's distance from the observer.

People differ greatly in their ability to judge movement. A

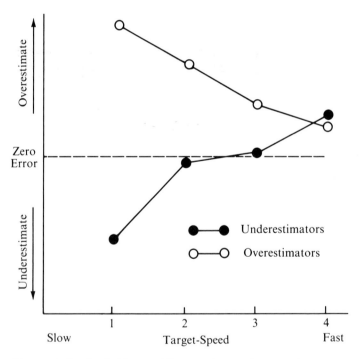

Figure 4-10. Individuals differ in their ability to judge the rates of movement of targets that are moving at various speeds. Some individuals, at slower target-speeds, tend to consistently underestimate the speed while others tend to overestimate. It can be seen from the figure that at the higher target speeds subjects were more accurate but with a tendency toward overestimation (Ellingstad & Heimstra, 1968).

study by Ellingstad and Heimstra (1968) found that human observers perceived movement in one of two ways. In this study subjects estimated the speed of targets that moved across a screen in front of them. Their task was to estimate when the target would reach a particular point on the screen. When the target was moving very slowly, some subjects tended to underestimate the target's speed; other subjects overestimated the speed. As the speed of the target increased, the subjects' judgments became similar to one another (see Figure 4–10). Perhaps two separate perceptual processes are employed in the judgment of a target's speed; the process used by a given individual may be determined both by previous experience in judging moving objects and by differential learning of the perceptual process. This is an area in which a great deal of additional research is necessary, however.

Apparent Movement

The essential condition for the perception of movement is that the image of the stimulus object sequentially excites different retinal receptors. With a real moving target, sequential excitation occurs when the retinal image of the stimulus object moves across the retina. However, sequential excitation of different receptors can also be produced under experimental conditions without a real moving stimulus object. Exposing a subject to two successively illuminating stimulus lights that are a short distance apart fulfills the requirement of sequential excitation. If the pause between illumination of one light and illumination of the other is short enough that the lights are not perceived as two discrete stimuli, but long enough that they are not perceived as a single stimulus, the observer receives an impression of a moving stimulus. This type of apparent movement is called the *phi phenomenon*. Apparent movement results when the pause between illumination of one light and illumination of the other is about 60 milliseconds. Shorter pauses result in the perception of a single stimulus, and longer pauses give the observer the impression of two discrete stimuli. Other important determinants of the illusion of movement include the duration of the stimulus exposure, the distance between stimuli, and the relative intensity of the two stimuli.

The System So Far

The primary functions of the sensing subsystem are to transform physical energies into nerve impulses and to deliver these impulses to the brain. The identifying, or perceptual, subsystem is responsible for giving meaning to these bits of sensory data once they have arrived at the brain via the sensing subsystem.

There is still some question as to how this process of "giving meaning to sensory data" takes place. We have chosen to describe it as an identifying and categorizing process whereby a stimulus input is placed in a certain class because of its defining attributes. It is important to note that the identifying function depends on the interaction and interdependence of several subsystems. (See Figure 4–11.) In one way or another, these subsystems

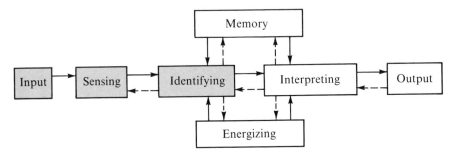

Figure 4–11. The system so far. Note that in addition to the input from the sensing subsystem, the identifying function also depends on inputs from the memory, energizing, and interpreting subsystems.

may alter the relationship between the physical attributes of the stimulus object and the perceived attributes.

In the first place, the process of identifying and categorizing (perception) depends to a large extent on *models* that enable us to place a stimulus object in a category or class with equivalent "somethings" and to exclude it from other categories. Although some models may be innately determined, most are learned and are stored in the memory subsystem. Consequently, memory is an integral part of the identifying function. Perception is also affected by attitudes, beliefs, and many other motivational factors, such as the organic state of the organism. Thus, the energizing (motivating) subsystem, which will be considered in detail in a later chapter, is also important to the identifying function. Finally, the interpreting subsystem, which will also be discussed later, contributes directly and indirectly to the identifying subsystem.

The identifying function is thus a complex process that depends on inputs from the other subsystems. It can also be seen from Figure 4–11 that there are feedback loops from the identifying subsystem to the other subsystems. This implies that the other functions, such as memory and energizing, are themselves dependent upon the identifying function. Similar interactions among subsystems characterize all human functions.

Summary

1. Perception is the process by which sensory data are organized and given meaning. It is the process of identifying and categorizing the stimulus input according to its defining attributes.

2. One important determinant of what we perceive is attention, and attention is determined both by stimulus factors such as size, intensity, contrast, repetition, and change and by personal factors such as organic needs, interests, and perceptual readiness, or set.

3. Our perceptions are organized in that we perceive a meaningful unity. Among the stimulus factors that influence the organization of perception are: (a) figure and ground, (b) similarity, (c) proximity, and (d) closure.

4. In addition to stimulus factors, there are a number of personal factors that affect perception. One of the most significant personal factors is the past experience of the individual. It appears that some perceptual achievements are a part of man's biological endowment; other achievements have to be learned.

5. Other personal factors that affect perception are organic needs, motives, emotions, attitudes, and values.

6. Along with stimulus and personal factors, social factors also are important in perception. Thus, a person in a group may perceive a stimulus situation differently than if he were alone. Cultural factors also tend to influence perception.

7. Due to perceptual constancies, the physical nature of the stimulus input may vary considerably without disturbing the identifications that are made by the individual. Shape constancy, size constancy, color constancy, and brightness constancy tend to stabilize man's perception of the world.

8. We are capable of perceiving depth even though the retina of the eye is two-dimensional and the image cast on the retina is two-dimensional. There are a number of stimulus cues that help us perceive depth. These cues are linear perspective, clearness, light and shadow, and interposition. In addition, there are internal cues to depth perception. These are accommodation, convergence, and retinal disparity.

9. The auditory cues utilized in estimating the distance of a

sound source are the intensity and the frequency composition of the stimulus. Man needs two ears to determine the direction of a sound. Cues to the direction of a sound are provided by the binaural effect, the intensity differential, and phase differences.

10. There are two types of perceived movement: apparent movement and real movement. In the latter case, the perceived object actually moves through space and retinal elements in different locations on the retina are stimulated. With apparent movement, the stimulus conditions are such that movement is perceived even though the stimulus object is not moving through space.

Selected Readings

Dember, W. N. *The psychology of perception.* New York: Holt, Rinehart and Winston, 1965.

Hochberg, J. E. *Perception.* Englewood Cliffs, New Jersey: Prentice-Hall, 1964.

Leibowitz, H. W. *Visual perception.* New York: Macmillan, 1965.

Weintraub, D. J., & Walker, E. L. *Perception.* Monterey, California: Brooks/Cole, 1966.

5

The Memory
Subsystem I

Kinds of Learning

Introduction

Of all the behavioral subsystems that contribute to the total human-system output, the memory subsystem plays a particularly important role in determining how a person behaves in a given situation. In discussing the memory subsystem in this chapter and the next, we will be considering three primary functions, or processes: learning, remembering, and forgetting. Each of these processes helps determine the output of the memory subsystem. This output, which in turn serves as an input to other subsystems, is dependent upon the learning process—the process that determines, at least initially, what is stored in memory. It is also dependent upon the process of forgetting, which, in a not completely understood fashion, removes some or all of the stored material from memory. Basic aspects of learning are considered in this chapter; human-skills learning, remembering, and forgetting are dealt with in Chapter 6.

A Definition of Learning

Most people underestimate the pervasive nature of learning, and many of us tend to think of it as being associated with textbooks and with academic performance; however, learning plays a much broader role in our everyday existence. From the time you were born you have been learning, and, as a matter of fact, what you learned as an infant or as a child may be an important determinant of your present behavior as an adult. Your interactions with friends and other people are instances of learned behavior. Your attitudes, beliefs, and morals; the way you eat; the manner in which you drive your car; the way you react to stress and to pleasant or unpleasant situations; your unique responses and adjustments—all these and many other forms of behavior are learned. It is no wonder that so many psychologists consider learning the most important process in human behavior.

Learning is commonly defined as *any relatively permanent change in behavior which takes place because of experience or practice.* Although changes in behavior might result from factors such as motivation, fatigue, drugs, and so forth, these changes would not be "relatively permanent" changes. Similarly, changes in behavior result from maturation, from physical growth and disease, and from injury. Although such changes may be permanent, they do not result from "experience or practice." According to this definition, moreover, a "change in behavior" need not be a "good" change. Thus, a behavioral change might be of such a nature that a person becomes less rather than more efficient than he had been previously in coping with his environment.

Several other aspects of this definition of learning deserve consideration. In the first place, a change in behavior may be either an actual change or a *potential* change. In other words, through learning we acquire the capability to make certain responses, but this capability may remain *latent*. Learning may not result in an immediate behavioral change. Secondly, we must distinguish between *learning* and *performance*. Due to the process of learning, an individual has the relatively permanent capability for making certain responses, and these responses are available as the occasion demands. When we refer to *performance*, we refer to the actual observable response. Put somewhat differently, learning is a process that cannot be directly observed, whereas performance can be observed and measured. We typically assume that our measures of performance provide a more or less accurate indication of learning.

However, performance may also reflect factors other than learning —for instance, fatigue, motivation, and stimulus conditions. Consequently, in studies on learning it is important that attempts be made to understand and control these other factors that may affect performance.

In dealing with the learning process, then, we are concerned with an input, an output, and some activity of the behavioral subsystems which relates the two—that is, transforms the input to an output. The input to the system is generated by the *stimulus situation* (S) and consists of the changes in physical energy which are transduced by the receptors of the sensory subsystem into nerve impulses. The output, or *response* (R), is usually some form of motor or verbal behavior. It is some behavior that we measure and call *performance*. In the typical learning situation, both the stimulus situation and the response can be identified, described, and measured. This is not the case, however, with the activity of the behavioral subsystems that underlie the learning process: we know relatively little about the neural activity that results in learning, although studies dealing with the biology of learning (Pribram, 1969) may soon give us a better understanding of what actually takes place between the S and the R.

A number of times we have stated that the function of the behavioral subsystems is to transform an input to an output—that is, to some kind of behavior. However, these transformations take place constantly, and while something that we have learned previously may affect the transformation process, we are not necessarily learning something new. In other words, we may have an S-R situation without learning taking place. Recall that learning was defined as a relatively permanent change in behavior which takes place because of experience or practice. If a given stimulus situation results in some particular response, we can assume that a *transformation* has taken place; however, we can infer that *learning* has occurred only after a number of presentations of the stimulus situation has resulted in a consistent change in performance. In considering the activity of the behavioral subsystems in the learning process, another point should be kept in mind. There are different kinds of learning, and the various subsystems will not be involved to the same extent in each of these different types. For example, the interpreting subsystem may play a greater role when one learns a new language than when one learns how to hit a golf ball.

Although it would be helpful if we could be more specific about the functions of the behavioral subsystems in the learning process, this information is not available. One must remember, however, that these subsystems are dependent upon each other and that they interact constantly. They are characterized by numerous feedback loops, with the functioning of one subsystem modifying the functioning of one or more of the other subsystems. Feedback from the various subsystems is particularly important to the learning process. Thus, feedback from these subsystems will modify the learning process, and this process, in turn, may modify the functioning of the subsystems.

Some Factors that Influence Learning

The quantity and quality of a person's learning is influenced by several factors. Basically, these can be classified as conditions within the learner and conditions within the learning situation, the most important of which include the person's motivation, the type of material to be learned, the practice conditions, and the person's prior learning. Although these factors and their relationship to learning will be discussed in some detail later, they merit brief consideration here as an introduction to our discussion of the various kinds of learning.

Motivation

There is evidence that, at least up to a point, the efficiency of learning improves as the strength of motivation increases. However, increased motivation does not always result in improved learning; in some cases, it may actually retard learning. For instance, a person who is too strongly motivated to learn may suffer anxiety over the thought of failure and thus learn less than someone who is less motivated.

Motivation in a learning situation may be either extrinsic or intrinsic. For example, laboratory animals may be motivated for correct performance of some task if they are provided with an extrinsic reward such as food. They may also be motivated extrinsically by punishment for an incorrect response. In either case—whether the animals are rewarded or punished—the motivation is *extrinsic* to the task to be learned or performed. Human learning or performance can be motivated extrinsically—for instance, by report cards, by gold stars for attendance at Sunday school or for performance in military battles, and so forth—but *intrinsic* motivation appears to be more important in human learning than extrinsic motivation. That is, human learning seems to be motivated more often by learning for its own sake—by rewards that are inherent in, or intrinsic to, the learning task. Whether motivation is extrinsic or intrinsic, however, it is an important factor in the learning process.

Material to Be Learned

Learning is affected by both the amount of material and the meaningfulness of material to be learned. An increase in the length of material to be learned usually results in an increase in the total amount of time required for learning; however, it also results in an increase in the average amount of time that is required to learn each item or unit of the material. It has also been demonstrated in many studies that the meaningfulness of material to be learned is an important factor in learning and that meaningful material is learned more rapidly than material that has low meaning.

Practice Conditions

Since what we learn is usually acquired through some form of practice, psychologists have long been interested in determining the "practice conditions" that are most effective for efficient learning. One important condition is *knowledge of results* (KR), or feedback. Learners who are kept informed about their progress usually learn more effectively than subjects who are not informed. The distribution of practice over time may also affect learning. Practice may consist of a number of short, spaced learning periods (*distributed practice*), or it may entail long, concentrated periods of practice (*massed practice*). Although distributed practice is often considered the most desirable procedure to follow, massed practice may have advantages in some types of learning situations.

The manner in which the learner *organizes* the material to be learned is also a factor that will influence learning. Is it better to divide the total material into parts and learn these or to go through all the material and then repeat the cycle? There is no simple answer to this question, since the best approach appears to be dependent upon the nature of the material involved.

Prior Learning

In many situations, a person's prior learning may influence his efficiency in learning new material or in performing new tasks. If what has been learned before facilitates the new learning, we say that *positive transfer* has taken place. For example, a person who has learned to drive one automobile usually has little difficulty in learning to drive one of another make. In some cases, however, prior learning interferes with the learning of something new. In such cases, we say that *negative transfer* has occurred. Negative transfer accounts for the difficulty one might experience in shifting from a car that has mechanical brakes to one that has power brakes or in visiting a country where one is required to drive on the left rather than the right side of the road.

Kinds of Learning: The Cumulative Learning Model

Much of what psychologists do is concerned with some aspect of learning. In fact, the psychological literature on learning has become so voluminous that it is no longer possible for anyone to know everything about the subject. Thus, learning psychologists have tended to specialize and have limited their research to a particular "kind" or "type" of learning.

How many "kinds" of learning are there? Psychologists have yet to agree on an answer to this question, and perhaps many of them would even argue that the question is inappropriate. Some psychologists are satisfied that there are at most only two or three kinds of learning, while others argue for a larger number.

Recently, Robert Gagné (1965) has proposed a scheme that categorizes learning according to eight types. Gagné's comprehensive categorization includes the various types of learning that have been discussed by other learning psychologists; thus, it is a useful model of learning for our purposes in this chapter because it presents a relatively broad, although admittedly general, overview of the field of learning.

Gagné's model, which he refers to as a *cumulative learning model* (1968), contrasts with most other models in its proposal that new learning depends primarily on the combining of previously learned and recalled capabilities. Each of the eight types of learning begins with a different state of the learner and ends with a different capability for performance. The capabilities acquired in one type of learning are necessary prerequisites for a succeeding type of learning; that is, learning can be considered as a cumulative process. The general sequence for cumulative learning can be stated as follows (Gagné, 1965, p. 60):

Problem solving (type 8)
   requires as prerequisites:

Principles (type 7),
   which require as prerequisites:
Concepts (type 6),
   which require as prerequisites:
Multiple discriminations (type 5),
   which require as prerequisites:
Verbal associations (type 4) or other chains (type 3),
   which require as prerequisites:
Stimulus-response connections (type 2).

While it is tempting to suggest that stimulus-response connections (type 2) require signal learning (type 1) as a prerequisite, it is not possible to draw this conclusion with complete confidence from presently available data.

The hierarchical nature of the cumulative learning model is illustrated by the flow chart in Figure 5–1. As the arrows in the figure indicate, stimulus-response (S-R) connections are required both for chaining and for multiple-discrimination learning, and each of the higher types of learning is dependent upon one lower on the chart. There is another point about the cumulative learning model which should be kept in mind as we consider each of the eight types of learning: Gagné's model is not a physiological or neural model of learning. Although it is assumed that neural changes are associated

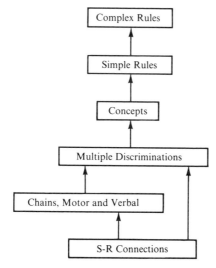

Figure 5–1. The general sequence for cumulative learning. In this figure, the stage labeled "simple rules" corresponds to the "principle learning" stage discussed in the text; the "complex rules" stage corresponds to the "problem-solving" stage. From R. M. Gagné, Contributions of learning to human development, 1968, **75**, 177–191. Copyright 1968 by the American Psychological Association. Reproduced by permission.

with the different types of learning, we will not attempt to discuss these changes.

Type 1: Signal Learning
(Classical Conditioning)

A more common name for what Gagné calls "signal learning" is classical conditioning; however, Gagné's term is more descriptive of the process that takes place in this particular kind of learning. Signal learning can occur in numerous types of organisms and in a variety of situations. The conditions for signal learning are basically simple. The first requirement is that there be a stimulus (S) of some sort that regularly elicits a response (R) from the organism. In duplicating and studying S-R situations in the laboratory, psychologists use a variety of experimental techniques. Figure 5–2 shows one standard apparatus that is used to study this kind of

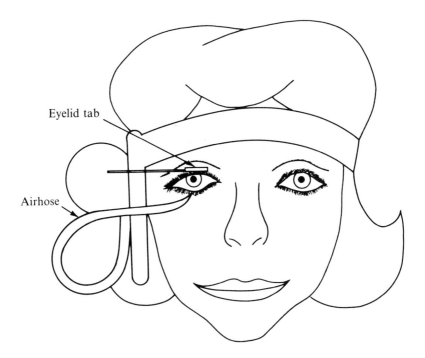

Figure 5–2. Basic apparatus for eyelid conditioning. A puff of air (US) delivered to the eye results in a blink (UR) which is recorded by means of the eyelid tab. The puff of air (US) is paired with another stimulus (CS), such as a weak light, for a number of trials. Eventually, the CS alone results in an eyelid movement (CR).

learning. When a puff of air is blown into a subject's eye, the air (the stimulus) elicits an eye blink (the response). This particular response is not learned, and normally it occurs the first time a puff of air is blown into the subject's eye. Once the subject has been exposed to the puff of air, the experimenter selects a stimulus that *does not* normally elicit the eye blink—for example, an auditory stimulus such as a click or a visual stimulus such as a weak light. A subject who is exposed to one of these stimuli normally would not respond with an eye blink; if he did, it would only be a coincidental response.

The next step in signal learning requires that the puff of air and the second stimulus—say, the click—be *paired* and presented to the subject. Actually, pairing the two stimuli typically means presenting the click about one-half second before the puff of air so that the S-R sequence is as follows: click-puff-blink. In other words, the click can be thought of as a *signal* that alerts the subject to the forthcoming puff of air. The two stimuli are presented together to the subject a number of times, and each such presentation, or trial, is referred to as a *reinforced* trial. During the reinforced trials, the subject could be expected to blink each time because of the presence of the puff of air. After a number of the paired trials, however, the click by itself elicits the eye blink. When this occurs, we say that signal learning, or classical conditioning, has taken place.

The study of signal learning (conditioning) originated with Ivan Pavlov (1849–1936), who introduced the concept of conditioning and established most of its basic principles. In Pavlov's classic study, food was used as a stimulus to elicit a salivary response on the part of a dog. The dog was given food either in a pan or by means of a special apparatus that enabled food powder to be puffed into the dog's mouth. When the food stimulus was presented, the dog salivated. In the second step of Pavlov's study, a bell was sounded each time the food stimulus was presented. Eventually, the dog secreted saliva at the sound of the bell alone.

The type of learning demonstrated in Pavlov's study and in the eye-blink studies is generally referred to as *classical conditioning*. The qualifying adjective "classical" has been used for a number of years to differentiate this particular kind of conditioning from another type, which involves some major departures from Pavlov's model. There is some rather specialized terminology that has become associated with classical conditioning. The stimulus that initially elicits a response (such as food or a puff of air in the preceding examples) is called the *unconditioned stimulus* (US), and the response (saliva flow or eye blink) is called the *unconditioned response* (UR). The stimulus that does not initially elicit a response (bell or click) when it is paired with the US is referred to as the *conditioned stimulus* (CS), or the *signaling stimulus*. Finally, the response that results when the US is terminated and only the CS is presented is called the *conditioned response* (CR). As pointed out earlier, the conditioned response is very similar to the unconditioned response (eye blink or saliva flow).

Signal learning (classical conditioning) has been studied in a wide variety of organisms, and numerous stimuli have been used to elicit unconditioned responses. Some of these unconditioned responses, as well as the stimuli that have been used to elicit them, are shown in Table 5–1. Certain conditions are common to all in-

Table 5–1. Examples of some of the unconditioned responses and the stimuli used to elicit them that have been used in various studies. This list by no means exhausts the responses that have been utilized.

Responses	*Stimuli*
Eyelid reflex	Air puff, shock
Knee jerk	Tap on patella
Eye movements	Rotation
Salivation	Acid, food
Nausea, vomiting	Morphine
Gastro-intestinal secretions	Food
Change in GSR (skin resistance)	Electric shock
Change in heart rate	Electric shock
Change in respiration	Electric shock
Change in pitch of voice	Electric shock

stances of signal learning. These conditions can be thought of as those within the learner and as those within the learning situation in which the learner is placed. In the former case, there must be a natural response of some sort (UR) that can be evoked by a stimulus (US). In the learning situation, the conditions are: (1) the signaling stimulus (conditioned stimulus), which does not initially elicit the unconditioned response, and the unconditioned stimulus (US) must be presented in close proximity to each other, and (2) there must be a number of repetitions of these paired stimuli. When these conditions are met, signal learning can occur in a variety of situations with many different kinds of organisms as subjects.

Since Pavlov's initial studies in classical conditioning, psychologists have done a tremendous amount of research on the various parameters of this kind of learning. A number of researchers, for instance, have studied the importance of the temporal relationship between the US and the CS during training. The object of these studies has been to determine whether the course of signal learning is affected by presenting the CS at different times in relation to the US. For example, what happens if the US is given first and removed before the CS starts? Under these circumstances, learning is almost impossible. Other variations in the temporal relationship between the US and the CS include: (1) presenting the CS well before the US and continuing it until the response occurs, (2) presenting the CS first and removing it before the US starts, and (3) beginning the CS shortly before the US and continuing it along with the US until the response takes place. This latter technique, which is called *simultaneous* conditioning, is the most efficient—particularly when the CS lead time is about half a second.

Other studies have been concerned with what is called *generalization*. It has been found that once the CS→CR relationship has been firmly established, the original CS is no longer required and stimuli that are similar to the CS in some respect will then elicit the CR. In other words, the subject generalizes from one CS to another that is similar. Typically, the more similar the new stimulus is to the original CS, the more effective it will be in eliciting the CR —although an organism may respond to new stimuli that are not very much like the original CS. There are methods of training the subject so that the degree of generalization is limited. This involves a procedure called *conditioned discrimination*. Basically, the subject is trained to discriminate between two stimuli by reinforcing (with food or by other means) his response to one stimulus and not to the other. For example, every time a tone (CS) of a given intensity is presented to a dog in a Pavlovian conditioning experiment, the dog is rewarded with the unconditioned stimulus of food. Then, when another tone (possibly very close in intensity to that of the initial tone) is presented, the dog is not given food. Eventually, saliva flow occurs only when the first tone is presented. In other words, the dog learns to discriminate between the two tones.

While many studies have dealt with the various factors affecting the acquisition of a CR, other studies have tried to determine what happens to the CR after it has been established. We have already stated that, after signal learning has taken place, the CR is elicited by the CS alone. The US is no longer required. After repeated presentation of the CS alone, however, the strength of the conditioned response eventually decreases until, after a number of these *nonreinforced* trials, the conditioned response disappears. This operation is referred to as *extinction* of the conditioned response. As might be expected, a conditioned response that has been very strongly established by many reinforced trials (CS and US paired) resists extinction longer than a weakly established CR. Some studies have used the rate of extinction of a CR as a measure of the strength of the original learning.

After it has been extinguished, a CR can be reestablished by again pairing the CS and US. Typically, it is much easier to reestablish a CR than it is to establish it originally. Sometimes the CS→CR relationship reappears after extinction even though no additional training has taken place. When this occurs, *spontaneous recovery* is said to have taken place.

One should not assume that signal learning is restricted to laboratory situations with well-defined stimuli and responses. There are many examples of this type of learning in everyday life, although the conditions involved cannot be as easily defined as those in the laboratory. For example, it may be that many of our emotions are conditioned responses to stimuli such as voices, faces, or particular types of behavior. Similarly, the meanings of words such as "good" and "bad" may be learned through this type of conditioning. It is probable that many of our fears are acquired by classical conditioning, and there is considerable reason to believe that this kind of learning plays an important role in determining much of our other behavior.

Type 2: Stimulus-Response Learning (Instrumental Conditioning)

The second kind of learning in Gagné's classification scheme is *stimulus-response learning,* which is a form of conditioning whereby a subject learns to make a response as a means of achieving some goal or reward. The response may result in some positive reward, such as food, or it may be a means by which the subject escapes some sort of punishment. In either case, the subject's response is instrumental in satisfying some motive. Consequently, many psychologists refer to this kind of learning as *instrumental conditioning.* Sometimes the term *operant conditioning* is also used, although it is not quite synonymous with instrumental conditioning.

Stimulus-response learning differs from classical conditioning (signal learning) in several important respects. In the first place, in instrumental conditioning the environmental event (food, escape from punishment, etc.) is dependent upon the response. The subject must make the response in order to get the food or escape the punishment. In classical conditioning, however, the environmental event—whether favorable or unfavorable—occurs no matter what response the subject makes. Also, in instrumental conditioning the response is not elicited initially by a specific stimulus, as is the case in classical conditioning; rather, the animal must "discover" that the rewarded response is associated with a particular stimulus situation. There may be many responses that can be made in the situation, but the subject must discover the correct response and then learn to select that response and drop the others.

Gagné suggests that the term "stimulus-response" emphasizes two important characteristics of this kind of learning. First, such learning involves a *single* connection between a stimulus and a response and not multiple or chained connections. Second, in stimulus-response learning the stimulus and the response appear to become bound together in a manner that does not take place in signal learning. Thus, in signal learning the tone serves only as a signal for the eye blink. In stimulus-response learning, the relationship between the stimulus and the response is more complex.

The stimulus-response relationship involved in this type of learning can be demonstrated in lower animals by means of an apparatus called a Skinner box, which is named after the psychologist, B. F. Skinner, who designed it. There are many versions of this apparatus, since studies of instrumental conditioning have been conducted with human subjects as well as lower animals. Shown in Figure 5–3 is a very basic version of a Skinner box used for research with rats. Typically, researchers use a much more elaborate apparatus, such as that shown in Figure 5–4, which automatically presents stimuli to the animal and records its responses. Regardless of the complexity of the apparatus, researchers generally follow certain procedures that result in the development of a predictable pattern of behavior on the part of the rat.

Note on the illustration of the Skinner box (Figure 5–3) that there is a lever, or bar, protruding from the wall of the box. Beside the bar is a food cup. When the bar is pressed lightly, a small pellet of food drops into the cup. When a hungry rat is placed into a Skinner box of this type and is allowed to explore the apparatus, the rat eventually presses the bar by accident. When this happens, a pellet of food is delivered to the food cup. The rat usually eats the food and continues its wandering until it accidentally presses the bar again and releases another food pellet. After several of these accidental bar pressings, the rat begins to "connect" the bar with the food so that the time between bar presses eventually decreases. Soon, without interruption, the rat presses the bar, eats, presses the bar, eats, and so on, until it is no longer hungry.

Actually, in most cases the investigator does not wait for

Figure 5-3. An illustration of a standard version of the "Skinner Box." When the animal presses the bar located beneath the light, a food pellet is released into the food cup. Photo courtesy of the BRS-Foringer Company. Reprinted by permission.

the rat to learn to press the bar purely by accident. Instead, he *shapes* the animal's behavior. That is, he rewards the rat first for any behavior that approximates the bar-press response—for instance, merely being close to the bar—and then only for the bar-press. A skilled investigator can "shape" various responses quite quickly. Shaping can also be used to produce some rather bizarre behavior on the part of an animal. For example, pigeons have been taught to play a miniature piano, and chickens have learned to play basketball on miniature courts.

Reinforcement

A critical question is: Why does the rat continue to press the bar? The answer, in this case, is clear-cut—it presses the bar for the food reward. In psychological terms, we say that the rat's response is *reinforced*. There is considerable confusion and ambiguity among psychologists as to just what is meant by reinforcement. For our purposes, we will consider reinforcement to have occurred when a response is followed by a reward (food, water, etc.) or when the response allows the subject to escape or avoid a noxious stimulus of some sort (shock, pain, etc.).

Figure 5-4. Some programming and recording equipment that is used in association with the "Skinner Box." When equipment of this type is used in research, it is frequently automated to such an extent that the experimenter merely places the rat in the box and later returns for his data. Photo courtesy of the BRS-Foringer Company. Reprinted by permission.

Schedules of Reinforcement. What happens if the rat is *not* reinforced for pressing the bar? If no food at all is presented for a number of trials—that is, if there are a number of *nonreinforced* trials—then the response may be extinguished. The rat's rate of responding in this situation will decrease gradually until it makes no more responses than the "accidental" type it made before training. We can then say that *extinction* has taken place. Suppose, however, that we establish a *schedule of reinforcement* whereby some, but not all, of the bar presses are reinforced with the food pellet. Obviously, we could establish any kind of schedule ranging from 100% reinforcement, as was the case in the learning situation discussed previously, to no reinforcement, where we would expect extinction to occur. A schedule somewhere between these two extremes is referred to as a *partial reinforcement* schedule. In other words, the rat will only occasionally receive the food pellet after pressing the bar.

Studies of instrumental conditioning use a variety of partial reinforcement schedules. In some cases the pellet of food is delivered after a predetermined number of responses—for example, after every ten bar presses—regardless of how long it may take the animal to make that many responses. Another common approach involves delivering the reinforcement (pellet) after a predetermined amount of time, regardless of how frequently the animal may have pressed the bar. A third partial reinforcement schedule consists of a random variation in the amount of time or the number of bar presses required for a pellet. Keeping the subject "guessing" with a random reinforcement schedule of this type tends to keep him working. Anyone who plays the slot machines will recognize the efficacy of a random varying partial reinforcement schedule of this type.

Results of studies involving partial reinforcement, in contrast to 100% reinforcement, have typically shown that responses are learned more slowly in the partial reinforcement situation. However, it is interesting to note that the response acquired under a partial reinforcement schedule is maintained far longer after reinforcement is removed than a response acquired under a 100% reinforcement schedule. The former schedule appears to establish an increased resistance to extinction.

In considering the general topic of reinforcement, we have been concerned primarily with reinforcement that serves as a reward to the subject. Instrumental conditioning can also involve a situation in which the subject learns to make a response that allows it to avoid or escape something painful or fearful.

Avoidance and Escape Learning. In avoidance learning, a correct response permits the subject to *avoid* some form of noxious stimulation, usually electric shock. In escape learning, the subject learns to make a response that allows it to *escape* from a painful or unpleasant stimulus. The difference between the two, then, is this: in avoidance learning, the correct response permits the animal to avoid the noxious stimulation completely; in escape learning, the rat does not avoid the stimulus—it learns to escape from the stimulus as quickly as possible by making a correct response.

The Skinner box technique, with minor modifications, can be utilized to demonstrate both avoidance and escape learning. The apparatus is constructed with an electric grid on the floor so that electric shock can be delivered to the feet of the subject—usually a rat. In escape learning, the shock is turned off when the rat presses the bar. As was the case in reward learning, the rat does not immediately learn that the shock can be turned off by a bar press. Initially, when the shock is presented the rat leaps, squeals, bites at the grid, urinates, defecates, and becomes very agitated. In the course of this activity, the rat sooner or later presses the bar by accident. After a number of trials, the rat learns to press the bar very quickly in order to *escape* the shock. Generally, the rat learns this response faster than it would learn to press the bar for a food reward.

The technique is modified somewhat for avoidance learning. In this situation, a signal of some sort precedes the onset of the shock. With this approach, initially the rat still engages in escape behavior in that it receives the shock. Eventually, however, the rat learns to press the bar when the signal is presented and thus learns to *avoid* the shock completely.

Performance Measurement
in Instrumental Conditioning

One could obtain a considerable amount of data by simply watching a rat in a Skinner box and recording the number of times it presses the bar in order to receive a food pellet or to avoid or escape an electric shock. However, there are somewhat more sophisticated procedures for recording the performance of subjects in instrumental conditioning situations.

The basic piece of apparatus used for recording the performance of a subject is called a *cumulative response recorder*. Most cumulative recorders, like the one in Figure 5–5, have three main parts. There is a paper chart, which is fed from a roll at a constant rate of speed under two recording pens. One of the pens, called a response pen, moves upward a small amount each time the subject makes a response. If the subject makes a number of responses, the result is a "staircase" effect such as that shown on the figure. The second pen, an event recorder, moves whenever a given event occurs—for instance, when the signal occurs or when the shock begins.

With a cumulative recorder of this type, low rates of response on the part of the subject result in a cumulative response record with a shallow slope; high rates of response result in steep slopes. For example, in Figure 5–6 two slopes are shown. In one situation, represented by the steep slope, the rat pressed the bar about 50 times in approximately five minutes. In the situation repre-

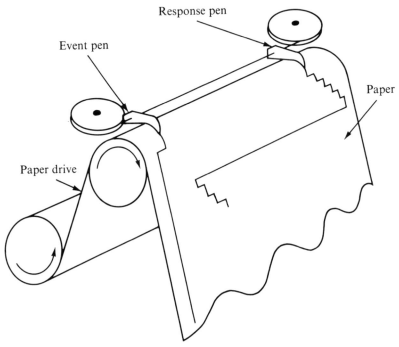

Figure 5-5. The essential components of a cumulative recorder.

sented by the shallow slope, the rat pressed the bar only about 20 times in five minutes.

Cumulative records of this kind are affected by the type of reinforcement schedule and by many other variables. Careful analysis of the records by an experienced investigator can reveal a great deal of information about the performance of the animal in the test situation. Certain aspects of the cumulative record are indicative of various behavioral characteristics of the subject. It has been found, for example, that different drugs—even in very small amounts —cause performance differences that show up clearly in cumulative records.

*Practical Aspects
of Instrumental Conditioning*

Relatively pure examples of instrumental conditioning, or stimulus-response learning, are not easy to find. Many behaviors that, at first glance, appear to be cases of instrumental condition-

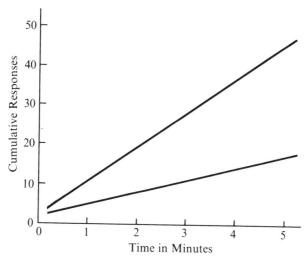

Figure 5–6. An illustration of two cumulative response records, one with a steep slope and the other with a shallow slope. At the end of the five minute period, the animals whose responses are represented by the steep slope had pressed the bar about 50 times. The other animal had pressed the bar only about 20 times.

ing turn out on closer examination to represent somewhat more complex forms of learning. Gagné suggests, however, that stimulus-response learning is generally involved in the acquisition of voluntary motor acts such as speech utterances and that "simple learned acts of the motor sort may be readily identified in young children, and perhaps come as close as any human behavior does to being pure cases of stimulus-response learning" (Gagné, 1965, p. 84). The special significance of stimulus-response learning is that it forms a substructure for the "higher" forms of learning, which we will discuss later. The many simple motor acts that are acquired through stimulus-response learning provide the foundation for the learning of much more elaborate responses.

Type 3: Chaining

Stimulus-response learning results in the acquisition of a large number of simple motor acts—such as picking up a key, placing it in the ignition, turning it, and so forth—which, by themselves, may not seem of particular importance in the response repertoire of the organism. However, simple motor acts are prerequisites for other kinds of learning—in this case, learning how to start an automobile.

One form of learning that depends on these motor acts is *chaining*, which is the acquisition of a series, or sequence, of simple motor acts that have been established previously through stimulus-response learning. Although chaining is considered a relatively simple type of learning, it can result in some rather complex patterns of behavior such as those required in the operation of various man-machine systems.

In this type of learning, connections are formed between a series of successive events or motor acts, each of which can be thought of as a link in a chain. A given response provides the stimulus for a succeeding response. Obviously, if chaining is to take place, each link, or motor act, in the chain must have been learned previously. Chaining consists of the organism's learning to place simple motor acts, or links, in some prescribed order that is required to perform a particular task. Thus, gripping a golf club, swinging it back, stopping the backswing at the correct point, starting the downswing, and so forth represent links in the chain required for properly hitting a golf ball. In order to place these motor acts in the proper order so that an attempted drive does not end up as a putt, the individual must learn to discriminate certain aspects of the kinesthetic feedback (information the brain receives from the muscles and joints when they are moved) from the previous motor act in the chain. Consequently, chaining involves more than an acquisition of a number of motor acts that, in total, make up a more complex response. Additional learning is required in order for one particular motor act to serve as a stimulus for the next motor act in the chain. The course of this learning becomes apparent when you watch a novice attempting to develop a good golf swing, an amateur musician learning to play an instrument, or a new driver attempting to operate a motor vehicle.

Type 4: Verbal Association

Through chaining, man is capable of a wide variety of motor responses. However, it is not these responses that set man apart from other species, since many animals are capable of elaborate forms of motor activity. It is only in his ability to make use of verbal behavior that man is clearly superior to other species.

Because verbal behavior is so important to man, the question of how this behavior is learned has been of interest to psychologists for many years. Numerous investigations, involving a wide range of experimental approaches, have dealt with various aspects of verbal learning. The term "verbal learning" refers to relatively simple processes such as verbal conditioning or to much more complicated processes such as the role of language in the acquisition of concepts and principles. At present we will be concerned with an elementary form of verbal behavior—the learning of verbal associations. It will become apparent later, however, that these associations play a role in more complex forms of verbal behavior.

Although the individual sounds that man can make are relatively few in number, the patterns and combinations that can be formed from these sounds are tremendous. Some of these patterns and combinations are learned as *verbal chains,* or *verbal associations.* In verbal chaining, words or sounds rather than motor acts form the links in the chain of learned responses. Verbal chains can be quite simple or extremely complex. As is the case with nonverbal chains, one link serves as a stimulus for the next succeeding link, and so on.

The two methods most commonly used in the study of verbal associations are the serial method and the paired-associate method, and the types of learning studied by these methods are referred to as *serial learning* and *paired-associate learning.*

In serial learning, a subject learns to reproduce certain responses in a prescribed order. The experimental procedure used to study serial learning is a simple one. A number of verbal items are presented to the subject one at a time. These items are usually words or nonsense syllables, which are meaningless syllables constructed according to certain prescribed rules about the location and frequency of consonants and vowels (usually, consonant-vowel-consonant). In serial learning, then, a list of these syllables—for instance, TAJ, ZIN, VEC, BIP—is presented to the subject. Each item, or syllable, on the list is presented in a set order, and the subject must learn to reproduce the items in the order in which they were presented. Typically, an item on the list is presented, and the subject is asked to give the next item on the list. Then this item is presented, giving the subject feedback as to the correctness of his response. Once he has been given feedback, the subject gives what he thinks is the next item on the list. Depending upon the nature of the study, this process may be repeated many times until the subject can recall all the items correctly in their serial order. Thus, serial learning is a chaining process in which each item on the list serves both as a response to the preceding item and as a stimulus that elicits the recall of the following item on the list.

When the paired-associate procedure is utilized in studies of verbal association, the subject initially is presented with paired items such as TAJ-ZIN, VEC-BIP, and so forth. On subsequent trials he is presented with only the first item of a pair (for example, TAJ) and is asked to reproduce the second item (ZIN). Thus, the subject learns a series of stimulus-response associations in which the first item of the pair serves as a stimulus and the second item serves as a response. The paired-associate procedure is familiar to anyone who has tried to memorize vocabulary in a foreign language by using flash cards to pair an English word with its foreign equivalent.

Psychologists who study serial and paired-associate learn-

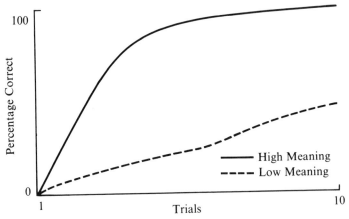

Figure 5–7. Curves that might be expected in a paired-associate learning study comparing high- and low-meaning material.

ing generally try to examine the factors that are important in either the *acquisition* or the *retention* of various kinds of verbal material. In studying acquisition and retention, the psychologist must decide what performance measures should be used. These measures may differ depending upon the nature of the study. For instance, in serial-learning studies, one presentation of a serial list generally constitutes a trial. The number of errors made during each trial can thus be considered one measure of the subject's performance. When the number of errors per trial is used as the criterion, each succeeding trial usually results in an improvement in performance. When the number of errors is plotted, learning curves similar to those shown in Figure 5–7 will result. In some cases, rather than being concerned with the subject's performance on a trial-to-trial basis, the investigator may establish a criterion for learning before the study begins. Thus, he may arbitrarily decide that the criterion will be one complete trial (or perhaps two or three trials) without errors. In this case, he is primarily interested in the number of trials a subject requires in order to reach the established criterion. Other measures of performance may be utilized—depending upon the requirements of the study—but those mentioned above are most typical of serial and paired-associate learning.

Several factors affect both the acquisition and retention of the materials. For instance, the *amount* of material to be learned is an important variable. The greater the amount to be learned, the longer is the time required for learning. Similarly, the *organization* of the material may increase or decrease the speed with which it is learned. The most important variable affecting serial or paired-associate learning is *meaningfulness* of the items or words that make up the serial list or the pairs. In general, the more meaningful the material, the more easily it is learned and retained. In most studies of verbal learning, the material to be learned consists of lists of words or items. The meaningfulness of each word or item on the list is measured by the *association value* each word or item has for the subject. A word has a high association value, or high meaningfulness, when its presentation results in a subject's thinking of a number of other words or items in response—that is, when a subject associates a number of words with the particular stimulus word. For instance, in a given period of time a subject can think of more associations to the word "car" than he can to a nonsense syllable such as "TAJ." The word "car," then, has a higher association value than the syllable "TAJ."

Shown in Figure 5–7 are two hypothetical learning curves that might be expected from a paired-associate learning study comparing the acquisition of material of high meaningfulness with the acquisition of material of low meaningfulness. If the figure also showed retention curves, one would expect to find that the material with a high level of meaning would be remembered longer than that with the low level.

Laboratory investigations of verbal learning have led to a better understanding of a process that is an important part of our everyday behavior. Memorization of a variety of materials is still required in our educational systems, although verbal memorization is not nearly as important as it once was in American schools. Regardless of the value of memorization in education, much of our use of language is based on memorized verbal sequences, and serial and paired-associate learning are important in the acquisition of these sequences. Although the utilization of effective speech depends on the understanding of grammar as well as on other factors, it also requires the recall of a tremendous number of verbal sequences that have been memorized. These sequences can be included in the language in a variety of forms and patterns.

Type 5: Multiple-Discrimination Learning

Once the organism has learned basic stimulus-response connections, whether verbal or nonverbal, these connections can be arranged in sequential fashion to form more complex responses. That is, stimulus-response connections enable the organism to form chained responses. In the chaining of either simple motor acts or verbal links, some part of the response aspect of one link serves as the stimulus for the next link in the chain. Although the organism must discriminate the stimulus generated by the previous response in order to make the next response, the process of chaining entails a *single discrimination* that is relatively easy to make. The learner responds to a single stimulus in a given way. But what happens when the individual is confronted by a set or collection of stimulus objects or events and must make different responses to the different objects or events? In this situation, *multiple discriminations* are required: the learner must learn to distinguish each stimulus in the set from the others and to respond to each stimulus in a prescribed manner. Multiple-discrimination learning of this kind is more difficult and complex than the previous types of learning that have been discussed. Not only must the learner have acquired a number of chains, verbal or otherwise, but he must also continually learn new chains as a result of the discrimination process.

The acquisition of multiple discriminations is of considerable importance to the individual. At a very young age the child learns to distinguish between many classes of objects that he encounters in his environment. For example, he learns to discriminate between people and to respond to different people in different ways. He also learns to discriminate between various sounds and to respond to these in a particular way. He is required to learn distinguishing names for a great many things and events. For a young child some of these discriminations are relatively easy—for instance, discriminating one parent's face from the other's—but other discriminations may be quite difficult. As he grows older, he is faced with the necessity of acquiring more and more new discriminations of stimulus objects, and he learns to make different responses to various printed symbols—numbers, letters, words, signs, and so forth. The process of multiple discrimination continues throughout the individual's life, since he must continually learn new discriminations between novel symbols, new faces, and many other objects and events in his environment.

Multiple-discrimination learning is important in that it plays a role in the more complex types of learning such as concept learning, principle learning, and problem solving. Although these three kinds of learning will be briefly discussed in this chapter, they will be taken up in more detail in Chapter 8.

Type 6: Concept Learning

In multiple-discrimination learning, a person learns to respond to a collection of stimuli by distinguishing or discriminating among them and responding to one of the stimuli. He may also learn to respond to all the stimuli in a collection by responding to them as a *class* rather than singly. When a person learns to do this, we say that *concept learning* has taken place. Concept learning permits the learner to respond to things or events as a collection rather than as individual events or things.

The differences between multiple-discrimination learning and concept learning can be illustrated by considering two experimental techniques that have frequently been used to study learning in subhuman primates. One technique requires the subject (usually a monkey or an ape but sometimes a child) to discriminate among numerous stimulus objects such as blocks of different colors, small toys, objects of different shapes, and so forth. A number of these different stimuli are simultaneously presented to the subject—say, a monkey—until he learns to discriminate among them and to find the reward that is always associated with a certain stimulus.

A second technique, which is used to study concept learning, requires the monkey to make discriminations among stimuli in such a way that he learns to find the "odd" object in any class of three stimuli. A monkey performing an "oddity problem" is shown in Figure 5–8. Through trial and error, the monkey learns to obtain the reward by moving the odd object of the three presented. Moreover, he learns to do this for *any* set of objects with which he might be confronted, even though he has had no previous experience with the objects. It can then be said that the subject has learned to use a concept—more specifically, that the monkey has developed the *oddity concept*.

This example of concept learning, which requires a trial-

Figure 5–8. A monkey solving an oddity problem. Regardless of the nature of the stimuli, the monkey will always go to the "odd" object of the three if he has learned the oddity concept.

and-error approach, is only one of the ways in which concepts can be learned. Concepts can also be learned in other fashions; however, concept learning is based on capabilities that have previously been established by means of multiple discriminations. Thus, in the development of the oddity concept, the monkey first had to be able to discriminate among the stimulus objects. Similarly, individual chains and stimulus-response connections were required before multiple discriminations would occur.

Regardless of the process by which concepts are learned, the importance of concept learning in our everyday existence cannot be overemphasized. As Gagné (1965) points out, it is the acquisition of concepts that makes instruction possible. Thus, it would be impossible to prepare a student for all of the specific things or events that he may encounter. Rather, because of concept learning, the individual no longer needs to be subjected to control by specific stimuli. Concepts enable a person to generalize from a specific thing or event to a variety of other things or events in the same class. As a simple example, consider again the concept of "oddity." Regardless of the particular stimuli that might be present when one learns the concept initially, the learner thereafter responds to the "odd" object, even in the presence of completely different stimuli. Thus, the learner is able to generalize the concept to many specific instances that were not involved in the initial learning situation.

Type 7: Principle Learning

Through his formal education and his everyday experience, an individual learns a wide variety of concepts. Concepts provide the foundation for *principle learning,* in which a person establishes relationships between various concepts. Principles consist of chains of concepts. The primary prerequisite for this kind of learning to take place is that the concepts that constitute the principles are already known by the learner.

As a simple illustration of this kind of learning, let us consider an example used by Gagné (1965). If a child is told that "round things roll," he has been exposed to a principle consisting of two concepts. If the child is to learn the principle, he must know the concept of *round things* and the concept of *roll.* He must know that the concept *round* applies to a variety of objects such as discs, cylinders, marbles, and balls. Additionally, by means of multiple-discrimination learning, the child must be able to distinguish *rolling* from other events such as sliding, tumbling, or falling.

Even with the concepts established, telling a child that "round things roll" might simply result in his learning a verbal chain rather than a principle. Consequently, it would probably be necessary to give the child verbal instructions of some type to ensure that he learns a principle rather than a simple verbal sequence. To determine whether the principle has been learned, one could test the child.

In an ideal educational system, much of the testing would be over principle learning rather than concept or multiple-discrimination learning. Ideally, the student would be exposed to related sets of principles rather than to single principles. In other words, the process of learning principles would be hierarchical in nature. Thus, two or more concepts would be involved in learning a single principle, two or more principles in the learning of a higher-level principle, these principles in still a higher-level principle, and so forth. The result would be a hierarchy of principles—a hierarchy forming the structure of organized knowledge.

Type 8: Problem Solving

Once principles have been acquired, the learner can use them for a variety of purposes in dealing with his environment. By combining the principles that he has learned, he can *think.* Also, by combining old principles and thus forming new ones, he is able to *solve problems* that are new to him. Basically, problem solving involves the use of principles in order to achieve some goal. However, as pointed out by Gagné (1965, p. 157), problem solving is more than the achievement of a goal: "When problem solution is achieved, something is also *learned*, in the sense that the individual's capability is more or less permanently changed. What emerges from problem solving is a *higher-order principle*, which thereupon becomes a part of the individual's repertory."

The topic of problem solving will be taken up in more detail in the chapter dealing with the interpreting subsystem (Chapter 8).

Gagné's Model: Implications for Education

Gagné's cumulative model of learning has a number of implications for the development of effective procedures for education. While the varieties of learning described do not necessarily have to take place within the context of formal instruction, the fact that learning is a cumulative process allows the instructor to plan sequences of instruction for a particular content area. If a student is to solve problems, then the principles to be applied to the problem must have been previously learned. If principles are to be learned, then the concepts on which they are based must have been acquired previously, and so on. When formal instruction is considered in this fashion, the instructor can "map" out or plan the sequence of learning in such a fashion that essential steps in the acquisition of knowledge in a particular area are not left out.

> Without such a plan, mistakes of this sort are unfortunately easy to make. It would be pleasing to everyone, for example, if a learner could progress to the capability of extemporaneously composing sentences in a foreign language without previously learning to use individual words. But in fact such "skipping" cannot be done and, if it is tried, may result in serious "blocking" on the part of the student that may persist for a long time. Attempts to skip essential capabilities in mathematics can lead to similar consequences. The same is true of almost any content subject. Following a preplanned sequence, then, and thus avoiding omission of prerequisite capabilities along any route of learning, appears to be a highly important procedure to adopt in achieving effectiveness for instruction [Gagné, 1965, p. 173].

The System So Far

At this point in our consideration of the behavioral subsystems of man, we have dealt with the sensing and identifying subsystems and have discussed one of the functions of the memory subsystem—namely, the learning function. Two other functions of this subsystem—remembering and forgetting—will be taken up in the next chapter.

Learning results in a relatively permanent change in the output of the behavioral system. While the learning function depends

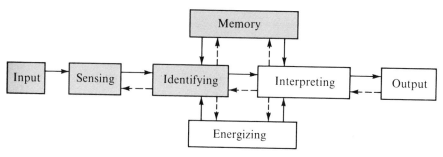

Figure 5-9. The system so far. We have now considered the input, sensing, identifying subsystems and part of the memory subsystem. In the next chapter the remembering and forgetting aspects of the memory subsystem will be discussed.

on inputs from other subsystems, it is also a source of input to other subsystems.

The learning process can be thought of as consisting of a number of progressively more complex "steps" with each higher step depending on lower steps. A step represents a particular "type" or "stage" of learning. These stages are hierarchical in nature, ranging from simple conditioning to complex problem solving. The latter type of learning is dependent upon a simpler type of learning, which in turn is dependent upon a still simpler form, and so forth. Thus, the learning function can be viewed as a cumulative process. At each step in the process, the capabilities of the subsystem are modified; that is, the subsystem is at one level of capability at the beginning of a stage of learning and at another level of capability at the end.

Summary

1. Learning is usually defined as any relatively permanent change in behavior which takes place because of experience or practice. Learning must be distinguished from performance, which is the actual, observable response. Learning cannot be directly observed but is inferred from performance.

2. There are a number of variables that have been shown to influence learning. Among these are: the learner's motivation, the nature of the material to be learned, the conditions under which the material or task is practiced, and the prior learning experience of the individual.

3. Gagné (1965) classifies learning according to eight types:

Signal learning (Type 1). The subject learns to make a general response of some type to a signal (bell, light, etc.)

Stimulus-response learning (Type 2). The subject develops a specific response to a discriminated stimulus.

Chaining (Type 3). The learner acquires a chain of two or more stimulus-response connections.

Verbal association (Type 4). While chaining involves learning chains of simple motor responses, verbal association involves the learning of verbal chains.

Multiple discrimination (Type 5). The learner develops the capability of making different responses to different objects or events. In other words, he learns to discriminate each stimulus in a set from the others and to respond to each stimulus in a prescribed manner.

Concept learning (Type 6). The person acquires the capability of making a common response to a class of stimuli rather than responding singly to the stimuli in the collection.

Principle learning (Type 7). Concepts provide the foundation for principle learning. In principle learning, the person learns to establish relationships between various concepts.

Problem solving (Type 8). By combining previously learned principles and forming new ones, the individual is able to solve problems. Principles are used to achieve some goal. As a result of problem solving, the individual learns something new.

Selected Readings

Gagné, R. M. Military training and principles of learning. *American Psychologist*, 1962, **17** (2), 83–91.

Gagné, R. M. *The conditions of learning.* New York: Holt, Rinehart and Winston, 1970.

Gagné, R. M. Contributions of learning to human development. *Psychological Review,* 1968, **3,** 177–191.

Pribram, K. H. (Ed.) *On the biology of learning.* New York: Harcourt Brace Jovanovich, 1969.

6

The Memory Subsystem II

Motor Learning, Remembering, and Forgetting

Motor Learning

Psychologists usually make a distinction between *verbal learning* and *motor learning*, although such a distinction is, in certain respects, artificial. Few, if any, tasks that are learned and practiced by humans can be considered "pure" motor tasks, since there are verbal components involved in the acquisition of nearly any motor skill. These verbal components may range from formal instructions regarding the performance of a task to "verbalizing," or talking to oneself, as the task is performed. In addition, feedback as to one's performance on a motor task may be verbal in nature. Similarly, an important motor element is involved in verbal learning, since one must learn muscular responses of the mouth and throat in order to enunciate effectively. Thus, human learning is neither completely verbal nor completely motor. Some forms of learning, however, are *predominantly* verbal while others are *pre-*

dominantly motor. It is the latter form of learning that concerns us in this chapter.

What Is a Skilled Response?

Many activities that we perform routinely every day consist of organized patterns or sequences of movements—that is, of *motor responses*. Often, these responses are so well established that we do not even consciously think about performing them. For example, we walk, talk, participate in sports, drive an automobile, ride a bicycle, use a typewriter, and engage in many other skilled activities without thinking about the motor responses that make up these skills. The complexity of skilled behavior becomes apparent, however, when we attempt to learn or to teach someone else, a new skill of some type.

Due to the importance of skilled behavior in man's interactions with his environment, *motor learning* (sometimes called skill learning, psychomotor learning, sensory-motor learning, or perceptual-motor learning) has been of interest to learning psychologists for many years.

Until recently, most definitions of a skilled response emphasized the coordination and the sequence of movements that are required in the performance of such a response. However, researchers have recently begun to think of motor skills as more than patterns of coordinated movements. For example, Fitts (1964, p. 244) defines a skilled response as ". . . one in which receptor-effector-feedback processes are highly organized, both spatially and temporally. The central problem for the study of skill learning is how such organization or patterning comes about." Generally, contemporary researchers describe skill learning as a system involving four components: input, information processing, output, and continuous feedback that can modify or reinforce the performance. An essential aspect of skill learning is the sensory-feedback component, which is based on kinesthetic cues that arise from the movements of the response member (hand, arm, leg, etc.). The nature of this type of feedback is discussed in more detail in Chapter 9.

The Acquisition of Skills

Generally, a person never begins the acquisition of a new skill without a background of many existing skills upon which to build. Adult human performance is based upon the utilization of a hierarchy of existing skills that are modified and organized in the acquisition of a new skill. Thus, an adult has available a vast number of sequences of movements which become fixed units within various kinds of complex motor activity. As Fitts and Posner (1967, p. 11) point out:

> These fixed units are quite automatic, and may be incorporated as components in many different activities. The timing and order of these units will vary with different skills and provide the unique character of each activity. Learning skills involves a new integration and ordering of units, many of which may be transferred as a whole from other activities.

If we assume that most of the discrete responses (fixed units) required for the learning of a skilled act are already available to the individual, then the integration and organization of these responses is the key process in acquiring a new skill. Just how this integration and ordering takes place is a question of considerable interest to the psychologists who specialize in motor learning or, for that matter, to anyone who is involved in teaching motor skills of any kind.

Fitts (1964) and Fitts and Posner (1967) discuss three phases of learning that appear to be involved in the acquisition of complex motor skills. The distinction between these phases is somewhat arbitrary, since there is no clear-cut transition between them. The three phases of skill learning are: (1) an early, *cognitive* phase, (2) an intermediate, *associative* phase, and (3) a final, *autonomous* phase.

Even in the early, cognitive phase of skill learning, the learner has available to him many of the individual responses that will be required in the task that is to be learned. In other words, most of the individual units that make up the new skill may not have to be learned. Of particular importance during the cognitive phase is that the learner develops an "understanding" of the task and what it requires; that is, he must establish the proper cognitive set for the task. In simple tasks this phase may be quite short; the learner may establish the proper set after he has had time to understand the instructions and to complete a few trials. In complex tasks, however, the cognitive phase may take some time. During the practice trials the learner is usually very much aware of the discrete responses that are involved in the new task. Generally, he needs to attend to kinesthetic and visual cues that he will not notice during later stages of learning. For example, consider for a moment how "aware" you were of all aspects of your first golf swings, tennis serves, or attempts at typing. In the later stages of learning, the various cues are usually not attended to in this fashion. In the cognitive phase of skill learning, "behavior is truly a patchwork of old habits ready to be put together into new patterns and supplemented by a few new habits" (Fitts & Posner, 1967, p. 12).

During the intermediate, associative phase of skill learning, the discrete responses that characterize the first phase become integrated and new patterns of motor behavior begin to emerge. The length of the associative phase depends on the nature of the task. Errors in performance are gradually eliminated during this phase; and, with practice, the integration and ordering of the individual responses involved in the new skill take place.

According to Fitts and Posner (1967, p. 14), with the transition to the final, autonomous phase,

> . . . component processes become increasingly autonomous, less directly subject to cognitive control, and less subject to interference from other ongoing activities or environmental distractions. In this phase, skills require less processing. This means that they can be carried on while new learning is in progress or while an individual is engaged in other perceptual and cognitive activities.

The last phase of skill learning may occur over a very long period of time. On many types of skilled activities, improvement in performance continues to be shown for months or even years. For example, consider the intensive practice one needs in order to attain championship performance in competitive sports. Typically, such performance requires years of practice; and even when an athlete's performance levels off, it may be due to loss of motivation or to physical factors rather than to the fact that he has no capacity for further improvement.

There is some experimental data available concerning the course of skill learning over long periods of time. In reviewing the research in this area, Crossman (1959) concluded that performance (in terms of speed) of simple perceptual-motor tasks increases gradually over very long periods of practice if the learner's motivation for improvement is maintained. Other studies have demonstrated that performance in skilled tasks improves over long periods of time if the learner is provided with knowledge of results.

The Study of Motor Learning

The kinds of apparatus used by psychologists in their studies of motor learning range from nothing more than a pencil and a piece of paper to elaborate pieces of equipment costing many thousands of dollars. An apparatus commonly used in these studies is the pursuit rotor, which is shown in Figure 6–1. This apparatus is used to gauge a subject's performance on a *pursuit tracking* task— a task that requires the subject to keep a controlled element on a moving target. As the turntable on the apparatus rotates, the subject attempts to keep the tip of the stylus (controlled element) on

Figure 6–1. An illustration of a pursuit rotor tracking apparatus. Photo courtesy Lafayette Instrument Company. Reprinted by permission.

the small metal disk (target). A pursuit rotor provides several measures of the subject's motor-skill performance—for instance, measures of the amount of time the subject is off (or on) target during a trial and the number of times the stylus is off the target. A *compensatory tracking* task imposes somewhat different requirements on the subject. The apparatus used in compensatory tracking consists of one moving element (instead of two, as in pursuit tracking), which the subject tries to hold stationary over a fixed target.

Since some type of tracking is necessary for the operation

of many man-machine systems, including the automobile, tracking performance has been subjected to a great deal of research. The equipment used in the research is usually much more complex than the pursuit rotor, although the task required of the subject may be quite similar. An example of a complex piece of apparatus utilized in tracking studies is shown in Figure 6–2. Much of the equipment

Figure 6–2. Console containing various items of equipment utilized in obtaining measures of tracking performance as well as other kinds of human performance. Photo courtesy of University of South Dakota, Human Factors Psychology Laboratory. Reprinted by permission.

on the console shown in this figure is used to measure performance of subjects who are engaged in various kinds of tracking tasks. With this kind of equipment, a variety of sensitive measures of performance can be obtained.

Regardless of the particular apparatus used in the study of motor learning, a great deal of the research on the topic falls into a few general areas. Irion (1969) lists these areas of research under the headings of (1) distribution-of-practice effects and the reminiscence phenomenon, (2) individual differences, (3) the whole-part problem, (4) feedback, (5) retention, and (6) transfer of training. Although a detailed discussion of these various areas would require numerous chapters, each area will be discussed briefly and the main research findings summarized.

Distribution of Practice and Reminiscence

Over the years, more studies have been conducted on the distribution of practice and reminiscence in performing a skill than on any other area of skills research. Early studies of the distribution of practice effects were primarily concerned with whether or not rest pauses during practice had an effect on performance. Typically, these studies compared the acquisition of some skill under two conditions. Acquisition of a skill through *massed practice,* in which many practice trials are given in a single session, is compared with acquisition through *spaced practice,* in which the same number of trials are distributed over a number of sessions with rest breaks between sessions. In most learning situations (but not all), distributed or spaced practice was found to be superior to massed practice. It was also found that long rest periods are usually better than short rest periods. Similarly, it was found that short practice sessions between rests result in better scores than do long practice sessions.

Figure 6–3 shows the results of a typical experiment involving conditions of massed versus spaced practice. The task involved pursuit tracking, which was described earlier. Note that performance under massed conditions was inferior to performance under spaced practice. Also note that immediately after a rest period there is an improvement in performance in the massed practice group. This finding is typical in experiments involving massed practice. The abrupt improvement resulting from a rest pause is referred to as *reminiscence.* The amount of improvement in performance due to reminiscence, however, is dependent upon such factors as the amount of massed practice that has taken place before the rest pause and the duration of the rest pause itself.

Early researchers in the field of motor-skill learning attempted to explain distribution effects by means of a "fatigue" theory. However, this notion had fallen from favor by the 1930s. A popular present view is that the results obtained from massed practice can be explained by means of a hypothetical process called *work inhibition.* According to this view, the inhibitory process builds up during massed practice and weakens the response (per-

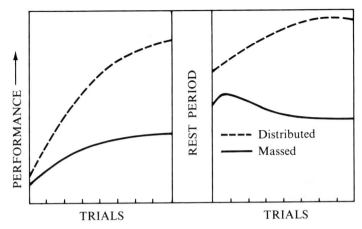

Figure 6–3. Hypothetical curves showing performance on a pursuit rotary tracking task under conditions of distributed and massed practice. Typically, in studies of this type, subjects in the massed practice group would complete a trial (perhaps one minute in duration) and then, with only a second or two of delay, would go on to the next trial. Subjects in the distributed practice group would be given several minutes between trials. The rest period shown in the figure would involve a considerably longer period of time.

formance), although it is thought to have no effect on learning. During rest periods, the inhibitory process diminishes. Thus, initial performance following a rest period will be markedly improved (reminiscence).

Individual Differences
in Acquiring Motor Skills

As is the case with any kind of behavior that can be adequately measured, differences between individuals in their ability to acquire and retain motor skills are quite apparent. There are a number of wide individual variations in performance that can be related to a variety of variables, such as age, sex, and motivation. These differences become obvious when individual performance curves are plotted rather than the group curves that are usually used. However, even though individuals differ, there are still a number of basic similarities that can be found when certain critical independent variables are employed.

The fact that wide individual differences do exist between individual abilities to master highly skilled tasks has inspired considerable research in the area of selection and training (Chapter

12). During World War II a great deal of effort was expended to develop methods for selecting personnel who could be expected to acquire necessary skills in a variety of complex man-machine systems. The tests were designed to select certain individuals and reject others based on their relative abilities—that is, their individual differences. Sometimes it was found that particular individuals who performed well on the selection tests performed adequately early in practice but not in later practice. Consequently, researchers became interested in the power of selection tests to predict psychomotor performance early and late in practice. The relationship between individual differences and changes in performance as a function of practice has been studied by a number of investigators.

The Whole-Part Problem

Researchers in motor-skill learning have been interested in whether *part training*, in which an individual practices on the components of a particular task, or *whole training*, in which the complete task is practiced, is most effective in mastering the skill. As pointed out by Irion (1969):

> The whole-part problem overlaps with a considerable number of other problems. For example, it tends to merge with the problem of distribution of practice in that each of the parts may be considered to be a shorter unit of practice than is the practicing of the whole task. . . . The fact that the parts must be practiced in some order also throws the whole-part problem into the category of transfer-of-training experiments . . . [p. 12].

From the experimental evidence that is available, it would appear that the whole method has some slight edge over the part method. However, many investigations have had ambiguous results, and it seems safest to conclude that each method has its advantages and disadvantages. Under certain conditions, one or the other approach may be more effective; sometimes either of the methods may be equally effective.

It appears that the part method is advantageous when the discrete responses making up the task are new and difficult for the learner. In this case, these responses can be acquired more rapidly through the part method and then integrated into the skill. Of course, the discrete response or "part" must be easily separable from the "whole." Often, a learner using the part method can feel successful sooner than with the whole method, since he can see some progress relatively quickly. This early success may be an important source of motivation.

We pointed out earlier that a skilled task involves the integration and coordination of a number of discrete responses. Consequently, one disadvantage of the part method, and therefore an advantage of the whole method, is that the performance of a single response by itself may be different from the performance of the same response as part of the complete task. Thus, practice of the individual response can result in a less efficient integration and co-ordination of the complete task than would be the case if the task were practiced by the whole method. The effectiveness of the part or whole method depends a great deal on how organized and complex the task may be. For example, Naylor and Briggs (1961) investigated the effects of task complexity and organization on the efficiency of part and whole methods of practice. They found that when tasks were unorganized the part method was best. However, under conditions of higher organization and complexity, the whole method proved most efficient. In a general statement concerning the whole-part problem, Annett and Kay (1956) suggested that a series of recurring events may be learned best by the whole method. If, however, the responses of the learner tend to alter the series of events in some fashion, then the part method will tend to reduce the variability or randomness of the series of responses.

Feedback (Knowledge of Results)

It is important to efficient learning and performance that the individual receive information about the consequences of his responses. In much of the literature on motor skills, this type of information is referred to as "knowledge of results." However, in line with current usage in control theory and cybernetics, many psychologists now call this information "feedback." Regardless of what it is called, it is a critical factor in motor learning. Thus, Irion (1966) states that "there can be small doubt that knowledge of results is the single most important variable governing the acquisition of skillful habits" (p. 34). Similarly, Bilodeau and Bilodeau (1961) point out that "Studies of feedback or knowledge of results . . . show it to be the strongest, most important variable controlling performance and learning . . ." (p. 250).

Assuming, then, that feedback is a critical factor in learning and performance, what do we know of its functions? First, research has shown that it can have at least three effects: it can strengthen responses, it can sustain performance, and it can eliminate previously established responses. These functions are generally accepted by most psychologists. However, there is some argument about the theoretical properties of feedback. In other words, *how* does feedback strengthen or eliminate responses and sustain performance? It is probable that these effects can be explained in terms of the *knowledge,* or information, provided the person by feedback and by its *motivating* and *reinforcing* characteristics. In providing the learner with knowledge about his performance, mistakes can be corrected and performance improved. Also, if behavior is goal directed—that is, if the individual wants to learn the task —then feedback can provide information about the present state of achievement in relation to his goal. In this way, feedback can serve as a strong source of motivation. And it is clear that motivation is necessary to sustain performance and to help learning to occur. In addition, feedback is a reinforcer, in that it is a stimulus that serves to strengthen responses that occur in close temporal proximity to it. It should be pointed out, however, that the theoretical status of feedback is somewhat obscure. Some psychologists accept all three properties, while others do not commit themselves to any theory of how feedback works.

In the development of skills, the individual is provided with two general types of feedback. *Intrinsic feedback* results from the response itself. For example, when we move our muscles, a system of receptors is activated, which in turn provides us with information about the movement. These kinesthetic receptors, located in muscles and joints, furnish cues to the movement and location of the hand, foot, or whatever other response member may be involved. Thus, when you throw an object such as a baseball, you have a good idea as to how far it will go based on the intrinsic feedback from the muscles in the arm. Intrinsic feedback, then, arises internally, as the result of the organism's response. Studies concerned with the distortion or reduction of normal intrinsic feedback have shown that there is a serious disruptive effect on performance, although improvement can occur as a result of additional learning. However, with reduced or distorted feedback it is almost like learning a new skill.

The second type of feedback—*extrinsic* or *augmented* or *artificial* feedback—arises from sources outside the organism. For example, feedback about performance on the pursuit rotor could be "augmented" in several ways. For example, a clock or counter could be placed in view of the subject so that he could see how much time he was "off target" or how frequently his stylus lost contact with the target. There are many other examples of extrinsic feedback. When you receive a grade on an examination, read the speedometer on your car, or watch your golf shot fall in the rough, you are experiencing extrinsic feedback.

Classification of Feedback. For the investigator who conducts research involving feedback as a variable, it is often not adequate to use only the intrinsic and extrinsic categories. Consequently, within these two general classes of feedback, there are other distinctions between various kinds of feedback. Holding (1965) presented one of the most comprehensive classification schemes for feedback. According to Holding's classification, both intrinsic and extrinsic (artificial) feedback can be divided into second-order types of feedback that are called *concurrent* and *terminal* feedback. Concurrent feedback is present all of the time that a person is responding, while terminal feedback arises only as a result of a completed response. In addition, concurrent and terminal feedback can be *immediate* (no gap in time between a response and feedback) or *delayed* (a gap in time between the response and feedback). Further, extrinsic feedback can be *verbal* (words, scores) or *nonverbal* (instruments, dials). And finally, feedback can be *separate* (for each response) or *accumulated* over several responses and presented at the end of a series. A particular situation can involve a number of these kinds of feedback. Thus, "accumulated, verbal, immediate, concurrent, artificial knowledge of results is given by a trainer shouting integrated error scores to a person trying to follow a moving target . . ." (Holding, 1965, p. 22).

Much of the early research on feedback was concerned with the effects of either giving or not giving feedback, but in recent years, there has been more interest in determining the effects produced by varying the ways in which feedback is presented. Thus, there have been a series of investigations dealing with the effects of distorted, diminished, or delayed feedback upon the performance of skillful acts.

Delayed Feedback. One interesting type of investigation has involved what is called "delayed auditory feedback" and its effects on speech. Speech, of course, is a complex skill involving a variety of muscles. It is dependent upon both kinesthetic and auditory feedback in that it is necessary not only to "feel" what the muscles are doing but also to hear the various sounds that are produced. In a delayed auditory feedback experiment, a subject speaks into a microphone, and special equipment "stores" the speech for a short period of time before the subject hears it through earphones. Thus, there is a delay between speaking and hearing, creating a kind of "echo" effect. With only a very short delay (a fraction of a second), the subject's speech is seriously affected. He may not be able to speak at all, or he may falter and stutter.

Another variety of delayed feedback studies has involved delayed visual feedback. K. U. Smith and his coworkers (Smith & Smith, 1962; Smith & Sussman, 1969) have conducted a series of studies on delayed visual feedback, as well as other types of delayed feedback. By means of equipment similar to that illustrated in Figure

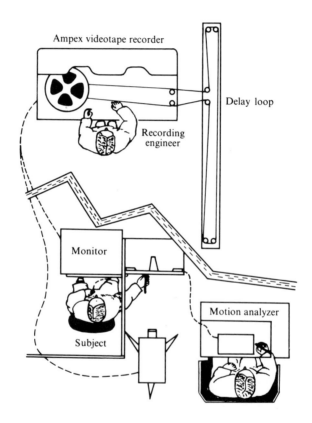

Figure 6–4. A system for introducing a delay between the time a subject makes a response, such as drawing a figure, and the time that he receives visual feedback. The subject cannot observe his own motions directly but sees only the image in the television monitor. Visual delay is brought about by means of the delay loop shown. From K. U. Smith & W. M. Smith, *Perception and motion: An analysis of space structured behavior.* Copyright 1962 by W. B. Saunders Company. By permission of W. B. Saunders Company.

6–4, it is possible to introduce a delay between the time a subject performs an act (traces a star or some other form) and the time he receives visual feedback from a television monitor. This is accomplished by means of a time-delay system, which imposes a time interval between the input to the camera and the output to the monitor. The subject thus sees his hands in the past. In such experiments, even very short delays resulted in jerky movements and a breakdown in coordination.

While delayed visual feedback studies have theoretical interest, they also have practical significance. An important factor in designing man-machine systems is the frequent lag between the time an operator initiates some sort of control movement and the time the machine responds. This lag was a particular problem, for example, in the early stages of the nuclear submarine development. When the operator initiated a control movement—such as pushing the stick forward for a dive—there was a considerable period of time before the submarine responded. Similar situations have been found in other systems with a consequent disruption of operator performance.

Behavioral Cybernetics. K. U. Smith (1966) refers to his approach of studying feedback and other aspects of learning and performance as *experimental behavioral cybernetics.* The basic assumption of behavioral cybernetics is that the organization of motor performance and learning is based on the feedback control that an individual maintains over his own behavior. The concept of feedback is essential in the science of *cybernetics,* which is defined as the science of control and communication in the organism and machine.

While an extensive discussion of the contributions of cybernetics to psychological thinking would involve us in areas such as computer simulation, information theory, and mathematical modeling of psychological systems, one of its primary contributions lies in its application of the concept of *servomechanisms* to human behavior. A servomechanism can be thought of as a machine that is purposeful or goal seeking. A servomechanism stands in contrast to machines that may be built for a purpose, such as a gasoline engine, but that do not have a built-in purpose or goal. Servomechanisms differ from other types of machines in that they are capable of "sensing" stimuli and responding to them in such a fashion that the "behavior" of the machine can be modified or corrected. The modification or correction is based on feedback.

While servomechanisms can vary considerably in complexity and purpose, there are four basic processes involved in these types

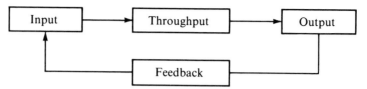

Figure 6–5. The basic processes involved in a servomechanism. These include an input, a transformation process (called throughput), an output, and feedback.

of machines. First, an input to the system is required. There is also a transformation process (called throughput) and an output. The fourth process is feedback. Figure 6–5 is a simple schematic showing the relationships among these operations. The similarity between this schematic and the schematics of the behavioral subsystems that have been presented in each of the chapters of this book should be quite apparent.

Retention of Motor Skills

The problem of retention will be discussed in more detail later in this chapter. It would appear that motor skills are remarkably resistant to forgetting. A number of reasons have been given to explain this resistance, although, since most studies have failed to find forgetting, it has been difficult to determine the variables that are responsible for the resistance.

Transfer of Training

The final area of research in motor skills that we will be concerned with is *transfer of training*. This area deals with the way in which new learning is influenced by previous learning. It has been found that things we have learned previously will sometimes help us learn new things, while at other times they will hinder new learning. The importance of transfer of training in our everyday existence cannot be overemphasized. Ellis (1965) has pointed out that "It is difficult to think of any adult learning that could not be affected by earlier learning. We might, in fact, regard all studies of learning beyond a very early age as studies of transfer of learning" (p. 5).

Basically, transfer of training refers to the fact that experience or performance on one task may influence performance on some subsequent task. If performance on the subsequent task is aided or facilitated because of the previous experience, we say that *positive transfer* has taken place. On the other hand, if performance on one task inhibits or disrupts performance on a second task, we call the process *negative transfer*. Of course, performance of one task may not influence performance of another task at all, in which case *zero transfer* takes place.

While research on transfer of training may involve elaborate experimental designs and a variety of variables, the basic research paradigm in this area can be rather simply illustrated. The simplest type of study of transfer requires two groups of subjects—an experimental group and a control group. It also requires two different performance tasks, which we will designate as Task A and Task B. The experimental design given below is then followed. The control group rests, or at least does not learn Task A, while the experimental group learns Task A. Both groups then learn Task B. If there is positive transfer, then the experimental group should perform better (learn faster with fewer errors) on Task B than the control group. However, suppose the experimental group's performance is inferior to that of the control group on Task B. We then assume that negative transfer has taken place. The learning of Task A has somehow disrupted the performance of Task B. Or, the control and experimental groups might perform Task B equally well, so that we have zero transfer.

	Original Task	*Transfer Task*
Control Group	(rests)	Learns B
Experimental Group	Learns A	Learns B

There are a number of factors that determine whether there will be positive, negative, or zero transfer from one task to another. One important variable is the degree of similarity between the original and transfer tasks. A generalization that is frequently made about transfer studies is that the greater the degree of similarity between two tasks, the greater the amount of positive transfer that will occur (*similarity concept*). The definition of "similarity" has sometimes presented problems. However, we can think of similarity between tasks in terms of the stimuli and responses associated with the tasks. Thus, if the stimuli and responses associated with two tasks are alike, the two tasks are considered as being similar. Much of the research in the area of transfer of training has involved the manipulation of these variables.

The relationships shown between these variables and transfer are complex; consequently, it is not possible to summarize in a brief statement the effects of stimulus and response similarity on transfer of training. Also, the vast majority of research has involved verbal tasks, so we have relatively little information on transfer in motor tasks.

In studies in which the response variable is held constant and stimulus similarity between tasks is varied, the usual result is that greater positive transfer is produced by similar stimuli than by different stimuli. When transfer is studied with identical stimuli but with varying responses, it has been found that making new responses to old stimuli will usually result in some degree of negative transfer. In some studies, both stimuli and response involved in the two tasks have been varied. It appears that if the responses in the transfer task are different from those in the original task, then transfer will decrease as similarity of the stimuli increases.

As pointed out above, our information about transfer with motor skills is limited. In studies dealing with transfer between skilled tasks, except under carefully controlled and arranged conditions, positive transfer is more likely to occur than negative transfer. Negative transfer effects are difficult to obtain in skill situations. Under conditions that might be expected to yield negative transfer (based on similar verbal learning situations) on motor tasks, positive transfer is found instead.

Based on the results of studies that are available, the use of the similarity concept in transfer on skilled tasks is questionable. However, despite the lack of evidence on whether transfer performance is systematically related to both stimulus and response similarity in motor tasks, the assumption is often made in training programs that similarity is a factor. Many programs involve the use of sophisticated simulators of one kind or another. Usually, considerable effort is made to make the simulator as "real" as possible on the assumption that positive transfer to the actual task will be increased. The more alike the simulated and real task, the higher the "fidelity of simulation." The simulators used to train the astronauts for their space missions are excellent examples of the level of fidelity that can be attained in simulator design and construction. However, "high fidelity" simulators have also been developed in other areas. In recent years a considerable amount of attention has been directed toward designing simulators that can be used to study driver behavior and that can be used in driver education.

A "High Fidelity" Driving Simulator. While there are a number of driving simulators currently available, a model presently being used in the authors' laboratory is particularly versatile. Basically, the device consists of two major subsystems—the mockup

Figure 6-6. A subject seated in mockup, operating the driving simulator. The scene in front of the subject changes as the subject operates the steering wheel and other controls. If she were to turn suddenly to the left, she would hit the car that is shown on the screen. Photograph courtesy of the *Minneapolis Tribune.* Reprinted by permission.

body and the display projection system. These subsystems are illustrated in Figures 6-6 and 6-7.

The mockup body is instrumented with standard automobile controls, including accelerator, steering wheel, gear shift, clutch pedal, and footbrake. The device has been modified to simulate automatic transmission if desired. The visual display is presented to the subject on a six-by-twelve-foot rear projection screen, which is located just ahead of the mockup body. The visual display is generated as the refracted image, produced when illumination from a high intensity point source of light passes through a transparent Plexiglass disk. The roadway scene is painted on the disk surface. The model road layout on this disk can be modified to suit the purpose of any experiment. It can include silhouette models of trees, hedges, signs, telegraph poles, buildings, and so on. Simulated movement is produced when the road disk is driven beneath the stationary point light

Figure 6-7. The projection system of the simulator. The large plastic disk moves as the subject operates the controls. As the subject increases the speed, the disk moves faster. When the subject turns, the entire disk swings. The disk moves under the light source which "projects" an image on the screen. Photograph courtesy of the *Minneapolis Tribune.* Reprinted by permission.

source. The movement of the disk is controlled by the subject's operation of the control elements in the mockup of the vehicle. The driver can drive at any rate of speed, can swerve off the road, hit other vehicles and, in general, do almost anything he could do in an actual car.

In terms of general operational characteristics, the chief advantage of a simulator such as this is that it can be operated in a completely nonprogrammed mode—that is, the driver controls what he sees on the screen—and that the fidelity of display response to control input is very high. While other types of simulators may produce visual displays of greater clarity, they are not capable of the same degree of nonprogrammed operation and display response that exists with the point light source simulator.

A number of studies have been conducted with this simulator. Because of the characteristics of the device, it might be expected that there would be a high degree of positive transfer from training in the simulator to actual driving. The amount of transfer that does take place is currently being investigated.

Remembering and Forgetting

It was suggested earlier that the memory subsystem involves three basic functions—the acquisition of responses, the retention or storage of the responses, and the loss of the responses. These functions can be labeled learning, remembering, and forgetting. While it is customary to discuss these functions separately, they are nonetheless closely interrelated. We do not remember something if it was not learned in the first place, and what we forget is simply the difference between what was learned and what is remembered.

Research in the area of memory is currently undergoing significant changes; there are new theories, new data, and new approaches. In our discussion of memory we will first consider some recent theoretical work and then describe experimental methods that are employed in the study of memory.

A Theory of Memory

When we remember a past event of some kind, there are a number of things involved. In order for the event to be remembered, information must first be acquired. After it is acquired, it must then be retained in a storage system. Finally, it must be retrieved when needed. Thus, we should consider all of its stages, if we are to understand the phenomenon of memory.

As a foundation for the discussion of a theoretical interpretation of memory, some brief comments on "kinds" of memory are necessary. Most studies dealing with memory have involved periods of time ranging from at least several minutes to weeks or longer. Such studies dealt with *long-term memory*, in which material is stored for long periods of time—even a lifetime. There is another kind of memory, however, which involves temporary storage of only a few seconds. This is called *short-term memory*. The question that has concerned researchers in the area of memory is whether similar processes are involved in the two types of memory. In other words, does looking up a telephone number and attempting to dial it immediately involve different processes from attempting to recall material that was learned months before? At present, a definite answer is not available, for some investigators have pointed out important differences between the two kinds of memory while others have argued that some of the processes operating in the forgetting of long-term memories are similar to those in short-term memories. Regardless of whether these processes are basically similar or different, an adequate theory of memory must take both into consideration.

The Shiffrin-Atkinson Theory

R. M. Shiffrin and R. C. Atkinson (1969) have presented a theory of human memory which, while still in its formative stage, has been applied successfully to a variety of commonly studied variables in the field of learning and memory. Their theory provides a general framework within which many of the specific aspects of memory can be considered. The following material is based on their theory of a memory system that is described in much more detail in their article called "Storage and Retrieval Processes in Long-Term Memory" (*Psychological Review*, 1969).

The major components, or subsystems, of the system are diagrammed in Figure 6–8. These consist of the sensory register, the short-term store (STS), and the long-term store (LTS). Note that the other subsystems include control processes and a response generator. The solid arrows indicate the directions in which information can be transferred between the various components of the system. However, it should be kept in mind that the "transfer" of information from one subsystem to another does not mean that it is removed from one storage and placed in another. Rather, the transfer can be thought of as a procedure in which information in one subsystem is "copied" by the next without affecting its status in the original subsystem. The dashed lines indicate connections that permit comparisons of information that reside in different parts of the system; they also represent connections that allow control signals that activate various processes within the system to be sent.

While a detailed discussion of the many aspects of this theory of human memory is beyond the scope of this book, we will briefly consider the components of the system and some of their interactions. It is suggested that students who are interested in pursuing

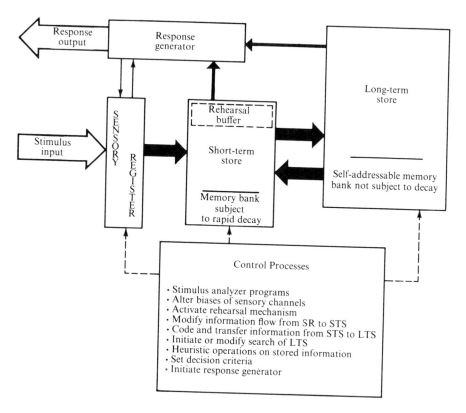

Figure 6–8. A flow chart of the memory system proposed by Shiffrin and Atkinson. The solid lines indicate information transfer pathways. The dashed lines show connections that permit comparisons of information arrays residing in different parts of the system. The dashed lines also indicate paths along which control signals may be sent which activate information transfer, rehearsal, and so forth. From R. M. Shiffrin and R. C. Atkinson, Storage and retrieval processes in long-term memory. *Psychologcal Review,* **76,** 1969, 179–193. Copyright 1969 by the American Psychological Association and reproduced by permission.

this area in greater depth read the original article by Shiffrin and Atkinson.

As you can see from Figure 6–8, the stimulus input to the system goes into the first of three memory stores: the *sensory register.* This store holds incoming sensory information for a very short period of time (measured in milliseconds) while it is initially processed. Information is then transferred to the *short-term store* (STS). If the person does not "pay attention" to this information, it will be lost from the STS in about 30 seconds or less. However, note the subsystem on the diagram that is labeled *control processes.* Control processes, such as rehearsal, retain information in STS for longer periods of time. Shiffrin and Atkinson describe the functions of the short-term store as follows:

> The short-term store serves a number of useful functions. On the one hand it decouples the memory system from the external environment and relieves the system from the responsibility of moment-to-moment attention to environmental changes. On the other hand, STS provides a working memory in which manipulations of information may take place on a temporary basis. Because STS is a memory store in which information can be maintained if desired, it is often used as the primary memory device in certain types of tasks; in these tasks the information presented for retention is maintained in STS until the moment of test and then emitted [pp. 180–181].

During the time that information is held in the STS, portions of it are transferred to long-term store (LTS), which is considered a permanent store for information. There are several mechanisms involved in this storage process, including *transfer, placement,* and *image production.* Since all of the information from short-term store is not transferred to long-term store, the individual must make decisions about *what* information to store, *when* to store it, and *how* to store it in LTS. For example, the decision about when to store information (and what to store) may be important, particularly if a great deal of information is coming into the STS. When the amount of information "overloads" the system in this way, the person is forced to select parts of the information for storage. How to store the information involves further decisions—should he store information via visual images or auditory storage, overt or covert rehearsal methods, organizational storage strategies, and so forth. These control processes, shown in Figure 6–8, are of key importance in the transfer process.

The placement mechanisms determine the locations where the particular information will be stored. The components of the ensemble of information will determine to a considerable extent the location of the storage. The ensemble of information, which is referred to as an "image," may be stored in more than one location. Just what locations are selected for the storage of the image is dependent upon a number of organizational and strategic factors that are beyond the scope of our discussion. The most critical aspect of the placement process is that it results in storage locations from which the information can later be retrieved. As we have indicated, not all of the information in STS will be transferred to a location in LTS. However, some portion of it will be stored as a permanent image in LTS. The proportion of information that is stored, which also is dependent upon a number of variables, is determined by the "image" production mechanism. The process of long-term storage takes place constantly from the information that is residing in the short-term store.

The content of the image that is stored may contain a wide range of information. Included may be characteristics of the item presented for study as well as some that have been added by the person. Thus, the image content could involve characteristics such as color, size, shape, sound, meaning, and so on (presented to the person), as well as codes, mnemonics, mediators, associations, and so on (which are added by the person). An image also contains links to other images or "sets of directions" to the locations of other related images that are stored in LTS.

A theory of memory must not only account for storage of information but also for the retrieval of this information once it has been located in LTS. In Shiffrin and Atkinson's theory of human memory, retrieval is thought to consist of three primary mechanisms: *search, recovery,* and *response generation.* Basically, the search mechanism involves a continually cycling process that successively examines locations of images in LTS. This search can be initiated by input information (which will also place certain restrictions on what to search for). Based on this input information, the person will look in some memory location and select an image for examination. The recovery process then determines how much information will be recovered from this image and placed back in short-term storage. This recovered information is then examined by means of the response generation process, and certain "decisions" are made. Based on the decision that is made, the search process may continue and the selection of another location or image for examination will be made. However, the search may have been "narrowed" because of the information that was already recovered by the previous search. The response generation process, however, may have arrived at another decision which involves termination of the search and emitting a response. Or, a decision can also be made to terminate the search without a response if, for example, the person decides that added search would not be useful. There are a variety of reasons why a search may be terminated before a response is made.

The above material represents a brief overview of a complex theory of human memory. In attempting to summarize and simplify, we have not been able to do full justice to the comprehensive nature of the theory as presented by Shiffrin and Atkinson. In addition to describing the theory, these authors also discuss a number of applications of the theory. Thus, within the framework of this theory, they discuss forgetting, interference, recognition, recall, and several other phenomena that a satisfactory theory of memory must take into account.

Measuring Remembering and Forgetting

In considering the measurement of remembering and forgetting, it should be kept in mind that we can directly measure only what has been retained by the individual. What is forgotten is the difference between what was learned and what is retained. Various approaches and methods have been employed in measuring the retention of what was learned. We shall be concerned with the three methods that are most commonly used and that you have encountered, in one form or another, many times. These are the *recall* method, the *recognition* method, and the *savings* method (sometimes called the *relearning* method). Each of these methods has its advantages and disadvantages, and the one selected for use will depend upon such variables as the type of material learned and the method used in learning.

Basically, the *recall* method compares performance at the end of training with performance demonstrated after some time interval. In other words, the person is called upon to reproduce something he has learned in the past. For example, suppose you memorized 100 words, and a few hours later you are able to recall only 80 of the original 100. You have recalled (retained) 80 percent and forgotten 20 percent. An essay examination is another example of a recall method of measuring retention. Of the various methods available, the recall technique typically yields the least amount of measurable retention, since it furnishes the minimum number of cues for remembering. The recall method is also sometimes referred to as the *reproduction* method.

Whenever you take a multiple-choice examination, your retention is being measured by means of the *recognition* method. You are required to "recognize" the correct item from a series of incorrect items. While this method is frequently used in the classroom because of its convenience, the amount of retention measured may not reflect the actual retention because of the "guess" factor.

The *savings* method requires that a task be relearned to some initial level of performance. Again, assume that you are required to memorize 100 words and that it took 50 repetitions (or a given period of time or number of errors) to learn the list perfectly. If, at a later date, it takes fewer repetitions (or less time or fewer errors) then there is a "savings" from the first learning. Perhaps the relearning involved only 25 repetitions instead of the 50 that were necessary for the initial learning. The savings, in this case, would be 50 percent. The savings method is used more frequently in research than the recall or recognition method because it is a more sensitive and reliable measure. Also, retention of a learned task may be demonstrated by means of the savings method long after the other methods fail to show that anything is retained.

Retention Curves

A retention curve is a method of graphically presenting the amount of material remembered at different points in time since it was first learned. Figure 6–9 is a "typical" retention curve with the

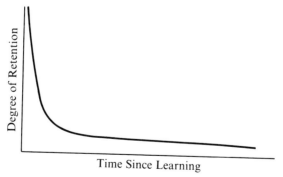

Time Since Learning

Figure 6–9. A typical retention curve. The degree of retention is plotted on the vertical axis and time since learning on the horizontal axis. The exact shape of the curve will depend on many factors.

degree of retention plotted on the vertical axis and the time since learning given on the horizontal axis. While this figure represents the usual shape of a retention curve, there are many other forms, which are dependent upon a number of variables. Generally, however, retention is characterized by a rather abrupt initial loss, followed by a much more gradual loss over time.

What are some of the factors that determine the form of a retention curve? An obvious variable is the manner in which retention is measured. We have mentioned that the savings method of measuring retention is more sensitive than either the recall or recognition technique. Consequently, we would expect a different retention curve for the various methods.

Several factors that have been shown to affect how efficiently initial learning takes place are also important to retention. For example, the meaningfulness of the material learned is a factor in retention, as well as in initial learning. Not only is meaningful material learned easier than nonsense material, it is also retained more easily. Similarly, it has been found that under a wide range of conditions, retention is greater after distributed (spaced) practice than after massed practice. However, as was the case with learning under spaced or massed practice, it cannot be stated that one or the other is best for retention under *all* conditions.

Retention is also influenced by the initial level of mastery of the material or task involved. As might be expected, when the original material is mastered at a high level, retention is improved. Thus, if you learn material to a level where you make no errors and then practice some more (overlearning), the material will be retained longer than it would be if it had not been overlearned. However, a point of diminishing returns is reached for overlearning—that is, for good retention there is probably an optimum amount of overlearning, after which it will do no good.

Why Do We Forget?

While it is not particularly difficult to measure how much we can retain over a period of time or to determine factors that affect retention, we still do not have a complete answer to the question of *why* we forget. Several theories have been advanced in an effort to explain "forgetting," but none can be considered complete. Recall from our earlier discussion of a theory of memory that in order for an event to be remembered it must be "retrieved" from the storage system. Assuming that the material was initially learned—that is, put into storage—then forgetting can be considered to be a problem of retrieval.

Interference Theory of Forgetting

One widely held theory of forgetting assumes that when we attempt to remember something, how much we remember is influenced by other learning that has occurred before or after the event we wish to remember. In other words, our ability to retrieve information is reduced because of other information we have learned— either before or after—that interferes with the retrieval process. This theory is called the *interference* theory of forgetting.

A number of studies have shown that learning something new will also interfere with the retention of material that was learned earlier. If the learning of something new (called *interpolated activity*) impairs the retention of the original material, we say that *retroactive inhibition* has taken place. Similarly, we find that the retention of newly learned material can be interfered with by material that was learned before the new material was acquired. This is called *proactive inhibition.* The interference of retention caused by retroactive or proactive inhibition is generally studied by means of the design shown in Table 6–1. As with the studies of transfer of training discussed earlier, a control group and an experimental group are required. Three steps or phases are involved in studying both types of inhibition. In retroactive inhibition, the control group learns Task A in the first phase, rests during the second phase, and is again tested on Task A during the third phase. The experimental group, however, does not rest during the second phase; instead it is required to learn a new task (B), after which it is again tested on the

Table 6–1. The experimental designs used to study retroactive and proactive inhibition.

	RETROACTIVE INHIBITION DESIGN		
Group	*Phase I*	*Phase II*	*Phase III*
Experimental	Learn A	Learn B	Retention test on A
Control	Learn A	"Rest"	Retention test on A
	PROACTIVE INHIBITION DESIGN		
Group	*Phase I*	*Phase II*	*Phase III*
Experimental	Learn A	Learn B	Retention test on B
Control	"Rest"	Learn B	Retention test on B

original task (A). Thus, the interfering interpolated activity (new learning) occurs for the experimental group but not the control group. If the experimental group does not demonstrate as much retention as the control group on the final test, then it can be assumed that the lower retention was due to the interpolated activity.

As you can see from Table 6–1, the design for studying proactive inhibition is somewhat different. It is intended to demonstrate the effects of an antecedent activity (Task A) on retention of a task (B) that comes *after* the activity. If proactive inhibition has occurred, subjects in the experimental group will not do as well on the final test as those in the control group.

If learning something new interferes with retention of previously learned material (retroactive inhibition), perhaps the best strategy in preparing for an examination is to sleep between the time you finish studying and the time of the test. Actually, it has been demonstrated that there is much better retention of learned material when it is followed by sleep than when other types of activity take place. Possibly, you might even want to sleep in a refrigerator since it has also been shown in a study with cockroach subjects that retention of maze learning is improved if the cockroaches are refrigerated between the time they learn the maze and are retested (Minami & Dallenbach, 1946).

Memory-Trace Theories

While all theories suppose that memory involves some change in the central nervous system, several theories are based on hypothetical changes that are assumed to take place in the brain. It is often assumed that memory involves a *trace* (sometimes called an *engram*) in the brain. The structural basis for this hypothetical trace is uncertain, although some related ideas will be discussed later. A number of people (but few psychologists) feel that the passage of time will automatically produce forgetting, because the memory trace will fade or dissipate with disuse. This is called the theory of *passive decay* or *disuse*. There is considerable evidence that forgetting is not merely an inevitable passive decay over a period of time. We certainly know that people can remember things over a lifetime.

Another theory, sometimes called the *qualitative-change* theory, is based on the assumption that the memory trace is not necessarily lost over time, but it may be distorted. If the distortion is severe enough, the "image" may be sufficiently changed so that the search process (in the retrieval function) does not "recognize" it. If it is recognized and retrieved, it may be so distorted and different from the image that was initially stored that it may actually appear as though the original image was lost. It has been shown that qualitative changes do take place in memory. For example, many details are forgotten in verbal narrative and in the memory of perceptual objects, even though the general "image" may be retained. However, even though qualitative changes do take place in memory, it is not certain whether this can be blamed on distortion of memory traces.

Other Reasons for Forgetting

According to Freudian theory, certain kinds of information will be "pushed" into the unconscious and will be retrieved only under unusual circumstances, such as hypnosis or drugs. This process, which is called *repression*, may take place for several reasons. Basically, however, it serves as a defense mechanism, keeping anxiety-provoking motives and memories out of the individual's consciousness. Thus, in some cases information may not be retrieved because we simply do not want it to be found—that is, we are motivated to forget. Forgetting can also occur when the stimulus situation under which the learning took place is quite different from the situation in which recall is attempted. While you obviously do not have to be in an identical stimulus situation in order to recall something that was learned, it does appear to help. For example, there is experimental evidence that if you are tested in the same room in which you learned material, you will recall more than if you are tested in another room. This phenomenon can be demonstrated without conducting an experiment, however. Have you ever visited a house where you lived years before or sat in an automobile that you once owned and sold? Both situations will result in a flood of memories about events that seemed to have been forgotten. While the memories might be quite different—for example, childhood memories in the home and possibly back-seat memories in the car—they are recalled because of the stimulus situation.

Finally, memory may be affected by the condition of the brain. There are a number of types of brain damage that will cause difficulty with memory. Depending upon their location, brain tumors affect memory in several ways. Difficulty with memory can be encountered after severe head injuries, after the oxygen supply to the brain has been interrupted (*anoxia*), or as a result of diseases such as encephalitis. Also, because of changes in the brain, old people may have problems with their memory. Often, they are incapable of remembering events that took place in the near past but can remember in great detail events that occurred many years before. This condition is referred to as *anterograde amnesia.*

It should be apparent from the above discussion that, at present, no comprehensive theory of forgetting exists. Rather, we have available several theories which account for certain aspects of memory, but none that can "handle" all of the facts that memory research has yielded. Possibly, some day we may be able to put all of these facts together into one complete theory of remembering and forgetting.

The Physiological Basis of Memory

A consideration of the physiological foundations of memory involves an attempt at answering one key question: What characteristics or properties of the neuron make possible the storage of information? While a number of theories have been advanced in an attempt to explain the neural basis of memory, none of them are founded on very solid evidence.

D. O. Hebb (1949) is the source of one popular theory on the physiological basis of memory. According to his theory, short- and long-term memory involve somewhat different neural processes. Immediately after sensory stimulation, there is thought to be short-term activity, which consists of nerve impulses "reverberating" through neural circuits in the brain. These *reverberating circuits* consist of "loops" of several nerve cells through which nerve impulses travel around and around for a short period of time. This circular type of activity, or *consolidation,* may form the basis for short-term memory. During this period, the activity is easily disrupted and, if a transfer to long-term storage does not take place, it will rapidly fade away. However, if these reverberations last long enough, they may lead to changes in the synaptic connections between the neurons that are involved. In this fashion, a relatively permanent reorganization takes place in the neurons and forms the basis for long-term memory. This *consolidation hypothesis,* then, suggests that there may be two different processes involved. The first is a short-term "consolidation" of recent experience, and the second is a long-term permanent storage of the "memory trace."

Assuming that memory involves relatively permanent changes in neurons, what kind of changes are involved? There is a popular idea that information storage in long-term memory is in some manner connected with RNA (ribonucleic acid), and there is some evidence that this may be the case. However, it has also been suggested that DNA (deoxyribonucleic acid) or protein and lipid molecules may be involved. While it is likely that the basis for long-term memory is biochemical (unlike short-term memory, which appears to involve only neuron activity) at present we cannot say with any degree of certainty just what is involved. The current status of our knowledge in this area is nicely summarized by Stevens (1966):

> We are just now, it would appear, on the threshold of making major advances toward discovering properties of neurons which serve as the basis for information storage in the nervous system. At present, however, and probably for the foreseeable future, understanding the neuronal mechanisms underlying learning and memory may be expected to constitute one of neurophysiology's central problems [p. 113].

The System So Far

The functions of the memory subsystem include learning, remembering, and forgetting. While we often tend to consider these

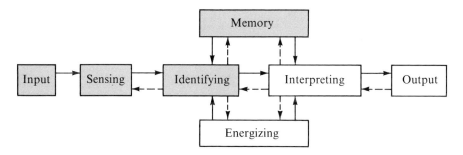

Figure 6–10. The system so far.

processes separately, each is involved in determining what the output of the memory subsystem will be at a given time. Thus, the output of the memory subsystem is dependent upon the learning process, which determines what is stored in memory, as well as the process of forgetting, which removes stored material from memory.

The interrelationships and interactions of the various behavioral subsystems are particularly obvious when the memory subsystem is considered. This subsystem is dependent upon inputs from the other subsystems which will modify its functioning and capabilities. However, in turn, the memory subsystem is essential for the functioning of the other subsystems and will modify their capabilities. As we have seen in the previous two chapters, the manner in which the memory subsystem operates is not completely understood, although it has been subjected to a great deal of research. Basically, we can say that when something is remembered, several prerequisite processes are involved. Thus, if an event is remembered, information must first have been acquired. After it is acquired, it must in some fashion be retained in a storage system. Finally, the information must be subject to retrieval when needed. Eventually, these processes will be understood, and we will be able to discuss the memory subsystem with more certainty.

Summary

1. Much of our behavior involves skilled responses of some type. A skilled response is one in which receptor-effector-feedback processes are highly organized. The acquisition of skilled responses is based on a background of many existing skills, and the key process in acquisition is the integration and organization of these responses.

2. It has been suggested that there are three phases of learning involved in the acquisition of a complex skill. These phases include an early or cognitive phase, an intermediate or associative phase, and a final or autonomous phase.

3. Most research in the area of motor-skills learning falls under the heading of (1) distribution of practice effects and the reminiscence phenomenon, (2) individual differences, (3) the whole-part problem, (4) feedback, (5) retention, and (6) transfer of training.

4. The memory subsystem involves three basic functions: the acquisition of responses, the retention or storage of the responses, and the loss of the responses. These processes are called learning, remembering, and forgetting.

5. It seems that there are at least two kinds of memory—short term and long term. Most theories of memory suggest that information is first held in short-term memory for a brief period of time and then either transferred to long-term memory or lost. A critical question in theories of memory is how the information is retrieved once it has been stored in long-term memory.

6. There are various ways of studying remembering and forgetting. Common methods include the recall method, the recognition method, and the savings method.

7. Several theories have been presented to account for the process of forgetting. One such theory is the interference theory. This theory explains forgetting in terms of learning that takes place

before and after the event that is to be remembered (retroactive and proactive inhibition). Other theories include the memory-trace theory and the qualitative-change theory. The process of repression can also explain some kinds of forgetting.

Selected Readings

Fitts, P. M., & Posner, M. I. *Human performance.* Monterey, California: Brooks/Cole, 1967.

Irion, A. L. Historical introduction. In E. A. Bilodeau (Ed.), *Principles of skill acquisition.* New York: Academic Press, 1969. Pp. 1–31.

Shiffrin, R. M., & Atkinson, R. C. Storage and retrieval processes in long-term memory. *Psychological Review,* 1969, **76** (2), 179–193.

Smith, K. U., & Smith, W. M. *Perception and motion.* Philadelphia: W. B. Saunders, 1962.

7

The Energizing
Subsystem

In previous chapters we discussed the sensing functions of the behavioral system, the identifying functions, and the functions of learning, remembering, and forgetting. We have repeatedly stressed the interaction of these subsystems in the process whereby input to the system is transformed to an output.

In this chapter we consider the subsystem that can be thought of as the source of "power" for man's other subsystems—the *energizing subsystem*. The function of the energizing subsystem is the activation or energizing of the complete behavioral system. Just as physical systems require a source of energy in order to operate, the behavioral system of an organism must also be energized. This is not a simple process, however, and the exact manner in which the behavioral system is energized or, to use a more common term, *motivated*, remains something of a puzzle.

In order to understand the functions of the energizing subsystem, we need to discuss a concept which, unfortunately, is difficult to define—namely, the concept of *motive*. As pointed out by Hall (1967), psychology is no closer to a definition of "motive" now than it was 30 years ago. Although psychologists attach many meanings to the term "motive"—a list of 200 meanings has been compiled by Littman (1958)—there is no one meaning or definition that pleases everyone.

One cannot directly measure or weigh a motive. The existence of a motive has to be *inferred* from observation of an organism's behavior. Thus, a person or an animal eats, and we infer that a hunger motive is active. Animals mate, and we assume a sex motive. An individual becomes the president of a corporation, and we infer an achievement motive. While a motive such as hunger or sex might be defined operationally in terms of hours of deprivation, we can only infer the presence of the motive by the behavior that is demonstrated. Thus, a motive can be defined as an *inferred entity that operates or functions to influence behavior in certain ways.* This influence can be manifested in several ways. A motive can (1) *energize* or *activate* behavior; (2) it can *direct* behavior by causing an organism to respond to certain stimuli and disregard others; and (3) it can cause behavior to *persist* toward a goal. Other motivational functions have been suggested but these three seem to be the most commonly accepted.

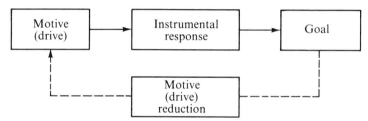

Figure 7–1. The motivational sequence. The motive brings about an instrumental response, which achieves the goal. This leads to a reduction of the initial motive.

Motivated behavior is *goal-directed* behavior. The influence of motives is such that the motivated organism attempts to achieve some goal such as food, water, sex, a promotion, a passing grade, and so forth. The classical model of motivated behavior, which involves a sequence of several events, is shown in Figure 7–1. While there are other models of motivation, the one shown in the figure is still popular among psychologists.

A motive, or drive—represented by the first block in the figure—arises from either biological or psychological causes. Because of the motive, some form of goal-directed behavior is instigated. This type of behavior is often referred to as *instrumental behavior,* since it is instrumental in achieving the goal. When the goal is attained, the motive is satisfied and the motivational sequence is terminated until the motive again builds up. For example, an individual may become hungry (motive) and look for a restaurant (goal-directed behavior or instrumental response). When he finds a restaurant, he eats (achieves goal) and is no longer hungry (motive reduction). The sequence is repeated when he gets hungry again, although there might be some variation in the behavior and in the nature of the goal.

This example, of course, consists of a very simple motivational sequence. Motives are often much more complex. In some cases, the motive may entail elaborate goal-directed behavior and may be satisfied by various goals. Thus, the satisfaction of an achievement motive may involve earning a college degree, becoming a star athlete or, perhaps, becoming a housewife.

Achievement of a goal does not mean that a person remains inactive until another motive develops. An individual has a number of motives active at any given time. When one is satisfied, another is not, and a new sequence of motivated behavior takes place. When there are several motives involved, the person may have to select from a hierarchy of needs or motives that are present and attempt to satisfy the one that, for various reasons, may be most significant at the time. Sometimes two different motives are incompatible so that they cancel each other. Similarly, one motive may prevent another from being satisfied. For example, a person camping near a stream may be very thirsty and yet, upon seeing that raw sewage is being dumped into the stream a few yards away, be unable to drink the water and reduce his thirst.

Psychologists have been "motivated" to classify or categorize motives in a variety of ways. Thus, they speak of acquired motives, learned motives, unlearned motives, fundamental drives, homeostatic drives, nonhomeostatic drives, physiological drives, psychological drives, intrinsically motivated behavior, extrinsically motivated behavior, and so on. However, it is common to divide motives into two broad categories or groups—those that arise from *physiological* conditions within the body and those that have a *psychological* basis. There are often various subcategories included under these two general headings. However, both types of motives— physiological and psychological—activate behavior, direct it, and cause it to persist.

Physiological Drives

When we refer to a drive as being "physiological," we assume that the drive has a direct physiological basis of some sort. While this assumption is easy to make, it is not so easy to determine the specific physiological mechanisms that are responsible for the drives. In some instances, research dealing with these drives has concentrated more on the behavior demonstrated than on the mechanisms involved. Thus, as Cofer and Appley (1964) point out, there is one group of bodily conditions that expresses itself in relatively consistent behavior patterns. It is these behavior patterns, which are organized around some physiological condition or state, that interest some investigators. Included in this group are activities such as maternal behavior, nesting, hoarding, sucking, migration, and sexual behavior. Temperature regulation, respiration, elimination, sleep, and fatigue might also be placed in this category.

On the other hand, there are some activities, which also reflect bodily conditions, where the interest of investigators is more on the conditions and mechanisms underlying the activity than on the behavior itself. Studies dealing with hunger and thirst drives are examples of this approach; and, in fact, a great deal of psychologists' knowledge about motivation has been derived from studies dealing with these particular drives. While these topics will be taken up in some detail shortly, we need first to consider an important concept in the area of motivation—*homeostasis.*

Homeostasis

The body's tendency to maintain a reasonably constant internal environment, despite events that tend to upset the equilibrium of this environment, is called *homeostasis.* Thus, when the sugar level in the bloodstream is reduced beyond a certain point, more blood sugar is secreted by various sources within the body so that the body's internal equilibrium is maintained. Similarly, other homeostatic mechanisms regulate the acidity/alkalinity of the blood, remove invading organisms from the blood, control metabolism, and perform many other functions that are essential for life. Homeostatic processes that automatically maintain the "steady state" of the organism can be thought of as a self-regulating system. Deficiencies in the system give rise to stimuli which, by means of feedback mechanisms, instigate self-correcting action on the part of the system. This action is *involuntary* in that the organism has no control over it.

Of more interest to psychologists, however, is the fact that homeostatic processes also give rise to physiological drives that require some *voluntary* reactions on the part of the organism. Thus, an imbalance in the system can lead to instrumental (goal-directed) behavior designed to reduce the drive and reestablish the balance. If the body needs food or water, the imbalance results in a physiological drive, which is reduced when food or water is obtained. The desirable equilibrium of the internal environment is again attained, but this time through voluntary behavior.

The homeostatic model has come to be considered by many as the basic framework for motivational systems. However, while homeostasis is an important concept, it does not account for all human activities. For example, what physiological imbalance is corrected when you study for your next examination, or go to a movie, or talk to your roommate? Obviously, all human activities cannot be explained with the homeostatic model.

Hunger

Most studies dealing with the physiological factors involved in hunger can be included in one of three general categories: (1) studies relating stomach contractions and distension to hunger sensations, (2) studies correlating various blood conditions with hunger, and (3) studies dealing with central nervous system factors in hunger. While it is beyond the scope of this chapter to review these areas of research in detail, an attempt will be made to summarize briefly some of the findings concerning factors that may be responsible for hunger.

Stomach Contractions and Distension

In a study conducted many years ago with human subjects, it was shown that a relationship exists between reported sensations of hunger and stomach contractions. The contractions were measured by means of a partially filled balloon that had been swallowed (empty) by a subject (see Figure 7–2). Contractions of the stomach changed the pressure on the balloon and these changes were recorded. Because the subject's reports of hunger correlated with the contractions, it was assumed that the contractions caused the hunger.

Prevailing opinion, however, is that gastric contractions do not provide a total explanation for hunger, even though they may provide the basis for the sensation of hunger. This opinion is based on data from several studies of hunger in rats. In none of these studies was there any change in rats' eating or food-seeking behavior when their stomachs were removed or when the nerve pathways from the stomach to the brain were cut. In a study by Tsang (1938), for instance, removal of 90 to 95 percent of a rat's stomach had no apparent effect on the animal's hunger behavior. Its behavior

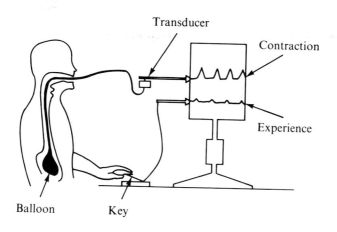

Figure 7–2. Sketch of apparatus utilized to record stomach contractions. The subject swallows the balloon, which is connected to a marker that records on a moving paper each time the stomach contracts. The subject depresses the key each time he experiences a hunger pang. Results show that there is a relationship between the contractions and the subject's experience of hunger pangs.

was nearly identical to that of control animals whose stomachs had not been removed.

Food intake may be regulated to some extent by the distension, or expansion, of the stomach. There is some evidence (Paintal, 1954) that distension may stimulate receptors in the smooth muscles of the stomach which, in turn, give rise to impulses that reach hypothalamic nuclei. Several studies have shown that gastric distension can lead to reduced food intake. However, psychologists have rejected as inadequate the view that the lack of distension causes the sensation of hunger.

Blood Conditions and Hunger

In some of the earliest experiments on hunger, blood was transfused from starving dogs into normal dogs to determine the effects of blood conditions on hunger. Several interesting findings resulted from these experiments. If the normal dog's stomach was showing some indication of contractions at the time of the transfusion, the contractions were greatly augmented. However, if no contractions were present in the normal dog's stomach, the blood transfusion from a starving dog did not initiate contractions. In another study, blood from a "satisfied dog"—that is, one that was not hungry—was transfused into a hungry dog. In this case, the hungry dog's stomach contractions were reduced. Studies of this sort have led some researchers to conclude that the blood contains a "hunger hormone" of some kind. Although it appears that blood factors can influence stomach contractions, nothing is known yet about the nature of these factors.

Numerous studies have attempted to establish a relationship between the blood sugar level and hunger contractions. These investigations have typically involved measuring the blood sugar level of subjects during fasting and obtaining reports of hunger and measurements of contractions. Other techniques involve inducing *hypoglycemia* (lowered blood sugar level) by means of insulin and obtaining subjective reports on hunger or measuring contractions and food intake. In general, attempts to relate blood sugar level and hunger have resulted in conflicting findings. At present, the data are not available to reach a firm conclusion as to the role of blood sugar in the phenomenon of hunger.

Many other factors contribute to the experience of hunger, including those factors related to the mechanisms of the central nervous system.

Central Nervous System Factors in Hunger

Several studies have demonstrated the role of the central nervous system in hunger. For instance, a study some years ago showed that hyperphagia (overeating) can be produced in animals by making lesions in certain areas of the hypothalamus. The hyperphagia arising from hypothalamic lesions typically consists of two phases. During the first phase the animal consumes tremendous amounts of food and rapidly gains weight. In the second phase the animal's weight stabilizes at a high level and there is some reduction in food intake. This pattern is illustrated in Figure 7–3.

Additional studies involving lesions of the hypothalamus and their effects on hunger have produced some interesting findings. It has been determined, for instance, that there are two centers in the hypothalamus that are important influences on an animal's eating behavior. It appears that one of the centers actively represses eating, and, when this center is destroyed by lesions, hyperphagia

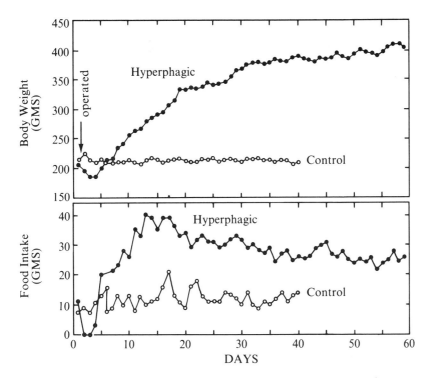

Figure 7–3. The daily food intake and body weight of a hyperphagic rat compared with that of a normal rat. From P. Teitelbaum, Sensory control of hypothalamic hyperphagia. *Journal of Comparative and Physiological Psychology*, **48**, 1955, 156–163. Copyright 1955 by the American Psychological Association and reproduced by permission.

results. In other words, when the inhibitory eating center is destroyed, its function of suppressing eating is also destroyed and the animal overeats. Another center appears to be critical in *causing* eating. When this center is destroyed, the animal stops eating (aphagia). Although it was once suggested that lesions in this center of the hypothalamus would prevent an animal from eating again, it has since been shown that eating behavior can be regained after a period of time if the animal is fed through stomach tubes.

There is no doubt that hypothalamic mechanisms are important determinants of eating behavior. However, it is not clear just what processes are involved in the control of these hypothalamic centers. Two hypotheses regarding their control have been advanced—the *glucostatic* hypothesis and the *thermal regulation* hypothesis. The former suggests that the centers are responsive to variations in blood glucose (sugar). Although the absolute blood sugar level in the system has not been shown to correlate with hunger, Mayer (1955) feels that the *ratio* of blood sugar in the arteries to that in the veins may be a factor in the stimulation of receptors in the hypothalamus. The thermal regulation hypothesis suggests that regulation of food intake is caused by the activity of receptors in the hypothalamus that are sensitive to temperature changes. It has been shown that heat production in the body increases after eating, and there is also a rise in central and peripheral body temperatures following eating. While there is some evidence supporting the thermal hypothesis, there is also some contradictory evidence.

About the best summary statement that can be made about hunger is that it is controlled by many variables. While we have briefly discussed some of the more important factors, it should be stressed that control of hunger is probably based on a complex interaction of all of these variables, as well as others that have not been mentioned.

The concept of homeostasis would suggest that animals whose systems require certain types of materials would be directed toward foods which contain the needed materials. This has been shown to be the case in a number of studies dealing with *specific hungers*. Similarly, we could spend some time discussing the role of learning in integrating the factors that appear to control hunger-related behavior. Indeed, an entire book could be devoted to just the topic of hunger. However, since such a discussion is not within the scope of this book, we will now turn our attention to another physiological drive—thirst.

Thirst

Research on thirst has paralleled the research on hunger. While a number of investigations of factors in thirst have been conducted, they have generally been concerned with thirst in relation to three factors: (1) dryness of the mouth and throat, (2) various conditions of the blood, and (3) central nervous system factors.

One cause of thirst is thought to be that the structures of the mouth, and of the pathway to and including the stomach, become dry and result in the sensation of thirst. While there is some research that supports this view, the greater amount of data disputes the idea that thirst is solely based upon dryness in the mouth and throat. Although dryness may be a factor, certainly it is not the only cause for thirst. Similarly, while certain conditions in the blood may play a role in thirst, again they cannot be considered the sole factors.

In our discussion on hunger, it was pointed out that areas in the hypothalamus are important in determining eating behavior. This seems true of drinking behavior, also. It has been found, for example, that small amounts of sodium chloride injected directly into the hypothalamus will produce drinking behavior, and electrical stimulation will bring about drinking behavior even more reliably than injections. Because injections of pure water will result in a decrease in water consumption, it would appear that there are cells in the hypothalamus that are sensitive to the nature of the fluid that bathes them. Changes in the characteristics of these fluids will result in changes in drinking behavior.

The state of our knowledge about thirst is nicely summarized by Cofer and Appley (1964):

> As with hunger, the local theory of thirst (local dryness in the mouth and throat) seems to have been superseded by findings emphasizing control by central hypothalamic structures. It appears that these structures must be sensitive to change in the distribution of body fluids and that a critical factor in thirst is cellular dehydration. Oral and gastric factors, no doubt, contribute to the control of drinking, perhaps because of learning, and there are hormonal regulations as well. Drinking occurs primarily to deprivation of water, but it is also influenced by experience, characteristics of fluids offered, and perhaps, by social factors [p. 258].

The Sex Drive

Our discussion of physiological drives would not be complete without some brief mention of the third drive with considerable implication for our everyday behavior. Unlike hunger and thirst, an individual's survival does not depend upon satisfying the sex drive, although life may not be as pleasant when this particular drive is not reduced.

In the lower species of animals, sex hormones are important determinants of sexual behavior. However, environmental stimulation, often based on certain characteristics of the mate's appearance and behavior, can also play an important role in the preparation for and the execution of the copulatory pattern. Thus, with lower species, reproductive behavior is controlled by both internal and external factors. In the higher species of animals, the internal hormonal factors are still important, but they play a less crucial role in sexual behavior than do many kinds of external factors. Cortical involvement in sexual behavior increases as we move from the lower to the higher species. Thus, in human sexual behavior, psychological factors are much more significant than physiological factors.

If we were to attempt to illustrate the motivational sequence for the human sex drive, we might add an extra feedback loop, as shown in Figure 7–4. This motivational sequence represents a

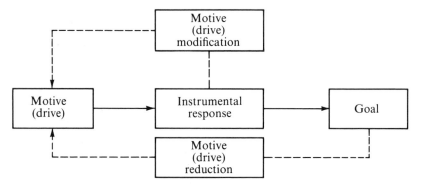

Figure 7–4. Motivational sequence for the human sexual drive. Note the feedback loop from instrumental response back to motive. Depending upon the situation encountered during the instrumental response, the strength of the drive can be increased or decreased.

situation in which the motive can be modified—that is, it can be enhanced or abolished without goal attainment. In other words, the instrumental response (goal-directed behavior) may serve to modify the motive (drive) before the goal is achieved. Depending upon the circumstances involved in this behavior, the sex drive may be diminished or enhanced. For example, the sudden appearance of a husband or boy friend during the "goal-directed behavior" part of the sequence can certainly alter the sex drive—possibly eliminating it for some time. Obviously, there are a number of other variables that might be encountered during the instrumental response that could have an effect on the initial drive.

The sexual behavior of humans has received an increasing amount of attention in recent years. It is likely that very few readers of this chapter have not at least made a cursory inspection of the Kinsey Reports and the Masters-Johnson studies. These studies have presented a vast amount of information about both the psychological and physiological aspects of sexual behavior.

Some Other Physiological Drives

Along with hunger, thirst, and sex there are other drives that are frequently listed under the heading of physiological drives. For example, *air hunger* is sometimes categorized as such. Under certain conditions, we can die from lack of oxygen without having received any "feedback" from the system about our lack of air to breathe. However, if carbon-dioxide collection in the lungs reaches a certain level, as when the breath is held, we become acutely aware of the lack of oxygen and make an instrumental response to obtain relief. Some psychologists consider *fatigue* and the need for *sleep* to be physiological drives and, indeed, there are demonstrable physiological changes in the body associated with these conditions. Finally, *warmth* and *cold* are often listed under this heading. It is known that the body must maintain its temperature within a fairly narrow range. It accomplishes this through such processes as sweating, shivering, increased or decreased activity, putting on or removing clothes, and so on. Some of the mechanisms by which temperature regulation is maintained are involuntary; others are voluntary.

There are other motives that are considered by some investigators to be in the biological or physiological class. However, at this point we will turn our attention to another major category of motives—the *psychological* motives.

Psychological Motives

While learning may play a role in some of the behaviors we discussed above, we tend to believe that they are primarily motivated by physiological drives.

A large part of behavior, however, is motivated by drives that have no obvious physiological basis. In many ways, these *psychological motives* may be more important than the physiological drives. This is particularly true of men in the more affluent societies whose physiological drives can be easily satisfied. However, physiological motives are likely to be stronger in countries experiencing widespread famine.

Motivation researchers are interested in additional psychological issues, such as whether motives are learned (acquired) or unlearned, what the role of reward and punishment is in their acquisition, and whether they are connected in some way with the basic physiological drives. For our purposes, it is sufficient to know that these issues exist. Rather than going into the results of such motivation research, it would be more helpful at this point to consider briefly some motives that are considered psychological.

Curiosity and Exploratory Behavior

A few years ago, psychologists began to pay some attention to the fact that an organism's behavior is often characterized by tendencies to explore, to investigate, and to seek out new varieties of stimulation (Fowler, 1965). For example, a hungry rat that is near food will often explore a new environment before eating. Monkeys, dogs, and many other animals actively explore. Indeed, anyone who has watched animals for any period of time realizes that curiosity and exploratory behavior represent a significant portion of their total behavior. As far as can be determined, these activities are not usually designed to maintain the organism's biological well-being. However, since animals, and man in particular, exhibit so much curiosity and exploratory behavior, a number of psychologists have concluded that these activities deserve as much investigation as those associated with physiological drives.

Most studies in the general area of exploration and curiosity have used subhuman animals as subjects and have focused on the animals' responses to novelty or to a change in the complex of stimuli they receive. It has been shown repeatedly that animals will respond to novelty or stimulus change with curiosity or exploratory behavior, which will persist for some time. However, as is the case with other drives, the curiosity drive does diminish after the animal has spent some time in the novel situation. Conversely, the curiosity drive also tends to increase with deprivation. The reinforcing properties of exploration have been demonstrated often in studies in which animals have learned to perform in mazes, to make discriminations, and to do other things in order to get an opportunity to "explore" for a short period of time.

Some investigators also refer to a *manipulative* drive, although it is questionable whether this drive should be differentiated from the curiosity or exploratory drive. Again, if you have watched animals, particularly primates, you probably have noticed that they may spend a considerable amount of time physically manipulating objects in their environment. A monkey, for example, may spend long periods of time handling some part of his cage. This particular drive has been studied in some rather clever ways. In some studies, monkeys have been presented with complex mechanical puzzles. Some groups of monkeys were rewarded with a raisin when the puzzle was "solved." Other groups of monkeys that did not receive a reward spent as much time working the puzzles, and were as successful in solving them, as were the animals that were rewarded. Apparently, the manipulation of the puzzle served as a reward in itself.

Affectional Drive

It is recognized that love or affection is a powerful motivator; however, not much research has been attempted in this area since it involves variables that are difficult to measure and to manipulate, particularly with human subjects. Professor Harry Harlow and his coworkers (1958) performed an important series of studies on the nature of love, using infant monkeys as subjects.

Harlow observed that infant monkeys that were separated from their mothers at birth developed a strong attachment to the soft cloth pads used to cover the cage bottoms. This observation led Harlow to develop a series of studies designed to investigate the drive for *contact comfort* and the development of affectional responses in infant monkeys. Harlow raised infant monkeys with two kinds of artificial mothers. One "mother" was designed to maximize comfort and was made of sponge rubber covered with cloth; the other was made of wire mesh with no cover. Both were equipped with a nipple from which the infant monkey could nurse. By varying the feeding conditions, the experimenters found that the baby monkeys preferred the "soft" mother regardless of where the food was obtained. In other words, the "contact comfort" was the variable of greatest importance; food was secondary. If affectional drives for a mother are learned because of her association with food (as is often thought to be the case), the infant monkeys that were fed only from the wire mothers should have preferred them to cloth mothers, which did not always provide food. However, this expectation was not borne out, for the infant monkeys spent more time with the cloth mother. Thus, it seems that there is an unlearned drive for "contact comfort." Other studies showed that the baby monkeys would run to the cloth mother for comfort and security when they were frightened. It was also found that the attachments to the cloth mothers that were formed early in life were quite enduring.

One particularly significant finding was that the satisfaction of the "contact-comfort" drive through the cloth mother was not adequate for normal social development (Harlow & Harlow, 1962). Certain forms of aberrant sexual behavior, play, and defensive behavior appeared in the animals raised with cloth mothers. However, infant monkeys reared without mothers but with other baby monkey "playmates" developed in a relatively normal fashion, although they were somewhat "retarded" initially. This suggests that peer relationships among infants may be more important than has often been thought.

Social Motives

Since man is a social animal, it should not be surprising that he has developed complex motives that determine much of his behavior in relation to society. Social motives are learned and modified throughout an individual's life. The manner in which these motives are acquired from infancy onward has interested not only psychologists but also sociologists, anthropologists, and others who are interested in the socialization process.

There are long lists of social motives that have been suggested by various investigators in this field. Because of the complex nature of these motives, it is difficult to arrive at a particularly meaningful list or classification, and we will make no attempt to present any of the classification schemes. Rather, we will list a few of the suggested social motives in order to give some idea of the kinds of motives that are considered in this category.

> *Affiliative:* The motive to seek and enjoy friends, to maintain social relationships, and to belong to the group.
> *Achievement:* The motive to succeed at difficult tasks, to achieve success, and to rival and surpass others.
> *Dominance:* The motive to influence, control, and direct others. The desire to be a leader.
> *Autonomy:* The motive to be one's own boss and to go one's own way.
> *Rejection:* The motive to keep others away by withdrawing or remaining aloof.

Not all psychologists agree that motives such as achievement, affiliation, and dominance are actually independent motives. These motives are often considered to be derived from the master motive—*anxiety.* In other words, these motives may not be independent; instead, they may identify behavior that is brought about by states of anxiety and fear. It is suggested that these kinds of behavior reduce fear and anxiety and are thus reinforced. There is some experimental work that supports this hypothesis, although it is still not completely accepted.

Motivation and Human Performance

You may have gathered from our discussion so far that a great deal is known about motivation. This assumption can be both true and false. Considerable research has been done in the area of motivation, and there is a great deal of data about drives, or motives, and behaviors associated with these drives. However, practical applications of these data are not so easy to come by. It is agreed that drives and motives are the "energizers" of the system and that this energizing subsystem interacts with the other behavioral subsystems to determine the output of the organism. Suppose, however, that we wish to improve performance on a tracking task, or operating a machine, or flying an airplane. Perhaps we want to develop new training procedures in a factory or in a technical school. We may want to develop more efficient learning techniques or to increase production on an assembly line. We assume, of course, that motivation plays a critical role in all of these endeavors. However, if we were to go to the literature on motivation in an attempt to shed some light on these practical problems, we probably would find it scant and not very illuminating.

There have, however, been a number of laboratory studies dealing with motivation and human performance. One of the most comprehensive studies concerned with the effects of motivational variables on performance was conducted by Mast (1966). Performance on a pursuit rotary tracking task was studied under a number of different motivational conditions. One group of subjects, designated as the *control* group, performed on the pursuit tracking task in isolation. Subjects in a *punishment* group performed in isolation and received moderate to heavy electrical shock whenever they failed to remain on target. Another group of subjects—the *social* group—performed in pairs, in full view of each other, on separate pursuit rotor tasks. Subjects in another group, called the *administrator* group, also performed with a partner (called a conspecific). However, when the subjects in the administrator group failed to maintain contact with the target, their partners (or conspecifics) received punishment in the form of an electric shock. In other words, the partner was punished each time a subject in the administrator group did not track in the proper manner. Subjects in the fifth group, designated as the *conspecific* group, were the partners of the subjects in the administrator group. The results of part of this study are shown in Figure 7–5. Note that in all cases the experimental groups' performances were superior to that of the control group. Subjects in the administrator group, who indirectly pun-

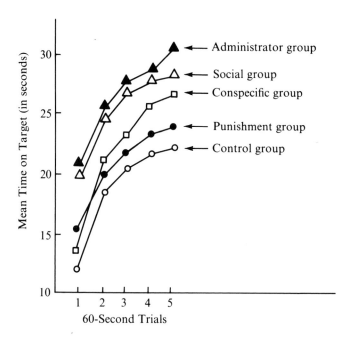

Figure 7–5. Mean time on target trials on a pursuit rotary tracking task. Subjects in the various groups were exposed to different motivational conditions (see text) which affected their performance. From T. M. Mast, Influence of motivational variables on prerest and postrest performance in rotary pursuit tracking. Unpublished doctoral dissertation, University of South Dakota, 1966. Reprinted by permission of the author.

ished another subject when off target, showed the highest level of performance. Subjects in the punishment group, who received shock when they were off target, were most similar to the control group in their performance.

   In another study, Ogden (1963) compared the performance of several groups of subjects on a vigilance task. The subjects were required to detect a faint periodic increase in the intensity of a light (signal). Subjects in the *control* group were simply placed in the test room, told what was expected of them, and the test session started. Subjects in a *reward* group were informed that they would be paid five cents for each signal detected and fined ten cents each time they reported a signal that, in fact, had not occurred (false response). In a third group, called the *individual competition* group, subjects were led to believe that they had been selected for the study because of "exceptional abilities," and they were told that they would be competing with other high-ability subjects. Subjects in the *group competition* were told that they were competing

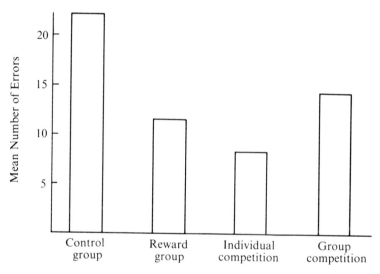

Figure 7–6. Mean number of errors (missed signals) on a vigilance task shown by subjects under different motivational conditions.

against other groups. For example, if a subject happened to be a freshman, he was told that the freshmen were competing against the sophomores, and so on.

The results of this study, which are shown in Figure 7–6, clearly indicate that subjects in the "motivation" groups performed better than those in the control group. While the differences in performance between the remuneration, individual competition, and group competition subjects were not great, they performed significantly better than subjects in the control group.

There are many similar studies that could be cited. In general, these studies have shown that when motivational variables are manipulated, changes in performance take place.

Motivation and the Worker

Possibly the first practical problems concerning motivation and performance centered on the relationship between the motivation of workers and their on-the-job performance. While a detailed discussion of this problem falls within the scope of an industrial psychology textbook, we will briefly consider some of the aspects of motivation within the context of a "job."

Some effort has been made, particularly in the last few years, to determine what factors are important in making a worker "happy." While it was once thought that money achieved this goal, it would appear that there are other factors that may be even more important. In one study (Herzberg, Mausner, & Snyderman, 1959), which represents an important effort to understand human motivation in industry, the experimenters attempted to determine aspects of job environments that are satisfying or dissatisfying to engineers and accountants. This study showed that "satisfying" jobs are characterized by opportunities to experience achievement and recognition, to advance into jobs that are of interest, and to have a sense of responsibility. Salary, as a motivating factor, was rated below these other factors. Feelings of dissatisfaction were attributed to such aspects of the job as incompetent supervisors or poor company policy. In a later study (Wernimont, 1966), *intrinsic* variables (recognition, achievement, responsibility, and so on) were compared with *extrinsic* variables (such as salary, company policies, or working conditions) in relation to the role they played in job satisfaction or dissatisfaction. Nearly twice as many extrinsic factors were reported for dissatisfying situations as for the satisfying situations. While the findings of this investigation corresponded closely with those of the Herzberg study in terms of the factors important in satisfying situations, the job factors contributing to dissatisfaction were somewhat different in the two studies.

In both of these studies, engineers and accountants were used as subjects. It might be expected that for blue-collar workers, extrinsic factors would be more important in providing satisfaction since these workers have less opportunity for achievement, recognition, and other intrinsic motivators. However, in one study that dealt with blue-collar workers, it was found that intrinsic factors as well as extrinsic factors were important in job satisfaction (Malinovsky & Barry, 1965).

It is possible, then, to list a number of factors that will tend to lead to satisfaction or dissatisfaction with a job. If the ultimate aim of industry is to employ vast numbers of satisfied workers, then this is good information to have. Of course, the assumption is often made that satisfied workers are *better* workers (better being defined by high production rates, improved quality, and fewer accidents) but, unfortunately, this assumption is based on very little evidence. Efforts that have been made to demonstrate relationships between the types of motives mentioned and actual job behaviors have usually ended with negative or inconsistent results.

Motivational Factors in Performance

Man's capacity to perform various types of skilled tasks is determined by the functions of all of the behavioral subsystems. Thus, his ability to receive sensory input relevant to the task, the identification of this information, what he has previously learned and remembered about the information, how the information is interpreted, and the capabilities of his effector system will all contribute to the output required for the task. Thus, the energizing subsystem, although important, is only one of several that determine performance.

A number of the motives that have been discussed earlier in this chapter could, of course, influence performance of a skilled task. Hunger and thirst, for example, may have an aversive effect on this type of performance. However, in our discussion we will be concerned with motivational variables that are more typically encountered and are important in determining human performance.

Performance Goals

In recent years, an increasing number of researchers have begun to study the effects of conscious goals and purposes on task performance. A conscious goal can be considered as something that the individual is trying to accomplish or to do. While this may seem like a rather obvious statement, not too many years ago much of the thinking in psychology was influenced by the doctrine of behaviorism, whose thesis was that behavior could be understood without concepts such as "conscious goals."

Just what determines an individual's goals in relation to a particular task probably involves a complex interaction of variables. Some of the variables are associated with the characteristics of the task, some with instructions the person may receive concerning his performance, and others with less tangible "intrinsic" factors such as personality, level of arousal, previous experience, and so on. These and other factors contribute to how a person "sets" his goal. One approach to studying the factors involved in the process of goal setting involves the *level of aspiration.*

Level of aspiration is not a simple concept. Basically, it can be thought of as a standard by which a person tends to judge his own performance. Based on his past experience with a particular task, the level of aspiration is the level of performance that the person undertakes to reach. Typically, if you ask a person what level he hopes to achieve on the task, he will generally cite a level somewhat higher than he usually reaches. In other words, the level of aspiration for familiar tasks is generally slightly higher than the person's typical performance. For example, a golfer who usually shoots twenty-five over par is not likely to set his level of aspiration for a par game, but he may hope to reduce his score to fifteen above par. His degree of satisfaction with his golf game is dependent upon how close his achieved score is to the score he is trying to make— that is, his level of aspiration.

There has been a considerable amount of interest in how a person's level of aspiration is affected by his consistent failure to achieve his goals. It is usually assumed that successful performance leads to an increased level of aspiration, while failure to achieve the goal leads to a reduced level of aspiration. Personality theorists have suggested that personal frustration, with resulting behavioral manifestations, may arise because of a discrepancy between the level of aspiration and the level of performance.

Recently, several studies have attempted to establish more clearly the relationship between the conscious goals of an individual in relation to a particular task and his performance on the task (Locke, 1968; Locke & Bryan, 1967, 1969). These studies, as well as others, have shown that goals can both energize and direct behavior on a task, that hard goals produce a higher level of performance than easy goals, that specific hard goals produce a higher level of output than a "do your best" type goal and that, in general, performance goals are related to, and can account for, the level of performance on a number of different tasks.

Helson (1964) has proposed an interesting way of viewing the relation of "goal setting" and performance that is based on the *concept of par or tolerance.* This concept maintains that an individual consistently sets his level of aspiration below a level of performance that he is actually capable of achieving. There is evidence from several studies that the level of performance shown by a person rarely reaches the level of which he is capable. One of the tasks of the psychologist who is interested in human performance is to determine what variables will bring the achieved level of performance closer to the potential level of performance.

Feedback

The importance of feedback, or knowledge of results (KR), in learning and performance has been discussed in detail in several of the previous chapters. The positive influence of feedback is well established and we will not belabor the point. However, in considering feedback as a source of motivation, an additional comment should be made.

In attempting to attribute motivational value to feedback, one must distinguish between the *information* or cueing function of feedback and the *motivational* function. The former refers to the information that a subject receives about his errors and the correct response required. The majority of studies dealing with the relationship between feedback and performance have dealt with this informational type of feedback. However, it is not clear how much "motivational" value this type of information feedback has, since it may tend to increase interest or reduce boredom and thus motivate the individual.

It is difficult to design a study in which one can be assured that he is working with either the informational or motivational aspects of feedback and not a combination of the two. However, it is possible to design studies in which the informational function of feedback can be minimized. One method is to give subjects feedback about their performance that cannot be used for correcting errors or improving responses. For example, on a pursuit rotor task a subject can be told the total time on or off target after a test session. While this is feedback about his performance, it does not give him specific information about a better method of performing. With a design of this sort, the effects of motivational factors in feedback can be more clearly determined. Studies attempting to reduce the informational value of feedback have usually found that feedback still improves performance. This improvement has been attributed to the motivational function of feedback.

Performance under Stress

Two kinds of stress are often distinguished—*systemic* and *psychological* stress. The former is of primary interest to physiologists and psychobiologists. It results from a failure of the normal homeostatic regulatory mechanisms and is manifested by actual changes in the biologic system. The agents (stressors), which can include neural, hormonal, and metabolic mechanisms as well as external events, are varied, and the determination of why, when, and the degree to which an agent becomes a stressor depends upon a number of factors. Psychological stress is not necessarily equivalent to systemic stress, although the two are closely related. Psychological stress is usually a broader term, which refers to a state of the organism that is brought about by an interaction with the environment. Psychological stress is considered to be a more extreme state than an ordinary motivated state, and it is similar to a state of extreme frustration or conflict. Despite the popularity of the stress concept in psychology, there is still considerable disagreement about how it should be defined, induced, or measured. Consequently, rather than spend more time at attempting a definition, we will turn our attention to some of the relationships that exist between stress and performance.

In designing a bridge or a machine, an engineer must consider not only their characteristics under normal conditions but also under stress conditions, such as increased load, high and low temperatures, vibration, and other stress variables. The human system is also exposed to conditions that exceed the normal range, and it must function under these conditions. Thus, we can consider stress in relation to the demands of the task or environment that the human encounters. When the demands exceed a certain limit or range, then the system is stressed. There are a number of characteristics of a task that can result in stress for the individual. As an example, let us consider a task in which the operator receives more information than he is capable of processing. In this case, information overload—that is, an excess of information beyond normal processing capacity—results in stress. Under this type of stress, what happens to the performance of the individual?

There are several ways in which a person can adjust when incoming information is beyond his capacity. Miller (1964) has suggested what responses can be made in a situation of this type. When encountering an input overload, the individual may tend to increase his rate of work, or processing, and *let errors increase.* He may also attempt to *filter out,* or disregard, part of the incoming information. What he filters out or selects will not necessarily be random, but rather it is likely to be based on priorities that he has established. A third mechanism, which is called *queuing,* essentially places incoming information in a line to wait its turn for processing.

This mechanism involves the use of short-term memory. Another possible response is that the person simply quits working for a time. This is probably the least desirable of the various methods used to cope with information overload.

Other overload conditions involved in performing a task may also be stress inducing. For example, in some situations task demands may change so that a person is required to work much faster than usual or, perhaps, exert a great deal more effort than normal. These, as well as other demands exceeding a normal range, may be stress inducing, and the person's performance can be affected.

While stress can arise because of an increase in input to the system that is relevant to the task being performed, it can also arise from increased input that is irrelevant to the task. Stress can also be induced under conditions in which all input to the system is greatly decreased, as is the case in sensory-deprivation studies. Environmental stress, in the form of increased irrelevant input, can arise from numerous sources. Thus, the situation in which a task is being performed may be extremely noisy, it may be very hot or cold, it may vibrate, and so on. While man is quite tolerant of these kinds of variables, when they exceed his tolerance for them they usually result in performance changes.

In considering the topic of stress and performance, one should not come to the conclusion that stress is all bad. Actually, there appears to be an *optimal stress* level at which the best performance can be expected. Above or below this level, performance may be impaired. What determines the optimal level at any given time is probably a complex interaction of task and personal variables. The optimal level concept will be discussed in more detail shortly.

Emotion as an Energizer

You experience emotion every day, you observe what you consider to be emotion demonstrated by others, but can you define the term *emotion?* If you try, it will quickly become apparent that defining an emotion precisely is a difficult task. In all likelihood your definition would include something about pleasant and unpleasant feelings that you experience, such as love, happiness, fear, or anger. Further, you would probably admit that these pleasant or unpleasant (and in-between) feelings play a part in determining how you behave.

For years, most psychologists considered emotions to involve concepts of affective states like pleasantness and unpleasantness that were difficult to specify and impossible to measure quantitatively. Emotions were considered to be transitory affective states that could be described introspectively or, perhaps, that could be correlated with a physiological response. In general, however, the relationship between these states and action (behavior) was not considered important. Thus, for a period of time the area of emotion was not of major interest for many psychologists, and comparatively few objective studies of emotion were undertaken. As a matter of fact, "a number of psychologists have taken the position that the concepts of affect and emotion should be deleted from the psychologist's lexicon" (Helson, 1964, p. 332). However, in recent years this situation has changed.

The reason for this change in interest was the realization that *emotions* play an important role in motivation. As it became apparent that emotions, as well as drives and motives, can activate, sustain, and direct behavior, emotions have been given a central role in theories of motivation.

A Current Theory of Emotion

There are a number of theories of emotion available. Most of them can be roughly categorized as dealing either with the subjective and cognitive aspects of emotion or with the relationship between emotion and physiological and biological factors. A theory in this second class, which is currently quite popular, is the *activation theory* of emotion.

Actually, the activation theorists' view of emotion can be put forth in quite simple terms. "An activation theorist states merely that a correlation exists between the amount of hormone, amount of neural excitation, and amount of emotional arousal. Considerable evidence can be marshaled in favor of the activation theory" (Pribram, 1967, p. 11).

We can think of emotions as involving two basic dimensions. They will vary qualitatively, as in the difference between fear and anger or love and hate. Or they will vary quantitatively from very mild to very strong. Arnold (1960) suggests that the quality of an emotion (fear opposed to anger) is dependent upon how we appraise a stimulus situation as positive or negative, helpful or harmful, and so on. She states that "The intuitive appraisal of the situation initiates an *action tendency that is felt as emotion*, expressed in various bodily changes, and that eventually may lead to overt action" (p. 177). However, the quantitative dimension can be explained most readily within the framework of activation or arousal theory.

What do we mean when we refer to a state of activation or arousal in an organism? When we think of activation of an organism in terms of observable behavior, we think of a continuum ranging from minimum activation (sleep or coma) to a maximum, such as wild excitement or other forms of strong emotion. These types of behavior reflect a continuum of activity of physiological processes, including neural and humoral activity, which is brought about by stimulation of the organism. Emotion is defined, essentially, as this physiological activation.

In Chapter 3, the reticular formation of the brain was discussed. This particular formation is of key importance in determining the arousal level of an organism. As you may recall, impulses from a sensory stimulus reach the cortex by two different routes—the traditional or "classic" pathways and through the ascending reticular activating system (ARAS). This system discharges a diffuse bombardment of impulses over wide areas of the cortex, which serves to "arouse" the cortex. Arrival of a stimulus over the traditional pathways alone is not sufficient to evoke a response, so the animal becomes somnolent or indifferent. The reticular system can also be aroused by means of stimulus inputs from the cortex, suggesting that mediational and memory responses can be arousing. Extensive research has been conducted on the mechanisms and functions of the reticular formation. In brief, there is no question that the reticular activating system is essential in bringing about an aroused or activated condition in an organism. Just *how* aroused or activated—that is, the activation level—will depend on a number of factors, both external and internal to the organism.

While the ARAS plays a critical part in the activation process, other components are also involved when physiological activation, or emotion, takes place. The role of some other components in this process can be seen in Figure 7–7, which is a hypothetical flow chart representing the activation theory of emotion. It is an incomplete chart in that the inputs from other behavioral subsystems, such as the identifying and memory subsystems, are not shown. For our purposes, these can be considered as being part of the subsystem labeled "cortex" on the chart.

An input, in the form of a stimulus with some emotional content, is transformed into neural impulses that are projected into the central nervous system by means of two routes. Some are sent by way of the ARAS, while others follow the direct or "classical" routes to the cortex. Projections from the ARAS to the cortex serve to arouse and activate the cortex. Similarly, impulses from the ARAS are also sent to the hypothalamus, which, as you will recall, is the part of the brain that is concerned with autonomic functions. You may also recall that there are a variety of autonomic visceral responses that are concomitants of emotion (or *are* emotions) that are brought about by impulses from the hypothalamus. Note that there is a feedback loop from the viscera to the ARAS that gives the ARAS information about the state of the viscera. Similarly, the ARAS receives feedback about what the organism is *doing* by means of a feedback loop from the "output" component. The output, or behavior, demonstrated by the aroused organism will typically involve skeletal muscles, and feedback to the ARAS is generated by sensory receptors in the muscle.

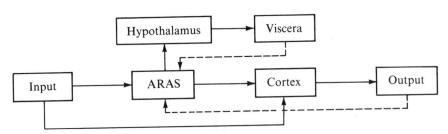

Figure 7–7. Schematic presentation of activation theory of emotion.

Activation, as depicted in Figure 7–7, is not of the "all or none" nature of a nerve impulse. Again, it should be stressed that activation theorists think in terms of a continuum of arousal, ranging from virtually zero to very extreme. The degree of emotion is thought to be correlated with points on this continuum of arousal or activation. One problem with this view, however, is that while it may explain the degree of emotion, it does not explain qualitatively different emotions. A more complete theory must take into account cognitive processes that are involved in determining the quality, as well as the quantity, of emotion. Steps in this direction have been taken by Schachter and Singer (1962) who, based on their research, suggest that there are two major components in emotional reactions. These interacting components are the *physiological arousal*, which we have discussed, and the individual's *interpretation* of the situation.

Activation Level and Performance

It has been suggested that an inverted U-shaped function represents the relationship between the level of arousal and performance (Malmo, 1957). This relationship is shown in Figure 7–8. This figure implies that performance improves up to an optimal level of arousal and then declines as the arousal level exceeds the optimal point. Bergum (1966) has attempted a taxonomic analysis

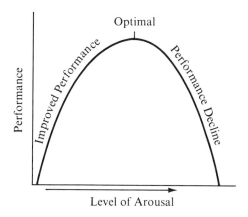

Figure 7–8. The hypothesized inverted U-shaped relationship between level of arousal and performance.

of performance as related to activation level. He presents a model of the hypothetical relationship between activation level and central nervous system stimulation. Bergum's conclusions are that:

> (1) level of activation represents a point along an assumed continuum of CNS stimulation ranging from very low (but never zero) to very high; that (2) for any given task there exists an optimum range of activation levels; that (3) levels below an assumed lower threshold for this optimal range will generally yield rapid declines in performance; and (4) levels above the upper threshold will generally yield changes in performance characterized by increased variability [p. 48].

Although some experimental evidence is available that supports this inverted U-shaped relation of behavioral efficiency to arousal, the available data deal with a relatively narrow range of behavior. Consequently, we cannot be sure whether this relationship holds for most kinds of behavior.

Some Other Aspects of Emotion

There are a number of other features of emotion that we could discuss at some length. For example, we have made no effort to attempt a classification of emotions. Various classification schemes are available, although none can be considered as complete. For example, one scheme can consider *primary emotions*, such as joy, fear, anger, and grief. Other classification schemes can focus on emotions involving *sensory stimulation* (pain, disgust, horror, delight), *other people* (love, hate), *moods* such as sadness, anxiety, or elation, and so forth.

Similarly, a number of researchers have been interested in how people express emotion. In other words, what overt responses of the body and face demonstrate emotion? What characteristics of speech express emotion? While there are certain cues to the emotional state of a person, which can be interpreted with some accuracy, the manner in which people express their emotions differs considerably. For example, contrast the individual who gets angry and pounds a wall with the person who is equally angry but simply turns slightly red faced.

Facial expression usually gives some indication of a person's emotions and provides us with some information on which to base future behavior. For example, the facial expression of a girl might warn a boy whether to "back off," proceed with caution, or go full speed ahead. While we can obtain some idea about emotions from facial expressions, there are definite limitations, which research in this area has indicated. *Vocal expression* can convey information about emotions through changes in inflection, loudness, pitch, or timbre. Thus, you can usually tell when someone expresses surprise or incredulity by changes in voice. Similarly, you can often tell when someone is angry by his voice. There are also a variety of *overt bodily responses* that give some indication of emotion. These can include running away from a feared object, attacking and destroying something in anger, approaching something, and many other overt activities.

Many attempts have been made to measure the various physiological activities that make up emotion. A long list of autonomic nervous system reactions has been studied and related to emotion. This list includes the electrical conductivity of the skin (called the galvanic skin response, or GSR), heart rate, blood pressure, finger temperature, respiration rate and salivary output, to mention only the most prominent measures. In Chapter 2, we already mentioned the work by Hess and Polt (1960) showing that pupillary dilation is produced in emotional stress and thus verifying the view that the eyes are the "windows of the soul."

A very useful tool in measuring the arousal level of the central nervous system is the electroencephalograph (EEG) technique, which is used to measure the electrical activity of the brain. By studying the EEG of subjects under various experimental conditions, it has been possible to obtain a considerable amount of information regarding the mechanisms of arousal and activation.

The System So Far

At this particular point in the analysis of the behavioral system of man we have considered several of the subsystems that

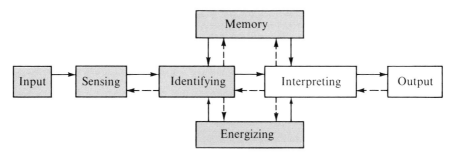

Figure 7-9. The system so far.

are responsible for the process by which input to the system is transformed to an output. The sensing subsystem, the identifying subsystem, and the memory subsystem have been discussed, and their roles in the transformation process have been considered. In this chapter, we have been concerned with a subsystem that can be thought of as supplying the "energy" for the functioning of these subsystems, as well as the interpreting subsystem that will be taken up in the next chapter.

We have seen that the energizing subsystem, as the name implies, will energize or activate behavior. This subsystem also serves to direct behavior in that it causes a person to respond to certain elements of his environment and disregard others. In addition, it can cause behavior to persist to a goal. The energizing subsystem, then, is an extremely important component of the behavioral system. Without it, we have a behavior system that cannot function because no "power" or energy has been applied.

Summary

1. The concept of "motive" is difficult to define. One definition states that a motive is an inferred entity that operates or functions to influence behavior in certain ways. Motives energize behavior, direct it, and cause it to persist.

2. Motives are often divided into two broad groups—those that arise from physiological conditions of the body and those that have a psychological basis. Hunger and thirst are examples of physiological drives, while curiosity, exploratory, manipulatory, and social drives are examples of psychological motives.

3. The body tends to maintain a reasonably constant internal environment in spite of events that tend to upset the equilibrium of this environment. This tendency is called homeostasis.

4. Hunger and thirst drives have been investigated extensively. Both appear to be complex drives that are controlled by many variables. Hunger research has centered on the relationship between hunger sensations and stomach contractions and distension, blood conditions and hunger, and central nervous system factors. Blood conditions and central nervous system factors, as well as dryness of the mouth and throat, have been related to the sensation of thirst.

5. Psychological motives are also important in determining how we behave. Complex social motives determine much of our behavior in relation to society. Numerous social motives have been suggested, such as affiliation, achievement, dominance, and rejection.

6. There are a number of motivational factors that can help determine how a person performs a task. One of the most important is the level of aspiration that the person sets for himself. Closely related to the concept of level of aspiration is the hypothesis of par or tolerance which suggests that an individual consistently sets his level of aspiration below the level of performance he can achieve.

7. Emotions play an important role in motivation and can also serve to activate, sustain, and direct behavior. There are various theories of emotion, one of the most recent being the activation theory.

Selected Readings

Cofer, C. N., & Appley, M. H. *Motivation: Theory and research.* New York: Wiley, 1964.

Fowler, H. *Curiosity and exploratory behavior.* New York: Macmillan, 1965.

Hall, J. F. Motivation and affectivity. In H. Helson & W. Bevan (Eds.), *Contemporary approaches to psychology.* Princeton, New Jersey: Van Nostrand, 1967. Pp. 223–271.

Harlow, H. F. The nature of love. *American Psychologist,* 1958, **13,** 673–685.

Harlow, H. F., & Harlow, M. K. Social deprivation in monkeys. *Scientific American,* 1962, **207,** 136–146.

Helson, H. *Adaptation-level theory.* New York: Harper & Row, 1964.

8

The Interpreting
Subsystem

Since all the various behavioral subsystems are required for behavior to occur, we cannot say that one is more important than another. Certainly, however, in terms of human behavioral systems, the *interpreting* function is of critical significance and is responsible for much of the behavior that we consider uniquely "human." When we speak of the interpreting function, we are referring to the processes that are usually labeled as thinking, problem solving, or, frequently, just "cognitive processes." In order to discuss the functions of the interpreting subsystem, it will be necessary to consider such terms as images, symbols, concepts, principles, and so forth. However, before taking up these topics we will briefly consider this particular subsystem in relation to the other components of the behavioral system that were discussed earlier.

In Chapter 4, it was pointed out that stimuli are organized into categories or classes and that this categorization is accomplished through a process of *identification*. In other words, identification involves placing a stimulus input into a certain class (category) on the basis of its defining attributes—that is, on the basis of its *appearance*. This identifying function is a necessary prerequisite for the interpreting function, for a person must *identify* (perceive) the stimulus situation before he can *interpret* it. As you will recall, the identification process is dependent on "models" that are stored in the long-term memory so that incoming information can be compared and categorized.

We can think of the basic function of the interpreting subsystem as giving *meaning* to the inputs from the identifying subsystem. In the identifying stage, stimulus inputs are categorized on the basis of their attributes, or appearance, but not in terms of meaning. The interpreting stage also involves a categorization process, but inputs are placed in categories that are based on possible courses of action in response to these inputs and the expected effects of these responses. Thus, the interpreting function involves identifying inputs on the basis of their expected effects rather than their appearance.

This categorizing or classifying on the basis of *expected effects* is accomplished by means of memory inputs from long-term storage. We refer to these memory inputs as *rules*. Many of the "rules" we use develop through prior experience with a particular input; they allow us a number of "courses of action" in response to the input.

As an example of the above functions, consider the following familiar situation. When driving on a hot day the red light on the dashboard goes on, indicating an overheated engine. Based on its attributes or appearance it is identified (perceived) by the identifying subsystem, but no meaning is yet attached to the onset of the light. This attachment of meaning to the red light (overheated engine) is the function of the interpreting subsystem, which uses previously acquired "rules" to do so. The driver has also stored a whole set of rules that determine possible courses of action (responses) that can be taken. Thus, the red light on the dash may cause him to stop the car, drive to a service station, drive slower, or any of a number of courses of action based on "rules" that are available from long-term storage.

This, of course, is a simple example of interpreting. In this chapter we will be concerned with a more complex process, in which interpreting takes place in a step-by-step fashion. We call this process *problem solving*, and it represents one of the most important functions of the interpreting subsystem.

Symbols and Concepts

The capability of man's interpreting subsystem is the basis for his uniqueness among animals. While a few animals appear to have some capacity for reasoning and communication, none ap-

proach man in these abilities. One primary reason for this difference
is that man has a well-developed capability of using *symbols* and
concepts in his thinking and his communications with others.
Symbols and concepts form the groundwork for all of the so-called
"higher mental processes" that we associate with the interpreting
subsystem.

Symbols

A symbol can be defined as a stimulus which, because of
learning, has come to stand for, or represent, something else. As
such, a symbol can be almost anything. Thus, words are symbols,
as are many pictures, movements, gestures, signs, and so forth. The
thing that a symbol stands for or represents is called its *referent*.
Obviously, the symbol is not the same as its referent; for example,
the word "man" is not at all like an actual man. However, an important aspect of human behavior is the tendency to respond to
symbols and their referents in a similar manner.

In order for a symbol to represent something—that is, have
a referent—it is necessary that a person learn the relationship between symbol and referent. From infancy onward, much of a
person's learning experience involves establishing these relationships. A child, during a relatively short period of time, learns
countless symbols and their meanings. For example, a child's
transition from babbling to communicative speech takes place
because he has learned words that symbolize events or objects in his
environment. At the same time that he is learning verbal symbols,
he is learning many other kinds of symbols that are necessary for
his effective interaction with his environment. He learns that some
symbols represent danger and that others represent desirable objects or events. As he grows older he continues to learn new symbols
as his language develops and as he is exposed to an increasingly
large and more varied environment.

While learning the relationship between symbols and their
referents is not a particularly complex type of learning, it should
be kept in mind that this kind of learning is based on several even
simpler forms. For example, in order to use symbols a tremendous
number of discriminations must be learned, and, as you may recall
from Chapter 5, discrimination learning is based on still simpler
forms. If a person could not discriminate between the referents,
then symbols would be of no use. Thus, if the symbols "car" and
"airplane" are to have any meaning, the individual must be able to
discriminate between an actual car and airplane. Obviously, this

represents a rather gross discrimination. However, consider all of the various types of cars within the general category of "cars." Finer and finer discriminations may be required if the symbol is "Brand X Car" or "Model Z of Brand X Car." We learn to discriminate among thousands of objects and events and also among the thousands of words in the language itself.

An important feature, then, of the interpreting subsystem is that it can utilize symbolic inputs that represent actual inputs from tasks or other environmental situations. Thus, the red light on the dashboard of the car is a symbolic input that represents a condition of the motor. You react to this red light in the same way you would react if you could actually see the motor overheating. Something *is* a symbol because it and its referent are responded to in a similar fashion.

Internal Symbols

There is another important characteristic of symbolic behavior. Our definition of a symbol as a "stimulus" representing something else at least implies that the symbol must be *external* to the organism—that is, it involves a sensory input by means of the visual, auditory, or some other sensory modality. This, of course, is the case with a great many of the symbols that we deal with. However, much of our symbolic behavior involves symbols that can be considered as *internal* symbols. In other words, a person can generate his own symbols and then respond to them.

An image, which is a "mental picture" of various objects of actual sensory experience, is one type of internal symbol. The role of images in thinking has been, at least historically, an issue in psychology and, around the turn of the century, there was some argument about whether *imageless thought* was possible. While it is apparent that much thinking can go on without images, they do function as symbols in many cases and are thus important in the thinking process.

Most of our images are visual, although auditory imagery is also frequent. In fact, some people may be stronger in this type of imagery than in the visual type. A few individuals even report that their images of smell, taste, touch, or muscle movement are stronger than the auditory or visual images. Actually, many of our images can be thought of as "composites," in that they involve several of the sensory modalities. For example, imagine yourself in what you would consider an interesting situation with your boy or girl friend. You will probably have a visual image of your partner but the image may also include auditory, smell, and touch components. While most of you are able to generate an image of this sort, not everyone's image will be equally vivid or will have the same content since people differ a great deal in their imagery. This difference is particularly apparent when we consider the individual who possesses *eidetic imagery.*

An eidetic image is a visual image that is so strong that a person almost seems to actually view the imagined object or scene. Relatively few people possess this type of imagery. They are capable of feats of memory that, to most of us, are remarkable. Some individuals with eidetic imagery can glance at a page of a book and then "read it back" from a visual image of the page. They can glance at a scene and give a complete description including minute details. People with "photographic memories" of this type represent one extreme of vividness and clarity of imagery. While few of us have this type of capability, there are few of us on the other end of the extreme where only the faintest of visual images are generated.

Distortion of Symbolic Input

When so much of the input to the interpreting subsystem is in the form of symbols, a critical question arises as to whether the *intended* meaning of the symbol and its *understood* meaning are the same. As we have indicated, a stimulus must be identified before it can be interpreted. In Chapter 4, it was pointed out that there are a number of variables that may affect the identifying function and result in a distortion of the input. These variables include factors associated with the stimulus situation and personal characteristics of the observer. Although some discrepancy between the intended and understood meaning of a symbol usually may not be of great significance, in some cases it may have serious consequences. This is particularly true when the symbol is meant to warn of some type of danger.

As an example of symbols of this type, consider the new product warning symbols that are now used in Canada. It is required that these labels, which are shown in Figure 8–1, be placed on poisonous, flammable, explosive, and corrosive products sold for everyday household use. Note that each symbol is placed inside an outline that shows the degree of severity of the hazard. An octagon means "Danger," a diamond means "Warning," and a triangle means "Caution." As adults, with considerable experience with symbols of this type, we have little trouble regarding the intended and understood meaning of these symbols.

Consider, however, the situation with someone who has not had this kind of experience. For example, many children ingest poison even though the container may have a clear warning symbol in the form of a skull and crossbones. Analysis of children's interpretation of this particular symbol revealed that many of them thought the symbol represented a "pirate" plaything of some sort while others thought it represented a "bone medicine." In other cases, children have been found to interpret warning signs on

Figure 8-1. Hazardous product symbols now used in Canada. By permission of Canada Department of Consumer and Corporate Affairs.

streets or pedestrian crosswalks as meaning it was safe to run across the street at that point without looking for cars. Obviously, in many instances when a discrepancy exists between the intended meaning of a symbol and the understood meaning, the results may be serious.

Concepts

You may recall from Chapter 5 that concept learning permits the learner to respond or react to things or events collectively, rather than as individual events or things. Thus, when a person learns a concept, he has acquired the capability of making a common reaction to a collection of things that have some property in common, regardless of how dissimilar they may be otherwise. The person reacts to the collection of things or events as being equivalent in certain ways. He may react to the collection as being equivalent by calling it by a common name, such as houses, cars, trees, and so on. He may also treat a collection of events or things as being equivalent by making the same kind of nonverbal response to them. Thus, we respond to scotch, bourbon, vodka, or gin as being equivalent in that we drink them.

Most symbols are concepts in that they do not stand for a unique thing or event but rather for a general class of things or events that are linked by some common characteristic. Thus, as one learns the discriminations that are necessary for the acquiring of symbols, he also, in many instances, learns concepts. However, concepts vary in their level of abstraction, so some are much more readily learned than others. For example, concepts based on common elements of objects or things, such as "boys," "books," "red objects," "cars," and so on, are relatively easy to learn. These are called *conjunctive* concepts. There are also *relational* concepts, which are based on common relationships between objects or events, such as bigness, smallness, and so on. The concept of oddity, which was discussed in Chapter 5, is another example of a relational concept. These types of concepts may become quite complicated, as in mathematical rules. A third type of concept is called a *disjunctive* concept. In the other two classes of concepts, universal common features are found and the concept is attained on the basis of these features. However, in disjunctive concepts there are no such universal common features. As an example of a disjunctive concept, consider the concept of "strike" used in baseball (Bruner, Goodnow, & Austin, 1956). A strike is a pitch that goes across the plate and somewhere between the batter's knees and shoulders, *or* it is a missed swing, *or* a foul ball if the batter does not already have two strikes. Disjunctive concepts, as you might expect, are considerably more difficult to attain than conjunctive or relational concepts.

Acquiring Concepts

Considerable research has been directed at determining factors that are important in concept formation. Investigators encounter some difficulties in studying this kind of behavior in that they cannot deal directly with a concept—that is, the internal behaviors that form the concept. Rather, one must infer the existence of a concept based on some external and measurable pattern of behavior. There are, however, a number of techniques that are common to this area, and the process of concept formation has been studied with some degree of success.

A number of studies that have been conducted deal with concept formation in children. One of the leading researchers in this area is Jean Piaget who, along with some coworkers, has developed perhaps the largest repository of knowledge about the cognitive development of children that is available. Although Piaget's approach to studying cognitive development (Phillips, 1969) is criticized by some because it is primarily clinical and relies on observing the child in his surroundings, he has nonetheless gathered a great deal of information about the cognitive development of children.

Piaget suggests that a child goes through three stages of cognitive development. These stages are thought to be hierarchical, with each successive stage being dependent on the mental organization of the preceding stage. The first stage, which is labeled the *sensorimotor stage*, extends from birth to about two years of age. The *concrete operations* stage extends from about two to eleven years, while the *formal operations* period extends to about fifteen years of age. While concept development is involved in each of the stages, there is a concrete operations subperiod (ages seven to eleven), during which a great deal of the child's concept formation behavior takes place. During this stage, the child will integrate symbolic processes into classes and relationships and will arrive at concepts that tend to be concrete and based on physical characteristics of the stimulus situation. For example, a child at this stage can group objects on the basis of similarity, such as, all blue objects in one class and all red objects in another class. Further, he is able, at least to some extent, to classify according to characteristics of the objects or events that do not depend solely upon what they look like. However, what can be considered as genuine abstract thinking takes place at the next higher stage of development.

While much of the research dealing with concept formation has been concerned with children, other studies have been conducted dealing with concept formation in the adult. We will now turn our attention to some of the characteristics of concept formation involving the human adult.

It appears that concept formation, as well as the application of a concept, does not require conscious effort on the part of the individual. As Leeper (1951) points out in his article on cognitive processes:

> Several experiments show that concepts may be formed, retained, and used "unconsciously." This statement does not imply that the subjects are not conscious of the perceptual materials before them. It implies merely that sometimes the subjects do not consciously recognize what properties they use to group or classify the materials [p. 743].

Leeper further suggests in his article that concepts can be formed, retained, and used without the person being aware of the process at any step.

Typically, however, concepts are consciously attained and consciously utilized. We have already indicated that some types of concepts are much more difficult to learn than other types. For example, the disjunctive type is more difficult to acquire than the conjunctive. Basically, it appears that the more "concrete" the concept, the more easily it is acquired. Thus, concepts based on physical characteristics of objects are relatively easily learned. Acquisition becomes more difficult when the concept must be based on abstract form, color, or numbers.

We could spend a great deal of time discussing concept formation, as well as other aspects of concepts. However, our interest in this chapter is directed more at the problem-solving function of the interpreting subsystem. This particular function requires that concept learning have taken place previously and that the concepts have formed the foundation for the learning of principles or rules. These, as we shall see, are particularly important in the problem-solving process.

Problem Solving

Problem solving is one of the key functions of the interpreting subsystem. While problem solving has always been of some interest to psychologists, it is a good deal easier to talk about than to investigate. There have been studies conducted in this area for many years, although much of the research has tended to concentrate on only certain aspects of the problem-solving process. Recently, there has been an upsurge of interest in investigating problem-solving behavior. This increased interest has been due, at least in part, to new concepts developed in the information-processing and computer-programming fields (Newell, Shaw, &

Simon, 1958; Simon & Newell, 1964), as well as concepts involving mathematical models of human problem-solving behavior (Luce, Bush, & Galanter, 1963). In this section we will consider some approaches used in investigating problem solving, as well as some current thinking on the nature of the problem-solving process.

What Is a Problem?

Since we all have had and currently have problems, it would seem that a definition is not required. A large portion of our behavior is concerned with solving problems. Some problems are quickly solved, while others can take long periods of time or perhaps are never actually solved. Although psychologists have presented various definitions of "problems," most agree that *problem solving involves the discovery of a correct response to a situation that is new and unique to the individual.* In other words, a person does not have a "rule" stored in long-term memory that can handle the particular situation. If he did, then the problem would not exist. Consequently, either a new rule must be developed, or a series of previously learned rules must be combined in a unique fashion so that he is able to solve the problem. Just how the new rules are developed or how old rules are combined is one of the basic questions that researchers in this area must deal with.

Some "Problems" for Problem Solvers

Many problems that we encounter in our everyday existence are very real and meaningful to us but, for various reasons, would not be very satisfactory for psychologists to study as examples of problem-solving behavior. First, it is necessary to measure problem-solving performance in some way—not an easy matter, even in carefully controlled laboratory studies. Thus, it is necessary to design "problems" that will allow a criterion of performance to be established. In addition to the performance that is measured (dependent variable), independent variables that may affect problem-solving behavior must also be considered. Thus, the effects of stimulus variables and instructions to the subjects on problem-solving behavior must be determined. Consequently, not just "any problem" is suitable for use in research in this area.

Studies of problem solving with humans have, as we have indicated, involved many different techniques. At the turn of the century, particular interest was shown in determining how subjects could solve puzzles of various kinds, including linguistic, mathematical, logical, and mechanical puzzles. Studies of how puzzles were solved gave some indication of what took place in the problem-solving process. Having subjects "think out loud" was once a popular means of obtaining data on these processes and it is still sometimes used. When a subject was presented with a problem he was instructed to "think aloud" and report the objects with which he was dealing, the situation as he saw it, and what he was trying to accomplish. This technique was designed to give the experimenter some idea of the steps and processes used in arriving at a solution. Other techniques, however, have replaced the "think aloud" approach in most problem-solving studies.

A number of practical problems have also been employed in studying problem-solving behavior. Typically, these problems require that a subject use materials in new ways or that he abandon some old "rules" and make use of new ones. More recently, there has been a tendency to study problem solving by means of elaborate computerized approaches that attempt to build "models" of the problem-solving processes.

While we will make no attempt to exhaustively cover the different techniques used in problem-solving research, or even to give a representative sample, we will describe several studies in order to give some idea of how researchers have approached this area. In a sense, the studies that are cited can be considered as "classics," if for no other reason than that they are described in virtually all introductory psychology books. They are important, however, in that they called attention to certain aspects of the problem-solving process and generated a considerable amount of research that has led to a better understanding of problem-solving behavior.

The Maier Studies

During the early 1930s, N. R. F. Maier conducted a series of "classic" studies investigating problem-solving behavior of adult humans. The problems that he used in these studies are called the Pendulum Problem and the Two-String Problem. The Pendulum Problem involved constructing two pendulums that would make chalk marks on specific points on the floor as they swung. The subject was furnished with two burette clamps, eight sections of metal tubing, four pieces of chalk, a table clamp, two lengths of wire, two one-yard poles, two two-yard poles, and a heavy wooden table (shown in Part A of Figure 8–2).

Three experimental groups received different degrees of

instruction in various subtasks which could be used in solving the problem. One group of subjects received no instructions. Another group was shown how to (1) construct a plumb line by attaching a clamp to a length of wire, (2) make a longer wooden strip from two short sticks, and (3) wedge a vertical stick in a doorway by using a second stick lodged horizontally across the doorway. Slight modifications of these subtasks represented a partial solution to the problem, although the subjects were not informed of this. A third group of subjects was also shown how to execute the subtasks but, in addition, was given hints regarding the "direction" of the solution of the problem. For example, subjects were told the problem could be solved if the two pendulums were suspended from the ceiling.

The solution to the problem is shown in Part B of Figure 8–2. While several of the subjects in the group receiving "direction"

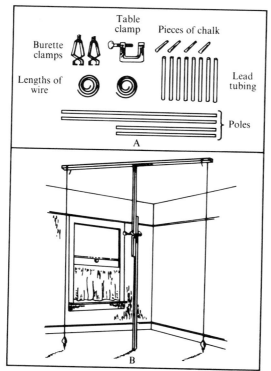

Figure 8–2. The pendulum problem. Part A of the figure shows the materials that were available to a subject, while Part B shows the correct solution to the problem. From *Recent Experiments in Psychology* by L. W. Crafts, T. C. Schneirla, E. E. Robinson, and R. W. Gilbert. Copyright 1950 by McGraw-Hill Book Company, Inc. Used with permission of McGraw-Hill Book Company.

hints solved the problem, only one of 62 subjects in the other two groups was successful in solving the problem. These results are somewhat puzzling in light of the fact that all the subjects were either graduate students or had Ph.D's in chemistry, physics, or psychology. Almost all subjects assumed that the walls and/or the table had to be used in the construction of the pendulum system. This illustrates what is called *functional fixedness*, meaning that an object that has a customary function is not easily seen to be suitable for another and quite different function.

Men tended to blame their inability to solve the problem on lack of appropriate materials, while some woman subjects tended to "shrug" off the failure by stating they were not mechanically inclined. The fact was, a majority of both men and women did not exhibit insight, nor did they utilize and synthesize subtask information in executing the problem-solving task.

In the Two-String Problem, the subjects were required to tie together the ends of two strings that were suspended from the ceiling. However, the strings were too short and too far apart, so that it was not possible for the subject to hold the end of one string and walk over and seize the end of the other. Among the materials available to the subject was a pair of pliers. The solution to the problem, which again is quite simple, consisted of tying the pliers to the end of one string and swinging it. By holding on to one string and swinging the other into reach, the other end could be reached and the two ends tied together. Many subjects were unable to solve the problem by using the pendulum principle, which was the simplest solution. Failure to use the pliers as a pendulum bob is another example of functional fixedness—that is, most subjects did not separate the concept of pliers from its typical functional context as a tool.

Luchins' "Water Jar" Problem

In Maier's studies it was shown that functional fixedness will interfere with the solving of a problem. Other studies have been concerned with the effects of a *set* or *Einstellung* (the German word for *mental set*) on problem-solving behavior. Possibly the best known of these types of investigations is the "water jar" experiment of Luchins (1942).

Shown in Table 8–1 are a number of problems that a subject can solve by using available "empty" jars to obtain a prescribed volume of water. For example, consider the first problem shown in the table. The subject has a 29-quart jar, a 3-quart jar, and all the water he needs. How can he measure exactly 20 quarts of water? The solution for the first problem is relatively simple: fill the 29-quart jar and then fill the 3-quart jar three times from the large jar; 20 quarts remain in the large jar.

The second problem can be solved in an equally simple way. The 127-quart jar is filled and from it the 21-quart jar is filled once and the 3-quart jar twice. This will leave 100 quarts in the large jar. All of the problems, with the exception of number nine, can be solved with the formula, $B - A - 2C$, that is, by filling the large jar and then pouring off the A jarful once and the C jarful twice.

Table 8-1. Some of the problems in the Luchins' "water jar" experiment.

Problem No.	Jars Regarded as Given			Required Amount (quarts)
	A	B	C	
1	29	3		20
2	21	127	3	100
3	14	163	25	99
4	18	43	10	5
5	9	42	6	21
6	20	59	4	31
7	23	49	3	20
8	15	39	3	18
9	28	76	3	25
10	18	48	4	22
11	14	36	8	6

After working several of the problems, the typical subject develops a *set* (*Einstellung*) for solving the problem by means of the formula given above. Thus, he continues to work the problems in this way, even though a simpler solution may be available. For example, consider the seventh problem on the list. Again, the problem can be solved by following the formula and filling the 49-quart jar and, from it, filling the 23-quart jar once and the 3-quart jar twice. This, of course, leaves the desired 20 quarts. However, study this problem for a moment. Do you see a simpler solution? If you were to fill the 23-quart jar and fill the 3-quart jar from it, you would have the 20 quarts.

Luchins' studies showed that set had a direct effect on this type of problem-solving behavior. Subjects ranging from grade-school children to graduate students exhibited the same lack of ability to extract the less complex solution. The original response pattern was highly resistant to extinction.

Katona's "Match-Stick" Problems

In addition to functional fixedness and set on problem-solving behavior, investigators have been interested in a number of other variables. For example, is memorization of rules and applying them routinely more effective in solving problems than understanding the principles involved? Katona's (1940) match-stick problem study is an example of an investigation that contrasted the relative merits of memorization versus the understanding of principles in solving problems.

In Katona's study, subjects were presented with a number of squares formed by match sticks and told to increase or decrease the number of squares by relocating a certain number of sticks. For example, a subject might be confronted with the match-stick patterns labeled "A₁" in Figure 8–3 and told: "Here are five equal

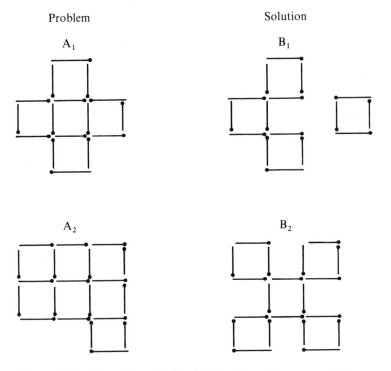

Problem   Solution

A₁   B₁

A₂   B₂

Figure 8–3. Examples of the kinds of problems used by Katona in his "match-stick" studies of problem-solving behavior. In problem A₁ the subject is told to make four squares by changing the position of three sides. In problem A₂ the subject is instructed to make five squares by moving three sides.

squares. You are to make four squares by changing the position of three sides." Similarly, with pattern "A₂" the subject is told to make five squares by moving three sides. Katona utilized a large number of similar problems in his investigations.

The results obtained by Katona were interesting. He found that the *least* effective method of training subjects on problems of this kind was to show the subjects how to solve several problems by actually moving the matches and having the subject memorize the moves. The more effective methods involved training the subjects to understand principles involved in solving the problems. Subjects trained by memorizing moves were less able to solve new match-stick problems than subjects trained to understand principles.

The Maier, Luchins, and Katona studies are but a few of many investigations that have been conducted by researchers in attempting to better understand problem-solving behavior. Many more could be cited, but space does not permit. Rather, we will now turn our attention to a more detailed discussion of the problem-solving process.

The Problem-Solving Process

It should be pointed out that many researchers in this field are really not concerned about what goes on "inside" the person when he solves a problem. Currently, there are two general classes of theories dealing with problem-solving behavior. One class can be labeled as an S-R (stimulus-response) or a behaviorist class, while the other includes the information-processing theories. The S-R theorists argue that problem-solving behavior is really no different from simple discrimination learning, and, on this assumption, they have attempted to analyze problem-solving behavior in terms of operant conditioning, chains of associations, and other concepts from S-R theory. Generally, S-R theories of problem solving do not take into account the processes that occur between the stimulus and the response. Behaviorists view the organism as a "black box," and they are concerned primarily with the inputs to the box, its outputs, and the relationships between the two.

Information-processing theorists differ from the behaviorists in that they are interested in what goes on inside the "black box." The information processors are interested in the organization that takes place within the "box" and the processes that intervene between input and output. Simon and Newell (1964) are representative of the contemporary school of problem solving, which emphasizes information processing and computer programming. Theories of this sort begin with the assumption that both man and computers organize and interpret information similarly. Thus, these theories assume that human thinking can be formulated in computer-programming languages and can be tested by simulating the predicted behavior with computers. Simon and Newell demonstrate this assumption by means of a hypothetical chess game, which represents the "macroscopic organization of thought in a particular task environment." The programmed instructions required by the computer are assumed to be similar to some problem-solving processes that guide human problem solving. Hopefully, with a technique of this sort it may be possible to delineate the mental processes and strategies involved in winning the game.

There are a number of fundamental differences between the behaviorists' and the information processors' theories of problem solving, and a discussion of these would quickly become quite technical. However, in considering a classification of theories of problem solving, a point raised by Green (1966) in his discussion of these theories should be kept in mind. He suggests that ". . . in fact, the identification of two opposing schools of thought has perhaps been premature. Plainly, there are many points of agreement . . ." (p. 18). While it is true that there are points of agreement, it is equally true that there are a number of points of disagreement. Consequently, lively arguments between advocates of the two schools have arisen and continue to arise. These arguments range from basic disagreements about the theory of problem solving to arguments over what may often appear to be minor points. We will now consider one of these arguments that deal with the nature of the problem-solving process.

Stages of Problem Solving

In dealing with the problem-solving processes, it has been traditional to think of these processes in terms of *stages* or steps. In other words, when an individual is confronted with a problem, it is thought that he goes through a series of distinct stages in solving the problem. While the number of stages in the process may vary somewhat, there are usually at least four listed. These often include *preparation, incubation, inspiration,* and *verification.* Sometimes a fifth stage, called *revision,* is included in this *stages model* of problem solving. Preparation involves studying the elements of the problem and collecting the facts and materials the person thinks may be necessary for the solution. During the incubation stage, the problem solver turns away from the problem and engages in other activities.

Hopefully, during the incubation stage he may learn something that will help solve the problem, or he may lose some ideas that were interfering with a solution. At some point, the individual may suddenly have the "Aha!" experience in which the solution suddenly "pops into his head" either spontaneously or after he has again directed his attention to the problem. Finally, during the verification stage the person determines whether his solution is indeed the correct one. It may or may not be. Sometimes the solution will require some modification or revision, which is the last stage. Other "stages" models present somewhat different hypothesized stages that an individual goes through while solving a problem.

Green (1966) has several pertinent comments to make about the stages model of problem solving. As he points out, the model has come largely from researchers who are dealing with the solving of difficult problems, and, consequently, the model is only relevant to such special cases. It tells us very little about the problem-solving behavior involving the ordinary problems that we encounter so frequently. Thus Green states:

> The salient feature of the model is incubation followed by inspiration. If a problem is solved in a straightforward manner by the solver, there is neither incubation nor inspiration, and the model is empty. Further, the nature of incubation is obscure. If incubation is merely leaving the problem, we have all incubated many problems that have never hatched. Probably the subject must return to the problem intentionally, and cases of unconscious inspiration are exaggerated. . . . The stages model has been accepted passively but has led nowhere [p. 12].

This statement would be challenged by many researchers who feel that the stages model is most appropriate and best suited to explaining the processes that take place during problem solving. Probably, most investigators would agree that stages of some sort are involved. The question, then, seems to be whether the stages, as defined by a particular model, serve as rigid segments of the problem-solving sequence. Few investigators would argue that the stages in a problem-solving sequence are so well defined that one could draw brackets around them during a given time period and state that only "stage 1 or stage 2" took place during this period of time. Most stages models are more flexible than this and, consequently, present a convenient way of summarizing the results of a particular part or segment of the problem-solving process. When stages models are viewed as flexible, rather than as rigid models stating that "such and such" occurred during a given time period in the problem-solving sequence, many more investigators are willing to accept them. However, there are some theorists who would argue that the stages notion is not necessary to understand the problem-solving process and that a person can proceed on a problem from start to finish without going through stages of any kind.

Obviously, an introductory psychology book is no place to attempt to resolve an argument of this kind. This is just one of several areas of controversy in the field of problem-solving research, and one is almost forced to "pick sides" somewhere along the line. We will elect to go along with the stages model in our discussion of problem-solving processes. You should keep in mind, however, that this is a controversial issue and that those who argue against stages models are convinced, based on their data, that the stages concept is not necessary. Possibly the research that is currently being conducted in this area will, in the near future, give us an answer to this question. Until then, we can expect to see a continuing argument between the advocates of "stages" or "no-stages" in the problem-solving process.

Before we go further into the stages model, however, another important question related to problem solving will be considered. What is the role of learning in problem-solving behavior?

Prior Learning and Problem Solving

Recall from the discussion of learning presented in Chapter 5 that learning was viewed as a hierarchical process with simple conditioning at one end of the hierarchy and problem solving at the other end. Learning was described in terms of a cumulative model, with new learning dependent upon the combining of previously learned and recalled material; each type of learning starts with a different state of the learner and ends with a different capability for performance. With a model of this type, in order for problem solving to take place, it is necessary that *principles* (rules) have been learned earlier. Principle learning is based on previously learned *concepts* which, in turn, require that *multiple discrimination* learning has taken place and so forth. In other words, if problem solving is to take place, it must have been preceded by a number of simpler types of learning.

Concept learning involves learning to respond to a *class* of stimuli rather than to one stimulus in a group (as is the case with multiple discrimination learning). Concept learning, as you may recall, permits a person to respond to things or events as a collection rather than as individual events or things. We have also indicated that in principle, or rule, learning, which is dependent upon concept learning, the person learns to establish relationships between various concepts. In other words, a principle can be considered as a chain of concepts. For example, the principle "hot things burn" consists of two concepts—hot things and burn—which must be understood in order for the rule "hot things burn" to be learned. Principles, then, form the basis for thinking and problem solving. Principles, or rules, of varying complexity can be manipulated and combined in the process of *thinking*. By combining old principles, and thus forming new ones, the person is able to *solve problems*. The basic assumption, then, is that if problem solving is to occur, it must have been preceded by a number of simpler forms of learning.

If we consider problem solving in these terms, then we must make a second assumption. We must assume that problem solving is an act of learning that results in a change in performance of the individual. We infer from this change in performance that solving a problem has brought about a change in the *capability* of the person. The question, then, is what kind of change in capability occurs in problem solving? What takes place in a person who has solved a problem? We will attempt to answer these questions by presenting a model of problem-solving behavior.

Solving the Problem

We can consider the following discussion of the problem-solving process to be a continuation of our earlier discussion of Gagné's cumulative learning model (1965; 1968). You may recall that this model had a hierarchical arrangement of types of learning, ranging from the simple conditioned response to complex problem solving, which was at the top of the hierarchy. In other articles, Gagné (1964; 1966) has discussed problem-solving behavior in considerable detail and has presented a theoretical model of the processes involved in this kind of behavior. While his model is a stages model, it is flexible and useful in describing the internal processes that are thought to occur during problem solving.

Basic to this particular model of problem solving is the assumption that the individual, when confronted with a problem-solving situation, has available to him a variety of previously acquired rules, or principles. Whether or not he has these learned capabilities will determine whether a solution to the problem is achieved. Again, it must be emphasized that for the individual to have acquired these rules, he must previously have acquired concepts which, in turn, were based on multiple discriminations and so forth.

Figure 8–4 is a diagram of Gagné's (1966) model of the in-

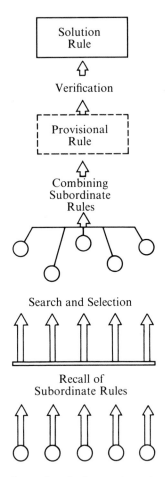

Figure 8-4. A schematic of the various internal stages involved in human problem solving. Adapted from Gagné, R. M.,
Human problem solving: Internal and external events. In B.
Kleinmuntz (Eds.), *Problem solving: Research, method, and
theory.* Copyright © 1966 by John Wiley & Sons, Inc. Reprinted by permission.

ternal processes that are inferred as necessary to problem solving.
The bottom of this figure represents an assortment of previously
learned rules, such as those mentioned above. The first step, then, in
the problem-solving process is the recall of some of the rules that an
individual has retained in long-term storage. At this step, rules that
are both relevant and irrelevant to the problem situation may be recalled. Various factors can influence the individual's ability to recall
these rules both in terms of the number of rules recalled and their
relevance. For example, instructions or other information from out-

side sources may stimulate recall and make more rules available.

Thus, among the rules that are recalled there will be rules that are relevant and those that are not. For example, the Maier pendulum problem situation, which was discussed earlier, could give rise to a variety of previously acquired rules regarding strings, sticks, clamps, tables, and so on. However, the fact that the individual recalls a rule that string can be used in fishing, or that a stick can be used to hit a ball, will not be very helpful in solving the problem at hand. Consequently, the second step of the problem-solving process involves "search and selection" on the part of the problem solver. At this stage, the person searches for and selects rules (called subordinate rules) that are relevant to the problem situation. Those rules that will not help him are rejected. Thus, rules relating to how two sticks can be fastened together with a clamp, how an object such as a piece of chalk can be held by a clamp, and other such rules would be retained, while the rule that a piece of string can be used to catch fish might be rejected.

At this point, then, the problem solver still has a number of relevant but independent rules about the problem situation. The next step involves combining these subordinate rules. This particular step is sometimes thought of as the hypothesis-formulating stage. As can be seen from Figure 8–4, the combining of the subordinate rules leads to the development of what is called a *provisional* rule which the person thinks might solve the particular problem. The provisional rule, however, must be verified. The final step in the problem-solving process is the verification step, in which the provisional rule is checked to see if it "works." If it does, then the *solution* rule has been acquired; if it does not work, then the person "retreats" and goes back to trying new combinations of rules.

The outcome of the problem-solving process just described gives us a somewhat more specific definition of problem solving than the general definition that was given earlier. The definition of problem solving presented by Gagné (1966) is as follows: "Problem solving is an inferred change in human capability that results in the acquisition of a generalizable rule which is novel to the individual, which cannot have been established by direct recall, and which can manifest itself in applicability to the solution of a class of problems" (p. 132).

Some Factors Affecting
Problem Solving

In concluding our discussion of problem-solving behavior, it should be pointed out that there are a number of factors that have an effect on how efficiently a person solves a problem. For example, information or instructions that are given to the problem solver during the course of problem solving can greatly modify his performance on the task. Instructions can help the person recall relevant rules and concepts and can also guide the thinking process in appropriate directions. Similarly, the problem-solving situation itself can influence the solving process. Thus, the physical stimuli that are employed as part of the problem-solving situation must be "identified" and interpreted. These stimuli are often symbols, and the information conveyed by them must be processed. The nature of these stimuli, then, may affect problem-solving performance.

One particularly critical variable in determining whether a problem will be solved efficiently, or even solved at all, is the characteristics of the problem solver. As is true with all abilities, individuals differ considerably in their capabilities in problem solving. While the topic of individual differences will be dealt with in detail in Chapter 10, some of the differences that are important to problem solving will be briefly considered. If you refer to Figure 8–4, it will become apparent that individual differences may be an important variable at each stage of the problem-solving process. For example, one can assume that people will differ with respect to the number of rules that are stored and that are necessary to recall in order to solve a problem. Similarly, the ease with which people can recall these rules may vary considerably. Possibly, one individual can recall many more rules than another and also recall them without confusing them with each other. At each of the other steps in the problem-solving process, individuals will differ in the manner in which they are capable of performing the step. Because of these individual differences, we find that a given input to the system, in the form of a problem situation, may result in transformation processes that bring about a variety of outputs.

Decision Making

Another very important function of the interpreting subsystem is *decision making*. While in some cases the distinction between problem solving and decision making may be hazy, we can nonetheless think of them as being different functions. We have suggested that problem solving involves the *discovery* of a correct response to a situation that is new and unique to the individual. Decision making, however, is the interpreting process that leads to the selection of a response from among a number of "known" alternative responses. Decision making, then, involves the "weighing" of alternative responses to a situation in terms of their desirabilities and potential costs and payoffs. Worded somewhat differently, "decision making is defined as the selection of an alternative response to an inferred environmental situation about which complete certainty is lacking" (Schrenk, 1969).

As was the case with problem solving, we all make so many decisions each day that we tend to view this process as a simple and uncomplicated act. Sometimes, however, we encounter a decision that is not so easy to make, and we begin to appreciate the many complexities involved in selecting the appropriate response. Since decision making is one of the most complex and pervasive aspects of human behavior, it is not surprising that this topic has received considerable study. There is an enormous and diverse literature dealing with decision making. For example, Edwards (1969) compiled a comprehensive bibliography of reports dealing with behavioral decision processes and ended up with over 1300 studies. However, despite the literature in this area, we are just beginning to understand human decision processes.

Man as a Decision Maker

Schrenk (1969) reviews some of the characteristics of the human as a decision maker in man-machine systems. Due to a number of investigations by various researchers, we are getting some idea of the capabilities of man in this role. While even a brief discussion of the many investigations dealing with man as a decision maker is beyond the scope of this chapter, we will summarize some of the relevant findings in this area.

The most common finding in decision making is that there are considerable individual differences between people in their ability to make decisions. It also appears that there is a tendency for people to require too much information, rather than too little, before making a decision and that they tend to delay too long in arriving at a decision. Although persons tend to require too much information, they still appear to be unable to use all the information that they have at their disposal. When new information becomes available, they are usually conservative in revising opinions even if the data warrants a revision. There is also research that suggests a person may develop and consider too few courses of action (Schrenk, 1969).

Although these findings can be considered limitations of the human as a decision maker, people usually perform quite well in this role. Because man can make decisions based on a variety of variables, his prime function in most man-machine systems is decision making. Since this is a critical function of man, from a practical point of view it is important that the decision-making performance of the human, as an element in a system, be maximized. There have been several approaches to improving decision-making performance.

Improving Decision Making

There are three basic methods by which the performance of the decision maker in a system can be improved. First, since individuals differ a great deal in their decision-making ability, selection of good decision makers for a task requiring this type of performance is a logical first step. However, adequate criteria of "good" decision making are not available for many complex operational tasks. Consequently, it is difficult to establish selection batteries that can "tap" decision-making ability.

Another method of improving decision-making performance is to train a person to be a good decision maker. However, in order to effectively train for decision making, a better understanding of all the variables involved in the decision process must be available. Although this approach may eventually be effective, further research is needed in the development of procedures and in the validation of the training.

A third approach is to provide the decision maker with "tools" that may make the decision-making process simpler. There have been a number of studies dealing with computer-aided decision making and, in laboratory settings, it has been found that better decisions are achieved with this type of assistance than by unaided decision making.

The Decision-Making Process

Most ideas about how decision making occurs fall into two classes—either they are very general or highly abstract. In either case, they tend to be irrelevant to many of the real decision problems.

Schrenk (1969) has presented a detailed, although admittedly tentative, definition of an idealized decision process. Because it represents a model that is neither too general nor too abstract, we will consider it in some detail. The model is divided into three phases consisting of the problem recognition phase, the problem diagnosis phase, and the action selection phase. Each of the three phases is further made up of a number of steps. In considering the phases of Schrenk's decision-making model, we will be concerned primarily with the final, or *action selection* phase.

Problem Recognition Phase

This phase of the decision-making process determines whether a problem requiring a decision actually exists. There are four steps in this phase, which include the receipt of information input, consideration of the decision maker's own objectives in light of the information received, the perception of the need for a decision, and finally an assessment of the problem urgency and importance.

Problem Diagnosis Phase

During this phase, which includes nine steps, the individual determines and evaluates the situation that is producing the problem. Much of this phase is concerned with deciding whether more information is needed, reevaluating the information and, on this basis, reevaluating hypotheses, and so forth.

Action Selection Phase

The action selection phase of the decision model, as the name implies, includes the steps that are required by the decision maker in choosing a course of action. Figure 8–5, which is a conceptual model of the action selection process, shows that the process is rather lengthy and consists of seventeen steps. It will be necessary to refer to this figure frequently during the brief discussion of these steps.

You will note that there are two inputs. In one case, the input is the process labeled as "define action goals." This is the input from the previous phases of the model that raises the question "Given the situation, what must be done?" The objectives and alternatives that were developed in the previous phase may be too broad. Consequently, this step provides for establishing subordinate objectives that are still consistent with the broader objective. The other input shown on the figure is the "operating doctrine input." This input provides the type of information that is necessary for a person to take action in situations that are guided by operating rules or doctrine.

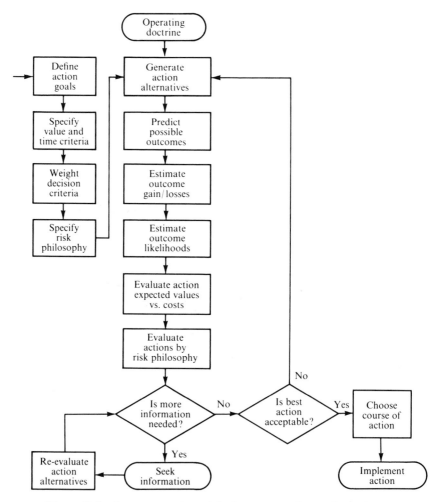

Figure 8-5. A conceptual model of a process for action selection in decision making. Refer to the text for a discussion of the various steps involved in the model. From Schrenk, L. P., Aiding the decision maker—a process model. *Ergonomics,* 1969, vol. 12, No. 4, 543–557. Reprinted by permission of the author and the publisher, Taylor and Francis, LTD., London.

After defining action goals, the next step is to specify value and time criteria. Since goals are usually multidimensional, relevant dimensions and time factors that may limit alternatives must be specified and these criteria must be "weighed." On the basis of these two steps, the decision maker must specify his *risk philosophy;* he must select an alternative based on all the possible outcomes. Thus, "should one choose an alternative which provides the possibility of a very desirable result along with some risk of a disastrous outcome or should one choose a more conservative, safer course of action? This question, which is basic and often perplexing, has been the subject of considerable concern to decision theorists" (Schrenk, 1969, p. 553).

The next step is to generate action alternatives. Frequently, there are a number of possible alternative actions, and the definition of what can be considered as a "reasonable" set may present problems. As Schrenk points out, care must be taken not to generate too many alternatives and overload the decision maker. Typically, however, the decision maker tends to consider too few courses of action rather than too many. After generating action alternatives, the possible outcomes of all of the alternatives must be predicted, each must be considered in terms of possible gains and losses, and the probabilities of the various outcomes occurring are estimated. At this point, the expected value for each action is arrived at and compared against the "cost" of the action. The expected value of an action is reduced by the estimated "cost" that is expected if the action is taken. The person is then prepared to evaluate the alternative actions based on his previously established "risk philosophy." The decision maker may then decide that he needs more information or that he has enough information in order to forecast action outcomes.

At this step, then, if the decision maker decides he needs more information, he seeks the information and reevaluates action alternatives. If he decides that enough information is available, he must then decide if the course of action is acceptable. As Schrenk points out:

> As a final check, the course of action which seems most desirable should be reviewed to ensure that it satisfies the desired goals and value criteria and to determine if the expected gain is worth the cost of action. There should also be a check to ensure that any possible adverse consequences can be accepted or avoided. If not, then some new alternative may have to be developed [p. 554].

As can be seen from Figure 8–5, if the course of action is not acceptable, then the process can be started again at the step at which action alternatives are generated. If, however, the action is acceptable, then the course of action is selected. It is at this point that the "decision" occurs, usually resulting in an irrevocable commitment of resources.

The final step in this model is the implementation of the action. Included in this step is defining the procedures for carrying out

the action, communicating the decision to other components of the
system that will execute it, taking precautions against potential adverse outcomes, providing for information feedback, and monitoring the progress of action (Schrenk, p. 554).

This discussion represents a rather cursory overview of an
interesting decision process model. The model, as Schrenk points
out, is tentative and needs further development, particularly to in-
corporate additional data on human decision processes. However, in
its present form the model can serve as a useful guide in structuring
the decision-making tasks in many kinds of man-machine systems.

In recent years, research in the area of decision processes
has been applied to the problems of sensory psychophysics. The theory of signal detectability incorporates decision theory with psychophysics and represents a more powerful approach to psychophysical
data than do the classical techniques. Because of the current importance of signal-detection theory, we will consider this area in some
detail.

Theory of Signal Detectability

Two factors are involved in a human subject's response to
stimuli in a psychophysical experiment—the subject's sensitivity
to the amount of stimulus energy and his decisions about that stimulus energy. The subject's sensitivity is of interest in terms of establishing sensory thresholds. The classical theory of sensory psychophysics, which was discussed in Chapter 2, assumes that the human
sensory system works in an all-or-none manner. That is, if a stimulus is below threshold in value, it will not produce a sensation;
similarly, with the difference threshold, if a second stimulus is not
the required amount greater than the first it will not be detected as
being different. The variations in threshold level from trial to trial
in the same observer are explained in terms of chance variations in
attentiveness or transient differences in the state of the sensory system from moment to moment. To handle these variations the classical theory utilizes the various psychophysical methods to yield average threshold values.

This first approach ignores or attempts to "average out" a
second aspect of the subject's response, which is his decision, based
on stimulus information available to him, whether a stimulus has
been presented (in the case of the absolute threshold situation), or
whether two stimuli are different (in the difference threshold task).
However, a new theoretical position, which first appeared in 1954

(Peterson, Birdsall, & Fox, 1954; Van Meter & Middleton, 1954), has given sensory psychologists a means of treating both aspects of a subject's response to stimuli of various intensities. This *theory of signal detectability* (TSD), is based on statistical decision theory and principles of electrical engineering. This theory distinguishes between the sensitivity of an observer and the decision-making process associated with his response to a stimulus. It suggests that psychologists should attempt to measure *response thresholds* rather than *sensory thresholds*. Before examining the concept of a response threshold, however, let us briefly put this theory in context.

Signal vs. Noise

TSD was originally designed for situations in which the observer's job was to detect weak *signals* (meaningful stimuli) in a background of *noise* (irrelevant stimulation). Such tasks are usually referred to in psychological jargon as *detection tasks* or, more generally, *vigilance tasks*. An example of such a task, and a situation which prompted some of the initial research in this area, is the task of a radar operator whose job is to recognize small "blips" on his screen (which represent the positions of aircraft) and to discriminate these signals (meaningful blips) from a background of nonmeaningful visual noise (interference or "snow" on the radar screen). Of course, in order to recognize the meaningful blips from the visual noise, it is necessary that the signal be physically different from the noise. This difference might be in intensity levels between signal and noise, shape, and so on. In situations of this type, the observer must decide, during a given time interval, if noise alone is present on his display or whether a signal accompanies the noise. It may be helpful to conceptualize this situation graphically as in Figure 8–6. The circle at the left in this figure represents the stimulus situation consisting of noise alone, and the circle on the right represents a stimulus situation of signal plus noise. The shaded area represents the overlap of the two stimulus situations—that is, a condition that might arise from noise alone or from signal plus noise. X_1 in this figure is a single observation made by a subject during a given time interval. This observation is drawn from the noise distribution, and we would expect the subject to say "no" if asked whether or not a signal was present. On the other hand, X_2 is an observation drawn from the pure signal-plus-noise area and we would expect the subject to report "yes, a signal is present." The situation is much more ambiguous in observation X_3 however. In this case, the observation might be from the noise area or it might be

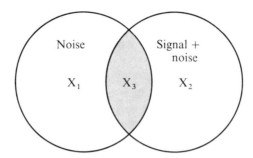

Figure 8–6. **A** simplified model of the noise, and signal-plus-noise distributions. Observation X_1 is from the noise distribution, X_2 is from the signal-plus-noise distribution, and X_3 may be from either.

from the signal-plus-noise area, and we need to know more about the way an observer makes his "yes" or "no" decisions to determine whether or not he would report a signal to be present.

Although TSD originated in research on detection tasks, in which noise competed with the signal for the subject's attention, the theory is also applicable to typical psychophysical experiments, in which noise may not be specifiable in physical terms. It may be helpful to consider noise as representing any background within which a signal stimulus may occur. Thus, noise may in some instances be extraneous stimuli which are sometimes confused with the signal, and at other times it may just be "static" in the sensory system, not due to specifiable stimuli.

The observer's task, in terms of TSD, is to decide upon the basis of stimuli presented to him and a rule for making decisions, whether a given observation (X) is from the noise distribution or the signal-plus-noise distribution.

The Decision Rule

The fundamental signal detection problem is often referred to as a yes-no experiment (Coombs, Dawes, & Tversky, 1970). In this situation there are two possible stimulus situations that may form the content of an observation: noise alone present, or signal plus noise present. Similarly, there are two possible responses for the subject to make. In such a situation, four outcomes are possible on a given experimental trial. These outcomes are summarized in the *payoff matrix* in Figure 8–7.

Two of the four cells in this matrix represent correct decisions on the part of the observer; if he says "yes" when a signal is

Subject's Response

	Yes	No
Signal	hit +	miss −
Noise	false alarm −	correct rejection +

Figure 8–7. The signal detection payoff matrix showing the types and values of outcomes as a function of the observer's response (yes or no) and the true situation (signal or noise).

present in addition to noise, he has made a correct decision; and if he says "no" when the observation is from the noise distribution, he is also right. In the language of TSD, the first of these correct decisions is referred to as a *hit*, and the second as a *correct rejection*. On the other hand, there are also two possible types of errors indicated in this matrix. The first error, called a *miss*, occurs when the observer says "no" when a signal is present. The second type of error is a *false alarm*, which occurs when the subject reports "yes" when the observation is from the noise distribution.

Unlike classical sensory psychophysics, TSD takes into account the value associated with each type of an outcome and the probability, or chance, that a signal might occur. The value consideration is reflected in the name which is given to the matrix in Figure 8–7, the *payoff matrix*. Correct responses—a hit or a correct rejection—are associated with a positive value. Negative values are, however, associated with false alarms and misses. In some tasks, such as a laboratory experiment, the cost, or size of the negative value, for false alarms and misses may be equal. In this case it is no worse to report a signal present when it is not than to report that no signal is present when in fact a signal is present. In practical detection tasks, however, different values are often attached to the two types of errors. For example, if the "blips" the radar operator is trying to detect on his radar scope represent enemy planes flying bombing missions, there will certainly be different costs associated with the two types of errors. If he makes a false-alarm error, the cost may be the expense of "scrambling" interceptor aircraft for a futile search. On the other hand, if he misses a signal, the cost may be the destruction of a city. It is obvious in this situation that the operator will try to adopt a decision-making rule that will be more likely to yield false alarms than misses. Thus, the value of an outcome is taken into account by TSD as a variable which may have an effect upon the subject's willingness to make one or another type of response.

In addition to considering the value of the various outcomes of a response, TSD also makes provision for the probability, or chance, that a given observation will be from the noise or signal-plus-noise distributions. In the language of TSD, the observer is able to compute a *likelihood ratio* upon which he will base his decisions. The likelihood ratio reflects the amount of confidence an observer has that a given observation is from the signal-plus-noise distribution, divided by the certainty that it is from the noise-alone distribution. TSD assumes that the observer, based upon stimulus information he receives in his observation, can compute a probability that signal plus noise is present. If the observer did not really know which was present, he would, for instance, calculate that there was a 50 percent chance that noise alone had occurred and similarly a 50 percent chance that signal plus noise had occurred (the sum of the two probabilities must equal 100 percent). In this case, a likelihood ratio of 1 would result (.50/.50). Likelihood ratios larger than 1 occur, however, if the observer computes the chance of signal plus noise as being greater than the chance of noise alone. On the other hand, a likelihood ratio of less than 1 indicates that the observer's estimate of the chance that a signal has occurred is less than the probability that noise alone was presented. For example, a likelihood ratio of .25 indicates that for a given task the observer was 80 percent sure that noise alone had occurred; while a likelihood ratio of 4 would indicate that the observer was 80 percent sure that signal plus noise had occurred.

In classical sensory psychophysics it might be assumed that any time the likelihood ratio was greater than 1, the observer would report that a signal had been presented. TSD, however, makes provision for the influence of other factors on the observer's judgment and provides a more precise treatment of his decisions relative to "yes" and "no" responses.

The Response Threshold

According to TSD, the prior odds and the payoff matrix determine a *response threshold* which is usually designated as β. The response threshold represents a criterion level that separates "yes" from "no" responses in a signal detection task. β is calculated in

TSD by multiplying the prior odds of a signal occurring by the relative value of a hit or correct rejection as opposed to a miss or false alarm. The prior odds represent the overall chance or probability that a signal will occur on a given trial. It is assumed by the theory of signal detectability that the observer, after exposure to several trials, will figure out the basic chance of a signal being present; or in some instances he will be told that 20 percent of the trials, for example, will be from the signal-plus-noise distribution. For those interested in the mathematics of the response threshold the following equation is calculated by the subject:

$$\beta = p(n) \,/\, p(s) \times [(V_{c.r.} + V_{f.a.} \,/\, V_{hit} + V_{miss})].$$

In this formula, $p(n)/p(s)$ is the prior odds and represents the ratio of the chance of noise alone to the chance of signal plus noise ($p(s)$ = probability of signal). The term at the right of this equation is calculated from the payoff matrix. $V_{c.r.}$ is the value associated with a correct rejection, $V_{f.a.}$ is the value, or cost, of a false alarm, V_{hit} is the value of a hit, and V_{miss} is the cost of a miss. The numerator of this expression is often referred to as the *importance of noise* and the denominator as the *importance of signal*. β represents a number, calculated by the subject, which takes into account the prior odds, or relative chance of receiving a signal, and the relative costs associated with the possible outcomes of the observer's decision (hit *vs.* miss; correct rejection *vs.* false alarm). According to TSD, the observer will, on every trial, calculate the likelihood ratio and β, and compare the two values. If the likelihood ratio is greater than the response threshold, he will say "yes, a signal was presented," and if it is smaller than β, he will say "no, a signal was not presented."

According to the concept of the response threshold, if the prior odds are 1 (signal and noise are equally probable) and the values in the payoff matrix are equal, the observer will respond "yes" whenever the likelihood ratio is greater than 1, and "no" otherwise. It is possible, however, that β may be either less than or greater than 1 if the chance of noise or if the values for various outcomes are different (as in the case of the radar operator attempting to detect enemy bombers). In these cases the observer's judgment will be influenced both by his degree of confidence that a signal has been presented (likelihood ratio) and by the response threshold.

The ROC Curve

In the "yes-no" type of experiment we have been discussing, there are basically two types of measures that describe an individual's performance. The first measure is the proportion of "yes" responses on trials that contain a signal; this represents the hit rate. The second measure is the number of "yes" responses when noise alone was present and, from this, the false-alarm rate is calculated. Ordinarily a signal detection experiment will consist of several series of trials, with each new series requiring the observer to adopt a different response threshold. The response threshold (β) is altered, as you recall, by either changing the chance that a signal will be present (prior odds) or by changing the payoff matrix. Each trial within a series will then physically contain either signal or noise, and the intensity of the signal, on those trials which contain one, may vary from strong to weak.

The performance of an observer in a signal detection experiment of this type is usually described by drawing a *receiver operating characteristic* (*ROC*) curve. To construct a ROC curve, the hit rate is plotted against the false-alarm rate for each of the series of trials conducted with different response thresholds. The hit rate is, once again, the percentage of "yes" responses when a signal was present, and the false-alarm rate is the percentage of "yes" responses when noise alone was present. Figure 8–8 illustrates a ROC curve.

Point 1 on this curve represents a situation in which β, the response threshold, is very high and in which the observer is unwilling to say "yes" unless he is very sure (the likelihood ratio is very high) that a signal has occurred. In this case, both the hit rate and the false-alarm rate are low. This type of situation could arise if false alarms were very costly, or if the chance of a signal occurring was very low. Point 2 on Figure 8–8 represents a more neutral response threshold situation. In this case β may be equal to 1, or the situation is such that both misses and false alarms are equally costly and the chance of a signal is about the same as the chance of noise. In this case, the hit rate is slightly higher than the false-alarm rate. Point 3, on the other hand, represents a β level of a trigger-happy observer. In this situation, the response threshold is very low, either due to a high chance of a signal being present or to a high value of a hit and a small cost of a false alarm. This means that the observer makes a "yes" response on most of the trials.

A Measure of Sensitivity

Psychologists using the theory of signal detectability have been able to arrive at a statistical index which represents the sensitivity of an observer. This index is called d' and is obtained by con-

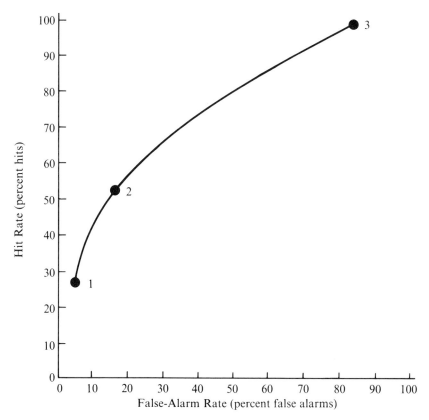

Figure 8–8. A hypothetical ROC curve. Points 1 to 3 represent decreasing values of the response threshold.

sulting appropriate statistical tables (Swets, 1964). Although a complete description of the mathematics involved in calculating d' is beyond the scope of this book, basically what this number represents is the shape of the ROC curve over various β values. In Figure 8–8, we indicated that the points representing the relationship between hit rate and false-alarm rate correspond to different β levels, and that β became smaller as we moved from left to right on this graph (point 1 represents a larger response threshold than point 2, and point 2 a larger β than point 3). The mathematical operations that are taken into account in determining d' involve the relationship between hit rate and false-alarm rate. The index of sensitivity (d') becomes larger as the observer becomes more sensitive to the presence of a signal, which can be seen graphically in the shape of the ROC curve. Figure 8–9 illustrates two theoretical ROC curves from two subjects who differed in their sensitivity. The first curve is

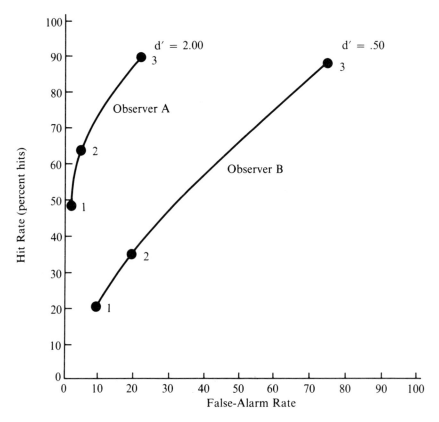

Figure 8-9. Two hypothetical ROC curves which illustrate different levels of sensitivity between observers A and B. The sensitivity index (*d'*) increases as sensitivity increases.

much steeper than the second, and it can be seen that as the response threshold changed (β is largest at point 1 and smallest at point 3) the more sensitive observer's hit rate increased faster than his false-alarm rate. Observer B responded with a higher percentage of hits at the smaller response threshold levels but also committed an increasing number of false alarms.

TSD thus provides two measures of the observer's performance. The response threshold (β) indicates the decision factors involved in judgments, while the sensitivity index (*d'*) allows a measurement of observer sensitivity independent of β.

Applications of TSD

The theory of signal detectability has been utilized in most situations that were previously investigated with the methods of classical sensory psychophysics. Most of the sensations that humans respond to have been explored with TSD, and it has been found that more consistent results are obtained with TSD than the methods of sensory psychophysics when different senses are investigated.

Perhaps the most outstanding advantage of TSD over the classical methods of threshold determination lies in the capacity of TSD to take into account, and to measure, both the observer's sensitivity to signal stimuli and the decision processes that are involved in an observer's judgments. Classical psychophysics can provide a measure of sensitivity in terms of the sensory threshold, but it cannot separate this measure from the response threshold that the subject may use on different trials. If the observer operates with a low response threshold (β), his sensory threshold will appear to be very low (he says "yes" most of the time whether a signal is present or not—his false-alarm rate is high). On the other hand, if he operates with a high β, his sensory threshold will appear to be very high, since he will be cautious about saying "yes" and will try to avoid false alarms. All the classical approach can do is to average out the differences, or attempt to correct the data for guessing, but it cannot separate the response threshold from the sensitivity of the observer (Corso, 1967).

"Risky" Decisions

An important step in the decision-making process is the specification of a *risk philosophy*. Basically, the decision is determined by the decision maker's answer to two questions that he asks himself: what is at stake, and what are the odds? Generally, the person is able to assess what is at stake quite accurately. On the other hand, a person's assessment of odds, or probabilities, is often not influenced sufficiently by the available evidence. Thus, a person combines his assessment of the odds, or probabilities, with his estimation of the stakes when he makes his decision. Depending upon the relationship of "odds" and "stakes," the decision can be more or less "risky."

Risky decision making has been studied by means of research ranging from abstract laboratory investigations to studies in operational systems. Typically, however, studies of risk-taking behavior have taken one of two general directions. Many studies have dealt with the parameters of the risky situation that affect a subject's decision, while others have included consideration of personality variables. Variables involved in studies of risky situations have included, among others, the effects of different levels of probability of an outcome occurring, whether the outcome is dependent upon skill or chance, whether the subject receives feedback concerning the results of his actions, and the amount of "payoff" that is involved. Almost all of these variables have been shown to influence decision making.

In those investigations that have combined the relationship of personality variables and risk taking in addition to the above-mentioned variables, findings have come in conflict. Some investigators report relationships, while others report negative findings. Other studies have dealt with the difference between risky decisions based on group decisions and individual decisions. These studies have shown that there is often a tendency for a group to take greater risks than members of the groups would take on their own. This has been called the *risky shift* (Wallach & Kogan, 1965).

Even though there is a considerable amount of research literature dealing with risk-taking behavior, we actually know very little about this kind of behavior in everyday activities. For example, consider an activity that most of you engage in every day—driving a car. In the course of a short drive, you make a number of decisions, some of them that could be considered risky. What variables are involved when you abruptly decide to pass a car on a hill without knowledge of whether another car may be coming over the hill? What kind of processes influence your decision when you get behind the wheel after a half dozen beers or mixed drinks?

One can discuss this type of behavior in terms of decision-making variables, but, as it turns out, they do not have much meaning in this case. Thus, in decision making, one assumes that the person "weighs" the odds and stakes. If the stakes are low and the odds of an undesirable outcome are high, then the individual will select an alternative course of action, if one is available. At best, when a dangerous driving decision is made, there is a small probability of a very great penalty and a high certainty of a small gain. Thus, by passing the car on a hill without a clear view ahead, there is a small possibility that you might be killed—a severe penalty to most people. The gain, in this case, would be a few minutes saved. In many instances, the probability of a severe penalty is much greater and the dangerous decision is still made. The question, of course, is why? Unfortunately, we do not have very good answers to this question.

As you might expect, risk-taking behavior is of particular interest to those who are involved in accident-prevention research. While we still know very little about the relationship between risky decisions and the event that we label as an accident, research in this area is beginning to shed some light on the many factors that may be involved in decisions that lead to accidents. For example, in order to weigh the outcome of a course of action, one must understand the risk involved in pursuing the particular course of action. This requires that some evaluation of the risk factor be made. The question, however, is whether people are always equipped to make this evaluation. For example, a child might not perceive a situation as being risky, while an adult, based on a considerable amount of past experience, might recognize the risk. Recently, in our laboratory, this problem was subjected to systematic research (Martin, 1970).

In this study, the manner in which children of various ages perceived the amount of risk or hazard in a variety of situations was determined. As might be expected, a number of variables were found to influence the degree of risk involved in different situations. For example, children from low socioeconomic backgrounds perceived certain situations as involving more or less risk than did children from higher socioeconomic backgrounds. Differences were also found between sexes as well as between rural and urban backgrounds. The age of the child was also an important variable. There is some indication that the way a child perceives hazard or risk may be related to the probability that he will have an accident at some time or another. Other studies along these lines promise to yield more information about risk-taking decisions in everyday behavior.

Thinking

Symbols, concepts, problem solving, and decision making are all aspects of the process that we label as thinking. However, there are other points concerning thinking, some of which we will briefly discuss in this section.

Kinds of Thinking

Some people consider the process of thinking to range between two ends of a continuum—*autistic* thinking and *realistic* thinking. Autistic thinking is the type of thinking that is largely determined by personal desires or needs and is relatively unaffected by conditions external to the person. At the extreme end of the autistic-realistic continuum is dreaming, in which environmental factors are reduced to a minimum and autistic determinants can exert their full force, so to speak. Fantasy and wishful thinking are other examples of autistic thinking.

In this chapter, in dealing with problem solving and decision making, we have emphasized realistic thinking. This type of thinking is determined almost exclusively by external or "realistic" factors. A situation that a person is exposed to presents certain objective requirements, on which realistic thinking is based. Actually, most thinking falls between the two ends of the autistic-realistic continuum, in that there is an interplay of autistic and realistic factors involved in the thinking. Thus, realistic thinking can be, and often is, distorted by personal desires and needs, while autistic thinking can be brought about by problems that are real and correctly perceived by the individual.

Some Physiological Correlates of Thinking

While we generally consider thinking an "invisible" process, researchers have been interested for many years in whether there are movements or physiological changes that are visible or that can be measured when thinking takes place. While a number of studies have been conducted in this area, we know a great deal more about *what* a person can do in the way of thinking than we know about the physiological correlates associated with thinking.

In man, the thinking that we know about depends upon the cerebral cortex, although, as we stated previously, the lower centers of the brain are necessary for the cortex to function.

A variety of investigations have shown that when certain areas of the cortex are damaged or destroyed, thinking suffers. However, while this tells us that the cortex is responsible for the deficit in thinking, it does not tell us what activity of the brain is responsible for thinking. Other types of studies have attempted to correlate electrical activity of the brain and thinking with varying degrees of success. We know, for example, that there are some characteristic electrical patterns associated with vivid imagery and other patterns with abstract thought. In recent years, a number of studies have been conducted which deal with electrophysiological correlates of learning. Most of these studies have attempted to establish a relationship between certain patterns of brain waves (EEG) and learning. However, as Grossman (1967) points out: "Although the many EEG studies of the past 25 years have provided much provocative and interesting information, no clear relation between specific electrophysiological response patterns and the conditioning process has become evident" (p. 670). Thus, while we can be quite certain that the cortex is a critical element in the thinking process, just how it functions in this role is not so certain.

In addition to the cortical activity that is involved during thinking, thinking also involves slight movements of groups of muscles. For example, when we think of a word, there are minute muscular responses that are similar to the movements we make when actually speaking the word. There is a general increase in muscular tone, and the more concentrated the thinking, the greater the general muscular tension. While the muscle tension is often recorded in muscles that are related to the content of the thought, this is not always the case, and, frequently, tension is found in specific muscles that are completely unrelated to the thought.

While an increase in muscle tone has been found to be associated with thinking, it has also been shown that muscle tension will facilitate thinking. For example, it was found in one study that learning of nonsense syllables was facilitated when muscular tension was introduced by having the subject squeeze a spring-loaded grip. However, it would appear that artificially induced tension works only up to a point since it was also found that if the subjects squeezed as hard as they could on the grip, memorization performance dropped below normal. Other studies have shown that action potentials can be found, as well as microscopic muscle contractions, in muscles that subjects are told to imagine are moving. Other lines of experimental evidence have also shown that thinking is accompanied by muscular contraction.

The System So Far

Because of the nature of the functioning of the interpreting subsystem of man, the human is capable of a variety of responses that are more elaborate and complex than those of other animals. It is the capability of this particular subsystem, then, that distinguishes man from other animals. The interpreting subsystem is responsible for all of the higher level mental processes, such as thinking, decision making, problem solving, and the other cognitive processes that are so important to man.

We have seen that a stimulus situation must be identified (perceived) before it can be interpreted. Thus, the interpretation subsystem is dependent upon an input from the identifying subsystem. We have also seen that interpreting is dependent upon an input from the memory subsystem. Although in this chapter we have not stressed the importance of the energizing subsystem in relation to the interpreting function, this subsystem also furnishes an important input. As can be seen from Figure 8–10, the interpreting subsystem in turn has feedback loops to all of these subsystems and thus will influence their functioning and capabilities.

In this chapter we have not considered all of the functions of the interpreting subsystem but have dealt with several of the more important ones. We have seen how the interpreting subsystem makes use of symbols and concepts and that the manipulation of symbols and concepts form the basis for most of the functions of this subsystem. Two particularly important functions—decision making and problem solving—were discussed in some detail. While there is

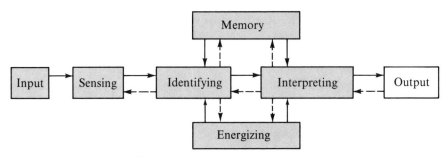

Figure 8-10. **The** system so far.

some question as to just how the interpreting subsystem "handles" these functions, no one questions the significance of these functions in our everyday existence.

Summary

1. Symbols and concepts form the groundwork for all of the cognitive processes that are associated with the interpreting subsystem. Symbols are stimuli which, because of learning, have come to represent something else. Symbols can be "external," involving a sensory input from the external world, or they can be "internal." An image is an example of a symbol that is generated internally by a person.

2. Concepts permit a person to react to stimuli as a collection rather than individually. When a person acquires a concept, he is developing the capability of making a common reaction to a collection of things that have some common property. There are different kinds of concepts, such as conjunctive, relational, and disjunctive concepts.

3. Attempts at understanding the problem-solving process have involved a number of different approaches. These approaches range from presenting a subject with puzzles or problems and

determining how he solves them to computerized approaches that attempt to build "models" of the problem-solving process.

4. The problem-solving process is often thought to consist of stages. Typical stages that are thought to be involved are those of preparation, incubation, inspiration, and verification. Other problem-solving models have somewhat different stages. Some investigators in this field would argue that problem solving can be considered without resorting to stages models of any kind.

5. Decision making is the interpreting function that leads to the selection of a response from among a number of known alternative responses. It involves the "weighing" of alternative responses in terms of their desirabilities and potential costs or payoffs. There are a number of models of decision making that have been developed. A three-stage model of decision making was considered in this chapter, including (1) the problem recognition phase, (2) the problem diagnosis phase, and (3) the action selection phase. Each of these phases consists of a number of steps.

6. The theory of signal detectability provides a method of studying psychophysical relationships which has distinct advantages over classical techniques of sensory psychophysics. TSD allows the investigator to distinguish between the sensitivity of an observer and the decision processes that influence his judgments.

Selected Readings

Coombs, C. H., Dawes, R. M., & Tversky, A. *Mathematical psychology: An elementary introduction.* Englewood Cliffs, New Jersey: Prentice-Hall, 1970.

Edwards, W. Information processing, decision making, and highway safety. In J. O'Day (Ed.), *Driver behavior—cause and effect.* Washington, D.C.: Insurance Institute for Highway Safety, 1968, 165–180.

Gagné, R. M. Human problem solving: Internal and external events. In B. Kleinmuntz (Ed.), *Problem solving: Research, method, and theory.* New York: Wiley, 1966, 128–148.

Green, B. F. Current trends in problem solving. In B. Kleinmuntz (Ed.), *Problem solving: Research, method, and theory.* New York: Wiley, 1966, 3–18.

Manis, M. *An introduction to cognitive psychology.* Monterey, California: Brooks/Cole, 1971.

Phillips, J. L. *The origins of intellect: Piaget's theory.* San Francisco: W. H. Freeman, 1969.

Schrenk, L. P. Aiding the decision maker—a decision process model. *Ergonomics*, 1969, **12**, 543–557.

9

The Output
of the System

In the preceding chapters, we have dealt with how an input to the system can be transformed by means of the various behavioral subsystems. This chapter is concerned with the end result of the transformation process—that is, the *output* of the system. The output of our human system, which is based on the interactions and outputs of the various behavioral subsystems we have discussed, is *behavior*. Broadly defined, behavior refers not only to the observable physical reactions and responses (motor behavior or motor responses) of people but also to mental reactions and responses, which are more difficult to observe and measure.

Think for a moment of all the "things" you do or are capable of doing. Obviously, a complete description of this continuing stream of activity cannot be accomplished in one chapter. Consequently, the present chapter will be concerned primarily with motor responses, although verbal behavior as a form of system output will also be considered. In dealing with the processes of thinking and problem solving in the previous chapter, we were in fact dealing with kinds of behavior that are also considered as outputs of the system. As a matter of fact, it is the superior ability of the human behavioral subsystems to make transformations necessary for these kinds of outputs that distinguish the human from other animals.

Figure 9-1. A representation of the somatic nervous system.

Even though we have greatly limited the range of human behavior by restricting ourselves to motor responses, there is still a vast repertoire of behavior included within this category. These responses range from discrete and finely coordinated movements involving just a few muscles to gross movements utilizing much of the body's muscular capabilities. Contrast, for example, the motor responses required of a watch repairman and those required of a fullback.

In order for motor responses to take place, the relevant muscles must receive nerve impulses from the central nervous system. The neural and muscular components that are responsible for the motor responses are considered part of the somatic nervous system that was discussed in Chapter 3. You will recall that the somatic nervous system was conceptualized as consisting of a number of subsystems as shown in Figure 9-1. In earlier chapters, the subsystems involving the receptors, afferent (sensory) fibers, and central processing were covered in some detail. However, in discussing the neural and muscular basis for motor responses, we are primarily interested in part of the central processing subsystem and the subsystems made up of the efferent fibers and effectors. These make up the *motor system,* as contrasted to the *sensory system.*

The Motor System

When we speak of the "motor system" of man, we are referring to several neural and muscular components, or subsystems, that are responsible for the various motor responses of which man is capable. At a different level of analysis, the motor system itself can be considered as a subsystem within the schema that have been utilized in the previous chapters. For our purposes, we will define the motor system as consisting of a particular type of muscles, called *striated muscles* (effectors), the nerves that innervate these effectors, and various structures of the spinal cord and brain. Before discussing these latter structures, we will first consider the effectors and their innervation.

Effectors

The term *effectors* generally encompasses all organs of response and, as such, refers to both muscles and glands. Further, there are several varieties of muscles and glands. There are the *striated*, or *skeletal*, muscles, whose contractions result in movement. There are also *smooth muscles*, which are located in the visceral organs of the body, and highly specialized muscles that make up the heart. The three major types of muscle fiber are shown in Figure 9–2. We will limit our discussion of effectors to striated muscles, although it should be remembered that glands are also of great importance as effectors.

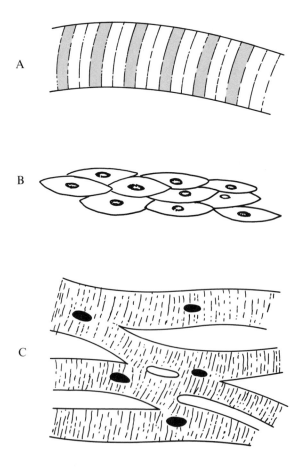

Figure 9–2. The three major types of muscle fibers. These are striated muscle (A), smooth muscle (B), and heart muscle (C).

The smallest independent units of skeletal muscle are called striated fibers. These fibers are specialized to contract; when they are stimulated by a nerve impulse, they become shorter and thicker. The fibers are referred to as "striated" because, when viewed through a microscope, they look like they consist of alternating dark and light bands. A skeletal muscle is made up of a large number of these striated fibers gathered together in a bundle. It is because of these muscles, working together or in opposition, that the diverse movements of our body and limbs are possible.

All of the striated muscle movements are controlled by nerve impulses that come from either the *motor neurons* of the spinal cord or by means of the *cranial nerves.* A motor neuron has its cell body in the ventral horn of the spinal cord (see Figure 9–3), but it synapses with other neurons, including those that convey impulses from the brain. In turn, these motor neurons are responsible for innervating the muscles and causing them to respond by contracting. While the motor neurons are located in the spinal cord, there are other nerves that enter and leave the brain rather than the spinal cord. There are twelve of these cranial nerves, and some of them are

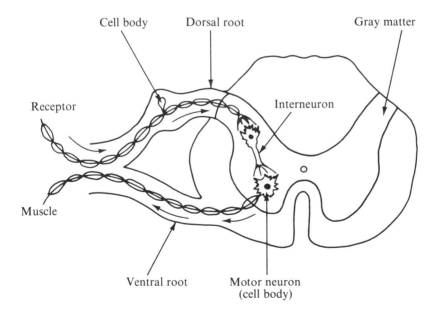

Figure 9–3. A schematic of a simple sensory-motor arc. Note the sensory (afferent) neuron with its short axon and long dendrite, a short interneuron, and a motor (efferent) neuron with its cell body in the ventral horn of the spinal cord.

responsible for the movements that are associated with the head, face, and mouth. While we are primarily concerned with the muscles as effectors, it should be remembered that sensory information is also transmitted to the central nervous system from muscles. Thus, there are receptors located in the muscles that are sensitive to various stimuli, and information (feedback) from these receptors helps give us a comprehensive picture of the state of our environment. Because these receptors are particularly important in relaying information about movement of the muscles, they are very critical in precise and coordinated movements. This type "feedback" will be discussed in more detail later in this chapter.

Motor Units

Although the cell bodies of the motor neurons are located in the spinal cord, axons from these neurons go out to various muscles of the body. Prior to reaching a muscle, however, the axon divides into a number of *axon fibrils* which, in turn, terminate upon a muscle fiber. Recall that a muscle is made up of a number of muscle fibers. Because of the manner in which a single axon divides into a number of fibrils, a single motor neuron may innervate a large number of muscle fibers. A *motor unit* is defined as a single motor neuron and the muscle fibers that it innervates. In some cases, a single motor neuron may innervate only a few muscle fibers, while in other cases a large number of fibers may be innervated by a single axon. In the former case, we say that the axon has a low *innervation ratio*, while in the latter situation there is a high innervation ratio. These ratios are important because an impulse in an axon with a high innervation ratio will result in a relatively large muscle contraction, while one with a low innervation ratio will produce only a small contraction. We find the large innervation ratios associated with the large muscles that are involved in walking and gross movements, while the ratio is low in the small muscles required for fine, delicate movements.

Innervation of Muscle Fibers

The point at which an axon fibril terminates on a muscle fiber is called a *neuromuscular junction*. Each nerve fibril terminates at a specialized region of the muscle fiber called the *end plate*. The events that take place at the neuromuscular junction which transform a nerve impulse into a muscle contraction are complex and beyond the scope of this book. In brief, when the nerve impulse arrives, it brings about the release of a chemical substance which is stored in tiny vesicles at the nerve ending. Release of this chemical, which is called acetylcholine (ACh), is followed by an active process whereby the ACh acts on the surface of the muscle fiber. The end result is that the muscle fiber is activated and contracts. The muscle fiber has its own supply of energy, and the nerve impulse only "triggers" the response of the fiber. Another chemical, acetylcholine esterase (AChE), breaks down and deactivates the ACh. This results in a relaxation of the muscle following a period of contraction. Many studies have been conducted which show that compounds that block ACh will block neuromuscular transmission, while others that deactivate AChE will cause prolonged activation of muscle fibers because the ACh will continue to work. South American Indians have used one ACh-blocking chemical, curare, effectively as an arrow poison for hundreds of years. An animal hit by one of these arrows will be paralyzed in a very short period of time.

Although most of us have some idea of the force that can be exerted by muscles in pushing and pulling, we tend to underestimate just how much force can be developed by the human musculature. It has been estimated that if all the muscles in the human body, which contain about 2.7×10^8 individual fibers, were to exert their combined tension in the same direction, a force of at least 25 tons would be developed.

Motor Areas of the Cortex

The area of the cerebral cortex that has special importance in movement and motor functions is located mainly in front of, or anterior to, the central fissure. This area is called the motor and premotor area (see Figure 9–4). The location of the "primary" motor cortex has been known for over 100 years and was first demonstrated in a study by Fritsch and Hitzig (1870). These investigators showed that stimulation of this portion of the cerebral cortex of a dog elicited muscle movements on the opposite side of the body. Studies have also shown that electrical stimulation of the "premotor" area will generally produce body and limb movements that are somewhat more complex than those which are produced by stimulation of the primary motor area. Motor functions are also represented in the area of the cortex located behind the central fissure, which is called the somesthetic or somatic area. Thus, electrical stimulation of the primary somatic sensory area of the cortex will also elicit movement. For example, when the region of the sensory area representing the hand is stimulated, the hand moves. However, it has been

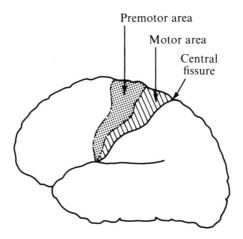

Figure 9–4. Diagram of brain showing general location of the motor and premotor areas. There are no sharp lines of demarcation between these areas and this figure merely illustrates their approximate locations.

shown that a considerably stronger electrical stimulus is necessary to elicit movement by stimulation of the somatic sensory area than is the case when the motor or premotor areas are stimulated (Woolsey, 1958).

Actually, a number of other areas of the brain will elicit body movements when stimulated. In the normal animal, electrical stimulation of virtually any region of the cortex may result in movement. However, to refer to all such areas as "motor areas" would be somewhat absurd. It is more meaningful to use the term "motor area" to refer to those regions of the brain that are concerned with "output" and that have connections with the spinal and cranial nerves that connect with the effectors. With this limitation in mind, we can say that our interest is primarily with the motor and premotor area of the cortex.

Motor Pathways

Impulses arising in the neurons of the motor area of the cortex pass down through various efferent pathways, the result being movement of some part of the body. It should be pointed out that these impulses do not actually "originate" in the motor cortex since, presumably, the motor area must receive afferent impulses from somewhere else. Thus, it is probable that the neurons in the motor area do not spontaneously emit efferent impulses but instead act as "connectors" between afferent and efferent impulses.

Impulses sent out by the motor areas of the cortex descend by various pathways that are generally classified into two general groups—the *pyramidal* and *extrapyramidal tracts*. Impulses traveling through both of these tracts eventually converge upon lower motor neurons which, in turn, innervate the muscles. Thus, it was highly appropriate when Sherrington (1897) termed the motor neurons "the final common path."

We will not be overly concerned with the specific pathways followed by the nerve fibers in the pyramidal and extrapyramidal tracts. The fibers of the pyramidal system originate in the cortex and follow a rather direct route to the spinal cord. However, the route followed by the extrapyramidal fibers is more complex and involves synapses with various subcortical centers before influencing the motor neurons. While fibers from both the pyramidal and extrapyramidal tracts influence the activity of the motor neurons, they work in somewhat different ways. We find, for example, that pyramidal impulses are necessary for willed activation of the motor neurons and are essential for any type of voluntary movement. However, while impulses from the pyramidal fibers are sufficient to produce small, discrete movements, execution of large, coordinated movements also requires an input of extrapyramidal impulses. Thus, in general terms, the pyramidal system is important in the precise regulation of voluntary muscle control, while the extrapyramidal system serves to regulate more gross movements, of an automatic nature, which involve larger groups of muscles.

The Cerebellum

We have already briefly discussed the cerebellum in our discussion of the hindbrain in Chapter 3. Because of its importance in the coordination of muscular activity, we should now look at the cerebellum in more detail.

The current evidence indicates that the cerebellum is important in coordinating and timing the activity of various groups of muscle fibers. In order to accomplish this, the cerebellum requires input from all of the receptors concerned with position and movement of the body. In addition, since visual control of movement is very important, the cerebellum receives impulses from the eyes. Auditory impulses also reach the cerebellum.

In addition to the impulses from the various sensory pathways, the cerebellum receives many impulses from the cortex. Of considerable importance, however, is the fact that the cerebellum also sends impulses back to the motor cortex, which will tend to maintain or enhance the excitability of neurons in the cortex. In this fashion, the cerebellum can alter the rate of discharge of these neurons and, consequently, modify muscular activity. Output from the cerebellum can also act through other parts of the brain to alter the excitability of the motor neurons. The primary thing to remember about the cerebellum is that it serves to coordinate incoming sensory information with incoming motor information; and, through a complex arrangement of feedback loops, it helps to regulate and modify motor responses. Although at this point we are interested in the motor functions of the cerebellum, there is considerable evidence that this structure is also important for many visceral activities, such as respiration and control of blood pressure.

Motor Activities

The particular type of system output that we categorize as "motor behavior" is highly important to all of us in our everyday existence. Indeed, we only have to lose a small part of our motor capabilities through injury or disease to become aware of just how important they are to us. While some of the responses we make may be of more importance than others in interacting with our environment (such as responses involving the hands and vocal mechanisms), all responses of which we are capable can and do serve useful purposes. A statement made over 100 years ago by Sechenov is still applicable. He pointed out that "All the endless diversity of the external manifestations of the activity of the brain can be finally regarded as one phenomenon—that of muscular movement" (Sechenov, 1935). While there are some who would consider this an overstatement, it is worth keeping in mind in our discussion of human motor activity.

It is not possible to describe or even systematically categorize all of the motor responses that an individual is capable of making. As a matter of fact, a person may never make two responses that are exactly identical—that is, a given movement may never be repeated identically (Paillard, 1960). Obviously, at best, any attempt to comprehensively categorize all types of motor behavior will result in rather gross categories whose meaningfulness can be questioned. However, psychologists are frequently called upon to attempt to analyze motor responses that are required for successful performance of specific tasks, particularly in various man-machine systems. Depending upon the task, an analysis of this kind may require only gross descriptions of certain types of motor responses or a very detailed specification of responses. Often an analysis of this sort is necessary before a particular machine is built and, if the analysis is not conducted, problems develop later when human operators are placed in the system. The problems involved in designing equipment to best suit the human operator are discussed in Chapter 13.

In order to illustrate how certain types of behaviors that may be required of a human operator in a man-machine system can be categorized, we will consider a relatively comprehensive classification of behaviors. The classification scheme shown in Table 9–1, which was utilized as part of a study concerned with performance evaluation in simulated environments, classed specific behaviors under (1) perceptual, (2) mediational, (3) communications, and (4) motor processes (Berliner, Angell, & Shearer, 1964). While this particular scheme involves more than just motor behavior, it is presented in order to give an idea of one method of analyzing the behavior required of a human within a man-machine system. While other systems of categorizing behavior will differ in particular categories, typically the intent of any categorizing scheme is to attempt to add some sort of structure to the "stream of activity" called behavior.

Types of Motor Activities
in Man-Machine Systems

If you look at Table 9–1 you will see that a number of specific behaviors are classed under the general category of "motor processes." Note that in a categorization scheme of this sort you must infer the actual type of motor activity, or movement, that is required. For example, what specific motor activities are necessary to connect, disconnect, or align? Another method of categorizing the motor activities that may be required of an operator in a man-machine system is to list the type of movement necessary to perform a task. McCormick (1970) lists several classes of movement that may be involved in various motor activities. These include *positioning* movements, *repetitive* movements, *continuous* move-

Table 9–1. One method of classifying various types of behavior which may be of importance in a man-machine system.

Processes	Specific Behaviors
Perceptual Processes	Detects Inspects Observes Reads Receives Scans Surveys Discriminates Identifies Locates
Mediational Processes	Categorizes Calculates Codes Computes Interpolates Itemizes Tabulates Translates Analyzes Chooses Compares Estimates Plans
Communication Processes	Advises Answers Communicates Directs Indicates Informs Instructs Requests Transmits
Motor Processes	Activates Closes Connects Disconnects Joins Moves Presses Sets Adjusts Aligns Regulates Synchronizes Tracks

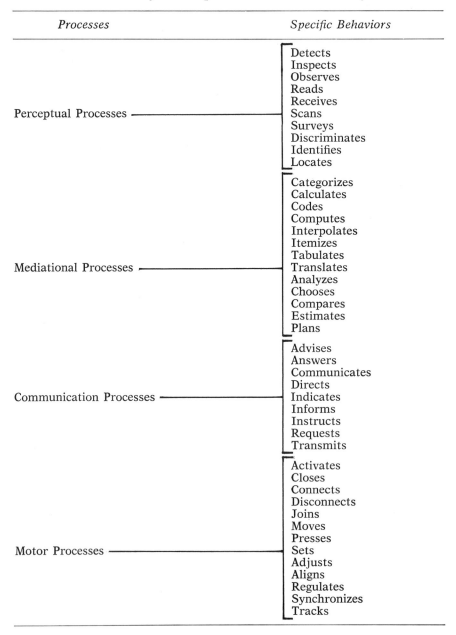

ments, *sequential* movements, *static* adjustments, and *manipulation* movements.

When a person throws a light switch or moves the shift of an automobile, he is making a *positioning* movement. In other words, he has reached for something and moved something from one place to another. In this type of movement, a body member is moved from one position to another position. As the name suggests, *repetitive* movements are those in which a movement is repeated. An example of a task requiring repetitive movements is the operation of a telegraph key. *Continuous* movements are defined as those in which a person must make continuous adjustments of some type in response to a changing situation. A very common example of continuous movement is operating the steering wheel of an automobile.

Sequential movements are more complex and consist of a number of more or less independent movements that are performed in a sequence. McCormick points out that the separate movements may be of the same type, such as typing or operating a calculating machine, or they may be quite different and consist of a sequence of various kinds of movements. *Static* reactions require muscle functions even if they do not involve movement. A static reaction, or adjustment, involves maintaining a body member in a fixed position. *Manipulation* movements involve using or handling tools, parts, various types of control mechanisms, and so on.

There are, of course, other ways of classifying motion or movements. For example, another classification scheme has two primary types of movement—*tense* and *ballistic*. Tense movements are those which fixate a part of the body or regulate its course of action. These movements are usually relatively slow compared to ballistic movements, which throw a part of the body, such as a foot, in a free-swinging arc.

In reading the brief descriptions of the various types of movements, it should be apparent that most skilled acts require combinations of several or all of the movements listed. For example, consider the operation of an automobile. Assume you are in the driver's seat and wish to start the car. You reach (positioning movement) for the ignition, turn it and, since it is dark and raining, also turn on the lights and windshield wipers (sequential movements). You place the car in gear (positioning movement), hold your foot over the brake for a moment (static adjustment), put your foot on the brake pedal (positioning movement) and then adjust the amount of brake pressure (continuous movement). You might then remove your foot from the brake, depress the accelerator and, by means of the steering wheel (continuous movement), control the car as you drive away. Tasks far more simple than operating a car will require combinations of movements.

A considerable amount of research has been conducted in an effort to better understand man's capabilities and limitations in regard to the various movements we have listed. In general, most of these studies have been directed at three particular character-istics of motor activities—the *timing or speed* of motor responses, the *precision or accuracy* of the responses, and the *strength* of re-sponse. Theoretically, there could be almost any combination of these three factors. Thus, there are activities, such as shoveling snow, which involve slow, nonprecise, but powerful motor re-sponses. Other activities might require very fast, but not precise or powerful responses. In some responses, all three factors may be very important, while in others, such as talking, neither speed, precision, nor strength is crucial. We will consider each of these factors in more detail.

Speed of Response

The speed with which we are able to respond in a particular situation is dependent upon a number of variables. These include not only the stimulus situation that elicits the response but also the functioning of all the various behavioral subsystems that we have discussed. Because the functionings of these various subsystems are not instantaneous, there is a certain irreducible delay between the onset of the stimulus and the operator's responses. In a man-machine system, this period of time is referred to as *operator delay* or *lag* (Wargo, 1967). Figure 9–5 is a schematic showing where these delays or lags take place within the human system.

It can be seen from Figure 9–5 that the first point at which a delay can occur is at the receptors. Recall that the receptors are specialized sensors that are sensitive to various types of physical energies (Chapter 2). The receptors transform, or transduce, the physical energies, which make up the appropriate stimuli, into neural impulses. These neural impulses are then transmitted via afferent nerves for processing by the central nervous system. The transformation process itself takes a short period of time for any receptor. However, there are differences among the various re-ceptors in the amount of time required to make the transformation. For example, the eye has a considerably longer receptor delay than does the ear. Research with animals and subhuman primates indi-

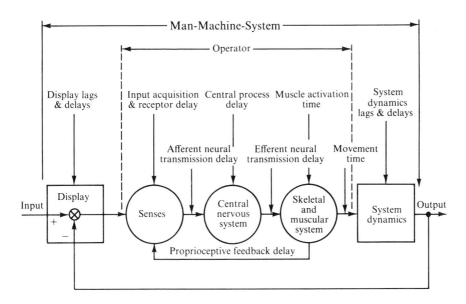

Figure 9–5. Various points in a system responsible for lag or delay. In the case of the operator, delay takes place at the receptors, during the transmission of the afferent impulses to the central nervous system, within the central nervous system, during efferent transmission and during the period that the muscles are being activated by the efferent impulses. From Wargo, M. J., Human operator response speed, frequency, and flexibility: A review and analysis. In *Human Factors*, 1967, **9**(3), 221–238. Reprinted by permission of the Human Factors Society.

cates that the transformation process of the eye may be about fifteen times slower than that of the ear.

A second source of delay within the system is in the transmission of the neural impulse. This delay occurs in both the afferent nerves (from receptor to cortex) and in the efferent nerves (cortex to effector). As has been pointed out, transmission speed will depend on factors such as nerve composition, diameter, and, of course, length. Thus, one important factor in response time is how far away the receptors and effectors are from the brain. Delays that are due to the functioning of the organism's identifying and interpreting subsystems are generally referred to as central process delays. These central delays are typically the longest and the most variable of the operator delays. It has been estimated that about half of the entire delay in a simple reaction time task is made up by central process delay.

The final source of delay or lag is in the effector itself. Following the release of ACh at the neuromuscular junction, the beginning of a reaction by the muscle is actually quite rapid. However, there is a brief period of time before the peak of the muscle tension is reached. Muscle contraction time varies as a function of muscle mass, the type of muscle, and the innervation ratio.

Some research has given us a picture of the magnitude of delay involved in each of the subsystems. The delays associated with the receptor, nerve, central, and muscle processes are shown in Table 9–2. The reaction time or total delay is dependent upon the

Table 9–2. Summary of operator lags and delays in a simple one-choice reaction time task and in a disjunctive reaction time situation. From Wargo, M. J., Human operator response speed, frequency, and flexibility: A review and analysis. In *Human Factors*, 1967, **9**(3), 221–238. Reprinted by permission of the Human Factors Society.

Delay Basis	Delay in Milliseconds	
	One-Choice	Disjunction
Receptor delays	1 – 38	1 – 38
Afferent transmission delays	2 – 100	2 – 100
Central process delays	70 – 100	90 – 300
Efferent transmission delays	10 – 20	10 – 20
Muscle latency and activation time	30 – 70	30 – 70
Reaction time or total delay	113 – 328	133 – 528

stimulus situation. Thus, when there is only one stimulus there is less central process delay than when there is more than one stimulus (or several states of the same stimulus) associated with a particular response. When the latter situation exists, it is referred to as *disjunctive reaction time*. The estimates shown in the table are presented in milliseconds (ms). (A millisecond is a thousandth of a second.)

Enhancing Response Speed

With the development of many highly complex man-machine systems, the response speed of the human operator has, in some cases, assumed considerable importance. Consequently, interest has arisen in possible techniques for increasing man's response speed (decreasing reaction time). In designing equipment, attempts are made to utilize displays that will make use of sense modalities with "fast" receptors. Thus, presenting the required information to an operator by means of the auditory or cutaneous sensory modalities will result in a faster reaction than if the information were presented visually (Chapter 13). Similarly, simultaneous input to several sense modalities may result in a greater response speed on the part of the operator. This is referred to as a cross-modality input. Figure 9–6 shows a device that gives feedback information about the subjects' performance over three sensory modalities—visual, auditory, and electrocutaneous. Not only can such a method

Figure 9–6. A device that gives feedback information over three sensory modalities. This device has been used to study the relative efficiency of three kinds of feedback—visual, auditory, or electrocutaneous—either individually or in various combinations on a compensatory tracking task. When the subject is "on target" he receives no stimulation. As he makes errors in either the left or right direction he receives feedback from either the left or right light, electrode, or earphone. This apparatus is tied in with the equipment shown in Figure 6–2. Courtesy of the Human Factors Laboratory, University of South Dakota. Reprinted by permission.

enhance speed of response but it also can increase the accuracy of response. Another method suggested for increasing response speed is to use response members that are closer to the cortex. Thus, in a study comparing the reaction time of the jaw, hand, and foot to an auditory signal, it was found that the jaw reaction time was faster than that of the hand, which, in turn, was faster than the foot reaction time (Seashore & Seashore, 1941). Obviously, some practical considerations are involved, however, when the design engineer attempts to put control devices in a system that could make use of the jaw as a response member.

Accuracy of Response

Many of an individual's motor responses require a combination of speed and accuracy. In some situations, speed may be more important than accuracy; in other cases the reverse situation may exist. However, we typically think of a motor response as involving both an accuracy and speed component. Under certain conditions, even for the same type of response, one or the other component may assume more importance. For example, when driving an automobile you may depress the brake pedal as you approach an intersection. This will require a reasonable amount of accuracy on your part as you move your foot and place it on the brake. This response will also have to be accomplished in a reasonable amount of time, so speed of response is also a factor. However, suppose another vehicle crossed your path in such a fashion that a collision seemed imminent. In that case, your response would have to be very rapid and also accurate. However, in many kinds of tasks the human operator has the option of trading speed for accuracy. Frequently, he can perform at various levels of accuracy depending upon the rate, or speed, with which he must act. This speed-accuracy trade-off is an important consideration in any type of skilled performance. In situations in which accuracy is critical, speed may have to be sacrificed.

The accuracy of a response is determined by a variety of factors. One important determinant is the part of the body involved in the response. We have already discussed innervation ratios—that is, how many muscle fibers are activated by one motor neuron. The grossness or fineness of the coordinations in which the muscle is involved is dependent upon its innervation ratio. In the large muscles of the body there may be as many as a hundred or more muscle fibers that are activated by only one neuron, while in the fingers there may be only three or four muscle fibers associated with a single neuron. Thus, the innervation ratio of a particular set of muscles is an important factor in determining how accurately an individual can use the muscles in making a response.

The precision of a response will also be limited by the ability of the person to make use of the feedback that is generated by the movement itself. There is a flow of information from the muscles and joints back to the central nervous system. We have pointed out previously that there are receptors within the muscles and joints that respond to the stretch and contraction of the muscle itself. The impulses generated by these receptors pass through sensory or afferent pathways to the central nervous system and convey information about the magnitude and direction of the movement. This feedback is important for the proper regulation of movement; without it, as sometimes occurs because of disease, movement is jerky and uncoordinated. Assuming that the feedback is normal, the precision of the motor response is limited by the accuracy of the individual's evaluation of this feedback. In other words, it is necessary for a person to discriminate and identify the sensory information coming in by this "route," just as he must for sensory information from other modalities. Some investigations have shown that by increasing the amount of feedback and, consequently, increasing the ease of discriminability of different movements, the ability to make precise movements increases.

The role of the human in many man-machine systems requires that he make accurate responses of one type or another. Thus, a question that often arises in the design of systems is how the response accuracy requirement can be met. Actually, there are a number of ways in which this can be accomplished. First, the operator can be selected for the task and then trained (Chapter 12). By means of proper selection, we start with an operator who will be more capable of making an accurate response than many other individuals. Because of the manner in which the various human behavior subsystems function, we can expect individual differences in motor capabilities as in intelligence, personality, and other human characteristics. Thus, when a quarterback is drafted by a professional team, it is because he has demonstrated that he is more capable of making an accurate motor response, such as throwing a football, than most other quarterbacks. Even though this particular motor response may be highly developed, it is refined even more by the training he receives as a professional. The same situation can apply to the human in a man-machine system. He may be selected in the first place because he is capable of making accurate responses. He is then subjected to various training procedures that will further

increase the precision of the responses required by the system. Even
if the initial capability is not very high, proper training and practice
will still result in marked improvement of performance. Selection
and training has developed into a major area of psychology with
many psychologists engaged in these activities. Specific details of
how men are selected and trained for various tasks will be taken up
in a later chapter.

The accuracy of the operator's response can also be improved by designing equipment with the limitations and capabilities
of the operator in mind. Research has shown that the accuracy of
several types of movements (such as continuous and positioning)
may depend on such factors as the direction or length of the required movement. For example, it has been found that positioning
movements can be made with greatest accuracy if they are straight
ahead and below shoulder height. Positioning movements toward the
side are least accurate. Similarly, when positioning movements were
evaluated in terms of accuracy for different distances, it was found
that there is a tendency to "overshoot" when short distances are
involved and to "undershoot" longer distances. However, the percentage error is greater for short arm movements, and it decreases
considerably when longer movements are involved. Accuracy is also
dependent upon the direction of the movement in continuous movements. In designing equipment, accuracy of these movements can
be maximized by placing controls in positions that take into consideration the operator's limitations in direction and length of
movements. Proper placement of controls with these factors taken
into account is one of the tasks of the human factors engineer
(Chapter 13).

Strength of Response

Although the strength of a response may be important in
some types of tasks such as shoveling snow or digging a ditch, in
most man-machine systems it is no longer an important requirement. Most machines are now designed to substitute mechanical
power for human power and thus require only limited force from
the human. However, in cases in which it is not practical to replace
human force, information about this aspect of human capability is
important. Also, this factor must be considered in machines in
which an emergency might require that human force be substi-
tuted for mechanical force. For example, the force required by the
human operator if power steering fails in an automobile is considerable.

A considerable amount of information has been collected over the years concerning the strength of response of the human under a variety of different conditions. As might be expected, there are a number of variables that affect the strength of response. Not only are physiological factors, such as fatigue, involved but also the position of the body, the body member utilized, and the direction and extent of the required movement are important. While we will make no attempt to review the data that are available dealing with strength of movements, a few examples will be included in order to illustrate the kinds of information that have been collected. For example, the force that a person can exert on a pedal from a seated position is usually greater than his body weight. In one study, it was found that about two thirds of over 500 subjects were able to exert between 465 and 665 pounds force on an airplane rudder pedal. When a man is seated, he can make movements involving greater force by means of straight ahead horizontal pushing than by horizontal pulling movements. Data are also available concerning grip strength, strength of hand turn, elbow and shoulder strength, lifting action, as well as the strength of other movements (McCormick, 1970). Information of this type is available to design engineers in various publications.

Verbal Responses

We have seen that one way of considering motor responses is in terms of their speed, accuracy, and strength. Without a great deal of searching we could find subhuman animals that could make these responses faster, as accurately, and with more force. However, in the area of verbal behavior, the human is clearly superior to any other animal. While human verbal behavior may have some primitive counterparts at the subhuman level, it is a skill that is considered characteristic of man. Efforts to teach animals to use words have been interesting but not particularly successful.

Verbal behavior can be considered an especially complex form of behavior and, as such, it can be studied from a number of points of view. Thus, we find that there are various disciplines that have developed whose aims are to study the different aspects of language. For example, *semanticists* are concerned with the meaning of words or other signs and how the human responds to these signs and words. *Phoneticians* are mainly interested in how the sounds of speech are made and how these sounds can be related to the written word. *Linguists* study the structure and sets of rules

that are applied to language, while many psychologists are interested
in how verbal behavior is learned. In recent years, a new field,
called *psycholinguistics,* has developed. Specialists in this field are
not only concerned with the nature of the communication or
message but also with the characteristics of the communicators.

There is now available a great deal of information in scientific journals and books dealing with the many facets of language
and verbal behavior. You may recall that certain aspects of language
were briefly discussed in previous chapters. For example, when
the interpreting subsystem was taken up, it was pointed out that
words are used as symbols and labels for concepts and are thus
involved in our higher thought processes. We have seen how higher
mental functions, such as problem solving, depend at least in part
on language. The interest of many psychologists in verbal learning
has also been mentioned earlier. However, these researchers have
given us relatively little information about language function since
their emphasis in verbal learning has typically been on the "learning" part of the phrase.

Although we will touch upon material associated with these
various methods of studying language, we will be primarily concerned with verbal behavior in the context of a communication
system and will deal mainly with variables that enhance and limit
the transmission of information by means of the system. When we
consider verbal behavior in this way, we can view the system as
comprising at least four elements or subsystems: (1) the message
to be transmitted, (2) the talker, (3) the transmission subsystem
through which the message is carried (air, telephone, radio), and
(4) the listener. Thus, we can analyze the communication process
in terms of the functions of these components. In our discussion,
however, we will be concerned mainly with the message and talker
components of the communication process.

The Message

The message element in the communication system transmits information from the speaker to the listener. The effectiveness
of this transmission is dependent on a number of characteristics
of the message. In this case, "effectiveness" refers not only to the
amount of information transmitted but also the ease with which
the listener can obtain the information from the message—that is,
the intelligibility of the message. We find that there are several
language factors that can increase or decrease the intelligibility of
a message. For example, the information content of individual words

is a factor. Other things being equal, words that occur frequently in everyday usage are more likely to be correctly identified when transmitted over a speech communication system. In other words, because of its frequency of use, a word may have more information content than other words. The size of the message set is also important; in general, the smaller the set, the greater the intelligibility of the message. Thus, the message set in the communication between air control and aircraft is deliberately limited. Because of the familiarity of both the pilots and aircraft controllers, the uncertainty of a message such as "Friendship tower: this is Navy 325 over Baltimore. Request landing instruction" is greatly reduced. Sentence or phrase structure is also a factor in message intelligibility. We learn to expect that certain "rules" will be followed in pronunciation, grammar, and the kinds of words that are appropriate in a message. In other words, the manner in which the message is "put together" may increase or decrease its effectiveness. There are also certain physical characteristics that may be of importance. For example, if a message is not spoken loud enough to be clearly heard, then it will still not be effective, no matter how many "rules" are followed in putting the message together.

The Structure of the Message

What about the structure or "putting together" of the message? Everyone at some time has heard a foreign language spoken. It may have sounded like a confused babbling with no apparent meaning or order; however, if you were to study the language it would soon be reduced to order. Actually, the sounds that are characteristic of a language are relatively few, although they may recur repeatedly in different combinations. These sounds can be considered the basic units of a language and, when combined in certain sets or patterns, they give a definable structure to the language.

When the structure of the language making up the message is subjected to analysis, we find that it has two major aspects— *phonological* and *grammatical*. When we refer to phonological structure we mean the finite number of distinctive sounds that the speakers of the language employ. The grammatical aspect of a language refers to the fact that there are certain meaningful arrangements in which the utterances of the language are placed. We find that the phonological and grammatical patterns of a language, such as English, are quite rigid. Thus, deviations from what we have learned to expect from the phonology and grammar of a message may reduce its effectiveness. Even when the phonological and grammatical patterns are adhered to, there is a considerable amount of information processing required of an individual to understand even relatively simple messages.

The basic unit of the phonological structure of language is a *phoneme*. Phonemes are combined in certain sequences in a given language and are the lowest common denominator of a spoken language. It is a unit of distinctive sound, actually quite complex, that is used in making syllables and words. There are relatively few phonemes in the English language—linguists list about forty. However, some are used much more frequently than others; there are nine phonemes that make up more than half of the sounds that we produce. The most frequently used phoneme is *i* (as in *bit*), while the least frequently used sound is *z* (as in *azure*). Also, vowel sounds tend to occur less frequently than consonant sounds in the English language.

Grammatical analysis of a language makes use of two basic concepts—the *morpheme* and *arrangement*. A morpheme is the minimal unit of *meaning* in a language. While a morpheme is often a word, it does not have to be. For example, the ending *er* is a morpheme, and the word *worker* has two morphemes—*work* and *er*. In this case, the *er* is referred to as a *bound morpheme* since it only occurs in an utterance as part of a larger word. Morphemes that can be used by themselves as a word—that is, a unit of language that makes up the content of an utterance (Go! Come!)—are called *free morphemes*. The arrangement aspect of grammatical analysis becomes important when morphemes are combined to yield even larger units—that is, when morphemes are combined in phrases and sentences.

Thus, we can see that the structure of a language is determined by its phonemes, morphemes, and a set of arrangements for combining these basic units. Any utterance heard in a particular language can be described in terms of the phonology and grammar of the language.

In discussing speech at the "formal" or message level, we have neglected a very important aspect of the speech process—the production aspect. While we will not go into the vocal trace configurations involved in speech production, it should be kept in mind that this process involves a complex motor response on the part of the speaker. For example, each phoneme requires a unique constellation of articulator positions. Thus, some aspect of the motor control of the vocal mechanism needed to produce each phoneme will differ from that required of any other phoneme. It has also been found (MacNeilage & DeClerk, 1969) that the motor control required will also differ depending on the identity of the previous and following phoneme. Consequently, when the production of a phoneme is considered along with the many phonemes that could precede or follow it, we are soon involved with many thousands of motor patterns necessary for speech. Research and theories of the motor control of speech are reviewed by MacNeilage (1970) in a comprehensive article calling attention to the complexity of this process.

We have, of course, just touched upon the structure of the language that makes up the message component of our communications system. Actually, it is a fascinating area, although some of you who have had phonology and grammar forced upon you in certain courses might disagree.

The Characteristics of Speech

We have seen that the effectiveness of a message will depend, at least to some extent, on whether the rules governing the structure of the language of the message have been followed. From a practical point of view, however, there are several characteristics of speech that are also important determinants of a message's effectiveness. Knowledge of these characteristics is important to the design of communication systems in which intelligible transmission is critical. The four primary characteristics of speech that determine the intelligibility of a message are: (1) intensity, (2) frequency, (3) harmonic composition, and (4) time characteristics. The subjective counterparts (sensations) associated with these characteristics are loudness, pitch, quality, and time perceptions, respectively. We discussed several of these variables in Chapter 2 on the sensing subsystem. In relation to a communication system, probably the most important characteristic of speech is its intensity or loudness.

If speech is too soft (too low in intensity), there may be various types of unwanted sound (noise) in the system that will be loud enough to mask the speech. The noise may surround the speaker or listener (*ambient noise*), or it may be noise in the transmission system itself (*system noise*), such as static on a radio. Consequently, it is important that the overall intensity of the speech be such that it can be heard and understood. All of us have encountered individuals who talk so softly that they can barely be heard. We have also encountered those who talk so loudly that they are annoying. The variation in intensity of speech is considerable between people.

In one study, the telephone-speech levels of a large number of people were determined (Fletcher, 1953). In this investigation it was found that the speech of a person talking as softly as possible was about 46 decibels. When talking as loudly as possible, the decibel level was about 86. While talking too softly will result in ineffective communication, speech that is too loud may also reduce the effectiveness. It may "overload" the system—that is, the design of the system may have some upper limit for intensity of speech. Thus, if speech is not loud enough it may be masked by the noise in the system; if it is too loud, it may overload the system. *Dynamic range* of a system refers to the difference, in decibels, between the intensity level at which overload occurs and the level of noise in the system. In most cases, the dynamic range at the listener's ear is most important. It has been found that for high-quality communication the dynamic range should be about 60 decibels but that with practiced talkers and listeners, communication can be effective in systems that have a dynamic range of only about 20 decibels.

While the intensity (loudness) characteristic of speech is probably of greatest significance in most communication systems, the other characteristics may also be of some importance in determining the effectiveness of the system. For example, the *frequency* of speech (whose subjective counterpart is *pitch*) can be varied by an individual. Each phoneme has a spectrum of frequencies, and a person may shift up and down this spectrum depending upon the circumstances. Thus, the pitch of a person's voice may be relatively low when talking quietly, but it may be considerably higher when shouting at a football game. The *harmonic composition*, or *quality*, of speech refers to the nature of the spectrum of sound waves that make up the speech. Actually, the quality of speech is dependent upon the mixture of pitch and loudness. The speech of various individuals can be recognized as being different because of the quality. Finally, *time characteristics* of speech, which are not actually physical characteristics such as those mentioned above, can help in determining the intelligibility of a message. Thus, the rate at which a person speaks (words per minute) and the ratio of speech time to pause time (speech sounds/pauses between sounds) may be important.

Speech Intelligibility

We have mentioned several variables that may affect speech intelligibility in a communications system. In many systems it is important to know just how intelligible a message will be under various conditions. Consequently, two procedures are available for measuring speech intelligibility. One procedure, which is quite complicated, involves the calculation of a predictive measure of intelligibility. In brief, by relating several of the characteristics of the communication system, such as the noise and speech level, it is possible to arrive at what is called an *articulation index*. Use of the articulation index makes possible the evaluation of some systems without resorting to more elaborate and time-consuming intelligibility testing.

The second procedure involves measuring intelligibility directly through some form of testing. There are various ways of conducting tests of this type. The simplest method has a talker present some type of material to a listener, who is asked to repeat or write down what he hears. Usually, one of three types of tests will be used: nonsense-syllable tests, monosyllabic-word tests, and sentence tests. Items in nonsense-syllabic-word tests are usually random combinations of fundamental speech sounds in a consonant-vowel-consonant pattern. *Monz, nihf, dayth, deeg, moog, pehp,* and *faz* are examples of nonsense syllables used in intelligibility testing. The listener attempts to repeat the words as he hears them and is scored on the number of component sounds of a syllable he gets correct. In a monosyllabic-word test, the items are usually drawn from lists of words in which the frequencies of occurrence of the basic speech sounds are proportional to their frequencies of occurrence in everyday speech. For example, a speaker utters words like *smile, strife, are, cleanse, ford, plush,* and so on, and the listener is scored on the basis of his phonetic agreement or disagreement with the speaker. In the sentence test, questions such as those listed in Table 9–3 are read to a listener who is required to respond

Table 9–3. Some questions used in the sentence test of intelligibility.

Question	Answer
1. What letter comes after C?	D
2. What is the opposite of narrow?	Broad, wide
3. Which is higher, a hill or a mountain?	Mountain
4. Does a man wear a hat or a table?	Hat
5. What do you chop wood with?	Axe
6. What country is Moscow in?	Russia
7. What number comes after three?	Four
8. Does an owl lay books or an egg?	Egg
9. Do palm trees grow in Alaska?	No
10. What is the opposite of dry?	Wet

appropriately. His answer determines whether he got the essential sense of the sentence. These tests can be used in procedures involving face-to-face communication, telephone, radio, and so on. The effects on intelligibility of a number of variables, such as ambient noise, system noise, and speech characteristics, can also be determined.

The Talker

Indirectly, when discussing speech characteristics, we have been concerned with the talker as a component of communication systems. Obviously, the intelligibility of a message will depend to a considerable degree on characteristics of the speaker's voice such as intensity, frequency, pronunciation, accent, and so on. In many systems, however, the most critical role of the speaker is originating the message. In other words, the content or meaning of the message may depend upon the speaker, although in some systems, he may just repeat a message that originated elsewhere. Thus, it is quite likely that a message is the end result of activity of all of the behavioral subsystems that have been considered in earlier chapters—sensing, identifying, memory, energizing, and interpreting. The content of a message, of course, is situation specific and may involve the behavioral subsystems to a greater or lesser extent depending on the situation.

Regardless of the role of the talker in formulating the message, we do know something about speech characteristics of good talkers. Research has shown that the speech of highly intelligible and extremely unintelligible talkers differed in certain characteristics. The intelligible speakers tended to have longer average syllable duration, spoke with greater intensity, used more of the total time with speech sounds and less with pauses, and varied the pitch of their voice more. Information of this type is of practical use since it can be used initially in selecting and training people who will serve as talkers.

The Transmission System

In face-to-face communications, the message is transmitted through the air. There are several variables that can affect this type of transmission. Obviously, the distance between the speaker and the listener will be of considerable importance. Ambient noise may make face-to-face communications impossible or extremely difficult. In other types of transmission systems, such as radio or telephone, system noise may be an important factor in determining the intelligibility of a message. Thus, static on a radio may make a message very difficult to understand.

The Listener

The listener, of course, is a key element of the communication system. Much of what we have been discussing is concerned with making the message more intelligible for the listener. In the typical system, we can assume that the listener has the physical (hearing) and mental capabilities to receive and understand the message. Depending on the situation, we may want certain types of individuals who have been specifically trained as listeners. This training may involve development of abilities to pay attention to only certain aspects of a message, to properly interpret the message, and to respond properly to the content of the message.

The System So Far

With this chapter we conclude our examination of the individual behavioral subsystems that are represented in Figure 9–7. In previous chapters we saw how these subsystems function and how they interact so as to transform an input to an output. This chapter discussed the output of the system—or behavior. While two types of outputs were discussed—motor responses and verbal behavior—it must be kept in mind that mental reactions and responses that lead to overt behavior can also be considered outputs. As we shall see in succeeding chapters, many of these mental responses are measurable through various tests and are of extreme importance to an individual's interactions with his environment. However, a significant amount of the output of the system—that is, behavior—is

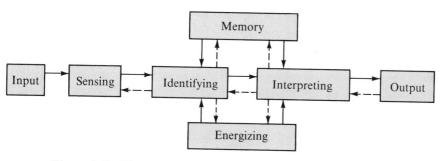

Figure 9–7. The system so far.

represented by either verbal or motor responses, and, while we recognize that these responses are based on mental reactions, we tend to analyze them in terms of observable characteristics. Thus, we consider the speed, accuracy, and strength of motor responses and such factors as phonology, grammar, physical characteristics, and intelligibility of verbal responses.

In considering "the system so far," we have reached a stage where we will no longer be primarily concerned with specific behavioral subsystems but, rather, will be dealing with the complete behavioral system. In other words, we have completed our systems analysis of the behavior system of man and will now be concerned with some of the characteristics of this system. In the following chapters we will discuss such characteristics as intelligence and personality and how these differ between systems. We will also view man as a subsystem functioning within many varieties of larger systems. While the behavioral subsystems will be considered from time to time in explaining certain aspects of behavior, our emphasis from now on will be with the *behavioral system* rather than the subsystems.

Summary

1. The smallest unit of skeletal muscle is called a striated fiber. Striated fibers are innervated by spinal motor neurons or by cranial nerves. Prior to reaching a muscle, the axon of the nerve cell divides and may innervate a number of muscle fibers. A motor unit is defined as a single motor neuron and the muscle fibers innervated by it. Generally, the fewer the fibers innervated by a neuron, the finer the movement capability of the muscle.

2. When a nerve impulse arrives at a neuromuscular junction, it releases acetylcholine (ACh), which acts upon the muscle fiber and activates it. In turn, the ACh is broken down by acetylcholine esterase (AChE), which deactivates the muscle.

3. Several areas of the cortex are involved with motor activities. However, the primary motor area is located in front of the central fissure. Impulses arising in the motor areas of the brain pass down two primary efferent pathways—the pyramidal and extrapyramidal tracts. The cerebellum is an important subcortical center that helps coordinate these activities.

4. As a form of human output, motor activities can be classed and analyzed in a number of ways. The types of movements required in various motor activities have been classed as position-

ing, repetitive, continuous, sequential, static, and manipulatory. Motor responses are also frequently analyzed in terms of the speed, accuracy, and strength of the response.

5. Speed of response is determined by operator delay or lag. Operator delay takes place at the receptors, during afferent transmission of nerve impulses, during central processing of the information, during efferent transmission, and in the effector itself. Accuracy of response is due to a number of factors, including the body member utilized, utilization of feedback, muscle innervation ratio, and practice.

6. Verbal behavior is a type of system output that can be analyzed in a number of different ways. The structure of language can be viewed as having two major aspects—phonological and grammatical. Phonology is concerned with the sound of a language and grammar with the meaningful arrangements in which the utterances are placed.

7. A phoneme is the basic unit of a spoken language. It does not necessarily have meaning by itself. A morpheme is the basic unit of meaning in a language. Morphemes, which are usually words, are further combined to form phrases and sentences.

8. There are a number of physical characteristics of speech that help determine the intelligibility of a message. These include intensity, frequency, and harmonic characteristics. Time characteristics of speech are also important. Speech intelligibility is measured by two procedures—determination of an articulation index and intelligibility testing.

Selected Readings

Bolinger, D. *Aspects of language.* New York: Harcourt Brace Jovanovich, 1968.

McCormick, E. J. *Human factors engineering.* New York: McGraw-Hill, 1970.

10

Differences among Systems

In viewing human behavior from a systems point of view, we have seen that a number of behavioral subsystems are involved. These subsystems work together and interact in such a fashion that the end result is the complex array of capabilities and characteristics that we associate with human behavior. We have also seen that the functioning of these subsystems can be modified or influenced by such factors as past experience and motivation. Thus, we find that, for a number of reasons, the subsystems of a given individual may function differently at different times. Similarly, we find that the subsystems of no two individuals function and interact in exactly the same fashion. In other words, the subsystems may function differently both *within* and *among* people.

The fact that the behavioral subsystems do differ among individuals has a number of implications. Let us assume for a moment that they did not differ. If this were true, then any given stimulus input to the system would be transformed in an identical fashion by all individuals and an identical output would result in each case. The task of the psychologist, who is interested in understanding, predicting, and controlling behavior, would be greatly simplified. His primary job would be defining the stimulus configuration and, once this was accomplished, he would have no problem in predicting behavior. Control of behavior would simply involve changing certain elements of the stimulus configuration.

However, since the functioning of the various behavioral subsystems does vary among people, we find that the situation is much more complex. Instead of transforming an identical input in a similar fashion with a consequent identical response, various individuals will make different transformations which will result in different responses. As we will see in the next chapter, sometimes the transformations of a particular individual are so different that so-called abnormal or deviant behavior will occur. However, even if this is not the case, the variations in the behavioral subsystems are such that people differ considerably from one another in any capability or attribute that we care to measure. In the terminology of the psychologist, these differences between people are referred to as *individual differences.*

The study of individual differences is an important part of the psychologist's job. Not only has this study developed into a major area of research, but it has also led to the development of the field of *psychological testing,* which is aimed at measuring and quantifying individual differences. Tests have been developed for measuring such psychological attributes as intelligence, aptitudes, attitudes, and personality, as well as many other attributes and capabilities. The theory and technology of psychological testing will be discussed in detail later in this chapter.

Studies concerned with individual differences have shown that on any capability or attribute people differ among themselves. Furthermore, when a sufficiently large number of people are tested, these differences tend to follow a prescribed pattern. For example, if a number of people were tested on a simple reaction time apparatus, the results would show that a few are capable of very rapid reactions, a few have very slow reaction times, but most of the individuals are somewhere between the two extremes. Similarly, if we were to measure the height of a number of people, we would find that some are very tall, others are very short, while most would be somewhere in between. Individual differences of these types are found for every human characteristic.

Thus, if the instrument available for measuring the particular attribute or capability is adequate, we find that the attribute will be present in varying degrees in different people. When we quantify or attach numbers to an attribute, such as IQ, we find that if the group measured is large enough and randomly selected, then we can expect a few extremely high scores, a few extremely low scores, with most of the scores being about "average." A convenient way of illustrating such data is shown in Figure 10–1. In this figure, the attribute being measured is plotted on the hori-

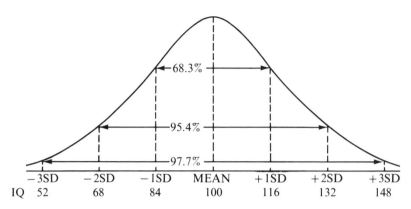

Figure 10–1. The normal distribution of IQ scores for a large number of children. The mean of the distribution is 100 and the standard deviation (SD) is 16. On this distribution, 68.3% of the children tested fall within ± 1 SD, 95.4% between ± 2 SD and 97.7% between ± 3 SD.

zontal axis, while the number of individuals having a given value of the attribute are represented on the vertical axis. Plotting the data in this fashion results in a bell-shaped curve, which represents a *normal distribution.* It can be seen from this figure that the scores of most of the individuals fall near the middle of the distribution and that only a few fall near the ends. When your instructor tells you that he is grading "on the curve," he is referring to a distribution of this type. If you are fortunate, your score will fall on the upper end of the distribution and you will receive an A grade. Most of the scores, however, will fall in the middle, or "average" area of the distribution, with resulting grades of C. Other scores will be found to fall at the low end of the distribution, and grades of D or F will be assigned to these scores.

We find, then, that the study of individual differences is based on the assumption that, for any given attribute, differences between individuals will be found and that these differences, when measured appropriately and plotted, will result in a distribution similar to that shown in Figure 10–1. Individual differences for many attributes, capabilities, and characteristics have been subjected to systematic study, and a considerable amount has been learned about the nature and extent of these differences. However, we will be concerned with two particular characteristics of individuals that are of extreme importance for adequate adjustment and achievement in our society—*intelligence* and *personality.* While at this point we will not deal with the instruments that are available to assess these characteristics, it should be kept in mind that over a long period of time a great deal of effort has been expended in the development of tests designed to measure personality and intelligence. Some of the features of these instruments are discussed in the psychological testing section of this chapter.

Intelligence

What Is Intelligence?

The question of what "intelligence" means is older than the science of psychology; it was discussed by philosophers and biologists for many years before psychology emerged as a discipline. However, despite this lengthy consideration of the question, there is still a great deal of disagreement about just what intelligence is and how it should be defined. Indeed, concepts of the nature of intelligence and definitions making up these concepts are found by the dozens.

In considering the nature of intelligence and in attempting to arrive at some sort of definition, it will pay us to consider for a moment an early definition put forth by E. G. Boring (1923). Boring stated that ". . . intelligence as a measurable capacity must at the start be defined as the capacity to do well in an intelligence test." In other words, intelligence is whatever is measured by intelligence tests. While this definition may appear somewhat facetious, it does illustrate an important point. Intelligence, as such, should not be thought of as a physical substance or as an attribute or mental power that is possessed by people in varying amounts or degrees. Rather, it should be considered as simply a word that is applied as a description of the extent to which people are capable of performing certain types of tasks and problems that make up "intelligence tests." Thus, when we refer to individual differences among people in "intelligence," we are referring to differences in their ability to perform the problems that make up the test. Some psychologists prefer to think of intelligence only in these terms, while others refuse to make any attempt at definition.

If you wish to "shop around," there are a number of ideas of the nature of intelligence available, since this has been a favorite topic of contemplation and argument for centuries. In 1897, Ebbinghaus defined intelligence as the ability to "combine" and, based on this definition, he suggested that a sentence completion test should be a good measure of intelligence. Terman (1921) felt that intelligence was the power to think abstractly, while Thorndike (1921) thought that intelligence was made up of a number of specific but independent abilities, including linguistic, manipulative, and social. Thurstone (1921) thought of intelligence as "that which can be judged by the degree of incompleteness of the alternatives in the trial and error life of the individual."

A number of other typical definitions have emphasized learning ability and the ability to adapt to new situations. Swift (1969) suggests that the "general ability to learn from all life experiences" can be considered the most practical and meaningful definition of intelligence. Wesman (1968) argues that intelligence should be defined as the summation of learning experiences. Wesman also believes that intelligence is unstructured and that it is differently comprised in every individual. It is the sum total of all the learning experiences the individual has uniquely had up to any moment in time.

In considering the nature of intelligence, most psychologists do not think of intelligence as a single ability or attribute. In other words, they do not feel that intelligence is a unitary thing or that there is a single underlying factor of general ability that accounts for intelligence. Rather, it is assumed that there are several primary mental abilities as well as several more specific abilities. This view of intelligence has developed largely through the utilization of a statistical procedure called multiple-factor analysis. This technique, which is discussed in more detail later, permits a researcher to identify the relative importance of various underlying factors that make up or contribute to a complex ability such as intelligence. A great deal of research on the structure of intelligence by means of multiple-factor analysis has been conducted by Guilford (1967).

It would be both appropriate and desirable if we could summarize this section with a concise and meaningful definition of intelligence. However, it should be apparent from our brief discussion that this is not feasible. While it might be convenient to consider intelligence as no more than "what the test measures," this pragmatic view begs the question since it gives no clue as to the "what" that is being measured. It appears that the other definitions of intelligence also have drawbacks. Basically, the definition of intelligence that one accepts depends a great deal upon particular orientations and preferences. The particular definition that appeals most to the authors is that of Wesman (1968), who considers intelligence to be a summation of learning experiences.

Individual Differences
in Intelligence

Regardless of how we define intelligence, we know that the output of the various subsystems is such that when we measure many individuals on intelligence tests we find that their performance on the tests differs greatly. We also know that there is a very strong correlation between how people perform on these tests and their educational and occupational achievements in life. Consequently, whatever it is that these tests measure is an ability that is important to our everyday existence.

This ability is distributed over a wide range. In attempting to quantify it, various methods are available for attaching numbers to the performance demonstrated by an individual on an intelligence test. In the case of children, the so-called intelligence quotient (IQ) was used for many years and is still used by some psychologists.

In this system, the *mental age* (MA) of the child is determined, based on the level of difficulty of items that he is able to pass on the test. Previous testing with other children has established the average difficulty level which children of various ages can successfully complete. The MA is divided by the *chronological age* (CA) and multiplied by 100 in order to arrive at an IQ score. Thus:

$$IQ = \frac{MA \times 100}{CA}$$

The purpose of multiplying by 100 is to eliminate the need for using decimals. Thus, if we tested a child and found that his MA and CA were identical, the resulting IQ would be 100 or average. On the other hand, if the MA turned out to be 10 and his CA only 8, then he would have an IQ of 125. His performance is being compared to other children's performance. Since he performed better, his MA is higher than average for children of his own CA. If his MA was less than his CA, his IQ would be somewhere under 100. He would not be performing as well as children of his own CA. When the relationship between CA and MA is used to determine the IQ, as is the case on the *Stanford-Binet* test, we find that the ratio of MA to CA is reasonably constant up to a CA of around thirteen years. After that the mental age increases more slowly and levels off at about eighteen. Thus, we would not expect a 25-year-old man to be higher in mental age than he was at eighteen. While the mental age of a ten-year-old is approximately twice that of the same child at five years of age, the mental age of a 36-year-old person is not twice that of the person at the age of eighteen. Consequently, IQ must be computed in a different fashion for adults; it is also more meaningfully interpreted if computed for children in this alternative manner.

The *deviation IQ* is used to measure intelligence independent of the MA/CA relationship. When using this technique, the average level of performance is measured for each group to which the test is meant to apply (for example, the Wechsler Intelligence Scale for Children, the *WISC*, is given to a number of groups of children). The *standard deviation*, which is a measure of the spread of scores around the mean (see Chapter 15), is also obtained for each group. When an individual IQ score is then compared with the group, the score can be placed in the distribution, and its deviation from the average can be computed. Using this technique, the IQ level for an individual should remain roughly constant over years of measurement. If the child is compared with other children of the same CA, he can be placed above or below the average for the children of the same CA. He is not being compared with older or younger children. As an example, if the standard deviation of a group is 16, and the mean (average) is 100, a child one standard deviation above the mean would have an IQ of 116. This level should remain roughly the same as an adult, unless his intelligence changes differently from the intelligence of other group members. He should still perform, as an adult, one standard deviation above the mean. If measured in this manner, an IQ always means the same thing: the deviation of the individual's IQ from the average IQ of his membership group.

An approximation of the distribution of IQ's, as measured by the Stanford-Binet test, for a large number of children was shown in Figure 10–1. Note that this is a normal distribution with a mean score of 100 and a standard deviation of 16. With a distribution of this type, the majority of children will be within one standard deviation of the mean. More specifically, 68.3 percent of the children would have IQ's falling between 84 and 116. These are considered as average. Toward the upper end of the distribution we have in the second standard deviation (13.6 percent) scores that represent superior intelligence, while those in the third standard deviation, with an IQ above about 135, represent 2 percent of the population. These are the "gifted" children. Conversely, toward the lower end of the distribution we find scores representing children classed as dull, normal or borderline and, in the third standard deviation, children considered as mentally deficient or feebleminded.

With tests devised to measure intelligence of adults, we find the same type of distribution of scores. One form of adult intelligence test that has been administered to a very large number of people is the Army General Classification Test (AGCT), which was used during and after World War II. The AGCT was constructed in such a fashion that the average score was 100 with a standard deviation of 20. Some interesting studies were conducted establishing the relationship between performance on the AGCT and civilian occupations. As we have already indicated, there is a relationship

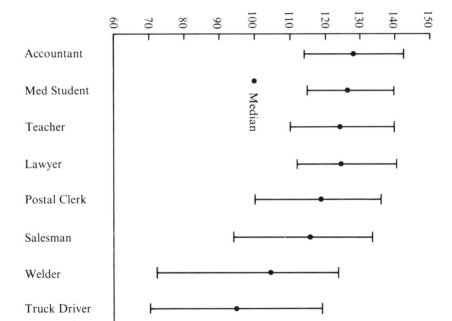

Figure 10–2. Distribution of AGCT scores for a number of different occupations. The median represents the score above and below which 50 percent of the scores fall. The distributions shown in the figure end at the 90th and 10th percentiles. Thus, in the case of the accountants, 80 percent of the scores fall between 114 and 143 while the median score was 129. Note the overlap of scores between occupations. Based on data from Stewart, N. G., AGCT scores of army personnel grouped by occupation. *Occupations*, 1947, **26,** 5–41.

between the ability to perform on an intelligence test and occupational achievement. This relationship is apparent from Figure 10–2; however, when considering this figure it must be kept in mind that there is a great deal of variability represented on the graph. Thus, some people in every occupation scored high, while some in each occupation also scored low. While there is an average difference between occupational groups in intelligence, there is also a great deal of overlap.

Why Do People Differ in Intelligence?

We have already pointed out that if the various behavioral subsystems functioned identically for all people, there would be no individual differences to be concerned about. All people would behave identically and all could do equally well on intelligence tests. However, the fact remains that these subsystems do function differently; consequently, there are some people who are mentally retarded, many more who are considered average in intelligence, and a few who are gifted. We are concerned with why these subsystems do function differently among people.

We know, of course, that there are transient factors that will result in a change in the functioning of the subsystems. For example, various motivational and physiological factors result in considerable short-term modification. However, we are interested in factors that can account for long-term or permanent differences in performance of the subsystems of different people. These long-term factors are generally classed under two headings—environmental factors and hereditary or genetic factors. While there is still a great deal that we do not know about the genetic component affecting the functioning of the subsystems, we know it is important. We also know that environment is important. In this instance, we utilize the term *environmental* to include more than the social and cultural factors that may influence the individual. Biological influences, such as prenatal environment and nutritional deficit early in life, may also result in modifications of the subsystems.

Heredity or Environment?

Because of the tremendous advances in the field of genetics in the last half century, a great deal is known about the inheritance of various physical characteristics of the human organism. However, we are on much less certain ground when we attempt to discuss the inheritance of behavior patterns or such attributes as intelligence. While we might safely state that "Jane inherited her mother's good looks," we would have much less basis in fact for stating that "John inherited his father's intelligence." However, because of the emergence of the field of *behavior genetics,* which is concerned with the contributions of heredity to behavior variation, data are being accumulated that may eventually establish the genetic foundations of behavior. At present, however, many questions remain unanswered.

The relative contributions of heredity and environment to intelligence have been argued for years. If one views these arguments from a historical framework, we see that for about the first half of this century, the genetic or hereditary view prevailed, and environmental influences on intelligence were largely ignored. In recent years, however, for a number of complex reasons, some of them social and political, it has been popular to take the environmentalist stand on intelligence.

What evidence do we have that heredity plays a major role in determining an individual's intelligence? Conversely, what evidence do we have that environment is important? Studies aimed at answering these questions are difficult to design, particularly when we are concerned with human beings rather than lower animals. Typically, the type of study that will yield the most information requires selective breeding and, of course, we are not prepared to undertake studies of this kind with humans. Results of investigations involving selective breeding with animals, however, shed some interesting light on the role of heredity in determining the organism's behavior.

Findings of selective breeding studies involving various species of mammals reveal that a number of behavioral characteristics, just as some physical characteristics, can be modified by means of genetic selection. For example, rats have been bred for maze-learning ability. By selecting rats that learn a maze very quickly (maze-bright) and others that learn slowly (maze-dull), and by selectively breeding these animals, it has been found that after a few generations the offspring of the maze-dull rats are quite poor maze learners. Since animal experiments have shown that a number of behavioral traits can be changed by genetic selection, it seems safe to assume that many behavioral traits in humans can also be modified in this fashion.

While studies at the human level have not been as dramatic as those involving genetic selection in rats, evidence concerning the importance of hereditary factors in intelligence has been accumulated. If intelligence is inherited, we might expect to find a strong correlation between the IQ of children and the IQ of their parents. Investigations that have involved testing parents and children have shown that this is the case—that a good positive relationship between the intelligence of children and their parents does exist.

Another approach has been to attempt to hold heredity constant while the environment is varied or, conversely, to hold the environment constant while heredity is varied. This approach can be used in studying identical twins who have been separated at a young age and reared in foster homes (heredity constant—environment varied) or by studying different children adopted into the same foster homes (environment constant—heredity varied). Unfortunately, research of this type is handicapped by the small number of cases available for study and the difficulty in controlling variables. However, based on these kinds of studies, one can tentatively conclude that intelligence is primarily genetically determined. While environment can accentuate or reduce the hereditary influence on intelligence, heredity is probably the more significant influence of the two. It must be realized, however, that development of intelligence is the result of a complex and not completely understood interaction between hereditary and environmental factors, and this interaction is the subject of investigation by some researchers today.

Class and Race Differences in Intelligence

A discussion of class and race differences in intelligence could just as appropriately have been taken up under the heading of heredity or environment. Obviously, when we deal with differences in performance on intelligence tests—differences that occur between groups occupying different positions in the social hierarchy of America, or by different races—we are still dealing with the question of heredity or environment. In recent years, this particular question has become emotion laden. Arguments have raged not only among psychologists but also among legislators, who have spent vast sums of money based on the concept that enriched scholastic programs can correct educational deficiencies and, consequently, increase intelligence test scores. A number of government-financed programs have had this objective in mind. Unfortunately, evidence is beginning to accrue that casts serious doubts on the success of these programs.

It has been shown that groups occupying different positions

in the status hierarchy of American society perform differently on intelligence tests. Figure 10–2 can give an idea of the differences in IQ between occupations and, indirectly, between socioeconomic levels. It is a well-documented fact that children's IQ's are correlated with the socioeconomic status of their parents. One would immediately assume that these differences in children's intelligence, associated with parents' socioeconomic status, can be attributed to environmental factors. Investigators have expended a great deal of effort to show that the environment and culture associated with the various levels of parental status account for the differences. However, Jensen (1969) argues that there are a number of reasons to believe that groups differing in socioeconomic status will also differ, on the average, in their genetic endowment of intelligence. In other words, Jensen suggests that it may not be socioeconomic status per se that is an environmental variable responsible for IQ differences. It may be that over the years a form of selective breeding has taken place and that genetic factors may be important for understanding social class differences.

Regardless of the factors responsible for the differences in IQ shown by various socioeconomic classes, we know they exist. Similarly, we know that differences exist between races in their ability to perform on intelligence tests. Again the question is raised—is it heredity or environment or, possibly, a function of the tests employed? It is well recognized that Negroes and American Indians have not had the same opportunity as whites to learn intellectual skills required to score high on intelligence tests. Environmentalists argue, and with some justification, that unequal educational and cultural advantages can account for the differences. Such conclusions are important from a sociological point of view in that they justify the efforts being made to improve the scholastic environment of Negro children. However, not all investigators are convinced that environment is the prime factor accounting for IQ differences shown between races, and some (Jensen, 1969) argue that hereditary factors may be equally important.

Sex Differences in Intelligence

While we can state that sex differences in intelligence do exist, we must immediately qualify that statement. Recall that one of the views of intelligence is that it is composed of what can be called primary or general abilities, as well as various specific abilities. When tests that "tap" these several abilities are utilized, then differences between sexes begin to emerge. For example, it appears that boys are better than girls on test items dealing with spatial relationships between objects and most items dealing with various kinds of problem solving. Girls are better than boys in numerical ability, reasoning, word fluency, and memory. However, when we view intelligence as a composite of all these various abilities, we find that there is no difference between the sexes. Since boys are better in some areas and girls in others, the differences tend to cancel each other out with the result that no differences are found in the overall level of intelligence. However, it should be pointed out that most tests are constructed to insure this outcome. Items clearly favoring males or females are not included in the tests.

We have seen, then, that despite years of argument and research dealing with intelligence, there are some questions that have been answered but many more that remain unanswered. We do not even have a good definition, let alone an understanding, of what intelligence actually is. Possibly we should not worry about definitions and understanding and settle for the statement that "intelligence is what intelligence tests measure." Whatever it is that these tests do measure, it differs considerably between individuals. Differences in intelligence are found to exist between socioeconomic classes and between races. We do not have a satisfactory answer to the question of "why" these differences exist. Some would argue that the explanation rests in environmental factors. Others feel equally strongly that heredity is the most likely explanation. Regardless of why these differences exist, it has been clearly demonstrated that intelligence is related to occupational and educational success. Thus, intelligence is of great importance if we wish to achieve certain levels in our society.

Another characteristic that is important for adequate adjustment and achievement will be considered next. This trait or characteristic is referred to as *personality*. You will see that many of the problems encountered in discussing intelligence, such as definitions, measurement, and understanding, will also be encountered in our consideration of this topic.

Personality

What Is Personality?

In an exhaustive search of the literature, Allport (1937) found nearly fifty definitions of personality. This is not surprising since there are very few words which have such a fascination for most people. Everyone uses the term, and in various ways. In some instances, the word is used to define or describe an individual's social skill or adroitness. If the person is capable of "getting along" with people, he is thought to have a good personality. If he is a "troublemaker" and does not develop positive reactions in his associates, he has a "bad" personality. In other cases, a particular characteristic of a person may be such that his personality is defined in terms of the characteristic. Thus, we may refer to someone as having an "aggressive personality" or, perhaps, a "friendly personality." There is virtually an endless variety of words that are used to describe an individual's personality. As a matter of fact, there is an immense collection of words descriptive of personality (called a psycholexicon) which consists of 17,953 words (Allport & Odbert, 1936).

Biosocial Definition

While there is a profusion of definitions of personality, most are encompassed within a relatively limited number of broad definitions, one being the *biosocial definition*. This definition equates personality to the "social stimulus value"—that is, the effect he has upon others—of the individual. In other words, it is the reaction of others to a person that defines his personality. This reaction is determined by the many characteristics and qualities of the person that will serve as stimuli to others. These stimuli range from physical characteristics such as height and weight to the way the individual behaves. While there is some merit to considering personality in these terms, a person's social stimulus value does not give us much information about the structure of personality. Obviously, the way that an individual appears and acts may conceal quite a different psychological makeup. In other words, personality can be organic as well as perceived. Definitions that take this point of view are referred to as biophysical definitions.

Biophysical Definition

According to biophysical definitions, personality can be linked to specific qualities of the individual that are susceptible to measurement and description. Personality structure is made up of *traits*, and a cluster of traits makes up what is called a *personality type*. Traits are defined as patterns of behavior that can be labeled with such adjectives as honest, sociable, brave, zealous, cynical, and so forth. There are actually several thousand words that might be accepted as trait names; further, any given individual may demonstrate a large number of personality traits. In general, however, traits are divided into two types—*surface traits* and *source traits* (Cattell, 1950). Surface traits are those that characterize the individual's behavior—that is, those that are observable and that we label with trait names. Source traits, on the other hand, represent underlying variables that may be the "source" or cause of the overt surface traits. Source traits are, theoretically at least, fewer in number than surface traits and are not as easily identified; however, source traits may be more important in accounting for personality. Cattell (1950) suggests that source traits can be divided into those reflecting the hereditary factors of an individual and those reflecting environmental conditions.

Any description of personality that made use of only trait names would result in very long, complex lists of trait names describing each person. One way to simplify the description of personality is to "combine" a number of traits to form a *personality type*. This is essentially what we are doing when we refer to someone as being an "aggressive type." Unfortunately, this type of characterization is oversimplified and generally incorrect since it is difficult to reduce the many traits making up a complex personality to one simple personality type. However, the concept of personality type has been with us for centuries. Hippocrates, for example, discussed choleric, melancholy, phlegmatic, and sanguine types. A choleric type was irascible, a melancholy type was depressed and slow, the phlegmatic type was apathetic, while the sanguine type was cheerful and active.

Possibly a more familiar scheme is that which reduces personality differences to the two basic types of *extroversion* and *introversion*. These personality type descriptions were first advanced by the famous Swiss psychiatrist Carl Jung, who described an extrovert as a person who is oriented toward the external, objective world and away from himself. The introvert is oriented toward the inner, subjective world; he looks within himself for the most important part of his experience. Jung felt that both introversion and extroversion orientations exist within a person but that one or the other will be dominant. Although Jung's ideas were theoretical, a large-scale study by Eysenck (1947) supports Jung's theories. Eysenck, using about ten thousand normal and neurotic subjects, factor analyzed a large number of traits that had been obtained through physicians' ratings. The analysis revealed two primary dimensions of personality that Eysenck identified as extroversion and introversion. Eysenck considered his findings in this area to represent a confirmation of the theoretical ideas that had been put forth by Jung.

The primary problem with personality type descriptions is that we are dealing with an organism whose actions and experiences are tremendously varied and unpredictable and, consequently, irreducible to a simple type description. People are characterized by a variety of traits, and only rarely do they all fit the pattern of any single personality type.

Concept of Self

We have considered personality to be defined as the social stimulus value of the individual (biosocial definition) or as a complex of interacting traits (biophysical definition). Biophysical definitions might also be considered "structural" definitions because they are concerned with the structure of personality. There is another class of definitions that could be considered "biophysical" but which we will take up separately because of their prominent role in today's personality theory. These are the definitions of personality which, in one way or another, involve the concept of "self." There are several ways in which the term *self* is employed by personality theorists. Some theorists are concerned with the individual's self-perception—that is, his *self-concept*. In this case, the self is conceived of as a cluster of attitudes and feelings that a person has about himself. Other theorists use the term *self* to refer to a group of psychological processes that will shape or determine a person's behavior. The self is thought of as some unobservable internal process that causes a person to behave in a certain fashion.

When the self is considered from the self-perception or self-concept point of view, the assumption is made that the manner in which a person perceives himself is an important determinant of his personality. He acts or behaves in terms of the kind of person that he perceives himself to be—aggressive, kind, stupid, hostile, and so on. Thus, the self is what a person thinks of himself. Generally, when we attempt to find out just what a person does think of himself, we have to rely on what he will "say" about himself either verbally or by agreeing or disagreeing with some statement such as "I am honest or kind, or stupid, or sociable," and so on. Consequently, most studies dealing with self-concept use various techniques designed to make a person reveal his notions about himself. With one method—the so-called Q-technique—a person is given a packet of statements on cards such as "I am a hard worker," "I am a submissive person," or "I am likeable." He is asked to sort the cards according to whether or not they are characteristic of the way he sees himself at that particular time. An interesting variation of this approach is to ask the person to sort the statements not in relation to how he sees himself at the present time but rather in terms of how he would *like* to see himself. In other words, he sorts the statements in such a fashion as to describe his *ideal self*. The Q-technique, as well as other methods, has given psychologists a considerable amount of information about the ways people view themselves.

A good deal more time could be spent in attempting to define personality. However, the above information should be sufficient to give the reader some understanding of the manner in which many psychologists view personality. Actually, when attempting to arrive at a definition of personality, it should be kept in mind that the way in which a given individual defines personality will depend very much upon his theoretical preference. Regardless of the definition we choose, the fact remains that there are psychological characteristics demonstrated by an individual which we think of as "personality," and these characteristics may differ widely between individuals.

Individual Differences in Personality

If we wish to think of personality as a person's external behavior and appearance, as a pattern of surface or source traits, or the manner in which a person views himself, the fact remains that people differ. As was the case with intelligence, we can suggest that these differences are due to the manner in which the various behavior subsystems function. Again, we must raise the question of why these subsystems do not function in an identical manner for all individuals. Once again, underlying the answers to this question is the problem of the contributions of heredity and environment.

While almost no one denies that genetic factors play a role in personality, many theorists feel that heredity is definitely of secondary importance to environment in determining the nature of an individual's personality. Although the role of genetic factors is typically played down and some form of environmentalism emphasized, it is possible that new developments in the field of behavior genetics may change thinking in this area. Thus, although most explanations today of why personalities differ are based on environmental factors, it should be kept in mind that there is an interaction between environment and heredity. For example, a hereditary defect of some sort may very well contribute to a person's self-concept, to his behavior and external appearance, and to the pattern of traits that he demonstrates. In other words, the defect may have considerable influence on his personality regardless of the way in which personality is defined. Basically, in considering the genetic factors to personality, we can say that personality is not inherited. Rather, a *predisposition* for personality to develop in a certain fashion may be genetically determined. Tendencies toward a particular type of personality are inherited, but what actually develops will be greatly influenced by environmental factors. Assuming, then, that there is a genetic foundation which will interact with environmental factors in determining personality, what environmental aspects appear to be most important?

Learning and Personality Development

Psychologists have long been aware that individual experiences are critical in shaping personality. Certain kinds of experiences, such as those associated with the culture the person is reared in or the family in which he grows up, may be of more significance in determining personality than other experiences. Some theorists feel that a child's *early developmental experiences* are the most important and that the key to adult behavior is to be found in experiences that occur in the earliest years of development. Others emphasize *contemporaneous experience* as the primary factor involved in personality. Regardless of the particular point of view of the personality theorist, when he considers the environmental factors that are important in personality development, he is either directly or indirectly concerned with the learning process of the individual. When we talk about the role of "experience" in shaping personality, we are, in fact, talking about learning.

In emphasizing the importance of learning in explaining personality, it must be pointed out that there is some disagreement among theorists about its relative importance. A few personality theorists see in the learning process the key to complete understanding of personality. Their view is that the description of personality can be accomplished in terms of learning principles. Others recognize that learning is important but consider it secondary to other processes. They feel that psychologists who employ learning principles as the primary explanation for personality oversimplify the description. While a comprehensive discussion of these views would carry us deeper into personality theory than is warranted, keep in mind that a basic distinction between theories has to do with the extent to which the learning process must be considered in explaining personality.

In the following pages several environmental situations that shape personality will be discussed. In each of the situations, rather than spending considerable time showing how and why learning principles are applicable, we will rest on the basic assumption that learning is associated with all the experiences the individual encounters with his family, in school, and so on and that the personality development of the individual is primarily a function of his own learning history. What we view as an individual's personality is determined to a considerable degree by his past experiences.

Early Experience and Personality
Development

To many psychologists, the experiences that are encountered by an individual during his infancy and childhood are the most critical in shaping the adult personality. Since most experiences that an infant or child encounters occur within his family, it is not surprising that there is a great deal of interest in the role of the family in personality development. Whether or not a child is loved or rejected, underprotected or overprotected, exposed to a permissive or controlled atmosphere are only a few of the family variables that are thought to determine personality. However, the particular experiences that a child might have within the family are prescribed, to a large extent, by the culture or subculture of which the family is a part. A given culture will have its own distinctive behavior patterns, morals, and values and will establish the rules that govern the rearing of children. Thus, the family may be the unit in which the actual rearing of the child takes place but the manner in which the child is trained is very much determined by the culture. The process whereby personality traits characteristic of a given culture are acquired is called *socialization.* Zigler and Child (1969) present a simple definition of socialization when they state that it "refers to a practical problem which is old and pervasive in human life—the problem of how to rear children so that they will become adequate adult members of the society to which they belong."

While the culture determines certain standards that the family tends to impose and follow, a good deal of difference exists between families in any culture in their child-rearing methods. We will first consider some of the cultural differences in child-rearing practices and then discuss how family differences in these practices can affect personality development.

Cultural Differences

Any given culture will prescribe certain ways of rearing an infant. Thus, we find that in some cultures an infant will be nursed whenever it cries, while in others feeding takes place only at specified hours. Nursing may be a leisurely or hurried affair. Similarly, a child may be allowed to cry without being punished in one culture, but the same behavior may be severely punished in another. There are numerous differences between cultures in child-rearing practices, and a great deal of information about these differences has been gathered by anthropologists. While any and all of the various practices may help shape personality, some psychologists have emphasized two as primary determinants of personality—*toilet training* and *feeding practices.*

An account of the differences between cultures in their approaches to these practices makes interesting reading. For example, among the Alorese in the Dutch East Indies no attempt at toilet training is made in the prewalking period, and efforts are first made only when the child is old enough to understand explanations. While the child may be nursed regularly for a few days after birth, shortly thereafter the mother goes back to work and the child is left with some older sibling. He is often deprived of food since he receives only what food the older children will give him—generally in response to begging and screaming. In other cultures, toilet training may begin very early and be quite severe, while feeding may be on a very regular basis by the mother and involve much affection and attention.

At this point, you might be wondering "So what?" What effect can the toilet training and feeding of an infant have on his adult personality? A possible answer to this question can be found in some of the *psychoanalytic theories* of personality. According to some theorists, infantile experiences, such as those associated with toilet training and feeding, can lead to the development of certain types of *complexes* in the adult. For example, an oral complex is derived from early feeding experiences. One type of oral complex is manifested by compulsive eating and drinking, while another type may be manifested by a low need for food, fear of oral infection and injury, and the need to reject, to name only a few. Anal complexes are derived from events associated with early toilet training. Again, depending upon the type of early training, this complex may manifest itself in activities involving disorder, dirtying and smearing or, on the other hand, in apparent prudishness. While the psychoanalytic views of the relationship between early experience and adult personality are interesting, we have available very little evidence that supports these views. It is a good deal easier to explain the effects of early experiences in learning-theory terms. In other words, the cultural experiences that a child is exposed to will modify various behavioral subsystems in such a fashion that, as an adult, he will demonstrate personality characteristics that are related to these modifications.

Family Differences

While the culture will establish the general rules for child rearing and for family relationships, these rules are subject to modification by the family. Consider, for example, the differences shown between families in our own culture in child-rearing practices. In one family the child may be given a great deal of affection, involving much fondling and "fussing" over. In another family, this type of affection may be almost completely withheld. In terms of later personality characteristics, there is some evidence that in the first case the child will develop more emotional responsiveness than the child from the family with little or no affection.

In his interactions with his parents, a child quickly learns that certain types of behaviors will be reinforced and others will be punished. Development of personality will depend to some extent on which behaviors are tolerated or reinforced and which are not. For example, if a mother lets a child have his own way when he loses his temper and pounds his head on the floor, the child may very likely attempt behavior of this type with his other contacts. While it may not be as successful, the child has learned that he can get his way sometimes by throwing a temper tantrum. Milder forms of this same type of behavior may be demonstrated as an adult. Children who grew up in a family where tantrums were not tolerated will probably develop different patterns of behavior in their contacts with other people. There are many other examples of this kind that could be listed. The importance of the family as a learning situation for the child cannot be overemphasized since it is here that behavior patterns that may carry into adulthood are learned.

Toilet training and feeding are, of course, only two types of experiences to which an infant or child is exposed. While these may be of considerable importance in his personality development, he also encounters a wide range of other kinds of experiences that may also affect his later personality. We have already mentioned the toilet training and feeding patterns of the Alorese culture. What other kinds of experience does a child in that particular culture encounter? One of the striking characteristics of the culture is the inconsistent manner in which children are treated by adults. Children are teased, ridiculed, praised, rewarded, or neglected in an absolutely unpredictable fashion. As soon as the child can walk, he is ordered about by any adult and forced to run errands. Later, more demanding tasks are required of the child. Following an adult's order may in one instance result in praise and in another instance result in ridicule or a scolding. It is no wonder that a five-year-old Alorese is capable of fluent cursing. It is also not surprising that this inconsistency leaves a child distrustful of his environment and other individuals. However, since much of the valued activity of the adult culture involves financial bickering in which bargaining, chicanery, and deceit are important, this type of training of a child seems functional.

Not only does the family determine what kinds of specific behavior will be reinforced or punished, it also helps shape the child's personality in many other ways. As children get older they are quite likely to develop many of the same attitudes that are held by their parents. This occurs because they are more familiar with the particular attitudes their parents hold and because holding similar attitudes is a method of obtaining a favorable response— love, admiration, attention—from their parents. Attitudes are, of course, an important part of the adult personality and help determine the way a person acts toward other people, groups, and social institutions. In the family situation, attitudes may be learned by imitation. The parents serve as *models,* which the child imitates. Not only are attitudes learned in this fashion but also more specific behavioral responses. For example, a boy tends to imitate his father and learns to behave like a man, while a girl imitates her mother. Other forms of behavior, such as aggression, can also be learned from models.

Psychological Testing I

We have indicated that psychological testing involves the *quantification of individual differences.* Two major areas within the field of psychological testing, or *psychometrics,* can be defined by the purposes that are served by the quantification of individual differences. The first major area involves the differences in the abilities possessed by various individuals. The quantification of abilities, aptitudes, or intelligence generally serves the purpose of defining the functions individual human systems are capable of performing. Ability can thus be defined as the human capacity to perform various tasks. In our discussion of abilities we will consider both the measurement of abilities required in the performance of specialized human functions and the tests and measures designed to evaluate general ability or intelligence.

The second major area of psychological testing involves the evaluation of differences in other aspects of system function. The tests are usually aimed at determining the degree to which individuals deviate from "normal" or average standards of behavior. The principal types of tests in this area involve the assessment of various characteristics of personality, and the application of these tests often occurs in conjunction with attempts to evaluate "abnormal" behavior, or system malfunctions. This topic will be taken up in Chapter 11.

The Nature of Human Ability

Historically, psychological theories of intelligence have ranged from viewing intelligent behavior as the result of many independent human abilities, or mental *faculties*, to considering human intelligence a completely general quality. The first point of view would argue that human abilities are highly specific and that mechanical ability is completely independent of verbal reasoning ability, which in turn, is independent from mathematical ability. The generalists, on the other hand argue that all human ability originates from a single quality of intelligence, each being dependent upon this general quality of ability.

Factor Analysis

The development of the statistical technique of factor analysis has helped to resolve the conflict between these two opposing points of view, and it now appears that the actual situation lies somewhere between the two early positions. Over the years a large number of ability tests have been constructed to assess human performance in a wide variety of test situations. We will examine specific examples of these tests later in this section. For the time being, however, keep in mind that the different tests attempt to measure human performance on many different types of problems. Some tests, for example, attempt to measure the ability of individuals to solve deductive reasoning problems, which involve the drawing of logical conclusions from information presented to the subject. Other tests have been designed to measure the capacity to memorize lists of items, while still other tests present the individual with problems designed to determine his capacity to coordinate eye and hand. There are, of course, dozens of other possible types of tests.

If human intelligence is composed of many separate, independent abilities, we would expect there to be little relationship between the various kinds of "mental" tests; on the other hand, if intelligence is a single general quality, we would expect a high correlation, or relationship, between all of the various tests since they would all reflect, in one way or another, a general *unitary* human ability. The evidence produced by hundreds of psychometric investigations does not clearly support either point of view. Instead, if we administer a large number of tests to a large number of people and compute the correlation coefficients (which are numerical indications of the degree of relationship between two measures or tests) between each pair of tests, we find that the tests tend to form clusters. Within each cluster of tests the correlations are fairly high, indicating a strong relationship, but ordinarily the correlations between tests from different clusters tend to be relatively low, with little or no relationship. Table 10–1 presents a theoretical *corre-*

Table 10–1. A hypothetical correlation matrix which shows the intercorrelations among nine tests. The entries on the diagonal line running from top to bottom—left to right—are all 1.00 since these points represent the correlation of each test with itself. The three clusters of highly correlated tests are indicated with dashed lines.

	A	B	C	D	E	F	G	H	I
					Tests				
A	1.00	.95	.97	.05	.10	.03	.01	.05	.11
B	.95	1.00	.92	.12	.06	.15	.02	.08	.06
C	.97	.92	1.00	.11	.09	.03	.13	.09	.07
D	.05	.12	.11	1.00	.96	.98	.05	.04	.03
E	.10	.06	.09	.96	1.00	.91	.07	.04	.01
F	.03	.15	.03	.98	.91	1.00	.10	.15	.02
G	.01	.02	.13	.05	.07	.10	1.00	.94	.97
H	.05	.08	.09	.04	.04	.15	.94	1.00	.90
I	.11	.06	.07	.03	.01	.02	.97	.90	1.00

lation matrix illustrating this typical result. A correlation matrix is simply a collection of correlation coefficients, ranging from +1.00 to −1.00, which presents the correlation of each test with every other test in a simple tabular form. Both the rows and columns of a correlation matrix are the tests, and the diagonal elements of the matrix are all 1's since these represent the correlation of each test with itself. It should also be noted that the numbers contained in the column associated with a given test are the same as those contained in the row associated with that test. This is true since the correlation of test 1 with test 2 will be the same value as the correlation of test 2 with test 1.

In our example, there are three clusters of three tests each. The correlations among the three tests within each cluster are fairly high, and the correlations among tests from different clusters are fairly low. If our nine tests represented most, or all, of the various types of ability tests, we might be led to believe that there were three types of intelligence—that the first type or factor was involved with the things measured by tests A, B, and C, the second factor with abilities measured by D, E, and F, and the final type of ability by the content of tests G, H, and I. Unfortunately, however, the real situation is not quite as simple as our example. There are, as we indicated, literally hundreds of different ability tests, and in actual practice the clusters of correlations are not quite so neat as the arrangement in our example. It is at this point that the important statistical tool, called *factor analysis,* comes to our rescue.

Factor analysis statistically inspects the correlation matrix obtained when we compute the correlations between each of a large number of psychological tests, and it mathematically identifies the important clusters of tests. At the heart of factor analysis is the assumption that a given test, no matter how specific it appears, may actually measure more than one type of ability. Thus, this statistical tool first determines the number of mathematically independent abilities that are measured by a given set of tests and then determines the relative contribution of each of these tests to each of the abilities. This job is accomplished by developing a set of *factor loadings* for each test on each attribute. Table 10–2 contains a set of factor loadings for our nine theoretical tests and three factors of ability. The factor loadings represent the correlation of a given test with a particular factor of ability. In the table it can be seen that the loadings of tests A, B, and C on Factor I are relatively high, while the loadings associated with tests D, E, F, G, H, and I on this factor are relatively low. Although tests D through I are not strongly related to Factor I in our example, the fact that the loadings

Table 10–2. Hypothetical factor analytic results from data like that contained in the correlation matrix of Table 10–1. The entries in the table are *factor loadings,* which represent the correlations between each test and each factor. The factor loadings of the three tests that primarily contribute to each factor are shown in italics.

	Factors		
	I	*II*	*III*
A	*.90*	.04	.05
B	*.87*	.12	.10
C	*.93*	.10	.16
D	.10	*.89*	.09
E	.18	*.95*	.05
F	.07	*.93*	.02
G	.03	.02	*.94*
H	.09	.08	*.89*
I	.12	.10	*.96*

are not zero indicates that they contribute something to this factor of ability. Thus, even the tests that are principally involved with Ability (Factor) II do measure a small amount of Ability I.

The Structure of Intellect

The application of factor analysis to the field of psychometrics has demonstrated the existence of many factors or types of abilities. Some of the important factors are verbal, numerical, reasoning, memory, spatial, and perceptual factors of ability (Nunnally, 1970). Each of these factors of ability are, in practice, measured by several types of tests.

In actual practice, psychologists have on some occasions been interested in testing individuals for specific ability factors and at other times the interest has been in securing a more general measure of ability. This has essentially consisted of determining the average of an individual's ability across several types of ability factors.

Measures of General Ability

The most familiar intelligence tests are those which seek to provide an overall evaluation of an individual's ability. Ordinarily these tests are composed of a variety of subtests that represent some of the more important ability factors. Although summarizing an individual's level of ability with a single number such as an intelligence quotient (IQ) may be somewhat misleading, the tests of general ability do serve a useful purpose. One of the primary applications of these tests has been, and probably will continue to be, the educational placement of students. The information sought from intelligence tests is the general or average ability level of the individual, rather than a more detailed evaluation of specific abilities, or types of ability. The tests for specific abilities are more commonly employed in selecting individuals for particular types of jobs.

A large number of tests have been designed to provide for the evaluation of intelligence or general ability. Basically, these tests can be classified as either individual or group tests. The former category of tests requires the examiner to test one individual at a time, while the latter type of test is designed so that several people can be tested simultaneously.

The Stanford-Binet

The Stanford-Binet is the oldest and one of the most widely used tests of general intellectual ability. This test was first devised by two Frenchmen, Alfred Binet and Théophile Simon, in 1905, for use in the French school system to identify intellectually subnormal children (Binet & Simon, 1905). The test was quickly adopted in the United States, principally at Stanford University. The revised and translated form of the test thus came to be known as the Stanford-Binet, and the most recent form of the test is the 1960 revision (Terman & Merrill, 1960).

Originally, the Stanford-Binet used an *age scale* with which the intelligence quotient (IQ) was determined as the simple ratio of mental age to chronological age. However, this method of determining IQ has been replaced by the *deviation IQ*, which allows the examiner to refer to tables provided with the test to determine the IQ value associated with a particular test score and chronological age.

The Stanford-Binet may be used for individuals from two years of age to the adult level. The test is designed so that at each age level the subject is presented with six subtests. Between the ages of two and five, each half-year interval represents a different age level, between five and fourteen the age levels represent yearly intervals, and for ages fifteen and above there are four adult levels. The subtests are designed so that the tests become increasingly difficult at each successive age level.

The examiner using the Stanford-Binet test is provided with

a kit containing the materials necessary to administer the test, and the subtests presented represent both verbal and performance abilities. Examples of the subtest used at two different age levels are presented below:

Three-Year Level

Subtest 1: Stringing Beads. A box of large beads and a shoe-string are used for this subtest. Sixteen of the beads are round, sixteen are square, and sixteen are cylindrical, but all are the same color. The child is required to string as many of the beads as he can within a two-minute time limit. The child is judged to pass this subtest if he strings at least four beads in the time limit.

Subtest 2: Picture Vocabulary. In this subtest the child is presented with eighteen pictures of common objects and asked to name as many as he can. The child passes the subtest if he can name ten or more of the objects.

Subtest 3: Block Building. In this subtest the materials required are a set of common one-inch blocks. The examiner constructs a simple bridge with three of the blocks and asks the child to make one just like it.

Subtest 4: Picture Memories. A set of four cards with pictures of animals is used as materials for this subtest. The child is shown a card containing a picture of a given animal; then the card is put back with the others and the child is asked to find it again. The child passes this subtest if he gets at least one correct.

Subtest 5: Copying a Circle. A printed circle is shown to the child and he is asked to draw one like it. If the child accomplishes this task in three tries, he is judged to pass the subtest.

Subtest 6: Drawing a Vertical Line. The examiner draws a vertical line and instructs the child to make one like it, allowing only a single trial.

Eight-Year Level

Subtest 1: Vocabulary. The child at this age level is asked to tell the meaning of a list of words that are both read aloud to him by the examiner and presented on a list that is given to the child. If the child correctly responds to eight of a possible 45 words, he passes the subtest.

Subtest 2: Memory for Stories. In this subtest the child is read a short, simple story and then asked questions about the story's content.

Subtest 3: Verbal Absurdities. The child is asked to tell the examiner "what is foolish" or absurd about a series of statements such as: "Walter now has to write with his left hand because two years ago he lost both his arms in an accident."

Subtest 4: Similarities and Differences. In this subtest the child is presented with a list of pairs of items such as "baseball and orange" and asked to tell how they are alike and how they are different.

Subtest 5: Comprehension. This subtest requires the child to

demonstrate comprehension of abstract ideas by answering questions such as "What makes a sailboat move?"

Subtest 6: Naming the Days of the Week. To pass this subtest
the child must name the days of the week in correct order.

In administering the Stanford-Binet test, the examiner will
usually start at an age level slightly below the chronological age of
the child. Thus, if a three-year-old is being tested, the examiner may
start at the two-year-and-six-month level. The testing will proceed
through each successively higher age level of tests until the child
no longer passes any of the tests at the upper age levels. Thus, for
our three-year-old we may find that all of the two-year-and-six-month
level and three-year level tests were passed, three of the three-year-
and-six-month, and one of the four-year level tests were passed.

The score on the test is determined by adding all of the tests
passed at each age level. The IQ can then be determined by consulting the deviation-IQ tables for the particular chronological age
of the child (or adult) and the score achieved.

The Wechsler Tests

The other major individually administered intelligence tests
in common use are the *Wechsler Adult Intelligence Scale* (Wechsler,
1955), and the *Wechsler Intelligence Scale for Children* (Wechsler,
1949). These tests are commonly referred to as the WAIS and WISC.

The WAIS is a particularly important test since it was specifically designed as an adult intelligence test. The WAIS contains both
a verbal intelligence scale and a performance scale, although ordinarily only a single full-scale IQ value is obtained. Six subtests are
contained in the verbal scale, and five subtests in the performance
scale of the WAIS. These subtests correspond roughly to some of the
more important factors of ability that were mentioned earlier. The
eleven subtests of the WAIS are briefly described below:

Verbal Scale

Subtest 1: General Information. In this subtest the individual is
asked to answer twenty-five general questions that are designed
to evaluate general levels of knowledge.

Subtest 2: General Comprehension. There are ten items on this
subtest that are intended to evaluate knowledge of rules and problem solving.

Subtest 3: Arithmetical Reasoning. The items on this subtest
involve simple arithmetic operations.

Subtest 4: Similarities. In this subtest the individual is asked to
indicate similarities between pairs of terms.

Subtest 5: Digit Span. This subtest is designed to evaluate immediate memory. The examinee is asked to repeat, in correct order, series of digits that are read to him by the examiner.

Subtest 6: Vocabulary. This subtest asks the individual to give the meanings of a list of forty words.

Performance Scale

Subtest 7: Digit Symbol. The individual is shown a list of symbols, each of which has a number associated with it, and another list of randomly ordered numbers, and he is required to match the appropriate symbols to the numbers in the second list.

Subtest 8: Picture Completion. In this subtest the subject is required to identify a missing part in each of a series of fifteen incomplete pictures.

Subtest 9: Block Design. This subtest requires the subject to assemble a set of colored blocks so as to reproduce seven different block designs presented on picture cards.

Subtest 10: Picture Arrangement. The examinee must arrange a set of pictures in the correct order to form a cartoon story.

Subtest 11: Object Assembly. This subtest involves the assembly of three jigsaw puzzles.

The WAIS is a *point scale*, rather than an *age scale*, and the IQ is determined by adding the weighted score from each of the eleven subtests and consulting a table supplied for that purpose.

The WISC is very similar in content to the WAIS, although the particular items on this test are designed to be more appropriate for children. The WISC contains approximately the same subtests as the WAIS, and it is also a point rather than an age scale. The WISC is appropriate for use with children between five and fifteen years, eleven months of age, while the WAIS is used with children over fifteen and adults. In general, psychologists prefer the WAIS over the Stanford-Binet for the testing of adults, but neither the Stanford-Binet nor the WISC holds a clear-cut preference for testing children.

Group Tests

A variety of group tests of general ability have also been devised and are widely used, particularly in school situations. The chief advantage of the group test lies in ease of administration, since a large number of people can be tested at one time. Another major advantage of group tests over individual intelligence tests, such as the Stanford-Binet and Wechsler scales, is that they generally require only minimally trained examiners. Most group tests are "paper-and-pencil" tests, with standardized instructions, and they can be administered and scored by anyone who can read and add. The individual tests, on the other hand, should be administered and scored by trained personnel since the judgment of the examiner is frequently required in deciding whether or not a given subtest was passed or failed.

The content of group intelligence tests is usually restricted to verbal material that tests factors such as comprehension, reasoning abilities, and numerical abilities (Nunnally, 1970), although some nonverbal tests are available.

Before leaving our discussion of ability tests we should briefly consider two extremely important characteristics of any test—the *reliability* of a test, or the extent to which the test measures the same thing from one occasion to the next, and its *validity*, or the extent to which the test measures that which it sets out to measure.

Reliability of Intelligence Tests

The determination of the reliability of any given test can be approached in several ways. Perhaps the most common measure of the reliability of a test is the *test-retest* technique. To compute the test-retest reliability, the test is administered to a given group of individuals on two different occasions, usually separated by a sufficient amount of time to rule out the possibility that individuals will remember the test items at the second testing, but short enough to reduce additional learning. The correlation is then computed between the two test administrations. If the test is measuring the same thing on both occasions, we would expect a high correlation; this correlation can be taken as an estimate of the test's reliability.

Another way to estimate reliability is to administer two equivalent forms of the test to a given group of subjects. Again the correlation between the two forms of the test is computed and is used as the reliability estimate. This technique is known as the *alternate-form* reliability method.

Another means of determining test reliability, which is closely related to the alternate-form technique, is the *split-half* method. In the case of the split-half reliability the correlation between two halves of the same test is calculated. Often the test is divided, for this purpose, by scoring the odd-numbered items separately from the even-numbered items and then determining the correlation between the odd and even items.

All of the commonly used intelligence tests have been subjected to reliability studies, and most of them report very high *reli-*

ability coefficients. The split-half reliability of the Wechsler scales, for instance is about .95 (Nunnally, 1970), which is a strong indication that the tests are reliable or stable.

Validity

The validity of a test represents the degree to which the test measures the things it is designed to measure. The two most important types of validity in connection with intelligence or ability tests are *predictive validity* and *concurrent validity.*

Predictive Validity

The correlation coefficient is also used to measure the validity of a test. In the case of predictive validity the psychologist is interested in the correlation between his test and some *criterion* measure. Usually, the appropriate criterion measure is taken to be the quality of educational achievement. It is assumed that more intelligent or able individuals will succeed better in terms of educational achievement and that a good test will predict this achievement. To establish the predictive validity of a given test, the test scores will be correlated with subsequent educational achievement and the resulting correlation coefficient will be taken as a measure of the predictive validity of the test. The major tests that we have discussed have reported relatively substantial correlations with this criterion, and consequently, they appear to be valid on this basis.

Concurrent Validity

Another means of estimating the validity of an intelligence test is to evaluate the correlation of that test with another test that is assumed to be valid. The Stanford-Binet, being perhaps the oldest and most widely accepted test of intelligence or general ability, is often the standard test against which other tests are compared for this purpose. To measure the concurrent validity of a new test, a large number of individuals will be tested on both the new test and, for instance, the Stanford-Binet. If the correlation between the two tests is high, the interpretation will usually be made that the new test is also a valid test. A correlation of .85 has, for example, been reported between the WAIS and the Stanford-Binet tests (Freeman, 1962). This is an example of a reasonably high indication of concurrent validity.

The System So Far

We have seen in previous chapters how the contributions of the various behavioral subsystems are combined into a complete behavioral system. However, because these subsystems do not function identically and are modifiable, differences between systems exist in all behavioral characteristics. These differences exist because of two primary influences—genetic, or hereditary, and environmental. The hereditary influences are such that the subsystems are predisposed to function in a particular fashion and, in some cases, limitations on the functioning may be established genetically. The environmental factors are considered by many to be the most important determinants of the differences that exist between people. Thus, the experiences that an individual encounters as he develops and, to a lesser extent, the experiences he encounters after attaining adulthood are thought to be critical factors in establishing individual differences.

Individual differences are shown between individuals in any behavioral characteristic that we can measure. However, in terms of adequate adjustment and achievement in our society, the two characteristics of intelligence and personality are of most significance. In this chapter, we have considered these characteristics and attempted to explain what they are and how they develop.

Summary

1. The study of individual differences is based on the assumption that for any given attribute differences between individuals will be found and that these differences, when properly measured and plotted, will result in a distribution of measurements called a normal distribution.

2. There are a variety of definitions of intelligence. Most definitions view intelligence as consisting of several abilities or attributes. This view has developed from studies involving factor analysis. However, a more basic definition is that which considers intelligence as a summation of all learning experience.

3. People differ widely in intelligence. Both heredity and environment contribute to these differences. Class and race differences in intelligence have been demonstrated frequently. Differences in environment have generally been used to explain class and

race differences in intelligence but some argue that heredity may be an important factor. While sex differences in intelligence exist, these differences are a function of testing for specific abilities. When overall level of intelligence is considered, there are no differences of any significance.

4. There are many definitions of personality, including those that can be considered as biosocial and others that are biophysical. The former equates personality to the "social stimulus value" of an individual, while the latter links personality to specific qualities of the individual that are susceptible to measurement and description.

5. The biophysical view of personality defines personality structure as being made up of traits. In general, traits are thought to be of two kinds—surface traits and source traits. A combination of traits determines the personality type. While there are many types of personality listed by various writers, a more familiar scheme reduces personality differences to two basic types—extroversion and introversion.

6. The concept of self is an important factor in several personality theories. Some theorists are concerned with the individual's self-perception—how he views himself in relation to others. It is felt that this perception is an important determinant of personality. To other theorists, "self" is defined as some unobservable internal process that will cause a person to behave in a certain fashion.

7. People differ considerably in terms of their personality characteristics. While there are genetic factors involved in determining personality, there are many environmental factors that are important. Thus, learning contributes a great deal to the personality of an individual. Learning that takes place during the early developmental stages is particularly critical. Cultural and family influences are key determinants of personality.

8. Psychological testing involves the quantification of individual differences. Individuals possess differing degrees of ability which can be defined as the human capacity to perform various tasks. One purpose of psychological testing is to evaluate these abilities. A second major purpose of testing is to determine the degree to which individuals deviate from "normal" or average standards of behavior.

9. Application of a statistical tool called factor analysis has led to a better understanding of the structure of intellect. There are many factors, or types, of abilities that make up "intelligence." These include such factors as verbal, numerical, reasoning, memory, spatial, and perceptual.

10. A number of instruments have been developed for meas-

uring intelligence. The most popular include the Stanford-Binet test and the Wechsler tests (WAIS and WISC).

11. There are two important characteristics that must be present with any test—reliability and validity. The former refers to the extent to which the test measures the same thing from one occasion to the next. Validity is the extent to which the test measures what it is designed to measure.

Selected Readings

DuBois, P. H. *The history of psychological testing.* Boston: Allyn and Bacon, 1970.

Guilford, J. P. *The nature of human intelligence.* New York: McGraw-Hill, 1967.

Jensen, A. R. How much can we boost IQ and scholastic achievement? *Harvard Education Review,* 1969, **39,** 1–123.

Nunnally, J. C. *Introduction to psychological measurement.* New York: McGraw-Hill, 1970.

Pervin, L. A. *Personality: Theory, assessment, and research.* New York: Wiley, 1970.

Zigler, E. & Child, I. L. Socialization. In G. Lindzey and E. Aronson (Eds.), *The handbook of social psychology.* Vol. III. Reading, Massachusetts: Addison-Wesley, 1969. Pp. 450–589.

11

System Malfunctions

We omitted one very important characteristic when we discussed characteristics of systems earlier. Any system, whether it is man or machine, tends to develop malfunctions. You encounter these malfunctions on an almost daily basis in various systems that you come in contact with—your automobile does not start, the light does not work in your room, the water in the shower is cold, and so on. These are minor system malfunctions. Sometimes a malfunction may be much more serious and the attention of the world is drawn to it, as was the case in the Apollo 13 flight. In this situation the malfunction was not serious enough to destroy the system, but the goal or purpose of the system was not accomplished. System malfunctions are so common, of course, that they support a significant percentage of our population who are engaged in correcting, or attempting to correct, malfunctions.

The human system is also prone to a wide variety of malfunctions. For example, we could fill a number of pages simply listing the labels that have been attached to the various diseases that man may suffer from. These malfunctions are so frequent that their treatment involves many thousands of physicians and supports a vast medical industry involving hundreds of thousands of people and billions of dollars. We also encounter malfunctions in the behavioral system of man, and it is these types of malfunctions and the methods employed in their correction that will be dealt with in this chapter.

We have seen that an input to a system will be transformed, by means of various subsystems, to an output. In a machine system, if the input is specified and all the subsystems are working properly, then we can accurately predict the output. This is true because machines are typically constructed so that the various subsystems operate in a prescribed manner at all times. Further, when several machines of the same design are involved, then the output of one should be identical to the output of another. If, however, there is a malfunction in one of the subsystems of a machine, then we can no longer expect the prescribed output. The output is no longer "normal" but rather it is "abnormal" in some respect.

Attempting to predict the output of the human system is much more complicated than is the case with a machine. Not only do the behavioral subsystems of a particular individual function differently at various times but the subsystems of no two individuals will function identically. Consequently, output (behavior) cannot be predicted perfectly on the basis of an understanding of the input to the system. Thus, even if we were able to very carefully control the input we would still find people differing on any behavioral response that we could measure.

While the transformation process between input and output is such that we cannot be completely accurate in predicting the behavior of a person in a given situation, we usually have some idea of what kind of behavior to expect. For example, what kind of behavior might be expected from a group of students who received failing grades in a psychology test? First, the behavior would be determined, at least in part, by a number of situational variables. How many students failed? Was the test "fair"? How much does the test count on the final course grade? With some understanding of the circumstances, we might expect responses ranging from quiet acceptance of the failing grade to an argument with the instructor. However, suppose a student physically attacked the instructor or, perhaps, went back to the dormitory and shot himself. Either of these responses would be considered highly inappropriate for the particular situation—that is, they would not be considered "normal" responses. Thus, while we accept the fact that differences in the functioning of our behavioral subsystems will lead to various kinds of responses in a particular situation, we also expect that these responses will fall within a certain range.

While we have suggested that a malfunction in the behavioral system will result in an "abnormal" output, our knowledge of the etiology of abnormal behavior is such that we cannot be very specific about what particular subsystem might be involved. It is not quite as simple as diagnosing a malfunction in an automobile as a problem arising from the carburetor. However, we can classify the malfunction as being one of two types. One form of malfunction involves actual damage to the system, such as brain damage of some sort, which causes the abnormal behavior. When this situation exists, we refer to the behavior as *organic* or *somatogenic* in origin. The second type of malfunction is not caused by any recognized physical damage and results in *psychogenic* or *functional* disorders. Although most forms of abnormal behavior are of this type, the nature of the malfunction is much more difficult to specify than is an organic malfunction. About all we can say of these kinds of behavior is that the "behavioral system is just not functioning properly." Regardless of the causes, the improper functioning results in behavior that we consider abnormal.

This brings us to an important question. When can we say that the behavioral subsystems are not functioning properly and that their output is distorted? In other words, when do we consider the output of the behavior system to be "abnormal" rather than "normal"?

What Is Abnormal Behavior?

In previous chapters we have seen that there are problems in defining such terms as "intelligence" and "personality." Once again we are confronted with a problem of definition when we attempt to answer the question "What is abnormal behavior?"

There are a number of reasons why it is not easy to arrive at a definition of abnormal behavior. In the first place, there is usually no sharp dividing line between behavior that might be considered as abnormal and that which is normal. Abnormal behavior grades into normal behavior in such a fashion that it is difficult to state when one type begins and the other ends. Nevertheless, the fact that most people do behave quite similarly, allowing marked deviation to become apparent, is the basis for what is called the *statistical definition* of abnormality. The person who is most normal by this definition is the individual who behaves most like other people. With this type of definition, normality comes close to being equated with conformity, and, for this and other reasons, the statistical definition does not please everyone. Definitions of this kind require the adoption of value judgments of some sort on the part of whoever labels the behavior as "abnormal" and raises the problem of who selects the values and what values are used to define abnormality.

The difficulty of adequate definition is increased by the fact that behavior considered abnormal in one culture may be viewed as perfectly normal in another culture. Thus, in one culture it may be normal to shout, tear your hair, and jump up and down whenever a slight frustration occurs. In another culture, you might be locked up for engaging in the same type of behavior in a very similar set of circumstances. The types of behavior that are called "abnormal" are those which, for various reasons, are not approved of by a particular culture. This presents a problem, of course, for arriving at a definition of abnormality that can be valid beyond a given culture.

The task of defining abnormality is further complicated by the fact that there are a number of professions interested in the problem of abnormality; each of these professions arrives at a somewhat different definition because of its frame of reference. For example, a psychiatrist, who is interested in treating and attempting to correct a form of abnormal behavior, may define it quite differently from a judge, who is primarily interested in whether the person knew right from wrong when committing an unlawful act.

We have stated that no completely adequate definition of abnormality is available. What are the requirements of an adequate definition? First, according to Ullmann and Krasner (1969), a definition of abnormality should be such that it includes all the people who are indeed abnormal and none of the people who are not. Second, a definition should be such that it can be consistently applied by different people or by the same person at different times. In other words, the definition should specify characteristics of abnormality that can be attended to and recognized by the person who is labeling the behavior, and these same characteristics should be recognizable by other observers. Unfortunately, we do not have available a definition that meets these criteria.

Possibly, there has been an overemphasis on the development of various concepts of abnormality. There has been an increased tendency among psychologists to question the concepts of abnormality that currently exist and to even question whether there is a need for these concepts. For example, Ullmann and Krasner (1969) wonder what would happen if these concepts were abandoned entirely. They believe that "professionals can describe, understand, measure, predict, and alter behaviors called abnormal more effectively without the concept of abnormality than with it." In brief, Ullmann and Krasner believe that if a behavior is learned, it should be considered normal. While a person may demonstrate behavior that an observer views as unexpected, bizarre, or deviant, that behavior may be a reasonable outcome of the particular individual's heredity and environment. In other words, the behavior is not "abnormal" to the person who is behaving but rather it is seen and labeled as abnormal behavior by the observer. Whether or not the observer considers the behavior as abnormal depends upon specific situations and includes such factors as the age, sex, social class, and race of the person being observed. Thus, the labeling is based upon the past experience of the observer just as the behavior that is labeled may be a product of the past experience of the person demonstrating the behavior. The view that many kinds of abnormal behavior are forms of learned behavior is significant from the point of view of the therapist who attempts to correct these behaviors. This aspect will be considered in more detail later.

Recognizing that any definition of abnormality that we might arrive at would not be completely satisfactory to everyone, how shall we define this kind of behavior? One common definition —the *medical model* of abnormality—identifies abnormality with a biological disorder. The individual's abnormal behavior is considered a symptom of some nervous, mental, or personality process that is "disordered." In other words, abnormality, or behavior pathology, is defined as a disturbance in normal processes. Conversely, normality is the absence of pathology. Clearly, our view of abnormality as a malfunction that occurs between input and output falls within the general category of "medical definitions" of abnormal behavior.

We have by no means exhausted the supply of definitions of abnormal behavior or the arguments, pro and con, concerning the definitions. However, regardless of the problems of definition, the fact remains that there are certain patterns of behavior that are labeled as abnormal in our culture. We will now consider some of these kinds of behavior.

Labeling Abnormal Behavior

One might wonder why so much effort has been made to label "abnormal" behaviors. Why not just label someone who demonstrates abnormal behavior as "abnormal" and let it go at that? We do not do this, of course, for the same reason that we do not use the label "sickness" for all of the variety of diseases that exist. Rather, a much more specific label is used to identify and distinguish a particular disease. The label is useful in communicating information about the disease and in suggesting possible treatment.

Over the years, several systems of labels have been used and abandoned. The most current system is that of the American Psychiatric Association (1968) which is described in the *Diagnostic and Statistical Manual of Mental Disorders* (abbreviated to DSM-II). As you might expect, not everyone is satisfied with this particular scheme. Some argue that this system is purely descriptive and that its classificatory principle is organized about symptom manifestation. They further argue that a system of this type tells very little, if anything, about cause, treatment, or prognosis. Regardless of the criticisms of the system, it is the most widely used. It contains ten major categories of disorders, each of which is further divided into a number of subcategories. The major categories of the DSM-II are listed in Table 11–1.

Table 11–1. Major categories of mental disorders listed in DSM-II.

1. Mental retardation
2. Organic brain syndromes
   A. Psychoses associated with organic brain syndromes
   B. Non-psychotic organic brain syndromes
3. Psychoses not attributed to physical conditions listed previously
4. Neuroses
5. Personality disorders and certain other non-psychotic mental disorders
6. Psychophysiologic disorders
7. Special symptoms
8. Transient situational disturbances
9. Behavior disorders of childhood and adolescence
10. Conditions without manifest psychiatric disorder and non-specific conditions

The Disorders

It is beyond the scope of this chapter to consider the behavioral patterns associated with all of the mental disorders listed in Table 11–1. For diagnostic purposes, each of the major categories shown in the table is further divided into a number of subcategories, each with particular behavioral characteristics.

Mental Retardation

We have seen that intelligence, as measured by the available instruments, is distributed in such a manner that most people fall in the middle range of the distribution, with some found at either end. At the one end these individuals are called "gifted" or "genius," while at the other end of the distribution they are called mentally retarded. An obvious problem, of course, is the point (or score) on the distribution at which someone is classified as retarded. Unfortunately, there is no convenient gap on the IQ distribution that can be used to distinguish between normal and retarded. Consequently, an arbitrary cutoff must be decided upon. This has been done on the basis of the amount of care and supervision typically required for individuals with IQ scores in certain ranges. Based on various estimates, there are thought to be between five and six million individuals in the United States whose IQ's place them in the retarded range.

While IQ is frequently the primary criterion in making a diagnosis of mental retardation, other criteria should also be involved. As is pointed out in the DSM-II (p. 14), the judgment "should also be based on an evaluation of the patient's developmental history and present functioning, including academic and vocational achievement, motor skills, and social and emotional maturity." Thus, a person who is classified as retarded based on IQ may very well be capable of assuming an active and worthwhile role in society based on other criteria. Most of us would find it difficult to call a person "mentally retarded" who has an IQ of 65 but successfully manages his own business and, possibly, employs a number of high IQ college graduates. An individual who has an IQ that would place him in the retarded class but who manages to adjust to society does not get into trouble with the law and, in general, assumes the role of a self-supporting citizen, should be considered as "normal." In other words, the overt social behavior demonstrated by a person should take precedence over the IQ measure in the classifying process.

Whether or not a person is designated as retarded based on IQ also depends upon the duration of the defect. For example, if a person with an IQ of 120 is injured or suffers from some disease and, afterward, has a measured IQ of 60, he would not be categorized as retarded. Rather, he would be placed in the organic brain syndrome category. To be classified in the mentally retarded category, the defect must have existed from birth or shortly thereafter.

When mental retardation is defined in terms of IQ, the DSM-II lists five categories or classifications of retardation—borderline, mild, moderate, severe, and profound.

Most individuals in the borderline category are rarely recognized as retarded and generally function as "normal" in their social and vocational roles. Similarly, a mild retardate is typically capable of vocational and social adjustment although some supervision may sometimes be needed. The amount of supervision and guidance that is required increases with moderate retardation although these individuals can perform satisfactorily in unskilled types of work. Virtually complete supervision is necessary in the case of the severely retarded and, with profound retardation, nursing care is generally required.

Etiology of Mental Retardation. There are numerous conditions, both psychogenic and somatogenic, that can result in mental retardation. For example, mental retardation can be caused by such somatogenic factors as infections, trauma or physical agents, disorders of metabolism, growth, or nutrition, various brain diseases, and chromosomal abnormality. While we cannot discuss all of these, we will consider some of the more common somatogenic origins of retardation.

One possible cause of retardation that we hear a great deal about is maternal infections, particularly *rubella* or *German measles*. There is a very good chance that a child will be retarded if the mother contracts German measles during the first three months of pregnancy. If the infection is contracted during the first month of pregnancy, there is nearly a 50 percent chance that the infant may be abnormal in some way. While this percentage is reduced considerably if the infection occurs in the second month of pregnancy, and even further reduced in the third month, there is still a significant chance of abnormality. This is the reason why many women consider abortion if they contract German measles during the early stages of pregnancy.

Another type of maternal infection that can cause mental retardation in offspring is *syphilis*. Not too many years ago it appeared as though this would no longer be an important factor in mental retardation since the incidence of syphilis had been reduced greatly by effective countermeasures. However, at the present time there is a great deal of concern on the part of various government agencies because of the tremendous increase of venereal disease in the United States. Consequently, an upsurge in retardation caused by syphilis infection of mothers should not be surprising.

Difficulties may also occur because of metabolic disorders of the child, such as *phenylketonuria* (PKU). In this particular disorder, incomplete metabolism results in injuries to the brain and consequent retardation. When this condition exists in a newborn infant, phenylpyruvic acid can be detected in the urine by means of a simple test. If detected, the infant can be fed on a special diet and the retardation prevented.

Mental retardation may also result from several kinds of chromosomal abnormalities. One of the most common types of somatogenic retardation is associated with a condition of chromosomal aberration involving one too many chromosomes (47 instead of the normal complement of 46). However, the reason for the occurrence of the extra chromosome and how it might produce the disorder is not completely understood. The common name for the type of retardation encountered in this situation is *Mongolism* although it may also be called *Down's syndrome* or *trisomy-21 anomaly.* Along with the mental retardation, there are a number of distinctive physical characteristics associated with Mongolism. The typical child with this syndrome would have a round face with slanting eyes, small chin and ears, a large fissured tongue protruding from a small mouth, as well as other distinctive physical features.

A question that has been asked frequently, and one to which we have no complete answer, concerns the effects of prenatal usage of drugs on the offspring. There have been, of course, some glaring examples of what prenatal drug use can do—for example, thalidomide—but there may be many other kinds of drugs with more subtle effects. Considerable concern has been shown, for example, regarding the possible effects of prenatal use of LSD on offspring. An increasing body of evidence (Cohen, Hirschhorn, & Frosch, 1967; Egozcue, Irwin, & Maruffo, 1968) has linked LSD with chromosomal damage and congenital birth defects. Experiments with animals have indicated that this hallucinogen passes through the placental barrier and, especially during the early stages of pregnancy, produces both morphological and chromosomal anomalies. Auerback and Rugowski (1967) found that rats given a single injection of LSD tartrate during early stages of pregnancy produced embryos that exhibited abnormal development and gross deformities in 57 percent of the cases. Offspring of animals that received LSD typically were stunted in their growth and had nervous-system defects. Even the animals that appeared normal often exhibited a retarded rate of development when compared to controls.

In human beings, research has produced equivocal results concerning LSD (Loughman, Sargent, & Israelstam, 1967; Irwin & Egozcue, 1967). Most studies, however, lend support to two observations. First, there is typically a degree of chromosomal damage in LSD users similar to that observed in leukemia or in persons surviving high amounts of irradiation. Second, offspring of LSD users exhibit chromosomal abnormalities at a rate significantly higher than that in the general population. Thus, it would seem that there is evidence that LSD produces birth defects.

As yet, no direct evidence associating marijuana with birth defects has been accumulated. However, the National Institute of

Mental Health is currently supporting research projects designed to investigate a possible link between the active constituent of marijuana (tetrahydrocannabinol) and congenital birth defects.

While the evidence that prenatal drug use may result in retarded offspring is sparse, if it is true we can certainly expect a major problem in the near future. The wide current usage of a variety of drugs almost guarantees that a large number of children will be born to mothers who are drug addicts or users.

We have by no means exhausted the somatogenic factors that may be responsible for mental retardation. While physiological syndromes of some type account for a large percentage of the retardates with very low IQ's, nonetheless we find that somatogenic factors are involved in far fewer cases of mental retardation than are the psychogenic factors.

Probably about 75 percent of the mentally retarded do not reveal any known somatogenic factor that would account for their deficiency. Most of these are simply individuals who score below the "cutoff" on IQ tests and, consequently, are classed as retarded. Why people differ in their ability to produce the behavior required on an intelligence test was discussed in the previous chapter. About all that we can say concerning this ability is that it is determined by a complex interaction of genetic and environmental factors, with the former generally considered as being most important.

In some instances, however, retardation can be directly related to some unusual environmental conditions. For example, the DSM-II has a category of retardation associated with deprivation of normal environmental stimulation in infancy and early childhood. While this type of retardation tends to be mild or marginal, it does suggest the possible importance of some kinds of environmental factors. In this vein, Bijou (1966) has presented some interesting ideas about retarded behavior. It is suggested that there are patterns of learning that lead to a limited behavioral repertoire and designation as a retardate. In other words, the retarded child may be capable of a larger behavioral range but does not possess it because he has not had adequate opportunity to learn. This idea, of course, has considerable implication for the training of retarded children, as Ullmann and Krasner (1969) point out:

> It is right and proper to ask if there are patterns of learning that have led to a limited behavioral repertoire. On the basis of such an analysis, testable programs may be developed to determine whether new experiences may lead to the generation of the serviceable behavior not previously learned. The focus of interest is shifted from a search for "intelligence" to a search for the conditions of "intelligent behavior" [p. 566].

The Neuroses

When the behavioral subsystems are operating properly, the individual is able to adjust to, or cope with, fears, conflicts, and anxieties without impairment of his functioning or his ability to deal with reality. There are, however, many individuals who are not capable of adjusting to themselves or their environment and consequently demonstrate certain patterns of behavior, or symptoms, that constitute a class of disorders called the *neuroses* or *psychoneuroses*.

There are several basic theoretical premises that have been put forth to explain the source of the behavior that is labeled as neurotic. A psychologist with a Freudian orientation would explain the origin of neurotic behavior in different terms than a psychologist with a learning-theory approach. While these theories make interesting reading, a discussion of them involves more detail and becomes more technical than is appropriate for an introductory text.

Unlike the psychoses, which will be taken up later, the neuroses do not result in gross distortion or misinterpretation of reality. Neither do they exhibit marked disorganization of personality. Further, unlike the situation that often occurs with psychotics, the neurotic is aware that his mental functioning is disturbed.

Anxiety—that is, generalized feelings of apprehension and worry resulting from lack of adjustment—seems to be the distinguishing characteristic of the neurotic disorders. These disorders are often manifested in the form of specific patterns of behavior that are frequently repeated over and over. However, instead of helping the neurotic solve his problem, this behavior often enhances the problem. The particular behavior that is demonstrated can range from that which interferes very little with everyday living to behavior that virtually incapacitates the person. While the neurotic's behavior may vary from time to time, there is usually a pattern present that can be observed and that can assist in determining the particular type of neurotic disorder that is involved.

The DSM-II lists a number of types of neuroses, including anxiety neurosis, hysterical neurosis, phobic neurosis, obsessive compulsive neurosis, hypochondriacal neurosis, as well as several other forms. Each of these has certain symptoms, some of which will be briefly discussed.

Anxiety Neurosis. Everyone is frightened or apprehensive at times, and this is perfectly normal assuming there is something to be frightened about. However, the individual with an anxiety neurosis is frightened and anxious much of the time, but his anxiety and fear is not directed at any specific object or situation. Rather, it is generalized and diffuse and not associated with any particular source as is the case with the phobic neuroses. He feels something terrible is going to happen to him but he does not know what. The anxiety is often accompanied by somatic symptoms, particularly during acute anxiety attacks, which may occur frequently. The somatic symptoms include cardiac reactions, such as rapid heart beat and palpitations; feelings of nausea; increased sweating; difficulty in bladder and bowel functions; disturbances in muscular reactions (tremors), as well as various other symptoms.

Hysterical Neurosis. This type of neurosis is characterized by an involuntary loss or disorder of some bodily function. There are two forms—the *conversion* type and the *dissociative* type. In the former, the special senses or the voluntary nervous system is affected, resulting in a variety of symptoms such as loss of sight, deafness, and various motor disturbances. Frequently the patient shows little concern about these symptoms "which may actually provide secondary gains by winning him sympathy or relieving him of unpleasant responsibilities" (DSM-II, p. 40). The dissociative type of hysterical neurosis is manifested in alterations in the person's state of consciousness or in his identity. This results in symptoms such as amnesia, sleepwalking, and multiple personality, such as the "Three Faces of Eve" type situation.

Phobic Neurosis. When a person is intensely afraid of an object or situation and consciously recognizes that there is no danger involved, he has a condition known as phobic neurosis. There are many objects and situations at which these types of irrational fears are directed—heights, open spaces, closed spaces, dirt, animals, and so on. The technical term for these conditions involve adding an appropriate prefix to the stem "phobia" resulting in words such as claustrophobia, hydrophobia, and so on.

Other Neuroses. There are several other forms of neuroses. For example, the *depressive neurosis* is manifested by an extreme reaction of depression because of an internal conflict or an external event such as the death of a loved one. In *obsessive compulsive neurosis*, there are repeated, unwanted, inappropriate thoughts and activities. These activities can range from simple movements to rather complex rituals. Repeated handwashing, for example, may be a form of obsessive compulsive behavior. *Neurasthenic neurosis* (neurasthenia) symptoms include complaints of fatigue, exhaustion, and chronic weakness, while the *hypochondriacal neurosis* is characterized by fear of presumed diseases.

When reading about the various categories of neuroses and the associated symptoms, you should be cautioned that the neuroses rarely occur in what could be called a "pure" form. Often the symptoms that are manifested tend to be "mixed," and it may be difficult for the diagnostician to arrive at a label that best fits the patient. In any particular case, a mixture of several types of symptoms will be the rule rather than the exception. This is also true of the psychoses which will be discussed next.

The Psychoses

While there is no clear-cut dividing line between the neuroses and the psychoses, it is generally believed that the two can be differentiated on the basis of the severity of the disturbance. The neurotic is considered to be less severely disturbed than the psychotic, who is usually markedly disoriented with gross distortions of perception and thought. According to the DSM-II:

> Patients are described as psychotic when their mental functioning is sufficiently impaired to interfere grossly with their capacity to meet the ordinary demands of life. The impairment may result from a serious distortion in their capacity to recognize reality. Hallucinations and delusions, for example, may distort their perceptions. Alterations of mood may be so profound that the patient's capacity to respond appropriately is grossly impaired. Deficits in perception, language and memory may be so severe that the patient's capacity for mental grasp of his situation is effectively lost [p. 23].

Psychotics, then, can be expected to show a loss of contact with reality and gross disturbances in behavior and thought processes. There are certain symptoms that tend to be manifested with the psychoses, either singly or in various combinations. Frequently, the patient will suffer from *delusions*, which are false beliefs of some sort that the individual maintains despite all evidence that they are not true. A psychotic may also experience *hallucinations*, which can be thought of as false perceptions—that is, sensory impressions of objects when there are no appropriate stimuli present in the environment. Finally, the psychotic patient may suffer from severe *disturbances of affect* characterized by extremes of gloom, elation, fear, anger, and so on.

A question that has often been raised is whether the neuroses and psychoses are basically similar forms of mental disorders that differ only in degree of severity or whether they represent two separate and distinct disease processes. This question has not been satisfactorily answered, and there are a number of supporters for both points of view. If the neuroses and psychoses are, indeed, similar forms of disorders that are distinguished from each other by the severity of the behavior demonstrated, then the situation depicted in Figure 11-1(A) would exist. With the "one-continuum" theory shown in this figure, the neurotics fall between the normal subjects and the psychotic subjects in terms of the behavior shown. However, both neurotics and psychotics are different from the normals. This is also the case in the second theory that neuroses and psychoses

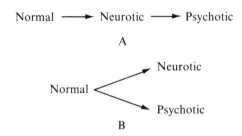

Figure 11–1. Part A of the figure represents the "one-continuum" theory of neurosis and psychosis. In this instance, the two are thought to be similar forms of disorders and are distinguished on the basis of severity. Part B represents the "separate-continua" theory, with neuroses and psychoses representing different processes.

represent separate and qualitatively different processes. In this case, the situation shown in Figure 11–1(B) would pertain. In other words, in the first instance the subsystem malfunctions are similar but differ in degree, while, in the situation illustrated in Figure 11–1 (B), the malfunctions are different for the neuroses than for the psychoses.

Some of the psychoses have an *organic* basis and are listed in the DSM-II as "psychoses associated with organic brain syndromes." Under this category are included psychoses that result from senile brain damage and various types of psychoses that are due to alcohol, as well as some caused by other conditions that damage the brain. A larger category of psychoses are those that are called *functional* and which are not attributed to an observable or recognized physical condition. However, just because a physical cause has not been isolated for the so-called functional psychoses, the possibility of a chemical or physiological origin should not be completely discounted. Considerable research has been, and continues to be, conducted in an effort to determine whether or not there may actually be some type of physical condition underlying various functional psychoses. For example, there is some evidence that the blood chemistry of certain types of psychotic patients differs from that of normal subjects. However, a key question in studies of this type is whether the difference is due to cause or effect. In other words, perhaps the difference in the blood is caused *by* the psychotic condition and not the other way around. Other differences in body chemistry have also been found, but the problem of interpretation of these differences is important. As an example of a problem of interpretation, consider a study done a few years ago.

In this investigation, analysis of the urine of psychotic patients and normals (ward attendants, and so on) revealed that there was a significant difference between the two groups in the amount of a particular chemical that was found in the urine. These results were reported and caused some excitement because of the implication that the chemical might be a factor in the psychoses. However, subsequent research revealed that the difference was due to the fact that the control group drank substantially more coffee than the patients.

Before we discuss some of the psychotic disorders, the same point that was made about the neuroses should again be stressed. Very rarely are psychotic disorders seen that can be considered "pure" or "textbook" cases. Consequently, when a list of symptoms for a particular disorder is given, keep in mind that it would be rare to find a psychotic showing just those symptoms. Rather, the symptoms would probably be mixed and difficult to neatly label.

Schizophrenic Reactions. Schizophrenia is the most common psychosis. At least 20 percent of all first admissions to mental hospitals are classified as schizophrenic. Also, patients diagnosed as schizophrenic tend to remain in the hospitals for very long periods of time so that a sample of the population of a mental hospital at any given time would reveal that about 50 percent of the patients are schizophrenics.

As indicated, there is no "typical" or "textbook" case of schizophrenia since the condition is characterized by a very wide range of symptoms which are not all found in any one person. Actually, there are a number of subtypes of schizophrenic reactions, four of which are considered "classic" forms—the *simple, hebephrenic, catatonic,* and *paranoid* forms of schizophrenia.

No attempt will be made to describe the many kinds of behavior that may be associated with this disorder. Our reason for not attempting to describe the many kinds of behavior associated with schizophrenia can be found in the following statement by Ullmann and Krasner (1969): "In general, any behavior of which a human being is capable may, when emitted inappropriately, i.e., not under the control of culturally acceptable discriminative stimuli, be called schizophrenic" (p. 360). Thus, we will briefly describe what some consider to be the four basic symptoms of schizophrenia: *association, affect, ambivalence,* and *autism.* These are sometimes referred to as "Bleuler's four A's" because Bleuler, a researcher in the field of mental disorders, thought that these were the fundamental symptoms. However, there are some who would be inclined to subtract an "A" or two and perhaps add a "B" or "C" to the list.

Sometimes the speech or writing of a schizophrenic may be jumpy and connected in such a fashion that a listener or reader cannot make sense out of the message. The patient does not make clear the *association* or links between the ideas that he attempts to express, and the result may be a "word salad." To illustrate the "word salad" that can result in schizophrenic communication, two excerpts from some correspondence from a schizophrenic are given below.

> I finally saw a man upside down in the bathroom at the state hospital. This I don't understand but I rather isolate myself under good supervision next time I try. It is connected with sex.

> Love and sex are the unity agents. A constant can vary constantly, time for me physically, has stopped outwardly meaning my body's surface. Please send the Queen Mother of England my regards. I respect those who acknowledge they were wrong.

In addition to failing to associate ideas in his communication, a schizophrenic may also show feelings or emotions that are highly inappropriate for a particular situation; this is called an *affective* disturbance. The patient may be completely indifferent to an event that would be tragic to a normal person. The patient might even laugh gaily about it. Sometimes the schizophrenic may have impulses that run opposite to each other and be emotionally pulled in different directions. This situation is called *ambivalence. Autism,* in which a person is largely dominated by his own wishes and needs and is little influenced by logic or reality, may also be a symptom of schizophrenia.

In combination, these four symptoms provide for an almost limitless range of behavior manifestations. Consider, for example, a short description of what schizophrenic behavior can be (Ullmann & Krasner, 1969):

> Some schizophrenics emit bizarre behavior. They giggle, grimace, assume strange postures, or perform repetitive rituals and strange movements. They may be extremely agitated, pace, and move their arms, or they may be almost immobile and actively resist movement. They may be mute and assume a posture such as huddling in a fetal position. Other motor symptoms shown by the schizophrenic may be an automatic obedience to commands, letting the psychiatric staff mold his body into strange postures which he then maintains (waxy flexibility). He may repeat what is said to him (echolalia) or mimic what others do (echopraxia). There may be a disregard for conventional behavior ranging from slovenly personal habits to public masturbation [pp. 359–360].

Affective Reactions. This group of psychoses is characterized by exaggerated states of mood ranging from extreme depression to elation. These are the *manic-depressive* psychoses consisting of three major subtypes: the manic type, the depressed type, and the circular type. In the depressed subtype of manic-depressive psychoses, the disorder consists exclusively of depressive episodes and mental and motor retardation that will sometimes progress to stupor. In the manic subtype, the disorder consists entirely of states of elation with associated talkativeness, accelerated speech and motor activities. In the circular subtype, the patient may have periodic depressions and periodic states of elation.

Paranoid Reactions. According to the DSM-II, paranoid reactions are "psychotic disorders in which a delusion, generally persecutory or grandiose, is the essential abnormality. Disturbances in mood, behavior and thinking 'including hallucinations' are derived from this delusion" (p. 37).

We have stated that a delusion is a strong belief that an individual maintains that is impervious to change by any evidence that it is not true. When an individual is experiencing delusion of persecution, he feels that he is surrounded by enemies who are "going to get him." These "enemies" may be people that the patient knows, or they may be imagined Martians who are using ray guns to attempt to kill him. Often the paranoid person will construct elaborate and quite logical systems to "prove" that someone is out to get him. The delusion of grandeur, which is also frequent among paranoids, is characterized by beliefs that the individual is God, the President, a millionaire, a famous scientist, writer, and so on. Frequently, these patients are easy to get along with and their only apparent "hangup" is the delusion. Problems may be encountered, however, if the same ward contains two Napoleons or Presidents. Sometimes the patient may combine delusions of persecution and grandeur in some complex fashion. For example, he may feel that he is being persecuted because he is some famous person.

Origins of Psychotic Reactions. Psychoses can have an *organic* basis, with brain damage of some sort, or they can be *functional*, with no observable physical condition. While there is no agreement about the causes of the functional psychoses, there are several factors that have been assumed to contribute to these disorders. Again, one's theoretical orientation will affect his explanation.

Evidence suggests that both hereditary and environmental factors are of some importance in the functional psychoses; thus, physiological factors cannot be completely ruled out. Numerous studies have indicated that psychotic disorders run in families, although few would go so far as to say that these disorders are directly inherited. Rather, it would appear that there is a genetic predisposition toward these disorders which renders a person more susceptible if certain environmental conditions are encountered. An important environmental factor, for example, may be the parent-child relationship in a family. A number of studies have found that faulty family relationships are associated with the appearance of psychotic disorders later in life. Studies have also shown that children who lose their mother or father will be more likely to manifest mental disorders later in life than children who live with both parents. It is quite likely that the hereditary, environmental, and, possibly, physiological factors may all interact in a complex way to cause the disorder.

Regardless of the probable causes of the psychoses, it will simplify thinking about them if we once again consider disorders in terms of system malfunctions. Thus, if the behavioral system does not function properly (functional disorder) for any number of possible reasons, again the output is distorted and the result is behavior that may be labeled as disordered. It is recognized, of course, that this approach does not tell us *why* the behavioral system malfunctions but, at present, there are no adequate explanations.

Other Forms of Mental Disorders

Of the ten major categories of mental disorders listed in the DSM-II, we have considered three: mental retardation, the neuroses, and the psychoses. We will conclude the material on the disorders with a brief comment or two about several of the other disorders.

Personality disorders are forms of maladaptive behavior that differ from psychotic and neurotic patterns of behavior for various reasons. Included in this category are such forms of behavior as sexual deviation (which is further broken down into subcategories such as homosexuality, fetishism, pedophilia, and so on), alcoholism, drug dependence, antisocial personality, as well as several others. The antisocial personality (once labeled the psychopathic personality) is a particular problem because his behavior patterns bring him into frequent conflicts with society. While most of the other personality disorders involve individuals who would just like "to be let alone," the antisocial personality actively seeks trouble.

Psychophysiologic disorders, which are often called psychosomatic disorders, involve real physical symptoms that are the result of emotional factors. The symptoms usually involve organs of the involuntary, autonomic nervous system. Some common symptoms of psychophysiologic disorders include ulcers, hypertension, asthma, and infections of the skin. However, in considering these types of symptoms, it should be kept in mind that they may not always be based on emotional (or behavioral) factors.

There are also behavior disorders that are associated with childhood and adolescence. Included in this category are a number of types of disorders whose labels are descriptive of the symptoms. Thus, there is a hyperkinetic reaction characterized by overactivity, restlessness, distractibility, and short attention span. There is also a withdrawing reaction, manifested by seclusiveness and shyness; an overanxious reaction with chronic anxiety, excessive fears, and sleeplessness; a runaway reaction (child runs away from home); unsocialized aggressive reaction; and a group delinquent reaction.

From our brief overview, several problems associated with the topic of mental disorders should be apparent. In the first place, how does one define abnormal behavior? What is the etiology of mental disorders? These questions, and many more, confront the psychologist who works in the field of abnormal psychology.

We will now shift our attention to another important question which, in one way or another, concerns more psychologists than any other problem in the field of psychology. How can the mental disorders that we have listed be prevented or treated? How does one go about correcting malfunctions in the behavioral system? While it is well beyond the scope of the present chapter to deal with all of the treatment methods that are currently in use, we will briefly mention several and then describe in more detail a method that is becoming more and more popular—behavior therapy.

Correcting the Malfunction

Regardless of the method that is selected by a therapist in attempting to correct the malfunction in the behavioral system, the ultimate goal is usually the same—to eliminate the disordered behavior and to replace it with a normal output. Some approaches, which come under the heading of *somatic therapies,* involve physical or physiological modification of the system. Other approaches attempt to modify the system by means of various communication techniques and training procedures. These include the *psychotherapies* and a relatively new approach which is called *behavior therapy.* While the former, called *evocative psychotherapies,* are concerned with, and focus on, the patient's feelings and motivations, behavior therapy deals more directly with the actual disturbed behavior.

The type of therapy selected will vary depending upon the particular case. However, the primary factor determining the therapy used is the orientation of the person conducting the treatment. Just as the way in which a psychologist views the etiology of mental disorder is determined by whether he is inclined toward Freudian theory or some other theory, what he considers as the proper approach to treatment also depends upon his theoretical leanings. Any attempt to list all of the different techniques of therapy advocated for use with mental disorders would be a formidable task. For example, Ellis (1955) surveyed the various techniques and found over forty major techniques under which could be included over three hundred more specific methods. Further, under the more specific methods of therapy there were literally hundreds of still more specific types. Obviously, if we wished to consider the approaches to psychotherapy in any depth, several volumes would be required.

Somatic Therapy

There are three main forms of somatic therapy that are used in the treatment of mental disorders. These include convulsive shock therapy, psychosurgery, and chemotherapy. While the other forms of therapies are used by nonmedical professionals, the use of the somatic therapies is restricted to physicians.

Shock Therapy

Although convulsive shock therapy was a popular form of treatment for a period of time, it has become less common in recent years. This type of therapy involves inducing convulsions which are followed by periods of unconsciousness or coma. The convulsion can be induced in several ways. One method makes use of an overdose of *insulin*. A drug called *Metrazol* was used for a time but, because of very dangerous side effects, it is seldom used today. A third method, and one that is used most frequently because of its simplicity and safety, is *electroconvulsive shock*. This method involves passing a carefully controlled amount of current through the brain of a patient. This brings about a convulsion followed by a period of unconsciousness.

In some cases shock therapy has been successful, particularly when severe depression was involved. Sometimes patients responded favorably enough to be discharged after a series of shock treatments. Also, shock therapy will often bring a patient to a point where he can benefit from psychotherapy. Just how or why shock therapy works in some instances remains open to speculation.

Psychosurgery

At one time a number of people were excited about the treatment of certain cases of mental disorders by means of surgery. While several types of surgical manipulations were tried, the most publicized was the *prefrontal lobotomy*. This operation involves cutting the nerve fibers that connect the prefrontal lobes of the brain with lower centers. In some instances this technique has been successful in relieving the symptoms of some types of disorders. However, in many cases, while the surgery did correct one type of disorder, the resulting personality and behavior changes shown by the patient were as undesirable as the initial disorder. For this reason, as well as the development of drugs which can be used to modify behavior in the same manner as surgery, psychosurgery is rarely, if ever, used in hospitals today.

Chemotherapy

A major advance in the treatment of mental disorders came about with the discovery of various drugs that could be used to alleviate the symptoms of some of the disorders. While there are numerous drugs that are routinely used in chemotherapy, they are generally categorized as either *tranquilizers* or *energizers*. Drugs in the former category, while differing in their modes of action, in general tend to have a calming effect on the patient. There is often a lessening of anxiety, a reduction in aggressive behavior and in hallucinations and delusions. The energizers, which have essentially the opposite effect of the tranquilizers, have been used, sometimes with dramatic effects, on severely depressed patients.

It should be emphasized that these drugs do not *cure* mental disorders since they treat the symptoms and not the illness itself. However, they are effective enough in this role so that a patient can often be discharged from the hospital and can continue on the medication at home. Generally, however, if the medication is stopped the symptoms return and the patient again must enter the hospital. Even if the patient must remain in the hospital, drugs may calm him enough so that he becomes amenable to other forms of therapy. Drugs have also been useful in terms of custodial problems. Hospitals are able to do away with many forms of physical restraints that were once required for agitated patients. Similarly, more patients can be discharged, with a consequent reduction in overcrowding and operating costs.

Currently, extensive research programs are underway that are aimed at developing a better understanding of the biochemical and physiological changes in the nervous system resulting from drug administration. Also, the interest concerning the effects of drugs on behavior has led to the emergence of a new discipline called *psychopharmacology*, which makes use of the tools and concepts of both psychology and pharmacology to investigate the behavior actions of drugs. To evaluate systematically and thoroughly the behavioral effects of a drug requires elaborate experimental designs involving a number of independent variables, which must be systematically varied or controlled, as well as careful selection of the dependent variable. For example, after some form of behavior has been selected to be studied, factors such as dosage level, length of time after drug administration that the behavior is measured, characteristics of the experimental situation (heat, light, and so on), characteristics of the subjects (age, sex, weight, and so on), must all be taken into account in the design of the study.

While there has been a tremendous increase in research in psychopharmacology in recent years, there are still many questions that remain unanswered or, at best, have incomplete answers. Some critical areas have been largely neglected. For example, at the human level there is relatively little research dealing with the effects of various social conditions on a person's response to a drug. It has been shown in several studies with animals that the effects of a given drug might be quite different in social situations than when administered to the animal in isolation. Thus, amphetamine is much more lethal to mice in aggregate than in isolated conditions (Mast & Heimstra, 1962). Similarly, there is a paucity of research in developmental psychopharmacology. It is known that children respond differently to some drugs than do adults. For example, adults will typically show increased activity after amphetamine treatment, while hyperactive children will often show reduced activity after this drug (Bradley, 1950). Findings of this sort have also been reported in studies with animals. A study by one of the authors (Heimstra & McDonald, 1962) suggested that the response of juvenile rats to amphetamine differed from the response shown by adult animals.

These are only two examples illustrating how complex drug behavior interactions may be. A great deal more research is needed in order to obtain some grasp of all the variables that may determine how a person responds to a particular drug.

Psychotherapy

To most people, the word "psychotherapy" immediately brings to mind a couch, a reclining patient, and a bearded therapist complete with pipe and notebook. While this image is not an incorrect one and not too many years ago would have been typical, currently there are many therapists who do not even own a couch or, if they do, it is in their home. Psychotherapy, which had its beginnings in the work of Sigmund Freud, has come to be viewed differently by different psychologists, and presently many diverse approaches are employed. However, the various types of evocative therapies have certain elements in common. For example, the motivating force for a particular disorder is thought to lie within the individual. The internal condition responsible for the disturbance may be in the form of unconscious motivational conflicts, emotional problems, memories, and so on. The task of the therapist is to modify, in some fashion, these internal conditions or processes so that there is a consequent change in observable behavior. When the therapist is successful—that is, when he is able to provide the conditions that bring about internal changes in the processes responsible for the disordered behavior—it is assumed that some sort of internal mediating event has taken place. This hypothesized event results in the patient gaining insight or awareness of his problem. In other words, evocative therapy is based on a process of self-realization through which the individual becomes more aware of unconscious factors that help determine his behavior and, as a result, he may be able to modify his behavior.

The evocative psychotherapies involve several different approaches but, basically, all concentrate on developing the process of insight or self-realization in the individual being treated. We will consider two of these approaches—psychoanalysis and client-centered (nondirective) therapy.

Psychoanalysis

Psychoanalytic therapy is based on the theory that much of human behavior is determined by unconscious motives or memories which have been *repressed*. Repression is a process that forces anxiety-provoking or threatening memories and motives out of consciousness and does not permit them to reenter. However, at the unconscious level these are assumed to influence an individual's perceptions and behavior. A primary aim of psychoanalytic therapy is to assist the person in "bringing back" this unconscious material to the conscious level where he will be able to deal with it in a more rational manner. In other words, once the person is "put wise to" the origins of his disorder, he may be able to handle it.

Bringing the repressed material back to the conscious level may be a time-consuming (and expensive) affair. Psychoanalysis often involves weekly sessions with the analyst that may extend over many months or even years. During these sessions, the analyst uses various approaches to "probe" at the patient's unconscious. One of the most common methods is that of *free association*.

When the patient is told "Just say the first thing that comes to mind," the stage is set for free association. However, "saying the first thing that comes to mind" is not as easy as it may seem since the normal impulse is to attempt to "edit" before speaking. The ability of a patient to say whatever he thinks, regardless of how indecent or absurd it may be, requires some time to learn. After the patient learns to free associate, the analyst is often able to interpret the material and gain some insight into the underlying motives and memories that may be responsible for the patient's behavior.

Another important technique of the analyst is *dream interpretation*. The assumption behind dream interpretation is that an individual may permit material to make an "appearance" during dreams that would be unacceptable to him when awake. While not all types of repressed material will be "permitted" to surface during a dream, it is thought that certain kinds might. In psychoanalysis, the relating of dreams is an important feature, and the analyst makes a very careful and thorough interpretation of the dreams described by the patient. Interpretation of the dreams may give the analyst a better understanding of the material that has been repressed by the patient.

During the course of analysis, a process referred to as *transference* occurs. This is another, and possibly the primary tool, that the analyst utilizes. In the process of transference, the patient will unconsciously attribute certain characteristics to the analyst that are based on characteristics of other significant persons in the patient's past. He will then respond to the analyst as he did to his father or mother or someone else who was important to him. The nature of the overt emotions or feelings directed at the analyst can reveal a great deal about the unconscious derivatives of the behavior. Thus, the interpretation of the transference reactions of the patient is a critical part of the analysis and is a means by which the analyst can demonstrate to the patient how unconscious material helps shape his present behavior.

The relationship between the patient and the analyst may become somewhat complex because of the transference reactions. Thus, while the analyst might become a "father figure" during the analysis (and this would be encouraged as part of the transference process), the transference must be "worked through" or resolved before analysis is complete; the analyst must again become the doctor rather than the father.

Free association, dream interpretation, and transference, then, represent three tools of the psychoanalyst. How he uses these tools, and others that he might employ, depends upon his own training and biases. However, the goal of the analyst is to give the patient an understanding of the origins of his problems and, in this way, allow him to more effectively deal with his environment.

Before leaving the topic of psychoanalysis, some general comments about this approach are in order. In the first place, it is a time-consuming and very costly procedure. Consequently, most of the patients who make use of this form of therapy are relatively affluent, are typically better than average in terms of education, and come from the middle or upper classes. While these patients have the resources to seek help through psychoanalysis, there are many millions of other people with similar problems who cannot afford this kind of treatment. Thus, psychoanalysis may serve a useful role in helping a limited number of people but has little to offer in the way of giving help to the vast number of mentally disturbed people. Second, the psychoanalytic approach is effective with a relatively limited number of mental disorders and is ineffective with the more severely disturbed patients. Because of these reasons, psychoanalysis has actually had little impact as a weapon against mental illness.

Client-Centered Therapy

In psychoanalysis, the analyst represents an authority figure who offers active interpretation, suggests solutions, and, in general, directs the course of the therapy. In *client-centered therapy*, which is also called *Rogerian* or *nondirective therapy*, the approach is quite different. The therapist does not explain, interpret, or advise. Rather, he serves as a "sounding board" for the patient (usually called a client). In this type of therapy, the key element is a permissive atmosphere in which the client can express his feelings and attitudes *without* direction or active interpretation by the therapist.

The therapist does not attempt to uncover repressed material or to actively probe the unconscious of the client. Rather, the primary role of the therapist is to "reflect back" or summarize what the client has expressed or the feelings he has shown. In other words, the therapist responds to the client in a manner that will clarify and emphasize something the client has expressed. For example, after a client has talked about some event in his life, the therapist might respond with a comment such as: "You felt you were too easily persuaded" or "You wished that you had not given in quite so easily." Much of the time the response of the therapist may be only an "H-mm" or other noncommittal sound. The comments that the therapist does make are intended to clarify the client's statements or feelings but not to judge them or to explain them.

The basic assumption underlying the nondirective type of therapy is that an individual, given the opportunity to talk freely, will eventually begin to develop an insight into his problems that will help him deal with them.

While this method may appear to be quite simple and, indeed, in principle it is simple, its application is far more difficult. The client, for example, may often demand answers to questions or active help from the therapist. It may be quite difficult for the therapist to withhold the answers or the help. It is also difficult for most therapists, at least initially, to refrain from becoming "directive" and giving authoritative advice. Maintaining a continuous permissive and nondirective relationship may not be easy in many situations.

Effectiveness of Evocative Psychotherapy

Considering the effort of the many therapists who are engaged in practicing evocative psychotherapy, very little evidence exists that it is effective. We find that much of the therapy research is still attempting to demonstrate that the process of therapy will change disordered behavior more effectively than no treatment at all. After reviewing the available data in this area, one prominent investigator (Eysenck, 1961) was led to conclude that psychotherapy fails to improve on the recovery rate that is obtained through everyday experiences and nonspecific treatment.

Because of this uneasiness about evocative psychotherapy, other procedures have developed. While the next type of therapy that we will take up—behavior therapy—developed independently, the recent upsurge in research and use of this technique is due, at least in part, to the questions regarding the usefulness of evocative therapy.

Behavior Therapy

With the evocative therapies there is an assumption, either stated or implicit, that the patient suffers from some sort of disorder that is reified as neurosis, psychosis, behavior disorder, or some other concept. The behavior to be changed is considered symptomatic of some underlying difficulty in much the same way that a physician considers a fever symptomatic of, or caused by, some physiological malfunctioning. Treatment of only the symptoms, or outputs of the system, is considered superficial. Without treatment of the underlying cause the patient will be vulnerable to *symptom substitution*, whereby new symptoms will be developed to replace those previously removed as manifestations of the underlying disorder.

When psychologists started to assume responsibility for changing malfunctions in the system, they initially used the concepts, terminology, and techniques of existing psychotherapists, usually physicians, and the concepts of a system based on the medical model outlined previously. However, being psychologists, they were not satisfied with the concepts and terminology of medical science, and they wished to use their own from the science of psychology. Therefore, many of the early behavioristic psychologists continued to use the medical model, which was all they had, but they rationalized or explained their procedures by use of the concepts and terminology of the psychological laboratory. At this stage psychologists were using techniques identical to psychoanalysis, or other evocative techniques, but substituting generalization for transference, extinction for working through, response or behavior for symptoms, and other learning terms for the terminology of the medical model.

In the next phase of adapting behavioristic concepts to the medical model, efforts were made to start with the facts of behavior, as learned in the laboratory, and to derive techniques appropriate to those facts. Concepts such as the underlying reified disorder, symptom substitution, and the desirability of insight were questioned. Therapists who started with the laboratory and derived their techniques had no need for such explanatory concepts and no fear of subjecting them to rigorous scientific scrutiny. The concept of underlying disorder was found to add nothing but confusion to the system, symptom substitution was repeatedly found to be a myth, and a new kind of thinking evolved in which the output of the system, or the behavior to be changed, was considered the disorder and *not*, as formerly believed, merely a manifestation of the disorder. With all of the esoteric mystery of the medical model stripped away, behavior was behavior, terms such as normal, abnormal, neurotic, and psychotic added nothing, and the new behavior-modification techniques came into being.

The first and most obvious change occurred in the area of diagnosis. With abandonment of the concept of the underlying disorder, traditional diagnostic procedures designed to yield data consistent with the medical model appear to be entering a period of deemphasis. The term *functional analysis* has been coined to refer to case formulation with relatively objective data, such as defining the target behaviors to be changed, the stimuli eliciting them, and the reinforcers maintaining them. Functional analysis identifies the nature of the disordered output in objective and parsimonious terms and, at the same time, dictates the goals of behavior modification and the appropriate techniques to achieve them. Thus, diagnosis, if this be diagnosis, at last serves a useful purpose of describing and determining treatment rather than of merely naming some hypothetical psychological entity whose very existence is at best only inferred.

Once the target behaviors are identified and understood, the goal of behavior modification is to replace those behaviors with nondisordered behaviors. The behaviors to be replaced are weakened by extinction, punishment, and reactive inhibition; new behaviors then are shaped and instated by operant and classical conditioning, modeling, and other well-understood behavior-changing operations. Thus, behavior therapy is not a unitary technique, such as psychoanalysis or nondirective therapy, but rather a way of proceeding using learning principles derived from the laboratory. The desired techniques are extremely varied and to some extent identified with particular practitioners. For example, Wolpe (1958) has developed *reciprocal inhibition*, the essence of which is the conditioning of a state of calmness and relaxation to stimuli formerly evoking a state of anxiety and tension. Sipprelle (1967) has developed a technique called *induced anxiety* in which subjects are operantly conditioned into a state of anxiety, identify the stimuli they associate with that state, and are then reciprocally inhibited to those stimuli through the Wolpe procedure. Stampfl (1967) *implodes* subjects by exposing them to extremely anxiety-provoking stimuli in the absence of primary reinforcement until their anxiety response to those stimuli is extinguished. Other practitioners have used modeling, aversive conditioning, and a wide variety of other applications of learning theory to the direct manipulation of behavior.

Behavior therapy is still in its formative stages, with new techniques and applications constantly appearing in the literature and considerable controversy occurring between advocates of the evocative and behavior therapy camps. The research on outcome is extremely promising, with authorities such as Eysenck (1967) concluding that the approach does yield demonstrable changes in behavior. Whether it will replace, or supplement, the more traditional approaches remains to be seen.

Psychological Testing II

The second major area of psychological testing, in addition to intelligence and ability tests, is the area of tests of personality. Although tests of this type are occasionally used in fields such as personnel selection, their biggest impact is in the field of *psychodiagnostics*. Psychodiagnostics is an area within the field of clinical psychology that is concerned with the determination of the *types* and *degree* of the system malfunctions present in particular individuals. Personality tests and inventories are the principal tools of the psychodiagnostician in accomplishing this purpose. The application of personality tests by the clinical psychologist is aimed at the goal of providing the correct label for the malfunction suffered by a given individual.

There is a major difference between the majority of the personality tests and ability tests. Intelligence testing allows one to define, with some degree of precision, the various abilities that collectively make up intelligence. These abilities can be described, and levels of superior performance can be defined, independent of the individuals who take the test. In other words, with tests of ability or intelligence, the concept of "high ability" has meaning no matter what the average level of ability is when a large number of people are tested. Thus, our concept of ability is such that ability is an *absolute quality*.

Personality, on the other hand, is a *relative quality*, and the notion of a "high personality" has very little meaning unless, perhaps, we are talking about drug users. "Good" personality is usually defined as normal, or average behavior, and deviations in either direction from this normal range may be indicative of deviant or abnormal characteristics. Personality tests are consequently designed to compare an individual's way of thinking, attitudes, emotions, or personal characteristics with average or normal ways of thinking, feeling, and behaving.

There are three basic types of psychological testing procedures that have been applied to the area of psychodiagnostics, and also to other personality testing situations. These three types of personality tests are: (1) rating scales, (2) personality inventories, and (3) projective techniques. We will briefly review some representative examples of each type of testing procedure. It should be remembered, however, that all of these techniques attempt to evaluate an individual in relation to normal or average behavior, feelings, and attitudes.

Rating Scales

Obviously, a description of personality is a prerequisite to designing tests to measure it, since we cannot measure an indeterminate quality. A general description upon which most of the various personality tests have been based is provided by Freeman (1962):

> Personality is *described* in terms of an individual's behavior—his actions, postures, words, and attitudes and opinions regarding his external world. But personality may be more basically de-

scribed in terms of the individual's covert *feelings* about his external world; feelings that may not be apparent or discernible in his overt behavior. It is described also in terms of one's feelings about *oneself* [p. 520].

Rating scales, as personality tests, attempt to measure the impressions of persons with whom an individual has come in contact. Thus, this type of personality test attempts to measure primarily the overt behavior of the individual and to compare this behavioral reflection of personality to normal standards. Central to the rating-scale technique is the concept of a personality trait, which can briefly be defined as a relatively specific aspect of an individual's personality that represents his characteristic way of behaving in a given situation, or the specific characteristics of his behavior and thinking. Some personality traits that are commonly evaluated are generosity, cooperativeness, introversion, and emotional control.

In some instances the rating-scale technique will be completed by associates of the individual being evaluated, as is typical when the rating-scale approach is used in industrial settings or in school situations. In the assessment of system malfunctions of more serious nature, however, the rating scale is often completed by a trained observer such as a psychologist, physician, or social worker.

Some Examples of Rating Scales

Although a complete coverage of the various types of rating scales would require an entire book, or perhaps several volumes, a brief examination of two typical and widely used rating scales will serve to demonstrate this technique.

Wittenborn Psychiatric Rating Scales

The Wittenborn rating scales (The Psychological Corp., 1955) are designed to be used by professionally trained personnel, such as psychologists and psychiatrists, to aid in the diagnosis of the nine psychiatric conditions of acute anxiety, conversion hysteria, manic state, depressed state, schizophrenic excitement, paranoid condition, paranoid schizophrenic, hebephrenic schizophrenic, and phobic compulsion (Freeman, 1962). As you might imagine, this rating scale is designed for the detection of relatively severe system malfunctions. The scale consists of a list of 52 different symptoms, which are rated from 0 to 3. One item pertains, for instance, to the difficulty a patient has in sleeping at night. On this item the rater evaluates the patient by recording a *0* if the patient has no difficulty in sleeping, or as high as a *3* if the person suffers from extreme insomnia. Values of *1* or *2* are assigned for sleep difficulties in between these extremes. High scores on these rating scales are taken as indications of particular types of malfunctions, depending upon the scores for the nine different sets of items that are rated.

The Alcoholism Scale

The rating-scale technique has also proved to be useful in diagnosing alcoholism (Jenkins & Davis, 1957). The *University of Tennessee Alcoholism Scale* is a very short rating scale, consisting of eight items, which is used by professional psychologists in evaluating the drinking behavior of individuals suspected of being alcoholic. This scale requires that the examiner record either a *1* or a *0* depending upon the eight characteristics of the individual's drinking behavior that are examined. A *1* represents a "poor" rating, and an individual who receives a high score on this scale is likely to be an alcoholic. One of the items, for instance, refers to the amount of alcoholic beverage consumed by an individual. The examiner is instructed to score a *1* for the individual if he ordinarily drinks three pints of "hard" liquor plus a case of beer a week, or if the individual doesn't drink beer but drinks five or more pints of "hard" liquor a week. Other items on this scale relate to the variety of alcohol consumed, the rate and frequency of drinking, and other aspects of an individual's drinking behavior.

In general, the rating-scale approach to personality testing cannot claim the reliability associated with personality inventories, or other types of personality tests. The approach does, however, serve an extremely useful purpose, particularly as an aid to the professional psychodiagnostician.

Personality Inventories

While rating scales are usually confined to the measurement and quantification of individual behaviors that may reflect system malfunctions, other testing procedures have been developed in an attempt to evaluate deviant *feelings* and *attitudes* which may reflect system malfunctions. Personality inventories are structured, objective tests that require the individual to answer questions designed to evaluate his feelings and attitudes.

Factor analysis has been an extremely valuable and helpful tool in the development of these types of psychological tests. Through the application of this statistical technique, a variety of personality traits which have proved to be useful in the diagnosis of abnormal behavior, or system malfunctions, have been identified. Similarly, factor-analytic techniques have assisted in the refinement of tests and subtests that more adequately measure the various personality traits.

However, we should emphasize again at this point that in the area of personality testing the psychologist looks for behaviors, feelings, and attitudes that deviate from the average. The personality inventories compare an individual's "score" on each personality trait with average scores obtained from individuals who do not show symptoms of system malfunctions in order to obtain an indication of abnormal behavior patterns.

There are two principal ways in which personality inventories have been constructed. Tests constructed according to the first technique use items that are characteristic of symptoms reported by individuals already known to suffer from a particular type of system malfunction. Thus, to develop a scale to detect hypochondriacs, questions such as "Do you frequently feel ill?" might be used. In actual practice, the items would probably be considerably more subtle than our example, but it does illustrate the technique by which items are selected.

The other major method of constructing personality inventories has involved "testing" large numbers of questions, some of which would appear to have no bearing on any type of system malfunction or abnormal personality condition, on different groups of individuals. Some of the groups would ordinarily be considered normal, while others would be classified as abnormal, or mentally ill, according to a variety of different neurotic and psychotic classifications. The test is developed by finding the items that discriminate between the various diagnostic groups. If, for example, a question such as "What is your favorite color?" would always produce a response of "blue" for normal subjects, "black" for schizophrenics, "green" for alcoholics, and "purple" for some other diagnostic category, this would be a useful item. The important point in connection with this method of constructing a personality inventory is that the items need not relate directly to the different symptoms of abnormality, but only to the fact that normal individuals will tend to consistently answer the questions differently from various "abnormal" subjects. For illustrative purposes, we will briefly discuss a personality inventory of each of the two types we have discussed.

Bell Adjustment Inventory

The Bell Adjustment Inventory (Bell, 1939) is a relatively old personality inventory that was designed to measure an individual's level of adjustment in different areas: the home, health, social adjustment, emotional adjustment, and occupational adjustment (Freeman, 1962). This inventory was developed according to the first technique discussed, and the questions are representative of the commonly reported symptoms of a variety of psychological disorders. This inventory presents the subject with a series of questions such as "Do you daydream frequently?" and requires a "yes-no-undecided" response from the subject. The pattern of an individual's responses to the questions on this inventory are used by the psychologist in placing the subject in the proper diagnostic category.

The MMPI

Perhaps the most well known and extensively researched personality inventory is the *Minnesota Multiphasic Personality Inventory* (Hathaway & McKinley, 1951). This personality inventory was developed according to the second technique we discussed. As an initial step in the development of this instrument, a large number of items were compiled and administered to several different groups of individuals, including normal subjects and a variety of psychological-psychiatric classifications of abnormal behavior groups. Those items which distinguished between the various groups were retained for the final form of the test, while those which could not discriminate between people in the various diagnostic categories were omitted. The MMPI can be administered in either individual or group form. The individual form consists of 550 statements, printed on separate cards, which the subject is required to sort into three piles. The three piles correspond to the subject's judgments of whether each statement is true of himself, or not. The three categories are "true," "false," and "cannot say." The group form of the MMPI consists of the same 550 statements arranged in a printed booklet in a multiple-choice format. The three choices are the same in this version, but the subject indicates his response by marking an answer sheet instead of sorting cards into piles. The items contained in the MMPI are grouped to form nine primary scales corresponding to the nine different clinical diagnoses of hypochondria, depression, hysteria, psychopathic deviate, masculinity-femininity, paranoia, psychasthenia, schizophrenia, and hypomania. In addition to these scales the MMPI also contains a "lie" scale, which is designed to detect subjects who deliberately try to answer questions falsely to give a favorable impression. Another scale, the "K" scale, is also included to indicate essentially the opposite tendency. This scale represents a correction factor that indicates that subjects are too critical in evaluating themselves.

In his use of the MMPI the clinical psychologist will ordinarily construct a *profile* for a given subject. The profile simply represents the subject's score on each of the nine scales of the MMPI relative to the average score for normal subjects. Diagnosis is then made on the basis of the pattern of a given subject's scores across all nine scales.

Projective Techniques

The final major type of personality test that is widely used by clinical psychologists is the projective technique. In contrast to the rating scales and the personality inventories, which are highly structured objective instruments, the projective techniques deliberately present the examinee with an unstructured test situation. The tests in this category all depend on the concept of psychological projection. According to Freeman (1962), *"projection* is an unconscious process whereby an individual (1) attributes certain thoughts, attitudes, emotions, or other characteristics to other persons, or certain characteristics to objects in his environment; (2) attributes his own needs to others in his environment; or (3) draws incorrect inferences from experience."

The rationale common to all projective tests is to present the subject with a given stimulus and to record and interpret the subject's responses to that stimulus. It is assumed that the subject will "project" himself into the stimulus situation and that his responses will reflect his inner self-concept, needs, feelings, and attitudes. Again, the aspects of the subject's personal makeup, which are revealed in his responses to the stimuli of the projective tests, are interpreted in relation to the responses of normal-average individuals.

The Rorschach Inkblots

The Rorschach Test is one of the oldest and most widely known of the projective techniques. The test consists of a set of 10 cards, each of which contains a bisymmetrical inkblot. In administering the Rorschach Test to a subject, the examiner will present one card at a time and ask the subject to tell him what the inkblot looks like. The examiner will then record, verbatim, the responses of the subject. The test is scored according to a number of factors involved in the subject's responses. The scoring of this test is an extremely complicated procedure, and the test is only used by highly trained professionals, who take into account the particular part of each inkblot that stimulated a given response, the types of objects that are reported as being present in the inkblots, and a variety of other aspects of the subject's responses to the ambiguous stimuli. The Rorschach Test was designed to reveal, to the highly trained psychologist, the underlying structure and organization of a subject's personality. There have been suggestions, however, to the effect that at least this aspect of clinical diagnosis is as much "art" as science.

The Thematic Apperception Test

The Thematic Apperception Test or, as it is more commonly known, the TAT (Morgan & Murray, 1935), is another projective technique that requires the subject to respond to relatively ambiguous stimuli. In the TAT the stimuli are pictures representing people in a variety of social settings. The subject is instructed to make up a story about each picture, and this story is recorded by the examiner. The test was designed to reveal to the trained examiner the various drives, needs, and conflicts that make up the examinee's personality structure. It is assumed that in making up a story about the ambiguous situation represented by the various pictures, the subject will project his own personality into the situation and reveal aspects of his personality that he might not directly admit to the psychologist.

As with the Rorschach Test, the scoring of the TAT is a complex process which depends upon the content of the stories given by the subject, the kinds of drives and motives the subject projects into the story, and a variety of other aspects of the subject's responses to each picture.

A variety of other projective techniques are available to the psychodiagnostician. The common element in all of these tests is an ambiguous stimulus situation to which the subject is required to make a relatively free response. All of these testing techniques require highly trained personnel for both test administration and scoring, and their use is consequently restricted.

The System So Far

An input to a system will, by means of various subsystems, be transformed to an output. In the case of the behavioral system, the output is called behavior. When all behavioral subsystems are functioning properly, it is possible under most conditions to predict with reasonable accuracy the output of the system. However, sometimes the transformation process between input and output is distorted because of a malfunction in one or more of the behavioral subsystems and the output deviates in an unpredictable manner. When this takes place, it is customary to refer to the output of the system as being "abnormal." The subsystem malfunction can be due to one of two causes. One kind of malfunction, involving actual physical damage to the system in brain damage, is an organic or somatogenic malfunction. Sometimes, however, the malfunction is not due to any recognized physical damage and is labeled as a psychogenic or functional malfunction. System malfunctions that result in an "abnormal" output are common, and a significant number of psychologists are engaged in diagnosing and attempting to correct these kinds of malfunctions.

Summary

1. There is considerable disagreement among psychologists about the appropriate definition of abnormality. A variety of definitions presently exist, including statistical definitions, medical model definitions, and others. However, regardless of the problems involved in arriving at definitions, the fact exists that there are certain patterns of behavior that are labeled as abnormal in our culture.

2. Several systems of "labeling" abnormal behavior have been developed. The most current is that of the American Psychiatric Association, which contains ten major categories of disorders that are further divided into numerous subcategories.

3. Mental retardation, which is one major category of dis-

order, involves individuals who fall below a certain score on intelligence tests. Depending upon the IQ level attained, mental retardates are classified as borderline, mild, moderate, severe, and profound. Retardation can be caused by many etiological factors, including infections, trauma, disorders of metabolism, brain disease, improper nutrition, and chromosomal abnormality. These are somatogenic factors. However, about 75 percent of the mentally retarded do not reveal any known somatogenic factors that would account for their retardation.

4. The neuroses represent disorders that prevent people from adjusting to themselves or their environment in a normal fashion. Anxiety seems to be the distinguishing characteristic of the neurotic disorders. The most common of these disorders are anxiety neurosis, hysterical neurosis, phobic neurosis, obsessive compulsive neurosis, and hypochondriacal neurosis.

5. The psychoses are disorders in which the person is usually markedly disoriented, with gross distortions of perception and thought. A psychotic often shows a loss of contact with reality and marked disturbance in behavior and thought processes. Schizophrenia is the most common of all the psychoses. Another group of psychoses is characterized by exaggerated states of mood, ranging from extreme depression to elation. These are the manic-depressive psychoses. Another group of psychoses involves paranoid reactions.

6. In addition to the neuroses and psychoses, there are several other forms of mental disorders. These include, among others, the personality disorders, the psychophysiologic disorders, and several types that are associated with childhood and adolescence.

7. There are a number of approaches to correcting the malfunction. Some approaches involve physical and physiological modification of the system. These approaches, called somatic therapies, make use of shock therapy, surgery, and drugs in an effort to eliminate the disordered behavior. Other approaches attempt to modify the system by means of various communication and training techniques. These include the evocative psychotherapies and the behavior therapies. Psychotherapies include psychoanalysis and client-centered therapy, as well as others.

8. Because of the questioned effectiveness of evocative psychotherapies, there has been an increased interest in behavior therapy, which uses various conditioning techniques in attempting to correct the malfunction.

9. Psychodiagnostics is concerned with determining the types and degree of system malfunctions that may be present. The

three main types of instruments used to assess personality are rating scales, personality inventories, and projective techniques. Rating scales are used in an attempt to obtain the impressions of persons about the overt behavior of another person. It is assumed that this behavior may tell something about the personality of the person being rated.

10. Personality inventories are typically structured, objective tests which attempt to evaluate the feelings and attitudes of a person. The Minnesota Multiphasic Personality Inventory (MMPI) is the best known and most widely used test of this type. Projective techniques deliberately present a person with an unstructured test situation in which he "projects" himself so that his inner needs, feelings, and attitudes are reflected in his response to the test situation.

Selected Readings

Eysenck, H. J. The effects of psychotherapy. In H. J. Eysenck (Ed.), *Handbook of abnormal psychology.* New York: Basic Books, 1961. Pp. 697–725.

Kaplan, B. (Ed.), *The inner world of mental illness.* New York: Harper and Row, 1964.

Ullmann, L. P., & Krasner, L. *A psychological approach to abnormal behavior.* Englewood Cliffs, New Jersey: Prentice-Hall, 1969.

Wenrich, W. W. *A primer of behavior modification.* Monterey, California: Brooks/Cole, 1970.

Zax, M., & Stricker, G. *The study of abnormal behavior: Selected readings.* (2nd ed.) New York: Macmillan, 1969.

12

Man as a Subsystem I

Selection and Training

We have emphasized in our earlier discussion that an analysis of a system can be carried out at a number of different levels. Thus, while we may be concerned with a particular system, we recognize that it is composed of a number of subsystems. We also recognize that, at a different level of analysis, it can be considered a subsystem within still larger systems. This concept of "systems within systems" is, of course, basic to any systems analysis approach.

In our analysis of the behavioral system of man, we have considered in some detail the various behavioral subsystems, including sensing, identifying, memory, energizing, interpreting, and output. In the previous two chapters we saw how the output of the system will differ among individuals and how, on occasion, it may become so different that it is labeled as abnormal. That is, our level of analysis was changed from the various subsystems to the behavioral system as a whole. In the remaining chapters, we will deal with another level of analysis, in which man is viewed as a subsystem within a larger system.

Man, as a subsystem, functions within a wide variety of other systems. For example, as a student you are an element of some type of educational system. The particular institution that you attend may possibly be a subsystem within a still larger state system. As an individual, you can be considered a subsystem within a broad cultural system, within a smaller social system, and within a number of even smaller groups and organizations. You may be employed and thus be an element within an industrial or commercial system. Obviously, we could arrive at a substantial list of systems within which you function as a subsystem. It is equally obvious that we cannot begin to discuss your role in all of these systems. However, regardless of the particular role of man in a system, there are certain procedures that are followed in many systems that affect how a person becomes part of the system and how he is modified to function more efficiently in the system. In some cases, particularly in a man-machine system, not only is an effort made to fit man to the machine but also to fit the machine to man. In considering man as a subsystem, we will be particularly concerned with these two aspects —fitting the man to the task required of him and, conversely, fitting the task to the man.

The requirements that various systems impose upon the human element vary greatly. Within a given system, requirements may range from those needed for successful ditch digging to those required for complex decision making by executives of the system. Because of these diverse requirements, most organizations make some attempt to *select* an individual who, because of certain attributes or abilities appears to be more likely to succeed in a particular job than other individuals. Similarly, most organizations make some effort to *train* a person after he is selected.

Most of you have probably already encountered several selection procedures as well as some training procedures. For example, most educational institutions require some form of entrance examination which usually serves as a selection device. If you have held a job of some type, it is likely that you were interviewed and, perhaps, required to complete a battery of tests. If you met certain criteria during the interview and in completing the tests, you were selected for the job. It is also likely that some training was required before you undertook the job or while you were on the job. This training might have ranged from being shown how to properly hold a broom or paintbrush to some fairly intense classroom and on-the-job training. In most organizations selection is followed by a training program of some sort, but this is not always the case. Frequently, elaborate selection procedures are not followed by adequate training; in other cases, a weak selection program may be followed by excellent training programs. In considering the problem of fitting the man to the job, it should be kept in mind that there are two important facets—selection and training.

Selecting the Job

Before we can select a man for a job, it is necessary that we know a good deal about what requirements the job will impose on the individual. We must have information about specific objectives, the duties required, the work situation, and the characteristic patterns of behavior that will be necessary to get the job done. In order to obtain this kind of information, we make use of a procedure that is called *job analysis.*

Job Analysis

What is a job? Although we usually use this term in a casual fashion, we can present a more formal definition of a job. *"A job is a relatively homogeneous cluster of work tasks carried out to achieve some essential and enduring purpose in an organization"* (Dunnette, 1966, p. 69). Typically, the tasks making up the job have some meaningful relationship in that they are similar in kind, or content, or they have similar requirements of some type. A job analysis is a study of the various tasks making up the job in order to discover the behaviors necessary for successful job performance. While at present our interest in job analysis is determining qualifications and behaviors for selection purposes, job analysis can serve a number of other purposes within an organization. For example, job analysis yields information that is necessary for establishing training programs, for improving job efficiency, and, in some cases, for establishing wage structures.

Later in this section we will discuss a procedure that is referred to as *task analysis.* There is frequently some confusion generated by the manner in which the terms "task" and "job" are used, sometimes interchangeably. Customarily, the "job" is thought to consist of a number of "tasks" or, put another way, tasks are often defined as the individual human activities that, taken together, make up a job.

The usage of these terms has changed somewhat in recent years. In the terminology associated with complex man-machine systems, one typically does not talk about the "job" that the human performs but rather about the "task" that he performs. A task, in this type of situation, may consist of a larger number of subtasks. Sometimes it is convenient to refer to a task as involving a primary task and a series of subsidiary tasks. The purpose of a task analysis, basically, is to describe the behavior required of a human in performing his task in a man-machine system. In this respect, the purpose of the task analysis is quite similar to that of the job analysis. However, as you will see, the approaches to the problem are quite different. The contrast between the task analysis and the traditional job analysis, with its often unsystematic procedures and poorly defined terminology, is frequently quite striking.

Methods of Job Analysis

There are a number of different methods of job analysis that are used to determine the kinds of behavior associated with particular jobs. The methods range from relatively simple questionnaire techniques to rather elaborate procedures that gather information about a job from a number of sources. Some of these techniques are described below.

Interview Methods. In one type of interview method, a job incumbent is extensively interviewed about his job. He is asked detailed questions about the tasks that he must perform and other questions that are relevant to his job. The interview is usually carefully structured so that valuable information can be gained. A variation of this *individual interview method,* which is called the *observation interview method,* actually takes place on the job. The interviewer talks to the job incumbent as he works. The interviewer observes the worker and questions him about his various duties. After interviewing a number of workers, the job analyst combines the data into a single job analysis. These methods can supply a relatively complete picture of a given job, but they are time consuming and costly.

The *group interview method* involves questioning a number of workers simultaneously. While they might be asked questions similar to those in the individual interview techniques, the advantage of this method is that it is much less time consuming than the individual interviews. Again, the analyst attempts to draw all the information together for a single job description.

The *technical conference method,* which is also an interview approach, brings together a number of "experts" in place of the actual job incumbents. These experts, who are individuals with a high degree of knowledge about the job in question, meet with the job analyst and attempt to provide him with all the characteristics of the job. The analyst then writes his job description from this information.

Questionnaire, Check List, and Diary Methods. These three methods have in common the requirement that the job incumbent attempt to analyze his job and put it down on paper. The *questionnaire* approach requires the person to answer a number of questions about his job and write the answers down in his own words. While this method can be effective, individuals vary a great deal in their ability to write answers down "in their own words." With the *check list method*, the requirement for writing answers is eliminated and the incumbent checks the tasks that he performs from a long list of possible tasks. With this technique, the analyst is confronted with the problem of preparing an extensive list of task statements for use by the job incumbents. The *diary method* requires that the incumbents record all of their daily activities in a logbook or diary. Again, the problem of the ability of the incumbent to adequately record this type of material may be encountered. This method is more often used with higher level jobs.

Work Participation Method. While this method is not used very frequently, it is an interesting approach to job analysis. In this case, the individual who is performing the analysis actually performs the job himself. This allows him to gain firsthand information about the behaviors required to perform the job. By systematically recording everything that he does on the job, the analyst is able to arrive at a very complete picture of the job. However, if the job is very complex, the analyst must receive considerable training before he attempts to "go to work" and, consequently, this procedure can be quite time consuming and expensive.

Critical Incident Method. With this method, supervisors, employees, and others that are familiar with a particular job make statements concerning *critical incidents* of job behavior. The incidents asked for are examples of either outstandingly *good* or *bad* performance on the job in question. The good or bad occurrences are typically recorded in anecdotal form and include material describing what led up to the incident, exactly what the person did that was so good or bad, the consequences of the good or bad behavior, and whether the consequences were actually within the control of the job incumbent.

While this approach can provide information to the analyst

about various critical aspects of a given job, it does not give him a complete picture of the entire task. Obviously, in most jobs not all of the behavior required can be considered critical and may still be important for successful performance on the task.

System Design and Task Analysis

At one time when complex man-machine systems were designed and built, the design engineers were interested in the equipment components and little else. The requirements that might be imposed on the human component were scarcely considered. Consequently, some systems required capabilities of the human that he did not possess. For example, we discussed in a previous chapter the problem of sensory overload and what can happen under this condition. With the realization that the human component must be considered in the same way as the equipment components, efforts were made to determine, during the design stages, just what requirements would be imposed on the man after the system was operational. This led to the procedure called *task analysis.* While there are a variety of techniques used for task analysis, they typically result in an organized listing of the tasks that are required of the human in the system.

System Design. The process of system design requires, essentially, two sets of specifications. One set is required for the equipment that will be part of the system and another set defines the human tasks in the system. Based on the equipment specifications, certain decisions related to the design of the system are made. However, just as the equipment specifications determine the development of the equipment components, the specification of human functions is required for the decisions that will determine just what will be required of the human in the system.

Thus, it is necessary for efficient system design that the interactions of men with machines and with their system environment (including other men) be defined. The definitions of these interactions constitute what is called a *task description.* A task description, essentially, specifies what functions men and equipment will be required to perform in the system. The design engineer must decide, based on a number of factors, the allocation of functions. Part of his decision will be based on an understanding of the requirements imposed on the human component. Thus, if it is apparent that the human's capabilities have been exceeded, it will be necessary to allocate more functions to equipment. Task descriptions are continually revised and redefined as the development of a system progresses.

In the design of a system, the task description takes place before the task analysis. A task description is a statement of *requirements,* whereas the analysis specifies what capabilities are needed by the man to meet the requirement. Before we discuss task analysis, let us consider an example that will clarify the difference between task description and analysis. While our example will be an extremely simple one, it should serve to illustrate the type of information, or statements, associated with a task description and with a task analysis.

The *task description* might read: "Operator must start car." The *task analysis* might read: "This requires the operator to set the gearshift lever. If automatic shift, he places it in park or neutral position. He depresses accelerator to set choke or, if no automatic choke, pulls out manual choke slightly. He releases accelerator and then depresses slightly. He inserts key into ignition and turns to 'on' position and checks that oil and generator warning lights are on. Turns ignition key until starter is heard. He holds key in starter position until engine starts. He releases key and listens for sound of engine."

When an analysis of a task as simple as starting a car requires as much detail as this, imagine what a task analysis of an astronaut landing a space vehicle on the moon would look like!

Task Analysis.   After it has been determined what functions men will be required to perform in the system, a *task analysis* is conducted. The task analysis is an attempt to describe the activities that take place at the interface of the human operator and the equipment and environments with which he will interact in the system. The analysis is aimed at determining the kinds of abilities, skills, and knowledge that are needed by the man in order to carry out the specified tasks. The results of the task analysis yield information that is useful in selecting a person for the task and also in designing training programs that will be needed to train the man for the task.

In the example of the task analysis of starting a car, a number of activities required of the operator were listed. In listing these activities, no attempt was made to describe the capabilities of the operator that were necessary for performing these activities. In many kinds of task analyses, these capabilities must be considered. For example, what capabilities are required for the first step listed in the analysis of car starting—setting the gearshift lever?

We can answer this question within the framework of the

model that we have used throughout this text. Thus, in addition to stating that the gearshift lever must be set, we could attempt to specify the requirements in terms of the sensing, identifying, memory, energizing, interpreting, and output subsystems that make up our model of the behavioral system. For example, information about the current position of the gearshift lever must be sensed, identified by comparisons with stored models, interpreted, and so on. The output is represented by moving the lever to a different position.

Thus, the task analyst is generally interested in input and output of the "human system" and the processes that take place in between. Usually, attempts are made to specify stimulus events that serve as input to the system, the identifying requirements of this information are considered, retention of task information in long- and short-term memory is taken into account, and the interpretation requirements, including problem solving and decision making, are determined. Obviously, this is a tall task. As Miller (1962) points out: "The source information to the task analyst is task requirements information plus all that is known and much that is conjectured in the full area of experimental psychology" (p. 204). If you contrast this approach with those described for job analysis, it should be apparent that a task analysis is capable of yielding a considerable amount of information that the job analysis methods cannot.

Selecting the Man for the Job

After the tasks that men must perform and the jobs that they must fill in the system have been defined and analyzed, the next step is to identify the men to occupy these jobs through *personnel selection*. The technology of personnel selection is aimed at identifying those individuals who have the capabilities, interests, and motives to succeed at particular jobs or tasks. Efficient selection is a nonrandom process in that those individuals who are selected are assumed to be a better "risk" at succeeding on the job than those who are rejected. In order to make sure that this assumption is valid, it is necessary that the individual who does the selecting utilize objective and scientific procedures and instruments. If selection is based on subjective and biased judgments, rather than on objective methods, it may become, for all practical purposes, a random process which will not accurately predict the success or failure of a particular individual.

The importance of efficient personnel selection procedures in an organization cannot be overemphasized. Placing a person in a job at which he cannot perform effectively can be an expensive situation for an organization. While it is difficult to estimate costs involved in replacing the individual, it is even more difficult to compute costs of reduced production, accidents, expensive "incorrect" decisions, and so on. Also, because of various types of union-management agreements, it might be difficult to fire a person who is found to be unsuitable for a particular job.

While the need for good selection is generally recognized, changes in technology over the last few years have made the selection process more difficult than ever. At one time, many of the jobs were simple and had obvious requirements. Consequently, selecting people for these kinds of jobs was not particularly difficult. However, jobs have become more and more complex and the requirements needed for these jobs are both hard to specify and hard to measure. More and more workers are "knowledge" workers, such as teachers, engineers, scientists, and accountants. Selection of these kinds of workers is much more difficult than selection for simple jobs.

Individual Differences and Personnel Selection

Obviously, if people did not differ in ability and in other attributes, there would be no problem selecting a person to fill a job. If everyone had the same abilities, it would be a matter of hiring the first person available. However, since differences do exist, personnel selection is aimed at identifying those workers who demonstrate the abilities, or potential abilities, that will make them a better risk for job success.

In attempting to accomplish this objective, a number of methods of selection are employed, including various types of psychological tests—such as aptitude, achievement, interest, and personality tests—as well as such other methods as biographical inventories, personal references, and interviews. Basically, all of these methods are aimed at evaluating individual differences which would make some individuals more or less likely to succeed at some job. We will discuss some of these methods in more detail shortly. However, before considering specific methods of selection, we will briefly discuss what might be called a basic selection model.

The Selection Model

As we have said, the selection process is based upon the fact that individual differences exist among workers. The rationale behind the selection is that persons who possess the required capabilities or attributes for a job be selected and those that do not possess these capabilities be rejected. While this may seem like a relatively straightforward objective, it is not so easily accomplished. In order for the selection process to be reasonably effective, a number of factors must be taken into account. Two of the most important factors are the selection of *predictors* and *criteria.*

Assuming that the first step of job analysis has been accomplished, the next step in the selection model is to choose some sort of indicator of "success" on a particular job. This *criterion* for success can sometimes be expensive and difficult to determine. For example, considerable effort is directed at the selection of men for training as military aircraft pilots. However, what determines "successful" performance as a pilot? In many less complex tasks, such as those involved in secretarial work or in running a lathe or drill press, it is not so difficult to arrive at a criterion of some sort of "good" performance. Along with the selection of a criterion, it is necessary to choose a measure that can successfully predict how the individual will do on the particular job. This measure is called a *predictor* or selection device. Tests, interviews, references, and so on are examples of predictors.

After choosing a predictor and criterion, one must obtain measures on both from a group of workers on the job. Suppose, for example, that "successful" performance on a particular job required soldering at least fifty electronic units per hour with only five rejections. We could attach a score to this performance and call it the criterion. Also suppose that we have a psychomotor test that we think will predict successful performance on the soldering job. We then administer the psychomotor test (predictor) to a number of individuals who are already hired and working on the soldering job. The performance score (criterion), based on the number of units soldered per hour and the number of rejects, is also obtained for each worker.

The next step in the process is to relate the predictor to the criterion. This step determines whether a real and meaningful relationship exists between the scores obtained on the predictor and the criterion. This step generally involves the correlational techniques that will be discussed in detail in Chapter 15. Correlation coefficients between two sets of scores could range from +1.00 to −1.00. The coefficient of +1.00 represents a perfect positive correlation, meaning that the worker with the highest score on the predictor measure would have the highest score on the criterion measure, the worker with the second highest predictor score would have the second highest criterion score, and so on, with the worker

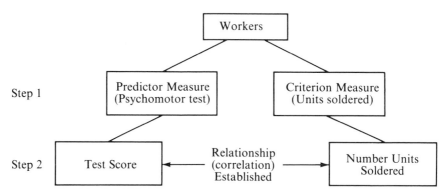

Figure 12–1. A model of the validation strategy for determining concurrent relationships between predictor and criterion measures. In the first step of this model, workers are
administered the two tests either together or very close in
time. The second step involves determining whether a relationship, usually in the form of a correlation, exists between the two scores obtained from the measures. In this
example, a score on a psychomotor task was used as a predictor score while the number of units soldered in a given
period of time was utilized as the criterion score. Obviously,
the particular job or task would determine the type of measures that would be utilized.

having the lowest criterion score also obtaining the lowest predictor score. While this sort of relationship never occurs in actual
selection procedures, a high positive correlation between the predictor and criterion measures is generally thought to indicate that
the predictor measure will probably be successful.

This procedure is called *assessing the validity* of a predictor.
The procedure outlined would assess what is referred to as *concurrent* validity. A schematic representation of this type of validation design is shown in Figure 12–1. Dunnette (1966) makes the
following point about this type of validity:

> It is not strictly correct to infer predictive usefulness for a test if
> it has been submitted only to concurrent validation. . . . A con-
> current study tells us only what the present relationship may be
> between the test behavior and other concurrently observed be-
> haviors. Nothing is necessarily implied about the usefulness of the
> test for predicting later nontest behavior, although investigators
> commonly imply that they have demonstrated predictive utility
> by carrying out concurrent validation strategies [pp. 114–115].

In some situations the predictor test is given to newly hired
employees and then a period of time is allowed for the new hires to
establish themselves as either successful or unsuccessful. The par-

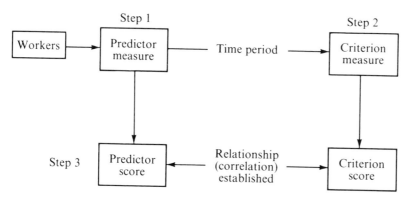

Figure 12–2. A validation strategy for determining predictive relationships between predictor and criteria measures. The first step involves testing a group of newly hired workers on the predictor measure that has been selected. After a period of time, possibly many months, the same workers are tested on the criterion measure (Step 2). The third step consists of determining the relationship between the predictor scores and the criterion scores.

ticular validation strategy involved here is called *predictive* validation and is represented in Figure 12–2. This validation strategy requires that all job applicants be tested on the predictor measure and that all are hired regardless of their performance on the measure. The worker's performance on the job is carefully evaluated in various ways (criterion measure) and, at some later date, the relationship between the predictor measure and the criterion measure is established. Again, Dunnette (1966) points out about predictive validation that:

> The predictive strategy is the preferred strategy for any personnel selection study because it is always our intention in the operational use of psychological tests to infer from the test results *future* job behavior outcomes. The predictive strategy also has the advantage of including test and job behavior information about *all* the applicants rather than a restricted sampling of them, as in the concurrent strategy [p. 116].

There are, then, several steps involved in the basic selection model. First, the job must be analyzed. Next, the selection of the criterion and predictor must be made. Once these are selected, it is necessary to obtain measures on both from workers on the job and then, statistically, relate the criterion and predictor measures. Obviously, these various steps may be more or less difficult depending upon the nature of the jobs or tasks that are involved. As we have indicated previously, it is one thing to use a model of this sort in establishing a selection procedure for secretaries or lathe workers and something quite different for attempting to select men for complex man-machine systems. Each step in the model would be much more difficult.

The steps described in the selection model are, of course, not undertaken each time a man is hired for a job. This model is used as a method of determining suitable predictor tests for regular utilization in hiring new employees. Once the predictor has been validated it would be used to select employees and, unless some researcher wanted more data, the measure of criterion performance and its relationship with the predictor would no longer be obtained.

Some Predictor Devices

As we have indicated, a number of methods of selection are commonly used. These involve psychological tests of various kinds, selection interviews, personal references, and biographical inventories. Sometimes only one or two of these methods are used but, often, the selection process involves the use of all of these methods.

The Interview

Although the selection interview is a relatively expensive procedure, it is one of the most common. While many personnel men have considerable faith in their ability to determine from an interview whether the applicant for a job will be a "good bet," their faith is largely unfounded. Most available data on the validity of this particular technique suggest that there is little relationship between predictions of job success made on the basis of interviews and actual job success. Actually, however, there is so little research on the effectiveness of interviews that we cannot fairly evaluate this technique. Smith (1964) says: "The interview may not be as useless as it seems; too few interview situations have been explored, too few research studies have been made, and too many studies have used poor experimental methods or produced ambiguous results" (p. 68). However, Smith also goes on to say that if we cannot assume the interview is useless, neither can we say it is useful; the evidence suggests that it should be judged guilty of wasting time and money.

It is possible that the interviewing technique could be improved. For example, most organizations make little or no effort to select and train their interviewers. Too often, the person assigned to conduct interviews is someone who could not succeed at another job in the organization and, for various reasons, was not fired but instead given the job of interviewer. We do not have sufficient data to state what would happen if a systematic effort was made to train interviewers. Similarly, it is possible that multiple interviewing might be more effective than single interviewing techniques. If several persons interviewed each applicant, their combined prediction might be more valid than that of one person. Again, data are lacking in this area.

Biographical Inventories and Personal References

Along with the interview, biographical inventories of some sort are part of the selection process in nearly all companies. There are two basic criticisms of these types of inventories. First, the responses are easy to bias in favor of the applicant. Also, even when the respondent is being "honest," it is often difficult to recall accurately items requested on the inventory. However, when properly designed, these inventories can provide data about age, previous employment, education, and so on that may be of value. For example, in one detailed study of biographical inventories, Fleishman and Berniger (1960) found that certain types of items differentiated between employees who remained on the job and those who quit. Members of the long-tenured group differed on a number of items from the short-tenured group. However, there are few studies that test the validity of the biographical inventory and, consequently, we can say little about its effectiveness as a predictor.

While at one time letters of reference were part of the selection procedure for most organizations, their popularity has dropped considerably. When they are required, typically some sort of standardized questionnaire is now requested rather than an open-ended letter. Several studies have shown that references, even the standard questionnaires, have little value in predicting success in most types of jobs. There are, of course, some obvious reasons for this. Many of you have, at one time or another, required a letter of reference for a job or perhaps for admission to college. You undoubtedly listed as a reference someone who you knew had a good impression of you and would write a favorable letter. There are very few unfavorable letters of recommendation written. There are also very few accurate letters of recommendation written.

Basically, there are four major reasons why letters of reference are not accurate in content. Often the person who is asked to write does not have adequate knowledge of the person who requests the letter. For example, as faculty members, both authors are frequently requested to write various types of letters of recommendation for students who took one of our courses. The particular course might have involved a large number of students and may have been offered several years previous to the request. Obviously, our knowledge of the particular student is not sufficient to write a letter of reference. A second reason for inaccurate content of letters of reference is the inability to assess the particular person involved. Even if the letter writer had some contact with the individual, it is often difficult to get an accurate impression of the person. A third problem involves describing the individual. Even if the individual is known and can be evaluated, it is often difficult to adequately describe the person in a letter. Finally, there is the problem of willingness to be accurate. Most of us want to be "good guys" and, consequently, are somewhat reluctant to list the unfavorable aspects of someone who has asked for a letter of reference. In some instances, the reluctance to be truthful about an incompetent person is overcome and an honest letter is written. However, most of us who read a number of letters of recommendation (for example, concerning applications for graduate school) realize that this reluctance is seldom overcome, and we learn to read between the lines. For example, "damning with faint praise" is a standard technique. Thus, a letter might read: "Although John's gradepoint of 2.3 may seem somewhat low and he is quite obnoxious, he did an excellent job in building a rat maze in his Experimental Psychology course." Obviously, the abilities required for building a rat maze do not compensate for the 2.3 gradepoint and the fact that John is obnoxious.

Tests as Predictors

There are many different tests that are routinely used as part of a selection procedure. One way of classifying these tests is to distinguish the type of behavior they are designed to measure. It is either assumed, or has been demonstrated, that the particular kind of behavior measured is behavior that is important to the particular job for which the person is being selected. For example, if personality factors of some sort are important for success at a job, part of the selection procedure would involve the administration of a personality test. If a high level of intelligence is necessary for this job, an IQ test will be given. If good vision is required for the job, a vision test will be included in the selection process. There are many behavior-specific tests, such as mechanical tests, interest tests, art tests, music tests, and so on, that may be administered individually or as part of a battery of tests.

Because of the tremendous number of tests available, we will make no attempt to describe any specific tests. Rather, we will consider several ways of classifying tests based on certain characteristics of the tests. Blum and Naylor (1968) list a number of ways in which psychological tests can be categorized into various groupings. Some of these groupings are described below.

Achievement and aptitude tests: An aptitude test is assumed to measure and predict a person's potential in some area whereas the achievement test is assumed to measure the person's level of skill or ability at the time the test is taken. In many cases, a test can be considered *both* an achievement and aptitude test since the measure of present skill level can also be used to predict future performance.

Paper-and-pencil tests and performance tests: As the name implies, the paper-and-pencil test requires that the testee record his response to some test item or question on a piece of paper or answer sheet that is supplied for that purpose. On the other hand, the performance tests, which may involve anything from driving a car during a license examination to manipulating or assembling mechanical objects, do not require written responses.

Speed and power tests: In some types of tests, accuracy is not as important as speed. For example, a *speed* test would require a person to complete as many items as possible in a given period of time. While the number of errors will usually be recorded and possibly be included in the final score, the primary weight is placed on the number of responses. In some other types of tests, called *power* tests, items may be quite difficult and the testee is given as much time as needed to finish the items. The score is based on the accuracy of the responses.

Individual and group tests: In Chapter 10, we discussed the uses of individual and group tests. As you will recall, group tests are more economical to administer and do not require a well-trained examiner, as do individual tests.

As one might expect, the effectiveness of tests as selection devices will vary considerably depending upon the nature of the criterion for using them as predictors. Many tests have turned out to be quite useful as predictors, while others are less useful or even useless. The effectiveness of a test is generally the result of a long developmental procedure, part of which we have already considered in our discussion of concurrent and predictive validity. Although it is beyond the scope of this book to deal with test construction, you should be aware that this endeavor requires sophisticated procedures and considerable effort. Throwing together a batch of questions, as is done in many "psychological" tests you sometimes see in popular magazines and newspapers, does not constitute a psychological test.

Legal Aspects of Testing

Social changes in America have raised questions about testing in industry that had never been seriously considered until recently. For example, are selection tests discriminatory? Are they designed for the individual in a white, middle-class culture? Are they designed so that they discriminate against women? In other words, are the tests constructed in such a fashion that a white male has a better chance of making a high score than a member of a minority group or a woman? Do some types of tests constitute an invasion of privacy? More and more legislative bodies are becoming interested in questions of this kind. It is quite likely that the answers to these and similar questions will be determined in the courts.

Training the Man for the Job

The selection process is only the first step in fitting the man to the job. In most cases, individuals are not ready to step out of the selection office into the operating system. Usually, the selected person does not yet possess the particular knowledge, skills, and attitudes needed to perform the job or task. These skills are developed by the process of *training*. There are a variety of training techniques used that are based on principles and findings of psychology as well as on a steadily expanding body of training technology.

The importance of training has been recognized for a number of years and there has been a considerable amount of research conducted in this field. While much of this research has taken place within various industrial settings, a significant amount of what we currently know about training methods and their effectiveness is based on research conducted by or for the military. Because of the nature of military training, which often requires training large numbers of men on complex tasks in a short period of time, new concepts in training have been developed, which have been demonstrated to be effective.

Before discussing training concepts and procedures, we will attempt to answer a question that often arises concerning training: What is the difference, if any, between *education* and *training?* Are you, as a student, being educated or trained? Traditionally, "education" has been thought of as a process by which an individual is developed not only intellectually but socially and physically as well. Training, on the other hand, has been viewed as a process for teaching particular skills for a particular purpose. However, the word *training* is now acquiring a much broader meaning and refers to activities ranging from the acquisition of simple motor skills to the development and change of complex socioemotional attitudes (Bass & Vaughan, 1966).

Developing a Training Program

Earlier in this chapter, the steps involved in developing a selection procedure were discussed. Development of an effective training program also requires a number of somewhat similar steps. The model of a training development project that we will consider is based on procedures that have resulted from military training research (Crawford, 1962). However, this model is equally suitable for utilization with civilian organizations and industries.

A sequence of the various activities required in the development of a training program is shown in Figure 12–3. While the various steps represent somewhat arbitrary divisions of the procedures required in developing the program, efforts of the kinds indicated at each of the steps must be made in order to develop the program and determine its effectiveness.

The first step in this model is *analyzing the system* and defining the objectives of the system. Tasks are defined and task descriptions, discussed earlier, are formulated. Then, within the framework of the whole system, the particular job that the training program is concerned with will be studied to determine the inputs from the rest of the system and the required outputs. The *task* or *job analysis* (also discussed previously) leads to the *specification of knowledge and skills* that are required for performing the task or job.

The next step involves the *determination of training objectives.* From the knowledge and skill specification and from the assessment of the existing capabilities of the trainees, it is possible

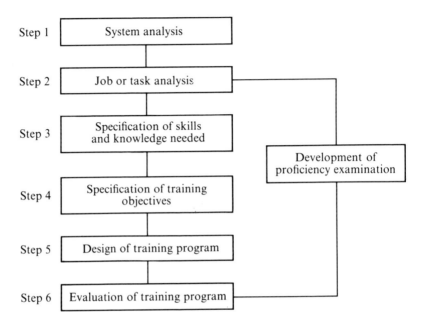

Figure 12–3. The major steps required in the development of a training program. See text for discussion of the various steps.

to define quite precisely the objectives of the training program, as Crawford (1962) points out:

> The goals may be limited to the specific job or may contain elements furnishing preparation for other jobs later in a man's career. In terms of the specific job, it is at this point that decisions may be made about the optimum combination of school and on-the-job training, and on the kinds of aids, such as manuals and check lists, which will be made available for use on the job [pp. 315–316].

The *construction of the training program* involves selecting specific subject matter, deciding how and when it will be presented, what selection and training devices and simulators will be utilized, what achievement tests will be used at various points in the training program as a measure of the trainee's progress, and what special techniques could be designed to motivate the trainee.

The military training programs have definite advantages over civilian counterparts in special techniques designed to motivate trainees. For example, some years ago when one of the authors was in the Navy, he was assigned to a school for a number of weeks of training. This particular school had a system that virtually guaranteed a high level of motivation. On the day of graduation all of the names of the students in a class were posted in order of their gradepoints. At the same time, the various worldwide assignments for the class were also posted. The top man of the class had his pick of all the various assignments, the second man then had his pick, and so on. Obviously, the choices of the last man or two in the class were quite limited. While it may be questioned whether motivation techniques of this kind are appropriate, they certainly are effective in maintaining a high output from a class.

Note on Figure 12–3 that a proficiency examination is developed from the information available about the inputs and outputs of the job that were determined during the job analysis. The construction of a proficiency examination is an important part of the development of a training program since it serves essentially the same purpose that the criterion measure served in the development of the selection program. The proficiency examination may be paper and pencil, performance, or a combination of both. Considerable care must be exercised in the construction of this test since it represents the means by which the entire training program is evaluated.

The last step in the model is the *evaluation of the program*. The proficiency examination is used for this purpose and can be used in a number of different ways. It can be used to compare the performance of equivalent groups of trainees who were exposed to different training techniques. For example, in the construction of the training program, groups of trainees may have been exposed to training procedures A, B, and C. All groups are subsequently tested on the same proficiency examination. If the trainees in group C did significantly better than those in the other two groups, it would suggest that procedure C is the most effective. In some cases, a training program may be designed to reduce the amount of time needed for training. Groups trained under the "long" and the "short" program can then be tested on the proficiency examination. In this situation, however, it would probably only be necessary to show that those trainees in the short training program were about equal to those completing the long program. There are various other aspects of training programs that are evaluated by means of the proficiency examination. Obviously, this examination is an important factor in establishing a training program. Criterion measures in training will be discussed in more detail later.

Objectives of a Training Program

We have already stated that one objective of training is to impart the necessary knowledge, skills, and attitudes for successful performance on the job. There are also other objectives. Often the objective of training research is to develop a shorter training program that is consequently less expensive (usually) than an existing program. Sometimes reduced cost is a secondary consideration and a shorter training program may be even more expensive than a longer program. However, in some systems, such as the military, time may be of the essence during a national emergency, and every day saved in preparing a military unit for operational readiness is critical. A considerable amount of the training research conducted by the military has been aimed at reducing the length of training required without subsequent reduction in performance capability.

Another objective of training can be to decrease the aptitude requirements for certain kinds of jobs. One aim of selection research is to establish certain "cut-offs" on various aptitude tests below which the probability of a person succeeding on a particular job is low. For example, in the military a person must have a certain score on an electronics aptitude test before being considered qualified to attend certain types of military schools that provide electronics training. When the manpower supply is unlimited, requirements of this sort present no problem since high-aptitude personnel are available. However, when the supply of personnel is limited and trainees with aptitude scores high enough to qualify for admission are in short supply, an important objective of training research may be to develop programs that can successfully train lower-aptitude personnel.

As an example of this type of training research, consider a project that was conducted for the Army that was to develop a training program that could effectively train personnel whose aptitude scores were below the level normally acceptable for admission to the training program (Goffard, Heimstra, Beecroft, & Openshaw, 1960). Basically, this project followed the steps outlined in Figure 12–3 in that the task was analyzed, specifications of knowledge and skills were determined, a proficiency test was constructed, and a training program was designed. The training program involved an experimental approach as well as the standard approach to training. The basic design called for comparing graduates of the experimental course with graduates of the standard course on the proficiency examination. This was a comprehensive basic electronics test battery (BETB).

At the time the study was conducted, the "cut-off" on the Electronics (EL) Aptitude Area of the Army Classification Battery was 100. For purposes of the experiment, however, a number of trainees with aptitude scores lower than 100 were admitted to the program. These, along with students who met the aptitude requirements, were assigned randomly to either the experimental training program or the standard program. Thus, a given class in either program contained a number of low-aptitude personnel along with the usual number of higher-aptitude men.

The experimental training program was quite different from the standard approach. Electronics information was consistently presented in a whole-to-part, concrete-to-abstract, operational-to-theoretical order. Properties, principles, and procedures were taught in terms of their functions, in contexts which had already been made familiar to the trainee. Components were taught as parts of familiar circuits, circuits as parts of familiar operating equipment. Knowledge was analyzed *out* of functional devices, not synthesized into them. The general approach was labeled the *functional context* method.

The results of this study are shown in Figure 12–4. Trainees from both the standard instruction groups and the experimenal groups were tested on the proficiency test (BETB). Note that only in the two groups with the highest electronic aptitude scores was the standard method of instruction superior. For the trainees in the lower aptitude groups, the experimental method was superior. As a matter of fact, low-aptitude students, whose scores of 100 or below would normally keep them out of the electronics training programs, did as well as students in the 110–119 aptitude score range. With this particular training program, then, the Army was able to include a number of men with EL scores below 100 in their pool of prospective electronic school trainees. Suppose that the Army obtained most of its trainees from a population with EL scores of 130 and above. Would the experimental course still be the best course to use?

Selection of Training Methods

The individual who is responsible for setting up a training program in either a civilian or military setting has a variety of different training methods available to him. His selection of an appropriate method should be based on such considerations as *who* is to be trained and *what* is to be taught. Too often the selection of a method is based on a personal bias, fascination with a particular

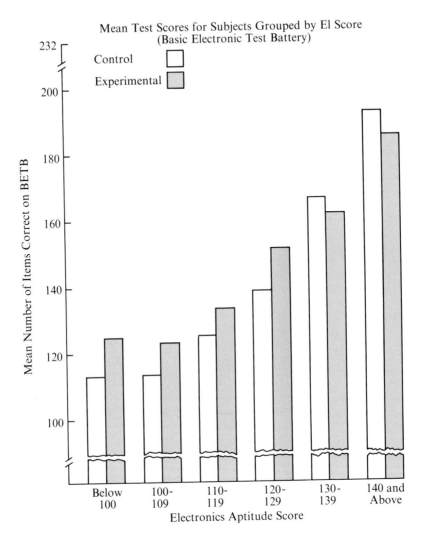

Figure 12–4. Subjects in the experimental group were exposed to a special form of instruction. Note that the experimental subjects with low electronics aptitude scores benefited more from the instruction than subjects with high aptitude scores. (From Goffard et al., 1960. By permission of the Human Resources Research Organization.)

method, or the training staff's personal experiences and limitations rather than on a consideration of the advantages and disadvantages of a particular method.

What constitutes an adequate training program? Bass and Vaughan (1966) suggest that a method will be adequate to the degree that it appears likely to do the following (based on the principles of learning):

1. Provide for the learner's active participation.
2. Provide the trainee with knowledge of results about his attempts to improve.
3. Promote by means of good organization a meaningful integration of learning experiences that the trainee can transfer from training to the job.
4. Provide some means for the trainee to be reinforced for appropriate behavior.
5. Provide for practice and repetition when needed.
6. Motivate the trainee to improve his own performance.
7. Assist the trainee in his willingness to change [p. 86].

It might be mentioned that not all psychologists agree with the idea that a training program is adequate to the extent to which it conforms to the principles of learning. Gagné (1962), in an article concerned with training and principles of learning, lists such principles as reinforcement, distribution of practice, meaningfulness of material, as well as several others. He asks how one fares if he seriously attempts to use such principles to design effective training situations. His answer: not particularly well. Gagné gives examples of situations in which these principles do not appear to be effective in military training.

Assuming that a training need exists, what methods does the training director have to choose from? While we cannot consider all of these methods, several of the most common will be discussed.

On-the-Job Training

On-the-job training (OJT) is by far the most common type of training in industrial settings. A survey of more than 500 industrial establishments revealed that over 50 percent made use of some type of on-the-job training. There are some definite advantages to OJT but there are also some disadvantages.

From the point of view of management, OJT appears to be a highly practical method of training. The new employee produces and earns while he learns. Management assumes that the employee is paying at least part of his own way as he learns. Thus, OJT is usually considered one of the most economical training methods. Actually, adequate statistics concerning the economy of OJT are lacking, and it may not be as economical as it is often assumed to be. Factors such as quality of production of the trainee, accidents, or loss of production by personnel who must supervise the trainee may make this a more expensive method than it would appear to be to management.

Usually in OJT, the trainee works on the machines or in the situation in which he will be working after his training period is over. Consequently, the problem of transfer of training is greatly reduced or even eliminated. OJT permits the trainee to practice the same operations during training that he is expected to perform upon completion of the training. Not only does he learn to perform the required job operations, he may also learn a good deal about the social factors involved in the job. He may meet the people that he will be working with after training and thus facilitate the transition from training to job.

Although OJT is a method that is often used, it is also often abused. In some organizations, the trainer who supervises the OJT may be far from a qualified instructor. Frequently, he may just be a "nice guy" type who is assigned what is often considered a "soft" position. The personality characteristics of the trainer, along with his capabilities and instructional techniques, may play an important role in how effective OJT will be. Also, many companies make no effort at establishing a systematic and organized program of OJT. The new employee is frequently told upon reporting on the job that he should "work with John Smith for a few days and learn the ropes." After a few days it is assumed that he has been trained and he is assigned a work station.

Apprentice Training. Apprentice training is, of course, a form of OJT. It is one of the oldest training methods and some of the problems that were associated with it 500 years ago still exist today.

Typically, apprentice training involves a relatively prolonged period during which the apprentice works with a skilled journeyman and learns by observing and assisting. This period may range from one year to six or seven. Too often, the apprentice program in an organization serves primarily as a method for obtaining inexpensive help. While an apprentice may be fortunate in being assigned to a craftsman who takes an interest in helping him, frequently this is not the case and he is forced to pick up information as best he can. However, in recent years there has been an increased interest on the part of labor organizations in setting up apprentice programs with good standards for training. Although it is estimated that less than one percent of the total working force are presently apprentices in training, this still represents a large number of individuals.

There are several other types of training methods that could be considered "on-the-job" training (in contrast to "off-the-job" training). Typically, the OJT procedures are most likely to be used for the blue-collar workers, although this is not always the case. Often, a period of OJT is required of supervisory and managerial personnel. Typically, however, OJT is just a first step that is followed by other kinds of training. Since most of you are in college to obtain some of the abilities required for white-collar jobs, what sort of training methods might you expect to encounter after being selected for such a position?

Leadership Training

The need for specialized training for supervisory personnel has gained more and more recognition in the last twenty years or so. Research in training for supervisory skills gathered momentum when industrialists realized that supervisors needed special abilities, which could be acquired through training, to cope with their problems in the same way that the assembly-line worker needs training to handle his job.

Generally, supervisory or management training, which we will refer to as *leadership* training, is aimed at developing skills in decision making and human relations. While the abilities to make correct decisions and to "get along" with others are both important in terms of leadership behavior, it should be emphasized that the essence of *any* supervisory or managerial position is decision making. If a position does not involve decision making, it is not a leadership position. Although human relations ability is desirable in that it may make a leader more effective, decision making ability is the most important.

The methods of leadership training that will be discussed generally take for granted that the trainee already has a considerable amount of technical knowledge about a given area. This knowledge may have been gained by years of experience in a particular company, by on-the-job training, or by preparation in an off-the-job setting such as a university. Technical knowledge about an area is essential if effective decisions are to be made by a leader.

While the methods of training described below do not exhaust the many types that are available and used, they represent the approaches that are most common in training for leadership behavior.

Case Study. The case-study approach is based on the assumption that the behaviors required of leaders can best be attained through detailed study and discussion of particular "real" problems associated with actual organizations. In this technique, a "case problem" is prepared by the training supervisor and presented to the trainees. Usually, the problem is written out in considerable detail so that the trainees have available to them enough information on which to base sound decisions about the problem.

Typically, after sufficient time to study the case, the trainees are brought together for a conference and individual trainees present their ideas and solutions to the case problem. This discussion period is the crucial element of the case-study method. When this method is properly used, trainees are able to better understand the problem-solving process and the steps required in arriving at a decision. The solution itself is of secondary importance.

There are several different forms of the case-study method of leadership training. While the detailed case history is generally used, in some other training situations only a brief sentence or two about a particular incident will be given the trainee. Prior to the training session, trainees are required to "think through" their solution based on the material given them. At the session, they obtain further information from the session leader and, as they gain additional information that they consider to be important, the trainees may progress toward various solutions.

An important aspect of this technique is that it reveals what kind of information a trainee thinks is important. For example, some trainees may be primarily interested in what rules, regulations, and policies are available to solve the problem, while other trainees may be more interested in obtaining information about the individuals involved in the incident, such as feelings, background, work history, and so on. This procedure leads the trainee to an understanding of how the solution was attained. This technique also emphasizes the solution itself.

Role Playing. In role playing, a problem situation is set up and trainees are assigned "roles" to play. For example, the hypothetical problem may involve a stubborn foreman and a supervisor who is attempting to get something done. One trainee will be assigned the role of the foreman, another the role of the supervisor. Generally, the role playing is carried out in front of a group of fellow trainees. The trainees who are playing the roles of foreman and supervisor "play out" solutions that they think might develop in the actual situation. For example, the supervisor might lose his temper and fire the foreman, he might try to reason with him, and so forth.

After a role-playing session, the "audience" of fellow trainees can discuss and comment on the various solutions that were obtained. Under the proper circumstances, the role-playing technique can be an effective training method.

Training by Simulation. Few of you who watched the television presentation of the moon shots could fail to be impressed by the occasional views of the elaborate simulators in which the astronauts were trained before undertaking the mission. Sophisticated (and very expensive) simulators have been used for a number of years to train military and civilian aviators. The military also makes use of simulators to train tank and submarine crewmen, as well as operators of many other man-machine systems. Some aspects of this type of simulation will be discussed in more detail later in this chapter.

In recent years, simulation has developed into a useful and effective method of training organizational behavior. Various types of situations are "simulated," and trainees are placed in these situations. While the simulated situations can vary considerably, Bass and Vaughan (1966) list the typical features of simulation as a training device in organization behavior as follows:

1. The essential characteristics of a real-life organization or activity are abstracted and presented as a case—not to be studied and analyzed as in the usual case method, but to be experienced by the trainee as a realistic, life-like circumstance.
2. Trainees are asked to assume various roles in the circumstance and to solve the problems facing them. They are asked to be themselves—not to act.
3. A simulation often involves a telescoping or compressing of time and events; a single hour may be equated with a month or a quarter of a year in real life, and many events are experienced in a relatively brief period of time.
4. Trainees are required to make decisions that have a real effect in the simulation and about which they receive rapid feedback.
5. The simulation is followed by a critique of what went on during the exercise [p. 105].

In-basket simulation: While first developed as an executive performance appraisal method, the in-basket technique is also useful as a training method. The trainee is given appropriate background material about the organization as a frame of reference, along with a series of letters, memos, notes, and so on, that might be expected to be found in an executive's "in-basket." Basically, the task of the trainee is to transfer the material from the in-basket to the out-basket. He "handles" the material as he would in the real situation by attempting to solve the problems that may be presented, answering letters, writing memos, setting up agenda for meetings, and so forth. A number of trainees can be handled simultaneously with this method. Typically, a group critique takes place after the trainees have responded (individually) to the material presented in the in-basket.

Gaming: This is another simulation training technique that is popular in both civilian and military organizations. Actually, it was out of the procedures developed for "war games" by military training establishments that games for training business executives have developed.

Most business games attempt to simulate a business environment that may include several competing companies. Usually, groups of trainees act as teams with each team representing a particular company and making decisions related to the running of the company. These games can range from relatively simple types to elaborate computer games. The consequences of decisions the teams arrive at concerning finance, marketing, production, research, personnel, and so on are fed back to the teams as quickly as possible, often by means of computer printouts, and this feedback is utilized in making subsequent decisions. At the end of the next period of "play," additional feedback is given, and so on, until the game is finished.

There are many advantages to games as training techniques. Games are motivating and offer challenges to the trainees involved. The trainees can learn a great deal about managerial skills that are difficult to learn by other techniques. Very real decision-making and risk-taking situations can be employed in the game that could not be used in other training methods. Bass and Vaughan (1966) point out:

> Probably the single greatest advantage of the business game over more traditional training techniques is its dynamic quality. Trainees are actively involved in decision making that has real consequences in the immediate environment. Because of the telescoping of time and events, they are able to experience the effects of many more decisions than would normally be possible in on-the-job training. Furthermore, the simulated environment is a nonpunitive one as compared with real life: the trainee will not lose his job or receive other serious reprimands for any bad decisions he makes in the game. Thus, he is encouraged to experiment—to try out new behaviors and new strategies for decision making—without the risk of the serious consequences that may attend real-life circumstances [p. 108].

The training methods that have been described represent but a few of the techniques that are commonly employed. There are important training considerations that we have not touched upon. For example, we have not discussed the problem of *team training*, which is particularly important in situations in which groups of men interact with machines or other men as a distinguishable operating subsystem within a larger system. In this type of situation, a group will be considered a subsystem and must be trained as a group. This presents some unique training problems that are not encountered in the other training methods. Usually, the team members bring to the training situation the prerequisite skills, and the team training focuses on the required *interplay* of the group members that will be needed for operating within some system.

Another training method that has become extremely popular in the last few years is *programmed instruction*. Many of you may already have encountered various types of programmed instruction in new textbooks. Programmed instruction is made up of a graduated series of items (questions or problems) that require some form of response from the trainee. The material is structured so that the trainee receives immediate feedback on the results of his response. He receives one item at a time, answers it, receives feedback, and, if he is correct, goes on to the next item. The advantages of this method are that each trainee is given new material at a rate that suits him, feedback is immediate, mistakes can be quickly corrected, and progress is visible to both the trainee and trainer. Some rather elaborate "teaching machines" have been developed for the programmed-instruction method of training and a considerable amount of money has been spent by organizations in establishing training programs of this type. There is, however, a rather sizable group of skeptics who are not convinced that this type of training is as effective as its advocates claim it to be.

Most of the developments in programmed instruction concern verbal learning of one kind or another. However, there is a new approach in motor learning that borrows some of its concepts from the area of programmed instructions—the *adaptive-training* approach.

Basically, adaptive training is a training procedure in which the problem, the stimulus, or the task is varied as a function of how well the trainee performs. In a report dealing with adaptive training, Kelley (1969) states that: "The primary requirements of adaptive training are that performance be continuously or repetitively measured in some way, and that the measurement be employed to make appropriate changes in the stimulus, problem, or task" (p. 549).

In many respects, the usual training that a person receives can be considered adaptive training in that a skilled instructor will vary the difficulty of the task depending upon how well the student has been performing. *Machine-controlled* adaptive training simply represents the automation of a function that is normally performed by the skilled individual instructor.

Shown in Figure 12–5 is a schematic comparing fixed, or standard, training with adaptive training. Note that the essential feature of the adaptive-training procedure, as contrasted to the fixed-training procedure, is the feedback loop. By means of this feedback, the problem, stimulus, or task is changed as a result of the trainee performance. Thus, an adaptive-training system can be thought of as a closed-loop feedback system. In adaptive training, because of this feedback, as the trainee performs better, the task becomes more difficult; if he performs poorly (in contrast to a previous level of performance), the task becomes easier.

It can be seen from Figure 12–5 that machine-controlled

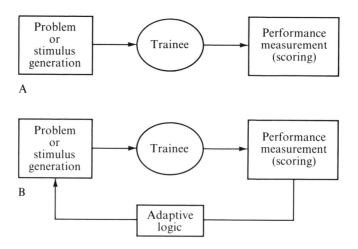

Figure 12–5. Schematic showing fixed (A) and adaptive (B) training procedures. In adaptive training, by means of the adaptive logic feedback loop, the problem, stimulus, or task is changed as a result of the output (performance) of the trainee. As his performance improves, the task becomes more difficult. From C. R. Kelley, What is adaptive training? In *Human Factors*, 1969, **11**(6), 547–556. Reprinted by permission of the Human Factors Society.

adaptive training has three elements. First, a means for measuring the performance of the trainee is necessary. For example, in an adaptive tracking trainer, the system would require a means of continually (or at least very frequently) measuring how well the trainee was tracking. The system would also require a way of adjusting the difficulty level of the tracking task as a function of how well the trainee was performing. A simple method might involve increasing or decreasing the speed with which the target in the tracking task was moved. Finally, some sort of adaptive logic, which automatically changes the task difficulty level as a function of the performance measurement, is required. Thus:

> Machine-controlled adaptive training automatically gets harder as the subject becomes more skilled. As a consequence, the same training equipment can be effective for the entire range of skills, from those of the neophyte to those of the expert. Whatever the level of skill of the trainee, the system will adjust itself so that he is receiving stimuli or problems or tasks that are suitable to his skill level [Kelley, 1969, p. 548].

Adaptive training has been found to be a very efficient method of training. However, the effectiveness of this type of training is dependent upon a number of variables. If a training device has poor transfer to the operational system, making the device an "adaptive trainer" is probably not going to improve the transfer characteristics. In some cases, training devices can be made less effective by being made adaptive than they were originally. When carefully designed, however, an adaptive trainer is much more effective than an otherwise similar system where the difficulty level is held constant throughout the training period.

The Criterion Problem in Psychological Research

In this chapter, the importance of the criterion measure was mentioned several times. For example, in validating the predictor measures in personnel selection, it was necessary to relate these measures to some criterion measure. Similarly, it was pointed out that in evaluation of a training program it is necessary to make use of a criterion, such as a proficiency examination, in order to determine the effectiveness of the training program. In discussing the criterion, however, we have not emphasized just how important it is. As Blum and Naylor (1968) point out:

> The criterion is basic to all measurement in industrial psychology. To overstate its importance would be literally impossible. Without adequate criteria, industrial psychology is ineffective and ceases to be a science. In other words, the magnitude of the contribution of industrial psychology is *completely* determined by the adequacy of the criterion measures evolved [p. 174].

Obviously, then, one of the most important aspects of the researcher's job in developing selection and training procedures is the design of criteria against which he can evaluate his procedures. Although considerable work has been done on the criterion problem in relation to man's performance and effectiveness on a job, it is a continuing problem; the need for new and more effective criteria develops as the requirements imposed on man in various systems change.

There are various definitions of a criterion. We have already said that a criterion is some sort of indicator of what "success" on a particular job involves. In this sense, it is an *evaluative standard* that can be used to measure the performance, attitudes, motives, or other factors that are important for a person to be successful on a job.

Some Classes of Criteria

Certain defining labels have been attached to criteria based on particular characteristics associated with a criterion measure. For example, criteria can be *proximal, distal,* or *immediate.* They can also be *actual* or *ultimate* criteria as well as *internal* or *external* criteria.

Suppose that we administer a test designed for predicting purposes to one or more potential employees. In some cases, we might also obtain criteria information at the same time the prediction instruments are used. Those criteria measures that are obtained at the same time that the predictor measures are administered are called *immediate criteria.* If the criterion measures are obtained shortly after the predictor measures, they are called *proximal criteria,* while *distal criteria* are obtained sometime (usually a year or more) after predictor measures.

We can also view criteria in terms of whether they are actual or ultimate measures of success.

> By definition, whatever measure of success one actually uses is the *actual criterion.* The *ultimate criterion,* on the other hand, is a theoretical and ideal criterion that usually exists only in the psychologist's mind. It is the "true" criterion of success, while our

actual criterion is the measure we have been forced to adopt simply because we can do no better [Blum & Naylor, 1968, p. 176].

In a training program, criteria are frequently labeled *internal* or *external*. The former refers to a criterion that measures improvements or changes within the training program itself, while an external criterion is one which is outside the program. For example, examinations in a course or the skill shown in the use of a simulator during a training program are internal criteria. The skill shown by a pilot in flying a plane after completion of training, the combat efficiency of military personnel, and success on the job in an industrial setting are examples of external criteria.

Usually, some form of external criterion is considered desirable as a means of evaluating the effectiveness of a training program. Often, however, internal criteria can be used. Suppose that the training situation corresponded very closely to the actual work situation. In that case, the internal criterion might resemble very closely the external criterion that would be used. An example of this type of situation is illustrated in secretarial training programs. A test of typing speed in the school (internal criterion) might be very similar to one given on the job (external criterion). Sometimes an internal criterion must be used because there is no satisfactory external criterion available for the researcher to use. Thus, if he is concerned with developing training programs for combat aviators, he can hardly start a war in order to have an external criterion available.

It is important for researchers, however, to demonstrate the equivalence of internal and external criteria and not just assume that they are equivalent. When the researcher does use an internal criterion, he should recognize that it is a substitute and should not make claims about the effectiveness of the program that are not warranted.

The Development of Criteria

A psychologist does not just reach into a desk drawer and pull out a criterion measure. Development of criterion for use in either selection or training research is a time-consuming and often difficult procedure. Typically, in order to construct a criterion measure, a thorough job or task analysis is first required. Once an understanding of the behaviors required in the task is obtained, the behaviors that constitute success on the job or task must be determined. It is often extremely difficult to define success at a particular task. What, for example, would we define as "success" in the case of a pilot or a combat infantryman? Once the "successful" behavior has been defined, methods for measuring the elements of successful behavior must be developed. This step can result in a *composite criteria*—several individual measures of job success that are combined into a single composite measure—or it can result in *multiple criteria*, meaning that each of the several "success" measures obtained will be used separately. Whether composite or multiple, the criteria can then be used to evaluate the effectiveness of the selection or training program.

We have suggested that it is one thing to list the steps required for the development of criteria and another thing to actually follow these steps. In order to illustrate the difficulties associated with criterion development, we will consider in some detail the criteria for a training program that most students encounter in high school—the driver training program.

Driver Training: A Search for a Criterion

Since its inception more than 35 years ago, high school driver education has grown to include the training of more than two million high school students each year. Although this number accounts for only about 54 percent of the total population of eligible students, it has been estimated that by the 1972–1973 school year, nearly 100 percent of the eligible population will be enrolled in driver education programs, at an expense to the taxpayer of about 330 million dollars (Nichols, 1970). One might naturally assume that a program of this magnitude would have a number of excellent criteria available with which to evaluate the success of the training. Nothing could be further from the truth. There are *no adequate* criteria to determine whether driver education programs are effective or a complete waste of money. Consequently, whether or not driver education programs are actually worthwhile is currently being subjected to considerable debate among experts in the field (Heimstra, 1970b).

We have seen that development of a criterion is dependent on a definition of successful performance on a job or task. What constitutes successful driving? What criteria can be used that reflect successful driving performance? Let us consider several criteria that, at first sight, might appear to be indices of "good driving."

Accident Rates. Some studies have shown that graduates of driver training programs have fewer accidents than drivers who learned to drive on their own or were taught by parents or friends. Thus, accident rates might be an indication of driving ability and could be considered a criterion. However, in these studies, accident records of trainees and nontrainees were usually obtained from police files. What these records do not show is the number of miles the person drives (quantity of exposure) or the conditions under which he drives (quality of exposure). There are some research findings which indicate that students who enroll in driver training programs drive significantly fewer miles than students who do not enroll in such courses. There are also indications that students who enroll in driver training drive under safer conditions than those students who do not enroll. Obviously, these factors would cast some doubt on the use of accident rates as a criterion of "good" driving.

Violation Records. There is some evidence that persons who have completed driver training programs have fewer traffic violations than those who do not enroll in such programs. The same criticisms that are leveled against using accident rates as a criterion can be used in the case of violation rates. Quality and quantity of driving exposure are both factors. Also, there is evidence that various personality traits are related to the frequency of traffic violations and that it is the individuals with these personality patterns that typically do not enroll in driver training programs. Again, this would result in a criterion measure that actually does not reflect the effectiveness of the training program.

Other Criteria. An obvious criterion for determining whether a driver training program is effective is to take the trainee out in a car and let him drive. Most of you have taken a driving test for licensing purposes and should have some idea about how adequate this procedure would be as a criterion. It is possible, however, with recent developments in instrumented research vehicles, that a driving test in a car of this type might eventually prove to be a good measure of driving performance. (An illustration of an instrumented research vehicle was presented in Figure 1–7.) With this type of device a number of different measures of driver performance can be obtained. Some of these measures have been shown to differentiate between experienced and inexperienced drivers and drivers with high and low violation records. While more research will have to be conducted with this particular type of vehicle before it can be considered for wide use as a testing device for driver training programs, it does have promise.

Another possible technique for criterion measurement is to

use driving simulators. In recent years there has been considerable research and development involving driving simulators (Schori, 1970b). If it could be assumed that a simulator, which was properly instrumented, would measure the types of behavior required for successful driving, then this kind of device would serve the same purpose as an instrumented vehicle. However, this type of measure is a step further away from the *external* type of criterion that is desirable. Before a simulator could be used, it would be necessary to determine whether measures obtained in the simulator were related to measures obtained in an actual vehicle. In other words, the simulator measures would have to be validated against actual "on-the-road" measures. A step in this direction has been taken in the authors' laboratory where a simulator has been instrumented in the same manner as the research vehicle discussed above. In one study (Hagen, Ellingstad, & Kimball, 1970) a large number of subjects were tested in both the simulator and the research vehicle, and a correlation was computed between the measures obtained in the simulator and in the car. Significant relationships were found between some of the measures, suggesting that the simulator measures are capable of providing measurement of driver performance similar to that provided by the instrumented research vehicle.

We have seen the difficulty that can be encountered in developing a criterion measure for a task that most of us take for granted. The problem, of course, is not always this difficult and adequate criteria may not be hard to come by in many cases. However, think for a moment of the many tasks that are much more complicated than driving a car and the difficulties that might be encountered in the development of criteria for these tasks. It is apparent that not only is criterion development a critical aspect of selection and training research, it is also the most difficult aspect.

Evaluation of Training Effectiveness

Before we can attempt to evaluate how effective a training program is in increasing efficiency, decreasing time and costs, or decreasing aptitude requirements of trainees, we must have a criterion. Assuming, then, that we do have an adequate criterion, what are some of the considerations in evaluating a training program?

Suppose that we take a group of trainees and administer our criterion test before they start their training. They are then trained for a few weeks and once again tested on the criterion. The average score on the second testing is significantly higher than the score on the first test. Can we then state that the training program is effective?

We *cannot* make that statement since we do not know for sure whether the higher scores on the posttest are due to factors that had nothing to do with the training. While we can be reasonably certain that the training received is responsible for the improvement, it is necessary that the change in performance of a group receiving training be compared with the change in performance of a group that does not receive training—that is, a *control group*—before we can be sure.

Control Groups

In previous chapters the importance of control groups in psychological research has been mentioned several times. Control groups are equally important in experiments that are designed to evaluate training programs. However, how a control group is used in training-evaluation programs may be dependent upon a number of factors.

In some evaluation experiments, a new training program may have been developed, meaning that there is no other program against which it can be compared. In this case, a control group would probably receive no training whatsoever during the period that the experimental group of trainees were being exposed to the new training program. In most cases, however, a new or experimental program is designed to replace an existing program of some sort. In this type of situation, the control group would be trained on the old program while the experimental group was trained on the new program.

Before beginning an experiment involving a control group, the researcher must decide whether he wants to *equate* his control and experimental groups. Essentially, this means that the experimenter will attempt to make sure that both groups are equally capable before the experiment begins. He might do this by testing all subjects on a pretest and then assigning them to the experimental and control groups so that the average test scores of the two groups are nearly identical. Often, however, attempts are made to equate groups on many other factors, such as age, education, IQ, or race. If this procedure is followed, then the effectiveness of the training would be evaluated as shown in Figure 12–6.

Sometimes, for various reasons, equating groups is not feasible. In such cases, a somewhat different method of evaluating the effectiveness of a training program is used. Rather than directly

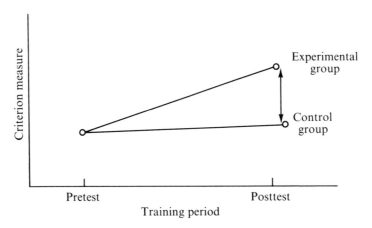

Figure 12-6. Illustration of method used to determine effectiveness of training with equated groups of subjects. The difference between the scores of the two groups on the post-test determines the effectiveness of the training. Various statistical tests would be conducted to determine whether the differences between the posttest scores of the two groups were significant.

comparing the performance of the two groups, the *degree* of change for each group between the pre- and posttest is of primary interest. For example, if the control group showed a 10 percent improvement on the posttest as compared to the pretest, while the experimental groups showed a 30 percent improvement, we would assume the experimental group was exposed to a more effective program.

The System So Far

At one level of analysis, man's behavior can be thought of in terms of a number of behavioral subsystems, all of which interact and contribute to system output. At a different level, we can think of man as a complete system and discuss such aspects as differences between systems and malfunctions of systems. Again, at a third level of analysis man can be viewed as a subsystem within a larger system. As a subsystem, man functions within a wide variety of other systems. However, one of the most important systems in which man is an element is the particular one in which he works. This chapter has dealt with the procedures and techniques involved in attempting to fit men to a system. In the next chapter, we will be concerned with the efforts that are made to fit the system to man.

Summary

1. Selection and training are two primary methods used to tailor a man for a job. However, before selection and training procedures can be developed, a job or task analysis is required. These types of analyses involve studying the job in order to determine the kinds of behaviors necessary for successful performance. There are several methods of job analysis, including interview methods, questionnaire, check list, and diary methods, the work-participation method, and the critical-incident method.

2. The process of system design requires specifications about the human component as well as the equipment components in the system. The human components are obtained through task descriptions and task analyses. A task description is a statement of human requirements, whereas the analysis specifies what capabilities are needed by man to meet the requirements.

3. After the job or task analyses have been conducted, selection procedures can be designed. The basis for personnel selection is the concept of individual differences. Personnel selection is aimed at identifying those workers who demonstrate the abilities, or potential abilities, that will make them a better risk for job success.

4. A selection "model" involves several steps. After job analysis is completed, some indicator of "success" on the job must be selected. This is called the criterion. Along with the selection of the criterion, it is necessary to choose a measure that can successfully predict how a person will do on the job. This is called the predictor. A critical element of the model is establishing the relationship (correlation) between predictor and criterion measures.

5. There are a number of predictor devices in use, including interview techniques, biographical inventories, personal references, and various kinds of tests. Tests, if properly designed and used, are generally the most valid predictors of job success.

6. After selection, most organizations expose the new employee to some type of training. Development of an effective training program can be time consuming and expensive. Several steps are typically involved, including job or task analysis, specification of knowledge and skills required, determination of training objectives, construction of the training program, and evaluation of the program.

7. There are several kinds of training methods. On-the-job

training is very common. Leadership training uses different techniques, such as the case-history method, role playing, and various simulation methods. Adaptive training is a relatively new technique that appears to be quite effective.

8. The development of the criterion measure to be used in training and selection is of critical importance. There are various classes of criteria, such as proximal and distal, actual or ultimate, and internal or external. While the development of adequate criteria is often difficult, they are absolutely essential if effective selection and training programs are to be designed.

Selected Readings

Bass, B. M., and Vaughan, J. A. *Training in industry: The management of learning.* Monterey, California: Brooks/Cole, 1966.

Blum, M. L., and Naylor, J. C. *Industrial psychology: Its theoretical and social foundations.* New York: Harper and Row, 1968.

Dunnette, M. D. *Personnel selection and placement.* Monterey, California: Brooks/Cole, 1966.

Holding, D. H. *Principles of training.* New York: Pergamon Press, 1965.

Kelley, C. R. What is adaptive training? *Human Factors*, 1969, **11**, 547–556.

13

Man as a Subsystem II

Human Factors Engineering

In the previous chapter we saw how man, in his role as a subsystem within a larger system, is selected and trained and thus modified to meet the demands of the parent system. Through selection and training the human subsystem can be made a more efficient component of the system, resulting in the improved overall efficiency of the system. In some cases, however, efficiency can be improved still further by modifying the system itself. In the case of man-machine systems, this can be accomplished through human factors engineering.

Unlike the personnel worker or human relations expert, who stresses adapting the *man to the machine* or to the job by means of selection and training, the human factors engineer stresses *adapting the machine and the job to the man*. He attempts to do this by applying his knowledge of human behavior to the design and structuring of machines and work environments. While the engineering capabilities of modern technology have often been astonishing, it is also true that in many instances an engineer's dream has been a nightmare for the human operator. This situation occurred in World War II when machinery was manufactured that required too many arms, legs, and in some cases too many heads for a man to operate such equipment. As a result human errors mounted and were responsible for gross malfunctions, with sometimes devastating results. Thus, engineers were joined by psychologists, physiologists, and other professionals in an attempt to design hardware subsystems so that human abilities could be complemented and human limitations compensated for.

The elimination of human error in systems in which man and machine must interact requires first that the designer understand which task must be performed by the operator and, second, that he understand the human functions that such tasks entail. Equipped with knowledge of what the human operator is really doing in interaction with a machine, the engineer can then adequately and intelligently design the particular features of the system that require interaction between man and machine. *Man-machine compatibility* is thus maintained.

The goals of human factors engineering are twofold: they involve the design of machines and work environments that will (1) permit optimal human functioning in the kinds of tasks performed by the operator; and (2) at the same time provide maximum system efficiency in attaining the goals for which the system was conceived.

In the pursuit of such goals, human factors engineering has become both a science and a technology. It has involved research into human behavior, as well as into the application of known behavioral principles. Consequently, human factors engineering has involved the efforts of professionals from several disciplines and has been given many names, such as engineering psychology, biomechanics, ergonomics, applied experimental psychology, biotechnology, as well as others. Some of the specific provinces of this discipline have included the distribution of functions between men and machines, the design of controls and displays, the design of safety, survival, and training equipment, and the integration of entire work environments to meet the needs of the human operator.

While psychology is only one of the several disciplines involved in human factors engineering, it has been a prime contributor to the field, both in laboratory and applied situations. The psychologist involved in human factors engineering is generally one who has been trained in human performance measurement, statistics, and laboratory research. Generally, his function has been to provide research findings concerning human behavior in specific system environments and to make system design recommendations on the basis of such results. In addition, the human factors psychologist performs an integral role in the specification of work-space layouts, normal environmental conditions of illumination, atmosphere, noise and vibration, and in determining the effects of unusual environmental conditions upon performance, as in space flight and underwater exploration.

Why a Systems Approach?

A systems or engineering model approach to describing human functions in a man-machine situation is particularly valuable for several reasons. First, by giving some insight into man's position in the system, a systems approach can provide for more precise direction of research efforts and a more organized collection of available research results. For example, once it has been determined that a man must perform a quality control function, such as detecting faulty products in a continuous assembly line, it can then be specified that certain criteria affecting man's detection and identification functions must be met. Such criteria may include adequate lighting, ventilation, optimal speed of assembly line, adequate rest periods to reduce fatigue, and so on. While much research has been conducted on the effects of these and other variables on human performance, a systems approach helps organize such information into a meaningful data structure.

In addition to the organizational attributes of a systems approach, engineering models furnish a system of mathematics which has already proven valuable when applied to the inanimate components of the man-machine system and which may turn out to be useful for describing the human element as well. However, it should be kept in mind that man differs in several significant ways from the hardware components of the system. One of the most important characteristics that differentiates man from a machine is man's *non-linearity of performance*. Non-linearity of performance implies that one cannot mathematically describe or predict man's future performance as a direct function of his present performance. Several variables such as fatigue, hunger, lack of sleep, or a quarrel with a fellow employee may influence human performance to such an extent that it would be unpredictable by any prescribed criteria. However, mathematical functions have been moderately successful in describing man's behavior under relatively normal conditions and have made the description and evaluation of man's activities relatively more precise.

Finally, both engineering and systems models have provided

the behavioral scientist with a new set of system-inspired concepts that have redirected his research inquiries. Consequently, behavioral data are more compatible with hardware data. Such models have forced the behaviorist to be more precise in his terminology and in his hypotheses, thus making research results less ambiguous. Instead of describing behavior in terms of stimulus, response, sensation, and so forth, behavior is now described in terms of inputs, outputs, storage, coding, and transfer functions. These designations fit more easily into the engineering terminology required for the design of the hardware components of the system and, consequently, enable the behavioral scientist and the engineer to work more effectively together.

Man's Role in the Man-Machine System

Obviously, the demands placed on the human subsystem in a man-machine system will vary depending on the type of system that is involved. Consequently, a complete description of man's role in man-machine systems is not feasible. However, there appear to be certain basic types of tasks that are characteristic of man's functions in different types of systems. We will consider two of these tasks—vigilance and tracking.

One of the human operator's primary roles in modern man-machine systems is to serve as a data transmission and processing link between the *displays* and *controls* of the machine. The human operator receives information from the displays in the form of signals, interprets such information, and transforms it into responses directed to the controls of the machine. Much of the human engineering in man-machine systems is concerned with modifying displays and controls to better suit the operator. Consequently, much of this chapter will deal with how controls and displays can be designed to enhance operator performance.

In addition to the direct influence on performance produced by the displays and controls of the machine itself, numerous environmental factors also have direct implications for the performance of the operator. Some of these factors, such as inadequate lighting, may have immediate detrimental effects upon performance, while others, such as moderately high temperature, may require more prolonged time periods before performance deterioration is noticeable.

Vigilance Tasks

One of man's basic system tasks is to monitor for system malfunctions or for detection of critical incidents, as in the detection of objects on a radar screen. This *vigilance* task generally requires infrequent responding on the part of the operator. Some of the problems involved in this type of task include (1) keeping the operator alert or sufficiently attentive so that critical detections are not missed; (2) reducing perceptual interference such as noise, static, and other distractions to a level at which the operator can detect the critical signals and can distinguish such signals from background noise; and (3) compensating for the detrimental effects of sensory underload, which cause the task to be extremely fatiguing or boring. Monitoring for infrequent critical signals often has the effect of reducing the level of sensory stimulation to a point where man cannot maintain his attention, and detection performance deteriorates. In some cases, this problem has been combated by (1) adding superficial tasks to keep the operator alert; (2) duplicating critical signals in additional sense modalities; (3) rest periods; (4) intermittent noise presentation; and (5) stimulants such as Benzedrine.

In a vigilance task, several human functions are required in order to perform effectively. These functions include (1) *detection* of the information signal; (2) *identification* of the signal; (3) *interpretation* of the signal's meaning; and, as part of the interpreting function, (4) making a *decision* about which responses are appropriate for such signals and (5) emitting the appropriate *response* as quickly and effectively as possible. While the problems we have discussed are primarily problems affecting the detection and identification functions of vigilance performance, somewhat different problems affect the interpreting and response-emitting stages of performance. It is particularly difficult for humans to respond promptly and accurately to a wide variety of signal types. As the number of signal possibilities increases, so the time needed for man to compare such information inputs with memorized decision rules and past experience also increases. Thus, a problem arises due to what Adams and Chambers (1962) call *stimulus uncertainty*. This phenomenon exists when the operator does not know which input signals to expect and thus does not perform as efficiently as when he *does* know exactly which types of signals will be presented. Conversely, *stimulus certainty* enables the operator to progress more quickly from detection to decision by eliminating much, if not all, of the identifying and interpreting functions. Stimulus certainty has been increased in some instances by (1) limiting the number of possible signal forms, (2) clearly distinguishing between different types of signals as in *color coding* or *size coding*, and (3) making the operator expectant or *set* for particular inputs through training.

In the response stage of human functioning, the human operator's performance can be enhanced through *response certainty*, which results when only a limited number of clearly distinguishable responses can be made. Responding can be further enhanced by designing the controls so that they are compatible with the displays (for example, an upward movement of the display indicator requires an upward movement of the control), by making the controls easily manipulative, and by placing controls close to the displays which they affect. These principles and others are discussed in more detail in the sections of this chapter dealing with displays and controls.

Tracking Tasks

The second basic type of task performed by the operator in a man-machine system is a relatively continuous manipulation of controls in response to constantly varying input signals. Such behavior, called *tracking behavior*, involves matching operator outputs to operator inputs. While much of this type of behavior has been replaced by machine functions in modern systems, there are still many situations in which the human performs such tasks. One particularly appropriate example is driving an automobile. In response to various input stimuli, such as the continuous change in the roadway and the change in distance between the operator's vehicle and other vehicles or objects, the operator must continuously manipulate the controls of the vehicle, such as the steering wheel, the accelerator, and the brake pedal, in order to maintain acceptable performance within the traffic system. In performing these tasks, the man is operating within a particular semi-independent man-machine subsystem involving his auto and himself, which in turn is operating within the much larger traffic system.

While many of the problems and human functions involved in the tracking task are similar to those involved in the vigilance task, some important distinctions should be made. In a tracking task, the detection and identification stages of human function, while still present, are less critical because of the relatively continuous characteristics of the input signal. In other words, in "pure" tracking performance, stimulus certainty is not a particularly critical aspect since the signal is relatively permanent, changing in quality and quantity rather than in type. The interpretation and decision functions on the other hand take on primary importance. Man is always handicapped by a *reaction time lag* in responding to system inputs. By enhancing the interpretation aspects of the input signal, decision time is also decreased, and as a result reaction time lag is kept at a minimum. In addition, where the future course of the signal input can be perceived or anticipated, decisions concerning future responses can be made in advance so that such responses can be emitted at the precise moment when they are appropriate. In this manner the operator output can most accurately correspond with operator input in a temporal dimension as well as in a spatial dimension.

Another important distinction between the characteristics of tracking and vigilance tasks concerns the types of controls required for the two tasks. In a vigilance task, *discrete responses*, such as deflection of a switch, or pushing of a button, are usually required. However, in most tracking tasks *continuous responses* are required, and the dynamic characteristics of the controls are more important. For example, friction coefficients, lag or deadspace in a control, the force needed to operate a control, and the position of the control all have important implications for how effectively the human operator can perform his task. Thus, the selection, placement, and dynamic properties of controls are of paramount importance to efficient tracking performance.

In systems that require simultaneous performance of tracking and vigilance tasks, particular care must be taken to avoid conditions of *sensory overload*. Sensory overload occurs when more input information is impinging upon the operator than he is capable of "processing." In such situations, the arrangement of controls and displays is particularly important, since man is incapable of simultaneously attending to more than one signal source at any given time. This property is known as man's *single-channel capacity*. The implication is that if man is to effectively perform more than one task simultaneously, he must be given sufficient time to alternate his attention between the two tasks without losing a significant amount of information in either task. In such situations, integrated displays, multisensory displays, and integrated controls have received much research attention.

The Effects of Automation
on Man's Role

Due to the present trends of ever-increasing automation, machines are fulfilling more and more of man's former functions in work situations. As a result, the human component in such systems is more frequently being assigned to equipment set-up and maintenance activities. Thus, even though many of his jobs are being filled by machines, man is often assigned even more responsible roles that require more problem-solving ability on his part and, consequently, more training.

However, while sensory overload is usually considered as a basic problem to be avoided in designing man-machine systems, automation has in some cases resulted in conditions of *sensory underload* for the operator. Both conditions are generally attributable to the indiscriminate assignment of man to positions in the system to which a machine has not yet been allocated. Thus, man in some cases has become the recipient of *wastebasket functions*, and he can find the resultant job either extremely difficult or extremely boring.

Some of the major job problems resulting from increased automation have been unchallenging jobs, high-anxiety jobs, night work, and disemployment which involves a reduction in the total number of jobs available due to increased output per worker. Smith (1964) has indicated that while executives, employees, and government have all generally favored automation, few have recognized the nature of the problems created by it, and virtually none have offered any satisfactory solutions.

Man-Machine Allocation

In the design of man-machine systems, one of the most important and most perplexing tasks of the human factors engineer is deciding when to use a machine and when to use a man to perform a particular job. Generally, after a complete functional description of system goals has been made, the system is divided into a set of subsystems, each of which makes its unique contribution to the total system output. It is at this point that the *allocation decision* is of primary importance, since only at the subsystem level can a relatively specific description of task requirements be made. Although such decisions are made at a subsystem level, they must involve consideration of possible effects on total system performance, and compromises or trade-offs must be made with regard to productivity, costs, maintenance, machine and labor availability, product demand, and so forth.

It has also become apparent that one must consider the effects of allocation decisions on the much larger social, political, and economic systems within which the system must function. For example, if machines that could completely replace all human components in man-machine systems were available, it would not be a wise decision to allocate all jobs to machines if it resulted in placing all humans into the ranks of the unemployed. Certainly, such a decision would have disastrous implications for the social and economic welfare of the nation, unless some revised means of distribution of wealth that provided for the constituents of the society could also be conceived. This redistribution would in turn become a political question.

On the other hand, if machines are to best serve man, they should be used in areas in which man is relatively deficient, and in which the need for efficiency is predominant. A recent joke tells of the labor foreman on a large excavation job who went to the contractor insisting that the excavating machinery was robbing jobs from a hundred men who could do the job just as efficiently with shovels. The contractor immediately agreed with the foreman and further assured him that he would consider completing the excavation by employing a thousand men with teaspoons. Such is the dilemma in job allocation. Machines were originally devised to aid man by extending his abilities. However, one must also insure that man is best served by machines, in a manner that complements his abilities rather than competing with them.

Allocation of Functions

For some time, it was thought that allocation decisions should be made primarily on the basis of performance criteria. In other words, the component that could best perform the task should be chosen for the job. As a result, human factors engineers set out to compare the relative abilities of men and machines for various tasks, and they developed lists summarizing such comparisons. Table 13–1 is an example of such a list. While such lists are informative, they are of little practical value as guidelines for allocation decisions, partly because they are fragmentary and extremely generalized. Also, trade-offs for pertinent factors such as cost, availability, demand, and so forth are not easily taken into consideration in the use of these lists. After years of investigating performance criteria, very little progress has been made in improving such lists, and researchers have begun to question their validity. Swain and Wohl (1961), for example, pointed out that, after ten years of research, there still was no adequate systematic methodology for allocating functions between man and machine. Jordan (1963) expressed his distaste for the entire allocation procedure by suggesting that men and machines are essentially incomparable and should

Table 13-1. Man versus machines.

Man Is More Capable	*Machines Are More Capable*
in situations which require improvisation or adaptation. at tasks which involve unusual or unexpected events. at tasks involving the detection of targets in high noise backgrounds. in performing tasks involving inductive reasoning. in the usage of entirely new solutions or those developed in related situations. in the usage of uncoded information. in the perception of complex stimuli in highly varied situations. in the use of subjective judgment based on previous experience. at anticipating stimulus input.	in the storage and retrieval of coded information. in the processing of large amounts of information in a short period of time. of reliable performance of highly repetitive tasks. by being relatively insensitive to extraneous factors. in the sensing of stimuli which are outside man's normal sensitivity range (sounds above 20,000 cps.). in the maintenance of a performance level over a long period of time. in the exertion of great force in a precise and consistent manner. in performing tasks involving deductive reasoning-recognition or categorization tasks involving previously experienced stimuli. by being able to simultaneously handle numerous inputs.

be thought of as being *complementary* to each other. Corkindale (1967) pointed out that man-machine comparisons are often misleading, since lists of machine limitations are likely to be out of date even before they are published. In addition, while it is generally known that machines are highly accurate and efficient at tasks like arithmetic computation, they can also fail as a result of overload or some unforeseen adversity and break down completely or make errors of a dramatic nature. Man, on the other hand, despite his speed and accuracy limitations, is characterized by *graceful degradation* under conditions of adversity. That is, man's output under such conditions will more closely resemble the correct output.

Corkindale also attributes the failure of performance comparison lists to the fact that performance is not the sole criterion on which to base such decisions. He points out some of the trade-offs that we have mentioned concerning cost, maintenance, social implications, and so on. Thus, he implies that a component that is adequate for a particular job may be a better overall choice for the job than would be a component that can do the job best.

Finally, Corkindale points out that there is a lack of adequate data on which to base task-allocation decisions. It is generally true that whenever man's functions can be understood well enough so that they can be mathematically described, it is possible to build a machine to perform such functions better. However, many of man's abilities and limitations are not understood well enough to make them comparable to machines in such a descriptive manner. For example, a man's inherent *flexibility*, his ability to reach the same goal by a variety of different methods, certainly is not easily describable, nor can any precise quantitative value be placed on this characteristic. Similarly, man's large repertoire of behavior resulting from many years of experience or *programming* provides him with a distinct characteristic that is not easily described or made comparable to mechanical characteristics.

Displays in Man-Machine Systems

Displays in man-machine systems link the machine to the man by presenting coded symbolic information concerning a particular aspect of the system's status. In turn, the man must process such information and make a decision to respond by manipulating the controls of the machine. Recall that before emitting a response directed at the controls, the man must first *detect* the information signal, *identify* it, *interpret* its meaning, and *decide* what the appropriate response would be. The type of display that is used to present such information to the operator will have a direct effect upon the speed and precision at which these functions can be performed.

To determine typical errors made in the use of displays, Fitts (1951) conducted a survey of pilot errors in responding to displays. The greatest number of errors in this survey involved the *interpretation* of display signals. The most frequent error was misinterpreting multirevolution instruments; the second most frequent was misinterpreting the direction of indicator movements. The third most frequent type of error in this survey was inadequate detection characteristics in the displays when the pilots failed to respond to warning lights or sounds. Finally, the fourth most frequent error was misinterpretation as a result of poor legibility of numbers and letters.

One of the first decisions to be made in the design of effective displays is which sense modality should be used. Generally, vision or audition are the senses employed for presenting information to the operator, due to the relatively wide range of information that can be received by the eyes and ears. However, even these modalities differ significantly in their information transmission capabilities and characteristics. For example, visual displays are most appropriate when (1) complicated or long messages must be displayed, (2) reference must be made to the message at a later time, (3) spatial orientations are involved, (4) the auditory modality is already being extensively used, and (5) the ambient noise level is so high as to interfere with auditory signals. Auditory displays, on the other hand, are most appropriate for warning the operator or attracting his attention to other displays. They should be used when (1) speed of reception is important, (2) advance preparation of the information is not possible, (3) the operator must have freedom to move around in the general work area, (4) signals are presented which vary over time, (5) the operator is susceptible to fatigue or inattention, (6) the visual modality is overloaded, and (7) environmental conditions exclude the use of visual displays.

While these lists do not exhaust all possible situations in which one modality is more effective than another, it does provide some insight into the problems that must be considered when selecting a particular modality by which a machine can communicate with man. In some instances, for example, it may be necessary to take special precautions to insure that the operator receives critical information. In such situations, it is not only desirable to use the most appropriate modality and provide maximal informational transfer characteristics in that modality, but it may also be vital to add another mode of information transfer (such as vision and audition simultaneously) to insure the reception of critical signals. Such display combinations are called *redundant displays.* Since visual displays are most predominant in man-machine systems, the most common means of providing redundant information is to add auditory and/or cutaneous displays. Generally, redundant displays are most appropriate for warning functions or for counteracting sensory underload.

Nonvisual Presentation
of Information

Certainly, the most common displays in man-machine systems involve the visual sensory modality. However, some displays that are important in presenting information involve other sensory modalities, such as auditory or cutaneous. Let us briefly consider these types of displays before taking up the visual displays.

Auditory Displays

Auditory displays have most often been used to warn the operator in a system that there is an emergency—that is, they serve a warning function. Other instances in which auditory displays are appropriate include situations in which (1) the visual sense is already overloaded, (2) critical or infrequent signals must be presented to the operator, (3) the operator must move around in his work environment, and (4) visual displays are incompatible.

In the many diverse situations in which auditory displays have been deemed appropriate, a number of devices have been used to communicate with the man in the system. Such devices have included loudspeakers, intercommunication systems, radios, earphones, buzzers, horns, bells, and sirens, among others.

There are, of course, a number of factors that must be considered in selecting the auditory display to be used. In general, however, the principles in selecting and designing an auditory display are standard for all types of displays, as well as controls. Some of the most important principles include (1) conforming to *population stereotypes*—that is, wailing signals associated with emergencies, high frequencies with up or high, and so on, (2) making the information presented by the device easily *discriminable* from other information signals and at the same time *understandable*, (3) *parsimony* with regard to presenting only information which is necessary for the operator or worker to carry out his functions, (4) *standardization* of a display's function and meaning, and (5) making the display *compatible* with the entire system including the human receiver.

Cutaneous Displays

Information can also be transmitted to the human by means of skin stimulation. Such displays are called cutaneous displays. Perhaps the most well-known form of cutaneous display is the Braille print used by blind persons. This form of display is called a *static tactual display* since it does not change its message over time. Those tactual or cutaneous forms of displays that *do* change over time are called *dynamic tactual displays*. There are two major types of such displays, which are classified according to the type of energy used to convey information—*mechanical* or *electrical*.

Geldard (1957) has conducted considerable research on the presentation of information to a human operator by means of a mechanical vibration unit. This vibrotactual device conveys information by means of three distinct types of information coding. The three codes involve five separate *locations* for stimulation, three different *intensities* of vibration, and three separate *durations* of stimulation. These combinations in turn are used to represent the twenty-six letters of the alphabet, the ten numerals, and four commonly used words. Research revealed that subjects are able to learn the codes and "read" by means of this method relatively well.

Another form of cutaneous information display presents information to the skin through electrodes that are attached to the arms, legs, chest, or neck, depending on the task the operator must perform. Research using electrocutaneous displays to present error information in tracking tasks has been conducted in the authors' laboratory by Hofmann (1968), Nichols (1970), and Schori (1970a). In these investigations, error information concerning the direction and, in some cases, the magnitude of deviation from a target course was presented to the operators by means of electrodes attached to the arms or to the neck. Stimulation to one side of the body indicated to the operator that he was in error on that side and that he should manipulate the controls in the opposite direction in order to get back on course.

These investigations revealed that for certain types of tracking tasks, electrocutaneous displays could be used as effectively as visual or auditory displays in presenting error information to the operator. In fact, there were some indications that the cutaneous modality was better than the visual modality for the presentation of such information. In a study comparing auditory, visual, and electrocutaneous displays in a vigilance task, the latter display was also found to be quite effective in comparison with visual and auditory displays (Damkot, 1969).

When using electrocutaneous displays, there are several dimensions possible for coding information. In addition to the various locations of the body that can be used, intensity, frequency, and pulse duration of the stimulus offer further dimensions for coding information. In some cases, when it is desirable to present continuous or semicontinuous information to the operator over a period of time, it is also desirable to have a comfortable stimulus. In other situations, in which a cutaneous display is intended as an arousal or warning device, a more aversive type of stimulation might be desirable. Electrocutaneous stimulation is very adaptable to these different situations.

Perhaps the greatest need for cutaneous information displays is in situations in which the visual and/or auditory modalities are already overloaded. In such situations, short uncomplicated signals can be presented quite effectively by means of cutaneous displays, either mechanical vibration or electrical shock. Like the auditory modality, the cutaneous modality offers an avenue of communication that cannot be "shut off" by the operator.

Visual Displays

The informational transfer characteristics of a particular modality can also be varied as a function of how the displays are designed and arranged. McCormick (1970) has discussed the extensive variety of visual display types that have been employed in man-machine systems, as well as the different types of information that can be conveyed by such displays. On a general level, McCormick distinguishes between two categories of visual displays: *dynamic* displays, which change over time (a temperature gauge), and *static* displays, which remain fixed over time (printed material and road signs). We will be primarily concerned with dynamic displays.

Dynamic Displays

McCormick suggests that at least three types of information can be presented in dynamic displays. These information types include *quantitative information* involving actual numerical values; *qualitative information* involving more general information classes such as hot, warm, or cold; and *dichotomous information* which indicates "on" or "off," "normal" or "not normal," and so forth. It is apparent that displays conveying these three types of information could also be categorized on the basis of the amount of information made available to the human receiver, with quantitative displays transmitting the greatest amount of information and dichotomous displays transmitting the least. It should also be apparent that these displays can vary significantly in the amount of interpretation or data processing required of the human operator. It must be kept in mind that more time will be required to decode, process, and translate quantitative information into appropriate manipulation of the controls than will be required for the translation of qualitative or dichotomous information. For this reason, quantitative displays should be used only when absolutely necessary and should be replaced by qualitative or dichotomous displays whenever possible.

Limiting information to only that amount which is needed or adequate conforms to a primary principle of system design—the principle of *parsimony.*

While the extra time required to monitor quantitative displays may not be critical to situations in which only one or a few displays must be monitored, it becomes extremely critical under complex job situations requiring that several tasks be performed simultaneously by the operator. The use of qualitative or dichotomous displays rather than quantitative displays also results in making the displays more *compatible* with the controls of the machine because the transition from the reception of signal to the emission of responses is simplified.

Following the selection of appropriate modalities, the substitution of auditory or cutaneous displays for visual displays when the visual modality is already overloaded, and the replacement of quantitative displays by qualitative or dichotomous displays whenever possible, what is the next step for improving the design of displays? This question can best be answered by considering the display factors that affect the various human functions involved in decoding displayed information.

Decoding Displayed Information

It should be pointed out that there are several varieties of quantitative displays, such as horizontal, vertical, open window, circular, semicircular, and counter. These displays are illustrated in Figure 13–1. As a rule, in situations in which the numbers would not be expected to change at an extreme rate, the counter and open window type displays are most easily and quickly read. However, in situations in which the quantitative values may be changing quite rapidly and direction of change is important, as in altimeters, circular and horizontal displays have been found to be most effective. Even in such cases a combination involving a counter for gross values and a circular display for smaller values subject to rapid change provides the best form of presentation. In all cases involving vertical, horizontal, or some form of circular dial, moving pointers are superior to moving background scales. This will be discussed further under decision attributes of displays.

Before embarking on a discussion of various display design principles in relation to the human functions they affect, it should be pointed out that the adequacy with which higher functions, such as those involved in interpretation, can be carried out is dependent upon the adequacy by which lower functions, such as detection and

Fixed scale, moving pointer

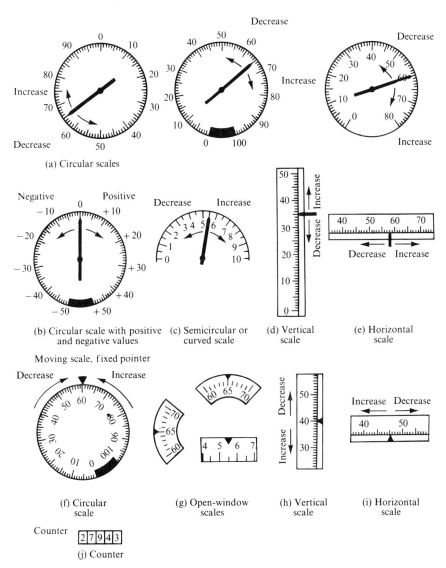

(a) Circular scales

(b) Circular scale with positive and negative values

(c) Semicircular or curved scale

(d) Vertical scale

(e) Horizontal scale

Moving scale, fixed pointer

(f) Circular scale

(g) Open-window scales

(h) Vertical scale

(i) Horizontal scale

Counter

(j) Counter

Figure 13–1. Examples of various types of quantitative displays. Certain features of these displays are discussed in the text. From *Human Factors Engineering* by E. J. McCormick. Copyright 1957, 1964, 1970 by McGraw-Hill, Inc. Used with permission of McGraw-Hill Book Company.

identification, can be performed. Consequently, it is difficult to make conclusions about where one process ends and another begins. Similarly, a particular design characteristic may affect several aspects of human function in varying degrees. Thus, many of the principles discussed in relation to detection and identification may be applicable in some degree to the interpreting function, just as some of the principles pertaining primarily to the higher mental functions will have varying degrees of influence upon detection and identification. Consequently, the paradigm followed in classifying design principles with regard to human functions in this chapter is somewhat arbitrary. The primary purpose of this classificatory scheme is to provide a more meaningful and sequential understanding of *why* various design principles are important.

Designing Displays for Maximum Detectability

The detection of displayed information primarily involves the principle of display visibility. Visibility in turn is affected by such variables as (1) the relationship between the size of the displayed information and the viewing distance, (2) the brightness of the displayed information, (3) the ambient illumination, (4) the color, and (5) the contrast attributes of the displayed information. In the following paragraphs, examples will be given of some of the principles that must be considered in display detectability. These examples are fragmentary and are meant only to give an insight into the problems which must be considered.

Size and Viewing Distance

Generally, a display 3 inches in diameter is sufficient for detectability at a *viewing distance* of 28 to 30 inches. For viewing distances greater than this, the size of the display should be increased so as to maintain a constant visual angle.

Brightness, Illumination, and Contrast

The *brightness* of the display should be determined according to the environmental conditions under which the display is to be viewed. For example, a brighter display is required for daytime detectability than for nighttime detectability because the eyes are not as sensitive when adapted to daytime conditions as when adapted to nighttime conditions. As a rule, illumination on the face of the display should be equal to the ambient illumination in order to provide maximum contrast within the display itself. Further, in situations requiring maximum dark adaptation of the eye, it is preferable to use monochromatic red display illumination so that the instruments can be read and dark adaptation can be preserved. This same principle is used in darkrooms for the developing of light-sensitive films. While it is controversial whether monochromatic light provides better visibility than light involving several wavelengths of all monochromatic lights, monochromatic yellow light provides maximum acuity.

Figure-Ground Relationship

Generally, the visibility of letters and numbers depends more upon brightness and contrast relationships than upon specific colors. However, it has become standard to use black figures on a white background for daytime viewing and white figures on a dark background for nighttime viewing (as in speed limit signs).

It should be pointed out that visibility is a very complex phenomenon that should be considered in view of the interaction of all of the variables mentioned here. Also, the principles presented are intended only as examples of some of the *many* factors affecting the detectability of visually displayed information.

Display Design and Human Identification Functions

The process of identification is dependent on the discriminability characteristics of displayed information, especially on the properties of *legibility* and *readability* of numbers and letters. Legibility is dependent on such factors as the stroke width of the letter or numbers (see Figure 13–2), the form of the characters, background, size, and illumination. Readability, which involves recognizing groups of letters or numbers (in contrast to legibility which involves identifying certain letters and excluding others), is more dependent on the spacing of the characters than the features of the individual characters.

Interpretation Aspects of Display Design

Interpretation of displayed information is directly influenced by the manner in which the information is presented. One of the most important factors in presenting such information is the ad-

Stroke-width to height ratio	Black on white	White on black

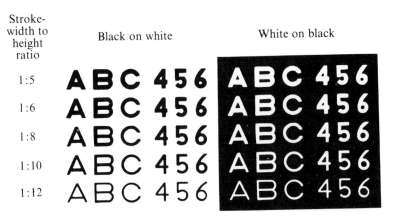

Figure 13–2. Illustration of various strokewidth-to-height ratios of letters and numerals. Strokewidth is typically expressed as the ratio of the thickness of the stroke to the height of the numeral or letter. With black letters on a white background the optimum ratio is about 1:8 while with white letters on a black background the optimum ratio is closer to 1:12. From *Human Factors Engineering* by E. J. McCormick. Copyright 1957, 1964, 1970 by McGraw-Hill, Inc. Used with permission of McGraw-Hill Book Company.

herence to *stereotypes* whenever possible. Stereotypes involve commonly accepted meanings given to directions of movement, figure-ground relationships, and colors. One of the most important stereotypes in interpretation of quantitative changes in displays involves the direction of indicator movement. Indicator movements to the right, up, or clockwise are naturally interpreted as indications of an increase in a quantitative scale, while indicator movements to the left, down, or counterclockwise are most easily understood as indicating a decrease on a quantitative continuum. Displays for presenting quantitative information, such as altitude, speed, or temperature, should be designed with considerations of such "natural" relationships in mind.

Figure-ground relationships are also important when the operator must obtain information concerning the status of his system with regard to some reference criterion (for example, the status of an airplane with regard to the horizon). Generally, displays in which the figure or indicator moves relative to the background or reference scale are more easily understood than displays in which the background or reference scale moves relative to the indicator. The former type of display is called an *outside-in* display and is preferable to the latter *inside-out* type of display. The principle in figure-ground relationships is that people have generally learned that most frequently they (or other figures) move within and relative to a much larger surrounding environment or background (for example, you travel within the nation, the nation does not move relative to you).

Another reason for having moving indicators and fixed-background scales is to provide for *control-display compatibility*. For the principle of stereotypes in movement, there are three general rules relating controls and displays: (1) scale numbers should increase in a clockwise fashion, or from bottom to top, or from left to right; (2) the direction of control movement should be the same as the direction of associated display movement; and (3) clockwise, left-to-right, or upward movement of a control should produce an increase in function, while counterclockwise, right-to-left, or downward movement of the control should produce a decrease in function. The only way all of these principles can be accomplished is by moving indicators relative to stationary scale backgrounds. Examples of various displays with fixed scales and moving pointers and with moving scales and fixed pointers were shown in Figure 13–1.

With regard to expectancy and set, it is a natural tendency for an operator to interpret a deflection on a display indicator as having the same quantitative meaning from one display to another. Thus, similar displays should be standardized as nearly as possible in direction of movement and the extent of movement requiring a compensatory response. On the other hand, in situations in which an increase in one display is desirable and an increase in another display undesirable, the displays should be designed in unlike manners to insure against interpreting the one display in the same manner as the other. Think, for example, of a temperature gauge and an oil pressure gauge in an automobile. It is perfectly acceptable for oil pressure to increase from a "normal" level when accelerating. However, if the temperature rises from a "normal" level during the same acceleration period, the change is undesirable and may be critical if the increase is extensive. This situation, however, involves the monitoring of only two displays. What would be the effect if five or ten or more displays had to be monitored? In such situations, it may be necessary to rescale the displays according to desirable or undesirable changes, thus standardizing the direction of indicator movement for this criteria. For example, all deflections to the left would indicate unacceptable deviations and all deflections to the right would indicate acceptable deviations or vice versa. Other implications of expectancy and set involve standardization of displays between similar man-machine systems, such as automobiles of different makes.

Generally, the design principles that have the most dramatic effect upon the decision-making functions are those which minimize interpretation. Interpretation can be minimized by (1) eliminating all unnecessary displays or unnecessary information presented by displays, and (2) by presenting information in the simplest, most useable form. While the first principle is relatively straightforward and requires no further explanation, there are several means by which the second principle can be accomplished. First, the substitution of qualitative and/or dichotomous displays for quantitative displays whenever possible is a primary means of minimizing interpretation time. Second, by color coding various areas on quantitative or qualitative displays and using colored indicator lights on dichotomous displays, interpretation can also be facilitated. Such color coding is most effective if the colors used conform to *stereotypes* of their meaning. This principle also applies to shape coding, in which various areas on quantitative and qualitative displays are coded by means of different visual configurations. Figure 13–3 illustrates the use of color coding in a quantitative display along with some of the common colors associated with particular conditions. Figure 13–4 illustrates some of the possible methods of shape coding in a qualitative display.

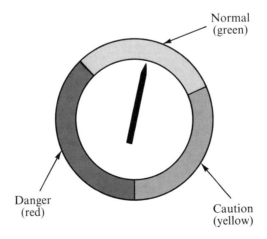

Figure 13–3. An example of a color-coded display. While the display shown is of the qualitative type, color coding can also be utilized in quantitative displays.

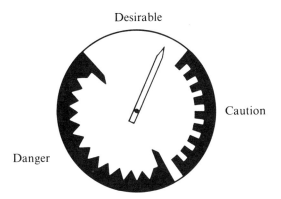

Desirable

Caution

Danger

Figure 13–4. The shape of the zone markings on a display can also indicate operating conditions.

Display Design to Enhance
Response Emission

While response-emission considerations are most appropriate in the design of controls, displays also have an important influence on the speed and accuracy of responses. Perhaps the most important factors affecting response tendencies are conformance to *stereotypes* already mentioned and to the *control-display compatibility* principle. Displays are more compatible with controls if (1) they are positionally located near their associated controls, and (2) they reflect the same direction of movement as do the associated controls. These considerations will be discussed further when we consider the problems of fitting the job to the man.

In summary, some of the more common considerations involved in display design include:

1. Eliminating all displays that are unnecessary.
2. Selecting appropriate sensory channels.
3. Substituting qualitative and dichotomous displays for quantitative displays whenever possible.
4. Making displays as legible and readable as possible with regard to such variables as figure size, spacing, type, figure-ground relationships, illumination, contrast, and color.
5. Preserving stereotype relations such as direction of movement, spatial locations, figure-ground relationships, and display-control compatibility.
6. Being consistent.

The Design of Controls

Many of the problems associated with controls are similar to those associated with displays. Such problems involve control-display incompatibility, controls which cannot be easily manipulated because they are out of reach or are not organized in a meaningful fashion, and overloading of manipulations by the hands as a result of too many manual controls. A survey of the control problems of Air Force pilots revealed that some of the most frequent control errors included (1) confusion of controls; (2) manipulation of a control in the wrong direction; (3) forgetting to use a particular control; (4) accidentally moving the wrong control; and (5) inability to reach a control (Fitts & Jones, 1961).

Just as the problems associated with controls are similar to problems associated with displays, so are the solutions similar. The principles of parsimony, compatibility, standardization, selection, and arrangement are involved in both fields of engineering endeavor.

McCormick (1970) has categorized controls as follows: (1) *Activation* controls, like dichotomous displays, involve only two possible states, such as on or off. (2) *Discrete setting* controls, on the other hand, offer any one of several positional settings and are analogous to qualitative displays. (3) *Continuous* controls and (4) *quantitative setting* controls offer a wide range of control positions anywhere on a quantitative continuum. The difference between the two is that a continuous control, as the name implies, is operated continuously, whereas the quantitative setting control, although it offers a continuous range of positions, is generally manipulated only discretely into one position or another (such as a thermostat control). Both of these types of controls are similar to quantitative dynamic displays in function. Examples of such control types are illustrated in Figure 13–5.

Selection of Controls

The first step in control design, as in display design, is based on the principle of *parsimony* and consists of the elimination of all unnecessary controls. Related to this process is the *integration* of controls in such a manner that controls which formerly required two hands for their operation (such as hand wheels) are replaced by controls which require only one hand for their manipulation (such as levers and joysticks). Such alterations, however, must be made

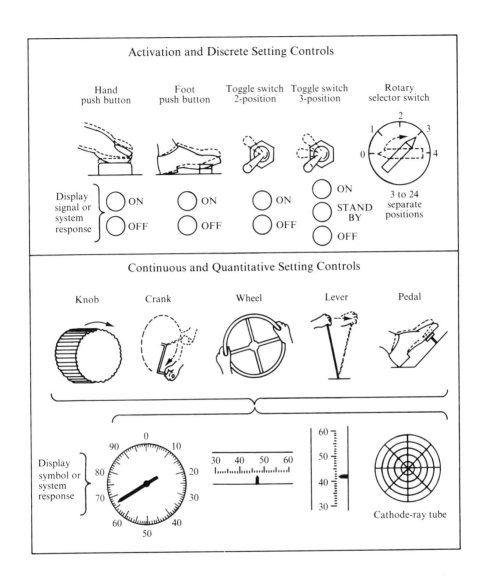

Figure 13-5. Examples of the various categories of control types and some of their uses. From *Human Factors Engineering* by E. J. McCormick. Copyright 1957, 1964, 1970 by McGraw-Hill, Inc. Used with permission of McGraw-Hill Book Company.

in view of such factors as the degree of accuracy and speed required and the characteristics of the particular controls involved.

While overloading of the visual modality can be a problem in display design, the problem of overloading the operator's hands confronts the control designer. Whereas in display design visual displays were omitted or replaced whenever possible, in control design, manual controls are omitted or replaced by foot controls whenever possible. Certainly the major factors that must be considered before replacing manual controls are the amount and extent of force, as well as the speed and accuracy of movement, required for adequate control manipulation. Foot pedals are appropriate for any manipulation that requires a large amount of force exerted over a long period of time (such as constant pressure on a braking device). Foot pedals are also appropriate for many tasks requiring repetitive types of movements of gross magnitude, such as pedaling a bicycle. Perhaps the most serious consideration when one allocates a particular movement to the legs or feet is the accuracy with which the movement must be executed, since foot controls often must be manipulated without the aid of visual feedback.

After relieving the hands of any overload, the next step is to replace controls requiring a continuous adjustment with those in which only positional or dichotomous movements must be made. This is similar to the process of replacing quantitative displays with qualitative and dichotomous displays. Positional controls include selector levers, such as gearshift control, indented rotary knobs, and so on. Dichotomous controls, on the other hand, consist of toggle switches, push buttons, and bat-handle switches.

Finally, after all unnecessary controls have been eliminated, manual controls have been minimized, and continuous controls have been minimized, the next step is the design of particular controls so as to optimize the manipulation characteristics of controls. Just as most display design effort has been directed to the more complicated quantitative displays, so most control design effort has been directed to the design of continuous controls.

Design of Controls

Standardization is one of the most important principles in control design. Standardization means that all controls that perform a similar function should be similarly operable. This principle of operation should also hold between similar machines. For example, how many times have you been unable at first to manipulate a particular dash control in a strange automobile because it was either not placed in the same position as in your own vehicle or operated by different principles? How many motorcycle accidents could possibly be attributed to the lack of standardization of the side on which the brake pedal is located?

Other important principles of display design involve a combination of highly related variables such as compatibility of control and display and conformation to stereotypes of movement. These principles have been discussed under display design, and it should suffice to say that such principles are of equal importance in the design of controls.

Coding Controls

Differentiability is a major consideration in the design of controls, especially when many controls must be manipulated as in piloting an airplane or in operating heavy equipment. There are several means of coding controls so that they will be more distinguishable. Some of the most frequently used methods are described below.

Perhaps the predominant method of control coding is labeling, in which printed abbreviations or words are used to identify various controls. While there is virtually a limitless number of possible designations and categories that can be coded in this manner, this method requires extra time for reading the labels and extra space for including such labels, and it cannot be used when the labels cannot be viewed directly or the illumination is very dim.

Shape and texture coding, on the other hand, uses different shapes and surfaces of controls or control knobs, which can be discriminated by touch as well as by visual recognition. Generally, in shape coding a control or control knob is constructed in the form of some attribute of the function with which the control is associated (see Figure 13–6) while in other cases, consideration is given only to forms that are easily differentiated, without regard to relating such forms to the functions of the controls (see Figure 13–7). In texture coding, only the surfaces of controls or control knobs are varied in order to enhance touch discrimination. These forms of coding can be used under conditions of minimal illumination and can aid in relieving an already overloaded visual channel. On the other hand, the number of discriminable shapes and textures that can be made meaningful to the operator is limited.

There are various other methods of coding controls. Color coding, for example, is popular. Size coding offers another avenue for enhancing control differentiability and involves discriminating

Design of Controls

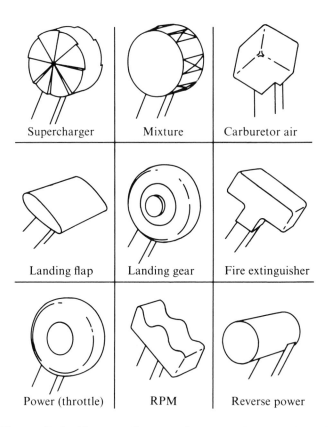

Supercharger	Mixture	Carburetor air
Landing flap	Landing gear	Fire extinguisher
Power (throttle)	RPM	Reverse power

Figure 13–6. Shape coding can improve visual and tactile identification of the controls. When possible, functional shapes are selected that suggest the purpose of the control. From *Human Engineering Guide to Equipment Design* by C. T. Morgan, J. S. Cook, III, A. Chapanis, and M. W. Lund (Eds.). Copyright 1963 by the McGraw-Hill Book Company, Inc. Used with permission of the McGraw-Hill Book Company.

between controls by varying their size. Another method, called location coding, enhances differentiation between controls by placing them in particular locations on the control panel. Location coding is another important consideration of the human engineer.

Arrangement of Controls

Perhaps the most important principles of location coding, or arrangement of controls, are the *frequency-of-use* principle and

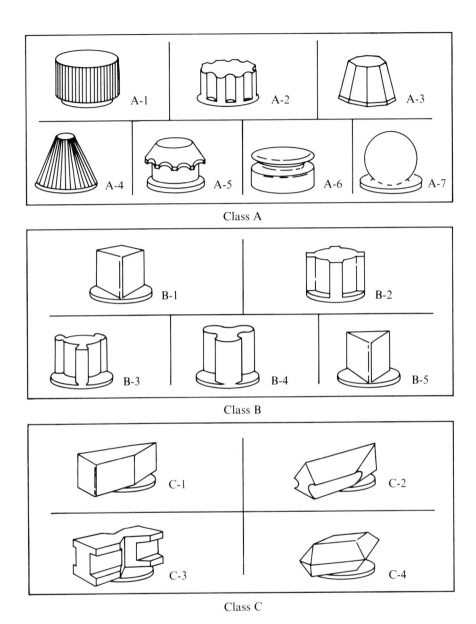

Class A

Class B

Class C

Figure 13–7. For shape coding purposes, knobs can be divided into the three classes shown. All of these knobs can be used together without confusing one with the other, except knobs of class A-2 should not be used with those of B-4, those of class B-1 should not be used with B-5 and those of class B-2 should not be used with those of B-3 or B-4. From *Human Engineering Guide to Equipment Design* by C. T. Morgan, J. S. Cook, III, A. Chapanis, and M. W. Lund (Eds.). Copyright 1963 by the McGraw-Hill Book Company, Inc. Used with permission of the McGraw-Hill Book Company.

the *sequence-of-use* principle. In the former, it is recommended that the controls used most frequently be placed in preferred locations and in relatively close proximity to each other. When considering sequence of use, on the other hand, it is recommended that the controls be placed in a proximal or spatial sequence that corresponds to the order in which they are to be used.

Other principles of control location include *functional* arrangements, in which controls with related functions are placed together; arrangements according to *importance*, in which controls with the most important functions are given prime locations; and *optimal location* arrangements, in which controls are arranged in such a manner that optimal manipulation of the total ensemble is achieved. It is apparent that while some of these location principles are complementary to each other, some are also contradictory. Consequently, in the design of controls and control panels, each of the principles should be evaluated in view of the total control functions. After trade-offs have been made and a decision has been reached, any effort to standardize the agreed-upon control arrangement inherently involves location coding.

Certainly, other considerations must affect control arrangement. For example, controls must be arranged to take into account the amount of force that must be applied and the environmental restrictions placed upon the operator. The safety of the operator and the reliability with which the operator can manipulate the controls adequately must also be considered.

Control-Display Relationships

The design of controls involves many of the considerations that are involved in the design of displays. For example, the principle of control differentiation is closely related to the detectability and identification principles of display information and efforts must be made to make controls as easily discriminable and accessible as possible. Also, controls must take into account the same factors that contribute to a "naturalness" of response in interpreting and decision making considerations in the design of displays. Such factors include standardization, conformation to population stereotypes, and control-display compatibility. Also, just as the more complex quantitative displays involved the most extensive design considerations, so the more complex continuous controls require the greatest degree of design sophistication.

For example, the design of continuous controls must take

into account the fact that proprioceptive feedback (for example, information from the receptors within human muscles) is an important source of information that affects the accuracy with which continuous control manipulations can be made. Although proprioceptive stimuli constitute a response factor that is difficult to observe or measure, it is quite evident that the human operator depends upon such internal stimuli, in addition to visual stimuli, for the moment-to-moment positioning of his limbs that is required in manipulation of continuous controls.

Control-Display Ratio

Another important factor in the design of continuous controls is the control-display ratio (C/D) of change—that is, the amount of display change for every unit of change in the control. A high C/D ratio indicates that a generous amplitude of control movement is required for any movement on the display. It has generally been found that C/D ratios around 1:1 are most desirable. If, however, a task requires gross movements of the display from one position to another and subsequent fine adjustment after the general location of the display indicator has been reached, research has indicated that two integrated controls should be used. The control for the *gross adjustment* should have a low C/D ratio to allow for rather large display movements and small movements of the controls, while the *fine adjustment* control would have a large C/D ratio so that a much smaller change in the display would result from a comparable movement of the control.

A low C/D ratio has the attribute of speed and the detriment of inaccuracy, while a high C/D ratio has the attribute of accuracy at the expense of speed. In situations requiring both speed and accuracy, *ganged* control knobs have frequently been used. In ganged controls, two or more control knobs are situated on a common axis, with one on top of another. Generally, there is a size progression of such knobs with the largest on the bottom and the smallest on the top. The bottom control is used for gross adjustments and has a low C/D ratio, while the top control is used for fine adjustments and has a high C/D ratio.

Before leaving the discussion of control and display design, it should be pointed out that it is very difficult to distinguish between the principles involved in the design of these two types of hardware components, since the input and output functions of the human being cannot be separated. The form of information input has a direct influence on how well the output response can be made. Both controls and displays must be designed to be compatible to each other—another important aspect of the systems principle. By thinking "system," a more smoothly functioning arrangement of components can be designed.

Adapting the Job to the Man

Design of Total Job Components

Many of the principles relevant to the design of total job situations have already been discussed in relation to the design of specific controls and displays.

The principles of *parsimony, standardization,* and *compatibility* are just as important in the final integration stage of system design as they are in the initial design of displays and controls. Generally, at this stage multiple components rather than single components are of primary interest. Thus, man-machine integration involves the design of total control-display consoles, arrangement of system components, and special considerations for the comfort and safety of the human operator. Some of the primary considerations in this process involve (1) matching inputs to outputs, (2) adjusting time constants, and (3) preventing overloads and underloads by means of meaningful job organization.

Matching Inputs to Outputs

This principle has already been considered as it is related to control-display compatibility. It was pointed out that designing controls and displays for compatibility entailed considerations of the most appropriate sense modalities for presenting information, the selection of appropriate controls, and the standardization of control-display relationships in conforming to population stereotypes. In the design of total job situations, compatibility is still concerned with the spatial, movement, and conceptual relationships between inputs and outputs and their consistency with human expectations. However, now we are interested in compatibility with regard to all the inputs and outputs involved in the entire system.

In this context, it must be remembered that since the system is composed of many individual subsystems, the output of one subsystem is in turn an input for another subsystem. Thus, individual input-output relationships should be considered as a series of such relationships, all of which must be compatible. This principle may be termed *subsystem compatibility.*

Adjusting Time Constants

Each component of the system must be able to function at a speed compatible with the rate of the total system. Here considerations of man's speed and accuracy characteristics are in order. It has already been pointed out that man is neither particularly fast nor accurate in his response capabilities. It should also be remembered that the faster man must perform the functions assigned to him, the less accurately he can perform such functions. If possible overload conditions can be foreseen in system design, a change in design should be considered, such as increasing the number of men responsible for a particular function.

Preventing Overloads and Underloads

The principles of parsimony, standardization, and compatibility are all appropriate for preventing *overload* conditions. However, the effects of such principles are limited in extreme overload situations and may require the addition of redundant human components that can divide their attentions and responses to achieve optimal system performance.

Underloads, on the other hand, can be counteracted by a variety of different methods including the use of redundant multisensory displays, stimulants, and rest periods. In addition to these methods, which are directed at the attention aspects of underload, other available methods are directed to the motivational aspects of total job situations. These methods include the enlargement of jobs, the creation of subtasks and subgoals, and the rotation of jobs within the system.

While much of the efforts of human factors engineers have been directed to the design of controls and displays, it has become more and more apparent that the optimization of a total system must involve a comprehensive view of personnel problems. That is, the human components of the system must be given the same integrated attention that is given to the composite of mechanical and electrical components of the system. The big difficulties involved in fitting jobs to men are not all technological. Many of the problems require social considerations for their solution. For example, the process of isolating employees who enjoy personal contact, forcing employees into positions of competition when they prefer to cooperate, and using men as replaceable cogs or links in an austere environment when such men need a sense of dignity and individuality certainly does not enhance the performance characteristics of the system. Human job satisfaction requires activities that demand the use of human skills, are meaningful, provide responsibility, and involve social contact.

Environmental Effects on Human Performance

No man-machine system operates in a vacuum, and the surrounding environment has a very real effect on the adequacy of human task performance. Some of the important variables in the job environment are the illumination, the atmospheric conditions, and noise effects.

Illumination

The level of illumination required for adequate human performance is task specific. There is no best amount of light for all tasks. Therefore, the problem is to provide as much light as is needed to adequately and comfortably accomplish a specific task. While generally it is more acceptable to have more rather than less illumination than is necessary, high levels of illumination can reduce the information transfer characteristics of visual displays. This results primarily from a reduction in the display's visibility characteristics due to excessively high illumination. Under conditions of high illumination, glare on the faces of visual display dials can make it difficult to read displays. Indirect lighting is a common solution to the glare problem, although localized illumination (illumination immediately over the specific work area) should be somewhat brighter than the ambient illumination. Also, as was mentioned in discussing display contrast characteristics, the greater degree of contrast between the displayed information and its immediate background, the less illumination necessary for adequate detection of such information. Generally, most industrial operations can be accomplished with an illumination intensity of about 10 foot-candles.

Ventilation

Ventilation is a complex variable involving temperature, humidity, and air movement. When the human engages in physical activity, the activity produces heat within the body that must be dissipated through pores of the skin. The effectiveness with which this process of perspiration can dissipate the heat buildup in the body is primarily dependent upon the three aspects of ventilation just mentioned. As a result, the interaction of temperature, humidity, and air circulation is an important factor determining the productivity level, accident rate, and morale of the workers.

Because the effectiveness of human perspiration in dissipating heat depends upon the interaction of all three variables, *effective temperature scales* have been developed which combine into a single value the effect of all three variables on the subjective feeling of temperature on the human body. Although other considerations such as individual preferences and amount of physical exertion must be taken into consideration, effective temperature scales are useful in determining optimal atmospheric conditions for various tasks. Usually temperature around 70 degrees Fahrenheit is considered most comfortable for jobs requiring moderate exertion. For heavy exertion, optimal temperatures are lower, and for light exertion temperatures as high as 80 degrees may be acceptable.

Noise

There have been conflicting opinions about the effects of noise upon work performance. Some maintain that noise is detrimental to task performance, especially in repetitive tasks, and others maintain that noise can in some situations enhance performance. Clearly, more research is needed on this matter. However, there is a considerable amount of evidence indicating that prolonged noise is detrimental to the work situation. Certainly, loud ambient noise levels interfere with speech communication, and there is growing evidence that prolonged exposure to such conditions may result in physiological damage in the form of a hearing loss. Also, due to an apparent increase in muscular tension and a consequent increase in expenditure of energy, it appears that workers in a noisy background become more easily fatigued, nervous, and irritable than those in a quiet background. Research suggests that noises of high intensity and/or frequency, intermittent noises, and reverberating noises are the most annoying. Thus, while noise may have little immediate effect on performance, it does appear that noise has definite effects for prolonged tasks.

There are, of course, many other environmental factors that can affect performance, such as vibration. However, consideration of all the varieties of environmental variables influencing man's behavior in a system is beyond the scope of this text.

Man in Unusual Environments

Man-Machine Systems for Space

Human factors engineers' involvement in man-machine systems for space flight is in many ways similar to their involvement in everyday industrial systems. The problems of designing displays, controls, and consoles involve many of the same principles. However, as a result of the unusual characteristics of the work environment in space-flight systems, additional factors must be taken into account, such as *acceleration, weightlessness* and consequent loss of traction, *disorientation,* and the effects of *prolonged confinement* in close quarters. Since the effects of these factors can generally be studied only by means of simulated situations, human factors engineers are also engaged in a considerable amount of research on simulation devices that attempt to approximate the conditions under investigation.

While simulation devices for investigating the effects of prolonged confinement are relatively straightforward and easy to produce, simulators that accurately reproduce conditions such as weightlessness and the control dynamics of a space module in flight require much more sophistication in their design and production. In addition, there is a considerable degree of variability in regard to the capability of these devices to reproduce the desired conditions. Generally, the effects of acceleration on human performance and human physiology have been investigated by means of centrifuges, rocket-propelled sleds, ejection seats, and in some cases real aircraft. Weightlessness has been simulated by aircraft trajectory flights that can produce up to 20 or 30 seconds of weightlessness, by water-immersion techniques, which reduce gravitational cues, and more recently by vertical-cable techniques, as illustrated in Figure 13–8.

Effects of Acceleration

Two primary considerations are the effects of acceleration upon human performance and upon human physiology. In terms of human performance, it is known that as the g forces due to acceleration increase, it becomes more and more difficult for man to move his arms and legs, and under extreme g force he may not be able to move any part of his body and blackouts may occur. It is also

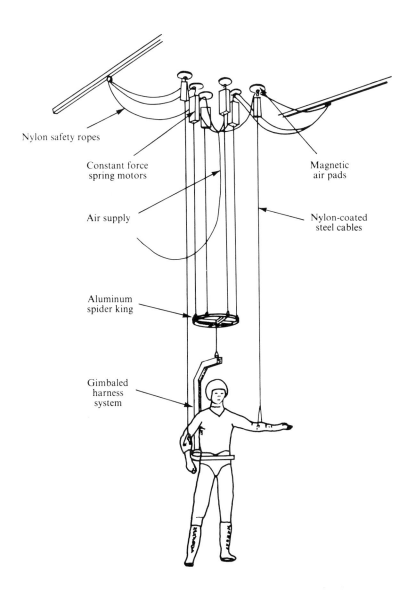

Nylon safety ropes

Constant force
spring motors

Air supply

Aluminum
spider king

Gimbaled
harness
system

Magnetic
air pads

Nylon-coated
steel cables

Figure 13–8. One method of simulating lunar-gravity conditions. By means of various cable and motor systems, the
subject can remain in a vertical position with about five-
sixths of his weight supported by the system. From Amos A.
Spady, Jr., Prototype of a new lunar-gravity simulator for
astronaut mobility studies. In *Human Factors,* 1969, **11**(5),
441–450. Reprinted by permission of the Human Factors
Society.

known that the direction of the acceleration, as well as the position of the body, are important factors in determining the extent of such debilitations and the extent to which the body can withstand such forces. While there are many other factors involved in designing the hardware equipment to permit optimal functioning under acceleration, the preceding examples are sufficient to point out the need for designing controls and support equipment so as to compensate for such abnormal forces upon the human body. For example, if it is particularly hard for the operator to lift his arms under extreme accelerative conditions, controls are limited to positions that do not require upward movement of the arms.

About the effects of acceleration on physiological organs and functioning, it is known that extreme acceleration causes distortion of body organs and affects blood circulation and heart rate, to name but a few. As a result of such effects, nausea may occur, vision may be temporarily lost, and total blackout or death may occur.

It is also known that particular directions of acceleration are more tolerable to the body than others. For example, vertical accelerations (that is, footward and headward acceleration) are the least tolerable, partly because they result in the greatest displacement of body organs. Horizontal acceleration (forward and backward acceleration) is the most tolerable to the human body. In addition, acceleration tolerance can be further enhanced as a function of the postural position of the operator, involving such factors as leg, arm, and torso positions. This knowledge can be applied to the design of seats and restraining devices.

Weightlessness

Prior to recent lunar missions, little has been known concerning the effects of prolonged weightlessness. Recent research findings, however, appear to indicate that while weightlessness has very real immediate effects upon task performance, proper equipment design can reduce such effects considerably. It also appears that prolonged periods of weightlessness have considerably fewer undesirable effects than was at one time anticipated. However, recent long-term orbits by Russians indicate that there may be some detrimental effects of long exposures to weightless conditions.

Some effects on performance in conditions of weightlessness result from the concomitant reduction of traction. As a result, the manipulations of the human operator suffer from lack of body support. Body movements are less efficient, manipulations like turning a wheel result in a turning of the body, responses are slower, and metabolic rate due to the resultant additional movements is higher. Wortz (1969) has indicated that while such effects are real, there is nothing particularly novel in solving such problems through engineering and design considerations. He also points out that the appropriate design of load transmission devices will eliminate problems due to the losses in traction and body support. In fact, appropriate design considerations can enhance performance to such a degree that manipulations can be carried out that require even less energy than under normal gravitational conditions. Some of the methods for eliminating the problems of load transmission are using console handles for body support, minimizing controls requiring twisting responses, and using adequate restraining and support devices in the design of operator seats and cockpits.

Man-Machine Systems Underwater

Human factors research in underwater exploration has involved the design of vehicles for prolonged submergence and underwater rescue as well as the equipment design principles of deep-sea diving. Some of the problems in the design of man-machine systems for underwater exploration are similar to those involved in space research. For example, the design of submergence vehicles must take into account provisions for life support, effects of such environments on human performance and physiological functioning, and the effects of prolonged confinement upon both the physical and psychological processes of the man.

Diving research has included investigations into the effects of cold, buoyancy, fluid resistance, and limited vision upon human performance. Bowen (1968) has reported two primary causes for human impairment in deep-sea diving. He reports a *water effect*, referring to the effects of water resistance in burdening the diver and limiting his attention. Other limitations resulting from this effect have been the reduction of the diver's sensory capabilities and of his mobility. Much of the lack of mobility, it should be mentioned, is a result of the cumbersome equipment needed for survival underwater. The second cause of impairment Bowen has termed the *temperature effect*, referring to the fact that extreme cold results in the impairment of peripheral functions such as movement of hands and legs. A study by Stang and Wiener (1970) of diver performance in cold water showed that performance on a number of tasks tended to decrease as water temperature decreased.

Other impairments such as reduced peripheral vision and narrowing of perception have been discussed by investigators such as Weltman and Egstrom (1966). As a result of their investigations, these researchers have made design recommendations for equipment such as full-face masks and modified breathing devices to widen the visual field of the diver. These authors also point out the communication problems resulting from narrowed perceptual fields.

Submergence-vehicle research has received considerable attention in recent years. Human factors investigators involved in such research have been interested in such problems as designing equipment and techniques for rescue operations, designing facilities for optimal recreation, exercise, and leisure-time activity during prolonged submergence, as well as the unique problems associated with control manipulation and display reading. Much of the research has been conducted through the use of sophisticated deep-sea simulators and vehicle mockups. Janousek (1970) discussed some of the problems investigated, which included (1) the design of pilot seating and restraint conditions to provide optimal performance under conditions of pitch and roll, (2) the handling of injured persons in rescue operations, and (3) provisions of power hoists and special slings and harnesses for the handling of rescues. Special tilting simulators were used for such studies.

Relevance of Laboratory Studies to Real-World Problems

Much of our information about human behavior has been obtained in carefully controlled laboratory studies. In these investigations, great effort is made to control and systematically manipulate independent variables and to accurately measure the dependent variables that have been selected for use. These kinds of investigations have greatly advanced our knowledge about behavior. Many of these studies have been "basic," in that they were designed to increase our knowledge in certain areas and were not "mission" oriented—that is, they were not designed to help solve some real-world problem. However, psychologists who are concerned with the application of psychological data to real-world problems must often make use of information that has been gathered in laboratories. Unfortunately, it has become apparent that all too often the data that were obtained so painstakingly in these studies have only limited application to the problems that confront the psychologist who is working in an applied setting.

In this section, we will be concerned with some of the reasons findings of laboratory research are often not relevant to practical situations. It should be emphasized, however, that it is not the intent of this section to detract from the value of laboratory research. The importance of this type of research has been stressed throughout this text. Rather, our aim is to call attention to certain characteristics of laboratory research that may reduce its generalizability to real-world problems.

Some Examples

On several occasions we have mentioned the problems encountered when an investigator attempts to apply learning principles, which have been largely acquired through laboratory research, to the training of men for functioning in man-machine systems or in other real-world situations. Laboratory research on learning processes represents possibly the largest single area of endeavor by experimental psychologists. Yet, as Mackie and Christensen (1967) point out: ". . . both academic and practically oriented psychologists agree that a very small percentage of findings from learning research is useful, in any direct sense, for the improvement of training or educational practices." We have already mentioned Gagné's (1962) comments on military training and the principles of learning in an earlier chapter. In concluding his article, Gagné states that if he were faced with the problem of improving training he would not look for much help from the well-known learning principles.

While much of the learning research that has been conducted was not designed to solve practical problems, vigilance research is usually conducted with practical applications at least a consideration. There are now a substantial number of laboratory findings dealing with vigilance performance and several sophisticated theories. Yet it turns out that these findings are not particularly relevant to contemporary monitoring problems (Kibler, 1965).

Chapanis (1967), in a thought-provoking article on the relevance of laboratory studies to practical situations, points out another dramatic example in which laboratory training did not generalize to the real-world situation. On the *Gemini 11* flight, one of astronaut Richard Gordon's tasks was to get outside the capsule and tie the capsule to an *Agena* rocket with a 100-foot cord. Gordon had been prepared for this task by many hours of training in the laboratory. You may recall how much difficulty this task presented to Gordon in space. He later commented that what he could do in about 30 seconds in the laboratory turned out to be a monumental 30-minute task in space.

There are many other examples of real-world situations that

do not correspond with laboratory findings. The critical questions, then, are: *Why* is this the case and *what* can we do about it? Chapanis (1967) gives us some answers to the *why* question. The remainder of our discussion will be based largely on Chapanis' analysis of the problem. Students who are interested in pursuing this topic, which is of considerable significance to psychology, are urged to read the original article, since our coverage, by necessity, will be somewhat cursory.

The Laboratory Experiment

There are, of course, many kinds of laboratory experiments. We will be concerned with the type of experiment discussed in Chapter 1 under the heading of "The Experimental Method." In this kind of experiment, the behavior of interest (dependent variable) is measured while various other variables (independent variables) are manipulated or controlled. Of primary interest is the change in the behavior that results from the manipulation of the independent variables. The problem, however, in relating laboratory findings to the real world is that, by their very nature, laboratory experiments are only rough and approximate *models* of the real-world situations that they might be designed to represent. Chapanis (1967), in suggesting that a laboratory experiment is a model of the real world, goes on to say:

> . . . as representations of the real world, models are *always* incomplete and so are *always* wrong. It follows, therefore, that in so far as they try to represent or model the real world, laboratory experiments are always wrong too. To put this another way, the results of laboratory experiments always fail to give us exact solutions to real-world problems. In some cases, to be sure, the results of a laboratory experiment may be *substantially* correct, that is, it may predict with reasonably good accuracy how people do indeed behave in life. At the other extreme, however, the results of laboratory experiments may not even come close to predicting human behavior. And, of course, one can get all possible gradations between these two extremes [pp. 561–562].

Independent Variables. In the typical experiment, there are usually many independent variables that can affect the dependent variable in some way. Out of the very large number of possible independent variables, the researcher usually picks no more than three or four for study. Some of the other variables will be controlled or held constant while all the rest are ignored. However, in

the real-world situation, the variables that may influence behavior
are not held constant, nor can they be ignored. In real life, these
variables may interact in such a fashion that they result in behavior quite different from that observed in the laboratory. Thus,
when one conducts a laboratory study in which only a few selected
independent variables are involved and attempts to generalize the
laboratory findings to a real-world situation in which dozens of
variables may influence behavior, it is obvious that this type of
generalization may be hazardous.

Another major difficulty encountered when we deal with independent variables in the laboratory is that not only are they reduced in number but they may also be different from those they are
supposed to represent in the real world. The very act of bringing a
variable into the laboratory usually changes its nature. A variable
in the real world contains a number of elements, and when you
bring this variable into the laboratory, you are likely to lose some
of the original elements as well as adding some that were not in
the original (Chapanis, 1967, p. 566). For example, consider the
problem of studying stress in the laboratory. The types of stress
that we can generate in a laboratory situation are probably quite
different from those in combat or major surgery, for example.
However, many studies use stress of some type as an independent
variable (Heimstra, 1970a). In this type of situation, then, the independent variable (stress) *loses* something when it is brought into
the laboratory.

One element that gets *added* to the independent variables
when they are brought into the laboratory is the experimenter himself. There is considerable evidence that the presence of an experimenter may modify the way in which a subject responds in a
particular situation. Even without an experimenter present, the fact
that the subject is in an experiment may modify his behavior. Thus,
it is quite likely that variables change when they are abstracted
from real-life situations and brought into the laboratory (Chapanis,
1967).

There is a third aspect of the independent variables involved
in laboratory studies that also affects the relevance of laboratory
findings to practical situations. In the laboratory, efforts are usually
made to control extraneous or irrelevant variables. Variables such
as noise, illumination, temperature, and time of day are generally
held constant for all subjects in the experiment (unless, of course,
one of these variables will be manipulated in order to determine its
effect on behavior). Holding these variables constant will increase
the precision of the experiment, and very small effects on behavior,

due to the manipulation of the independent variables, may be *statistically* significant. However, these small effects may have no *practical* significance. For example, suppose it is found under very carefully controlled laboratory conditions that a small amount of alcohol increases reaction time by a fraction of a second. When statistical comparisons are made between the reaction times of subjects receiving alcohol and control subjects, it is found that the difference between scores of the two groups is significant. However, what is the *practical* significance of this finding in terms of, for example, the ability of a driver to adequately handle a motor vehicle? A more detailed discussion of practical versus statistical significance is given in Chapter 15.

Dependent Variables. While the above factors related to the use of independent variables in laboratory experiments contribute to the problem of generalizing laboratory findings to real-world problems, the dependent variables selected for use also contribute. Generally, the dependent variables used in laboratory research are variables of convenience. Thus, the typical measures of reaction time, number of errors, number of targets missed or detected, number of trials needed to learn some task, and so forth, are selected for convenience rather than for their relevance to some practical situation. Thus, it may be difficult to translate laboratory findings on reaction time, or number of errors in a learning task, to a real-life problem.

Other factors contribute to the problem. Often the methods used to present the variables in the laboratory are both artificial and unrealistic. For example, we typically study reaction time in the laboratory by having a subject, who is seated at a table, press a key when a light goes on or a buzzer sounds. This situation bears little resemblance to real-life situations in which reaction time may be important. Chapanis points out another methodological factor that is characteristic of the laboratory study. In order to obtain enough data we often tend to overload the subjects in laboratory studies. The experimenter may speed up the presentation of stimuli, add distracting or irrelevant tasks and, in general, attempt to make the task more difficult than it really is. In other words, the experimenter might deliberately distort conditions in his experiment from what occurs in real life.

All of this, of course, is somewhat depressing for the psychologist who spends many hours in the laboratory and who may hope that his research has some applied value. Calling attention to the problem, as Chapanis has done, has been beneficial in that some researchers are now taking a harder look at the independent and dependent variables as well as the methods that they use in their experiments. Also, some investigators are beginning to consider alternatives to the typical laboratory experiment. It is important that the problem of the relevance of laboratory studies to practical situations has been recognized and, hopefully, steps *are* being taken to help solve it.

The System So Far

In this and the previous chapter, we have viewed man as a subsystem functioning within a larger system. We have seen how man as a subsystem is "fit to the task" by means of selection and training procedures. We have also seen how, by means of human factors engineering, certain aspects of the system can be "fit to the man" so that he is capable of more efficient functioning. The primary aim of selection, training, and human factors engineering is to make the human subsystem a more effective component of a system and, in this way, to enhance the overall efficiency of the system.

Summary

1. The goal of human factors engineering is to design machines and work environments that will permit optimal human functioning and provide maximum system efficiency.

2. One of man's primary roles in man-machine systems is to serve as a data-transmission and processing link inserted between the displays and the controls of the machine. Consequently, much of the effort expended by human factors engineers is in the design of more effective displays and controls.

3. While man performs many functions in man-machine systems, as a data-processing link he frequently performs two basic system tasks—a vigilance task and a tracking task. In performing these tasks, a number of human functions are required, including detection, identification, interpretation, decision making, and emitting the proper response.

4. A major design decision involves the allocation of functions between men and machines in a system. Men have certain unique qualifications as do machines. Generally, however, attempts

to list the functions performed best by machines and by men have not been very useful.

5. Displays are usually visual, but sometimes auditory and cutaneous displays are also used. Two general categories of visual displays are dynamic and static. The former changes over time while the latter remains fixed (for example, a road sign). Dynamic displays can be used to present quantitative, qualitative, and dichotomous information.

6. There are several factors involved in designing displays for efficient decoding. Physical characteristics of the displays themselves—round, horizontal, counters, or open-window types—are important variables. Other factors such as size, brightness, contrast, and figure-ground relationships also affect detection.

7. There are several types of controls, including activation controls, discrete setting controls, continuous controls, and quantitative setting controls. In the design of controls, factors such as the principle of parsimony and control integration must be considered. Coding of controls by means of color, shape, or texture is important when many controls must be manipulated. Arrangement of controls based on the frequency-of-use and the sequence-of-use principles must be considered. Control-display relationships must also be taken into account. In continuous controls, the control-display ratio is a particularly important factor.

8. Man is often required to work in environments that may affect his performance. Illumination of work areas, various atmospheric conditions, and noise effects have been of primary interest to researchers in the past. In recent years, however, factors associated with performance under weightless conditions and underwater conditions have become more important.

9. Although most of the data in human factors psychology and in other areas of psychology originate in the laboratory, the question of generalizability of these data to real-world situations has been raised. Too often the findings of laboratory experiments have been shown to have little relevance to real-world practical problems.

Selected Readings

Bennet, E., Degan, J., & Spiegel, J. (Eds.) *Human factors in technology.* New York: McGraw-Hill, 1963.

Chapanis, A. *Man-machine engineering.* Monterey, California: Brooks/Cole, 1966.

Chapanis, A. The relevance of laboratory studies to practical situations. *Ergonomics,* 1967, **10**, 557–577.

McCormick, E. J. *Human factors engineering.* New York: Mc-Graw-Hill, 1970.

Woodson, W. E., & Conover, D. W. *Human engineering guide for equipment designers.* Berkeley: University of California Press, 1966.

14

Man as a Subsystem III

Social Interactions

We have seen how man can be viewed as a subsystem within a variety of systems that range from simple to extremely complex and, at first sight, would appear to have very little in common. While the structure, function, and purpose of these systems may be quite different, virtually all do have one particular characteristic in common: man's behavior in these systems is influenced by other persons. It would be difficult to conceive of a system in which the behavior of the human elements is not determined to some degree by other people. While in some systems the influence of other people may be minimal and will have little effect on its functioning and output, in other cases interactions among the people in a system can be the basis for its very existence. Thus, in many types of social systems the effectiveness is determined by the nature and degree of the interactions among the people involved. Typically, in these social systems the individual will have an effect on the functioning of the system which, in turn, will also have an effect on the person.

In considering man's interactions with other men in a system, we must once again define our level of analysis. As subsystems, people can form political, social, and cultural systems, to name only a few. When considered at the system level, these areas are of interest to political scientists, sociologists, and cultural anthropologists, respectively, but are not of primary concern to the psychologist who is interested in man as a *subsystem* within these systems. The psychologist is concerned with man as an individual while sociologists, anthropologists, and political scientists are interested in the systems that are formed by these individuals interacting together. The psychologist is most concerned with the situation in which man is influenced by a system. Put somewhat differently, the psychologist and, in particular the *social psychologist*, is interested in how a given individual is affected by all of the social stimuli that surround him.

Social psychology is a discipline aimed at understanding and explaining how the thoughts, feelings, and behavior of *individuals* can be influenced by the actual, imagined, or implied presence of other individuals. (The term "implied presence" refers to the activities that are carried out by a person because of his role in social systems and membership in cultural groups [Allport, 1968].) Within recent years, possibly because of the types of problems that confront our society, social psychology has evolved at a very rapid rate. Its range is now so vast that we will not be able to give a satisfactory overview in one chapter. Consequently, we will select certain topics of social psychology for discussion that appear to be of particular interest currently.

Before considering these areas, however, some general comments about the field of social psychology are in order. Much of the data of social psychology were gathered in laboratories, usually with no thought to their applicability in real-world situations. Although many social psychologists have stepped out of the laboratory and into the real world, they usually find that the data gathered so painstakingly in the laboratory are not of much use to them in attempting to solve the staggering problems confronting society. For example, there is little in the way of laboratory data that tells us how to deal with the problems of the cities, with race relations, with the aggressive behavior that is currently manifested in riots, war, and murders or in the increasing deviant behavior shown by our society. While social psychologists are becoming more and more involved in problems of this kind, they often find that they do not have the tools to effectively deal with them. However, because of the realization that most of their data are irrelevant, much of the laboratory or experimental work that is being conducted by social psychologists today is "action oriented" in that the studies are aimed at real-world problems. The topics of social psychology discussed in the following pages are, for the most part, topics with practical applications.

Attitudes and Attitude Change

With due apologies to the reader, we must again begin by stating that we have here another psychological concept that is difficult to define. What is an attitude? There are about thirty or forty definitions from which to choose. Although we could argue for some time about the pros and cons of these various definitions, for our purposes we will consider an attitude to be *a mental state of readiness to respond that is organized through experience and will exert a directive influence on behavior*. Stated more simply, an attitude is a general predisposition to behave in a certain way.

Because attitudes are thought to shape so much of our behavior, both good and bad, psychologists have been interested in how attitudes develop, how they can be measured, and how they can be changed. In an earlier chapter we briefly discussed how attitudes develop and how a child's interactions with his family are of critical importance in this development process. While we have not discussed attitude measurement, there are a number of techniques that are used. However, any serious consideration of attitude measurement would rapidly take us into areas that are beyond the scope of this text. Consequently, in our discussion of attitudes we will be primarily concerned with approaches to influencing and changing attitudes.

Why Change Attitudes?

We generally consider attitudes to exert some influence on the way in which we behave, particularly toward some object, person, or group. Suppose that for some reason we wish to change the particular behavior that is demonstrated toward the object, person, or group. There are several ways in which we could do this. For example, we could employ certain learning principles and perhaps punish some kinds of behavior and reward other kinds as a means of modifying a person's behavior. However, if attitudes are generalized predispositions that influence a person's behavior, then it seems reasonable to assume that by changing attitudes one should also be able to produce changes in overt behavior. Much of the effort that is directed at attitude change is based on this particular assumption. It is assumed that by changing underlying attitudes, which are

Figure 14-1. The primary variables involved in attitude-change research. Most studies have been concerned with the source of the message, the message itself, the channel utilized, and the receiver.

thought to be relatively permanent, rather than just the behavior itself, the ensuing behavior change will be more enduring.

Changing Attitudes

As we have said, attitude change has been of interest to psychologists for a number of years and, consequently, we have available a considerable amount of data concerning factors that appear to be important in bringing about these changes. The primary variables that have been shown to be involved in attitude change can be presented within the framework, or model, shown in Figure 14-1. Most of the research conducted in the area of attitude change has been concerned with one or more of the variables shown in this figure.

Source Variables

When we consider source variables in attitude change, we are dealing with variables that are associated with the *communicator* of a particular message or communication that is designed to change attitudes. In other words, we want to know what aspects of the source of a communication are important in determining whether or not an attitude is successfully modified.

One important source variable is the *credibility* of the source. It has been shown that there will be more attitude change in the desired direction if the communicator has high credibility than if he has low credibility. While a number of factors are important in determining the "credibility level" of a source, it is based primarily on the expertise and trustworthiness, either real or perceived, of the communicator. However, the situation is complicated somewhat by the fact that credibility of the source is less important in attitude change later on than it is immediately after the first exposure to the message.

Another source variable in attitude change is the *attractive-*

ness of the source. At least three aspects of source attractiveness have been studied: familiarity, similarity, and liking (McGuire, 1969). It is probable that the three are interrelated in that similarity can lead to familiarity and familiarity to liking and so forth. In fact, they can be considered to make up a reverberating circuit in which they tend to mutually strengthen each other.

There is considerable evidence that a factor in determining the persuasiveness of a communication is whether the individual receiving it perceives the source as being similar to himself. As McGuire (1969) points out:

> Presumably the receiver, to the extent that he perceives the source to be like himself in diverse characteristics, assumes that they also share common needs and goals. The receiver might therefore conclude that what the source is urging is good for "our kind of people," and thus change his attitude accordingly [p. 187].

Generally, it also appears that if the receiver is familiar with, and likes, the source, then he is more likely to change his attitudes in the direction that the source is advocating. There are some interesting exceptions to this situation, however. One exception is the so-called "praise from a stranger" phenomenon. It has been found in several studies that social reinforcement influences children's behavior more when it comes from a stranger than from a parent or familiar person. It has also been shown that while praise from a stranger is more effective than praise coming from a friend, criticism from a friend is more effective than that from a stranger.

While there are several other source variables, we will mention only one more—the *power* that the source has over the receiver. Typically, the receiver evaluates "power" in terms of the extent to which the source can administer either positive or negative sanctions to him (perceived control), as well as how much the source cares whether or not he actually conforms (perceived concern). Finally, he evaluates whether or not the source can actually observe whether the source's position is accepted (perceived scrutiny). Depending upon the receiver's perception of the above contingencies he may, at least overtly, go along with the source's position (McGuire, 1969). Even though the receiver's attitudes may not have been changed initially, overt power-induced compliance may eventually bring about internalized attitude change. In other words, changing the behavior may result in attitude changes.

Message Variables

The second major class of variables that has interested re-searchers is made up of those variables involved in the message or communication itself. There are four types of message variables that appear to be of particular importance: (1) the types of persuasive appeals that are utilized, (2) inclusions and omissions from the message, (3) order of presentation within the message, such as should the strongest arguments come first or last, and (4) source-receiver discrepancy.

There are a number of factors that must be considered when studying the *type of persuasive appeal* that is used. Should the appeal be rational or emotional? What types of logical arguments should be used? Should the appeal arouse fear in the receiver? These as well as other questions have concerned social psychologists, who have found that there are no simple answers. Sometimes emotional appeals are more effective, sometimes factual ones. It all depends upon the characteristics of the receivers of the message. Similarly, sometimes fear appeals are effective while on other occasions they are not. Again, the effectiveness of this type of appeal depends upon the nature of the receivers, as well as on a number of situational variables. Some studies have shown a negative relationship between fear arousal and attitude change, while others have found positive relationships with higher fear arousals being associated with greater attitude change.

As an example of a fear-arousing message that many of you have encountered, consider some of the films you have seen dealing with automobile accidents. Possibly, as part of your driver-education training, you were shown movies involving gory car wrecks coupled with recommendations as to how the wreck might have been avoided. There is some evidence that such films, which produce a high fear level, are not very effective since the viewer tends to "avoid" the fearful message and ignore the recommendations the film may present. A mild fear-producing film, which does not bring about active viewer avoidance, may be more effective in changing the viewer's attitude.

A number of studies dealing with *inclusions and omissions* from the message have been conducted. Some investigators have attempted to determine whether it is better to use a message with explicit or implicit conclusions. In the explicit conclusion message, the conclusion is presented to the receiver, whereas in the implicit message he arrives at the conclusion "on his own." While we find studies supporting both explicit and implicit conclusion techniques, most of the evidence suggests that the explicit technique is most effective.

In determining what should be included or omitted from a message, one must also decide whether opposition arguments should be refuted or ignored. Should the content of the communication be one-sided and ignore the opposition, or should it be two-sided and refute the opposition's message? It appears that it is more effective to present one side of the argument when the receivers are friendly, when your position is the only one that will be presented (that is, the opposition will not have a chance to be heard), or when you want immediate temporary attitude change. On the other hand, presenting both sides of the argument will typically be more effective if the receivers disagree with your argument, or if they will hear the opposition's point of view.

The *order of presentation* of the material in the message has been shown to be a factor in influencing attitude change. Assuming that the conclusion of the message is to be explicitly stated, is it better to place it at the beginning or the end of the message? This question cannot be directly answered since there are advantages to both approaches. In what order should agreeable or disagreeable material be presented in a message? McGuire (1957) found that an agreeable-disagreeable order produced significantly more opinion change, a finding that has been supported by a number of other investigators. Suppose that we have two sources, each arguing for a different side on a given issue. Does the message espousing a given side have greater persuasive impact when it follows or precedes the message arguing for the other side? It appears that when opposite views are presented one after another, the one presented last will probably be most effective.

The last message variable that we will consider is *source-receiver discrepancy*, which refers to the difference between the position urged in the message and the position held by the receiver regarding some attitude. There is evidence that the greater the discrepancy between the position espoused in the message and the receiver's position, the greater the attitude change. This statement must be qualified, however, in that with extremely discrepant positions there may be a falling off in attitude change.

Channel Variables

Of practical interest to politicians, advertisers, and many others who wish to change attitudes is the communication modality that can be utilized most effectively to present their message. For example, politicians must decide whether to concentrate on the mass media to get their points across, whether to engage in a significant amount of face-to-face communication, or whether to combine the two approaches. Obviously, most politicians select the last alternative. There is considerable evidence to support the view that any impact that the mass media has on attitude change is less than that produced by face-to-face communications. This view holds up with both voting and buying behavior. Obviously, however, costs and payoffs must be considered. Vastly greater audiences can be reached by mass media at much less cost per receiver than is possible with the face-to-face approach.

Receiver Variables

Actually, all of the variables that we have been discussing can be considered "receiver" variables in that they must somehow operate inside the person in order to produce an effect. Under the heading of receiver variables, however, we are concerned specifically with the *state* of the individual when he receives the message and how a particular state might help determine whether the message effectively modifies attitudes.

Based on learning theory and on concepts from the area of psychotherapy, it has been predicted that the degree to which a receiver *actively participates* in the persuasive communication is important for attitude change. Social psychologists are interested in the nature of this participation. For example, what happens if the receiver is called upon to participate actively by improvising the content of a message rather than just passively reading it? Contrary to predictions that would be made based on learning theory and psychotherapy, it has been demonstrated that the communication is just as effective when the receiver merely reads it as when he must actively participate by drawing his own conclusion. Active participation has been studied by other approaches. Thus, it has been found that actively "role playing" an unacceptable position will tend to increase the acceptability of the position.

Considerable interest has been shown in the relationships among a wide variety of personality variables, as well as variables such as intelligence, age, sex, and susceptibility to attitude change. Studies in this area have shown that individual differences are important determinants of influenceability. Thus, personality traits have been shown to affect susceptibility to persuasion. For example, a receiver is more easily influenced when his self-esteem is low.

Similarly, the level of intelligence of the receiver will determine the effectiveness of certain kinds of messages. While the relationship between receiver age and susceptibility is not clear, there does appear to be a clear sex difference; females are more susceptible to persuasion than males.

There are a number of other important receiver variables that we will not be able to consider in any detail. Essentially, these variables can be summarized under what Zimbardo and Ebbesen (1969, p. 18) refer to as a psychological *process* model of attitude change. They suggest that change in opinion is a combined function of the receiver's *initial position,* his *attention* to the source and the message, his *comprehension* of its arguments, examples, appeals, and conclusions and, finally, his general and specific *motivation* for accepting its position. Each process is important and will help determine whether or not attempts at changing attitudes are successful.

Attitude or Behavior Change?

Earlier we stated that much of the interest in attitude change is based on the assumption that changes in behavior will follow changes in attitudes. The assumption is also made that if attitudes themselves are general and enduring, a change in attitude should result in an enduring and general change in behavior. However, research has shown that these assumptions are not necessarily true (Mischel, 1968). Thus, changes in attitude are often not accompanied by changes in behavior and, when changes in behavior do take place, they are seldom general or enduring. As Zimbardo and Ebbesen (1969) point out:

> It seems that we are faced with a real problem. Most practical situations in which we wish to induce change require that *both* attitude and behavior change be produced. If, however, behavior change does not automatically follow from attitude change, how can attitude change techniques help us solve the practical problems [p. 85]?

There are a number of psychologists who feel that attempting to change attitudes in order to change behavior reverses the procedure that should be used. Much of the current thinking in the area of attitude change is based on the concept that behavior change must be brought about *before* attitude change will take place. There are now techniques for producing and maintaining behavior change which may, in turn, produce changes in attitudes. Some of the behavior-modification approaches that were discussed in Chapter 11 have been particularly effective. These approaches have raised a number of interesting questions that have led to a reconceptualization, at least on the part of many psychologists, of the whole notion of "attitudes." It appears that we may be entering a period during which many of the accepted views of attitudes and attitude change may be challenged.

Performance in Groups

Over the past few decades, individual behavior and performance within a social context has been intensively studied. Generally, research has involved "small groups," consisting of about a dozen people or less. There are several obvious reasons for using small groups rather than large. First, small groups are simpler objects of study and can be subjected more easily to experimental control. More important, however, is the fact that so much of our social life actually takes place in small groups of one kind or another. "Getting together" with a limited number of people is a common event, and the bulk of our social interactions take place in such groups. Consequently, these interactions have been of considerable interest to social psychologists.

The Group Considered as a System

It was pointed out earlier that man, as a subsystem, will be influenced by the system but will, in turn, influence the system in some fashion. In dealing with small groups, researchers have been concerned with both of these aspects. They have investigated individual performance in a social context but they have also been interested in "group performance." Basically, in one case they are interested in the output of a particular individual within a group, and in the second instance they are concerned with the combined output of the individuals making up the group—that is, the group output.

We can view a group much as we have viewed other systems that we discussed in previous chapters. First a group can be thought of as having a number of *structural*, or formal, properties. It can be described in terms of such characteristics as number of members, how often it meets, its stated purpose, its leader or leaders, and so forth. While this type of information is necessary in order for the psychologist to study small groups, typically the *functional* properties, or the actual "goings on" of the group are of more interest. Thus, the interactions between members, the conflicts, pressures, problem solving, decision making, the type of leadership, and so on, are of more concern to the psychologist than are the structural characteristics.

We have also seen that a system involves more than just a group of components. These components must interact and be interdependent before we regard them as a system. The same is true in considering groups. To the psychologist, a dozen or so people gathered together (waiting for a bus, perhaps) does not necessarily constitute a group. While there are many definitions of groups, we will consider a group as some number of persons among whom there exists some observable or definable set of relations. "A group is a set of mutually interdependent behavioral systems that not only affect each other, but respond to exterior influences as well" (Davis, 1969, p. 4).

The Individual's Output in a Social Context

The primary focus in this area is an individual's performance as it occurs under social conditions in which he can be influenced in his activities by the presence of other persons. Typically, the output of interest in studies of individual performance in groups has involved tasks that are quite complex and that require abstract cognitive processes. However, there are a number of exceptions to this, and some investigations have made use of tasks requiring simple responses or routine psychomotor performance.

There are, of course, a number of social situations in which the individual's performance could be evaluated. For example, in some situations there may be a passive audience of some type. In this case, the question is whether the mere presence of others will affect the performance of a single individual. However, what is the effect if others are engaged simultaneously on the same task but working independently? How does interaction with other members of the group affect the performance of a single individual? These, as well as other questions concerning the individual's performance within the group, have been studied by social psychologists.

Audience Effects

Research has shown that individual performance is affected by the sheer presence of other persons. A number of studies have found that the presence of an audience will result in facilitation of performance on the part of an individual. However, other findings reveal that under certain conditions subjects will do worse when an audience is present. While we do not have sufficient data to predict with any high degree of certainty what types of tasks would benefit or suffer from an audience, we can make some "educated guesses." For example, if a task is well learned and the required responses can be produced with efficiency, then its performance will probably be facilitated by an audience. On the other hand, if the task is not well learned, an audience will probably have an adverse effect. If a task is to be learned in the presence of others, there is evidence that suggests the learning will be slower. If the performance task requires complex intellectual processes such as concept formulation, detecting relationships, or analogical reasoning, it is probable that performance will suffer since these kinds of processes frequently appear to be disrupted by the presence of others.

Coaction Effects

What happens if, instead of a passive audience, we have others who are also performers of the same, or related, task as is the individual being studied? Even though these "coactors" do not interact directly with the individual, they may have a significant effect on his performance. For example, a form of the coaction paradigm is illustrated in many kinds of athletic events. In track, for instance, a runner racing against "the clock" instead of other runners will usually have a slower time.

As was the case with audience effects, we find that coactors will have an effect on an individual's performance. Also, as was true with audience effects, there are some situations in which the presence of coactors will lead to better performance while, in other situations, poorer performance will result. Thus, coaction can be both inhibiting and facilitating. Whether it is inhibiting or facilitating depends upon a number of factors associated with the task that is being performed as well as with the characteristics of the individual performing the task.

What Causes Audience-Coaction Effects?

While it is clear that the presence of an audience or coactors will often have an effect on an individual's performance, it is not at all clear why. While a number of explanations have been advanced, it appears that no single explanation will explain all of the various findings in the area of audience-coaction effects. However, we will briefly consider an important explanatory notion that has recently been developed by Zajonc (1965) and that can account for some of the findings.

It was pointed out that the presence of others often facilitates an individual's performance on well-learned tasks but may inhibit performance on tasks that are not well learned or are being learned. The question, then, is what is the difference between well-learned tasks and the other types that would lead to this facilitation in performance? Performance on this type of task involves the emission of old responses—that is, responses that are "well learned" and dominant. Learning experiments have shown that high drive (or arousal or activation) favors the emission of responses that are dominant or well learned. Thus, Zajonc's suggestion that the presence of others is a source of general arousal or activation might explain why performance is facilitated on tasks that consist of well-learned (dominant) responses. The individual's activation level is high; this favors emission of dominant responses; the emission of these responses leads to improved performance. However, what about the inhibition of performance by the presence of others when the task is not well learned or is being learned?

Zajonc's explanation also fits these situations. During early stages of learning, or when a task has been learned but not "well learned," the dominant responses may be the *wrong* responses. In this type of situation, the high activation level brought about by the presence of others would increase the probability of these dominant (and wrong) responses being emitted. This leads to impaired learning in the tasks being learned and impaired performance on the tasks that were not well learned.

We have seen that an individual's output may be modified by the mere presence of other people. While individual performance in a social context is an important topic and one which we have by no means exhausted, we will now turn our attention to another aspect of performance in social situations—the output of the group as contrasted to the output of the individual.

The Group's Output

One of the major reasons that people get together in groups is to collectively pursue a particular end. Consequently, the effectiveness with which a group can arrive at its goal has been subjected to considerable research. Nearly all of this research has taken place in a laboratory setting but, as Davis (1969) points out:

> The laboratory investigation of small groups reached a peak in the late 1950's, but since that time has figured less prominently in the study of social behavior. It has become increasingly evident (a) that the laboratory group is still a complex and difficult thing with which to work, and (b) that the group in a "natural" setting still has much to teach us [p. 4].

In considering group output, we will restrict our discussion to a contrast between individual and group output. While there is a great deal more to small group research, as it is often called, than simply comparing individual and group output, this type of comparison is important from a practical point of view. Whether or not an individual or a group can most effectively solve problems or make decisions has implications for the military, industry, legislative bodies, as well as for many other situations. Our approach, then, in this section, will be to consider the group as a system, and our interest will be directed at its output. It should be kept in mind, however, that the output of any system is based on interactions and interrelationships of its various subsystems. The interactions of the human "subsystems" making up a group has been the focus of much of the research of social psychologists. Thus, research effort has been directed at communication networks within groups, at group structure, at how leaders develop within groups and, in general, how individuals "turn into groups."

Individual versus Group Output

At the outset, it must be pointed out that there are many variables that will determine the relative efficiency of group performance in contrast to individual performance. As you might expect, one of the most important variables is the type of performance task that is utilized. Another important factor is the level of ability of the people involved. Often these variables will interact. For example, let's consider some of the findings from studies involving group problem solving.

It appears that when the problems presented to a group are relatively easy, the more capable individuals in the group can solve all or most of the problems alone. Thus, in a situation in which all group members are capable and the problems are easy, individual and group performance would be the same. However, with more difficult items, each capable person may solve some but not all of the problems. By "pooling" their answers, the group output will be superior to the individual outputs. Suppose, however, that we have group members with low abilities who are presented with difficult problems. They do poorly alone and can contribute little to a "pool" so that individual and group performance both are at a low level. With easier problems, each of the low-ability individuals will master certain ones and a pooling effect will result. Thus, with easy problems and capable group members, there is little or no advantage for group problem solving while with difficult problems there is an advantage. When individuals of low ability make up the group, however, the situation is reversed. Easier problems are better solved by the group while solving more difficult problems does not benefit from group participation.

It is important, then, to understand that any broad generalizations about individual or group output being "better" or "worse" are risky since so much depends upon variables such as those mentioned. While at one time it was thought that groups were generally more successful than individuals, the relative proficiency of group output as compared to individual output depends very much on the characteristics of the problem, as well as on the distribution of ability among the group members. Groups are highly proficient on some types of problems and very inefficient on other types.

The term *efficiency,* in relation to group versus individual output, refers to more than whether or not a problem is solved correctly or a correct decision is made. In many practical situations, other variables may also be important. For example, there are numerous experiments that show that when groups and individuals are given standard tests to perform, groups are slower and require more time. Even when groups accomplish more in a given period of time, they may prove to be inefficient in terms of man/hour ratios of productivity (Kelley & Thibaut, 1969). Groups can also be more *uncoordinated* when compared with individuals, particularly on motor tasks. It has frequently been shown that on tasks requiring coordination of efforts, groups are inferior to individuals.

Group decisions or judgments also tend to be more *risky* than individual decisions or judgments. It has been demonstrated many times that individuals in a group are willing to accept more risk than they would as individuals outside the group context. This phenomenon has been labeled the "risky shift" and has been shown to take place under a variety of task conditions.

Much of the research on group versus individual performance has involved information-acquisition, information-processing, and decision-making tasks. The tasks and techniques used have been varied, and we will make no attempt to describe any particular studies. Rather, we will attempt to briefly summarize, in very general terms, what appears to be the existing evidence on the efficiency of group or individual output.

Information Acquisition. Not a great deal is known about how groups acquire and store information. From the few studies available, it appears that when differences are found between groups and individuals, the groups tend to make fewer errors in reaching a criterion and sometimes may reach the criterion faster than individuals. In general, differences between individuals and groups on information-acquisition tasks are usually negligible, but when differences are found they are usually in favor of the group.

Information Processing. More attention has been devoted to information-processing groups—problem-solving groups—than to groups facing either learning or decision-making tasks. The available data suggest that groups are usually better than individuals in terms of errors and proportion of correct responses. However, we have already indicated that groups may be slower than individuals in arriving at solutions. A group can be considered "slow but sure."

Decision Making. One of the most important functions of many groups is decision making. While the various factors involved in group decision making have been subjected to considerable study, there is relatively little information available comparing group and individual decision making. It is apparent, however, that whether a group decision is "better" than the decision of an individual is dependent upon a number of characteristics related to the composition of the group, ability of its members, group interactions, member motivation, and so forth. We have already pointed out an important difference between group and individual decisions when the "risky shift" phenomenon was discussed.

The complexities involved in making comparisons of group and individual products have become more thoroughly appreciated in recent years, as Davis (1969) points out: "The individual-group comparison is now coming to be regarded as a special case of the more important question of how individual products are combined into a group product through the interaction of the members" (p. 42). However, in an attempt to make a rather gross summary of comparisons that have been made between group and individual outputs, we can say that on most criteria groups are generally somewhat superior to individuals. This statement must be qualified, however, by again emphasizing that the existence and degree of superiority depends upon variables associated with the task to be performed and with the capabilities of the individuals involved.

Group Pressures and Conformity

Have you ever done something that you really didn't want to do and, perhaps, knew that you should not do, because you were a member of a group whose other members were engaging in that type of behavior? Most of us have. As a member of a group, an individual is exposed to a number of kinds of group pressures, some subtle and some very apparent, to change some of his beliefs and behavior patterns. The pressures are aimed at changing the individual's behavior to conform with the beliefs and standards of the behavior of the group. *Conformity* is defined as the change in behavior or beliefs toward a group that take place because of group pressure. When psychologists study conformity, then, they are studying the change of the individual toward the group—that is, his movement or change in beliefs and behavior toward those of other members of the group.

In recent years the term *conformity* has taken on an unfavorable connotation to many individuals who like to feel that they are "nonconformists" and, consequently, something special. Actually, of course, whether you consider yourself a conformer or nonconformer depends on whom you are comparing yourself with. Thus, if you are a hippie or a beatnik you may think of yourself as a nonconformist while, in reality, you are very much a conformist in that your behavior, and possibly beliefs, have been changed by various group pressures. Thus, labeling a person a conformist or nonconformist is misleading since conformity is group and situation specific. In order to actually label someone as a nonconformist, and be at all accurate, we would have to be in a position to analyze his whole psychological environment. Obviously, we are not usually in a position to do this.

How Do We Study Conformity?

Conformity has been studied by means of a number of different approaches and techniques. While we will not take time to discuss in any detail the nature of these various studies, we should point out that the key word in research in this area is *change*. Conformity is a change in behavior or beliefs of a member of a group because of various group pressures. Thus, investigations dealing with group norms and group standards in general are not really studies of conformity since they are not concerned with change in individuals brought about by group pressures. Study of individual behavior that just happens to coincide with the behavior of a group is not a study of conformity either, since behavior that is coincidental is not related to group pressures. In order to effectively study conformity, it is necessary to have experimental designs that allow us to quantify, in some fashion, the changes in beliefs or behavior of the individual that result from the influence of the group.

Again, we come to the importance of control groups, which are as useful in studying conformity as they are in any other type of psychological experiment. For example, suppose that we obtained measures of behavior, or beliefs, before a number of individuals became members of a group and then obtained measures after they were in the group for some time. If there were a change in these measures, could we really say that the change was due to group pressures? We could not, since all of the individuals might have changed because of factors unrelated to the group. Instead, we would attempt to compare the individual's behavior after group interaction with the behavior of others who were not in the group. We could then infer that changes, if they took place, were due to group influences. With this type of design, we are in a position to investigate other aspects of conformity besides behavior change. For example, we could take the two sets of individuals (one set belonging to a group of some kind and the second set consisting of nonmembers) and attack certain beliefs that are associated with the group. If the individuals who belong to the group are more resistant (or less) to the attack, we can infer change in beliefs.

Earlier we discussed Asch's "classic" study of conformity, in which naive subjects judged line lengths while other "confederates" gave different judgments. As you may recall, some subjects yielded to the group opinion which, of course, was actually wrong. Modifications of the Asch technique can also allow us to study a number of independent variables such as group size, status of group members, and so on.

In considering the results of conformity studies, an important aspect of conformity must be kept in mind. We can think of two kinds of conformity—*compliance* and *private acceptance*. Kiesler and Kiesler (1969) differentiate between compliance and private acceptance as follows:

> Compliance refers to overt behavior which becomes more like the behavior that the group wishes its members to show. The term

refers to outward actions without consideration of the private convictions of the actor. When we speak of "compliance only," we mean that the person is behaving as the group wants him to but does not really believe in what he is doing. That is, he is going along with the group without privately agreeing with the group. Private acceptance means a change in attitude or belief in the direction of group attitudes and beliefs. In this case, the person may not only act as the group wishes, but changes his opinions so that he believes as the group believes [pp. 3–4].

As you might expect, it is easier to study compliance in group situations than private acceptance. Since compliance involves overt behavior, in many cases the psychologist can obtain his data by means of observing and measuring behavior. It is usually more difficult to obtain data concerning the real beliefs of the individuals in whom we are interested.

Some Variables Influencing Conformity

Based on numerous studies dealing with conformity, it has become apparent that there are several variables that will influence this type of behavior. For example, certain variables in the experimental situation itself will determine whether group pressure is effective in bringing about conformity. In the Asch study, if there was a glaring discrepancy between the length of the standard line and the line chosen by the majority (stooges), the effectiveness of the majority opinion was less than if the difference between the lines was not very great. It appears that when an experimental situation is made more ambiguous, the subject will be more likely to yield to group pressure. *Stimulus variables,* then, are important in conformity studies. *Group variables* are also important. The size of the group (up to a point) and whether or not the members of the group are unanimous will have an effect on whether the subject conforms. If the group consists of several members and they are all in agreement, conformity by a subject is more likely to occur. Similarly, the status of the members of the group will make a difference. When the prestige of the members is great, there is more pressure on the individual to conform.

It has been shown that some individuals are more likely to conform than others. In most conformity studies, there are always a few "bullheaded" subjects who stick to their guns and refuse to conform to group opinion. This finding has led to the assumption that *personality variables* are important in conformity. Actually, while it has been shown that there are large and consistent individual differences in the tendency to conform or remain independent under group pressure, we cannot state that one individual has a "conforming" personality and another does not. As we have pointed out, conformity is situation specific, and a person who conforms in one situation may not in another. However, a study by Crutchfield (1955) sheds some light on personality factors that appeared to be related to ability to withstand group pressure. In this study, it was found that males with higher intelligence, originality, self-confidence, an absence of anxiety feelings and inferiority, as well as several other characteristics, tended not to conform.

Finally, *cultural variables* play an important role in conformity. While experimental data in this area are sparse, a study by Milgram (1961) involving French and Norwegian students, showed that the French subjects were less conforming than the Norwegians. It is probable that certain cultures reinforce conformity more than others and that this cultural influence would be revealed in experiments designed to measure conformity.

Group Pressure

Why do we conform? We have indicated that group pressure can be considered the motivating force behind conformity. What, then, is group pressure? How is group pressure "transmitted" to group members? Why is it effective?

Group pressure can be defined as a psychological force that operates on a group member to fulfill other group members' expectations of him. This psychological force is developed in several ways. A group member typically pays attention to other members of the group and cares about what they think of him. He wants the others to accept him and to like him. One way of accomplishing this is to conform and therefore avoid risking the rejection of the group. Similarly, it is important to the member that the group goal be successfully achieved. He recognizes that conformity will help achieve the goal. He also recognizes that conformity of group members is often necessary in order to ensure that the group will continue to function. These motives, as well as others, serve to establish a "psychological force" that effectively produces conformity. Group pressure is directed at changing behavior and beliefs that are salient to the group. In other words, the group is not concerned with all the behavior of a particular member. It is concerned only with behavior that is relevant to the group and its functioning. The member must conform to the norms of the group and play the role that is assigned to him as a group member.

Group pressures, or expectations, can be transmitted in a number of ways. In some instances they are quite explicit and may be in the form of written orders or commands by group leaders. Often, however, the expectations are transmitted in a much more subtle fashion. The individual group member may perceive that his behavior or beliefs are in disagreement with those of the other members of the group. Usually, disagreements of this type are relatively easy for the member to perceive. Whether or not the member acts on the apparent discrepancy, however, is dependent upon variables that we have discussed earlier.

Person Perception

Person perception, or interpersonal perception as it is often called, refers to "the processes by which man comes to know and to think about other persons, their characteristics, qualities, and inner states" (Tagiuri, 1969, p. 395). The study of person perception is important since the manner in which we perceive other people is one of the key determinants of how we behave.

In some respects, the perception of other people involves processes that are similar to those involved in the identifying subsystem (Chapter 4). As a physical object, a person is basically no different from other physical stimuli. As is the case with physical stimuli, we tend to perceive people as having physical attributes of various types and we tend to categorize and classify on the basis of these attributes. Similarly, we perceive the behavior of other persons and we identify and classify this behavior. However, person perception involves a great deal more than just classifying physical and behavioral attributes. We also make inferences about attributes that are *inside* the other person and are strictly psychological. Thus, the inferences that we make are often about the other person's intentions, emotions, ideas, attitudes, and so on. The social psychologist is interested in person perception because this process is not only one of the most important outcomes of social interaction but it is also one of the most important determinants of the nature of social interactions.

In considering the studies that have been conducted in the area of person perception, we find that most investigations fall into one of two classes or groups—those dealing with the perception of emotion and those concerned with perception of personality characteristics. In the case of perception of emotions, much of the research has focused on the stimuli, such as facial expressions, which elicit the perception that an individual is experiencing a certain emotional state. Research dealing with the perception of personality traits has often been concerned with accuracy of perception and with identifying the difference between accurate and inaccurate perceivers. While both these areas of research have interested investigators for many years, perception of emotions appears to have received the most attention, and we will be primarily concerned with this area in our discussion of person perception.

Recognition of Emotions

Historically, the study of person perception can be traced to Darwin (1872) whose book *Expression of Emotions in Man and Animals* stimulated others to look further into this area. While the problem of recognition of emotions was secondary in Darwin's work, his systematic treatment of this area provided a model for later researchers. Although interest in this type of research has fluctuated over the years, in the 1950s an upsurge in research in perception of emotion and other aspects of person perception took place. Currently, it is still a popular topic of study.

Methodological Considerations

In the typical study dealing with the recognition of emotion, a stimulus (an expression of emotion) is presented to an individual or to a group whose task is to identify the particular emotion being expressed. Tagiuri (1969) discusses a number of technical points which must be considered in evaluating the results of such studies. First, the stimuli utilized in emotion-recognition studies show tremendous variation. Some studies have used real persons who attempted to express various types of emotions that were labeled by observers. Other studies have made use of motion pictures of a real person, photographs of a person, or a diagram or drawing of a person. Sometimes the voice of a person has been presented to observers who were asked to label the emotion expressed in the voice.

The use of photographs or movies as stimuli in these types of studies again raises the question of the relevance of laboratory studies to real-life situations. As Tagiuri (1969) points out:

> All in all, one wonders about the significance of studies of recognition of "facial expressions of emotion" in isolation from the context. From the point of view of the adaptiveness of social behavior, it is rare that judgment of an emotion ever takes place

> in the same way as it does when one examines a photograph of a facial expression [p. 404].

In real-life situations, we are not limited to simple facial cues in recognizing emotional states in others. There are many other cues that are important, such as verbal cues, body posture and movement, and eye contact. It is probable that a number of such cues are combined to form a total impression of emotion.

Another factor involved in studies concerned with recognizing emotion is the nature of the discrimination that is required of the subjects who are attempting to recognize an expressed emotion. For example, it is more difficult to discriminate facial expressions related to fear and anger than those related to love and disgust. Similarly, the nature of the identifying labels that the subjects are allowed to use may make a difference. It has been shown that subjects reach a higher agreement about an emotion being expressed when they are allowed to make use of their own terminology than when they are forced to use labels furnished by the experimenter. These, as well as several other factors, are important considerations in the design of studies dealing with recognition of emotion.

Accuracy in Judging Emotions

Based on the laboratory data available, we cannot make any conclusive statements about our ability to accurately perceive emotions. Whether or not we can recognize expressed emotion in a laboratory setting is dependent on a variety of factors such as the stimuli conditions, the particular emotion being expressed, or the labels supplied the judges. In many studies it has been shown that accurate judgments can be made while in other studies, in which the variables mentioned were modified in some fashion, accurate judgments could not be made.

However, as we have pointed out, the laboratory studies of recognition of emotion do not tell us a great deal about our ability to recognize emotion in a real-life situation. It is quite possible that this type of judgment might be quite accurate when we have all of the cues available that exist in an "unposed" situation. At this point, however, we do not have enough data from the "real world" to know if this is the case.

Judgment of Personality Traits

Studies dealing with recognition of emotion have been concerned with whether transient states of the individual—that is, emotions—can be recognized from various cues exhibited by the person. What about the ability to recognize the more enduring characteristics and traits that are subsumed under the heading of "personality?" Considerable research has been directed toward answering this question. However, many of the studies in this area have been directed not so much at determining how accurately personality traits of others can be assessed, but rather at determining or identifying the kinds of perceivers who are particularly sensitive to the enduring characteristics of others (Hastorf, Schneider, & Polefka, 1970).

As with perception of emotion, there are a number of methodological problems involved in studies concerned with the perception of personality. While we will not consider these methodological points, it should be pointed out that in recent years questions have been raised that make the findings of many of the earlier studies difficult to interpret. Consequently, when we attempt to discuss the accuracy of judgments about personality and the differences between judges in this ability, there are a number of qualifications and restrictions that must be imposed.

It has been demonstrated repeatedly that one's accuracy in "judging others" depends on a number of variables. Possibly the most appropriate statement to make about accuracy is that it is difficult to draw any firm conclusions from the studies made to date. This view is held by a number of investigators (Tagiuri, 1969).

The question whether some individuals are better "judges" than others is also a difficult one to answer. Allport (1961) insists that some individuals are more accurate judges than others, and he lists a number of characteristics of the "good judge." It would appear, however, that the achievement of these "good judges" is not based on a unitary process or ability. Rather, when a person is able to make an accurate judgment it is the result of a "multitude of component processes and abilities relevant to understanding others" (Tagiuri, 1969).

While the problem of accuracy of judgments is still of interest to many investigators, others have become more concerned with the *process* of making judgments about others.

The Process of "Knowing Others"

How are we able to recognize the inner states and qualities of others? What are the processes involved? In other words, how does one get to know another person?

One explanation that has been popular for a number of years and has attracted considerable interest recently is the so-called *inference theory* of interpersonal perception. This theory suggests that we know about others through a very rapid process of inference or analogy. Through this process, which we are seldom aware of, we infer "the state or characteristics of another person because the circumstances, behavior, or sequence of events are similar to those we have met in previous situations, and with which we ourselves have had personal experience" (Tagiuri, 1969, p. 415).

There are other investigators, however, who feel that more direct processes than inference are involved. They suggest that there are certain external cues that have meaning and that are mediated by more direct physiological and psychological processes. Thus, the state of the other individual is reflected in various external cues that the observer recognizes. Actually, person perception may involve a combination of these explanations—that is, inference and analogy as well as sensory cues derived from responses of the person being observed.

Cues for "Knowing Others"

A person has two major external sources of information that tell him something about the state or characteristics of another individual. First, the other person furnishes certain cues. Second, the situation or context in which the observed person is located will also furnish a considerable amount of information. In the case of the other person himself, there are a number of aspects that we attend to and that may influence our judgment. Disregarding the situation or context variable, we make judgments about the state of a person based on such aspects as facial expressions, body posture and movements, eye contact, changes in voice, and so on. We have already indicated, however, that one can question the accuracy of these kinds of judgments.

Accuracy of judgment is increased when more information is available to the observer. For example, we would probably not find consensual judgments among a group of observers if a photograph of a face expressing some type of emotion was shown to them. However, suppose that some information was also available to the observers about the situation when the photograph was taken. For example, if the observers were told that the photograph was taken at a funeral, it is likely that there would be a higher level of agreement about the emotion being expressed. Other sources of information are also used in these judgments. For example, knowledge of the role of the person being observed increases the veridicality of the judgment of observers. Suppose photographs of two male faces taken at a wedding were shown to judges. If one face was identified as the groom's and the other as a former suitor's, the judges would probably be able to make more accurate judgments than they would if this role information was not known.

There is a great deal more that could be said about the approaches and theories associated with person perception. New techniques are being developed that will soon lead to a greatly expanded understanding of this very important form of human response and interaction. It seems likely that in the near future substantial progress will be made in this area. It is important that this progress be made since a science of interpersonal behavior will be based on an understanding of the process of "knowing others."

The Scope of Social Psychology

As we pointed out earlier in this chapter, the scope of social psychology is so broad that we cannot hope to discuss it in a meaningful fashion in only one chapter. Consequently, our approach was to briefly discuss several current areas of social psychology. In an attempt to give the reader some notion of the breadth of this field, let's consider a recent publication in the area of social psychology.

In 1969 a five-volume handbook of social psychology was published (Lindzey & Aronson, 1969), which was the second edition of a two-volume edition initially published in 1954. A partial listing of some of the chapter headings in these volumes will serve to illustrate the many topics that are considered within the field of social psychology. Volume I deals with the history and systematic positions of social psychology. Volume II is concerned with research methods. Volume III deals with the individual in a social context and includes, among others, chapters on social motivation, the nature of attitudes and attitude change, social and cultural factors in perception, person perception, socialization, personality and social interaction, and laughter, humor, and play. Volume IV is concerned with the phenomena of interaction and group psychology and includes chapters on group problem solving, group structure, leadership, cultural psychology, national character, and collective behavior, as well as others. The fifth volume deals with applied social psychology and takes up topics such as prejudice and ethnic relations, effects of mass media on communication, industrial social psychology, psychology and economics, political behavior, social psychology of education, of religion, and of mental health.

Obviously, then, a researcher in social psychology can involve himself in a variety of topics that are not only interesting but also meaningful in our everyday existence.

The Human Subject
in Psychological Research

By the time you read this section, most of you will have been a subject in a psychological experiment of some type. One of the favorite sources of subjects for psychological research is the introductory psychology course in which, by means of threats, promises, or pleading (and sometimes pay), students "volunteer" to take part in the research of faculty members or graduate students of the psychology department. If you have been a subject, you may have been shocked (electrical or otherwise), deceived, insulted, flattered, asked to judge the length of lines, the brightness of lights, had physiological recordings taken from different parts of your anatomy, asked to rate your fellow students on a variety of scales, asked to judge how you "feel" at the moment, and on and on. Possibly some of you were even lucky enough to find out what the purpose of the experiment was.

The use and misuse of the human subject in psychological research has been an issue for a number of years. The question, of course, is what constitutes "misuse." Obviously, no psychologist will undertake an experiment in which his subjects run much of a risk of actually being injured. In studies in which such physical stimuli as electric shock, noise, vibration, heat or cold are used, the psychologist exerts great care to design the equipment so that a subject will not be injured. In psychopharmacological research, subjects receive drugs only under the supervision of a physician. As an additional safeguard to the subject, the government granting agency that supplies most of the funds for psychological research requires that each research proposal involving human subjects be screened by a "human subjects" committee at the institution where the proposal originated. Thus, even if a psychologist designed a study in which a subject might be injured, it is doubtful that the proposal would get by the screening committee.

Consequently, there is very little chance that a human subject in a psychological study will actually be physically "hurt" although you may not have been easily convinced of this when you took part in an experiment. What has concerned some investigators, however, is the fact that in many studies it is necessary to deceive the subject. The degree of deception may vary considerably but, the fact remains, deception often takes place. Possibly, the research in the area of social psychology has employed deception more than any other area of psychology. This increasing use of deception in social-psychological experiments has, to many psychologists, taken on increasingly serious proportions. While subjects may be "debriefed" after taking part in an experiment and the purpose of the deception explained to them, some psychologists feel that this may not be sufficient to counteract the possible effects of the deception.

Some Kinds of Deception

Suppose that you took part in a study of the effects of motivation on performance. You might have been told that a friend or a member of another group did better on the task than you were currently doing. Actually, they might never have been tested, but you were told that they had been in order to increase your motivation to perform on the task. You had been deceived. This, and other mild forms of deception, goes on all the time in laboratories and not too many people object. However, let us consider another type of deception.

Suppose you are a young GI and have been told that you will be required to fly, along with a number of other soldiers, over the ocean in a military aircraft. When you board the aircraft a number of electrodes are attached to you and the others, and you are told that you are taking part in an experiment on the effects of altitude on various physiological responses. Suddenly, at 8000 feet altitude, one of the motors of the aircraft sputters and stops, a man runs out of the cockpit and shouts that the plane is not capable of making it back to land and that an ocean landing will be necessary. He further instructs everyone to remain seated and to prepare for a crash landing. The plane then begins a slow glide downward. About the time that it appears that a crash is imminent, the motor again "catches" and the plane rises. Actually, the whole episode has been faked. During this entire period the electrodes were attached and readings were being taken. The psychologists conducting the study were not interested in altitude effects but, rather, they were concerned with the effects of stress on physiological responses. Again, the subjects have been deceived.

As a further example of a study involving subject deception, let us consider a study published several years ago that received a great deal of attention—Darley and Latané's (1968) investigation of bystander intervention in emergencies. Interest in this topic arose after a young woman was stabbed to death in a New York City street while over thirty people watched from the safety of their apartments.

Darley and Latané arranged an experimental situation in which subjects, thinking that they were alone or that other "unseen" persons were present, overheard an "epileptic seizure" which, of course, was faked. The major dependent variable in this study was the length of time it took the subject to attempt to help. Some interesting findings were reported. With the presence of other by-standers, an individual's feelings of personal responsibility seemed to be reduced, lowering his speed of responding. As the authors report, however, whether or not subjects intervened, they believed the seizure to be genuine and serious. Again, the subjects were deceived.

We could cite numerous other studies involving deception of subjects. As a matter of fact, a significant percentage of the articles published in social psychology have, as part of the experimental design, a situation in which subjects are deceived. However, at this point we will consider some of the current views on this issue.

Some Views on Deception

In a very thought-provoking article concerned with the "human use of human subjects," Kelman (1967) discusses the many factors that must be considered when we employ deception in psychological experiments. While we can only summarize the main points made by Kelman, it is suggested that students who might be interested in pursuing this topic further read Kelman's excellent article.

Basically, Kelman's concern about the use of deception is based on three considerations: the ethical implications of deception, the methodological implications, and the implications of deception for the future of social psychology.

Ethical Considerations

Kelman (p. 4) asks an interesting question that points up the entire problem of the ethics of deception. He wonders if we have the right to add to life's little anxieties and to risk the possibility of more extensive anxiety purely for the purposes of our experiments. Many of the experiments in social psychology that involve deception may have potentially harmful consequences. For example, suppose that as part of a study you were told that tests you have taken indicate that you have homicidal tendencies. Even though you were told that you had been "deceived," some doubts might linger for a long period of time. The possible long-term effects of some types of deception can only be guessed at. However, even when harmful effects are not likely to occur, there are other considerations, which Kelman (1967) points out:

> Serious ethical issues are raised by deception per se and the kind of use of human beings that it implies. In our other interhuman relationships, most of us would never think of doing the kinds of things that we do to our subjects—exposing others to lies and tricks, deliberately misleading them about the purposes of the interaction or withholding pertinent information, making promises or giving assurances that we intend to disregard. We would view such behavior as a violation of the respect to which all fellow humans are entitled and of the whole basis of our relationship with them. Yet we seem to forget that the experimenter-subject relationship—whatever else it is—is a *real* interhuman relationship, in which we have responsibility toward the subject as another human being whose dignity we must preserve [p. 5].

Methodological Implications

The methodological implications must also be taken into account. We use deception in experiments because we assume that if the subject were actually aware of certain conditions of the experiment, we could not draw valid conclusions from the results. In utilizing deception, of course, it is important that the subjects be unaware that they are being deceived, or the purpose for using deception is defeated.

It is becoming more and more difficult to find naive subjects for psychological experiments, particularly among college students. Although they may be uncertain about what the experiment is all about, they generally take it for granted that it is not what the experimenter says it is. While psychologists don't always lie, many college students think that they do. The suspicion on the part of the subject that he is being deceived in some fashion may be a variable that will affect the results of the study. Thus, while it may be necessary to use deception in some types of studies, the psychologist who undertakes the study with the assumption that he has naive subjects is actually being naive himself.

Implications for the Future of Social Psychology

With obvious ethical and methodological implications in deception studies, what is the future of deception in social psychological research? Kelman, in considering the implications of deception for the future of social psychology, states:

> From a long-range point of view, there is obviously something self-defeating about the use of deception. As we continue to carry out research of this kind, our potential subjects become more and more sophisticated, and we become less and less able to meet the conditions that our experimental procedures require. Moreover, as we continue to carry out research of this kind, our potential subjects become increasingly distrustful of us, and our future relations with them are likely to be undermined. Thus, we are confronted with the anomalous circumstance that the more research we do, the more difficult and questionable it becomes [p. 7].

Thus, the use of deception in social psychological experiments is a matter of concern to many investigators. To deal with the problems of deception, it is necessary that researchers become more aware of the negative implications associated with the use of deception and to make use of this technique only when it is absolutely necessary. When they do use deception, they must consider methods of minimizing possible negative consequences. It is also necessary that more thought be given to developing new experimental techniques that do not require deception. These steps are being taken by more and more psychologists.

The System So Far

In this text, we have considered the behavioral system of man at several levels. At one level of analysis, we have viewed the behavioral system as consisting of a number of subsystems and have discussed the functions and interactions of these subsystems in some detail. Thus, the characteristics of the sensing, identifying, interpreting, energizing, and memory subsystems were considered as well as the processes by which these subsystems transform an input into output. We have also dealt with the behavioral system at a different level and discussed such topics as differences between behavioral systems and malfunctions of these systems. Finally, we have viewed man as a subsystem within larger systems and have seen how man is modified to fit a particular system, how a system is modified to better fit man, and, finally, how man interacts with other behavioral systems—that is, his social interactions.

In attempting to keep this text to a reasonable size, several important areas of psychology have been omitted or just touched upon. An obvious omission, for example, is the area of developmental psychology. The behavioral system that we know as "man" does not just come upon the scene fully developed and functional. Each of the behavioral subsystems that were discussed can also be considered in terms of how they develop and become fully functional. Other areas of psychology have also been touched upon in only a cursory fashion. However, it is not the intent of the authors to present another "encyclopedia" of psychology. Rather, it is our intent to show that the human organism can be viewed as a system in which numerous elements, or subsystems, are complexly interrelated and interact in such a fashion that all contribute to the output of the system. As a system, the human organism can be viewed in much the same manner as many of the nonhuman systems. While this "mechanistic" view of man may have offended some, it provides a means for discussing the complex functioning of a complex organism in a manner that a "humanistic" presentation often fails to do.

Summary

1. Social psychology has been defined as a discipline that is concerned with understanding and explaining how the thoughts, feelings, and behavior of individuals can be influenced by the actual, imagined, or implied presence of other individuals.

2. Much of the research of social psychologists has been concerned with attitudes and attitude change. An attitude is a mental state of readiness to respond that is organized through experience and that will exert a directive influence on behavior. In attempting to change attitudes, psychologists have been primarily interested in source variables, message variables, channel variables, and receiver variables.

3. Research with small groups has dealt with the individual's output as a member of a group and with the output of the group itself. Various factors influence an individual's performance in a social situation. The mere presence of others may modify behavior. Coaction effects are also obtained. There are many variables, however, that affect the individual's output and also the group's output.

In general, on most criteria, it would appear that when the output of individuals is compared with group output, the latter is somewhat superior.

4. Conformity is defined as the change in behavior or beliefs toward a group that takes place because of group pressures. Conformity can be labeled as either compliance or private acceptance and will be influenced by a number of variables, such as stimulus, group, personality, and culture.

5. Person perception refers to the processes by which we come to know and think about other persons. Much of the research on person perception has dealt with recognition of emotions and the judgment of personality traits of others. The accuracy of these types of judgments is affected by many factors and, in general, individuals cannot make these judgments very accurately.

6. In recent years, there has been considerable concern about some of the methods used by some social psychologists in their research. One important issue is the question of deception in these experiments, which involves both ethical and methodological considerations.

Selected Readings

Davis, J. H. *Group performance.* Reading, Massachusetts: Addison-Wesley, 1969.

Hastorf, A. H., Schneider, D. J., & Polefka, J. *Person perception.* Reading, Massachusetts: Addison-Wesley, 1970.

Kelman, H. C. Human use of human subjects: The problem of deception in social psychological experiments. *Psychological Bulletin,* 1967, **67,** 1–11.

McConnell, J. V. (Cont. Ed.) *Readings in social psychology today.* Del Mar, California: CRM Books, 1970.

Zajonc, R. B. *Social psychology: An experimental approach.* Monterey, California: Brooks/Cole, 1966.

Zimbardo, P., & Ebbesen, E. *Influencing attitudes and changing behavior.* Reading, Massachusetts: Addison-Wesley, 1969.

15

Research Methods in Psychology

It has been pointed out that when a psychologist observes behavior by means of a research method—such as naturalistic observation, case study, testing, or the experimental method—he must in some fashion quantify his observations. That is, he must measure behavior. He must also systematically organize and examine the data from his observations through the application of statistical techniques. While these topics have been touched upon in previous pages, they are of such importance in psychological research that they will be taken up in detail in this chapter.

Measurement

It is not possible to specify the behavior of an organism, or to assess the quality of this behavior, until we can decide on an objective measure of the performance in which we are interested. Quantification of observations is perhaps the most critical aspect of any scientific undertaking. Whether we are interested in investigating the range of audible frequencies for man, or the manner in which he utilizes the steering controls of an automobile, we must be able to attach a number to his performance.

The basic problems in the measurement of behavior are how to specify the particular attribute or quality to be measured and what rules to follow in assigning numbers to these qualities. The only measurement that can be made, in any system including man, are reflections of system output. We cannot, for instance, directly assess the way in which man perceives or senses information from his environment. We must, instead, make inferences about his perceptual and sensory capabilities by examining the way in which he responds to the environment. If we are interested in investigating the lowest intensity of sound that man can hear, we must structure the situation in such a way that the man will make a particular response when he hears the sound. If we then present him with a large number of trials, with each trial being a sound presentation at a different intensity level, we can determine which intensities are audible to the observer.

In this example, the response that is measured is a relatively artificial indicator of the attribute we are trying to measure (sensitivity of hearing), but it does possess the necessary quality of being an observable response. In other contexts, the response process itself is the object of measurement. In such instances, the performance measurement is more directly related to the task. If we are interested in quantifying the steering control activities of the operator of an automobile, for instance, we may measure the physical movements of the steering wheel. However, again we are faced with the problem of specifying what it is we are trying to measure. Do we measure the number of times the steering wheel is moved, the average degree of movement, or the ratio of degree of movement to number of movements? In short, we must determine the kind(s) of responses that are representative of the qualities or attributes we are trying to measure.

Scales of Measurement

When we have determined the response we will measure, we must decide what kind of measurement is applicable to that response. There are four basic types of measurement that can be used in the quantification of any attribute or quality. These four types of measurement, or *scales of measurement*, are defined by the rules which determine the manner in which numbers are assigned to observations.

Nominal Scale

The simplest scale of measurement, and the least powerful, is the *nominal scale*. The nominal scale of measurement is used when we merely classify objects or responses as being different from one another. The most common use of this scale is in the classification of objects or events into one or another of several mutually exclusive categories. The only mathematical operation necessary for the application of this scale of measurement is a determination of equality on the attribute of interest. As an example we might use the most common nominal classification scheme, and one with which we are all familiar: the sex classification. Given a large number of people, except for extremely unusual cases, there will be only two sex categories in which these people may be placed. To assign our observations to one or the other of these categories we determine if two people are equal, or unequal, with regard to their sex. We can then progress through our whole group of experimental subjects with this type of determination. When we have finished, we will have two groups. To one group we will arbitrarily assign the designation *male*, to the other the label *female*. The only information we have gained by this application of measurement is a determination of the group in which each subject falls, and the number of subjects which fall into each group. We cannot say that one male is more masculine than another or that he possesses a different degree of maleness, but only that they are both members of the male group.

The category designations or labels are relatively unimportant in the application of the nominal scale of measurement. We could have just as easily assigned numbers to the two groups instead of the labels male and female. The only statistical operation that is permissible with this scale of measurement is the operation of counting the incidence of observations within each classification. The *mode* is a summary statistic used with the nominal scale and is the label of the category into which the largest number of observations fall.

Ordinal Scale

A slightly more powerful type of measurement is provided by the *ordinal scale*. In using the ordinal scale, we specify not only differences in kind of object or response, but also a ranking of our categories. Ordinal measurement thus adds to the classification process the concept of magnitude. We frequently encounter ordinal measurement in psychological tests. In a test designed to measure a subject's attitude, for example, the individual might be asked to rate his feelings about a particular situation on some type of continuum. The subject might be asked to express his attitude toward a driver who fails to dim his lights by checking one of the following responses: "not annoying," "slightly annoying," "moderately annoying," "quite annoying," or "very annoying." The scoring of the subject's response to this item would probably assign a "1" to the "not annoying" category, a "2" to the "slightly annoying" category, and a "5" to the "very annoying" category. Again the assignment of numbers or labels to the attribute we are measuring is done by an operation of determining the equality of observations. In addition, however, we now determine the order of the categories from most to least. Consequently, each assigned number conveys more information than does a number assigned by the nominal scale of measurement, since it tells us not only the category but the rank of the category. Because of the increased *power* of the ordinal scale (that is, the greater amount of information contained in each number assigned by this scale of measurement), it is possible to introduce some mathematical operations to data collected with ordinal measurement which were not possible with nominal measurement.

The *median* is a summary statistic that is calculated from data collected on the ordinal scale of measurement. The median is the midpoint of a given set of ordinal observations—that is, the point above and below which one half of the scores fall. The median is a convenient way to summarize a large amount of data collected with the ordinal scale of measurement. In a sense it is the average of the responses made on this scale of measurement.

Interval Scale

Although the ordinal scale includes the concept of greater than, or less than, it is not possible to make statements about the amount of difference between two ranked categories. We cannot, for instance, infer that the same amount of difference exists between a "3" and a "4" as between a "2" and a "3" on our driving attitude question. All we know is that one person was more annoyed than another. To permit statements of relative magnitude between two observations, responses, or measures, we must take our performance measurement on the *interval scale*. To the categorization and ranking operations of the nominal and ordinal scales of measurement, the interval scale adds the concept of equal intervals. With measurement on the interval scale, the difference between a "5" and a "7" is the same as the difference between "105" and "107." Most experiments strive for interval measurement because it allows them both to gain more information from every observation and to utilize more powerful statistical techniques on the data they have collected. A common example of the interval type of measurement is the measurement of temperature. The numbers assigned to the lines etched on our thermometers are arbitrary numbers, but the spaces between the lines are equal. Thus, the difference between 20 and 30 degrees Fahrenheit is the same as the difference between 90 and 100 degrees Fahrenheit. It is apparent that the ability to make our measurement on the interval scale provides a substantial gain in the amount of information conveyed by each observation. Now we not only know that two observations are different, and that one is greater than the other, but also we are able to determine the size of the difference between any two observations.

With the interval scale of measurement we can introduce the *arithmetic mean* as a convenient statistic with which to summarize our observations. The arithmetic mean (or mean) is obtained by adding all of the observations of a given set, and dividing

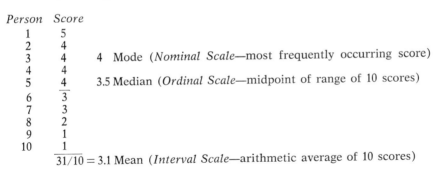

Person	Score	
1	5	
2	4	
3	4	4 Mode (*Nominal Scale*—most frequently occurring score)
4	4	
5	4	3.5 Median (*Ordinal Scale*—midpoint of range of 10 scores)
6	3	
7	3	
8	2	
9	1	
10	1	

$31/10 = 3.1$ Mean (*Interval Scale*—arithmetic average of 10 scores)

Figure 15–1. A comparison of the treatment of scores assigned by three different scales of measurement. The *nominal scale* has assigned people to one of five groups by determining equality between persons. The summary statistic for this operation is the *mode*, or most frequently occurring observation. The *ordinal scale* has ranked people from 1 to 5 on the possession of a particular quality. The summary statistic for this treatment is the *median*, or the category above and below which fall 50% of the observations. The *interval scale* has assigned numbers according to the possession of varying amounts of the quality being measured. The *mean* represents the arithmetic average amount of this quality for the entire group of 10 people.

by the number of observations in the set. By using this summary statistic we can describe the response of a large number of subjects with a single number. This operation was not possible with either the nominal or ordinal scales because these scales of measurement lacked the property of equal intervals.

Ratio Scale

Although the interval scale provides for the determination of relative amounts of a quality possessed by two observations, it does not refer this measurement to an absolute zero point or to a lack of any of the attribute we are trying to measure. In our measurement of temperature on the Fahrenheit scale, for example, we do not include the concept of no temperature or an absolute zero point. Measurement on the *ratio scale*, however, does reference the measurement of an attribute to an absolute lack of that attribute. This scale of measurement adds the concept of absolute zero to all of the advantages of interval scale measurement. The

Table 15–1. Scales of Measurement

Scale	Rules for Assigning Numbers	Examples
Nominal	Determination of the equality of observations.	Numbering of objects; sorting into classes.
Ordinal	Determination of equality + Ranking of classes or categories from most to least.	Rating scales; preference for foods, activities, etc.
Interval	Determination of equality + Ranking + Determination of equality of distance or difference between categories.	Measurement of temperature (Fahrenheit & centigrade); intelligence tests.
Ratio	Determination of equality + Ranking + Determination of equality of intervals + Reference to absolute zero point.	Measurement of length, weight, time, temperature (Kelvin scale).

measurement of weight is an example of the application of the ratio scale. On most scales, there is a zero point signifying the absence of the quality of weight. All measures of the weight of objects with such scales refer to this zero point in assigning weight numbers to the objects being measured on the weight attribute. A 12-pound sack of potatoes will thus weigh 12 pounds more than nothing. The designation "ratio scale" derives from the existence of a zero point in this scale of measurement. Since this scale contains an absolute zero point, the calculation of ratios between two measurements is permissible. Only with the ratio scale can we say that a "2" is twice as great as a "1" and one half as large as a "4." The most notable examples of measurement in psychological research that demand the ratio scale of measurement are measures of time taken to complete a response or of the physical magnitude of responses. Generally, it is necessary to measure physical energies to obtain measurement on this scale.

Statistical Methods

Statistical methods are extremely important not only to the field of psychology but to every scientific discipline that deals with empirical data. Statistical techniques allow us to describe psychological data and to make inferences about psychological processes on the basis of these data. It is important to realize at the outset, however, that statistics are used in psychology as a convenient and frequently necessary tool and that we should neither stand in awe nor become slaves to this tool. We might keep the following advice of J. P. Guilford (1936) in mind as we examine some statistical methods in the following pages:

> The sane attitude to take is to remember that statistical methods are merely helpful and significant tools and that the master craftsman remains the master of his tools; he never lets his tools become the master of him. If, too often we find that figures fool, it is because too often fools figure [p. 12].

Statistics serve two basic purposes for the psychologist. The first purpose is to describe and summarize scientific data. The second purpose of statistics is to interpret data and to draw inferences about particular psychological phenomena on the basis of data collected in various types of experiments.

Descriptive Statistics

Descriptive statistics are used to summarize scientific data. In this capacity, descriptive, or summary, statistics provide a simplified and less cumbersome means of understanding our data than would an inspection of a large list of individual scores on a test, for example. One means of summarizing and simplifying data is provided by the *frequency distribution*. A frequency distribution is simply a graphic means of presenting and organizing data. Suppose, for example, that we administered a paired associates test to 15 subjects and that the score obtained for each subject represented the number of correct responses out of a list of 20 pairs of words. The *raw data* might look like the second column of Table 15–2. It is possible to get some idea of how the subjects did on our test by inspecting this table, but we still do not have a very clear picture. It would be even more difficult if 150 subjects, rather than 15, had

Table 15–2. Summary of the data from the hypothetical paired associates test for 15 subjects. Raw scores, deviation scores, and squared deviation scores are shown, as well as the values of the mean, median, mode, variance, and standard deviation.

Subject	Raw Score	Deviation Score	Deviation²
1	17	+3	9
2	11	−3	9
3	13	−1	1
4	13	−1	1
5	14	0	0
6	14	0	0
7	16	+2	4
8	13	−1	1
9	14	0	0
10	14	0	0
11	15	+1	1
12	15	+1	1
13	15	+1	1
14	14	0	0
15	12	−2	4
	210	0	32

Mode = 14 (5 of 15 subjects had this score)
Median = 14 (5 subjects had scores greater than 14, 5 had scores less than 14, and 5 had scores equal to 14)
Mean = 14 (210/15)
Variance = 2.133 (32/15)
Standard Deviation = 1.46 ($\sqrt{2.13}$)

been tested. One solution to determining how our subjects fared would be to construct a *frequency polygon* like the one shown in Figure 15–2, or a *histogram,* or bar graph, as in Figure 15–3. The different scores obtained by the 15 subjects are placed, in ascending order, on the *horizontal axis,* or *abscissa,* of both figures; while the number of people (frequency count) is represented on the *vertical axis,* or *ordinate,* of both graphs. For the frequency polygon,

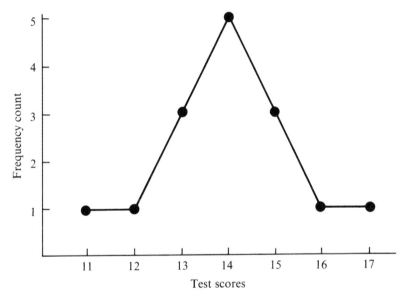

Figure 15–2. A frequency polygon depicting the data in Table 15–2.

each point on the graph represents the number of people who obtained each score given on the abscissa. In the histogram, a solid bar is drawn for each score shown on the ordinate, and the height of this bar indicates the number of people obtaining that score.

Frequency distributions can have a number of different shapes, depending upon the characteristics of the data they are drawn to describe. Perhaps the most common shape, and one which is approximated by our example, is the *normal distribution.* The normal distribution is characterized by a bell-shaped curve, in which the highest frequency counts occur in the center of the distribution, and the frequency falls off toward either extreme. Since many statistical methods and techniques are based upon the normal curve, we will consider it again later.

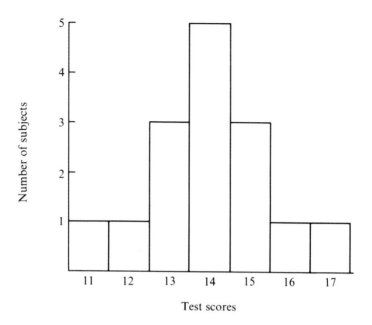

Figure 15–3. A histogram containing the same information as the frequency polygon.

Measures of Central Tendency

In our discussion of the four scales of measurement, we considered the various measures of central tendency that can be used to provide a single number to describe an entire set of scores. These measures are the *mode,* the *median,* and the *mean.* The mode is the most frequently occurring score, the median is the middle score or the score below and above which 50 percent of the scores fall; and finally the mean is the simple arithmetic average of the set of scores. In our example in Table 15–2 the mode is 14, the median is 14, and the mean is 14.

Measures of Variability

Although an appropriate measure of central tendency, such as the mean, provides one way to summarize a given frequency distribution of scores, we also need a measure to indicate how the individual scores are spread out around this mean.

The Range. The simplest measure of variability, or the spread of scores, is the *range.* The range for a given set of data is simply the difference between the highest and lowest scores. The range in our example from Table 15–2 is 6, which represents the difference between the scores of subject 1, the high-scoring individual, and subject 2, the low-scoring person.

Deviation Scores. Another approach to evaluating the spread or variability of scores is to calculate a deviation score for each individual. A deviation score is obtained by simply subtracting the mean of all the scores from each individual's raw score. Those subjects who score below the mean will have negative deviation scores, while those scoring above the mean will show positive deviation scores.

Although the deviation scores (column 3 of Table 15–2) give us a method of seeing how each individual's score differs from the mean, we are still left with a large number of scores in Table 15–2. It would seem logical to add up all of the deviation scores and divide by the number of people to get a single number to describe the deviations from the mean. If we do this, however, we will always come up with an answer of 0. This is true because, when we calculated the deviation scores, we subtracted the mean from each score. Since the mean is the middle value of the distribution, the sum of the scores above the mean will be equal to the sum of the scores below the mean and the positive and negative values of the deviation scores will cancel each other out and produce an answer of zero.

The Variance and Standard Deviation. The most useful measures of variability, or the spread of scores, are the *variance* and the *standard deviation*. These measures of variability get around the problem of the deviation scores summing to zero by squaring each deviation score and then taking the average, or mean, of the squared deviation scores. Column 4 in Table 15–2 contains the squares of the deviation scores shown in column 3. The variance, or *mean square deviation*, is simply the sum of this column divided by the number of people who were tested. The variance in our example is 2.13.

The *standard deviation* is the square root of the variance. In our example, the standard deviation is 1.46. This measure is usually taken as the best single indicator of the spread, or variability, of a distribution of scores. In our example there was little spread in the scores and 73.3 percent of our subjects (11 out of 15) had scores within one standard deviation of the mean (between 12.54 and 15.46).

Correlation

Up to this point we have been concerned with describing single sets of data which consisted of a single score for each of a number of subjects. Our interest in constructing frequency distributions, computing the mean, and standard deviation has been in describing how the subjects, as a group, did on a given test or in a particular experiment. These summary statistics are important and will be used in other treatments of data of this type. We frequently encounter a situation, however, in which there are two sets of scores for a given group of subjects, and we are interested in the relationship between the two sets of scores. Suppose, for example, that in addition to the scores on the paired associates test we had also recorded the age of each of our 15 subjects. We might be led to believe that age is related to proficiency on a learning test of this type and wish to determine the degree to which the two variables were related. The statisticians have provided us with a convenient tool, with which to examine the relationship between two variables, in the form of the *correlation coefficient*.

Just as we were able to describe the central tendency and the variability of a single set of scores with simple, descriptive statis-

Table 15–3. Two hypothetical sets of data consisting of the age and paired associates score for each of 15 subjects. The paired associates test scores are ordered from smallest to largest. Notice the direct relationship between paired associates score and age. Data like this would yield a perfect positive correlation.

Subject	Test Score	Age
1	11	14
2	12	15
3	13	16
4	13	16
5	13	16
6	14	17
7	14	17
8	14	17
9	14	17
10	14	17
11	15	18
12	15	18
13	15	18
14	16	19
15	17	20

tics, so are we able to describe the degree to which two different measures are related with a single, descriptive statistic.

Correlation is dependent on the statistical concept of *covariance* between two measures. In very simple terms, covariance is the degree to which two different measures tend to vary together in value. In the case of a perfect relationship (or correlation) between two measures, such as age and number of correct responses in our example, the two measures will vary, across individuals, in exactly the same way. In this case, as age increases so will the score on the paired associates test. Table 15–3 indicates what our scores might look like if there were a perfect positive correlation between age and paired associates score.

In this case higher scores are associated with higher ages. A perfect relationship is also possible, however, if an exact inverse relationship exists between the two measures (see Table 15–4). In this case, a high paired associates score is associated with a low age and low scores with higher ages. When such a relationship is present, we speak of a *negative* correlation.

The correlation coefficient, usually designated as r, is the descriptive statistic used to indicate the degree and direction of the relationship. The value of the correlation coefficient, in any given case, may range from +1.00 (a perfect positive relationship as in Table 15–3) to −1.00 (a perfect negative or inverse relationship as in Table 15–4). It should be emphasized at this point that $r = +1.0$ and $r = -1.0$ *both* represent a perfect correlation between two vari-

Table 15–4. Two hypothetical sets of data which illustrate a perfect negative correlation. Notice that, in this case, there is a perfect inverse relationship between paired associates score and age.

Subject	Test Score	Age
1	11	20
2	12	19
3	13	18
4	13	18
5	13	18
6	14	17
7	14	17
8	14	17
9	14	17
10	14	17
11	15	16
12	15	16
13	15	16
14	16	15
15	17	14

ables. Similarly, high negative correlation coefficients (such as
−.8 or −.9) indicate the same strength of relationship as do positive coefficients of the same absolute magnitude. The sign of the
coefficient merely indicates whether the measures are directly $(+r)$
or inversely $(-r)$ related.

Ordinarily, with actual data, the correlation coefficient will
not reveal a perfect relationship. In interpreting correlation coefficients, however, the closer the value is to $+1.00$ or -1.00 the
stronger the relationship, while the closer the value is to 0 the
weaker the relationship. In psychological research we find many
applications of correlation as a statistic describing the degree of
relationship between two measures.

Statistical Inference I: Samples and Populations

We have seen how descriptive statistics can be used to summarize psychological data and thus make the results of psychological experiments more manageable. Summary statistics do not,
however, test the validity of psychological theories or principles.
As the name implies, they simply describe what occurred in a given
experiment. Ordinarily the researcher is interested in more than
simple description. The majority of psychological experiments are
designed to yield information about general aspects of human behavior and not just the particular characteristics of a small sample
of individuals who happen to be the subjects for a given experiment.
Inferential statistics serve as the tools with which the psychologist
can generalize from his experiments with small *samples* of individuals to large *populations* of people.

Population versus Sample

The distinction between a population and a sample is probably the most important key to understanding the need for inferential statistics. A *population* is the entire group of individuals to
which the results of a given experiment are to be generalized. In
some instances the population may be exactly defined (for example,
the students presently enrolled in your college), while in others it
might be infinitely large (for example, all present and future college students in the United States).

Ordinarily a researcher cannot test all of the individuals included in the population to which he intends to generalize his findings. Assume, for example, that we are interested in evaluating the

problem-solving ability of the individuals in the two populations we have just mentioned. In the first case—the students in your institution—it might be possible to test every individual, but it would be a tremendously time-consuming process. In the second case, this testing would be impossible. Because populations are usually so large, the scientist must satisfy himself with *samples* from these populations. A sample can be defined as a relatively small number of individuals selected from a particular population. Samples are usually selected so as to accurately represent the population that is of interest to the investigator. On the basis of the results of a given experiment conducted with a sample of individuals, the experimenter will make *inferences* about the characteristics of the population.

Thus, in our study of problem-solving ability we might administer a test to only 225 students in your institution, and assume that these 225 students accurately reflect the entire population. Later in this chapter we will discuss techniques of sampling that are designed to make sure that this assumption is correct. However, for the moment we may assume that the 225 students tested are similar to the population. The important point to keep in mind is that while we can describe our sample exactly by employing the various descriptive statistics, such as the mean and standard deviation, we can only estimate or infer these characteristics of the population. The techniques of inferential statistics allow us to make estimations of this type and also to determine the probability that these estimates represent the true characteristics of the population.

Estimation of Parameters

This function of inferential statistics is formally known as the *estimation of population parameters*. A parameter, in statistical language, may be defined as the true value of a particular characteristic of a *population,* such as the mean and standard deviation. The mean and standard deviation of a *sample* from that population, on the other hand, are *statistics* that provide our best guesses about the true nature of the population. One function of inferential statistics is to provide an indication of the degree of confidence we can have that the *sample* mean, for example, is an accurate reflection of the *population* mean.

Standard Error of the Mean. There are two types of errors that are possible when we select a sample, perform our measurements, and compute an estimate of the population mean. An *er-*

ror of measurement may be due to a lack of precision in our measuring instruments or to mistakes on the part of the experimenter. The chief way in which this type of error can be removed from our data is in exercising maximum care in our measurements. The second type of error is called *sampling error*. To the extent that the sample of 225 students, for instance, is different from the population of your institution as a whole, our estimate of the population mean (the estimate is the sample mean) will be in error and will not reflect the true population mean. We can, however, introduce a statistical index that will give us an indication of the magnitude of the sampling error. This index is called the *standard error of the mean* and will be used later to compute a probability statement that reflects our confidence in the "goodness" of our estimation of the population mean.

The standard error of the mean is based on the fact that if we took repeated samples from a given population and computed a mean for each of these samples, we would have a new distribution of scores for which we could compute a mean and a standard deviation. This new distribution of scores is, however, a distribution of *sample means* and not individual scores. The extent to which these means differed from one another would be reflected in the standard deviation (the variability of the sample means about the mean of the means) and would represent the error associated with obtaining a sample mean. This standard deviation, or standard error of the mean, can be estimated, however, from our single sample by the following formula:

$$SD_M = SD/\sqrt{N},$$

where SD_M is the standard error of the mean, SD is the standard deviation of the sample scores, and N is the number of scores making up the sample.

Suppose, for example, that the standard deviation of the scores for our 225 students on the problem-solving test was 30. The standard error of the mean would then be equal to:

$$SD_M = SD/\sqrt{N} \text{ or } SD_M = 30/\sqrt{225} \text{ or } 30/15.$$

This gives a standard error of the mean equal to 2.

An important point is evident from this formula. As the size of the sample increases, the standard error of the mean becomes smaller. Thus, if we obtained the same standard deviation (30) with a sample size (N) of 25, the standard error of the mean would be $30/\sqrt{25} = 6$; while if we had taken a larger sample, such as 900, the standard error of the mean would be $30/\sqrt{900} = 1$.

Having obtained an estimate of the standard error of the mean for our sample, we are now in a position to calculate a precise index of the degree of confidence we can have that our sample mean accurately reflects the true value of the population mean. This index will be in the form of a *probability statement* about the value of the mean. Before proceeding, however, we will consider the nature of such probability statements, since an understanding of probability is essential to our discussion of inferential statistics.

Probability—The Language of Statistics. Everyone is familiar with the basic concept of probability—that is, the chance, or likelihood, that a given event will occur. We frequently hear, for example, that there is a 30 percent chance of rain. The entire area of inferential statistics is based upon the theory of probability since, when we attempt to make inferences about populations from information we have gained from samples, there are always sources of error that make it impossible to exactly specify population parameters. Consequently, statisticians have designed techniques that attempt to estimate the size of these errors of sampling and to specify the degree of certainty, or the probability level, that we can have that our results reflect the true state of affairs in the population. Most of these techniques of inferential statistics, including the standard error of the mean, are based on the *normal distribution*, which we considered briefly in our discussion of frequency distributions. An example of a normal distribution of scores is shown in Figure 15–4. In a normal distribution the mean, median, and mode are all equal, and the distribution is bell shaped—that is, tallest in

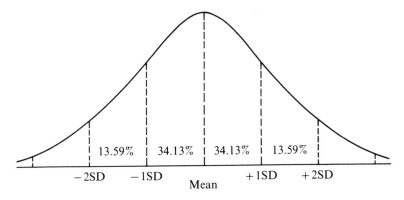

Figure 15–4. The normal distribution, showing the percentage of scores falling ±1 and 2 standard deviation units from the mean.

the center over the mean and sloping to either side of the mean. In a distribution of this type, the same number of scores fall below the mean as fall above the mean.

The most important feature of the normal curve, with respect to its usefulness for inferential statistics, is the fact that we can specify the percentage of scores falling under any part of the distribution by knowing the mean and standard deviation. For example, approximately 68 percent of the scores will fall within plus or minus 1 standard deviation from the mean, while approximately 13.6 percent of the scores will be between 1 and 2 standard deviations away from the mean of the normal distribution.

Knowing the proportion of scores that lie under any part of this distribution allows us to calculate the probability that we will obtain any given score, provided that we know the mean and standard deviation of our sample. To do so, however, we must standardize our scores.

Standard Scores. Standard scores can be computed by the following formula:

$$z = \frac{M - X}{SD}$$

where z is the standard score, M is the mean, X is the particular score whose probability we wish to compute, and SD is the standard deviation of our distribution of scores. The calculation of z scores allows us to make use of the tables of the normal distribution probabilities that are contained in most statistics books.

Let us return to our example of the problem-solving test we administered to a sample of 225 students. We obtained a standard deviation of 30 for this sample, and, let us assume, a mean of 100. Suppose that we wished to know the probability of obtaining a score of 160. Utilizing our formula, we have:

$$z = \frac{100 - 160}{30} = 2.$$

Now we can see that the score of 160 is two standard deviation units away from the mean and, by consulting a table of the normal distribution, we would find the probability of a score this large, or larger, to be approximately .02. In short, a score this large would occur only two times in one hundred observations and is relatively unlikely.

Confidence Intervals for the Mean

We now have all of the tools we need to determine the amount of confidence we have, in terms of a probability statement, that our sample mean is representative of the true population mean. To accomplish this task we will compute a *confidence interval* for our sample mean, using the normal distribution, the mean of our sample, and the standard error of the mean. The confidence interval is a range of scores, with the sample mean at the center, within which there is a specific probability that the true population mean will fall.

To determine the confidence interval within which we can be 95 percent certain that the true mean will fall we must use our sample statistics (the sample mean and standard error of the mean) to calculate the range of scores to be included in the confidence interval. To do so we will compute a value that, when subtracted from the sample mean, will give us the lower limit of this range of scores and, when added to the sample mean, will give the upper limit. Remember that the sample mean is at the center of this range of scores. This value to be added or subtracted from the mean is determined by multiplying the standard error of the mean by a coefficient taken from the tables of the normal distribution. This coefficient represents the probability level we have selected, in this case the 95 percent level. In the case of the 95 percent confidence level, the appropriate value from the table is 1.96. This number represents standard deviation units away from the sample mean, and 95 percent of the normal distribution will be between plus and minus 1.96 standard deviation units from the mean. The confidence limits for our mean of 100 are illustrated in Figure 15–5. The lower limit is obtained by subtracting:

$$1.96 \times SD_M \text{ or } 1.96 \times 2$$

from the mean. The 1.96 is the coefficient from the normal distribution table, while the 2 is the value of the standard error of the mean for our sample of 225 students. Thus, the lower limit is:

$$100 - (1.96 \times 2) = 96.08.$$

The upper limit is obtained by adding 3.92 to the mean of our sample:

$$100 + (1.96 \times 2) = 103.92.$$

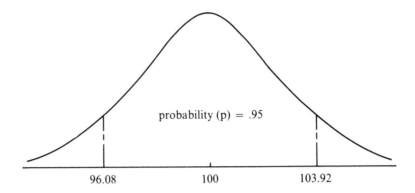

Figure 15–5. 95 percent confidence limits for the mean. The probability is .95 that the true population mean will fall between plus and minus 1.96 × standard error of the sample mean.

On the basis of these computations we can now make a statement that will reflect a precise degree of confidence in the true value of the population mean as inferred from our sample. This statement will say that we can be 95 percent certain that the real population mean will be a value between 96.08 and 103.92. You can readily see that reducing the size of the value that is subtracted from the mean to determine the lower limit of the confidence interval and added to the sample mean to determine the upper limit will decrease the range of scores within which the true population mean will lie. The two numbers that determine the size of this value are the coefficients found in the tables of the normal distribution and the standard error of the mean. The first number, the coefficient, can be reduced by selecting a lower probability value, which amounts to changing the statement about the confidence interval to a smaller degree of certainty. If, for example, we change our probability value, or our confidence level, from 95 percent to 75 percent, the coefficient from the table reduces to about 1.15. Using this value for the coefficient, the lower limit of the confidence interval will be:

$$100 - (1.15 \times 2) = 97.70$$

and the upper limit of the confidence interval is:

$$100 + (1.15 \times 2) = 102.30.$$

Now the range of scores making up the confidence interval is smaller, but we are only 75 percent certain that the true mean will fall within these limits.

A more useful way to reduce the range of scores making up

the confidence interval is to decrease the size of the standard error of the mean. If we can accomplish this, we can arrive at a narrower confidence interval and still be 95 percent certain that the true mean is within that interval. For example, if we had obtained the same sample mean and standard deviation with a sample of 900 students rather than 225 students, the standard error of the mean would be reduced by one half.

$$SD_M = SD/ \sqrt{N} = 30/ \sqrt{900} = 1$$

Now the lower limit of the confidence interval is:

$$100 - (1.96 \times 1) = 98.04$$

and the upper limit is:

$$100 + (1.96 \times 1) = 101.96.$$

In this case, we have reduced the size of the confidence interval, and we are still 95 percent certain that the true mean will be found within this interval.

In this section we have discussed just one function of inferential statistics, the estimation of population parameters. Next we will take up another important topic of statistical inference, that of hypothesis testing.

Statistical Inference II: Hypothesis Testing

Hypothesis testing is an area of inferential statistics which again involves inferences about populations based upon the data obtained from samples selected from these populations. In this case, however, the experimenter will ordinarily attempt to evaluate the truth or falsity of specific statements, or hypotheses, about some characteristic of the population of interest. An example of a particular hypothesis might be that a thirsty animal will run faster through a maze to obtain water than an animal that is not thirsty.

Scientific versus Statistical Hypotheses

A scientific hypothesis is usually a relatively general statement about the particular process under investigation. Our example is probably too specific to qualify as a typical example of a scientific hypothesis. In this case, the scientific hypothesis might state that thirst creates a high-drive level in an organism. Generally a scientific hypothesis is not, in itself, testable, because the statement is general. In this example we cannot measure drive level, for instance, and we have no guidelines that would indicate how long a period of water deprivation is required in order to develop thirst.

In contrast to the scientific hypothesis, the statistical hypothesis is specific to a given experimental situation, and it completely specifies all of the conditions of an experiment. Again our first reference to a hypothesis is probably not a good statistical hypothesis since it is too general a statement. A statistical hypothesis based upon the above scientific hypothesis might be as follows: Rats deprived of water for 24 hours will run at a significantly higher rate of speed through a straight alley maze than will rats who have had free access to water immediately prior to testing.

We can see that the statistical hypothesis does not mention the concept of thirst, or of drive level, but that it specifies certain conditions under which we believe rats will increase their running speed. The statistical hypothesis completely specifies the operations necessary to conduct a test of the hypothesis.

Statistical hypotheses are usually, if not always, based upon scientific hypotheses, and if the statistical hypothesis is borne out in an experiment, support is given to the scientific hypothesis. As we have stated, however, scientific hypotheses are not directly testable, and we must infer the correctness or incorrectness of this type of hypothesis from evidence gained from testing the statistical hypotheses they produce.

The Null Hypothesis

The various statistical tests used to test hypotheses generally involve a situation in which statistical evidence, in the form of probability statements, is computed. This evidence serves as the basis for a choice between two hypotheses. In most experimental studies the statistical hypothesis is stated in such a form that it is either true or not true, and the statistical test used will support a dichotomous decision—either accept or reject the statistical hypotheses. The *null hypothesis* in psychological investigations is the exact converse of the statistical hypothesis which is tested. Whereas our statistical hypothesis about running speed of thirsty rats stated that water-deprived animals would run faster than nondeprived rats, the null hypothesis in this case would state that water-deprived rats run as slow as, or slower than, nondeprived rats.

When we employ a statistical hypothesis test in this situation we will obtain evidence that will either lead us to reject the null hypothesis in favor of the original statistical hypothesis (usually called the *alternative hypothesis*) or evidence that will fail to reject the null hypothesis.

Significance Levels

When appropriate null and alternative hypotheses have been defined, and an appropriate statistical test selected, the researcher will determine the significance level for his statistical test. The *significance level* is a specific probability level that will be used by the experimenter in deciding between the null hypothesis and the alternative hypothesis. It represents the experimenter's degree of assurance that his data support the alternative hypothesis. In our example of the thirsty vs. the drinking rats, for example, we may decide that we must be 95 percent certain that the thirsty rats ran faster than nonthirsty rats before we will reject the null hypothesis. In this case the significance level is the .05 probability level or, in other words, the data must indicate that there was only a 5 percent chance that the nondeprived rats really ran as fast as the thirsty rats. Ordinarily the researcher will set a significance level relatively low (.05 or less) so that he can be reasonably sure that chance factors are not likely to influence his choice between the null hypothesis and the alternative hypothesis.

Deciding between Hypotheses. The experimenter employing statistical tests to aid him in selecting between the null and alternative hypotheses is faced with the same type of a decision process and payoff matrix that we discussed in connection with the signal-detection experiment in Chapter 8. In the hypothesis-testing situation, as in the yes-no signal-detection experiment, the experimenter has two ways in which he may be correct, and also two potential errors. Table 15–5 illustrates the experimenter's payoff matrix.

If he rejects the null hypothesis (and consequently accepts the alternative hypothesis) and the real situation is such that the alternative hypothesis is true, he will make a correct decision. Similarly, if he accepts the null hypothesis when it is true, he is also correct. On the other hand, if he rejects the null hypothesis when it is true, he will commit a *Type 1* error. If he falsely accepts the null hypothesis when the alternative hypothesis is true, he will commit a *Type II* error.

In selecting a particular significance level for his test, the experimenter determines the exact probability of committing a Type I error. In our example the probability of accepting a false al-

Table 15-5. The payoff matrix in the hypothesis-testing situation. Accepting the alternative hypothesis when it is true is a correct decision, while accepting it when false results in a Type I error, the probability of which is determined by the significance level. Rejecting H_1 (the alternative hypothesis) when it is true leads to a Type II error, while rejection when it is false is another correct decision.

		TRUE CONDITION IN POPULATION	
		H_1 *True*	H_1 *False*
DECISION	*Accept* H_1	Correct decision	Type I error $p = $ sig. level
	Reject H_1	Type II error	Correct decision

ternative hypothesis is .05—the significance level. The probability of committing a Type II error generally cannot be specified in an experiment, but it is usually true that when the probability of a Type I error is decreased (by selecting a smaller significance level), the probability of a Type II error increases. The converse is also true. Ordinarily, however, the researcher's prime concern is with the chance of a Type I error. Usually it is considered more acceptable to reject the alternative hypothesis when it is true than to accept it when it is false.

Choosing the Statistical Test

Statisticians have provided the experimenter engaged in psychological research with literally dozens of different statistical tests all designed to help him decide between the null hypothesis and his alternative hypothesis. The very fact that so many statistical techniques are available presents an important problem to the researcher. In order to do justice to his data, and to have maximum confidence in his findings and conclusions, the researcher must be sure that the particular test he chooses is appropriate to the types of measures he has obtained and to the hypotheses he is attempting to evaluate.

Perhaps the most important single consideration that should guide the choice of a statistical test is the types of measurements constituting the experimental data, more specifically the scale of measurement upon which the data are based. Two principal types of statistical tests are available to the researcher. *Nonparametric statistical tests* were designed primarily for data that represent measurement on the nominal and ordinal scales of measurement, although they may be used in some cases in which a more powerful scale of measurement is employed. *Parametric tests*, on the other hand, are suited primarily for data that represent measurement on the interval or ratio scales of measurement. In the remainder of this section we will discuss some examples of each type of statistical test.

Parametric Hypothesis Tests. The parametric hypothesis tests are the most powerful statistical techniques available to the researcher—that is, they are the most likely to indicate rejection of the null hypothesis when it is false. Unlike the nonparametric tests, however, the parametric techniques require the experimenter to make a number of assumptions about his data. First, as we indicated, he must assume that his measurements satisfy the requirements of the interval scale or the ratio scale of measurement, because the mathematical operations necessary in computing these statistical tests require the calculation of means and standard deviations, which is not permissible or meaningful with data having only nominal or interval scale properties. For the application of parametric tests it is also required that the measurements be taken from normally distributed populations. Generally, however, this assumption is not nearly so important as the first, since most of the populations used by the psychologists can safely be assumed to be normally distributed and, even when this assumption is not true, the effect on the accuracy of the parametric tests is not great. The important consideration, then, is that the measurements be interval or ratio scale measures.

The t test. There are several varieties of the widely used *t* test, but it is most commonly applied when the experimenter wishes to statistically evaluate the difference between means of two groups of subjects. In our example, for instance, we might select two independent groups of rats. The first, or experimental group, will be deprived of water for 24 hours and then tested in a straight alley runway. As a dependent variable we would then measure and record the time taken to run from the starting point in the maze to the dish of water at the other end. Knowing the distance between these two points, we can determine the running speed of the rats by dividing the distance by the time taken to cover that distance. If, for example, the distance between starting point to the water dish is five feet and a particular rat had a running time of 10 seconds, the running speed would be .5 feet per second. The second group of rats would have water available in their cages and would be tested under the same test conditions without being deprived of water. Again the running speed would be calculated for each animal.

Assuming that we tested 10 rats under each condition, we might find data similar to Table 15–6.

At the bottom of each column in Table 15–6 we have indicated the mean, variance, and standard deviation for each group.

Table 15–6. Hypothetical running speeds for two groups of rats—Group I deprived of water and Group II nondeprived. The computational steps in the calculation of the t test for significance of the difference between the mean running speed of the two groups are also shown.

Rat #	Group I (Deprived Rats) Running Speed (ft./sec.)	Rat #	Group II (Nondeprived) Running Speed
1	10.	1	8.
2	12.	2	7.
3	15.	3	10.
4	10.	4	5.
5	8.	5	6.
6	14.	6	5.
7	12.	7	15.
8	15.	8	12.
9	15.	9	4.
10	13.	10	6.

$$M_1 = 124./10 = 12.4$$
$$SD_1 = 10.21$$

$$M_2 = 78./10 = 7.8$$
$$SD_2 = 3.34$$

$$SD_{diff.} = \sqrt{(SD_1^2/N_1) + (SD_2^2/N_2)}$$
$$= \sqrt{(10.21^2/10) + (3.34^2/10)} = 3.40$$

$$t = (M_1 - M_2)/SD_{diff.} = (12.4 - 7.8)/3.40 = 1.35$$

These statistics and the number of animals in each group will be used in calculating the t test.

The mathematical procedure for conducting the t test is very similar to the one we used earlier in determining the confidence intervals for the mean. The t statistic is computed by the following formula:

$$t = (M_1 - M_2)/SD_{diff.}$$

The calculated value, t, is the test statistic, M_1 is the mean of the first group, M_2 is the mean of the second group, and $SD_{diff.}$ is the standard error of the difference between groups. The standard error of the difference ($SD_{diff.}$) is similar to the standard error of the mean we used to establish confidence intervals. $SD_{diff.}$ is calculated in the following manner:

$$SD_{diff.} = \sqrt{(Var_1/N_1 + Var_2/N_2)}$$

where Var_1 is the variance of the first group (SD_1^2), Var_2 is the variance of the second group, and N_1 and N_2 are the number of rats in each group.

   As we can see from the table, the value of t for our example is 1.35. Having calculated this value, how do we use it to determine whether or not we will reject the null hypothesis that thirsty rats do not run faster than rats who are not thirsty? As we saw earlier, the first step in the process was to select a significance level. In this case we will use the .05 level, and we will reject the null hypothesis in favor of our alternative hypothesis if, on the basis of our test, we can be 95 percent certain that the mean of the water-deprived group is really larger than the mean of the nondeprived group. The t test is based on the t distribution, which is very similar to the normal distribution. There are tables of the t distribution that indicate the probability of obtaining a score any particular distance from the mean of the distribution. In our hypothesis-testing situation, we assume that the null hypothesis is true and that the mean of the nondeprived group is the true mean.

   We then determine the probability of a score, represented by the mean of the deprived group, which is some amount different from the mean of the nondeprived group. As with confidence intervals, the t statistic represents the size of the difference between the means in standard deviation units. By consulting appropriate tables of the t distribution we can determine the probability that a difference as large as the one we have observed could occur if no real difference between groups existed. In our case the probability associated with a t value of 1.35, which is obtained with 10 rats in each group, is about .10. In other words, there is only a 10 percent chance that the means of the two groups are the same.

   Given this result, how do we decide whether or not to reject the null hypothesis? Here the decision is automatic. We have already said that we must be 95 percent confident that a real difference exists before we will reject the null hypothesis in favor of our alternative hypothesis. We have found that we are only 90 percent certain about this difference. Consequently, we must accept the null hypothesis and conclude that thirsty rats do not really run faster to a source of water than rats who are not thirsty.

   Ordinarily, however, the researcher does not let his hypothesis die so easily. If we come this close to finding a statistically signif-

icant difference we may decide that we really need another test before we will completely throw out our hypothesis. If this is the
case we might take a good, hard look at the way in which we conducted the experiment and see if our measurements were as reliable
as possible. We might also consider repeating the experiment with
larger groups of rats. The last alternative is sometimes a reasonable
conclusion since the standard error of the difference reacts in the
same way that the standard error of the mean does when we increase
the number of subjects. If more subjects are tested, the size of the
standard error of the difference will generally decrease. If the standard error of the difference can be reduced by testing a larger number
of subjects, the .05 significance level may represent a smaller t
value, and consequently a small difference between the two means
will be detected as a statistically significant difference.

Nonparametric Hypothesis Tests. As we indicated earlier,
the most important use of nonparametric statistical tests is in cases
in which we are unable to measure behavior on the interval or ratio
scale. An additional advantage of these tests, particularly to the researcher who dislikes mathematics, is that they are usually much
simpler and require fewer arithmetic operations. The last point is
true simply because most arithmetic operations, except counting
and ranking, are not meaningful or possible with nominal and ordinal scale data. To illustrate nonparametric statistical tests we will
briefly discuss one of the simplest and most popular of these techniques, the sign test.

The sign test: The use of the sign test to evaluate hypotheses
requires only that the measures of behavior used as experimental
data be taken on the ordinal scale of measurement. In other words,
our data need only indicate larger, equal to, or smaller than.

Suppose, for example, that we wished to evaluate the scientific hypothesis that married men have a stronger achievement motive than their wives. Again, the scientific hypothesis is not directly
testable, and we must formulate a statistical hypothesis that specifies the type of measure of achievement motivation and determines
the manner in which data are to be collected. Our statistical hypothesis in this case might read as follows: Scores on a written test
designed to measure "need for achievement" will indicate that married men score higher than their wives. Since we are dealing with
pairs of subjects, only one score is necessary for each pair. We can
administer our "need for achievement" test to 10 couples and for
each couple record a "plus" if the man scores highest, a "zero" if

the scores are the same, and a "minus" if the wife scores higher than the husband. The sign test is designed to test the null hypothesis that husbands and wives do not differ in terms of their scores on the "need for achievement test."

The data from our experiment might look like Table 15–7. Although the scores on the test are given in the first two columns, they are only used to determine the signs, which are indicated in the last column.

Since only the sign of the difference between the scores of husbands and wives is used in this test, it makes no difference at all how big a difference between any two scores actually occurred.

Table 15–7. Hypothetical scores of husband-wife pairs on the achievement motivation test, and the signs of the differences between the scores of each pair. The last column (signs) is the only data required in the nonparametric sign test.

| | Test Scores | | Sign of |
Couple Number	Husband	Wife	the Difference
1	58	50	+
2	47	45	+
3	40	41	−
4	100	32	+
5	96	85	+
6	72	68	+
7	40	99	−
8	30	20	+
9	62	61	+
10	10	100	−

The sign test does not take the sizes of differences into account because, with the ordinal scale of measurement, the only operation allowable is ranking of observations in terms of greater than, less than, or equal to.

In conducting the sign test we will again establish a significance level to use in our decision of whether or not to reject the null hypothesis in favor of the alternative hypothesis. Let us again use the .05 significance level; we must be 95 percent certain that the difference between the number of "pluses" and the number of "minuses" represents a real difference between the relative size of husbands' and wives' scores on the "need for achievement" test, and our result must not be due to chance effects if we are to reject the null hypothesis. As with the parametric test, there are statistical tables designed to indicate the probability of a particular proportion of "plus" or "minus" signs out of a given number of differences. Consulting such a table, we would find that the probability of obtaining as few as 3 minus signs out of 10, if the null hypothesis were true and there was no real difference between the husbands and wives, is .172. This result indicates that if there is no difference in achievement motivation, as measured by our test, the chance is only 17 percent that there will only be 3 out of 10 minus signs. Again, however, we must accept the null hypothesis and reject our alternative hypothesis, since we had already decided that we needed 95 percent assurance in our results before we would reject the null hypothesis.

The Design of Experiments

Sampling and Variables in Research

In previous pages we have reviewed some statistical techniques that are frequently used by psychologists in order to describe their data and to make inferences from them. However, all of these statistical methods must be applied to experiments that have been properly designed and executed if they are to be useful and valid. In this section we will discuss research design considerations that influence the validity of the conclusions reached by research investigations.

Recall that there are four basic research methods, or strategies, that psychologists can use: *naturalistic observation, case studies, testing,* and *experimental method.* Recall also that all psychological research involves three types of variables: *dependent variable(s), independent variables,* and *nuisance variables.* Whatever research strategy a psychologist uses in a particular investigation, his primary concern is to measure the effects of a particular independent variable(s) on a dependent variable, while eliminating the effects of nuisance variables. Experimental design, as a topic within psychological research, is concerned with the selection of dependent and independent variables and the control of nuisance variables. Experimental design does not refer specifically to the statistical analysis of psychological data, but it is the activity of formulating the specific plan by which the data are to be collected. The validity of the statistical tests and the conclusions they produce are influenced by the way in which an experiment is designed. Poor experimental design can render even the most sophisticated and carefully conducted statistical test completely meaningless.

Insuring the Generality of Research

One of the key issues in experimental design is the choice of an appropriate method of selecting a sample from a particular population. Any legitimate sampling technique must be designed to insure that the sample will accurately reflect the population. In this section we will discuss two types of sampling that are designed to accomplish this purpose.

Random Sampling. The first, and most common, sampling technique is simple *random sampling.*

> A method of drawing samples such that each and every distinct sample of the size *N* has exactly the same probability of being selected is called simple random sampling [Hays, 1963, p. 64].

Most men over 19 years of age reading this book are probably painfully aware of at least one technique whereby simple random sampling of subjects can be accomplished—the recently instituted draft lottery system. Two large drums, each containing 365 capsules, are repeatedly turned, and pairs of capsules, one from each drum, are drawn until the drums are empty. One capsule of each pair contains a draft number from 1 to 365, and the other contains one of the 365 dates of the year. This technique was used to insure that each date was equally likely to be assigned any of the 365 numbers, and to eliminate possible sources of bias in assigning the draft numbers.

It is possible to accomplish the same type of random selection without going to the trouble of drawing numbers from a mixing drum, however. Most statistics books contain *tables of random numbers* that can be used. These tables consist of long lists of numbers that have been selected in a manner similar to the draft lottery. The use of random number tables is actually the same as the lottery system except that the publisher of the tables has done the drawing for the researcher.

There is one major drawback to the use of simple random sampling to select a sample of experimental subjects from the population to which we wish to generalize our findings. To insure that each person in the population has an equal chance to be included in the sample, it is necessary that we be able to list all of the people in the population, and that they all be available to participate. This situation is usually impossible to achieve. If we wish to generalize the findings of a problem-solving experiment to the population of college students in the United States, for instance, it would be impossible to insure that the entire population would be available for testing in the experiment. We may, in fact, be restricted to the students in one single institution. In this case, which is reasonably typical of most psychological research, we can do one of two things. First, we can assume that the particular subgroup of the total population available to us is a random sample, or at least representative of the larger population. In many research applications we can make this assumption with a fair degree of safety. Our other option is to qualify our conclusions by restricting our inferences to the subgroup.

Stratified Sampling. Another strategy often used to insure the representativeness of a sample is known as stratified sampling. In this case, the researcher has some prior information about the characteristics of the population, and he may have more direct control over the representativeness of his sample. He may know, for example, that 10 percent of the college population comes from high-income families, 25 percent from moderately high-income families, 50 percent from average income, 10 percent from moderately low, and 5 percent from low-income homes. He would then select the same proportions of each of these income categories in our sample. Thus, we no longer provide that each individual is equally likely to be selected in the overall sample, but instead we attempt to obtain a sample containing the same proportions of each income category as the population as a whole.

Usually the researcher will combine random sampling techniques with the stratified sampling technique, and within each category (such as high-income students) random selection will be used. In our example, the researcher would actually select five random samples, one from each of the income groups. The size of each sample would, however, be dictated by the size of that income group in the total population.

Selection of the Dependent Variable

The selection of the particular behavior or response that is to serve as the dependent variable in psychological research is another extremely important facet of experimental design. Virtually all types of psychological research, from naturalistic observation to laboratory experimentation, are faced with the problem of deciding upon a particular index of performance that is relevant to the aims of the study. Although there are statistical techniques available to the researcher that can simultaneously treat more than one dependent variable, ordinarily an experiment is designed to consider a single measure of performance, and it is important that the measure selected be a meaningful index of performance on the task of interest. It is also important that the particular index selected be amenable to reliable measurement and quantification, preferably on a relatively powerful scale of measurement.

You will recall from our discussion of parametric versus nonparametric statistical tests that the principal determining factor in deciding between the two varieties of hypothesis tests was the scale of measurement employed. Thus, the selection of the dependent variable in an investigation will, in effect, determine the type of statistical treatment that can be applied to the data from an experiment.

Selection of the Independent Variable

There are basically two types of independent variables used in psychological experimentation. The first type involves characteristics of the experimental situation external to the person who is tested. Ordinarily in studies using an independent variable of this type, identical, or similar, groups of subjects will be exposed to different experimental conditions or, in some cases, the same subjects (one group) will be exposed to different experimental conditions on different occasions. If we are studying the effects of noise on target-detection performance of pilots, for instance, we might select two groups of pilots to serve as subjects. Through the application of random sampling, we will attempt to insure that the subjects in the two groups possess the same level of target-detection skill. We might then expose one group to an intense noise level during the experimental session and the second group to quiet during testing. Since we have attempted to insure that the two groups were equal, or both representative of the same population, prior to the experiment, any differences in performance can be attributed to the differential effect of noise. The independent variable in this case represents a condition of the experimental situation, and the various levels of the independent variable are determined by the experimental situation to which the subjects are exposed.

A second type of independent variable involves classification of the experimental subjects, rather than the characteristics of the experimental situation. In this instance, the experimental conditions might be exactly the same for both groups of subjects. Suppose, for example, that the purpose of our study was to determine the effect of age on the target-detection performance of pilots. We might select one group of young pilots and another group of old pilots and administer exactly the same test, under exactly the same experimental conditions, to both groups. Now any differences in the performance of the two groups could be attributed to the age variable, since this is the only characteristic that differs between the two groups.

In actual practice, both classificatory and environmental variables are used as independent variables in psychological experimentation.

The Control of Nuisance Variables

In addition to dependent and independent variables, any psychological investigation will contain some number of nuisance, or extraneous, variables. Nuisance variables, like independent variables, may be characteristics of the experimental environment or characteristics of the subjects. In either case, they may potentially affect the dependent variable in the experiment and either mask or accentuate the effects of the independent variable. If one of the two groups in our experiment on the effects of noise on target-detection performance came into the experiment with hearing difficulties, for instance, the test of the independent variable's effect upon performance would be contaminated by the operation of this nuisance variable.

There are two principal means of eliminating or reducing the effects of nuisance variables in an experiment. The first method is to hold the nuisance variable constant for all subjects in the experiment. Of course, the experimenter must first know exactly what all of the nuisance variables are, so that he can structure the experimental situation to allow all subjects to be tested under the same environmental conditions. He must also select his subjects so that all groups are equal in terms of the classificatory type of nuisance variables. In practice, however, it is generally not reasonable to assume that we have actually identified all potential sources of bias.

The second method of eliminating the nuisance variables, and one which is often used in combination with the first, is to randomly assign subjects to the various groups or experimental conditions. This procedure will tend to uniformly spread the effects of the nuisance variables over all experimental conditions so that they will not systematically bias the results. It is important to note that the nuisance variables will still be present in the experimental situation and that they are still affecting the dependent variable. The effects which they now have, however, are uniform over all conditions and do not influence just one or another experimental condition or group.

Interpretation of Results

So far in our discussion of the design of experiments and the application of statistical tests to the results of these experiments, we have been concerned with the objective and quantitative aspects of psychological research. Another major aspect of the research activity is, on the other hand, involved with the more subjective interpretation of research findings.

After having formulated a scientific, and then a statistical hypothesis, designed an experiment, collected data and, finally, utilized a statistical test, we must then interpret the result of the experiment in terms of the original hypothesis. With the statistical tests we have discussed, we will usually be provided with information that will favor either rejection or acceptance of our hypothesis. However, we must still consider the practical versus statistical significance of our findings.

Practical versus Statistical Significance

Assume, for example, that we find a statistically significant difference in the reaction times of young and old automobile drivers, and that the difference between the mean reaction time for the two groups is .05 seconds. It is entirely possible that a difference this small can be detected as statistically significant in actual experiments, particularly if the groups are relatively large. In the face of these experimental results, it might be very tempting to conclude that a hypothesis which states that "Young drivers can react to emergency situations faster than old drivers" is true. Are we justified in taking the statistical test at face value and making this interpretation of the results? Before answering this question, stop and think for a minute and try to conceive of a situation in which five one-hundredths of a second would make an appreciable difference in the reaction of a driver to an emergency situation. If we accept the scientific hypothesis on the basis of a significant test of a statistical hypothesis, which probably stated something to the effect that "drivers between the ages of 15 and 25 will respond more rapidly to a simple reaction time test than drivers between the ages of 40 and 50," we are, in effect, asserting the practicality of the resulting difference.

In interpreting the statistically significant outcomes of research we must take two issues into account. The first concerns the practicality of the result of our test. If, as in the example above, we have found a statistically significant difference between two groups, or between two experimental conditions, we must very seriously ask ourselves whether or not the size of the difference is meaningful. If we find a situation like our example, where a statistically significant difference is not large enough to have practical meaning, we may "pat" ourselves on the back for achieving very sensitive measurement in the experiment. We must, however, interpret our findings in light of their practical significance.

The second issue that must be faced in the interpretation of an experiment that produces a statistically significant result concerns the relationship between the scientific and statistical hypotheses. We should, at this point, review the statistical hypothesis to insure that it is an accurate reflection of the scientific hypothesis. Consider again the two hypotheses involved in the example:

1. Scientific hypothesis: "Young drivers can react to emergency situations faster than old drivers."
2. Statistical hypothesis: "Drivers between the ages of 15 and 25 will respond more rapidly to a simple reaction time test than drivers between the ages of 40 and 50."

We have defined young drivers to be between 15 and 25, and old drivers to be between 40 and 50 years of age. More importantly perhaps, we have specified, for the purpose of the experiment, that a simple reaction time test is an adequate measure of reaction to emergency situations. Most researchers in the area of driver behavior would argue that there is a great deal more than simple reaction time involved in the speed of reaction to emergency situations, even though reaction time is a factor. The impact of this discrepancy on our experiment might be that, since reaction time is only a part of the process of reacting to emergency situations, a rather large difference, perhaps on the order of 1 or 2 seconds, in reaction time would be necessary before the groups could be considered different from a practical point of view.

Although the example given to illustrate the concept of practical significance was somewhat extreme, there has been considerable psychological research published that could be criticized for ignoring these issues.

Nonsignificance: The Other Side of the Coin

It is common for a psychologist to find that, on the basis of a statistical test, he cannot accept his hypothesis. In these cases the statistical analysis clearly indicates, if we have followed the rules of experimentation, that we must reject the statistical hypothesis in favor of the null hypothesis. In *every* case, this means that we cannot show evidence of the validity of the scientific hypothesis. However, a nonsignificant result need not mean that we must abandon the scientific hypothesis. The researcher faced with this turn of events must consider a number of questions.

Again, one of the first possibilities he might consider involves the relationship between the scientific and the statistical hypothesis. Suppose, for example, that the reaction time of the young and old drivers had not produced a statistically significant result. One factor which might be considered in this case is the ages used to define young and old drivers (young = 15–25; old = 40–50). The researcher might, on second thought, feel that 40- to 50-year-old drivers did not really qualify as old drivers, and that he should have used 60- to 70-year-old drivers for this group. It is important to realize that finding disagreement between the statistical and scientific hypothesis cannot save the experiment. What the investigator can do, however, is to conduct a new experiment using what he has learned from the first study.

Another possible explanation for a nonsignificant result involves the precision of the measurement applied to the dependent variable. We have discussed the fact that parametric statistical tests are more powerful than nonparametric tests. Again, this difference in power is principally due to the scale of measurement upon which the data are measured. It is possible in psychological research to miss finding real differences between groups or conditions if we do not, or cannot, utilize a powerful scale of measurement. Thus, it may pay the researcher to reevaluate his dependent variable and attempt to devise a suitable measure that can meet the assumptions of the interval or ratio scales.

In discussing possible explanations for nonsignificant experimental results, we do not mean to imply that the researcher must always rationalize his failure to reject the null hypothesis. Regardless of the outcome of the statistical analysis, the researcher must interpret his results. This interpretive activity should include a reevaluation of the experimental design and statistical treatment of the data. In addition, the results should be evaluated in terms of their meaning and practical significance.

The Need for Replication of Research

The primary aim of psychological research is to establish general laws and principles that will serve to describe and explain behavior. We have discussed at some length the fact that particular experiments do not absolutely prove hypotheses but rather that they are designed to indicate the relative degree of confidence we can have in them. There is always a chance that error can enter into a hypothesis-testing situation and cause the experimenter to make a wrong decision. Similarly, there is always a chance that sampling errors will create a situation in which the sample of individuals we use as subjects do not accurately reflect the population to which we intend to generalize the results. Although statistical methods allow us to take these potential errors into account, they can never absolutely prevent their occurrence. To guard against the influence of these errors, psychological hypotheses do not win acceptance as laws or principles explaining or describing behavior until they have been demonstrated to hold up under a number of experimental tests. This replication of experimental research is generally held to be an essential aspect of good scientific methodology. If identical results are observed after a number of replications of a particular experiment, perhaps with minor variations in experimental design, our degree of assurance in the validity of the scientific hypothesis can be substantially increased. We might eventually be willing to accept the hypothesis as a demonstrated fact or principle.

Summary

1. There are four types, or scales, of measurement, which are defined by the rules determining how numbers are assigned to observations. These scales of measurement are the nominal scale, the ordinal scale, the interval scale, and the ratio scale.

2. Descriptive statistics are used to describe and summarize data. A frequency distribution is one means of summarizing and simplifying data. Measures of central tendency—the mode, median, and mean—are used to describe an entire set of data by means of a single number. Other measures provide information about how an individual score, in a set of scores, stands in relation to the other

scores. These measures, which are called variability measures, include the range, deviation scores, variance, and standard deviation.

3. Correlations are used to describe the degree to which two different measures are related. This description is embodied in a single score, called a correlation coefficient, which ranges from +1.00 to −1.00. A perfect positive correlation is +1.00, while a perfect negative correlation is −1.00. A correlation of zero indicates that there is no relationship between the two measures being correlated.

4. Inferential statistics deal with the mathematical tools used by researchers to generalize findings from relatively small samples of individuals to large populations. One of the principal functions of inferential statistics is to estimate population parameters, such as the true value of the population mean, from sample statistics.

5. The statements of the statistician are almost always made in terms of probability levels, which represent the degree of confidence that can be placed in a result. The calculation of these probability levels involves the normal distribution, the size of the sample, and the mean and standard deviation of the sample.

6. Hypothesis testing is a statistical process in which the experimenter follows particular statistical rules in deciding between a null hypothesis and an alternative hypothesis.

7. Statistical hypothesis tests require the experimenter to determine the significance level for each test. This represents the degree of assurance required before he will reject the null hypothesis in favor of his alternative hypothesis.

8. The choice between parametric statistics and nonparametric techniques is usually determined by the scale of measurement on which the experimental data is measured. Parametric tests, such as the *t* test, are appropriate for interval and ratio scale data, while nonparametric tests are principally useful with nominal and ordinal data.

9. The manner in which samples are selected is an important determinant of the degree to which we can make generalizations from psychological experiments. Random and stratified sampling techniques are used to insure that the sample accurately represents the population.

10. Aside from selecting a sample, the other main activities involved in the design of experiments are the selection of dependent and independent variables and the control or elimination of nuisance variables.

11. The interpretation of the results of research requires that the experimenter reevaluate his experimental design and statistical methods, and that he assess the results in terms of their meaningfulness and practical significance.

12. It is generally required by the scientific method that experiments be replicated before successfully tested hypotheses can be accorded the status of psychological laws or principles. This replication leads to increased assurance that experimental and sampling errors have not affected the results.

Selected Readings

Lorge, I. The fundamental nature of measurement. In D. N. Jackson and S. Messick (Eds.), *Problems of human assessment.* New York: McGraw-Hill, 1967.

References

Adams, J. A., & Chambers, R. W. Response to simultaneous stimulation of two sense modalities. *Journal of Experimental Psychology*, 1962, **63**, 198–206.

Allport, G. W. *Personality: A psychological interpretation.* New York: Holt, 1937.

Allport, G. W. *Pattern and growth in personality.* New York: Holt, 1961.

Allport, G. W. The historical background of modern social psychology. In G. Lindzey and E. Aronson (Eds.), *The handbook of social psychology* (2nd ed., Vol. I). Reading, Mass.: Addison-Wesley, 1968.

Allport, G. W., & Odbert, H. S. Trait names: A psycho-lexical study. *Psychological Monographs*, 1936, **47** (1, Whole No. 287).

Alpern, M., Lawrence, M., & Wolsk, D. *Sensory processes.* Monterey, Calif.: Brooks/Cole, 1967.

American Psychiatric Association. *Diagnostic and statistical manual of mental disorders* (2nd ed., DSM-II). Washington, D. C.: American Psychiatric Association, 1968.

Annett, J., & Kay, H. Skilled performance. *Occupational Psychology*, 1956, **30**, 112–117.

Arnold, M. *Emotion and personality.* New York: Columbia University Press, 1960.

Asch, S. E. Opinions and social pressure. *Scientific American*, 1955, **193**(5), 31–35.

Auerback, R., & Rugowski, J. Lysergic acid diethylamide: Effect on embryos. *Science*, 1967, **157**, 1325–1326.

Bass, B. M., & Vaughan, J. A. *Training in industry: The management of learning.* Monterey, Calif.: Brooks/Cole, 1966.

Békésy, G. von. *Experiments in hearing.* New York: McGraw-Hill, 1960.

Bell, H. M. *The adjustment inventory.* Palo Alto, Calif.: Consulting Psychologists Press, 1939.

Bennet, E., Degan, J., & Spiegel, J. (Eds.) *Human factors in technology.* New York: McGraw-Hill, 1963.

Bergum, B. O. A taxonomic analysis of continuous performance. *Perceptual and Motor Skills,* 1966, **23**, 47–54.

Berliner, C., Angell, D., & Shearer, J. W. *Behaviors, measures and instruments for performance evaluation in simulated environments.* Paper presented at the Symposium and Workshop on the Quantification of Human Performance, Albuquerque, N. M., August 17–19, 1964.

Bijou, S. W. A functional analysis of retarded development. In N. R. Ellis (Ed.), *International review of research in mental retardation* (Vol. 1). New York: Academic Press, 1966. Pp. 1–19.

Bilodeau, E. A., & Bilodeau, I. McD. Motor-skills learning. *Annual Review of Psychology,* 1961, **12**, 243–280.

Binet, A., & Simon, T. Méthodes Nouvelles pour le diagnostic du niveau intellectual des anormaux. *Année Psychologie,* 1905, **11**, 191–244.

Bishop, G. H. The peripheral unit for pain. *Journal of Neurophysiology,* 1944, **7**, 71–80.

Blum, M. L., & Naylor, J. C. *Industrial psychology: Its theoretical and social foundations.* New York: Harper, 1968.

Boer, A. P., & Sipprelle, C. N. Elimination of avoidance behavior in the clinic and its transfer to the normal environment. *Journal of Therapeutics and Experimental Psychiatry,* 1970, **1**, 169–174.

Bolinger, D. *Aspects of language.* New York: Harcourt, 1968.

Boring, E. G. Intelligence as the tests test it. *New Republic,* 1923, **34**, 35–37.

Boring, E. G. *A history of experimental psychology* (2nd ed.). New York: Appleton-Century-Crofts, 1950.

Bowen, H. M. Diver performance and effects of cold. *Human Factors,* 1968, **10**(5), 445–463.

Bradley, C. Benzedrine and dexedrine in the treatment of children's behavior disorders. *Pediatrics,* 1950, **5**, 24–37.

Broadbent, D. E. A mechanical model for human attention and immediate memory. *Psychological Review,* 1957, **64**, 205–215.

Bruner, J. S., & Goodman, C. C. Value and need as organizing factors in perception. *Journal of Abnormal and Social Psychology,* 1947, **42**, 33–44.

Bruner, J. S., Goodnow, J., & Austin, G. N. *A study of thinking.* New York: Wiley, 1956.

Bryan, W. L., & Harter, N. Studies on the telegraphic language: The acquisition of a hierarchy of habits. *Psychological Review,* 1899, **6**, 345–375.

Butter, C. M. *Neuropsychology: The study of brain and behavior.* Monterey, Calif.: Brooks/Cole, 1968.

Cattell, R. B. *Personality: A systematic theoretical and factual study.* New York: McGraw-Hill, 1950.

Chapanis, A. Color names for color space. *American Scientist,* 1965, **53**(3), 327–346.

Chapanis, A. *Man-machine engineering.* Monterey, Calif.: Brooks/Cole, 1966.

Chapanis, A. The relevance of laboratory studies to practical situations. *Ergonomics*, 1967, **10**, 557–577.

Chaplin, J. P., & Krawiec, T. S. *Systems and theories of psychology.* New York: Holt, 1960.

Cofer, C. N., & Appley, M. H. *Motivation: Theory and research.* New York: Wiley, 1964.

Cohen, M. M., Hirschhorn, K., & Frosch, W. A. (State U. of New York School of Medicine, Buffalo). In vivo and vitro chromosomal damage induced by LSD-25. *New England Journal of Medicine*, 1967, **277**(20), 1043–1049.

Coombs, C. H., Dawes, R. M., & Tversky, A. *Mathematical psychology: An elementary introduction.* Englewood Cliffs, N. J.: Prentice-Hall, 1970.

Corkindale, K. G. Man-machine allocation in military systems. In W. T. Singleton, R. S. Easterby, and D. Whitfield (Eds.), *The human operator in complex systems.* London: Taylor and Francis Ltd., 1967.

Corso, J. F. *The experimental psychology of sensory behavior.* New York: Holt, 1967.

Costanzo, P. R., & Shaw, M. E. Conformity as a function of age level. *Child Development*, 1966, **37**(4), 967–975.

Crawford, M. P. Concepts of training. In R. M. Gagné (Ed.), *Psychological principles in system development.* New York: Holt, 1962. Pp. 301–341.

Crossman, E. R. F. W. A theory of the acquisition of speed-skill. *Ergonomics*, 1959, **2**, 153–166.

Crutchfield, R. S. Conformity and character. *American Psychologist*, 1955, **10**, 191–198.

Dallenbach, K. M. Smell, taste, and somesthesis. In E. G. Boring, H. S. Langfeld, and H. P. Weld (Eds.), *Introduction to psychology.* New York: Wiley, 1939. Pp. 600–626.

Damkot, D. K. A comparison of auditory, visual, and electrocutaneous displays in a vigilance task. Unpublished doctoral dissertation, University of South Dakota, 1969.

Darley, J., & Latané, B. Bystander intervention in emergencies: Diffusion of responsibility. *Journal of Personality and Social Psychology*, 1968, **8**, 377–383.

Darwin, C. *Expression of emotions in man and animals.* New York: Appleton & Co., 1872.

Davis, J. H. *Group performance.* Reading, Mass.: Addison-Wesley, 1969.

Dember, W. N. *The psychology of perception.* New York: Holt, 1965.

DeValois, R. L. Analysis and coding of color vision in the primate visual system. In *Cold Spring Harbor symposium on quantitative biology*, 1965, **30**, 567–579.

DuBois, P. H. *The history of psychological testing.* Boston: Allyn & Bacon, 1970.

Dunnette, M. D. *Personnel selection and placement.* Monterey, Calif.: Brooks/Cole, 1966.

Eccles, J. C. *The physiology of nerve cells.* Baltimore: John Hopkins University Press, 1957.

Edwards, W. Information processing, decision making, and highway safety. In J. O'Day (Ed.), *Driver behavior—cause and effect.* Washington, D. C.: Insurance Institute for Highway Safety, 1968. Pp. 165–180.

Edwards, W. A bibliography of research on behavioral decision processes to 1968. *Univ. of Michigan, Human Performance Center. Memo. Rep. No. 7,* 1969.

Egozcue, J., Irwin, S., & Maruffo, C. (Oregon Regional Primate Research Center, Beaverton). Chromosomal damage in LSD users. *Journal of American Medical Association,* 1968, **204**(3), 214–218.

Ellingstad, V. S. Velocity estimation for briefly displayed targets. *Perceptual and Motor Skills,* 1967, **24,** 943–947.

Ellingstad, V. S., & Heimstra, N. W. Estimation of movement as a function of target speed, display distance, and concealment distance. *Technical Report No. 7,* April 1968, Driver Behavior Laboratory, University of South Dakota.

Ellingstad, V. S., & Heimstra, N. W. Velocity-time estimation as a function of target speed and concealment extent. *Human Factors,* 1969, **11,** 305–312.

Ellis, A. New approaches to psychotherapy techniques. *Journal of Clinical Psychology,* 1955, **11,** 208–260.

Ellis, H. C. *The transfer of learning.* New York: Macmillan, 1965.

Eysenck, H. J. *Dimensions of personality.* London: Routledge and Kegan Paul, 1947.

Eysenck, H. J. The effects of psychotherapy. In H. J. Eysenck (Ed.), *Handbook of abnormal psychology.* New York: Basic Books, 1961. Pp. 697–725.

Eysenck, H. J. New ways in psychotherapy. *Psychology Today,* 1967, **1,** 39–47.

Fitts, P. M. Engineering psychology and equipment design. In S. S. Stevens (Ed.), *Handbook of experimental psychology.* New York: Wiley, 1951.

Fitts, P. M. Perceptual-motor skill learning. In A. W. Melton (Ed.), *Categories of human learning.* New York: Academic Press, 1964. Pp. 243–285.

Fitts, P. M., & Jones, R. H. Analysis of factors contributing to 460 "pilot-error" experiences in operating aircraft controls. In H. W. Sinaiko (Ed.), *Selected papers on "Human factors in the design and use of control systems."* New York: Dover, 1961.

Fitts, P. M., & Posner, M. I. *Human performance.* Monterey, Calif.: Brooks/Cole, 1967.

Fleishman, E. A., & Berniger, J. One way to reduce office turnover. *Personnel,* 1960, **37,** 63–69.

Fletcher, H. *Speech and hearing in communication.* Princeton, N. J.: D. Van Nostrand, 1953.

Fowler, H. *Curiosity and exploratory behavior.* New York: Macmillan, 1965.

Freeman, F. S. *Theory and practice of psychological testing* (3rd ed.). New York: Holt, 1962.

Fritsch, G., & Hitzig, E. Ueber die elekrische Erregbarkeit des Grosshirns. *Arch. anat. Physiol. wiss, Med.,* 1870, **37,** 300–332.

Gagné, R. M. Military training and principles of learning. *American Psychologist,* 1962, **17,** 83–91.

Gagné, R. M. Problem solving. In A. W. Melton (Ed.), *Categories of human learning.* New York: Academic Press, 1964. Pp. 293–317.

Gagné, R. M. *The conditions of learning.* New York: Holt, 1965.

Gagné, R. M. Human problem solving: Internal and external events. In B. Kleinmuntz (Ed.), *Problem solving: Research, method, and theory.* New York: Wiley, 1966. Pp. 128–148.

Gagné, R. M. Contributions of learning to human development. *Psychological Review,* 1968, **3,** 177–191.

Geldard, F. A. *The human senses.* New York: Wiley, 1953.

Geldard, F. A. Adventures in tactile literacy. *American Psychologist,* 1957, **12,** 115–124.

Geldard, F. A. Some neglected possibilities of communication. *Science,* 1960, **131,** 1583.

Gibson, E., & Walk, R. The visual cliff. *Scientific American,* 1960, **202**(4), 64–71.

Gibson, J. J. *The senses considered as perceptual systems.* Boston: Houghton Mifflin, 1966.

Goffard, S. J., Heimstra, N. W., Beecroft, R. S., & Openshaw, J. W. Basic electronics for minimally qualified men: An experimental evaluation of a method of presentation. *Technical Report No. 61,* 1960, Human Resources Research Office, Washington, D. C.

Graham, C. H., & Ratoosh, P. Notes on some interrelations of sensory psychology, perception, and behavior. In S. Koch (Ed.), *Psychology: A study of a science.* New York: McGraw-Hill, 1962.

Green, B. F. Current trends in problem solving. In B. Kleinmuntz (Ed.), *Problem solving: Research, method, and theory.* New York: Wiley, 1966. Pp. 3–18.

Gregory, R. L. *Eye and brain: The psychology of seeing.* New York: McGraw-Hill, 1966.

Grossman, S. P. *A textbook of physiological psychology.* New York: Wiley, 1967.

Guilford, J. P. *Psychometric methods* (1st ed.). New York: McGraw-Hill, 1936.

Guilford, J. P. *The nature of human intelligence.* New York: McGraw-Hill, 1967.

Hagen, R. E., Ellingstad, V. S., & Kimball, K. A. A validation study of a driving simulator. *Technical Report 14,* Human Factors Laboratory, University of South Dakota, 1970.

Hall, J. F. Motivation and affectivity. In H. Helson and W. Bevan (Eds.), *Contemporary approaches to psychology.* Princeton, N. J.: D. Van Nostrand, 1967. Pp. 223–271.

Harlow, H. F. The nature of love. *American Psychologist,* 1958, **13,** 673–685.

Harlow, H. F., & Harlow, M. K. Social deprivation in monkeys. *Scientific American,* 1962, **207,** 136–146.

Hastorf, A. H., Schneider, D. J., & Polefka, J. *Person perception.* Reading, Mass.: Addison-Wesley, 1970.

Hathaway, S. R., & McKinley, J. C. *Minnesota multiphasic per-*

sonality inventory: Manual for administration and scoring. New York: Psychological Corporation, 1951.

Hays, W. L. *Statistics for psychologists.* New York: Holt, 1963.

Hebb, D. O. *The organization of behavior.* New York: Wiley, 1949.

Heidbreder, E. *Seven psychologies.* New York: Appleton-Century-Crofts, 1933.

Heimstra, N. W. The effects of "stress fatigue" on performance in a simulated driving task. *Ergonomics,* 1970, **13**, 209–218. (a)

Heimstra, N. W. Problems and issues in traffic safety research. In N. W. Heimstra (Ed.), *Injury control in traffic safety.* Springfield, Ill.: Charles C. Thomas, 1970. Pp. 3–22. (b)

Heimstra, N. W., & McDonald, A. L. Social influence on the response to drugs. III. Response to amphetamine sulfate as a function of age. *Psychopharmacologia,* 1962, **3**, 212–218.

Helson, H. *Adaptation-level theory.* New York: Harper, 1964.

Helson, H. Perception. In H. Helson and W. Bevan (Eds.), *Contemporary approaches to psychology.* Princeton, N.J.: D. Van Nostrand, 1967.

Hernández-Péon, R., Scherrer, H., & Jouvet, M. Modification of electric activity in cochlear nucleus during "attention" in unanesthetized cats. *Science,* 1956, **123**, 331–332.

Herzberg, F., Mausner, B., & Snyderman, B. *The motivation to work.* New York: Wiley, 1959.

Hess, E. H., & Polt, J. Pupil size as related to interest value of visual stimuli. *Science,* 1960, **132**, 349–350.

Hochberg, J. E. *Perception.* (Foundations of Modern Psychology Series) Englewood Cliffs, N.J.: Prentice-Hall, 1964.

Hodgkin, A. L. Ionic movements and electrical activity in giant nerve fibers. *Proceedings of the Royal Society,* Series B, 1958, **148**, 1–37.

Hodgkin, A. L., Huxley, A. F., & Katz, B. Ionic currents underlying the activity in the giant axon of the squid. *Arch. Sci. physiol.,* 1949, **3**, 129–150.

Hofmann, M. A. A comparison of visual, auditory, and electrocutaneous displays in a compensatory tracking task. Unpublished doctoral dissertation, University of South Dakota, 1968.

Holding, D. H. *Principles of training.* New York: Pergamon Press, 1965.

Irion, A. L. A brief history of research on the acquisition of skills. In E. A. Bilodeau (Ed.), *Acquisition of skill.* New York: Academic Press, 1966.

Irion, A. L. Historical introduction. In E. A. Bilodeau (Ed.), *Principles of skill acquisition.* New York: Academic Press, 1969. Pp. 1–31.

Irwin, S., & Egozcue, J. Chromosomal abnormalities in leukocytes from LSD-25 users. *Science,* 1967, **157**, 313–314.

Janousek, J. A. The use of mockups in the design of a deep submergence rescue vehicle. *Human Factors,* 1970, **12**(1), 63.

Jenkins, J. G., & Dallenbach, K. M. Obliviscence during sleep and waking. *American Journal of Psychology,* 1924, **35**, 605–612.

Jenkins, W. O., & Davis, H. C. *University of Tennessee alcoholism scale.* Knoxville, Tenn.: University of Tennessee Press, 1957.

Jensen, A. R. How much can we boost IQ and scholastic achievement? *Harvard Education Review,* 1969, **39,** 1–123.

Jordan, N. Allocation of functions between man and machine in automated systems. *Journal of Applied Psychology,* 1963, **47,** 161–165.

Judd, D. B., & Kelley, K. L. Methods of designating colors. *National Bureau of Standards Journal of Research,* 1939, **23,** 355–385.

Kaplan, B. (Ed.) *The inner world of mental illness.* New York: Harper, 1964.

Katona, G. *Organizing and memorizing: Studies in the psychology of learning and teaching.* New York: Columbia University Press, 1940.

Kelley, C. R. What is adaptive training? *Human Factors,* 1969, **11,** 547–556.

Kelley, H. H., & Thibaut, J. W. Group problem solving. In G. Lindzey and E. Aronson (Eds.), *The handbook of social psychology* (2nd ed., Vol. IV). Reading, Mass.: Addison-Wesley, 1969.

Kelman, H. C. Human use of human subjects: The problem of deception in social psychological experiments. *Psychological Bulletin,* 1967, **67,** 1–11.

Kibler, A. W. The relevance of vigilance research to aerospace monitoring tasks. *Human Factors,* 1965, **7,** 93–99.

Kiesler, C. A., & Kiesler, S. B. *Conformity.* Reading, Mass.: Addison-Wesley, 1969.

Lashley, K. S. *Brain mechanisms in intelligence.* Chicago: University of Chicago Press, 1929.

Lashley, K. S. In search of the engram. Symposium—Society of Experimental Biology, 1950, **4,** 454–482.

Lazarus, R. S., Yousem, H. R., & Arenberg, D. Hunger and perception. *Journal of Personality,* 1953, **21,** 312–328.

Leeper, R. Cognitive processes. In S. S. Stevens (Ed.), *Handbook of experimental psychology.* New York: Wiley, 1951. Pp. 730–757.

Leibowitz, H. W. *Visual perception.* (The Critical Issues Psychology Series) New York: Macmillan, 1965.

Lindzey, G., & Aronson, E. (Eds.) *The handbook of social psychology* (2nd ed., Vols. I–V). Reading, Mass.: Addison-Wesley, 1969.

Littman, R. A. Motives, history, and causes. In M. R. Jones (Ed.), *Nebraska symposium on motivation.* Lincoln: University of Nebraska Press, 1958.

Locke, E. A. Toward a theory of task motivation and incentives. *Organizational Behavior and Human Performance,* 1968, **3,** 157–189.

Locke, E. A., & Bryan, J. F. Performance goals as determinants of level of performance and boredom. *Journal of Applied Psychology,* 1967, **51,** 120–130.

Locke, E. A., & Bryan, J. F. The directing function of goals in task performance. *Organizational Behavior and Human Performance*, 1969, **4**, 35–42.

Lockman, R. F. An empirical description of the subfields of psychology. *American Psychologist*, 1964, **19**, 645–653.

London, T. D. Research on sensory interaction in the Soviet Union. *Psychological Bulletin*, 1954, **51**, 531–568.

Lorge, I. The fundamental nature of measurement. In D. N. Jackson and S. Messick (Eds.), *Problems of human assessment*. New York: McGraw-Hill, 1967.

Loughman, W. D., Sargent, T. W., & Isrealstam, D. M. (Univ. of Calif., Donner Lab. of Medical Physics and Biophysics, Berkeley). Leukocytes of humans exposed to lysergic acid diethylamide, lack of chromosomal damage. *Science*, 1967, **158**(3800), 508–510.

Luce, R. D., Bush, R. R., & Galanter, E. *Handbook of mathematical psychology* (Vols. I and II). New York: Wiley, 1963.

Luchins, A. S. Mechanization in problem solving: The effect of einstellung. *Psychological Monograph*, 1942, **54** (Whole No. 248).

Mackie, R. R., & Christensen, P. R. Translation and application of psychological research. *Technical Report 716–1*, 1967, Human Factors Research, Inc. (Santa Barbara Research Park, Goleta, Calif.)

MacNeilage, P. F. Motor control of serial ordering of speech. *Psychological Review*, 1970, **77**(3), 182–196.

MacNeilage, P. F., & DeClerk, J. L. On the motor control of co-articulation in CVC monosyllables. *Journal of the Acoustical Society of America*, 1969, **45**, 1217–1233.

Maier, N. R. F. Reasoning in humans. *Journal of Comparative Psychology*, 1930, **10**, 115–143.

Malinovsky, M. R., & Barry, J. R. Determinants of work attitudes. *Journal of Applied Psychology*, 1965, **49**, 446–451.

Malmo, R. B. Anxiety and behavioral arousal. *Psychological Review*, 1957, **64**, 276–287.

Marks, W. B., Dobelle, W. H., & MacNichol, E. F., Jr. Visual pigments of single primate cones. *Science*, 1964, **143**, 1181–1183.

Martin, G. L. The perception of hazard by young children. Unpublished doctoral dissertation, University of South Dakota, 1970.

Mashour, M. *Psychophysical relations in the perception of velocity*. Stockholm, Sweden: Almqvist & Wiksell, 1964.

Mast, T. M. Influence of motivational variables on prerest and postrest performance in rotary pursuit tracking. Unpublished doctoral dissertation, University of South Dakota, 1966.

Mast, T. M., & Heimstra, N. W. Prior social experience and amphetamine toxicity in mice. *Psychological Reports*, 1962, **11**, 809–812.

Mayer, J. Regulation of energy intake and body weight: The glucostatic theory and the lipostatic hypothesis. *Annals of the New York Academy of Science*, 1955, **63**, 14–53.

McConnell, J. V. (Ed.) *Readings in social psychology today*. Del Mar, Calif.: CRM Books, 1970.

McCormick, E. J. *Human factor engineering.* New York: McGraw-Hill, 1970.

McGuire, W. J. Order of presentation as a factor in "conditioning" persuasiveness. In C. I. Hovland (Ed.), *Order of presentation in persuasion.* New Haven: Yale University Press, 1957. Pp. 98–114.

McGuire, W. J. The nature of attitudes and attitude change. In G. Lindzey and E. Aronson (Eds.), *The handbook of social psychology* (2nd ed., Vol. III). Reading, Mass.: Addison-Wesley, 1969.

McLennan, H. *Synaptic transmission.* Philadelphia: Saunders, 1963.

Meister, D., & Rabideau, G. *Human factors evaluation in system development.* New York: Wiley, 1965.

Milgram, S. Nationality and conformity. *Scientific American,* 1961, **205**(6), 45–51.

Miller, J. G. Adjusting to overloads of information. In D. McK. Rioch and E. A. Weinstein (Eds.), *Disorders of communication.* Research Publications Assoc. Res. Nerv. Ment. Dis., 1964, **42,** 87–100.

Miller, R. B. Task description and analysis. In R. M. Gagné (Ed.), *Psychological principles in system development.* New York: Holt, 1962. Pp. 187–227.

Minami, H., & Dallenbach, K. M. The effect of activity upon learning and retention in the cockroach. *American Journal of Psychology,* 1946, **59,** 1–58.

Mischel, W. *Personality assessment.* New York: Wiley, 1968.

Morgan, C. D., & Murray, H. A. A method of investigating fantasies: The thematic apperception test. *Archives of Neurology and Psychiatry,* 1935, **34,** 289–306.

Naylor, J. C., & Briggs, G. E. *Long-term retention of learned skills, and review of the literature.* Laboratory of aviation psychology, Ohio State University & Ohio State Res. Found., 1961.

Newell, A., Shaw, J. C., & Simon, H. A. Elements of a theory of human problem solving. *Psychological Review,* 1958, **65,** 151–166.

Nichols, J. L. Driver education and improvement programs. In N. W. Heimstra (Ed.), *Injury Control in traffic safety.* Springfield, Ill.: Charles C. Thomas, 1970. Pp. 49–87.

Nichols, J. L. The effects of redundant multisensory information displays on the reduction of operator error in a compensatory tracking task. Unpublished doctoral dissertation, University of South Dakota, 1970.

Nunnally, J. C. *Introduction to psychological measurement.* New York: McGraw-Hill, 1970.

Ogden, L. E. Effects of incentive on the performance of a visual vigilance task. Unpublished Master's thesis, University of South Dakota, 1963.

Paillard, J. The patterning of skilled movements. In *Handbook of physiology,* Vol. III. Washington, D. C.: American Physiological Society, 1960. Pp. 1679–1708.

Paintal, A. S. A study of gastric stretch receptors. Their role in the peripheral mechanism of satiation of hunger and thirst. *Journal of Physiology*, 1954, **126**, 255–270.

Pervin, L. A. *Personality: Theory, assessment and research.* New York: Wiley, 1970.

Peterson, L. R., Birdsall, T. G., & Fox, W. C. The theory of signal detectability. *Institute of Radio Engineers Transactions*, 1954, **PGIT-4**, 171–212.

Pfaffmann, C. The afferent code for sensory quality. *American Psychologist*, 1959, **14**, 226–232.

Pfaffmann, C. Taste, its sensory and motivating properties. *American Scientist*, 1964, **52**, 187–206.

Phillips, J. L. *The origins of intellect: Piaget's theory.* San Francisco: W. H. Freeman, 1969.

Pribram, K. H. Emotion: Steps toward a neuropsychological theory. In D. C. Glass (Ed.), *Neurophysiology and emotion.* Rockefeller University Press and Russell Sage Foundation, 1967. Pp. 3–40.

Pribram, K. H. (Ed.) *On the biology of learning.* New York: Harcourt, 1969.

Rapoport, A. Foreword. In W. Buckley (Ed.), *Modern systems research for the behavioral scientist.* Chicago: Aldine Publishing Co., 1968.

Ross, S., & Lockman, R. F. *A career in psychology.* Washington, D. C.: American Psychological Association, 1965.

Royce, J. R. Psychology in the mid-twentieth century. *American Scientist*, 1957, **45**, 57–73.

Rushton, W. A. H. *Visual pigments in man.* Liverpool University Press, 1962.

Rushton, W. A. H. Color blindness and cone pigments. *American Journal of Optometry*, 1964, **41**, 265–282.

Schachter, S., & Singer, J. E. Cognitive, social and physiological determinants of emotional state. *Psychological Review*, 1962, **69**, 379–399.

Schori, T. R. A comparison of visual, auditory, and cutaneous tracking displays when divided attention is required to a cross-adaptive loading task. Unpublished doctoral dissertation, University of South Dakota, 1970. (a)

Schori, T. R. Experimental approaches and hardware for driving research. In N. W. Heimstra (Ed.), *Injury control in traffic safety.* Springfield, Ill.: Charles C. Thomas, 1970. Pp. 154–175. (b)

Schrenk, L. P. Aiding the decision maker—a decision process model. *Ergonomics*, 1969, **12**, 543–557.

Seashore, S. H., & Seashore, R. H. Individual differences in simple auditory reaction times of hands, feet, and jaws. *Journal of Experimental Psychology*, 1941, **29**, 342–345.

Sechenov, I. *Selected works.* Moscow and Leningrad State Publishing House, 1935.

Segall, M. H., Campbell, D. T., & Herskovits, M. J. *The influence of culture on visual perception.* New York: Bobbs-Merrill, 1966.

Sherif, M. A study of some social factors in perception. *Archives of Psychology*, 1935, (Whole No. 187).

Sherrington, C. S. The central nervous system and its instruments. In Sir M. Foster (Ed.), *A Textbook of physiology* (7th ed.). London: Macmillan, 1897.

Shiffrin, R. M., & Atkinson, R. C. Storage and retrieval processes in long-term memory. *Psychological Review*, 1969, **76**(2), 179–193.

Simon, H. A., & Newell, A. Information processing in computer and man. *American Scientist*, 1964, **52**(3), 281–300.

Sipprelle, C. N. Induced anxiety. *Psychotherapy: Theory, research and practice*, 1967, **4**, 36–40.

Smith, H. C. *Psychology of industrial behavior*. New York: McGraw-Hill, 1964.

Smith, K. U. Cybernetic theory and analysis of learning. In E. A. Bilodeau (Ed.), *Acquisition of skill*. New York: Academic Press, 1966. Pp. 425–482.

Smith, K. U., & Smith, W. M. *Perception and motion: An analysis of space structured behavior*. Philadelphia: Saunders, 1962.

Smith, K. U., & Sussman, H. Cybernetic theory and analysis of motor learning and memory. In E. A. Bilodeau (Ed.), *Principles of skill acquisition*. New York: Academic Press, 1969. Pp. 103–139.

Spady, A. A. Prototype of a new lunar-gravity simulator for astronaut mobility studies. *Human Factors*, 1969, **11**(5), 441.

Stampfl, T. G., & Levis, D. J. Essentials of implosive therapy: A learning theory based psychodynamic behavioral theory. *Journal of Abnormal Psychology*, 1967, **72**, 496–503.

Stang, P. R., & Wiener, E. L. Diver performance in cold water. *Human Factors*, 1970, **12**, 391–399.

Stevens, C. F. *Neurophysiology: A primer*. New York: Wiley, 1966.

Swain, A. D., & Wohl, J. G. *Factors affecting degree of automation in test and checkout*. Stamford, Conn.: Dunlop and Association, 1961.

Swets, J. A. (Ed.), *Signal detection and recognition by human observers*. New York: Wiley, 1964.

Swift, W. P. *General psychology*. New York: McGraw-Hill, 1969.

Tagiuri, R. Person perception. In G. Lindzey and E. Aronson (Eds.), *The handbook of social psychology* (2nd ed., Vol. III). Reading, Mass.: Addison-Wesley, 1969.

Terman, L. M. Intelligence and its measurement. *International Journal of Educational Psychology*, 1921, **12**, 124–127.

Terman, L. M., & Merrill, M. A. *Stanford-Binet intelligence scale: Manual for the third revision form L-M*. Boston: Houghton Mifflin, 1960.

Thompson, R. F., Voss, J. F., & Brogden, W. J. Effect of brightness of simultaneous visual stimulation on absolute auditory sensitivity. *Journal of Experimental Psychology*, 1958, **55**, 45–50.

Thompson, T., & Schuster, C. R. *Behavioral pharmacology*. Englewood Cliffs, N. J.: Prentice-Hall, 1968.

Thorndike, E. L. Intelligence and its measurement. *International Journal of Educational Psychology*, 1921, **12**, 124–127.

Thurstone, L. L. Intelligence and its measurement. *International Journal of Educational Psychology*, 1921, **12**, 201–207.

Tsang, Y. C. Hunger motivation in gastrectomized rats. *Journal of Comparative Psychology*, 1938, **26**, 1–17.

Ullmann, L. P., & Krasner, L. *A psychological approach to abnormal behavior.* Englewood Cliffs, N. J.: Prentice-Hall, 1969.

Van Meter, D., & Middleton, D. Modern statistical approaches to reception in communication theory. *Institute of Radio Engineers Transactions*, 1954, **PGIT-4**, 119–145.

Viteles, M. S. Postlude: The past and future of industrial psychology. *Journal of Consulting Psychology*, 1944, **8**, 182–185.

Wallach, M. A., & Kogan, N. The roles of information discussion and consensus in group risk taking. *Journal of Experimental Social Pschology*, 1965, **1**, 1–19.

Wargo, M. J. Human operator response speed, frequency, and flexibility: A review and analysis. *Human Factors*, 1967, **9**(3), 221–238.

Warner, H. D. Effects of intermittent noise on human target detection. *Human Factors*, 1969, **11**(3), 245–250.

Wechsler, D. *Wechsler intelligence scale for children.* New York: Psychological Corporation, 1949.

Wechsler, D. *Manual for the Wechsler adult intelligence scale.* New York: Psychological Corporation, 1955.

Weintraub, D. J., & Walker, E. L. *Perception.* Monterey, Calif.: Brooks/Cole, 1966.

Weltman, G., & Egstrom, G. H. Perceptual narrowing in novice divers. *Human Factors*, 1966, **8**(6), 499.

Wenrich, W. W. *A primer of behavior modification.* Monterey, Calif.: Brooks/Cole, 1970.

Wernimont, P. F. Intrinsic and extrinsic factors in job satisfaction. *Journal of Applied Psychology*, 1966, **50**, 41–50.

Wesman, A. G. Intelligent testing. *American Psychologist*, 1968, **23**(4), 267–274.

Wever, E. G. *Theory of hearing.* New York: Wiley, 1949.

Wever, E. G., & Bray, C. W. The perception of low tones and the resonance-volley theory. *Journal of Psychology*, 1937, **3**, 101–114.

Wittenborn psychiatric rating scales. New York: Psychological Corporation, 1955.

Wolff, H. G., & Wolf, S. *Pain.* Springfield, Ill.: Charles C. Thomas, 1948.

Wolpe, J. *Psychotherapy by reciprocal inhibition.* Stanford, Calif.: Stanford University Press, 1958.

Woodson, W. E., & Conover, D. W. *Human engineering guide for equipment designers.* Berkeley: University of California Press, 1966.

Woolsey, C. N. Organization of cortical auditory and motor areas of the cerebral cortex. In H. F. Harlow and C. N. Woolsey (Eds.), *Biological and biochemical bases of behavior.* Madison, Wisc.: University of Wisconsin Press, 1958. Pp. 63–81.

Worden, F. G. Attention and auditory electrophysiology. In E. Stellar and J. M. Sprague (Eds.), *Progress in physiological psychology.* New York: Academic Press, 1966. Pp. 45–116.

Wortz, E. C. Work in reduced gravity environments. *Human Factors*, 1969, **11**(5), 433.

Zajonc, R. B. Social facilitation. *Science,* 1965, **149**, No. 3681, 269–274.

Zajonc, R. B. *Social psychology: An experimental approach.* Monterey, Calif.: Brooks/Cole, 1966.

Zax, M., & Stricker, G. *The study of abnormal behavior: Selected readings* (2nd ed.). New York: Macmillan, 1969.

Zeigler, H. P., & Leibowitz, H. W. Apparent visual size as a function of distance for children and adults. *American Journal of Psychology*, 1957, **70**, 106–109.

Zener, K., & Gaffron, M. Perceptual experience: An analysis of the relations to the external world through internal processing. In S. Koch (Ed.), *Psychology: A study of a science.* New York: McGraw-Hill, 1962.

Zigler, E., & Child, I. L. Socialization. In G. Lindzey and E. Aronson (Eds.), *Handbook of social psychology* (Vol. III). Reading, Mass.: Addison-Wesley, 1969. Pp. 450–589.

Zimbardo, P., & Ebbesen, E. *Influencing attitudes and changing behavior.* Reading, Mass.: Addison-Wesley, 1969.

Zotterman, Y. Special sense: Thermal receptors. *Annual Review of Physiology*, 1953, **15**, 357–372.

Zotterman, Y. Thermal sensations. In J. Field, H. W. Magoun, & V. E. Hall (Eds.), *Handbook of physiology: Neurophysiology* (Vol. 1). Washington, D. C.: American Physiological Society, 1959. Pp. 431–458.

Author Index

Subject Index